The Act of Teaching

The Act of Teaching

Third Edition

DONALD R. CRUICKSHANK

The Ohio State University

DEBORAH BAINER JENKINS

The State University of West Georgia

KIM K. METCALF

Indiana University

Boston   Burr Ridge, IL   Dubuque, IA   Madison, WI   New York   San Francisco   St. Louis
Bangkok   Bogotá   Caracas   Kuala Lumpur   Lisbon   London   Madrid   Mexico City
Milan   Montreal   New Delhi   Santiago   Seoul   Singapore   Sydney   Taipei   Toronto

McGraw-Hill Higher Education

A Division of The **McGraw-Hill** *Companies*

THE ACT OF TEACHING
Published by McGraw-Hill, an imprint of The McGraw-Hill Companies, Inc. 1221 Avenue of the Americas, New York, NY, 10020. Copyright © 2003, 1999 by The McGraw-Hill Companies, Inc. All rights reserved. No part of this publication may be reproduced or distributed in any form or by any means, or stored in a data base or retrieval system, without the prior written consent of The McGraw-Hill Companies, Inc., including, but not limited to, in any network or other electronic storage or transmission, or broadcast for distance learning. Some ancillaries, including electronic and print components, may not be available to customers outside the United States.

This book is printed on acid-free paper.

domestic 4 5 6 7 8 9 0 QPD/QPD 0 9 8 7 6 5 4

ISBN   0-07-242666-7

Publisher: *Jane Karpacz*
Developmental editor: *Terri Wise*
Senior marketing manager: *Pamela S. Cooper*
Senior project manager: *Jean Hamilton*
Senior production supervisor: *Lori Koetters*
Media producer: *Lance Gerhart*
Senior designer: *Jenny El-Shamy*
Supplement producer: *Nathan Perry*
Photo researcher: *Brian Pecko*
Cover designer: *Donna Cambra*
Cover images: *Getty Images*
Typeface: *10/12 New Baskerville*
Compositor: *ElectraGraphics, Inc.*
Printer: *Quebecor World Dubuque Inc.*

Library of Congress Cataloging-in-Publication Data

Cruickshank, Donald R.
    The act of teaching / Donald R. Cruickshank, Deborah Bainer Jenkins, Kim K. Metcalf.—3rd ed.
       p. cm.
    Includes bibliographical references and indexes.
    ISBN 0-07-242666-7 (softcover : alk. paper)
    1. Teaching. 2. Lesson planning. I. Jenkins, Deborah Bainer. II. Metcalf, Kim K. III. Title.
LB1025.3 .C78 2003
371.102—dc21
                                                          2002070293

www. mhhe.com

About the Authors

Donald R. Cruickshank

Donald R. Cruickshank received his degrees from the State University College at Buffalo, New York, and the University of Rochester. After stints as a teacher, supervisor, and principal in the Rochester schools, he began a college teaching and administrative career that took him to SUNY Brockport, the University of Tennessee, Wheelock College, and The Ohio State University. Professor Cruickshank has been the recipient of Fulbright-Hayes senior scholar awards to Australia and Brazil and served in the Thai Ministry of Education and the United Nations' Bangkok office. Additionally, he worked for the Asian Development Bank in Indonesia and Manila. He has taught and lectured in Australia, Brazil, Canada, England, Scotland, Thailand, and Wales as well as throughout the United States and Puerto Rico. He has authored numerous articles and encyclopedia entries, and this is his eighth book. He is best known for his pioneering efforts in developing simulations and reflective teaching and his research on teacher clarity. His graduate students have won seven outstanding dissertation awards and have fashioned accomplished careers in teaching, scholarship, service, and administration.

Deborah Bainer Jenkins

Deborah Bainer Jenkins, formerly of the Ohio State University, is professor of curriculum and instruction at the State University of West Georgia. She received her B.S. in biology from Geneva College and her M.S. in environmental education and Ph.D. in Teacher Education from The Ohio State University. She taught middle school and high school science in the United States and in Asia and formerly chaired the education department at Biola University. Currently, her teaching responsibilities involve science methods, curriculum trends, research, and school improvement and reform. Dr. Bainer works extensively with school-based partnership programs aimed at enhancing science instruction. She has authored numerous articles and book chapters reflecting her research in teachers' professional development through partnerships, and effective multicultural instruction. She was awarded the distinguished teaching and scholarship awards from The Ohio State University and has received community service awards for her work with teachers.

Kim K. Metcalf

Kim K. Metcalf is director of the Indiana Center for Evaluation and an associate professor of education at Indiana University, Bloomington. He was awarded his M.A. and Ph.D. in teacher education and educational research and evaluation from The Ohio State University. Dr. Metcalf is a former music teacher and administrator who worked with students in grades K–12. As director of the Indiana Center for Evaluation, he oversees the conduct of large-scale evaluations of educational programs and policies throughout the U.S. and Europe. Among these projects have been examination of statewide class size initiatives, nationwide comprehensive school reform programs, and international programs for civic education. His current work is most widely known for the continuing evaluation of the voucher program in Cleveland, Ohio. He has been recognized for outstanding research and scholarship on teaching and teacher education by the Association of Teacher Educators and the Association of Psychological Type.

v

Contents in Brief

Contents in Detail

CHAPTER 7

Four Instructional Alternatives: Presentation, Discussion, Independent Study, and Individualized Instruction

Four More Instructional Alternatives: Cooperative Learning, Discovery Learning, Constructivism, and Direct Instruction 228

Evaluating Students' Learning 270

Preface

How This Book Was Developed

The decision about what content to include in this book on teaching derives from several sources: work done at Educational Testing Service (ETS) to determine what a competent *beginning* teacher should know and be able to do; work done by the National Board for Professional Teaching Standards to determine what a competent *experienced* teacher should know and be able to do; the advice of persons engaged in the preparation of beginning teachers; and our personal experiences as teacher educators and scholars.

What is a competent beginning teacher? Here we looked at both the recommendations made by ETS researcher Reynolds (1992)[1] and the ETS Praxis III standards.[2]

Reynolds reviewed the research literature on learning to teach and on the act of teaching itself. She concludes that on entering their first classroom, novices must have a thorough knowledge of what they will teach, a desire to find out about their students and their school, a solid grasp of instructional methodology, and a firm intention to reflect on their teaching actions and the behavior of their students. Soon thereafter, they should be able to plan and teach lessons that help students relate new learning to prior understanding and experience, develop rapport with students, arrange the physical and social conditions of the classroom in ways conducive to learning, assess student learning using a variety of measurement tools and then adapt instruction accordingly, and show improvement in their ability to reflect on teaching.

The Praxis III standards, or criteria set up for beginning teachers, require novices to become familiar with students' background, knowledge, and experience; articulate clear and appropriate learning goals; understand the connections among the content to be learned, content learned previously, and future content; be able to select teaching methods, activities, and materials appropriate to lesson goals and students; be able to create or select proper evaluation strategies; create a class climate that promotes fairness; establish and maintain rapport with students; communicate challenging learning expectations; establish and maintain consistent standards of student behavior; ensure a safe environment conducive to learning; make instructional goals and procedures clear; make content clear to students; encourage students to extend their thinking; monitor student understanding and provide corrective feedback; use time effectively; reflect on how well instructional goals have been met; demonstrate a sense of efficacy; build relationships with others; and communicate with parents and caregivers. Appendix A shows where the text meets requirements of Praxis III.

What is a competent experienced teacher? The **National Board for Professional Teaching Standards (NBPTS)**[3] was established in the late 1980s to set "high and rigorous" standards for experienced teachers. In order to do so, committees were set up composed mostly of distinguished teachers and complemented by experts in child development, teacher education, and subject matter specialists. Subsequently, standards have been developed for experienced early childhood, middle childhood, early adolescent, and adolescent and young adult teachers. For example, the standards for teachers of middle childhood (7 to 12 year-olds) expect teachers to know and/or be able to do the following: understand their students' abilities, interests, and aspirations; make sound decisions about what is important for students to learn; establish a caring, inclusive, stimulating, and safe community of learners; help learners respect differences; develop and use a rich, varied collection of learning materials; help learners integrate knowledge across subject fields and understand how what they study relates to the world around them; know and be

[1] Reynolds, A. (1992, Spring). What is a competent beginning teacher? *Review of Educational Research, 629*(1), 1–35.

[2] Educational Testing Service (1995). *The Praxis Series: Professional Assessments of Beginning Teachers. Praxis III: The Classroom Performance Assessments Orientation Guide.* Princeton, NJ: Author.

[3] http://new.nbpts.org/standards/framework.pdf

able to use a range of generic instructional alternatives so that students are provided with multiple paths to learn; understand the strengths and weaknesses of different assessment methods; create positive relationships with caregivers; regularly reflect on the quality and effectiveness of their practice; and work to improve schools and to advance education knowledge and practice.

Besides bearing in mind conclusions of the Educational Testing Service study and the NBPTS, we also listened to teacher educators' advice about what teachers should know and be able to do. Some of them shared course outlines with titles such as, "Principles and Methods of Teaching," and "The Teaching Process." Others reviewed previous editions of the book and offered comments and suggestions that were most helpful. Following is a partial list of our resource persons: Kay Alderman, University of Akron; Leo Anglin, Berry College; Leigh Chiarelot, Bowling Green State University; Gerald R. Dotson, Front Range Community College; Kathleen A. Gosnell, Duquesne University; Denise M. Grant, Kennesaw State University; Gail P. Gregg, Florida International University; Mary Lynn Hamilton, University of Kansas; Barbara J. Havis, Southern Illinois University; C. Michelle Hooper, Stephen F. Austin State University; Gae Johnson, Northern Arizona University; Karla Lynn Kelsay, The Florida State University; Catharine C. Knight, University of Akron; Philip McKnight, University of Kansas; Robert McNaughton, Cleveland State University; Robert McNergney, University of Virginia; Janice Nath, University of Houston; Jeanette Nunnelley, Indiana University Southeast; Lem Londos Railsback, Texas A&M University; Sherry Rulfs, Stephen F. Austin State University; Diane Sopko, The University of Memphis; Melba Spooner, University of North Carolina; Gary Stuck, University of North Carolina; Barbara Tea, Wright State University; Marie Tuttle, Brigham Young University; Patrick Walton, The University College of the Cariboo; Jian Wang, The University of Nevada at Las Vegas; and Kinnard White, University of North Carolina.

Finally, in order to determine the content of the book, we drew from our own combined experience as K–12 teachers, and as teacher educators and scholars, and from the numerous scholars and practitioners cited in the author index.

Of course, as authors we received welcomed assistance from our illustrator, Kathy Grossart, and from the several cartoonists. Our publisher, McGraw-Hill, also served us well. Among those who had an impact on this and earlier editions are Lane Akers, Beth Kaufman, and Terri Wise, who, respectively, edited the first, second, and this edition of the text.

Changes in the Third Edition

A great many changes have been made in this edition.

The contents of the text have been cross-referenced to the 19 Praxis III Standards on which beginning teachers are tested in 38 states. See Appendix A.

Chapter 2 has been made into two chapters, a new Chapter 2, The Challenge of Teaching in a Diverse Society, and a new Chapter 3, Teaching Diverse Students. All subsequent chapters are renumbered.

Many new research citations have been added and older ones updated.

New Web Resources have been added and are easily located using the @ icons that appear in the page margins.

Each text chapter has been updated and improved as described below.

Chapter 1 contains new sections on how student gender influences teaching, how teacher beliefs affect teaching, how teachers' past experiences affect teaching, and how small classes affect student learning.

Chapter 2 contains new sections on how parents can help their children succeed in school, steps to good teacher-family partnerships, children home alone, and how children spend their time.

Chapter 3 contains a new section on sexual preference differences, a new case study of a mainstreamed child, and guidelines for a good individualized education plan.

Chapter 4 has an added section illustrating reciprocal teaching.

Chapter 5 has added sections on motivating students to learn, research on motivating reluctant learners, and how to write anecdotal comments in student records.

Chapter 6 contains new sections on Chicago's provision of lesson plans for teachers, Sternberg's way of classifying educational objectives, how to evaluate a lesson plan, and resources useful when planning instruction.

Chapter 7 has illustrative lesson plans for the four instructional alternatives presented therein and added sections on how instructional variety matters, how student teachers want to learn about using classroom discussion, research on homework, a case study on how teachers individualize instruction, and a section on using technology in teaching.

Chapter 8 also has illustrative lesson plans for the four instructional alternatives presented therein and new sections on constructivist teaching and learning and how teachers use DISTAR.

Chapter 9 contains a new section on types of scores from standardized tests, enhanced coverage of authentic assessment, a new section on portfolio assessment, and

1 line short

substantially more information on teacher-developed classroom assessment methods.

Chapter 10 contains a new section on using portfolios to develop reflective activities.

Chapter 11 continues to focus on teacher characteristics that help students feel more comfortable and confident in the classroom, drawing on recent research and ideas that emphasize teacher attributes that are effective in today's diverse classrooms.

Chapter 12 remains committed to the importance of the teacher in helping students make optimal progress in the classroom. Revisions include a greater emphasis on student-directed classroom situations and teacher behavior associated with facilitating rather than directing student learning.

Chapter 13 contains new information on developing classroom rules, building prosocial behavior, managing technology in the classroom, handling aggressive students, and the dangers of overpraising students. More applications to secondary school students are made throughout the chapter.

Chapter 14's title has been changed to Challenges Classroom Teachers Face and new sections include preventing and resolving parent-teacher differences and research on how class size relates to teacher problems.

Text Supplements

New and vastly improved supplemental materials accompany the third edition. Contact your McGraw-Hill sales representative for more information.

A new **online learning center website** at *http://www.mhhe.com/cruickshank* features multiple valuable, book-specific resources for both instructors and students. For instructors, the site features teaching and presentation resources, links to professional websites and forms for field use. For students, the site features numerous study and research tools including chapter outlines, chapter quizzes, online vocabulary activities, links to lesson plans, case studies, video clips, and much more!

The **Instructor's Manual and Test Bank** have been updated and improved. The Manual contains a rationale for each text chapter, chapter objectives, a detailed chapter outline (summary), key concepts, additional teaching and learning activities, additional resources (both print and visual), and selected transparency masters. The Test Bank contains numerous multiple choice, vocabulary, and essay questions from which to choose.

A new **Diploma © dual-platform CD-ROM Test Bank** features a test generator, an online testing program, Internet testing, and grade management systems.

Each copy of the text is packaged with a free **PowerWeb** password, allowing students access to a wide array of online education resources including study tips with self-quizzes, links to related sites for the course, current readings from annual editions, weekly updates, current news, a Web research guide, and access to 6,300 premium sources via Northern Light.

Using **PageOut**, you can create your own course website! Simply plug your course information into a template and click on one of sixteen designs, and you can create your own professional-looking website. Powerful features include an interactive course syllabus that lets you post content and links, an online gradebook, lecture notes, bookmarks, and even a discussion board where students can discuss course-related topics.

Donald R. Cruickshank
Deborah Bainer Jenkins
Kim K. Metcalf

How to Use This Text Well

Please take sufficient time to become acquainted with this book. The following approach may be helpful:

1. Turn to the **Contents in Brief** on page vii. Note that the text contains four parts. **Part One, The Backdrop of Teaching,** permits you to better know yourself and to find out what is known about human learning. **Part Two, The Act of Teaching,** focuses on functions competent teachers must perform: instructional planning, instruction, assessment, and reflection. **Part Three, The Effective Teacher,** looks at the personal attributes and professional abilities that competent teachers need, including classroom management skills. Finally, **Part Four,** the **Practice Teaching Manual,** contains activities intended to increase selected classroom skills, your ability to reflect and learn from your teaching experiences, and your ability to be a better classroom problem solver. The text also contains a **glossary** and **indexes** (both subject and author).

2. Turn to the next page, **Contents in Detail.** Now you can see precisely what content is found in each chapter and in the Practice Teaching Manual.

3. Select and turn to any of the first several chapters to see how one is set up.

Note that in the side margins there are questions we refer to as **reflective questions.** These questions are intended to prompt you to consider your personal experiences and knowledge. There are no "correct" answers to them. You and your peers should find them provocative, and they should generate considerable class discussion of that section of the chapter, if time permits.

Next, note the figures, tables, cases, "Spotlight on Research" and "Highlight" sections. They serve to reinforce, summarize, or add new information. Occasionally you will see a cartoon that we think illustrates something text related.

At the end of each chapter is a **Chapter Summary** followed by **Issues and Problems for Discussion, Theory into Action Activities** and **References.**

Issues and Problems for Discussion contains questions for class debate or classroom problems that classroom teachers supplied. You should find many of these issues and problems challenging and thought-provoking.

Theory into Action Activities are critical and will help you to put what you have just learned into practice.

We suggest that before reading each chapter you go through it, reviewing all these elements, *but this time read the reflective questions, the chapter summary, issues and problems, and theory into action activities.* Doing these things will prepare you for the material ahead.

The Backdrop of Teaching

PART ONE

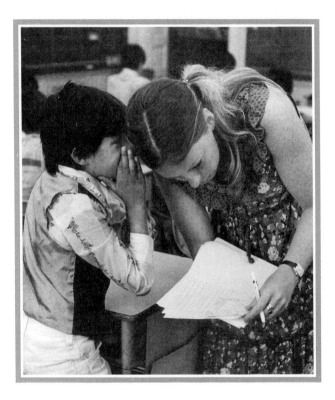

The five Backdrop of Teaching chapters will help you better know and understand yourself, your students, and the way you and they learn. In Chapter 1, Factors That Influence How We Teach, you will learn how your personal characteristics, previous experiences in schools, and the setting you will work in influence how you will teach. In Chapter 2, The Challenge of Teaching in a Changing Society, you will find out how societal changes are affecting America's population, families, children and youth, and schools. Chapter 3, Teaching Diverse Students, will help you understand many of the important ways students differ from one another. Chapter 4, Three Schools of Thought about Learning and Teaching, will enable you to understand several prominent theories about the way humans learn and about the values and uses these theories have for teachers. Finally, Chapter 5, Getting to Know Your Students and Motivating Them to Learn, will tell you how to find out about your students and encourage them to learn.

Factors That Influence How We Teach

Contents

Personal Characteristics

Experience and Preparation in Education

Context

Would you believe you have been a student in elementary, secondary, and university classrooms for over 15,000 hours? During that time, you have observed all kinds of teachers. Have you ever wondered how they became the way they are? Have you questioned why they teach the way they do? Have you thought about what kind of teacher you will be? In this chapter we will consider three sets of factors that have influenced your teachers and likely will affect your teaching as well (see Figure 1.1).

One set consists of your *personal characteristics*, such as gender, age, experience, personality, and beliefs. A second set consists of your *experience and preparation in education*. This set includes how you have been taught, how you prefer to be taught, how you prefer to teach, your knowledge of subject matter, and your teaching or pedagogical preparation. A final set of factors affecting teaching derives from the *context*, or setting, in which you teach. Context is determined by the kinds of pupils you have, class personality and size, availability of instructional equipment and material, time available for instruction, the nature of your lesson, and the dominant or prevailing views about the best way to teach.

Personal Characteristics

To a large extent, your personal characteristics dictate what you will be like as a teacher. These characteristics, mentioned in the previous paragraph and illustrated in Figure 1.2, include gender, age, experience, personality, and beliefs.

FIGURE 1.1   Factors That Influence How We Teach

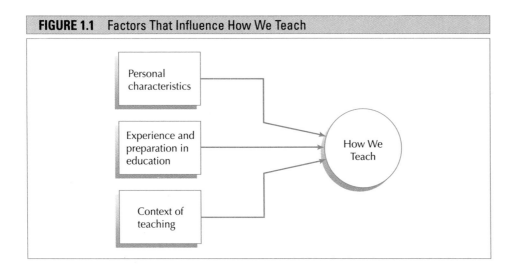

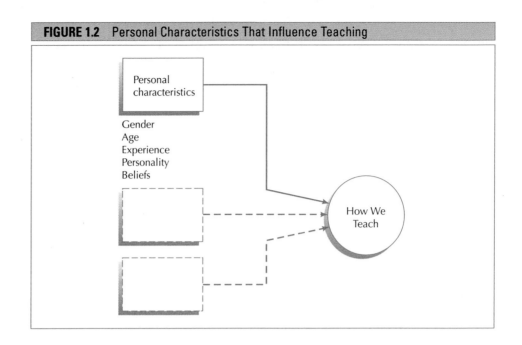

FIGURE 1.2 Personal Characteristics That Influence Teaching

Personal characteristics

Gender
Age
Experience
Personality
Beliefs

How We Teach

HOW GENDER INFLUENCES OUR TEACHING

A number of studies have been conducted to determine whether male and female teachers differ in terms of their classroom styles (Dunkin, 1987; Weiner, 1995). Although the results are inconclusive, male teachers appear to be more dominant and authoritarian than female teachers. Relatedly, their classrooms are more organized and teacher controlled. Conversely, female teachers more often appear to maintain "warmer" classrooms and they seem to be more tolerant of misbehavior. Furthermore, some investigators have reported that in classrooms with female teachers, students are more likely to initiate a question or statement, give more incorrect answers, and take risks by guessing answers. Female teachers, more than males, also seem to use praise more frequently and are more likely to provide the correct answer when students can't or don't.

Dunkin concludes that, on balance, female teachers' classrooms more often are warmer and more nurturing, while male teachers' classrooms are better organized and more task oriented. Coulter (1987) reports similarly on gender differences. He finds that female student teachers are more "tender-minded and pupil supportive and less authoritative than males." Moreover, he notes that these gender differences are more prominent among secondary than elementary student teachers (p. 591).

Kalaian and Freeman (1994) find female secondary education majors are more optimistic that their professional preparation will make them better teachers, more likely to use student-centered instruction, more likely to accept responsibility for teaching exceptional students, and more likely to have realistic expectations regarding teaching. Conversely, they are less confident in themselves as teachers, which may account for their more realistic expectations. Gender differences likely exist among your university professors too.

Now that we have seen some ways that *teacher* gender influences teaching, let's turn to a related question. How does *student* gender influence our beliefs and the way we interact with learners? Weiner (1995) reports that both male and female teachers pay more attention to boys, perceive that boys demonstrate more initiative and a greater capacity for independent learning, are more likely to chastise and criticize them, and hold boys to higher intellectual standards. He also notes that they hold lower expectations for girls and are more likely to reward them for good

1.1 Have your teachers shown any of the gender-related behaviors reported in research?

1.2 How do you think gender may influence your teaching?

behavior and tidiness. Hyun & Tyler (1999) tell us that female teachers of younger children consider boys more active, loud, and aggressive and perceive them as less teachable and more difficult to work with. Additionally, they find that female teachers describe girls as quiet, talkative, and sensitive.

HOW AGE AND EXPERIENCE INFLUENCE OUR TEACHING

Several studies have focused on how our age and experience seem to influence our teaching and students' perceptions of it. After reviewing studies of the effect of teacher age and experience on teaching, Barnes (1987) reports that teachers are perceived as being better at teaching during the first few years, leveling off, and then declining somewhat. However, a study by Martin & Smith (1990) suggests that middle-aged teachers are perceived by students as being more effective.

Barnes also reports that beginning teachers have a tendency to accept innovations and change more easily, although she cautions that ready acceptance may simply be a signal that newer teachers are less discriminating—everything looks good until you try it.

Fuller and Bown (1975) find beginning teachers more controlling and authoritarian, probably as the result of several factors. First, teacher educators, mentor teachers, and school principals often counsel novice teachers to be strict—"don't smile until Winter break." Second, novice teachers may well be a bit in awe in their first classroom and don't want to lose control. Finally and unfortunately, new teachers often are given very demanding assignments and are likely to "confront students who have less academic interest and a tendency to misbehave" (Kagen, 1992, p. 145).

Several investigators note that younger, less experienced teachers are more concerned with personal and social dimensions of teaching than with academics. They tend to work hard to develop a unique teaching identity and pay more attention to student interests than to involving them in instruction and monitoring their achievement (Artiles, Mostert, & Tankersley, 1994; Housner & Griffey, 1985; Szpiczka, 1990).

Coulter (1987) and Cruickshank (1990) find that many confident beginning student teachers lose a measure of self-assurance when they confront classroom life. This is to be expected when novice idealism meets reality.

HOW PERSONALITY AFFECTS OUR TEACHING

We use the term *personality* to mean the totality of character and behavioral traits peculiar to an individual. No two persons are alike in this respect, not even identical twins. Naturally, what we are like, our personality, affects everything we do, including our teaching.

Suppose that you are a warm person, sensitive, emotionally stable, enthusiastic, willing to take risks, persevering, curious, open to experiences, and tolerant of ambiguity. You have broad interests and value originality. How might each of these characteristics and behavioral traits influence your teaching behavior and your relationships with learners? How might the absence of these things play out in a classroom?

Our personality needs may be particularly influential when it comes to deciding how we will teach a particular lesson or lessons. For example, if we feel the need to dominate, we may choose ways of teaching that put us front and center, such as presenting or lecturing. If affiliation is our goal, then we may be prone to use discussions or discovery.

Several research findings relate to teacher personality. Coulter (1987) reports that education majors place more value on and have a stronger commitment to people and personal relationships than noneducation students do. Morrison and McIntyre (1973) report similarly that teachers are more people oriented than persons in most other occupational groups. Both the Coulter and the Morrison and McIntyre studies note that teachers correspondingly place less value than others on

1.3 Do you think it is better to begin teaching being strict or lenient?

1.4 What differences have you seen between novice and experienced teachers?

"Mirror, mirror, on the wall, who's the most sensitive, open, student-centered, and innovative teacher of all?"

economic success. As human service professionals, teachers seem to be more interested in establishing and maintaining helping relationships than in their level of income (Powell, 1992).

Coulter also found that education students, when compared with experienced teachers, are more liberal, idealistic, and supportive of K–12 students. As with self-confidence, however, these personal dispositions diminish for some students as they engage in field experiences such as student teaching. Once again, the shock of actual classroom experience probably accounts for this attitudinal change. Although disconcerting, reality shock probably occurs in every profession—a fact we should keep in mind.

Pigge and Marso (1987) find several things related to the attitudes of prospective teachers. They note that elementary education majors and students who make an early commitment to become teachers seem to share generally positive attitudes toward teaching. On the downside, Pigge and Marso find that education majors are anxious about such things as finding teaching satisfying, convincing pupils to follow directions, preparing lessons, and being able to control a class. Other concerns are that they will lack sufficient instructional materials and be unable to meet the needs of different pupils, a problem we will discuss in the next chapter.

HOW OUR BELIEFS AFFECT OUR TEACHING

Teachers hold a variety of beliefs about such things as their students, their subject matter, and teaching itself. Some beliefs may be well-founded. However, others are the result of personal bias, misconceptions, or untruths.

Since what we believe strongly influences our behavior in general and our teaching behavior in particular, many studies of teacher beliefs have been conducted. Some attempt to find out what teachers do believe. Others look for the relationship between what they believe and how they teach. Still others examine the extent to which teacher beliefs can be changed.

What are some teacher beliefs? Block & Hazelip (1995) report these: High-ability students pose fewer behavioral and intellectual demands; students should be organized homogeneously (i.e. students of like ability taught together); good learners can learn more complex and abstract ideas; different curriculum should be provided for good and poor learners; given more time and help, slower learners can learn as much as faster learners. Biehler and Snowman (2000) report these teacher beliefs: attractive children are brighter, more capable, and more sociable; girls' behavior is preferable to boys; and majority students can do better than minority students. Li (1999) finds that both male and female teachers tend to believe that math is a male subject, have higher expectations for boys in math, and overrate boys' math capability. Solomon (1996) states that compared with teachers in suburban communities, teachers in poorer communities tend to believe their school's climate is less positive and stimulating. They also are less trusting of students and more skeptical of their abilities.

Whether or not these beliefs are true, studies that look at the relationship between what teachers believe and do report that teachers tend to act on them. Teachers who believe students *can* learn teach more content and insist on higher student performance, and the reverse is also true (Ormrod, 1995). Teachers who hold some of the beliefs listed above put more emphasis on authority and control and provide less engaging kinds of classroom activities. Obviously, such beliefs can form immense obstacles to student learning and achievement.

Unfortunately, teacher beliefs are resistant to change even when attempts are made to clear up misconceptions or to counter negative beliefs that may, in fact, hold true (Nettle, 1998).

Obviously, you need to be aware of your beliefs about students, teaching, and learning and what effect they may have on your teaching and on student learning.

1.5 Are you surprised, encouraged, or disappointed by the findings regarding personality characteristics of teachers?

1.6 How do you think your personality may affect your teaching? What positive traits do you have? What negative traits must you overcome?

1.7 What beliefs about students, teaching, and learning do you hold that may have either a positive or negative influence on your teaching?

Experience and Preparation in Education

A second set of factors influencing how you will teach are your educational experiences. Those experiences include the way you were taught, your preferred ways of learning, your preferred ways of teaching, your proficiency in your chosen teaching or academic field, and the kind and amount of teaching preparation you are receiving (see Figure 1.3).

HOW THE WAY WE WERE TAUGHT AFFECTS OUR TEACHING

If it is true that "you teach as you were taught," then your teaching will model the teaching of your mentors, most of whom you encountered in K–12 schools. A number of investigators have observed K–12 teachers, and they have identified two dominant styles of teaching: direct and indirect. **Direct teaching,** also referred to as **expository teaching,** occurs when teachers dominate by presenting information to students, giving students directions, and using criticism (Dunkin & Biddle, 1982, p. 113). By definition, direct teaching is associated with a teacher-centered or teacher-controlled classroom in which the teacher decides what, when, and how to teach. Teachers with a direct style tend to (1) set definite academic goals, (2) use structured, sequential learning materials, (3) prescribe what students will do and how they will do it, (4) monitor and check student progress toward the goals and provide them with corrective feedback, and (5) allow sufficient time to learn the prescribed materials. Although direct teaching may sound cold and impersonal, it need not be. You may recall teachers who were direct but sometimes creative, stimulating, and humorous, too.

You have also witnessed **indirect** teaching, used by teachers who prefer to draw things out of their students. For example, these teachers may provide students with an experience or a block of information and then help them develop their own conclusions from it. A teacher with a direct style might present information about the worldwide refugee problem, encourage students to discuss the information, and then evaluate the solutions currently used. On the other hand, a teacher with an indirect style might ask students to find out about the worldwide refugee problem

 1.8 Have you mostly been exposed to direct or indirect teaching? Which style do you prefer, and why?

FIGURE 1.3 Educational Experiences That Influence Teaching

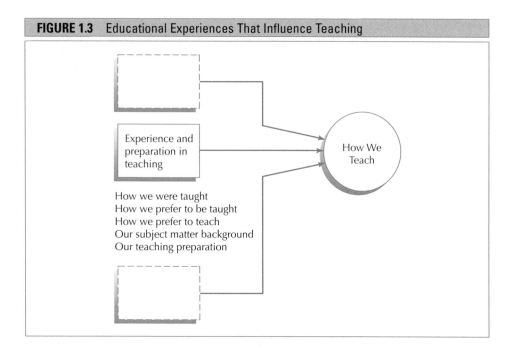

Experience and preparation in teaching

How we were taught
How we prefer to be taught
How we prefer to teach
Our subject matter background
Our teaching preparation

How We Teach

and to present additional suggestions regarding its resolution. Teachers with an indirect style seem to be aware of and to make the most of student diversity; they also tend to be more democratic and flexible (Dunkin & Biddle, 1982, pp. 97–98). Teachers with an indirect style (1) set general rather than specific goals, (2) use more, and more varied, learning materials, (3) may set a task to be accomplished but permit students to decide how to do it, (4) serve as facilitators or mentors when students need help, and (5) provide sufficient time to accomplish the task and to consider its merit.

You will learn more about direct and indirect teaching in Chapter 4, Three Schools of Thought about Learning and Teaching.

The way you will be inclined to teach depends in part on the teaching styles to which you have been exposed. Yes, experience teaches.

HOW THE WAY WE PREFER TO LEARN AFFECTS OUR TEACHING

1.9 Can you describe a teacher who taught in a way compatible with your learning style?

1.10 How do you *not* wish to be taught?

You no doubt recall some favorite teachers. You liked them for various reasons. For one thing, the way they instructed you probably made it easier for you to learn. They taught you in the way you preferred. For example, if you are visually oriented and like to read, they may have assigned a lot of reading. Or, if you are socially oriented and learn best by interacting with others, they may have given lots of group work. Said another way, your "best" teachers probably taught to your preferred learning style. Thus, it is likely that your future teaching will reflect both your own learning style and that of your past teachers. Of course, that could be problematic for your students whose learning styles may differ from yours. Little, however, has been recorded about how teachers as a group prefer to be taught. Skipper (1985) studied the preferences of education students and reports that elementary majors like to learn in a group, do not like individual oral presentations, like classes that are well organized, and believe the most important goal is the development of independent learners. Learning style is discussed further in Chapter 3.

HOW THE WAY WE PREFER TO TEACH INFLUENCES OUR TEACHING

As we have mentioned, your teaching preferences are probably influenced by how you enjoy being taught. For example, those of you who learn best from direct or expository teaching may consciously or unconsciously conclude that your students share your preference. Of course, as you will learn in Chapters 2 and 3, classrooms contain students of great diversity, including diverse learning styles. The question becomes whom to please: you, the students, or both?

1.11 What will your preferred teaching style be like?

1.12 What do you think of Zahorik's views?

Zahorik (1990) believes that each education major has a preferred way of teaching and that teacher educators should help you to determine your favored style and to become more effective with it. Thus, rather than help you acquire a varied repertoire of teaching skills and strategies, we should instruct you only in the ones you like best. Zahorik feels that to determine your preference, we need to discover your beliefs about education and teaching. Then we can determine which ways of teaching most closely support these beliefs.

To discover your beliefs about education and teaching, Zahorik would have you consider the following questions: (1) What do you believe about students? (2) What do you believe is the function knowledge should serve? (3) What is the role of a teacher in the classroom? And, consequently, (4) Which way of teaching seems most compatible with your present views?

HOW OUR KNOWLEDGE OF SUBJECT MATTER AFFECTS OUR TEACHING

It seems reasonable that we need extensive knowledge of the subjects we will teach. However, having substantial subject or content knowledge alone does not ensure good teaching or student learning. If it did teachers with the most advanced knowledge in their fields would have students who learn the most. Contrary to that expectation, studies of teacher subject or content knowledge have failed to find such a relationship. Yes, all of us have had teachers who knew their subject well but didn't or couldn't help us learn it.

However, Grossman (1995) suggests that teacher content knowledge affects both what and how we teach. For example, when deciding what to teach, we are more likely to give greater coverage to areas in which we are more knowledgeable and to skip or downplay areas about which we know less. (Many states require so many hours of instruction in certain subjects partly to ensure that they actually get taught.) Additionally, if we are content secure teachers, we are more likely to ask students more critical and challenging questions.

We presume that knowledge of our subject has other benefits too. It may enable us to create more interest in and enthusiasm for what we teach, show students how knowledge in the subject is developed (for example, what scientists do), show the relationship of that subject to others (for example, the relationship of mathematics to science), use both direct and indirect teaching, and function as a resource for learners. Additionally, knowledgeable teachers are less dependent upon textbooks and more aware of other learning resources.

1.13 To what extent are you master of the subjects you will teach? How can you increase your mastery?

HOW OUR TEACHING PREPARATION INFLUENCES OUR TEACHING

Another contributor to the way you will teach is the quality of the teaching or **pedagogical** preparation you are receiving. Professional education for teaching includes study of both the parent disciplines of education—such as psychology, philosophy, and sociology—and their offspring, the applied fields of educational psychology and sociology, child and adolescent development, and pedagogy (the way we plan and deliver instruction and evaluate learning). The extent and quality of the professional preparation you receive will influence both the quality and the style of your teaching. The more knowledge and skill you have in planning and delivering instruction and evaluating learning, the better your students should learn. Persons without sufficient pedagogical or teaching knowledge are forced to teach by instinct and are doomed to trial-and-error approaches. As noted earlier, Kagan (1992) finds that novice teachers, with little knowledge of pupils and teaching, "tend to grow increasingly authoritarian and custodial. Obsessed with classroom control, they may also begin to plan instruction designed not to promote learning, but to discourage children's misbehavior" (p. 145).

Although knowledge of and skill in teaching are critical to success, you also need positive attitudes toward teaching, schools, and students, attitudes that university and K–12 school personnel need to foster and reinforce (Cole & Knowles, 1993).

Student teachers and graduates of colleges of education are often distinguishable as a result of the teacher preparation they have received. It is not uncommon for public and private schools to favor student teachers or graduates from a particular university because they feel these persons are better prepared and that they will have a more positive, immediate impact on students.

1.14 Recall effective and ineffective teachers you have had. How did they differ with respect to knowledge of child development, knowledge of how to teach, or knowledge of how we learn?

Context

The final set of factors influencing you as a teacher encompass the context of your workplace. Several ingredients will affect your workplace and, consequently, the way you will teach: (1) the number and kinds of learners you have, (2) class and classroom size, (3) the availability of instructional materials and equipment, (4) time, (5) the nature of the lessons you must teach, and (6) national educational imperatives (see Figure 1.4).

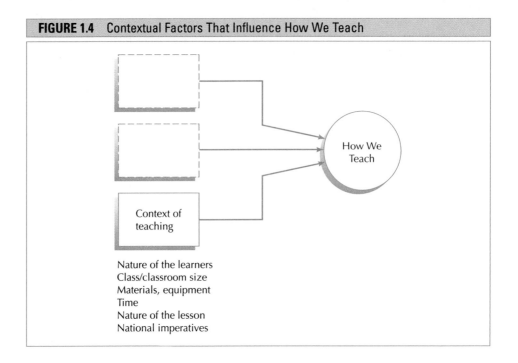

FIGURE 1.4 Contextual Factors That Influence How We Teach

How We Teach

Context of teaching

Nature of the learners
Class/classroom size
Materials, equipment
Time
Nature of the lesson
National imperatives

HOW STUDENT DIFFERENCES AFFECT OUR TEACHING

In Chapters 2 and 3 you will be reminded that student variability is a fact of life in all schools and classrooms. You as a teacher must recognize that diversity—whether economic, cultural, gender, developmental, or other—and take it into account.

Since you will have little, if any, control over the nature of the pupils placed in your care, you are well advised to discover who they are and accept them as they are. Unhappily, newer teachers are more likely to have difficulty recognizing and responding to student variability. They are more apt to see or to want to see the class as an entity, a whole—to view it as more homogeneous than it actually is (Cruickshank & Callahan, 1983). To novice teachers the class seems to have a single face rather than many faces. However, as you study child development and gain teaching experience, you are more likely to see, accept, and provide for differences among learners. At that point, individual learners will clearly have an impact on your instructional planning and on how you will teach.

Case 1.1, written by a first-year teacher, demonstrates that many teachers do accept students as they are and can learn from them.

HOW CLASS AND CLASSROOM SIZE AFFECT OUR TEACHING

Imagine yourself teaching a large number of students, perhaps forty or more, as is normal in many classrooms throughout the world. Class size, to some extent, dictates how you will teach. In such a crowded, complex environment it is more likely, all things being equal, that you may choose to teach the class as a whole and that you may use direct or expository teaching. Conversely, having fewer learners and teaching in a less complex environment permit more teacher–student interaction. Smaller classes, therefore, are more likely to be characterized by individual and small-group instruction. (However, the nature of learners within a class, regardless of size, also weighs on how you will teach. For example, a large or small class of achievement-oriented learners allows you multiple teaching options. Conversely, a large or small class of disengaged students limits your teaching options.)

Class size also seems to have a bearing on how well students learn. Generally, research on class size supports smaller classes (Bracey, 1999). Glass (1987) notes that "the relationship of class size to pupil achievement is remarkably strong. Large

1.15 What do you suppose it would be like to teach children of lower as opposed to higher socioeconomic status (SES); girls as opposed to boys; a child with a hearing impairment; a child with learning disabilities; Desmond from Case 1.1?

CASE 1.1
A Letter to Desmond

Dear Desmond,

Now that you are a young adult out in the world, you may not remember your first-grade teacher, but I remember you. I remember your blonde hair, big brown eyes, and freckles just as clearly as if you were standing here now. You were so tall and I can still see you looking down the row of heads in front of you after I'd sent you to the back of the line for something you swore you hadn't done. I remember your smiles, your tears, your fists, your heavy boots, and your angry, unhappy words.

You probably didn't know that I was a first-year teacher and that I had never experienced anyone like you before. Maybe you did know. I didn't know that working with you that year would become one of the most memorable experiences of my career. I didn't know that there were so many of you, at least one every year.

Do you remember greeting us each morning by throwing your books on the floor after finally making your way to your desk? Do you remember the range of responses that drew from me? Every day was a new challenge. I'd go home at night, often in tears, and plan my strategy for the next morning's book slam. One day, I'd be stern and take away

some privilege, and then the next day I'd try ignoring you. The day after that you might have been praised for not slamming the books as loudly as before. I'm sure it was great fun for you to try and guess what was coming next. However, I was determined to keep trying and, admittedly, I spent a lot more time trying to figure you out than I did making bulletin boards that year.

Maybe some of the other events of the year are starting to come back to you now. There were so many, and I know that I learned much, much more from them than you did. The one experience that stands out above all the rest was the day you shut yourself in the locker and you couldn't get out.

The class was coming in from recess in their usual noisy way. I remember watching the other classes walking in fairly quiet, straight lines and thinking how we really *should* work on this line stuff some. As most of the class sat down, we heard four muffled, high-pitched shrieks coming from the hall. The shrieks quickly turned into screams and by then I realized what had happened. I tried to get your locker open, but part of your coat was jammed in the door and I couldn't get the door to budge. I yelled for the custodian to

please help me and possibly remove the door. I noticed his sense of urgency subsided when he heard it was you in the locker. Remember how mad he was when you started the "How High Can You Shoot?" contest in the boys' restroom? Then, after a few long moments, you were out. When the door finally opened, you ran out and came straight for me and I hugged you easily. I felt you shaking, and for the first time I saw you as a child and not as the reason I was having doubts about my being a teacher.

So every year as I deal with others like you, I remember the locker. I remember learning that no matter how tough we act, we are *all* afraid of something. I also learned that this awareness of fear doesn't give me the right to hold it over your head but, rather, to keep your actions in perspective. I have since tried harder to find out why children do what they do instead of just dealing with their behavior afterward.

I hope you were lucky enough to have some teachers along the way that had learned these things before you came along. Thank you for teaching me.

Source: Kathy Tatham, Searforce Elementary School, Johnstown, Ohio

---

reductions in class size [by a third to a half] promise learning benefits of a magnitude commonly believed not to be within the power of teachers to achieve" (p. 544).

According to Robinson and Wittebols (1986), Finn and Voekl (1995), and Wenglinsky (1997), you are particularly likely to be successful when teaching reading and arithmetic in the early grades if class size is small; Finn and Voekl suggest thirteen to seventeen pupils. Robinson and Wittebols also report that small class size works well with students of lower academic ability.

In summary, what do we know and not know about the affect of class size on teaching and learning? We know that class size affects the way teachers teach. We also know that the way they teach small classes contributes to improved student learning. What we very much need to know is, what do teachers in small classes do that results in greater learner achievement?

A number of Internet sites focus on class size. They can be accessed at <http://ericir.syr.edu/cgi-bin/print.cgi/Resources/Educational_Levels/K-12_Education/Grouping/Class_Size.html>

1.16 How has class size affected teaching and learning in your experience? Has it impacted your learning?

Web Resource

A study conducted in Tennessee (Project Star) found substantial advantages for K–3 children in smaller classes (thirteen to seventeen students). Specifically, on average, they performed better on all tests of academic achievement. A follow-up study was done to see whether the benefit of having been in smaller classes carried over into later grades. Findings include that, on average, students who attended small K–3 classes for only one year performed no better in grades 4, 6, or 8 than students who had attended larger classes; students who attended for two years performed a bit better; and students who were in small classes for three years showed important carryover effects in the later grades (Finn, Gerber, Achilles, & Boyd-Zaharias, 2001).

California accepted that class size affects student learning and reduced primary classes from an average of 30 to 20 students. Evaluations confirm that students enrolled in those smaller classes perform slightly better than students in larger ones. Additionally, teachers say they spend more time teaching and less time disciplining (Strecher, Bohrnstedt, Kirst, McRobbie, & Williams, 2001).

The physical size of your classroom also has an impact on your teaching. The availability of space in a room permits you many more instructional options than does a crowded environment. A larger room also provides everyone more private space. It should be said that dedicated professionals find ways to be effective despite any restrictions imposed by class or classroom size.

HOW AVAILABILITY OF MATERIAL AND EQUIPMENT AFFECT OUR TEACHING

1.17 What educational resources will you likely need to be the best you can be?

Teachers are limited when there are insufficient resources. A well-stocked "larder," in your case the classroom, provides greater potential for instruction. A visit to so-called developing countries reveals that teachers without adequate educational materials, even textbooks, are severely limited in how or what they can teach. For example, Masai children of eastern Africa are mostly taught by educated tribesmen who have few if any resources to draw upon. In such countries and in poorer areas in America, students share desks and books, and have little paper and no audiovisual equipment. Compare this to other American classrooms where nearly every educational resource is available—multiple textbooks, reference materials, television, and computers. Thus, teachers in a poorer school often lecture out of necessity. By contrast, teachers in a wealthy school may choose to lecture but can employ other instructional alternatives.

"They meet in there. Some kind of support group."

HOW AVAILABLE TIME AFFECTS OUR TEACHING

There are limits to the amount of instructional time available to teachers. Therefore, time, or lack of it, has a real impact on how you will teach. If you have more time, you can employ more indirect learning strategies such as experimentation and discussion. When time is short, you may have to be more direct, telling learners what they need to know through lecture, since that is a reasonably efficient way of presenting large amounts of information in a short amount of time. Of course, the burden often is on the learner to process, understand, and remember it.

You must never forget that *how* you use instructional time is extremely important. An hour of instruction can be either beneficial or wasteful. If, in that hour, you can keep your students involved and engaged, they will learn (Smyth, 1987). Chapters 4, 11, and 14 provide an important perspective on time considerations.

1.18 How will you maximize the amount of time available for instruction?

HOW THE NATURE OF LESSON OBJECTIVES AFFECTS OUR TEACHING

In Chapter 6, Planning Instruction, you will discover that there are three kinds of learning outcomes: cognitive, psychomotor, and affective. Here is an example of each:

1. *Students know that 6 sevens are 42 (6 × 7 = 42).* This is a cognitive objective that primarily requires the use of mental processes.

2. *Students can hold a paint brush in order to create a particular brushstroke.* This is a psychomotor objective that primarily requires physical dexterity.

3. *Students enjoy listening to orchestral music.* This objective requires the learner to "feel" something. It is affective.

The nature of objectives will also influence the way you teach. Can you see that each kind of objective probably requires you to teach somewhat differently? For example, suppose your objective is to help students *understand* why 6 sevens are 42; you will need to use some kind of discovery or constructive experience. When you teach students how to hold and use a paint brush, demonstration seems appropriate. If you want students to enjoy orchestral music, you might rely more on listening and valuing experiences.

HOW NATIONAL IMPERATIVES AFFECT OUR TEACHING

During different periods in history, different kinds of teaching have been championed (Cruickshank & Haefele, 2001). Many of them resulted from events such as the former USSR's launching of the first spacecraft, Sputnik, in 1957. As a result of that event, the American public saw the need for U.S. students to learn more math and science to catch up with the Soviets. Consequently, programs of "new math and science" emerged. The new view required teachers to actively involve students in learning by encouraging inquiry, discovery, and problem solving through questioning, hypothesizing, experimenting, observing, and concluding. Discovery learning, or inquiry teaching as it was known then, became the instructional method of choice. (Chapter 8 will inform you about discovery learning.)

In the 1960s, due to widespread social unrest, a new national imperative emerged: to improve human relationships in general and race relationships in particular. This view required teachers to promote and celebrate diversity. Consequently, teachers were expected to engage students in activities intended to result in changes in personal attitudes and values. To accomplish this, teachers used a variety of instructional methods, including "inviting school success," "values clarification," "moral education," and "multiethnic education." (Chapter 4 will discuss humanistic approaches to teaching.)

With the arrival of the 1970s, another imperative arose, this time that schools should be accountable, that is, more productive and efficient. Here teachers were required to clearly define the goals of instruction by stating precisely what their students must know and be able to do. They also were urged to utilize learning incentives or rewards that were tied to student accomplishment. This led to rekindled interest in behavioral approaches to learning. Relatedly, teachers were expected to model the classroom behavior of effective teachers—those teachers able to raise student achievement more than other teachers working with similar students. (Chapter 6 will inform you about instructional goals, Chapter 4 about behavioral approaches to learning, and Chapters 11 and 12 about effective teachers.)

The 1980s and 1990s brought with them interest in approaches to teaching not unlike those of the 1950s—inquiry, discovery, and problem solving. This time, however, there was much less interest in "new math" and similar concepts. Rather, greater emphasis was placed on cognitive learning theory. Now teachers were expected to employ such concepts as reception learning, reciprocal teaching, discovery learning with a constructivist emphasis, and problem solving. These terms are discussed in later chapters and appear in the glossary.

What now? Things are still changing. The public has renewed its interest in accountability and many states are now requiring that students pass standardized achievement tests to attain grade promotion and eventual graduation. The effect on teachers is that they feel compelled to "teach to the test." The probable result of the perceived need to teach to the test is that teachers will be compelled to utilize more teacher-centered direct instruction and less student-centered approaches such as inquiry. (Chapter 8 describes direct instruction.)

1.19 Do your instructors seem to vary their teaching according to the learning objectives they have in mind?

1.20 How do you feel about the various results of national imperatives?

1.21 How might "teaching to the test" affect your teaching?

How do our experiences prior to entering a teacher education program influence how we think about teaching and how we teach? Powell (1992) conducted a study to find some answers. Forty-two education undergraduates participated in the study: seventeen traditional students were entering teaching as their first profession while twenty-five nontraditional students had had other jobs before deciding they wanted to teach.

On the first day of the general methods course, each completed an autobiographical questionnaire and then created a "concept map" of teaching. This means they were asked to write down and group terms that came to mind when they thought about teaching; for example, terms such as *preparation*, *motivation*, *presentation*, and *knowledge*. During the second week, participants were videotaped as they taught brief lessons to each other. Afterward, the teachers were asked to talk about why they did certain things as they taught; for example, why did they

ask particular questions of students? Thus, the teachers were asked to reflect on what they did and, more importantly, why they did it. Teachers were later interviewed to discuss their former work experience, to describe all prior nonclassroom teaching experiences, to further discuss their concept maps, and to explain the process used to plan the peer lesson. In this context, they were shown a part of their videotaped lesson and asked to recall what influenced them to do what they did.

The results of this study indicate that when we embark on a teaching career we will be influenced by the following:

- K–12 experiences and college experiences as a student; for example, the influence of prior teachers. Mark said that the way he presented his lesson was influenced by "teachers I had before."
- Teacher education; for example, Aaron said that he planned his lesson

using ideas he gained in an earlier education course.
- Beliefs and a value system; for example, Jill believed that "There is more to teaching than the student in a chair. That student is a real person with real needs."
- Personal learning style; for example, Christy used posters in her lesson and explained that "I feel more interested when I see something."
- Beliefs about students; for example, Shelly said, "Students have things to contribute to a classroom" and "the teacher needs to trust the students."

Other factors that students noted as influences on their thinking about teaching and how they taught included personal needs, prior work, nonclassroom teaching they had done (such as in church work), relatives who were educators, experience as a parent, and knowledge of the subject being taught.

Some Final Thoughts

Try Activities 1.1 and 1.2

Yes, the context in which you will work, your prior experiences in education, and your personal characteristics will influence your teaching. To the extent that you understand this, your insight into yourself and your teaching will grow. You will become more aware of who you are as a person and as a teacher and why you teach the way you do. As a consequence, your wisdom will grow, enabling you to address penetrating questions about yourself: How might my personal characteristics affect my teaching for better or worse? How might my prior experiences in education help or hinder me and my learners? How can I make the very most of my teaching situation? If you can answer these questions, you are well on your way toward becoming a reflective practitioner. Your teaching will be guided by insight rather than history, tradition, or compulsion.

CHAPTER SUMMARY

- Your personal characteristics, your experience in education, and the context in which you work influence your teaching.
- Personal characteristics that affect teaching include gender, age, experience, personality, and beliefs. Although men and women are not unlike in the way

they teach, men's classrooms seem to be more task oriented, businesslike, and organized, while women's seem to be more nurturing and accepting.

- Some teacher differences are related to age and experience. Many teachers appear to be at their zenith after a few years in classrooms. Novice teachers seem more controlling and authoritarian, perhaps because of admonitions from their university professors and teaching colleagues or perhaps because their insecurity makes students seem unruly.

- Your unique personality needs or traits affect your teaching. Because you have certain dispositions, you will teach in particular ways. At the same time, many teachers share common traits such as a commitment to others, a desire to have good relationships, and certain anxieties related to teaching success. In all cases, your traits and needs spill over into your classroom, making it unique.

- Your past experiences in education affect your teaching. The way you were taught is very important since beginning teachers often model or imitate their former teachers. Most of your teachers probably used a "direct style," so, for good or bad, you probably will tend to do so.

- Your personal learning preferences likely will cause you to presume that your students want to learn in the same way as you.

- As your knowledge of subject matter increases, so too does your confidence and competence in teaching and the likelihood that your students will learn and appreciate the subject matter you teach.

- Both the extent and quality of your professional preparation will affect your teaching. Professional knowledge and skill enable you to be wiser and more resourceful and less authoritarian and custodial.

- The context or setting in which you work will also affect your teaching. The ability to recognize and accept learner diversity and to adapt your teaching accordingly is becoming increasingly important.

- As class size increases it becomes more difficult to deal with individual students and overall class variability. Likewise, the physical size of classrooms, the availability of materials and equipment, and the instructional time available all affect the richness of any learning environment.

- Different kinds of learning objectives call for different ways of teaching and, often, for different teaching environments.

- Over the past several decades, many events have influenced prevailing approaches to teaching. During the late 1950s and early 1960s, teachers began using discovery and problem solving as instructional alternatives. During the 1960s, the emphasis shifted to teaching in ways that increased positive human interactions and tolerance, and multicultural education was born. In the 1970s teachers were expected to state teaching goals more clearly, to teach to them, and to be more accountable for pupil mastery. More recently, as a result of recent advances in cognitive learning theory, a renewed interest has arisen in discovery learning and problem solving. At the same time, increased interest in accountability and student academic achievement is affecting how we teach.

ISSUES AND PROBLEMS FOR DISCUSSION

1. Which factors influencing how we teach have a beneficial impact? Which have a negative impact?
2. How do you believe any of these factors will affect you?
3. How will you use what you have learned in this chapter to improve your teaching?

THEORY INTO ACTION ACTIVITIES

ACTIVITY 1.1: A Teaching Self-Portrait and Analysis Describe what you think you will be like as a teacher. As a teacher, I think I will be:

_____

_____

_____

Now describe how you believe some of the factors mentioned in this chapter or in other chapters may shape your teaching behavior.

ACTIVITY 1.2: Your Cooperating or Mentor Teacher's Self-Portrait If you are in a field experience, share your self-portrait with the cooperating or mentor teacher. Ask him or her to react. Perhaps your mentor would then be willing to talk about what he or she is like and the factors that seem to be influential in his or her teaching. Can you discover other factors that impact a teacher's classroom behavior?

REFERENCES

Artiles, A. J., Mostert, M. P., & Tankersley, M. (1994). Assessing the link between teacher cognitions, teacher behaviors, and pupil responses to lessons. *Teaching and Teacher Education, 10*(5), 465–481.

Barnes, J. (1987). Teaching experience. In M. J. Dunkin (Ed.), *International encyclopedia of teaching and teacher education* (pp. 608–612). Oxford: Pergamon Press.

Biehler, R., & Snowman, J. (2000). *Psychology applied to teaching.* Boston: Houghton Mifflin.

Block, J., & Hazelip, K. (1995). Teacher beliefs and belief systems. In L. Anderson (Ed.), *International Encyclopedia of Teaching and Teacher Education* (pp. 25–28). Oxford: Pergamon Press.

Bracey, G. (1999, November). Reducing class size. *Phi Beta Kappan, 81*(3), 246–247.

Cole, A., & Knowles, J. (1993). Shattered images. *Teaching and Teacher Education, 9*(516), 457–471.

Coulter, F. (1987). Affective characteristics of student teachers. In M. J. Dunkin (Ed.), *International encyclopedia of teaching and teacher education* (pp. 589–597). Oxford: Pergamon Press.

Cruickshank, D. (1990). *Research that informs teachers and teacher educators.* Bloomington, IN: Phi Delta Kappa.

Cruickshank, D., & Callahan, R. (1983). The other side of the desk: Stages and problems of teacher development. *The Elementary School Journal, 83*(3), 251–258.

Cruickshank, D., & Haefele, D. (2001, February). *Good teachers, plural! Educational Leadership, 58*(5), 26–30.

Dunkin, M. J. (1987). Teacher's sex. In M. J. Dunkin (Ed.), *International encyclopedia of teaching and teacher education* (pp. 606–608). Oxford: Pergamon Press.

Dunkin, M. J., & Biddle, B. J. (1982). *The study of teaching.* Washington, DC: University Press of America.

Finn, J. D., & Voekl, K. E. (1995). Class size. In L. Anderson (Ed.), *International encyclopedia of teaching and teacher education.* Second Edition (pp. 310–315). Tarrytown, NY: Elsevier Science.

Finn, J., Gerber, S., Achilles, C., Boyd-Zaharias, J. (2001, May). The enduring effects of small classes. *Teachers College Record, 103*(2), 145–183.

Fuller, F. F., & Bown, O. H. (1975). Becoming a teacher. In K. Ryan (Ed.), *Teacher education.* 74th Yearbook of the National Society for the Study of Education, Part II (pp. 25–52). Chicago: University of Chicago Press.

Glass, G. V. (1987). Class size. In M. J. Dunkin (Ed.), *International encyclopedia of teaching and teacher education* (pp. 540–545). Oxford: Pergamon Press.

Grossman, P. (1995). Teachers' knowledge. In L. Anderson (Ed.), *International encyclopedia of teaching and teacher education*. Second Edition (pp. 21–24). Tarrytown, NY: Elsevier Science.

Housner, L., & Griffey, D. (1985). Teacher cognition. *Research Quarterly for Exercise and Sport, 56,* 45–53.

Hyun, E., & Tyler, M. (1999). *Examination of preschool teachers' biased perceptions on gender differences.* Paper presented at the Annual Conference of the American Educational Research Association in Montreal, April 19–23.

Kagan, D. M. (1992, Summer). Professional growth among preservice and beginning teachers. *Review of Educational Research, 62*(2), 129–169.

Kalaian, H., & Freeman, D. (1994). Gender differences in self-confidence and educational beliefs. *Teaching and Teacher Education, 10*(6), 647–658.

Li, Q. (1999). Teachers' beliefs and gender differences in mathematics. *Educational Research, 41*(1), 63–76.

Martin, K., & Smith, L. (1990). *Effect of teacher age and gender on student perception.* (Eric Document Reproduction Center No. ED347162).

Morrison, A., & McIntyre, D. (1973). *Teachers and teaching.* Harmondsworth, Middlesex, England: Penguin Education.

Nettle, E. (1998). Stability and change in the beliefs of student teachers during practice teaching. *Teaching and Teacher Education, 14*(2), 193–204.

Ormrod, J. (1995). *Educational Psychology.* Englewood Cliffs, NJ: Prentice Hall.

Pigge, F., & Marso, R. (1987). Relationships between student characteristics and changes in attitudes, concerns, anxieties, and confidence about teaching during teacher preparation. *Journal of Educational Research, 81*(2), 109–115.

Powell, R. R. (1992, June). The influence of prior experiences on pedagogical constructs of traditional and nontraditional preservice teachers. *Teaching and Teacher Education, 8*(3), 225–238.

Robinson, G. E., & Wittebols, J. H. (1986). *Class size research.* Arlington, VA: Educational Research Service.

Skipper, C. (1985). *Instructional methods and course goals preferred by preservice elementary and secondary teachers.* Paper presented at the annual meeting of the American Educational Research Association in Chicago, March 31–April 4 (Eric Document Reproduction Center No. ED261031).

Smyth, W. J. (1987). Time. In M. J. Dunkin (Ed.), *International encyclopedia of teaching and teacher education* (pp. 372–379). Oxford: Pergamon Press.

Solomon, D. (1996). Teacher beliefs and practices in schools serving communities that differ in socioeconomic level. *Journal of Experimental Education, 64*(4), 327–47.

Stretcher, B., Bohrnstedt, G., Kirst, M., McRobbie, J., & Williams, T. (2001, May). Class-size reduction in California. *Phi Delta Kappan, 82*(9), 670–674.

Szpiczka, N. A. (1990). Display of self. Unpublished doctoral dissertation, Syracuse University, Syracuse, NY.

Weiner, G. (1995). Gender and racial differences among students. In L. Anderson (Ed.), *International encyclopedia of teaching and teacher education*. Second Edition (pp. 319–323). Tarrytown, NY: Elsevier Science.

Wenglinsky, H. (1997). *When Money Matters.* Princeton, NJ.: Educational Testing Service.

Zahorik, J. A. (1990). Stability and flexibility in teaching. *Teaching and Teacher Education, 6*(1), 69–90.

The Challenge of Teaching in a Changing Society

Try Activity 2.1

As a teacher you need to understand certain societal changes that are affecting teaching and learning. In this chapter we look at a few: how population is changing, how the family is changing, how the nature of childhood and youth is changing, and, how school is changing. To the extent you understand these four areas of change and are able to take them into account, you should be able to improve your students' chances for success and your professional satisfaction.

America's Changing Population (U.S. Census 2000)

America's population of 281 million in 2000 continues to grow, with Hispanic and Asian minorities leading the way. Thus there are and will be more students to teach in the United States and they will be more culturally and racially diverse. At the same time, the population is graying.

MINORITY POPULATION GROWTH

America is known as a place where immigrants of different cultures and races form an integrated society while maintaining their ethnicity. Each group of immigrants brings with it different fertility and mortality rates, which keep the racial and ethnic composition of the country in flux. In 1999, the racial, ethnic composition was as follows:

White	71.9%
Black	12.1%
Hispanic	11.5%
Asian, Pacific Islander, American Indian, Alaskan Native	4.5%

However, by 2025, it is expected the composition will be:

White	62 %
Black	12.8%
Hispanic	18.2%
Asian/other	7 %

During this time span what is expected to happen? First, the percentage of whites will decline by ten percentage points. Second, Hispanics will outnumber African Americans and account for 18 percent of the population. Third, the percentage of Asian/others will increase dramatically. Fourth, one-third of Americans will be members of minority groups. Overall, Hispanics and Asians will account for over half of the U.S. population growth every year for the next fifty years (Census 2000).

MINORITY POPULATION DISTRIBUTION

Over the next 25 years, minority concentrations are expected to increase in every section of the country. However, the greatest increases will be in the South, Southwest, and West. By 2025, minorities are expected to account for 50 percent or more of the populations of four states (California, Hawaii, New Mexico, and Texas) and the District of Columbia. Additionally, the minority population of several other states (New York, Maryland, New Jersey, Alaska, and Louisiana) will exceed 40 percent (U.S. Census 2000).

OTHER NOTEWORTHY POPULATION CHANGES

Lower Percentage of Children: Higher Percentage of Senior Citizens   The number of children continues to grow, but the percentage of children in the population is declining. Presently, children constitute about 26 percent of the total population. By 2025 that percentage is expected to dip to 24. However, just as minority populations are not distributed evenly, neither is the child population. Thus, some states and parts thereof will have a greater growth in the child population while others may experience decline.

The nation is also aging. Besides minorities, the other high-growth sector is people over age 55. This group, which includes the front edge of the baby boom generation, grew at a 40 percent rate from 1990 to 2000. Not only will the baby boom generation get older; its lifespan is expected to reach new highs.

Lots of population information is available online at <http://www.census.gov/main/www/subjects.html>

Web Resource

THE IMPLICATIONS OF POPULATION CHANGES FOR TEACHERS

Population changes, fueled by increases in racial and ethnic minorities and older Americans, create challenges for you as a teacher. You will be asked to educate a generation that is more ethnically and racially diverse than any in our history. Among other things, you will be asked to teach children who have limited English proficiency. One in five of these children will live in a household headed by an immigrant. Since the majority of minority children will live in certain sectors of the country and predominantly in urban areas, you may find more job opportunities in these locales.

2.1 How well do you think you are prepared to teach minority children?

2.2 How willing are you to teach in locales needing teachers the most?

2.3 How might you "invite" senior citizens?

Soon, 20 percent of Americans will be senior citizens living on fixed incomes with no children in school. Will they maintain a commitment to education? Will they approve school bond issues so essential to running our schools and paying our teachers? You will be expected to bridge the gap between your students and seniors in your community, showing them the strengths of the schools and the value of their educational programs.

For an excellent treatment of population changes and how they will challenge education, see Olson (2000).

The Changing Family

From time immemorial, the family has been the fundamental unit responsible for the health, education, and general well-being of children: indeed, the family has been the central organizing principle of societies everywhere. In the United States, the structure and function of families have undergone profound changes in the last 30 years (Hamburg, 1995). Let's look at some of them.

"Kim, this is Eddie. He only has one set of parents!"

FAMILY TRENDS

Since family is important in the lives of youths, it is useful to know something of what is happening with American families today. To begin with, they are smaller because women are bearing fewer children, and consequently children have fewer siblings. Second, parents tend to be older because more marriages occur later in life.

Third, family styles are changing. For example, there are fewer traditional families consisting of a working father, homemaker mother, and children and more single-parent families (Center for the Study of Social Policy, 1992). Some of the diversity in family styles is attributable to both parents working (thus no homemaker parent), but most is due to the approximately 50 percent divorce rate. As a result of divorce, the percentage of children living with two parents has declined to the point that over one-fourth of American families are now headed by a single parent. Two-fifths of white and three-fifths of African-American children will experience yet a second divorce, and divorce is associated with reduced school achievement and school completion and an increase in early sexual activity, childbearing, and marriage. The high divorce rate means that 30–40 percent of all marriages are remarriages, which often create blended families ("his, hers, and theirs"). Two-parent families do seem to be staging a modest comeback. Reports indicate that the proportion of children living with two married parents (including stepparents) remained constant during the late 1990s. Perhaps more importantly, the proportion of poor kids living with a single mother declined (Dionne, 2001). Other family styles, including single-adoptive (a single person adopting one or more children), are growing in number. Another growing phenomenon is grandparents raising grandchildren.

Hacker (1982) and Popenoe (1993) attribute a changing attitude toward the traditional family to our unwillingness to accept its obligations and constraints. Signs supporting this contention include our reluctance to remain in a less-than-ideal marriage and to invest time, money, and energy in family life. However, others maintain that the movement toward alternative family styles merely shows our acceptance of varying lifestyles (Suransky, 1982) and the shift of women into the paid labor market (Fraser, 1989).

2.4 How do you think the changes in families are affecting children and teachers?

The American Family: An Endangered Species?

The National Broadcasting Company (NBC) produced a ten-part film series with this thought-provoking title. Several of the portrayals follow.

The Edholms: Blended Family
(9 minutes, 16 mm, color)

Visits the home of Marg Van Horn and Chuck Edholm, who were both divorced and later married each other. Depicts the Edholms' new blended family, with five children from their previous marriages. Reviews the problems those children perceive and the problems the stepparents perceive. Family members discuss feelings of resentment, sibling rivalry, and jealousy but overall willingness to make their new family work.

The Hartmans: Mother Returns to Work
(8 minutes, 16 mm, color)

Maria Hartman returns to work because her husband Bill's pay doesn't cover the expenses for their seven children. The family discusses the situation and the adjustments to the mother's new job. Maria would rather be at home and does not like working. The children would prefer their mother be at home, although they feel they are learning to be more independent.

The Kreinik and Bosworth Families: Single Adoptive Parents
(8 minutes, 16 mm, color)

Views two separate families in which single persons have adopted children. Ms. Kreinik and Mr. Bosworth discuss their unique situations, their yearning for children, and their fulfillment through adoption. Kreinik adopted two and Bosworth three—one handicapped and two from the Saigon baby lift at the close of the Vietnam War.

The Marinos: Divorcing Parents
(9 minutes, 16 mm, color)

Rick, a policeman, and wife Dianne are in a bitter custody battle for their three young children. Focuses on the anger and pain as both parents make charges and countercharges. Both insist they are seeking custody as the best solution for their children.

Peggy Collins: Single Mother
(9 minutes, 16 mm, color)

Peggy, who married at 16, divorced after fifteen years. Her two sons live with their father and her daughter lives with her. Peggy and Linda, her daughter, reveal emotional problems the divorce has wrought.

Other films include

- *Sean's Story: Divided Custody* (12 minutes)
- *Shuster/Issacson: Lesbian Mothers* (9 minutes)
- *The Sorianos: Extended Family* (9 minutes)

2.5 What kind of family do you think is best?

Web Resource

Ultimately, the question becomes how well does each family type fulfill the traditional family functions of nurturance, caring, and intimacy; cultural transmission; and economic support? Some, including Hamburg (1992) and Fraser (1989), conclude that the transformed American family is largely unprepared to meet the challenges of raising a child and therefore calls upon government health care institutions, schools, and voluntary organizations to help. Others, such as Coontz (2000), feel that every kind of family has strengths that can be fostered and weaknesses that can be avoided. Canadian readers can learn about family trends in Canada at http://www.vifamily.ca/cft/cft.htm.

FAMILY INFLUENCE ON SCHOOLING

Most families have a substantial influence on their offspring. For example, an analysis of data collected from over 12,000 seventh through twelfth graders reveals the following:

2.6 How did your family and community affect your education and schooling?

- The more teenagers feel their parents pay attention to them, understand them, and love them, the less likely they are to have early sex, smoke, or abuse alcohol or drugs.
- The presence of parents at key times—before school, after school, and at dinner—is associated with less negative adolescent behavior of all kinds.

- Parents' expectations that teenagers get good grades and refrain from sexual activity have a powerful influence on youth regardless of family income, family type, or race (Resnick, 1997).

Other studies also report a strong relationship between family characteristics, children's behavior, and school achievement. The relationship between the **socio-economic status (SES)** of parents and their children's school achievement seems very strong. Children from higher SES families are much more likely to do better in school. They are more likely to be "advantaged" by their parents' positive experiences with and dispositions toward school and learning and also by the family's ability to provide educationally enriching opportunities, such as greater parent–child conversation that includes questioning, explaining, and positive feedback (Hart & Risley, 1999) and accoutrements such as computers, reading materials, and a place to study (Bracey, 1995; Jencks et al., 1972; U.S. DHEW, 1966; Walberg and Fowler, 1987). One way parents can help increase student academic achievement is by providing their children with rich learning experiences in the summer months. This is especially important for disadvantaged children who mostly keep up academically during the school year but fall increasingly behind more advantaged peers over each summer (Bracey, 2002). Additionally, it has been substantiated that parental involvement in schooling is related to students' better grades and greater enjoyment of school. A father's involvement seems particularly helpful while children are in grades 6 through 12 (National Center for Educational Statistics, 1997). The formula seems to be teacher effort + parent effort = greater student learning.

Whether a student is from a single- or a two-parent family also is associated with the child's achievement and behavior in school. Brown (1980) studied data comparing school achievement and school problems of over 8,000 low-income elementary and high school children of two-parent and one-parent families. He found, respectively, that 76 percent, 21 percent, and 3 percent of children lived in two-parent, one-parent, and other families. He reports that a substantially higher proportion of high achievers came from two-parent families and, conversely, that an inordinate proportion of children from one-parent families were low achievers. Further, Brown notes:

- A disproportionate number of elementary school students from one-parent homes were excessively tardy.
- Students living with one parent or a relative and students living in foster homes created a disproportionate share of elementary and secondary school discipline problems.
- Although K–12 students from one-parent and other category homes made up one-fourth of school populations, they were suspended at about twice the rate of students from two-parent homes.
- Students from one-parent homes and those living with no natural parents accounted for over half of school truancy.
- All students expelled were from one-parent families.
- One-parent and other category secondary students constituted 40 percent of the school dropouts.

Werner and Smith (1994) traced 200 high-risk Hawaiian children into adulthood. These born-into-poverty children were exposed to three risk factors: health problems at birth, parents without secondary education, and family histories of alcoholism or mental illness. Werner and Smith found that about two-thirds of these high-risk children had serious learning or behavioral problems by age 10, or delinquency records, mental health problems, or an unplanned pregnancy by their 18th birthday. However, they found delinquent children living with both parents were significantly less likely to become adult criminals. Relatedly, they discovered that those who recovered

How Parents Help Children Succeed in School

Thorkildsen and Stein (1998) reviewed studies that provide clues regarding how parents help their kids succeed in school. As a result, they offer the following suggestions, among others:

- Parents should hold high expectations for the educational success of their children and should provide them with a supportive home environment.
- Parents should reinforce education by encouraging reading, caring about what happens in school, and finding a place for their kids to study.
- Parents need strong, ongoing support from schools and teachers. This support is especially necessary for low-income parents.
- Where schools have formal parent involvement programs, parents must support them and get involved in them.

Additionally Thorkildsen and Stein find that:

- Children's academic achievement appears more strongly related to their parents' level of educational involvement than to their parents' level of education or income.
- Younger students are more influenced by parent involvement than older ones.

Source: R. Thorkildsen & M. Stein (1998, December). Is parent involvement related to student achievement? Research Bulletin. *News, Notes and Quotes. Newsletter of Phi Delta Kappa International, 43*(2), 17–20.

from mental health problems were twice as likely to have had two parents at home during their adolescent years. Although circumstances alter individual cases, it appears that family economic well-being and intactness are two factors having a considerable impact on K–12 student learning and social adjustment.

Another factor of considerable importance, according to Caplan, Choy, and Whitmore (1991), is family culture. For example, very poor immigrants to America with strong cultural and family traditions seem to engender in their children the attitude that success in education and life comes from hard work, rather than from luck or circumstances of birth. Caplan et al. cite the phenomenal school success of children from recently immigrated Vietnamese, Laotian, and Chinese families. These children have done remarkably well in our schools despite their attendance in low SES community schools and their limited English proficiency.

The lives of children and teachers are inextricably bound to families, parents, and other caregivers. Establishing and maintaining good relationships with such significant others is a prime concern of most teachers, as you will see in Chapter 14. Teachers are well aware of the impact parents and community have on student academic success and classroom behavior. A Metropolitan Life (1992) survey of the American teacher revealed that 65 percent of teachers say that lack of support or help from parents presents a problem (see Table 2.1). In a similar 1993 survey, 80 percent of teachers polled said that promoting parental involvement in education should be the first or second priority on the national education agenda (Richardson, 1993).

2.7 What might you do to increase parental interest?

Studies of secondary students confirm the importance parents play in their academic success. Among students who get As and Bs, 87 percent said their parents are available to help them with homework. On the other hand, students who get grades lower than C said parents are not involved, even in talking about school life (Metropolitan Life, 1998).

Columnist William Raspberry insists that parenting skills must be improved, especially for young persons less likely to have been exposed to good parenting themselves, for example "second and third generation 15 year old mothers" (Raspberry, 1998). Additionally, he argues that every community should have regular sessions where parents of young children learn tricks and techniques for getting children ready for school. Specifically, Raspberry feels parents should learn how to instill in children attitudes and habits that make school learning possible such as patience, persistence, and self-esteem. Instilling a love of reading and of learning are particularly important (Raspberry, 1993).

TABLE 2.1 Lack of Parental Support—The Most Serious Hindrance to Students' Ability to Learn

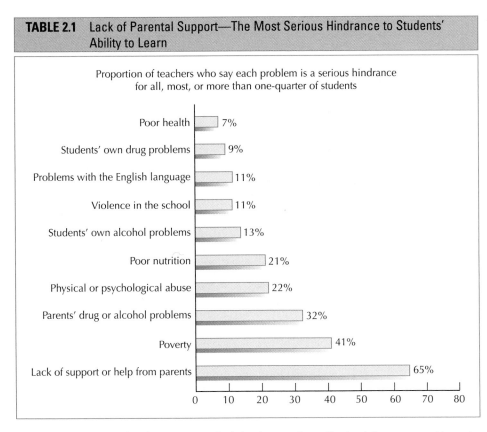

Proportion of teachers who say each problem is a serious hindrance for all, most, or more than one-quarter of students

Problem	Percentage
Poor health	7%
Students' own drug problems	9%
Problems with the English language	11%
Violence in the school	11%
Students' own alcohol problems	13%
Poor nutrition	21%
Physical or psychological abuse	22%
Parents' drug or alcohol problems	32%
Poverty	41%
Lack of support or help from parents	65%

Source: Metropolitan Life, (1992). *Ready or not: Grade level preparedness: Teachers' views on current issues in education.* New York: Metropolitan Life Insurance Company.

IMPLICATIONS OF FAMILY CHANGE FOR TEACHERS

We can draw a few implications for teachers from the data concerning family influence on schooling. As couples continue to marry later and more parents pursue full-time careers, more and more children have somewhat older parents who have less time and energy to give to child rearing. Many of these working parents will likely maintain busy schedules, spend less time than they would like with their children, and find it difficult to schedule time for themselves. Teachers need to understand such circumstances and do their best to facilitate family needs without negatively affecting a child's school success. Also, since more students will come to your classrooms having experienced parental separation, divorce, or remarriage, you must be sensitive to their need for emotional support and for help in thinking through related concerns. Finally, inasmuch as a large number of children now live in single-parent and blended families, you need to accept alternative family styles and to include them when referring to families in class. Sensitivity is especially important here.

Because a larger number of children live in single-parent families, you should take into account that they may have fewer financial resources and may also be less supervised. Such conditions usually result in less access to educational materials in the home and poorer homework performance. Those children who are most at risk with regard to school achievement and behavior are those who live in a single-parent family and are born into poverty, who have health problems at birth, whose parents lack a secondary education, and whose families have a history of mental illness or alcoholism. Also, because we know that parents and caregivers have a positive impact on schooling, you may need to show family members how to help their children succeed. Finally, since children represent a decreasing population, you need to be a child advocate in your community and argue for improved services for all children.

2.8 To what extent would you be willing and able to take on family functions such as nurturing and caring?

Seven Steps to Good Teacher-Family Partnerships

How can you go about establishing good relationships with parents and care-givers? Here are seven steps to follow (Patrikakou & Weissberg, 1999):

- Make establishing a partnership with parents a priority, something that has to happen.
- Plan for the partnership just as you would plan for anything else of importance. At the beginning of the year, let parents know that you must have a partnership with them. Find out how, in the past, they have been involved with the school or with classrooms. Find out what their present needs are with regard to involvement in their children's learning.

- Provide parents with regular, positive communications. Inform them of expectations and goals you hold for learners, class rules and routines, and how they can help at home. Use a variety of communications according to parents' preferences, such as notes, a home-school journal, phone calls, and e-mail. Follow up on all communications you receive.
- Find ways to communicate positive messages about learners since they solidify congenial relationships that are necessary when and if negative messages are required later.
- Provide personalized messages through home-school journals in which you inform parents of their

child's interests, strengths or weaknesses, and concerns and in which parents inform you likewise. Utilize parent conferences.
- Provide parents and caregivers with practical suggestions of how they can assist in their child's education. Specifically, tell them things they can do at home that will help the child learn.
- Reflect on your partnership plan and fine-tune it so that it results in improved parent involvement in student academic and social success.

Source: E. Patrikakou & R. Weissberg. (1999, February 3). The seven Ps of school-family partnerships. *Education Week 18*(21), 34, 36.

The Changing Nature of Childhood and Youth

Yes, America is changing, and so is the process of growing up in our nation. The following headlines unfortunately portray a bleak picture of being raised in America today: "More U.S. Kids Live in Poverty," "Study of 8th Graders Finds 20% at High Risk of Failure," "Latchkey Kids Are More Likely to Smoke, Drink," "Students Studying TV More than Books," "Fifth Graders Organize Rebellion," "Rapes by Children Expected to Rise."

You may feel that such headlines are sensational and exaggerated. However, in most cases the news stories are based upon governmental and scientific reports (Fuchs & Reklis, 1992). As you might suspect, the scenarios are worse for minorities and the poor, which are the most rapidly growing segments of a declining youth population. However, majority and more affluent youth, while less affected by these concerns, are more affected by others. Let's look briefly at some of the problems that affect childhood today.

ECONOMICALLY DISADVANTAGED CHILDREN

Lots of kids in the United States—an estimated 14 of 60 million children—live in poverty (Sack, 2000). The major contributor to child poverty is a problematic family that results from such things as unemployment, low wages, insufficient welfare benefits, single-parenting, and single teen-age mothers (Biddle, 1997). Furthermore, children of the poor are more likely to live in substandard housing, receive less medical and dental care, have an inadequate diet, wear cast-off and torn clothing, lack affordable day care, have fewer educational resources, and move frequently—all factors known to interfere with good school performance (Viadero 2000).

A disproportionate number of poor kids are minorities. Compared to white and Asian American children, Hispanic children are twice as likely and Black children three times as likely to be raised in low income families (Viadero, 2000).

2.9 How willing are you to teach children of the poor? What pluses and minuses would you bring to this task?

At issue is whether the schools and teachers can "save the poor." So far, the answer is elusive. Note the following statements made after an investigation by *New York Times* reporter Traub (Traub, 2000):

- There is little evidence that any existing [educational reform] strategy can close more than a fraction of the overall achievement gap separating children with low socioeconomic status from their wealthier, largely suburban counterparts.

- Educational reform programs that seem to work do not have a long-term, carryover effect.

- Spending more money is problematic. Many of the most catastrophic school districts in America spend far more per student than do nearby middle-class communities.

Traub concludes, "There is reason to believe that schools can make some kind of a difference, but right now they are not making nearly enough."

For more facts on child poverty visit http://cpmcnet.columbia.edu/dept/nccp/main4.html.

2.10 What do you think schools and teachers can do to help poor children have greater academic success?

Web Resource

CHILDREN WITH INADEQUATE SUPERVISION

About three-fourths of America's children live in two-parent families, mostly with their biological parents. However, many of these children, like those in single-parent families, are dependent upon self-care or day care. A number of factors seem to contribute to this situation. More than ever before, both parents in two-parent families work. Additionally, well over half of working-age women are now in the workplace. Of course, the increased number of single-parent families also contributes to the self-care/day care phenomenon.

For whatever reason, a majority of children do not have a parent at home full time (Center for the Study of Social Policy, 1992). This means that parents and guardians seek child care help from a variety of sources including relatives, friends, and day care providers. Many expect their children between the ages of about 7 and 13 to look after themselves. When children are regularly home alone, they are referred to as **latchkey children.** In fact, the frequency of day and self-care has become so great that today's children are often referred to as the "day care generation." Some even go so far as to argue that children today experience near abandonment (Louv, 1990).

At times, latchkey children seek refuge in libraries. A study of 125 librarians (Dowd, 1990) reports that 76 percent see significant numbers of unattended children in the library after school. On weekends, 50 percent report seeing unsupervised children. The librarians report that the 10- to 12-year-old age group seems to be using libraries most regularly as havens.

What are the effects of being supervised by someone other than a parent, or of not being supervised at all? While there is little conclusive data about the effects of day care, some express concerns. Babies or infants in day care seem to be at greater risk of developing insecure relationships with their mothers, the high rate of turnover among day care providers results in inconsistent supervision for developing children, and children cared for outside the home are at greater risk of sickness due to increased exposure to both adults and children (Wingert & Kantrowitz, 1990).

Likewise, there is little conclusive knowledge about the effects of self-care. However, a study of almost 5,000 eighth graders (Dwyer et al, 1990) raises concerns. Dwyer and associates reported that 68 percent of these children cared for themselves at least part of the time after school. When these latchkey children were compared with their supervised peers, they were twice as likely to be under stress, to feel conflict with their families, to indicate that their parents were gone too much, and to call themselves risk-takers. Additionally, they were angrier, skipped school

According to the Census Bureau, 7 million children age five to fourteen are regularly left unsupervised while parents work or are away for other reasons.

- Children caring for themselves spend an average of six hours per week doing so.

- Fifty percent spend less than five hours per week without adult supervision: 13 percent spend more than ten hours unsupervised.

- Self-care is more prevalent among middle school-age than elementary-age kids.

- Self-care increases with family income.

Source: K. Smith. (2000). *Who's minding the kids? Child care arrangements: Fall 1995.* Washington, DC: US Census Bureau.3

more, were more afraid when alone, and went to more parties. They were also twice as likely to drink alcohol, smoke, and use marijuana. Some of these findings might suggest that such children are better adjusted and more independent. Eighth graders who became latchkey children in elementary school were more likely to take risks (be independent) and go to parties (be social). However, such children were also three times more likely to abuse substances than their supervised peers. Children beginning self-care later, in junior high, were twice as likely to engage in substance abuse (Weisman, 1990).

Of course, children with a parent or parents at home are not necessarily adequately supervised. Furthermore, children differ in their need for supervision.

ABUSED AND NEGLECTED CHILDREN

2.11 What degree of responsibility do you think parents have for child supervision?

2.12 What experiences have you known of child abuse or neglect?

When we read newspapers or magazines or watch television, we are well aware that child abuse is all too common. It is estimated that almost 2 million children are either abused or neglected *each year.* Abuse and neglect are defined in Public Law 93-247 as "physical or mental injury, sexual abuse, negligent treatment, or maltreatment of a child under 18 by a person who is responsible for the child's welfare under circumstances which indicate that the child's health or welfare is harmed or threatened thereby" (Child Abuse Prevention and Treatment Act of 1974). Generally, abuse and neglect are associated with parents who were themselves abused as children; stress brought about by poverty, unemployment, marital problems, or isolation; low level of parental education; poor information concerning child rearing; and a violent environment (Kauffman, 2000; Gelardo & Sanford, 1987).

All fifty states have laws requiring teachers to report all suspected cases. Indicators of physical and sexual abuse and neglect appear in Highlight 2.3. Visit the National Clearinghouse on Abused and Neglected Children at http://www.calib.com/nccanch/ for more information.

Web Resource

"AT-RISK" CHILDREN

If students in your classroom are affected by circumstances that can torment childhood, they are at substantial risk of school failure and dropping out. Some of these circumstances, we already know, are poverty, lack of supervision, and abuse and neglect. Common characteristics of children at risk include:

- They live in a single-parent home.
- They are at home unsupervised for long periods of time.
- Their parent(s) have a low income.
- Their parent(s) have a low level of education.
- They have limited proficiency in English.
- They have siblings who have dropped out of school.

Indicators of Abused or Neglected Children

- Appear to be different from others in physical and emotional makeup.
- Parents describe them as different or bad.
- Child is afraid of parent(s).
- May have bruises, welts, sores, or other skin injuries that seem untreated.
- Receive inappropriate food, nutrition and/or medication.

- Receive inadequate supervision.
- Child is chronically unclean.
- Exhibit extreme behavior (e.g. often cry/never cry or aggressive/passive).
- Child is wary of physical contact, especially with adults.
- Exhibit a sudden change in behavior.
- Have learning problem that can't be diagnosed.

- Are habitually truant/late to school, may have prolonged absences due to injury.
- Often tired and may fall asleep in the classroom.
- Often dressed inappropriately to cover scars and bruises on arms and legs.

Source: http://members.toast.net/rculpepp/rcchild/anc.html

- They perform poorly in school.
- They have repeated a grade.
- They do not expect to graduate.

Case 2.1 describes a study of Aaron, a child at risk. What are some of the factors placing him at risk?

A national study of almost 25,000 eighth graders provides a snapshot of at-risk adolescents (*A Profile of American 8th Graders,* 1990). It reveals that nearly one of every two students is affected by at least one of the above listed at-risk factors! One in five students has two or more risk factors, and, the study notes, these youth are especially at risk. Of course, as the number of risk factors increases, the risk of failure and of dropping out increases.

Minorities are more often affected by one or more risk factors. For example, African Americans are twice as likely as whites to come from low-income and single-parent families. Hispanics are much more likely than whites to have limited English proficiency (LEP) and to have parents who did not complete secondary school.

Of course, some children are at risk even though they seem not to be afflicted by poverty, single parenthood, lack of supervision, and so forth. It is often difficult to understand why seemingly advantaged children do not achieve or underachieve. Eighth graders interviewed in the study may provide some answers: Half said they were bored in school and went to class unprepared, and nearly half said they hardly ever discussed schoolwork with a parent.

A study of over 9,000 6- to 17-year-olds reveals an additional risk factor. Regardless of normal risk factors such as poverty, having a single parent, or lack of parental supervision, children who move often—at least six times during grades 1 to 12—are 77 percent more likely to have more behavior problems and 35 percent more likely to fail a grade (Cohen, 1993).

Surprisingly, a number of at-risk children turn out all right. In the earlier reported study, Werner and Smith (1994) reported that one of every three such students developed into competent, confident, caring adults by the time they were 18. These so-called **resilient children** tend to have a nurturing adult in their lives (not necessarily a parent), and they had easy temperaments as infants. Masten, Best, and Garmezy (1991) found that resilient children are perceived as more appealing or attractive to adults. Moreover, they report that such children have good intellectual and problem-solving skills and that, as they mature, they have a knack for finding a good environment outside the home in a church, youth, or club group or in the family of a friend or relative that offers stability and support. Researchers at Johns Hopkins and Syracuse Universities (Winfield, 1991) report that resiliency may also

2.13 How do you think you might feel or behave when you discover a child may be "at risk?"

CASE 2.1

Aaron, A Child at Risk

Aaron Allen is an 11-year-old boy in the sixth grade. He has a small and slender build for this grade level. He comes to school well groomed and usually well dressed.

Aaron lives with his mother in a low-income area. They live in a little three-room house and receive public assistance. Aaron is an only child, and his parents are divorced. Mrs. Allen is willing to talk about Aaron. She appears to care very much about him, but admits she is losing control over him. She took a babysitting job this last summer for extra money.

Mr. Allen is in prison and has been out of the home since Aaron was six years old. This means that Aaron has been without a male figure in the home. As a result, he became very close to a 24-year-old uncle. This uncle did not work; he lived with his mother and received whatever he wanted. Constantly in trouble, the uncle was a very bad influence on the boy. Aaron's uncle was killed in a bar shooting last year. The tragedy left Aaron with no male figure to relate to at all.

Aaron gets whatever he wants at home and goes wherever he pleases. He rides his bicycle most places, but if his destination is too far, he takes a bus. He associates with older children and most of his close friends attend the junior high school, which is two blocks from the elementary school and one block from his house. Aaron is fairly well accepted by his peers. He has no juvenile record, but the police have talked to him and warned him for various actions. Mrs. Allen explains that he was caught stealing several times and was reported at the scene of a fire. When there is a problem, Mrs. Allen says she gets her son out of trouble, talks to him, and hopes he won't do it again. She explains that she threatens him, saying if he doesn't behave, "he will be taken away to a detention home in hopes that it will scare him and he will straighten up."

The information in Aaron's cumulative school folder states that he has an average IQ, but his performance is very much below the grade-level standards. He reads at a third-grade level. Aaron seems disinterested in school,

with a definite "I don't care about school" attitude. He has stated many times that he does not like school and that he would not come if he did not have to. His record shows increasingly poor attendance. When he loses interest, he becomes a problem for his teachers. He continually disrupts the class and is often sent to the office. So far, this does not seem to have improved his behavior.

Recently Aaron's behavior has gotten worse. He could not care less about school or what happens to him. When his mother was contacted, she said she felt helpless and had more or less given up. For the past five to six weeks, the regular teacher has been ill, and the room has had six different substitutes. This has affected all the students in the room, but Aaron is in trouble more than usual because the substitutes will not tolerate any behavior problems. School, with the room in such turmoil, presents a real problem for Aaron.

Source: Barbara Dahmke, Grandview Heights Middle School, Columbus, Ohio.

be fostered when young black males participate in sports. Werner and Smith (1994) tell us that certain schools and teachers also are instrumental in helping at-risk students to become resilient. For example, they report that if schools and teachers assist at-risk children to gain good reading ability by grade four, these children will have a much better chance at later success.

How could we do a better job teaching students who are at risk of school failure? Alderman (1990) provides us with some clues in Highlight 2.4. For further ideas visit the National Institute of At-Risk Students at http://www.ed.gov/offices/OERI/At-Risk/.

 Web Resource

"HURRIED" CHILDREN

Child advocates feel that children should be allowed to be children, that they should not be hurried into school and faced with formal learning requirements at very young ages. Elkind (1989) and Postman (1994) are among those who decry the shortening and even disappearance of home-based childhood in favor of early schooling. Among the factors that contribute to rushing children through childhood are working parents, television, and growing materialism. Working parents simply have less time to spend with their offspring, and the time they do share is often marred by the stress and exhaustion of the adults' lives.

Alderman (1990) notes that teachers must always be alert to the need to motivate students, especially when the students are at risk. She concludes that teachers of at-risk students have a particularly monumental task of helping these kids break the cycle of failure: low expectations and helplessness. After reviewing research on motivation, Alderman offers these suggestions:

- Have confidence in your ability to help these students learn.
- Hold high expectations for at-risk youth. Let them know you want and expect them to succeed.
- Assist at-risk students in establishing reachable and specific goals and in charting their own progress.
- Help children identify strategies for reaching their goals.

- Make sure children link their success to their effort.
- Let children know precisely what they did that made them successful.

Source: Alderman, M. K. (1990, September). Motivation for at-risk students. *Educational Leadership, 48*(1), 27–30.

Of course, television has its good and bad aspects, and those who study child development continue to debate its impact on childhood behavior. However, it is well known that children, as well as adults, imitate what they see. And what they often see is distorted teenage and adult conduct that exaggerates violence, cruelty, and sexual behavior. It has been said that television reveals all adult secrets that young children formerly could not easily discover. As a consequence, young children, who naturally try to imitate adult behavior, may be led into recreating acts of violence and sexual intimacy. Fortunately, there are efforts (although not well supported) to offer more television programming options that match children's normal developmental needs and interests.

Materialism is the doctrine that comfort, pleasure, and wealth are the highest goals and values one can aspire to. Society is deluged by reminders of materialistic needs, including better jobs, vacations, houses, cars, and entertainment. Parents who buy into materialism are more likely to expect their children to be achievers in all things so they, too, will obtain "the good life." Such children can be constantly on the run, participating in a variety of activities that may be undertaken more as means to an end (achieving) than as ends in themselves (fun). Thus, to some extent, children are hurried because adults are, too. However, child advocates like Elkind (1989) warn that we are so overvaluing adulthood and undervaluing childhood that adult pressures are harming children.

"That class ought to come with a warning: 'May cause drowsiness.'"

DISENGAGED CHILDREN

In the section "At-Risk Children," we learned that half the eighth graders in one study (A Profile of American Eighth Graders, 1990) said that school was boring. In another study of 20,000 high school students in California and Wisconsin, 40 percent say they are disengaged—bored and just going through the motions in school. Boredom can result from many things, including feelings of inadequacy (Reim, 1997). Signs of boredom in school include reading material unrelated to class, daydreaming, doing work for other classes, and talking with peers (Plucker & Omdal, 1997). Disengaged students report that friends influence school performance and drug use more substantially than parents' positive practices at home. However, researchers find that students who come from homes where parents are firm, loving, and respectful are more likely to be engaged in school learning.

Besides taking in the potentially negative influence of friends, disengaged students are often busy with nonacademic pursuits. Two-thirds of teens work: half more than fifteen hours per week. When not working, teens spend twenty to

2.14 How might you motivate a disengaged student to learn?

Motivating Disengaged Students

Plucker and Omdal (1997) note that when students are not challenged or do not see the relevance of what they are to learn, teachers can

- Determine the extent to which the students may already know the material.
- Find out the interests of such students and try to relate material to be learned to those interests.

- Help students apply or see applications of what they are learning: frame what is being learned in relationship to real-life situations/problems.
- Get students to think deeply, that is, analytically, critically, or creatively about what they are learning.

- Provide learners with options regarding their assignments—to the extent possible, let them learn in ways they prefer.

Chapter 5 provides more on motivation.

twenty-five hours weekly with friends (Steinberg, Brown, and Dornbusch, 1996). Highlight 2.5 suggests how teachers can motivate disengaged students.

The Changing School

For the past several decades, America has been trying to cope with an ever-increasing number of scientific, economic, and educational challenges. Several are depicted in Figure 2.1.

Whatever the challenge or its source, Americans expect their public schools to "fix whatever is broken." For the most part, America's schools have accepted these challenges and, as a consequence, have transformed themselves in a number of ways. Following is a brief description of selected challenges that our schools have accepted and how they have changed to meet them.

Challenge 1—To Foster Equity The pursuit of equity is transforming both our society and its schools. You have matured during a period when the concept of equal treatment and opportunity has blossomed. You are probably already familiar with some of the ways this concept has affected education: For example, it has triggered the desegregation of schools and classrooms, the elimination of most same-sex schools, the inclusion of special-needs students in regular classrooms, the development of

FIGURE 2.1   External and Internal Challenges That Have Changed Schools

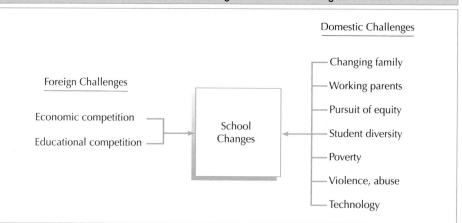

SPOTLIGHT ON RESEARCH 2.3

How Children 12 and Under Spend Their Time and How That Relates to School Learning

Compared with children in 1981, children in 1997 used their time somewhat differently (Hofferth 1998). In 1997 they spent more time in school, doing artwork, reading, studying, and engaging in sports. Conversely, they spent less time outdoors, playing, and watching television. Hofferth notes some advantages of these changes—there is a positive relationship between the amount of reading a youth does and higher scores in reading and math, and children who watch more television have lower scores.

After reviewing Hofferth's findings, professor of child study David Elkind notes that it is probably good that youths are watching less television and bad that they have lost more of their "free time" (Jacobson 1998). Elkind also wonders whether reduction of TV viewing has simply been replaced by time spent playing electronic games.

Source: S. L. Hofferth and associates. (1998). *Healthy environments, healthy children.* Ann Arbor, MI: Institute of Social Research, University of Michigan; L. Jacobson. (1998, November 18). Study tracks how children spend their time. *Education Week, 18*(12), 8.

special programs for children with no or limited English proficiency, the fostering of multiethnic education, and so forth. This equity challenge pervades each and every day of a teacher's life. It requires that you be proactive and vigilant to ensure that all students have equal opportunity and receive equal treatment.

Challenge 2—To Achieve World-Class Academic Standards   As a consequence of scientific and industrial achievements abroad, America is having a more difficult time providing its citizenry with the level of living they have become used to. America's declining position within this fierce global economic competition has been attributed in part to improved education abroad and declining education at home. Analysts frequently cite comparative student test scores that seem to show that American students are not achieving at a world-class level (Stevenson, Chen, & Lee, 1993). Schools are attempting to answer this challenge by introducing new, more rigorous curricula, by instituting the practices of our most effective schools into those with poor track records, and by utilizing more promising teaching practices. Further, you will find that students are taking many more tests in an effort to monitor their progress better.

Challenge 3—To Support Families   Throughout history, the family was expected to support the school. More recently, the school is being asked to support the family. The changing family has resulted in substantial changes at school. Increasingly, schools are asked to provide before- and after-school child care. Some schools literally begin their day before sunrise and conclude it after sunset. In addition, it is more difficult to communicate with working parents and fewer are available as school volunteers than before. On average, children are less likely to receive the nurturing they need, so you must be prepared to listen to them and, on occasion, to help them in nonacademic ways.

Challenge 4—To Celebrate Diversity   Given the changing demography of America, you will find students are more diverse. Since a section on the diversity of students follows, at this point it is sufficient to say that schools are responding to this diversity not only by accepting it but also by promoting its value and richness.

Challenge 5—To Utilize Technology   As society has become increasingly dependent on technology, schools are challenged to use that technology and to foster its use among students. Albeit slowly, schools have accepted the challenge. Some school districts conduct their own television broadcasts, teach broadcasting, and produce programs. Likewise, many schools have computer laboratories as well as computers

2.15   How important are the five challenges schools face? Which of these challenges might be most difficult for you?

2.16 Some would argue that schools cannot be all things to all people, that they are changing too much in order to meet such challenges. How do you feel? What do you think the role of the school should be?

in classrooms. Most schools, however, still grapple with the problem of how to help students become discriminating television consumers and sophisticated rather than game-playing computer users.

As a future teacher, you must keep abreast of these and other challenges facing schools today. Furthermore, you must work to respond appropriately to them. You can do so by getting behind school district and school building response efforts and, perhaps more importantly, by conducting your classrooms accordingly. More specifically, as you plan your curriculum and instruction, you must always be alert for opportunities to foster equity, celebrate diversity, provide for children's special needs, foster a high level of learning, utilize technology, and support your students' families and communities.

Some Final Thoughts

2.17 Which of these challenges are you most and least up to?

As teachers, we must know as much as possible about children collectively and about school-age children in particular if teaching is deserving of the label "helping profession." So many children are experiencing poverty that, on average, one of every five students is likely to be ill-nourished and in poor health, unprepared to learn, and, in some cases, homeless. Consequently, you must take your students' physical, mental, and emotional condition into account and, when necessary, be prepared to access child services supplied by the school district and community. Since poor children and their families are more poorly represented politically, teachers and schools must be visible, loud, and continuous in their support.

Unfortunately since some children have inadequate supervision, you must be prepared to have students who come to school ill, tardy, anxious, or lonely. Without unduly infringing upon family situations, you may need to keep track of children involved in self-care. Make sure they are not unnecessarily at risk due to their self-care arrangements and that they are knowledgeable about what to do in problem or emergency situations. Also, given the increased incidence of child abuse and neglect, you will need to watch for telltale signs and report suspected cases in accordance with school policy. Monitor the stressed-out children of high-pressure parents who want their children to hurry up and "make it" as well. Finally, try to find ways to engage the disengaged.

CHAPTER SUMMARY

- To be a more effective teacher you need to be more aware of and take into account the distinguishing characteristics of the changing society in which you work. Among those characteristics are a growing minority population; a lower percentage of children; an increasing variety of family styles; recognition that families influence school learning; and an awareness that too many children live in poverty, lack adequate supervision, and are neglected, abused, hurried, or disengaged from school and learning.

- America's minority population is fast growing. By 2025 it is expected that the percentage of whites will decline further, Hispanics will outnumber African Americans and the percentage of Asian Americans will close in on 10 percent. Over one-third of Americans will be non-white. Population changes create challenges for teachers who must educate a more ethnically and racially diverse student body, many of whom will have limited English proficiency.

- America's families are also changing. Parents start families later in life and families are smaller, less stable, and increasingly likely to be headed by one parent. A strong relationship exists among family background, income, educational level of parents, and achievement in school. Children from low-income, single-parent homes are more likely to be lower achievers and develop school problems. Children with multiple at-risk factors are most likely to have serious learning and/or behavioral problems. Additionally, if they live in single-parent homes, they are more likely to become involved in crime and less likely to recover from mental health problems.

- More children, particularly minority youth, are growing up in poverty; more lack parental supervision; more are reported abused and neglected; and more are being hurried to grow up.
- American families represent a variety of types including traditional, remarried, blended, and single-adoptive. Each presents different challenges to family members as they strive to meet family functions such as nurturance, caring, intimacy, cultural transmission, and economic support.
- Certain family factors seem to positively influence student learning: parent attention, parent presence, high parental expectations, parent socioeconomic status, and parent involvement in the school.

ISSUES AND PROBLEMS FOR DISCUSSION

ISSUES Here are some issues for you to debate.

1. To what extent do you think teachers should be concerned with the social and cultural context of teaching?
2. What kind of family do you think is best for children?
3. How can schools help families have a more positive impact on their children's education?
4. To what extent should schools and teachers assume any of the normal family functions such as nurturance, caring, or intimacy?
5. How can schools and teachers offset or overcome the effects of poverty, lack of home supervision, child neglect or abuse, low parental and child expectations toward education, gender stereotyping, crass materialism, or other negative factors?
6. How involved should teachers get when students are at risk?

PROBLEMS The following problems have been shared with us by teachers. How might they be resolved?

Problem 1: When school started today, one of the children came into the room in tears. She was so poorly dressed that she was just about frozen. She wore no gloves or boots and had a very thin scarf on her head. Her hands, ears, and feet were very cold. She came from a home without heat.

Problem 2: Today got off to a frustrating start. Many children had runny noses, red eyes, and seemed drowsy. Some children had no breakfast, since their parents are still out or are asleep when they leave home.

Problem 3: When the lesson began, many children were unable to provide a paper and pencil, since it was late in the month and their parents' welfare money had run out.

Problem 4: A student from a migrant family is having trouble with subtraction facts. The other students make fun of him. I think the student considers this a racial thing, and he has become resentful and defensive.

Problem 5:   There are several non-English-speaking children in class. They are well-behaved but need an inordinate amount of individual attention, which I don't have the time to provide.

Problem 6:   One boy refuses to leave the room, fearful that boys from another school are waiting to kill him. He says the problem is the result of an incident that occurred over the weekend.

Problem 7:   A boy came into the room in obvious pain with strips of cloth wrapped around his right hand. He says that his mother's boyfriend held his hand on a toaster.

Problem 8:   One of the girls in gym class is very upset that she cannot participate in square dancing. Her parents do not condone any kind of dancing.

THEORY INTO ACTION ACTIVITIES

ACTIVITY 2.1: Implications of population, family diversity, and family circumstances for teaching   After reading this chapter make a list of about five things you have learned and their implications for classroom practice. For example:

MAJOR LEARNING	POSSIBLE IMPLICATION(S)
1. Our population is increasingly diverse ethnically and racially.	1. I will need to be effective working with whites, blacks, Hispanics, and Asians so I will need to know how to interact with children of diverse cultural backgrounds.

ACTIVITY 2.2: Teaching in an ever-changing society   Prepare a paragraph or so on the topic "What I think it will be like to teach in a context filled with population and family diversity."

ACTIVITY 2.3: Preparation for teaching in an ever-changing society   Prepare a paragraph or so on the topic "What I need to know and be able to do to teach in a context filled with diversity and how I can gain that knowledge and skill."

ACTIVITY 2.4: Obtain teachers' views about teaching in a changing society   Talk with classroom teachers about teaching in an ever-changing society. Ask them the following:

- Have you noticed any changes in the population of the school neighborhood?
- Have you noticed changes in the families of students?
- If so, how do you think these things are affecting learners?
- How and how well is the school meeting the challenges resulting from changes in population and family?

REFERENCES

A profile of American 8th graders. (1990). Washington, DC: U.S. Government Printing Office.

Alderman, M. K. (1990, September). Motivation for at-risk students. *Educational Leadership, 48* (1), 27–30.

Biddle, B. (1997, September). Foolishness, dangerous nonsense, and real correlates of state differences in achievement. *Phi Delta Kappan 79*(1), 9–13.

Bracey, G. (1995, March). The myth of school failure. Paper presented at the Association for Supervision and Curriculum Development Conference, San Francisco.

Bracey, G. (2002, March). What students do in the summer. *Phi Delta Kappan, 83*(7), 497–498.

Brown, B. F. (1980, April). A study of the school needs of children from one-parent families. *Phi Delta Kappan, 62*(8), 537–540.

Caplan, N., Choy, M. H., & Whitmore, J. K. (1991). *Children of the boat people: A study of educational success.* Ann Arbor: University of Michigan Press.

Center for the Study of Social Policy. (1992). *What the 1990 census tells us about children.* Washington, DC: The Center for the Study of Social Policy.

Cohen, D. (1993, September 22). Frequent moves said to boost risk of school problems. *Education Week, 13*(3), 15.

Coontz, S. (2000). *The way we never were.* New York: Basic Books.

Dahmke, B. (nd.) Aaron, a child at risk. (unpublished).

Dionne, E. (2001, February 10). 2-parent families are in comeback. *Columbus Dispatch,* A10.

Dowd, F. S. (1990). *Latchkey children in the library and community: Issues, strategies, and programs.* Phoenix, AZ: Oryx Press.

Dwyer, K., Richardson, J., Donley, K., Hansen, W., Sussman, S., Bronnon, D., Dent, C., Johnson, C., Floy, B. (1990, September). Characteristics of eighth-grade students who initiate self-care in elementary and junior high school. *Pediatrics, 86*(3), 448–454.

Elkind, D. (1989). *The hurried child: Growing up too fast too soon.* Cambridge, MA: Perseus.

Fraser, A. (1989, Spring). The changing American family. *In Context, 21,* 2–7.

Fuchs, R. F., & Reklis, D. M. (1992, January). America's children: Economic perspectives and policy options. *Science, 255,* 41–46.

Gelardo, M. S., & Sanford, E. E. (1987). Child abuse and neglect: A review of the literature. *School Psychology Review, 16,* 137–155.

Hacker, A. (1982). Farewell to the family? *New York Review of Books, 29,* 37–45.

Hamburg, D. A. (1992). *The family crucible and healthy child development.* New York: Carnegie Corporation.

Hamburg, D. A. (1995). *A developmental strategy to prevent lifelong damage.* New York: Carnegie Corporation of America.

Hart, B., & Risley, T. (1999). *Meaningful differences.* Baltimore: Paul Brookes.

Hofferth, S. (1987, February). Implications of family trends for children: A research perspective. *Educational Leadership, 44*(5), 78–84.

Hofferth, S. L., and associates (1998). *Healthy environments, healthy children.* Ann Arbor, MI: Institute of Social Research, University of Michigan.

Jacobson, L. (1998, November 18). Study tracks how children spend their time. *Education Week, 18*(12), 8.

Jencks, C., Smith, M., Aclond, H., Bane, M., Cohen, D., Gintis, H., Heyns, B., & Michelson, S. (1972). *Inequality: A reassessment of the effect of family and schooling in America.* New York: Basic Books.

Kauffman, J. M. (2000). *Characteristics of emotional and behavioral disorders in children and youth.* Englewood Cliffs, NJ: Prentice Hall.

Louv, R. (1990). *Childhood's Future.* Boston: Houghton Mifflin.

Masten, A. S., Best, K. M., & Garmezy, N. (1991). Resilience and development: Contributions from the study of children who overcome adversity. *Development and Psychopathology, 2,* 425–444.

Metropolitan Life. (1992). *Ready or not: Grade level preparedness: Teachers' views on current issues in education.* New York: Metropolitan Life Insurance Co.

Metropolitan Life. (1998). *Survey of the American teacher.* New York: Metropolitan Life Insurance Co.

National Center for Education Statistics. (1997). *Fathers' involvement in their children's schools.* Washington, DC: Government Printing Office. (Document NCES # 98091).

Olson, L. (2000, September 7). Children of change. *Education Week, 20*(4), 31–41.

Patrikakou, E., & Weissberg, R. (1999, February 3). The seven P's of school-family partnerships. *Education Week, 18*(21), 34, 36.

Plucker, J., & Omdal, S. (1997, June 18). Beyond boredom. *Education Week, 16*(38), 32.

Popenoe, D. (1993). American family decline. *Journal of Marriage and Family, 55*(3), 27–42

Postman, N. (1994). *The disappearance of childhood.* London: Vintage Books.

A profile of American 8th graders. (1990). Washington, DC: U.S. Government Printing Office.

Raspberry, W. (1998, June 12). Parenting boost would help schools. *Columbus Dispatch*, 3B.

Raspberry, W. (1993, January 14). Parents must instill kids with will to learn. *Columbus Dispatch/Forum*, 13A.

Reim, S. (1997, April). An underachieving epidemic. *Educational Leadership, 34*(7), 18–22.

Resnick, M. (1997, September 10). Protecting adolescents from harm. *Journal of the American Medical Association, 278*(10), 823–832.

Richardson, J. (1993, May 19). Teachers in poll seek greater federal push for parent education. *Education Week, 12*, p. 10.

Sack, J. (2000, December 6). Number of poor children has dropped. *Education Week, 20*(14), 24.

Smith, K. (2000). *Who's minding the kids? Child Care Arrangements: Fall 1995*. Washington, DC: U.S. Census Bureau.

Steinberg, L., Brown, B., & Dornbusch, S. (1996). *Beyond the classroom: Why social reform has failed and what parents need to do.* New York: Simon and Schuster.

Stevenson, H. W., Chen, C., & Lee, S. (1993, January 1). Mathematics achievement of Chinese, Japanese, and American children: Ten years later. *Science, 259*, 53–58.

Suransky, V. (1982). *The erosion of childhood.* Chicago: University of Chicago Press.

Thorkildsen, R., & Stein, M. (1998, December). Is parent involvement related to student achievement? Research Bulletin. *News, Notes and Quotes. Newsletter of Phi Delta Kappa International, 43*(2), 17–20.

Traub, J. (2000, January 30). Schools can't save the urban poor. *Columbus Dispatch*, B1-2.

U.S. Census 2000. http://www.census.gov/main/www/cen2000.html.

U.S. Department of Health, Education and Welfare. (1966). *Equality of educational opportunity. Summary report.* (The Coleman Report). Washington, DC: U.S. Government Printing Office.

Viadero, D. (2000, March 22). Lags in minority achievement defy traditional explanations. *Education Week, 19*(28), 1, 18–22.

Walberg, H., & Fowler, W. (1987, October). Expenditure and size efficiency of public school districts. *Educational Researcher, 16*, 5–13.

Weisman, J. (1990, September 19). Latchkey 8th graders likely to possess emotional risk factors, study discloses. *Education Week, 10*(3), 6.

Werner, E. E., & Smith, R. S. (1994). *Overcoming the odds: High-risk children from birth to adulthood.* Ithaca, NY: Cornell University Press.

Winfield, L. F. (1991, November). Resilience, schooling and development in African-American youth: A conceptual framework. *Education & Urban Society, 24*, 3–14.

Wingert, P., & Kantrowitz, B. (1990, Winter–Spring). The day care generation. *Newsweek Special Issue*, 86–92.

Teaching Diverse Students

Contents

3

Chapter 2 examined selected challenges you will face as a teacher in our changing society. *First,* you will be challenged to meet the needs of children coming from an increasingly culturally diverse, growing minority population. *Second,* you will be challenged by changes in the nature of the family. Multiple family styles must be understood and reckoned with. *Third,* you must be ready to understand and work with economically disadvantaged children and children who are inadequately supervised, abused or neglected, at-risk of school failure, hurried, and disengaged. *Finally,* you will be expected generally to foster equity, achieve world-class academic standards, support families, celebrate diversity, and utilize technology.

In this chapter we look at perhaps the most important challenge of all—understanding and providing for student diversity. Consequently, among other things, you will learn how your students differ socioeconomically, culturally, in terms of gender, developmentally, in learning style, and in ability. Having such knowledge and understanding will enable you to accommodate, and even celebrate, your students' differences.

Student Diversity

> Why did I have to discover so much on the job? Have I messed up kids because I couldn't recognize some things I should have been able to see? Kids who needed attention, had poor nutrition, lacked good role models, never had a good school experience, had a messed-up family? How do I convey knowledge to these kids so they can understand it and have good feelings about themselves? So they can have success and build on it? I don't have the training to do it. I go home with these things troubling me. (Bower, 1978, p. 31)

Student diversity is a fact of life in all our schools and classrooms. And students differ in more ways than we can count. To be effective, teachers must be aware of some of the important ways students vary and consciously take that diversity into account when planning and instructing. We cannot successfully teach subject matter without teaching the child. Let's examine some of the kinds of diversity you will find. They are illustrated in Figure 3.1

3.1 What do you believe are the advantages of teaching diverse children? The challenges?

SOCIOECONOMIC DIFFERENCES

The gulf between rich and poor American families is wider now than at any time since the 1940s, when record keeping on the gap began. Presently, the wealthiest 20 percent receive nearly half of all income, while the poorest 20 percent earn less than 4 percent (Kozol, 1990). The effects are devastating for poor children. They are more likely to be born outside of marriage; to live in one-parent, female-headed

FIGURE 3.1   Six Ways in Which Students Differ

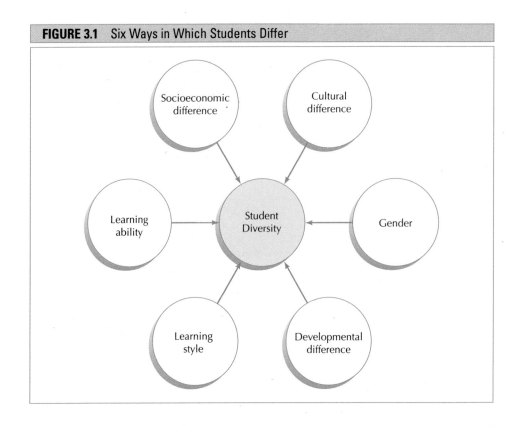

households; to live in rental housing or to be homeless; to have a working mother; to have medical and dental problems; to engage in sexual activity at an early age; and to become more involved in crime, violence, and drug abuse (Select Committee, 1989).

Low socioeconomic status (SES) children also are more educationally disadvantaged. They tend to live in communities and states that spend less on education, their teachers are often less well paid, they perform more poorly academically, they are more often identified as retarded, and they drop out of school at a higher rate. Additionally, they are more likely to enter school with experiential deficits, for example, not knowing letters, numbers, or colors (Select Committee, 1989).

In Chapter 2, we noted that 14 million of the approximately 60 million children in America fall below the poverty line. Even more critical, 500,000 are homeless. Kozol (1990) refers to these youngsters as "the new untouchables" who grow up in environments plagued by infectious illnesses such as whooping cough and tuberculosis, come to school so tired and hungry that they cannot concentrate, and carry "the smell of destitution with them—the smell of sweat and filth and urine" (p. 52). These children of poverty are the ones hardly anyone wants to teach, and since they more likely congregate in large cities and rural areas, schools in these locations have great difficulty attracting teachers. Only 6 percent of beginning teachers plan to teach in the low-income schools where homeless children are more likely to attend (You and the System, 1990).

Fortunately, advocacy groups with particular interest in economically disadvantaged youth exist. By far the largest is the Children's Defense Fund. Others are the American Agenda, the Committee for Economic Development, and the National Coalition for the Homeless. Related projects directed toward such children provide special supplemental food programs, prenatal care, child immunization, early education. Head Start is a preschool program for economically disadvantaged 3- and 4-year-olds, and compensatory education (Chapter 1 makes monies available to improve skills in reading and math).

Teaching Low SES Youth   Three things are fundamental to helping children who live in poverty. First, early intervention by communities and schools is essential. As Joan Beck, a syndicated journalist, writes in responding to a study reported in the *Journal of the American Medical Association*:

> How can I put this strongly enough? The surest way to help children to succeed in school is to increase their fundamental ability to learn . . . using the caring and family supporting techniques of early learning during the first few years of life. (1990, p. 11A)

Second, since children of the poor often feel they have little or no control over their lives, Herculean efforts must be made to generate a sense of **efficacy** in them— that is, the sense that they can control their own destinies. All children must feel that they are worthy, they matter, they count! Third, since children of the poor often have educational deficits, you can promote the achievement of low SES students if you

3.2   What experience do you have with children whose SES differs from yours? What further experience would help?

- Hold high expectations that they can and will learn.
- Respect each student's background, culture, and language style.
- Help them understand what they are learning.
- Teach thinking and problem-solving skills.
- Plan interesting and engaging learning experiences.
- Set and maintain high expectations for behavior.
- Maximize heterogeneous or mixed academic grouping.
- Provide individual help (Cruickshank, 1990; Knapp, Turnbull, & Shields, 1990).

For the most part, this is good advice for anyone teaching children, although the issue of heterogeneous versus homogeneous grouping remains undecided.

CULTURAL DIFFERENCES

When a group of people have many things in common—for example, language, ideas, values, traditions, and behaviors—they are said to share a culture. Although there is a dominant American culture, in reality America is made up of many subcultures. These subcultures or minorities may be like the dominant culture in some ways and differ from it in others. Beyond having a common language that may not be English, these ethnic groups may also have different modes of dress, food preferences, and ways of thinking and doing.

3.3   What experience do you have with children whose cultural backgrounds differ from yours? What further experience would help?

Being somewhat different from members of the majority culture—that is, being a so-called minority student, does not make a child disadvantaged. However, in cases where ethnicity and/or race are tied to low SES, minority students often do less well in school. This reflects the fact that, regardless of subculture, low SES families usually cannot or do not provide their children with the kinds of early stimulation and academic preparation more typically afforded by middle- and upper-class families. Headden (1997) provides an example. Hispanics have a drop-out rate close to 41 percent, but one-third of Hispanic children live in poverty and "start school at a substantial disadvantage: they rarely attend preschool, and their parents, often ill-educated or illiterate, don't read to them" (p. 64). Again, being disadvantaged is more a function of economics than of culture.

Osborne (1997) reports an oddity with regard to cultural differences in self-esteem. In general boys and girls who are white, Hispanic, or African American identify very positively with academics in the eighth grade. However, as they move through secondary school, both their self-esteem and their identification with academics drop off. After analyzing data collected from nearly 25,000 students, Osborne found, unexplainably, that black students continue to hold the most positive view of themselves even though their grades and test scores fall increasingly below those of students in the other groups. He notes, in general, that African Americans maintain the highest levels of self-esteem at all ages, but by twelfth grade, African-American boys, to a greater degree, detach their self-esteem from academics, and their self-esteem remains relatively high despite lesser school success. "They're removing school from their self-esteem equation as time goes on." Just why black males come to care less about academics than other groups is unclear. This underscores the importance of teachers tending to the academic needs of these youth.

A major problem when minorities encounter schools is that school policy, curriculum, and instruction normally reflect the majority American culture, which may be at odds with values and behaviors children learn at home. For example, Hispanics and Native Americans are accustomed to group learning and mutual assistance, while schools often are often organized around competitive, individual learning experience.

Teaching Minority Students   You probably know or have heard that minority students, on average (with the exception of Asian Americans and perhaps black students immigrating from Caribbean countries) do not do as well in school. These achievement differences appear at school entry. They widen in elementary school and then remain fixed in high school. Thus, raising minority achievement is a national priority. The question is, how? Some argue that minority kids have fewer educational resources, and less-qualified teachers, get poorer quality instruction, take fewer advanced placement and honors courses, and receive harsher discipline. However, the gaps still persist in integrated, largely middle-class and upper middle-class suburbs like Evanston, Illinois, Montclair, New Jersey, and Shaker Heights, Ohio, where the aforementioned handicaps are less evident. Others blame the achievement gap on parents. James Harris, president of the Montclair NAACP, notes, "There is a level of under involvement of black folks at every level of the education enterprise" (Johnston and Viadero, 2000). Kimberly Gibson, a black woman, feels it is the fault of low-income black parents—being black in itself is no excuse. Specifically, she is concerned that black students learn that academic achievement is "uncool and acting white." (Gibson, 2000). Cheryl Johnson, a black parent, feels part of the problem is that African-American kids are held to a lower academic standard (Viadero, 2000). Finally, many feel the achievement gap exists because minority and majority children fail to appreciate the worth of minorities and diversity.

Schools and teachers are making sincere efforts to respect and even encourage healthy diversity. Some of these efforts result from federal law, for example, the Bilingual Education Act. As the name implies, this law sponsors programs that, in the early grades, build upon a child's native language (for example, Spanish) and then gradually introduce English in second or third grade. In this way, students learn the dominant language but maintain and value their native speech. Schools are trying a great array of programs under the rubric of multicultural education. Cushner, McClelland, and Safford (2000) describe several, including:

- *Teaching the culturally different.* These programs primarily try to help students "develop and maintain their own cultural identity" while also helping them develop competence in the dominant culture. Development of a positive self-concept is a central goal.
- *Human relations.* The intention in such programs is to help "students of different backgrounds learn to communicate more effectively with others while feeling good about themselves."
- *Single-group studies.* These are primarily programs directed toward a targeted ethnic group. They celebrate that group's identity and achievements. Thus children engage in African-American studies, Native-American studies, and Hispanic-American studies.
- *Multicultural education.* In an effort to raise the consciousness of all students about various cultures and their contributions, multicultural programs have

Advocates of multicultural education feel that for too long schools have presented a narrow, Eurocentric viewpoint that focuses almost solely on the achievements of Americans of European descent. Therefore, a multicultural approach is needed. That approach, according to University of California–Riverside Professor Carlos Cortes, should focus on at least the five major American ethnic groups: Native Americans, blacks, Latinos, Asians, and Europeans. Additionally, says James Banks,

professor at the University of Washington, students must learn and explore certain concepts from multiple perspectives. These concepts include immigration, intercultural interactions, and racism.

Multicultural education also must utilize multicultural teaching. Banks and others feel that teachers must use a variety of instructional alternatives since students from different cultural groups may prefer different ways of learning. For example, G. Pritchy Smith of the

University of North Florida notes that Hispanic students tend to be field-sensitive learners. (This concept is presented in a later section of this chapter, Learning Style Differences.) Likewise Diane Boardly-Suber of Hampton University says that most African-American students respond well to collaborative, hands-on approaches to learning (see Chapter 7).

Source: S. Willis (1993, September). Multicultural teaching. *Curriculum Update*, 1–8.

emerged. They cut across subcultures, focusing on ethnic minority music, arts, or literature, and the history of minorities in America (pp. 154–155). Spotlight on Research 3.1 explains multicultural education in more detail.

For specific strategies useful when teaching minority children go to <www.ed.gov/databases/ERIC_Digests/ed435147.html>.

Web Resource

GENDER DIFFERENCES

The literature on gender differences addresses, among other things, gender roles, differences in male and female cognition, and the reactions of teachers to males as opposed to females.

Gender roles are learned early. Wynn and Fletcher (1987) report this as occurring during preschool and kindergarten. During this period, most boys begin to engage in outdoor, physical, and aggressive play, while most girls prefer art, doll play, and dancing (Carter, 1987). Although some amount of gender role learning is realistic and healthy, efforts are being made to avoid perpetuating the kind of gender role stereotyping that encourages girls to be dependent and passive and boys to be aggressive and reluctant to show emotion. Many hope that children will acquire a more balanced gender role that combines traits supposedly unique to one gender but valued by both—for example, assertiveness. Such children would supposedly possess high psychological androgyny and would be better adjusted than gender-typed persons. Evidence seems to support this position (Dusek, 1987).

Research shows that boys and girls differ in their cognitive characteristics; at issue is why and how much. Slavin (1999) reports that females generally exhibit greater verbal aptitude than males, while males usually excel in visual-spatial aptitude. Biehler and Snowman (2000) note that by the elementary grades, gender differences show up in boy-girl cognitive abilities and in overall performance. Girls frequently are superior in verbal fluency, spelling, writing, reading, and mathematical computation. Boys often excel in mathematical reasoning, spatial relationships, and insight problems. It is important to note, however, that the gender differences are not great and that individual differences within each gender are large. After examining 165 studies, Hyde and Linn (1988) conclude that gender differences in verbal ability are so small as to be insignificant, and the Educational Testing Service (1997), which examined an even greater number of studies, agrees.

Tannen (1991) and others have studied why males and females differ in the way they participate in classrooms. She suggests that boys speak in class more often because they have learned to use language more publicly in play and activity groups. In such groups, language is one way that high-status boys push low-status boys around. Conversely, girls speak in class less often since they have learned to use language more privately, with best friends and for sharing secrets. Good and Brophy (1990) believe that gender differences are not genetic but acquired, and conclude, "To the extent that society begins to expect equal achievement from boys and girls in different subject matter areas, we may begin to see it" (p. 604).

Teachers and schools seem to contribute to the maintenance of gender differences. Boys receive more disapproval and blame, while girls tend to be punished more promptly for aggressive behavior such as calling out answers without first being acknowledged (Slavin, 1999). Good and Brophy relate additional ways teachers respond differently to gender. Teachers give blander feedback to girls and more animated, detailed feedback to boys. They sometimes perform complex tasks for girls but merely coach boys to task completion. They encourage girls in grooming and manners but boys in academic striving and accomplishment. Overall, teachers tend to interact more with boys than girls.

Tannen (1991) offers the following advice to help promote gender equality in classroom interaction. Rather than asking students to "attack" an idea or a reading, sometimes ask them how they "feel" about the ideas or material being read. Rather than expecting them to raise hands, encourage students to sometimes jump in at will to express themselves. Also, occasionally have students work in homogeneous, single-gender groups.

Effective teachers are aware of gender differences and are able to establish classrooms that do not put either gender at a disadvantage. Certainly we do not want to exclude any students from participation or success in school activities because of gender. Brophy (1985) goes so far as to say that we must not only treat boys and girls the same in similar situations, but that we must overcompensate (for example, direct more math and science questions at girls) to counteract gender expectation differences.

SEXUAL PREFERENCE DIFFERENCES

You should be aware, especially if you teach adolescents, that some of those in your care may be homosexual or have concerns about sexual orientation. Therefore, according to the American Academy of Pediatrics (1993), you should be able to provide factual, current, nonjudgmental information to them in a confidential manner.

Additionally, as we know, gay and lesbian adolescents may be stigmatized, isolated, or targets of hatred by others, even parents and care givers. Peers may engage in cruel name-calling and even physical abuse. Parents and care givers may be critical, harass, and even reject. Such treatment by significant others may lead to isolation, runaway behavior, homelessness, depression and substance abuse. The difficulties homosexual youth face are reflected in their much higher tendency toward suicide. Accordingly, schools and teachers increasingly are searching for ways to deal with the sensitive question of homosexuality and to ensure that homosexual students enjoy a safe school environment.

Bickmore (1999) argues that it is important to discuss sexuality even with elementary students just as we might discuss other human differences and tolerance for them. She feels that homosexuality is readily visible to children through public images—television, film, newscasts—and cannot be easily overlooked since children are inherently interested in understanding their world. She also feels that the mini-society of elementary classrooms becomes more inclusive when all members respectfully interact with diverse individuals and unfamiliar ideas.

Clyde & Lobban (2000) provide an annotated bibliography that focuses on the issues of homosexuality in books for children. Most of the books are for adolescents.

3.4 How do you think student gender will affect the way you teach?

DEVELOPMENTAL DIFFERENCES

Students differ developmentally across and within age groups. In other words, 10-year-olds not only differ from 15-year-olds, they differ from each other. These psychosocial, cognitive, and moral differences are well documented in child development and educational psychology textbooks. Biehler and Snowman (2000) present selected theories of development and then draw implications for teaching. Each theory emphasizes that children must go through predictable developmental or growth stages, and effective instruction should aim at each student's appropriate developmental level.

Psychosocial Development Erickson (1963) suggests that our adult personal and social characteristics result from passing through certain life stages. During that journey, we resolve dichotomies and conflict between positive and negative traits—for example, between trust and mistrust, autonomy and shame, initiative and guilt, industry and inferiority, identity and role confusion, generativity and stagnation, and intimacy and isolation. A healthy personality results when we emerge with more positive than negative traits; that is, we are more trustful, more self-confident, more initiating, more productive, and clearer about our sexual and occupational roles.

Biehler and Snowman (2000) suggest we can facilitate development of more positive student personalities by

- Allowing young preschool children more free play and guided experimentation, and by not shaming them.
- Providing preschool children with activities that foster initiative and a sense of accomplishment, while not censuring them for their questions and actions.
- Presenting elementary students with tasks that are within their capacities and then rewarding accomplishment, and encouraging self-competition and cooperation.
- Assisting secondary students to consider who they are, accept their appearance, reflect on their sex roles, and explore and confirm occupational choice.

One trait that educators deem crucial to healthy personality is **self-esteem,** defined as our personal judgment of our worthiness or how favorably we regard ourselves. It was referred to in the earlier section on cultural differences. Unfortunately, although high self-esteem may be healthy, it does not by itself translate into better school academic performance (Kohn, 1994). Thus, school programs geared to raise self-esteem do not necessarily improve student learning. Improvement in learning is more specifically related to *self-esteem as a learner*, and that seems only to result from actual improved academic performance. Said another way, if we want students to have confidence that they can succeed academically, we must ensure they are having successful academic experiences. There is no simple fix.

Evans (1999) feels that the recent emphasis on raising self-esteem has, in some cases, gone too far and is harmful. He questions certain practices that teachers and parents use to make students feel good about themselves or to avoid hurting their feelings including excessive use of praise unrelated to accomplishment, failure to discipline, and not telling them when they are "selfish, mean, lazy or rude" or that their behavior is otherwise unacceptable. Evans notes that some teachers are now even unwilling to praise individual students for an accomplishment since that might make other students feel bad. As a consequence of shielding and even misleading children in this way, children lose the ability to feel shame on the one hand and true pride on the other.

3.5 What will be your approach toward balancing a child's self-esteem with reality?

Cognitive Development Piaget (1997) and his colleagues suggest that intellectual development has four stages: sensorimotor, preoperational, concrete operational, and formal operational. Furthermore, all youth proceed through all stages but at different rates. During the **sensorimotor stage** (birth to 2 years), the intellect develops primarily through using the senses and engaging in motor or physical activity. During the **preoperational, prelogical stage** (2 to 7 years), young learners develop knowledge from their personal experience, by exploring and manipulating real objects and by learning the three Rs and other basic knowledge and skills. In this stage, youngsters start to use symbols such as words and numerals to represent objects.

At the **concrete operational stage** (7 to 11 years), children become capable of logical thought. Among other things, they come to understand conservation (that matter is neither created nor destroyed, but merely changes shape or form). They also can arrange or classify objects into categories, and they can place objects in order according to characteristics such as size, length, or weight.

The **formal operational stage** (11 years and up) is achieved when children more regularly are able to deal in abstractions or perform activities mentally, or "in their heads." At this stage, students are capable of understanding more abstract mathematical concepts, such as ratio. They also now are able to use complex forms of language including proverbs, metaphors, sarcasm, and satire.

In order to utilize what is known about cognitive development, Biehler and Snowman (2000), suggest that you as a teacher

- Determine the stages of thinking of your students.
- Plan learning experiences in terms of these stages.
- Use lots of hands-on activities that allow children to manipulate objects.
- Mix more advanced with less advanced thinkers so that children can think with and learn from each other.
- Encourage students to share with others the mental processes they use for reaching concepts and conclusions.

Moral Development   Piaget (1997) and Kohlberg (1981) have ideas about how **moral development** occurs. Piaget claims that children are capable of two types of moral reasoning: morality of constraint and morality of cooperation. Typical 6-year-olds hold to **morality of constraint.** This means that they regard rules as sacred and unchangeable: Everyone should obey rules in the same way, with no exceptions. On the other hand, typical 12-year-olds hold to **morality of cooperation.** They have reached a point where they believe that rules are flexible and that there can be exceptions to them. Typical 6-year-olds, compared with 12-year-olds, are more adamant that punishment should follow rule breaking. Conversely, 12-year-olds like to take into account the circumstances causing the rule breaking. They are also concerned that misbehavior violates some mutual social agreement.

Kohlberg (1981), too, feels that children proceed through stages of moral reasoning. He originally identified three levels of moral reasoning development, each including two stages. In the earliest of Kohlberg's levels, children 9 or younger stay out of trouble only to avoid punishment or retribution. At the second level, youth 9 to 20 years stay out of trouble because they recognize that rules have been established in order to maintain security and order. At the highest level, reached only after age 20 and only by relatively few adults, people understand, accept, and adhere to the moral principles that undergird our social rules and conventions.

3.6   How will you take children's developmental differences into account?

As teachers, we can encourage moral development by engaging students in the discussion of moral dilemmas and moral issues (for example, capital punishment). Additionally, involving our students in the development and maintenance of classroom rules provides an excellent opportunity for children to model the thinking required to make moral decisions that govern many people.

Children with Special or Exceptional Needs   What does it mean to be exceptional? **Exceptionality** is a term that is used to describe children with special physical, social, emotional, and mental qualities. Such children may be either handicapped

Candy: A Mainstreamed Child

Candy is a child with cerebral palsy who was placed in Louise DeFelice's English class. DeFelice worried about a number of things: she had no experience with handicapped youth, she was apprehensive about Candy's ability to speak, and she wasn't sure how her classmates would react to her.

Candy, on the other hand, was neither worried nor self-conscious. She wasn't seeking sympathy or any kind of special treatment.

Ms. DeFelice soon became concerned about whether Candy could handle an upcoming oral report and asked her if she would rather substitute another assignment. Candy insisted that she could do it. On the day of the reports, when Candy's turn came, DeFelice was apprehensive as the girl "lumbered to the front of the classroom." She reports:

> It began much as I feared. The students sat looking down at their desks or giving one another embarrassed sidelong glances as Candy stammered and stuttered her way through the first few minutes . . . After a few more minutes each of the students began to whisper to each other (page 640).

However, just as the teacher was about to say something, Vince, a class leader, turned to his peers and told them "to shut up and pay attention." Afterward, the other kids began to look straight at Candy and concentrate on what she was trying to say. Wonderfully, at the conclusion of Candy's report the class applauded and her eyes gleamed tearfully.

Candy's belief in herself followed by what Ms. DeFelice terms "classroom magic" forever justified her faith in teaching and students.

Source: L. DeFelice. (1989, April). The Bibbidibobbidiboo Factor in Teaching. *Phi Delta Kappan, 70*(8), 639–641.

or gifted. As Good and Brophy (1994) point out, children who are either handicapped or gifted and talented may be less than successful students unless certain adaptations are made for them.

Individuals with **"handicaps"** or **"challenges"** are regularly categorized and labeled even though a stigma may be attached to them as a result. The intention of categorization is to spur efforts to meet their special needs, which are related to cognitive, perceptual, emotional, or behavioral problems. Special-needs categories include physical impairment (orthopedic handicaps, epilepsy, cerebral palsy); visual and hearing impairment (low vision, educationally blind); articulation disorders (stuttering, voicing problems); behavior disorders (conduct disorders, anxiety-withdrawal disorders, immaturity); hyperactivity; and learning disabilities and retardation. The term **challenged** is used increasingly to connote that these children are challenged—not handicapped.

Since learning in the early years is crucial, providing stimulating learning environments for young children is critical. The National Institute of Health argues that, in addition to your need to stimulate children, you need to identify those who need special education. Unfortunately, most children who might benefit don't go into special education until about 9 years of age (Pipho, 1997).

According to the Education for All Handicapped Children Act (Public Law 94-142), now known as the Individuals with Disabilities Education Act (Public Law 101-476; Public Law 105-17), children with handicaps are to be taught in the best possible—that is, the "least restrictive," or "most inclusive"—classroom placement and assisted by a team of specialists. A least restrictive environment is a setting that is as normal as possible. This often means that such children are placed in regular classes for all or part of the school day, a process referred to as *inclusion* or *mainstreaming*. See Case 3.1. The assisting team includes the child's teacher or teachers, the school psychologist or special education teacher, any persons providing academic or physical assistance or care, and the parents. A formal Individualized Educational Program (IEP) is developed by this team of specialists, including parents, and

- Must be based upon a careful assessment of the learner
- Must describe why the plan is necessary and contain objectives with a timetable for reaching each
- Must be developed by a team of individuals that work directly with the learner such as teachers, tutors, social workers, clinicians

- Should define what should be taught and how, who will teach it, where it will be taught, when the program will begin, how long it will last, when it will be reviewed, how special education and related service will be provided, and how the learner will be educated in the "least restrictive" or most normal environment possible

- Should be discussed and finalized at a meeting involving the regular classroom teacher, special education teacher, representative of the school district, and possibly the learner
- To the extent possible, parents or care givers should be involved.

followed in the classroom. As teachers, you will assist in developing IEPs for children with special challenges, care for such individuals in your classrooms, and be charged with helping them succeed in reaching goals outlined in the IEP. (See Highlight 3.1).

Biehler and Snowman (2000), Good and Brophy (1994), Slavin (1999), and Whitmore (1980) offer many suggestions for working with students with special needs. Since these children are so numerous and their problems so varied, prospective teachers are well advised and, in some states, required, to enroll in special coursework.

The second kind of student with special educational needs is labeled gifted and talented. Gifted and talented children are blessed with some combination of above-average ability, creativity, and task commitment. The Gifted and Talented Act describes such children as having intellectual, creative, academic, or leadership abilities. According to Whitmore and Maker (1985), as many as *5 percent of individuals with disabilities are gifted and talented as well.*

Unfortunately, not all children with such gifts are academically oriented or high achievers in school. Studies inform us that 42 percent of gifted high school students underachieve; 54 and 33 percent, respectively, of gifted boys and girls work below their capabilities (Alter, 1953; Gowan, 1955; see also Whitmore, 1980; Butler-Por, 1987). One study (HM Inspectors, 1978) notes that underexploitation of the gifts of children with special talents ranks as one of the most serious deficiencies in Great Britain's elementary schools. A parallel exists in America. As teachers, one of your challenges will be to meet the special needs of these students.

Here are some Internet sites on special education that you may find useful:

If you want to locate special education resources on the Internet, visit <http://seriweb.com/> or to <http://curry.edschool.Virginia.EDU/go/specialed/>.

If you want information on the Individualized Education Program, visit <http://www.ed.gov/offices/OSERS/OSEP/Products/IEP_Guide/> or <http://www.ldonline.org/ld_indepth/iep/legally_correct_ieps.html>.

Web Resource

LEARNING STYLE DIFFERENCES

We are well aware that we harbor preferences with regard to what we are interested in learning and how we wish to learn (see Chapter 1). Some of us enjoy studying the humanities (art, music, history, philosophy, language), others the social and behavioral sciences (sociology, anthropology, psychology), natural sciences, or mathematics. Further, we prefer to obtain and process information in distinctively personal ways. Some of us prefer to work alone; others enjoy group experiences. Some learn better when information is presented visually; others learn better by hearing the information. As the saying goes, "To each his own."

Children as young as age 4 or 5 begin to display such preferences. One child will enjoy solitary reading, another will enjoy group projects in social studies, while still another might relish science activities that require manipulating objects and experimenting with them.

For years, psychologists and educators have tried to better understand, describe, and measure individual learning preferences and styles. As a consequence, many different points of view have developed and a number of terms have been coined to describe these styles. Some of the terms are used quite loosely (Della-Dora & Blanchard, 1979). For example, our **learning style** can be thought of as our "learning personality." It is a consistent pattern of behavior and performance we use to approach learning experiences.

The most familiar way of measuring and describing a person's learning style is by exploring **cognitive style;** this term refers to the consistent ways in which an individual responds to a wide range of perceptual tasks (Dembo, 2000). Familiarity with the following cognitive style differences should help you plan and execute your lessons in a more flexible and responsive manner.

Conceptual Tempo   We all know both impulsive and reflective people. These people differ in **conceptual tempo.** Impulsive people like to work fast, make decisions quickly, and may do things without serious forethought. Consequently, they often rush through their work in what seems to be a careless way, perhaps completing the task incorrectly because they neglect to read the directions or do not persist long enough to complete the task. Because they rush, impulsive students tend to perform more poorly in school tasks requiring analysis and attention to detail.

While impulsive students like to work quickly, reflective students are likely to take considerable time in their work and in making up their minds, usually because they consider several alternative responses before arriving at their answer. Rather than speed, they are concerned about accuracy and about ensuring that they have a good answer. Reflective learners sometimes receive poor evaluations because they are so meticulous. Although they may not finish a task, what they have completed may be nearly perfect. Reflective learners may not participate in class discussions or respond when called upon. Quite literally, they are still thinking about their answer!

Woolfolk (2000) makes clear that not everyone who works fast is impulsive. "Some people are simply very bright and quick to understand" (p. 150). Nor are slow workers necessarily reflective; they might be less bright or able to understand. She notes that some people are fast-accurate or slow-inaccurate thinkers.

As part of normal development, children become more reflective with age. However, the tendency to respond either impulsively or reflectively remains fairly stable. Children can become more reflective by learning to think before they respond or by talking themselves through each step of a complex task (Meichenbaum, 1999).

Field-Sensitive versus Field-Independent Learners (Witkin et al., 1962, 1981)   Students also differ along this continuum, which is part of one's cognitive learning style. On the one hand are students who view situations in their totality, seeing a whole pattern, or gestalt. They "see the forest" as opposed to seeing individual trees therein. Such children are called **field-sensitive,** or **field-dependent.** Persons who have difficulty reading a diagram and putting together something requiring assembly may be field-sensitive.

Field-sensitive learners seem to share certain characteristics. They tend to be more gregarious or people-oriented. Second, they are better at learning material with social content such as social studies, social sciences, and literature. Third, they have difficulty noticing or picking out details and working with material presented to them in an unstructured way. For example, field-sensitive learners may have difficulty with math word problems because they do not identify and distinguish between relevant and irrelevant information. Finally, these learners are more responsive to praise and other kinds of reinforcement and more adversely affected by criticism.

On the other hand are **field-independent** learners. They focus more easily on "the trees," or the details. Their characteristics include being more curious and self-reliant, and less conforming and obedient. Furthermore, they are more task oriented, and they work better with unstructured tasks such as problem solving. On the downside, perhaps, field-independent students have more difficulty learning social content and working with others. Compared with field-dependent or field-sensitive students, they need less praise and are less affected by criticism.

Some studies (Fritz, 1992) indicate that boys are generally more field-independent, which may result from different child-rearing patterns. Furthermore, some believe that field sensitivity is related to one's cultural heritage. For example Mexican-American and African-American youth have been reported to be more field-sensitive than majority Americans (Ramerez & Price-Williams, 1974). Although, over time, persons may become more or less field-sensitive or -independent, each of us tends to remain one or the other and not to cross over.

Convergent/Divergent Thinking   A third aspect of cognitive style is convergence/divergence. Persons who tend to think in independent, flexible, and imaginative ways are considered more creative. Such persons are sometimes called **divergent thinkers** because they have the ability to come up with different ideas for accomplishing a task or solving a problem. Persons predisposed to think in conventional, typical ways are termed **convergent thinkers.** They search for a single, logical answer. When asked what a pencil might be used for, convergent thinkers reply that a pencil is for writing. Divergent thinkers may add that a pencil can be used for punching holes in paper, rolling clay into sheets, or as a handle for a slingshot.

Perceptual Modality Preferences/Strengths   This fourth dimension of cognitive style describes a learner's tendency to use different sensory modes to understand experiences and to learn (Keefe & Farrell, 1990). For example, some students prefer to learn visually, by seeing information. You may have heard a friend say, "I'm a visual person." Such persons learn most easily by reading material or seeing something demonstrated. Others are auditory learners who need to hear information in order to learn. Lectures with careful explanations or hearing a textbook on tape are effective ways for these students to learn. Kinesthetic, or tactile, learners need to be physically or even emotionally involved in order to learn. Students who need to count on their fingers to complete arithmetic computations or to manipulate objects or materials are often kinesthetic learners.

Dunn, Dunn, and Price (2001) believe we should determine the preferred learning styles of each of our students and adjust our teaching accordingly. Consequently, they have developed the Learning Style Inventory for this purpose. Kolb (1985) has developed another learning style inventory. You may find out what your learning style at http://www.learningstyle.com. (The report costs $5.00.)

Although the notion of learning styles is attractive to many administrators and educators, research supporting curriculum or teaching changes based solely on some aspect of learning styles is "murky at best" (O'Neil, 1990). However, research on learning styles has contributed some key understandings that can guide us as teachers. These include recognizing that people are different; that learners will respond differently to a variety of instructional methods; and that we need to respect and honor individual differences among the students who make up our classes (Brandt, 1990).

Finally and importantly, as noted in Chapter 1, we must realize that our personal learning style and teaching style generally match. Consequently, we often assume that all of our students enjoy the same kinds of learning experiences we do. Wrong! To be effective, we will have to provide many different kinds of learning activities. In the classroom, variety truly is "the spice of life."

3.7   What is your learning personality? Are you impulsive or reflective, field dependent or independent, convergent or divergent?

Web Resource

3.8   Are you a visual, kinesthetic, or auditory learner?

LEARNING ABILITY DIFFERENCES

We all know students differ in their academic performance: Some are outstanding, most are average, and some have difficulty. These differences are due to four factors, namely, aptitude, attention differences, the home-community environment, and classroom instruction.

Student Aptitude Normally, we think of students' aptitude solely as their mental ability or intelligence. We commonly accept the idea that this ability is demonstrated in how well they can perform verbal-language and/or mathematical tasks. However, some psychologists (Gardner, 1988, 1993, 1995 and Gardner & Hatch, 1989) remind us that students have multiple aptitudes. In addition to having linguistic or language ability and logical-mathematical ability, they also possess abilities (termed *intelligences*) in spatial matters, body kinesthetics, music, interpersonal relations, self-understanding, and pattern recognition (see Highlight 3.2).

To understand Gardner's **multiple theory of intelligence,** it is necessary to understand his definition of *intelligence.* Intelligence is the ability to solve problems or make something of value. That ability must meet three conditions: brain evidence must support its existence, persons must be particularly good or bad at it, and it must be possessed and needed by animals other than humans (Checkley, 1997).

Thus, Gardner and others want teachers to recognize and nurture the diversity of abilities different students have. Let's explore an example—interpersonal intelligence, or the ability to understand others.

As we know, understanding and getting along with others is an important human ability. Bell Laboratories, a high-tech think tank, reports that its most valued, productive electrical engineers excel in traits such as cooperation, empathy, rapport, and the ability to build consensus. This particular attribute is called interpersonal intelligence by Gardner but often is termed **emotional intelligence** or EQ (again, see Highlight 3.2).

Unfortunately, EQ is on the wane among American youth, and children with low EQ are more likely to be disobedient, to pick fights, to engage in unlawful activity, and to become pregnant (Goleman, 1997). To reverse this trend, the Yale Child Study Center is developing courses for K–12 teachers that promote student ability to control impulses, show empathy, cooperate with others, focus on a task, pursue goals, and resolve conflicts. You can learn a lot more about EQ from Elias et al. (1997).

"We studied genetics at school today. If you wanted a smart child, you should have adopted one."

HIGHLIGHT 3.2
Eight Kinds of Intelligence

- *Linguistic intelligence* is the capacity to use language, your native language and perhaps other languages, to express what's on your mind and to understand other people. Poets really specialize in linguistic intelligence, but any kind of writer, orator, speaker, lawyer, or a person for whom language is an important stock in trade highlights linguistic intelligence.

- People with a highly developed *logical-mathematical intelligence* understand the underlying principles of some kind of a causal system, the way a scientist, mathematician, or a logician does.

- *Spatial intelligence* refers to the ability to represent the spatial world internally in your mind—the way a sailor or airplane pilot navigates the large spatial world, or the way a chess player or sculptor represents a more circumscribed spatial world. Spatial intelligence can be used in the arts or in the sciences. If you are spatially intelligent and oriented toward the arts, you are more likely to become a painter or a sculptor or an architect than, say, a musician or a writer. Similarly, certain sciences like anatomy or topology emphasize spatial intelligence.

- *Bodily kinesthetic intelligence* is the capacity to use your whole body or parts of your body—your hand, your fingers, your arms—to solve a problem, make something, or put on some kind of a production. The most evident examples are people in athletics or the performing arts, particularly dance or acting.

- *Musical intelligence* is the capacity to think in music, to be able to hear patterns, recognize them, remember them, and perhaps manipulate them. People who have a strong musical intelligence don't just remember music easily—they can't get it out of their minds, it's so omnipresent. Now, some people will say, "Yes, music is important, but it's a talent, not an intelligence." And I say, "Fine, let's call it a talent." But, then we have to leave the word intelligent out of all discussions of human abilities. You know, Mozart was damned smart!

- *Interpersonal intelligence* is understanding other people. It's an ability we all need, but is at a premium if you are a teacher, clinician, salesperson, or politician. Anybody who deals with other people has to be skilled in the interpersonal sphere.

- *Intrapersonal intelligence* refers to having an understanding of yourself, of knowing who you are, what you can do, what you want to do, how you react to things, which things to avoid, and which things to gravitate toward. We are drawn to people who have a good understanding of themselves because those people tend not to screw up. They tend to know what they can do. They tend to know what they can't do. And they tend to know where to go if they need help.

- *Naturalist intelligence* designates the human ability to discriminate among living things (plants, animals) as well as sensitivity to other features of the natural world (clouds, rock configurations). This ability was clearly of value in our evolutionary past as hunters, gatherers, and farmers; it continues to be central in such roles as botanist or chef. I also speculate that much of our consumer society exploits the naturalist intelligences, which can be mobilized in the discrimination among cars, sneakers, kinds of makeup, and the like. The kind of pattern recognition valued in certain of the sciences may also draw upon naturalist intelligence.

Source: H. Gardner in Checkley, K. (1997, September). The first seven and the eighth. *Educational Leadership*, 55 (1), 8–13.

3.9 What kinds of intelligence seem to serve you?

Since Gardner recognizes at least eight kinds of intelligence, including EQ, he recommends teachers introduce and examine topics in a number of different ways (Gardner, 1995). For example, if the topic at hand is "conflict," teachers can introduce and examine it by telling a story about conflict, through formal argument about what conflict is, by engaging students in conflict creating a simulation such as Starpower, or by engaging students in artistic expression—"Picture 'conflict'. What does it look like?" These strategies facilitate personalized, multiple ways of knowing and understanding. Gardner characterizes a good school as one that takes learning differences very seriously. In such a school, teachers develop curriculum, teach, and assess learning in ways that serve the multiple intelligences children possess.

A number of Internet sites relate to multiple intelligences. Go to <http://ericir.syr.edu/Resources/General_Education/Learning_Theories/Multiple_Intelligences.html>.

Web Resource

Dusty, a Child with ADHD

Dusty Nash, an angelic-looking blond child of 7, awoke at 5:00 one recent morning in his Chicago home and proceeded to throw a fit. He wailed. He kicked. Every muscle in his body flew in furious motion. Finally, after 30 minutes, Dusty pulled himself together sufficiently to head downstairs for breakfast. While his mother bustled about the kitchen, the hyperkinetic child pulled a box of Kix cereal from the cupboard and sat on a chair.

But sitting still was not in the cards this morning. After grabbing some cereal with his hands, he began kicking the box, scattering little round corn puffs across the room. Next, he turned his attention to the TV set—or rather, the table supporting it. The table was covered with a checkerboard Con-Tact paper, and Dusty began peeling it off. Then he became intrigued with the spilled cereal and started stomping it to bits. At this point, his mother interceded. In a firm but calm voice, she told her son to get the dust pan and broom and clean up the mess. Dusty got out the dust pan but forgot the rest of the order. Within seconds he was dismantling the dust pan, piece by piece. His next project: grabbing three rolls of toilet paper from the bathroom and unraveling them around the house.

It was only 7:30, and his mother, who teaches a medical school course on death and dying, was already feeling half-dead from exhaustion. Dusty was to see his doctors that day at 4:00, and they had asked her not to give the boy the drug he usually takes to control his hyperactivity and attention problems. . . . It was going to be a very long day without it.

Source: C. Wallis. (1994, July 18). Life in overdrive. *Time, 144*(3), 50.

Student Attention Differences Students also vary in their ability to pay attention. Some are so adversely affected that they are referred to as having **attention deficit disorder,** or ADD. Persons with ADD may be hyperactive inattentive, hyperactive impulsive, or impulsive but not hyperactive (*Diagnostic and Statistical Manual of Mental Disorders,* 1980). The hyperactive variety of ADD, attention deficit/hyperactivity disorder (ADHD), is portrayed in Case 3.2.

Although the term ADHD was not well known two decades ago (such children were merely referred to as difficult or obstreperous), some say that up to 35 million children, mostly boys under 18 (about 4 percent) display its symptoms, which include extreme distractibility, almost reckless impulsiveness, and general difficulty in sitting or being still. In the Rochester, New York, area, 13 percent of boys ages 6 to 12 are medicated for ADHD. Indeed, ADHD is the most commonly diagnosed behavioral disorder (Coles, 2000). Some fear that adults are too willing to medicate children in order to make adult lives easier (French, 1996; Shute 2000).

Children with such characteristics may not function well in traditional schools unless schools make accommodations. Without special care, such children have an extremely high risk of school failure, substance abuse, and lawbreaking. Additionally, they often have few friends and their parents or caregivers frequently are blamed for failure to control them. Over time, such children may lose their sense of self-worth and may fall far behind academically.

Within the classroom, teachers are urged to consider giving such children stand-up desks, seating them near the teacher, and letting them take tests in a quiet area. Other ways you can assist such children include helping them to be organized, establishing a predictable schedule of activities, assigning them a location for school possessions, and using principles of behavior modification that are presented in the next chapter. (Additional suggestions are found in Armstrong, 1996a, and Pellegrini and Horvat, 1995, and at "Teaching Children with ADHD" http://ericir.syr.edu/cgi-bin/print. cgi/Resources/Specific_Populations/Disabilities/Specific_Disabilities-Disorders/ Attention_Deficit_Disorders.html). Furthermore, you are warned not to automatically label such kids as ADD or ADHD since their symptoms, if new, may be the result of some other problem such as anxiety, depression, or neurological dysfunction (Armstrong, 1996b). Highlight 3.3 lists some of the symptoms of the disorder. The

Web Resource

Does a Child You Know Possibly Have Attention Deficit Hyperactivity Disorder?

If eight or more of the following statements seem to characterize a child you know, he or she has traits common to ADHD. A medical diagnosis may be useful.

1. Often fidgets or squirms when sitting.
2. Has difficulty remaining seated.
3. Is easily distracted.
4. Has difficulty awaiting turns.
5. Often blurts things out.
6. Has difficulty following directions.
7. Has difficulty paying attention.
8. Often shifts from one incomplete activity to another.
9. Has difficulty playing quietly.
10. Often interrupts or intrudes.
11. Often doesn't seem to listen.
12. Talks excessively.
13. Often engages in dangerous play without considering consequences.

Source: Adapted from C. Wallis. (1994, July 18). Life in overdrive. *Time, 144* (3), 50.

Web Resource

Try Activity 3.1

Try Activity 3.2

American Academy of Pediatrics provides guidelines for ADHD diagnosis in children age 6–12; see http://www.aap.org/policy/ac0002.html.

Finally, students differ in their interest and self-concept. Those who are interested, who have a sense that they are in control and are "OK," are better able and more likely to learn. Thus, key factors contributing to student aptitude, or ability to learn, are intelligence, emotional maturity, interest, and self-concept.

IMPLICATIONS FOR TEACHERS

3.8 Are you up to the challenge of teaching students who have difficulty learning?

Teachers are effective in large part because they care about children enough to accommodate their seemingly endless diversity. Wang (1998) tells us that "what works is adapting instruction to students' diverse backgrounds and needs, an approach that determines how each child learns . . . and then tailoring instruction to meet those needs" (p. 39). Less effective teachers often have a difficult time either noticing or attending to the variability of students in their classes. They want and tend to see the class more as a homogeneous group. While this makes instruction less complicated, if you are to advance from a novice to a more expert teacher, you must learn to teach children who are socioeconomically, culturally, and developmentally diverse and diverse in terms of gender, exceptionality, learning style, and learning ability. To summarize, our schools need teachers who will

- Care about economically disadvantaged youth and be willing to work with them (this implies willingness to teach in rural and urban schools).
- Help students gain a feeling of efficacy or control over their destinies.
- Accept, appreciate, and promote culturally specific characteristics.
- Promote the best attributes of both genders in all children.
- Provide students with experiences that may help them develop positive personalities.
- Take into account students' varying levels of cognitive development when teaching.
- Encourage growth in moral development.
- Show concern for and work with exceptional students.

Try Activity 3.3

- Allow for students' learning, thinking, and cognitive styles and their multiple intelligences.

Some Final Thoughts

This chapter describes some of the many faces of student diversity and challenges they present. To the extent you recognize that your learners are unique and take that uniqueness into account, you are more likely to increase their academic and social success. Consequently, you will be remembered by them as a teacher who made a difference in their lives. Hopefully, you had one or more teachers who took a personal interest in you, who cared about you as an individual. Pass it on!

Try Activity 3.4

CHAPTER SUMMARY

- To be an effective teacher you must know the many ways learners differ and take those differences into account.
- Students differ socioeconomically, and the impact of socioeconomic status on poor children can be great. They are more likely to be born outside of marriage, live in a single-parent or care giver family in rental housing, be homeless, have greater medical and dental problems, engage in early sexual activity, and become more involved in crime, violence, and substance abuse. Low SES children also are more likely to enter school with experiential deficits and perform less well academically.
- In order to help low SES children you need to muster all the parent, care giver, and community support available, instill in the children a sense of efficacy (that they are adequate persons in control of their personal destinies), hold them to high learning and behavior expectations, offer interesting, engaging lessons, teach them thinking and problem-solving skills, help them *understand* what they are learning, provide individual help, and respect their cultural backgrounds.
- Students differ culturally. When ethnicity or race is tied to low SES, minority students often do less well academically, as described above.
- Unfortunately, the school curriculum often makes little of the contributions of certain minority cultures and the way we teach may be at odds with the values and behaviors minority children learn at home.
- In order to help culturally different children educationally and personally you may need to help them acquire greater English language proficiency while maintaining their cultural identity, celebrate the contributions their culture has made, develop or maintain a positive self-esteem, and keep them focused on academics.
- Children demonstrate real and healthy gender differences. However, avoid perpetuating gender stereotypes, for example that boys are aggressive and reluctant to show emotion and girls are dependent and passive. When boys and girls are treated differently, it may be to their disadvantage.
- Boys and girls do evidence some academic learning differences; however the differences on average are not great whereas individual differences within a gender are large.
- Sexuality preferences exist and begin to emerge during adolescence. You need to help students who are concerned and/or who may be stigmatized or isolated by peers, parents, or care givers. Since the media depicts homosexuality, it probably is wise to help children of all ages with questions about it.
- Students differ developmentally in a number of ways—psychosocially, cognitively, and morally. For example, psychosocially children differ in their self-esteem. Cognitively they differ in intellectual development. Morally they differ in how and what they think about rules. You need to know your learners developmentally and help them to grow each capacity further.
- Children differ physically, emotionally, and mentally. Learners who are blessed in such ways are referred to as gifted. Those who have deficits are considered handicapped, "challenged," or special needs persons. More attention is given to the latter, particularly to enhancing their school success through such things as providing stimulating learning environments, placing them in least restrictive environments, and utilizing carefully constructed individual education plans.

- Students prefer to learn different things and to learn in different ways. Some like one subject and not another. Some like to learn in groups, others individually. Some are impulsive, rushing to complete work; others are reflective taking lots of time to consider and complete a task. Some are field-dependent in that they are more gregarious, and learn certain subjects (social studies, social sciences, literature) better. Some are field-independent in that they are more curious and less conforming. They seem to enjoy problem-solving tasks.

- Children differ in terms of whether they are convergent or divergent thinkers and in terms of their perceptual modality preferences. Convergent thinkers search for a single best answer to a question while divergent thinkers prefer to explore many answers or solutions. Some prefer to learn visually; others learn by listening.

- Children have different learning abilities. In terms of intelligence they differ in multiple ways, for example linguistically and logically-mathematically. Another way children demonstrate differences in learning ability is through their emotional or interpersonal intelligence, that is, how well they can cooperate, show empathy, control impulses, and resolve conflicts.

- Students vary in their ability to pay attention. Those who cannot satisfactorily do so often are termed attention deficit. They are too easily distracted and have learning and sometimes social problems. You need to be alert for signs of attention deficit and make accommodations to increase the successful participation of attention deficit children.

- Students differ developmentally, that is, psychosocially, cognitively, and morally. Teachers can facilitate children's development by assisting them in building healthy personalities, providing educational experiences suitable to each child's cognitive level, and helping them think through moral issues and dilemmas.

- Students differ according to their physical, social, emotional, and mental needs. Some have exceptional abilities and talents, while others have exceptional needs. Some also seem to have preferences regarding how they like to learn. Teachers need to recognize these exceptionalities and learning preferences and adjust their teaching accordingly.

- Students differ in how well they do in school. Some have a high aptitude for school learning, live in a stimulating environment, and attend excellent schools. Others do not. Teachers can make a great impact by recognizing and rewarding students who possess different kinds of intelligence.

ISSUES AND PROBLEMS FOR DISCUSSION

ISSUES   Here are some issues for you to debate.

1. To what extent do you believe teachers can accommodate the many kinds of differences learners bring to the classroom?

2. What, in your mind, are the most important kinds of learner differences (socio-economic, cultural, gender, sexuality, developmental, learning style, learner ability) that teachers should try to accommodate?

3. To what extent should learners be grouped according to their likenesses and differences? For example, what might be the advantages and disadvantages of grouping learners according to cultural background, gender, development, learning style, or learning ability?

4. How well prepared are you to work with diverse children? How can you increase your ability to do so?

PROBLEMS   The following are some related, verbatim, day-to-day problems teachers have shared with us. How might you resolve them?

Problem 1:   Artis tells you that you don't like him.

Problem 2:   Tipp's mother feels he is developing a very negative self-esteem.

Problem 3:   Every lesson you assign seems to result in some children finishing ahead of others and some not doing the assignments well.

Problem 4:   The girls complain that you always call on the boys and give them special privileges.

Problem 5:   James is very upset with his report card. He comments, "I try real hard but all I get are bad marks. I give up!"

Problem 6:   Kimberly's mother doesn't want her in the low-reading group.

THEORY INTO ACTION ACTIVITIES

ACTIVITY 3.1: Personal Feelings about Teaching Diverse Students   Write a paragraph or so on the topic "What I think it will be like to teach diverse children." Compare your thoughts with others.

ACTIVITY 3.2: Five Student Types   Scholars (Good & Power, 1976) have identified five types of students. If you are in a field experience, with the help of your mentor teacher try to identify one of each type. How might you serve each?

1. *Successful.* These students are academically successful in school. They work hard and cause few problems. They like school and teachers.
2. *Social.* These students are more interested in the social aspects of school life than in the academic. They are popular and friendly. Their socializing can cause problems.
3. *Alienated.* These students may be openly hostile toward the school and teachers, or they may be passive and withdrawn.
4. *Dependent.* Such students are emotionally and/or academically insecure. They need approval and help.
5. *Phantom.* Such students are quiet, independent, and seldom seen or heard.

Names of students I have identified and how I would work with each:

1. Successful _____

2. Social _____

3. Alienated _____

4. Dependent _____

5. Phantom _____

ACTIVITY 3.3: Obtain Classroom Teachers' Views about Student Diversity   Talk with one or more classroom teachers about student diversity. Perhaps they would respond to questions such as

- What differences do you see among children from different SES backgrounds?
- What differences do you see among children with different cultural backgrounds?
- What is the difference between teaching majority and minority students?
- What is the difference between teaching boys and girls?

- In what ways do your students differ developmentally (e.g., in terms of their personalities, self-esteem, thinking ability, sense of morality)?
- What children have special needs and how do you meet them?
- How do your students differ in the way they like to learn? In their learning abilities?

ACTIVITY 3.4: The Implications of Student Diversity for Teaching After reading this chapter, make a list of five to ten *major* things you have learned and their possible implications for classroom practice. For example:

MAJOR LEARNING	POSSIBLE IMPLICATION
1. Students differ from one another in many ways.	1. To be effective as a teacher, I need to know how my students vary and how I can accommodate their differences. I certainly can't expect to teach them all successfully without using different approaches from student to student and from time to time.
2.	2.
3.	3.
4.	4.
5.	5.
6.	6.
7.	7.
8.	8.
9.	9.
10.	10.

REFERENCES

Alter, H. (1953). A study of high school students with scores of 130 and above on the California Test of Mental Maturity. Unpublished paper.

American Academy of Pediatrics. (1993, October). Homosexuality and adolescence: Policy statement. *Pediatrics, 92*(4), 631–634.

Armstrong, T. (1996a, February). ADD: Does it really exist? *Phi Delta Kappan, 77*(7), 424–428.

Armstrong, T. (1996b, February). A holistic approach to attention deficit disorder. *Educational Leadership, 53*(5), 34–36.

Beck, J. (1990, June 12). Getting to children early must be stressed. *Columbus Dispatch,* 11A.

Bickmore, K. (1999). *Why discuss sexuality in elementary school?* Paper presented at the Annual Meeting of the American Educational Research Association, Montreal, April 19–23, (ERIC Document Reproduction Services ED 434 893).

Biehler, R., & Snowman, J. (2000). *Psychology applied to teaching.* Ninth Edition. Boston: Houghton Mifflin.

Bower, E. M. (1978). *Teachers talk about their feelings.* Rockville, MD: Center for Studies of Child and Family Health, National Institute of Mental Health.

Brandt, R. (1990). On learning styles: A conversation with Pat Guild. *Educational Leadership, 48*(2), 10–13.

Brophy, J. (1985). Interactions of male and female students with male and female teachers. In L. Wilkinson & C. Marrett (Eds.), *Gender differences in classroom interaction* (pp. 115–142). Orlando, FL: Academic Press.

Butler-Por, N. (1987). *Underachievers in schools: Issues and intervention.* New York: John Wiley & Sons.

Carter, D. B. (1987). The role of peers in sex role socialization. In D. B. Carter (Ed.), *Current conceptions of sex roles and sex typing* (pp. 101–121). New York: Praeger.

Checkley, K. (1997, September). The first seven and the eighth. *Educational Leadership,*
55(1), 8–13.

Children's Defense Fund. (1992). *Child poverty data from the 1990 Census.* Washington, DC:
The Children's Defense Fund.

Clyde, L., & Lobban, M. (2000). *Out of the closet and into the classroom: Homosexuality in books*
for young people. Victoria, Australia (ERIC Document Reproduction Services ED 437 482).

Coles, A. (2000, May 10). Educators welcome guidelines for diagnosing ADHD. *Education*
Week, 19(35), 6.

Cruickshank, D. (1990). *Research that informs teachers and teacher educators.* Bloomington, IN:
Phi Delta Kappa.

Cushner, K., McClelland, A., & Safford, P. (2000). *Human diversity in education.* New York:
McGraw-Hill.

DeFelice, L. (1989, April). The Bibbidibobbidiboo Factor in Teaching. *Phi Delta Kappan,*
70(8), 639–641.

Della-Dora, D., & Blanchard, L. J. (Eds.). (1979). *Moving toward self-directed learning.*
Alexandria, VA: Association for Supervision and Curriculum Development.

Dembo, M. H. (2000). *Applying educational psychology in the classroom.* New York: Addison-
Wesley Longman.

Diagnostic and statistical manual of mental disorders. Third Edition (1980). Washington:
American Psychiatric Association.

Dunn, R. & Dunn, K. (1988). *Complete Guide to Learning Styles.* Boston: Allyn & Bacon.

Dunn, R., Dunn, K., & Price, G. (2001). *Learning style inventory.* Lawrence, KS: Price Systems.

Dusek, J. (1987). Sex roles and adjustment. In D. B. Carter (Ed.), *Current conceptions of sex*
roles and sex typing (pp. 211–222). New York: Praeger.

Educational Testing Service. (1997). *ETS gender study: How females and males perform in*
educational settings. Princeton, NJ: Educational Testing Service.

Elias, M., Zins, J., Weissberg, R., Fry, K., Greenberg, M., Haynes, N., Kessler, R., Schwab-
Stone, M., & Shriver, T. (1997). *Promoting social and emotional learning.* Alexandria, VA:
Association for Supervision and Curriculum Development.

Erikson, E. (1963). *Childhood and society.* Second Edition. New York: Norton.

Evans, D. (1999, October 20). The excesses of self-esteem. *Education Week, 19*(8), 47.

French, L. (1996, Fall). Haircuts and hyperactivity. *Rochester Review, 59*(1), 33.

Fritz, R. L. (1992). *A study of gender differences in cognitive style and volition.* (ERIC Document
Reproduction Services ED 354 379).

Gardner, H. (1993). *Frames of mind: The theory of multiple intelligences.* New York: Basic Books.

Gardner, H. (1988). Beyond the IQ: Education and human development. *Harvard*
Educational Review, 57, 187–193.

Gardner, H. (1995). Reflections on multiple intelligences. *Phi Delta Kappan, 77*(30), 200–209.

Gardner, H., & Hatch, T. (1989). Multiple intelligences go to school. *Educational Researcher,*
18(8), 4–10.

Gibson, K. (2000, August 5). Poverty is no excuse for a poor education. *Columbus Dispatch,*
A11.

Goleman, D. (1997). *Emotional intelligence.* New York: Bantam Books.

Goleman, D. (1995, September 17). Successful people demonstrate high "nice guy"
quotient. New York Times Wire Service. *Columbus Dispatch,* 6B.

Good, T., & Brophy, J. (1999). *Contemporary educational psychology: A realistic approach.* New
York: Longman.

Good, T., & Power, C. (1976). Designing successful classroom environments for different
types of students. *Journal of Curriculum Studies, 8,* 1–16.

Gowan, J. (1955). The underachieving gifted child: A problem for everyone. *Exceptional*
Children, 21, 247–248.

Hart, B., & Risley, T. (1999). *Meaningful differences.* Baltimore: Paul Brookes.

Headden, S. (1997, October 20). The Hispanic dropout mystery. *U.S. News & World Report,*
123(15), 64–65.

HM Inspectors of Schools. (1978). *Primary education in England.* London: HMSO.

Hyde, J., & Linn, M. (1988, April 5–8). Gender differences in verbal ability: A meta-
analysis. Paper presented at the annual meeting of the American Educational Research
Association in New Orleans.

Johnston, R., & Viadero, D. (2000, March 15). Unmet promise: Raising minority
achievement. *Education Week, 19*(27), 1, 18–23.

Kauffman, J. M. (2000). *Characteristics of emotional and behavioral disorders of children and youth.* Seventh Edition. Englewood Cliffs, NJ: Prentice Hall.

Keefe, J. W., & Farrell, B. R. (1990). Developing a defensible learning style paradigm. *Educational Leadership, 46*(2), 57–61.

Knapp, M. S., Turnbull, B. J., & Shields, P. M. (1990, September). New directions for educating children of poverty. *Educational Leadership, 48*(1), 4–8.

Kohlberg, L. (1981). *The philosophy of moral development.* New York: Harper and Row.

Kohn, A. (1994). The truth about self-esteem. *Phi Delta Kappan 76*(4), 272–283.

Kolb, D. (1985). *Learning style inventory (LSI).* Boston: McBer.

Kozol, J. (1990, Winter–Spring). The new untouchables. *Newsweek Special Issue,* 48–49, 52–53.

Maccoby, E., & Jacklin, C. (1974). *The psychology of sex differences.* Stanford, CA: Stanford University Press.

Meichenbaum, D. (1999). *Cognitive behavior modification: An integrative approach.* New York: Plenum.

O'Neil, J. (1990). Findings of styles research murky at best. *Educational Leadership, 48*(2), 7.

Osborne, J. A. (1997, December). Race and academic disidentification. *Journal of Educational Psychology, 89*(4), 728–735.

Pellegrini, A. D., & Horvat, M. (1995). A developmental contextualist critique of attention deficit hyperactivity disorder. *Educational Researcher, 24*(1), 13–20.

Piaget, J. (1997). *The moral judgment of the child.* New York: Free Press.

Pipho, C. (1997, September). Reshaping special education. *Phi Delta Kappan 79*(1), 5–6.

Poverty and Wealth Statistics Branch. (1991). Poverty in the United States 1990; *Money income of households, families, and persons 1990; Measuring the effect of benefits and taxes on income and poverty 1990.* Washington, DC: U.S. Bureau of the Census.

Ramerez, M., & Price-Williams, D. (1974). Cognitive styles of children of three ethnic groups in the United States. *Journal of Cross-Cultural Psychology, 5*(2), 212–219.

Select Committee on Children, Youth and Families. (1989). *U.S. children and their families: Current conditions and recent trends, 1989.* Washington, DC: U.S. Government Printing Office.

Shute, N. (2000, October 2). Pushing pills on kids. *U.S. News and World Report, 129*(13), 60.

Slavin, R. (1999). *Educational psychology: Theory into practice.* Fifth Edition. Boston: Allyn Bacon.

Tannen, D. (1991, July 19). Teachers' classroom strategies should recognize that men and women use language differently. *Chronicle of Higher Education, 37*(40), B1, B3.

Viadero, D. (2000, March 22). Lags in minority achievement defy traditional explanations. *Education Week, 19*(28), 1, 18–22.

Wallis, C. (1994, July 18). Life in overdrive. *Time, 144*(3), 50.

Wang, M. (1998, June 24). Comprehensive school reform. *Education Week, 17*(41), 52, 39.

Wang, M. C. & Gordon, E. W. (Eds.) (1994). *Educational resilience in inner-city America: Challenges and prospects.* Hillside, NJ: Lawrence Erlbaum Associates.

Whitmore, J. (1980). *Giftedness, conflict and underachievement.* Boston: Allyn & Bacon.

Whitmore, J. & Maker, C. (1985). *Intellectual giftedness in disabled persons.* Rockville, MD: Aspen Systems Corporation.

Willis, S. (1993, September). *Multicultural teaching.* Curriculum Update, 1–8.

Witkin, H. A., Dyke, R., Faterfon, H., Goodenough, D., & Korp, S. (1962). *Psychological differentiation: Studies of development.* New York: Wiley.

Witkin, H. & Goodenough, D. (1981). *Cognitive styles.* Madison, CT: International University Press.

Woolfolk, A. (2000). *Educational psychology.* Boston: Allyn & Bacon.

Wynn, R., & Fletcher, C. (1987). Sex role development and early educational experience. In D. B. Carter (Ed.), *Current conceptions of sex roles and sex typing* (pp. 79–88). New York: Praeger.

You and the system. (1990, April). *Teacher Magazine, 7*(1), 10.

Three Schools of Thought about Learning and Teaching

Contents

Have you been in classrooms where a teacher was teaching, but not all students were learning? This could happen to you when you teach. If it does, you will ask yourself, "what should I be doing that I'm not doing?" Hopefully, when you ask that question, you will have answers. Many of the answers come from learning theory—what we know about learning. That's why the information about learning contained in this chapter is so important to your success. You simply cannot fail at teaching if you put it to use.

Be warned at the outset that there is much to know about learning that cannot be included here. Since, as Wittrock (1987) notes, "models of instruction derive largely from the behaviorist, cognitive, and humanistic psychological perspectives" (p. 69), we limit ourselves to summarizing those major schools of thought. Figure 4.1 depicts them. Although the schools appear to be independent, you will see they share many beliefs.

After completing the chapter, you should be able to understand what each school of thought attempts to do, describe the beliefs and findings associated with each school of thought and their implications for teaching, denote some educational

4.1 What do you recall about how we learn from previous course work and experience?

FIGURE 4.1 Schools of Thought That Contribute to Our Knowledge of How Students Learn

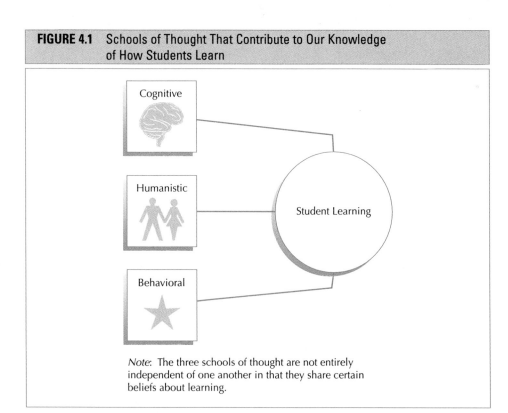

Cognitive

Humanistic

Student Learning

Behavioral

Note: The three schools of thought are not entirely independent of one another in that they share certain beliefs about learning.

practices with roots in cognitive, humanistic, and behavioral learning theory, compare and contrast the three schools of thought, and describe ideas you will use from each of them.

The Cognitive School of Thought

The first school of thought we will examine has its roots in cognitive science, a field that emerged in the 1960s to study how people think. Specifically, cognitive scientists try to fathom what goes on inside our heads when we are learning. They have contributed two important, wide-ranging ideas that help us understand how people learn and remember: information processing and meaningful learning.

Information processing refers to the study of how we mentally take in and store information and then retrieve it when needed. Thus, if we understand and use what we know about information processing, we should be able to help our students become better at taking in and remembering information. **Meaningful learning** involves the study of how new information can be most effectively organized, structured, and taught so that it might be used, for example, in problem-solving situations. Let's look at these two somewhat different and sometimes overlapping ideas.

INFORMATION PROCESSING

If you have taken a psychology or educational psychology course, you know that cognitive scientists—persons interested in information processing—study how we *attend to, recognize, transform, store, and retrieve information.* They develop models, such as the one shown in Figure 4.2, to illustrate how they believe information is processed. Essentially models such as this one suggest that although we encounter many stimuli, we pay attention to only some of them. Of the stimuli we notice, some will be discarded almost immediately, while the rest go into our short-term, or working, memory. **Short-term memory,** as the term suggests, is a storage system that holds only a limited amount and certain kinds of information for a few seconds. When these stimuli reach our short-term memory, the items we then use to any degree are transferred to our long-term, or permanent, memory and saved. As the

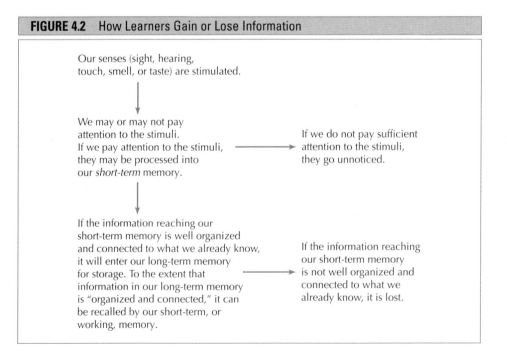

FIGURE 4.2 How Learners Gain or Lose Information

Our senses (sight, hearing, touch, smell, or taste) are stimulated.

We may or may not pay attention to the stimuli. If we pay attention to the stimuli, they may be processed into our *short-term* memory.

If we do not pay sufficient attention to the stimuli, they go unnoticed.

If the information reaching our short-term memory is well organized and connected to what we already know, it will enter our long-term memory for storage. To the extent that information in our long-term memory is "organized and connected," it can be recalled by our short-term, or working, memory.

If the information reaching our short-term memory is not well organized and connected to what we already know, it is lost.

name implies, long-term memory is where we keep information for a longer time. Information that we do not use to any degree, and that therefore does not reach **long-term memory,** is forgotten as if we had never been exposed to it in the first place. We're sure there are many things that, for lack of proper storage and use, haven't stuck in your memory.

Computers also have short-term and long-term memory. To illustrate, if we search the Internet using the keyword "learning theory," we may find there are three schools of thought about learning—cognitive, humanistic, and behavioral. If the computer is not told to "save" this knowledge before it is shut down, the information is lost since it existed only in its short-term memory. However, if the computer is told to save the information, perhaps placing it in a document or folder, then it is transferred into the hard drive or the computer's long-term memory.

As you might expect, cognitive scientists often try to answer questions that are very important to teachers, such as, What attracts and holds a student's attention? How can more information be placed into short- and long-term memory? How should we organize and present information to make it more memorable? and How can students best study or learn new information? Following are some major beliefs and findings of cognitivists that are related to such questions. These beliefs and findings should have direct bearing on the way you teach.

Beliefs about Attention   Getting students to "pay attention" to information is a very real, everyday teacher concern. Cognitivists suggest teachers use the following guiding principles to gain and hold learners' attention:

- Learning experiences should be as pleasant and satisfying as possible. Students are more likely to attend to something (mathematics, music, sport) when they have had previous positive experiences with it. If learners' previous experiences with that stimulus has been unpleasant, the experiences you give them must be especially good.

"First, you have to get their attention."

- Whenever possible, lessons should take into account the interests and needs of students. Students are more likely to pay attention to lessons that focus on what they want to know or what they want to be able to do. A major task for you will be to encourage or motivate them to attend to things they have little interest in.

- The attention of learners can be gained and held longer by making use of different sensory channels and change. A student is more likely to attend to lessons that employ a variety of stimuli, that is, when shifts occur from listening to talking to doing, and so forth. Novelty also helps. Avoid monotony!

- Learners can attend for only so long, and they differ in their ability to attend. Younger children and those with dyslexia (a reading impairment) and attention deficiency disorders (described in Chapter 3) have shorter attention spans.

- Since it is easier to maintain attention when learners are alert, schedule work that requires intense concentration during the morning and work that may be more intrinsically interesting and/or may require less concentration in the afternoon. For this reason, elementary teachers try to teach art, music, and physical education later in the day.

- Distractions interfere with attention. Therefore, find ways to eliminate the many interruptions to learning that students, other teachers, and administrators can cause.

- Learners can attend to only so much information at any one time. Students should not be overwhelmed or they may become so confused that they attend to nothing.

To the extent that you can get learners to pay attention by applying these guidelines, the information and experiences they have will enter their short-term memories.

4.2   Can you describe instances when your teachers either followed or violated one of the principles for gaining attention?

4.3   What will you most keep in mind about attention?

"I knew the answers. I just couldn't retrieve them from my memory bank."

4.4 Which beliefs about short-term memory have been most useful to you?

Beliefs about Short-Term Memory The stimuli we attend to find their way into short-term memory. But, how do we get some of this information beyond short-term and into long-term memory? Cognitivists believe the following principles to be true.

- Short-term memory capacity is severely limited. Estimates are that adult learners can hold only about 5 to 9 bits of new information at one time. Therefore, it is difficult to remember a meaningless series of numerals, such as a long-distance telephone number or a Social Security number. Young children's short-term memory is much more limited, usually 3 to 5 bits.

  To overcome the limited capacity of our short-term memory, new information can be both *organized* and *connected* to what we already know; for example, learners can be helped to combine, or "chunk," new information. Thus a 10-bit, long-distance telephone number is placed into three chunks, such as (614) 292–1280. Chunking a 9-bit-long Social Security number also aids short-term memory. Consequently, if it were important to remember the names of the first nine U.S. presidents, we might group them in threes: (Washington, Adams, Jefferson), (Madison, Monroe, Adams), (Jackson, Van Buren, Harrison). Short-term memory also is enhanced by using mnemonics, or systems to aid memory; for example, we more easily recall the names of the Great Lakes if we use the familiar word *HOMES* (*H*uron, *O*ntario, *M*ichigan, *E*rie, *S*uperior) to spur our recall.

- Information can be remembered better by connecting it with what students already know. Consider the following task. You are helping students learn multiplication facts. They know that six 6s are 36. You help them see that seven 6s is one 6 more.

- To forestall forgetting new information, we must manipulate it or, as cognitive scientists say, engage in active "rehearsals" with it. Such rehearsals can involve either practicing repeatedly or simply thinking about the information. When we engage in recurrent practice, we can move information to our long-term memory through sheer repetition or memorization. Many of us learned multiplication facts in this way, repeating $9 \times 7 = 63$ ad infinitum. Spaced rehearsal, however, seems preferable. Thus, repeating $9 \times 7 = 63$ every hour for five hours is better than repeating it five times in one minute. We might also think about the information, for example, questioning "How can we prove nine 7s are 63?".

Beliefs about Long-Term Memory As noted, information that learners process extensively, or use in a meaningful way, finds its way into long-term memory. Cognitivists believe the following to be true with regard to long-term memory:

- The capacity of our long-term memory seems to be limitless. We never run out of room to learn.

- We are best able to retrieve information from our long-term memory if that information relates to something we knew previously.

- We can call up, or recollect, related information from long-term memory when processing new information in short-term memory. For example, as you receive new information about how people learn, you can compare it with information you have already learned. In this instance, as you go along, you are able to compare what you already know about short-term memory with what you are learning about long-term memory.

- Reviewing information fixes it more firmly—think about how you have retained the multiplication facts.

General Beliefs about the Memory Process The general beliefs of cognitivists with regard to memory include the following:

- Information in short-term memory is lost either when that memory is overloaded or with the passage of time.
- When information in short-term memory is lost, it cannot be recovered. If we forget a telephone number, we must relearn it. In contrast, information in long-term memory can be retrieved and used when conditions are right.
- Retrieval, or remembrance, of information in our long-term memory is enhanced if we connected the information to something we already knew at the time we originally learned the new information. Additionally, retrieval is easier when the information is originally presented in an organized way.

Figure 4.3 depicts key concepts and key words associated with information processing.

4.5   Why do you forget?

MEANINGFUL LEARNING

While some cognitive scientists are interested in information processing (attention, short-term and long-term memory), others are interested in how information can be made more meaningful so that it can be better understood and used. These scientists address **meaningful learning.** As you will see, they use many of the beliefs from information processing, especially those about long-term memory.

There are a number of ways to teach that have their roots in meaningful learning. They include **reception learning, reciprocal teaching, discovery learning, constructivism,** and **problem solving.** Two of the most widely used, discovery learning and constructivism, are presented in depth in Chapter 8. The others are presented here as examples of meaningful learning.

COGNITIVE APPROACHES TO TEACHING AND LEARNING

Reception Learning   Reception learning refers to learning that takes place when teachers offer students new information that is carefully organized and structured. Such lessons are referred to as **expository lessons.** According to Ausubel (1977) and others, the better organized and structured the lesson, the greater likelihood it will be understood. Here are some structuring and organizational strategies that cognitivists believe increase learner understanding:

- At the outset of the lesson, share with learners what you are trying to help them accomplish: Tell them the lesson objectives. Now you and your learners are "on

"I know my seven-digit phone number, my nine-digit zip code, my four-digit address, and my three-digit area code. There's just one thing I don't know. What's a digit?"

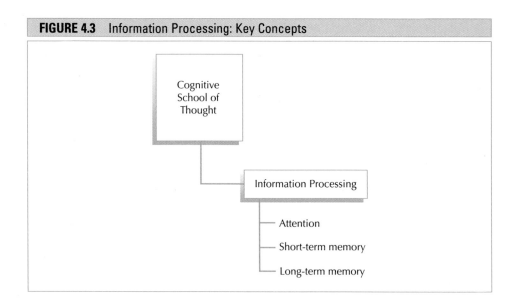

FIGURE 4.3   Information Processing: Key Concepts

Cognitive School of Thought

Information Processing

— Attention

— Short-term memory

— Long-term memory

the same page." Next make certain learners understand how accomplishing the lesson goals is of potential value to them. "Here is how this lesson will be useful." (Marzano, 2001, pp. 94–95).

- Prepare learners for the new information using an **advance organizer.** Ausubel (1977) and Leinhardt (1992) describe different kinds. The best preparation occurs when you relate new information to information your learners already know when you connect the new with the old. For example, "Yesterday we talked about the election process for choosing a president. What did we learn? . . . Today we are going to learn about the part the electoral college plays in the process." A second kind of advance organizer gives learners background knowledge needed in order to understand new knowledge. For example, "Today we are going to learn about word processing. However, before we can do that we need to know some things about how a computer works." A third kind of advance organizer prepares learners to focus their attention on specific things so as to notice and understand them better. For example, "In this basketball film, pay particular attention to the defensive players. Notice what they do in common." A fourth type of advance organizer helps learners follow your lesson. For example, if you give a lesson on rain forests, give them a skeletal outline to fill in as the lesson unfolds.
- Present the new information in a clear, sequential (step-by-step) manner.
- Proceed from the general to the specific. "First we will learn about the world's oceans in general. Then we will find out specifically how main currents affect shorelines."
- Involve learners during a lesson. Encourage questions and reactions since they increase understanding.
- Present positive examples and negative examples of what students are to know. "Good defense in basketball is characterized by . . . Poor defense is characterized by . . ."
- Review what learners should understand at the lesson's closure. "What have we learned about subcultures?"
- Have learners summarize what they learned. This causes them to engage in rehearsing-reviewing and analyzing.
- Have learners reflect on the use and value of what was taught. "How can what we have learned about ratio be useful to us?"

In summary, reception learning is characterized by (1) sharing with learners what they are expected to know or be able to do, (2) getting learners ready to receive the information, (3) presenting the information in an organized, sequential way, (4) proceeding from the general to the specific, (5) encouraging learner participation, (6) using examples and nonexamples, and (7) having learners summarize what they have learned and consider how it can be used.

Figure 4.4 illustrates key concepts associated with reception learning. In Chapter 7 much more attention will be given to use of principles of reception learning applied to the instructional alternative we call **presentation.**

Strong research support for many of the principles of reception learning can be found in Marzano and others (2001).

Reciprocal Teaching   **Reciprocal teaching** is a form of teaching wherein the teacher gradually shifts teaching responsibility to learners (Nuthall, 1995; Palincsar, 1986). Perhaps some of your teachers have done this. At first, the teacher models and/or explains to the learners how to do something, for example how to summarize. As the learners catch on, the teacher selects one or more to demonstrate or explain to others how to summarize and how *they* summarize. During this process, the appointed

FIGURE 4.4 Reception Learning: Key Concepts

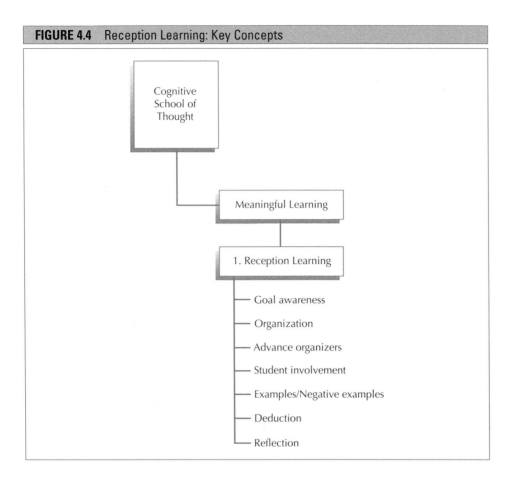

teacher asks learners questions to assure their understanding and, conversely, learners may comment and raise questions. Meanwhile, the teacher stands aside, ready to provide any encouragement or assistance needed. This teaching act is called "scaffolding" since it helps and supports learners. You probably remember when former teachers, after teaching a concept or process, asked class members to go to the chalkboard and demonstrate or describe how to do something such as multiplying fractions or diagramming a sentence. If, when those demonstrations and explanations occurred, student interchanges followed that increased understanding, then you have already experienced a variation on the theme of reciprocal teaching. Figure 4.5 (see page 72) depicts related key concepts.

Problem Solving   A third method of learning cognitive scientists advocate is problem solving. **Problem solving** requires that (1) a situation exists wherein a goal is to be achieved and (2) learners be asked to consider how they would attain the goal. Frederickson (1984) maintains there are different types of problems, and Biehler and Snowman (2000) describe two of them. One type, which is often encountered when studying mathematics or science, is a "well-structured" problem that can be solved by recalling and applying a mathematical or scientific procedure. Undoubtedly you can recall working on well-structured mathematical problems that required the application of an algorithm such as multiplication or division to obtain an answer: For example, if you have 18 apples and wish to fill gift boxes with 6 apples each, how many boxes can you fill? Preparing a lesson can be thought of as a well-structured problem, since there is a goal we hope to achieve (writing the plan) and there are specific procedures to be followed (described in Chapter 6).

4.6   Can you think of any "well-structured" problems in the subject matter you will be responsible for teaching?

(Notice how the teacher leads but shares teaching with student Claire. Notice how the learners interact, comment, and raise questions.)

Teacher, *reading from the text:* The pipe fish change their color and movements to blend with their surroundings. For example, pipe fish that live among green plants change their color to a shade of green to match the plants.

Claire, *child leading the discussion:* One question that I had about this paragraph is, What is special about the way that pipe fish look?

Keith, *clarifying:* Do you mean the way that they are green?

Andy, *elaborating:* It's not just that they're green—they're the same color as the plants around them, all around them.

Claire, *resuming her role as discussion leader:* Yes, that's it. My summary is, this part tells how the pipe fish looks and that it looks like what is around it. My prediction is that this is about its enemies and how it protects itself and who its enemies are.

Monty, *amplifying:* They also talked about how the pipe fish moves.

Keith, *summarizing:* It's always back and forth.

Teacher, *questioning:* What do we call it when something looks like

and acts like something else? The way that the walkingstick was yesterday. We clarified this word when we talked about the walkingstick.

Angel, *predicting:* Mimic.

Teacher, *reinforcing:* That's right. We would say that the pipe fish mimics the . . .?

Several students, *predicting:* Plants.

Adapted from A. Palincsar & A. Brown, (1989). Classroom dialogues to promote self-regulated comprehension. In J. Brophy (Ed.), *Advances in research on teaching.* Vol. 1: *Teaching for meaningful understanding and self-regulated learning.* Greenwich, CT: JAI.

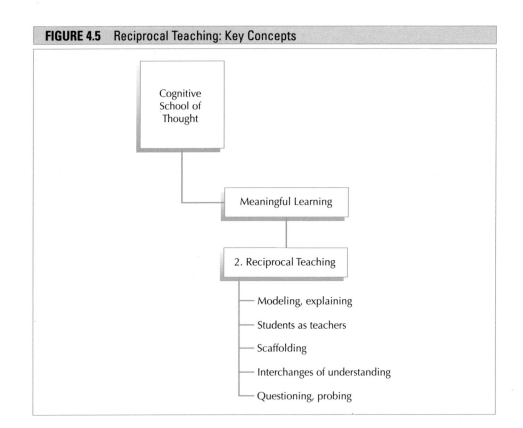

FIGURE 4.5 Reciprocal Teaching: Key Concepts

Cognitive School of Thought

Meaningful Learning

2. Reciprocal Teaching
— Modeling, explaining
— Students as teachers
— Scaffolding
— Interchanges of understanding
— Questioning, probing

4.7 What are some other "ill-structured" problems students face?

A second type of problem is "ill-structured or unstructured." It occurs more often in daily living, and comes up when studying people-oriented subjects like psychology or education. With these problems, no specific, simple procedure exists that can be applied to obtain a finite solution. Examples of ill-structured problems

Solving an Ill-Structured Problem

Dom Christoff was regularly assigned students who, for one reason or another, seemed to find school unpleasant. One morning, the school principal appeared at the classroom door with Gary Ross. Mr. Waters introduced Gary to Christoff and noted that Gary would reenter school the next day. Looking over his shoulder as he left with Gary, Mr. Waters suggested, "Let's get together before you leave this afternoon." Christoff acknowledged with a nod of the head.

Later, in the principal's office, Mr. Waters described Gary as a 13-year-old with school phobias. On several occasions he had run away from school, even jumping from classroom windows.

Christoff recognized this as an ill-structured kind of problem. He knew he was expected to keep Gary in school and, particularly, from leaping out the window. He recognized Gary's fear of school and flight syndrome. The next day Christoff talked with Gary, telling the boy that he wanted to help Gary enjoy school.

Christoff suggested that Gary give a signal, inconspicuously, by placing his arm across the top of his head whenever he felt he was about to panic. Further, he told Gary to sit next to the door and to leave the class at any time after he gave the signal. Gary agreed to this plan and promised that if he felt compelled to leave the building, he would inform the school office, which would notify Gary's parent.

To everyone's astonishment, Gary—perhaps secure that he could leave whenever he wished—never again did.

include questions such as these: How can I manage my time better? or How can I make this lesson meaningful to my students? Teachers face ill-structured problems when they expect students to achieve or to behave in a certain way and they don't. Students also face ill-structured problems such as How can I get the other kids to like me? or How can I pass math when I hate it?

To summarize, major beliefs about problem solving include the following:

- A major goal of education is to help students learn to solve all types of problems, both subject-matter-related (well-structured) and people- or life-related (ill-structured).

- Some problem-solving strategies tend to be subject-area-specific, such as procedures for solving mathematical or scientific problems. For example, we apply the quadratic formula in order to solve a quadratic equation, or a procedure for solving "train problems" involving distance-rate-time calculations (Schoenfeld, 1989, p.88).

- Other problem-solving strategies are more useful when dealing with ill-structured problems. A general problem-solving strategy might include the following steps: (1) State the goal to be achieved, (2) identify the obstacles standing in the way, (3) project alternative ways to achieve the goal, (4) consider the consequences of each possible solution, (5) decide how to implement the best proposed solution and do so, and (6) evaluate your degree of satisfaction with the problem resolution (Cruickshank & Associates, 1980).

4.8 How prepared are you to teach problem solving?

A classroom scenario illustrates how a teacher and student resolved an ill-structured problem (see Case 4.1). Figure 4.6 illustrates key concepts associated with problem solving and the place problem solving has in the cognitive school of thought.

4.9 What is your opinion of cognitive approaches to learning?

Try Activity 4.1

The Humanistic School of Thought

A second school of thought about learning and instruction is based upon humanistic education, which borrows heavily from social psychology. Persons who champion humanistic or affective education focus on the personal and social learning and development of students. While the humanistic approach recognizes the importance of cognitive learning, it feels that schools focus too much on accumulating knowledge and too little on helping students learn to become psychologically healthy persons.

4.10 What do you think about the criticism that schools are too academically oriented and too little interested in students' personal development?

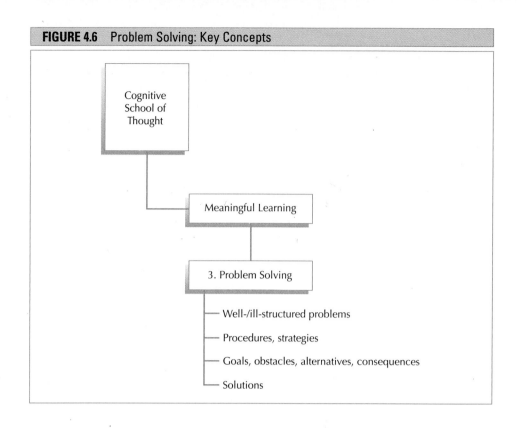

FIGURE 4.6 Problem Solving: Key Concepts

Cognitive School of Thought

Meaningful Learning

3. Problem Solving

— Well-/ill-structured problems

— Procedures, strategies

— Goals, obstacles, alternatives, consequences

— Solutions

Disciples of this school of thought mostly want to make children feel better about themselves and become more accepting of others. To accomplish these goals, followers say that first we need to accept each child as unique and as possessed of individual feelings and ideas, and that, second, we need to help him perceive himself and others as worthwhile and able. Teachers with such an orientation truly believe that "each child counts" and that "each child can do it in his own way."

BELIEFS OF THE HUMANISTIC SCHOOL

The humanistic school holds several core beliefs:

- Having good feelings about oneself is essential to positive personal development and may enhance academic achievement. Therefore, engender in students a sense of self-respect, self-worth, and **efficacy,** or having a feeling of control over one's life and destiny.

- Having good feelings about others is also essential to healthy development. Thus, aspire to help learners build respect for and accept others, even when their opinions and behavior may be different.

- "The school should be made to fit the child rather than that the child made to fit the school (Neill, 1969). Therefore, personalize education by giving learners considerable latitude in deciding what to do (learn) and how to do it. Relatedly, create an environment that provides choices and then help students make choices that seem wise to them.

- The school and classroom environment must help youth satisfy such essential human needs as personal safety and security, love, belonging, and achievement (Maslow, 1998); and autonomy, competence, and social relationships (Deci and Ryan, 1990). Failure to meet these needs will be counterproductive to personal development and will have a negative impact on learning.

- Accept learners as they are, that is, with their unique behaviors, feelings, and opinions (Rogers, 1983).

4.11 How will you help learners have confidence in and feel good about themselves and others?

- Place yourself "in the shoes" of learners in order to see and understand a learning situation from the students' perspective (Combs, 1965).

- Use techniques that help learners better understand their feelings and values. Such techniques include active listening, invitational learning, and values clarification—all of which are discussed in the following section.

4.12 How will you show you accept your learners as they are?

HUMANISTIC APPROACHES TO TEACHING

Advocates of the humanistic approach to learning often advocate specific programs and ideas that promote personal development; they include: Inviting School Success, values clarification, moral and character education, and multiethnic education.

Inviting School Success   Inviting School Success was developed to get teachers to communicate to learners that they are "responsible, able, and valuable" people (Purkey & Novak, 1996, p. 3). To convey this, **invitational learning** calls upon teachers to (1) know learners' names, (2) have individual contact with each learner, (3) show learners they respect them, (4) be honest with learners and themselves, (5) not take a student's rejection personally, and (6) respect themselves as teachers.

Values Clarification   Values clarification refers to techniques by which learners (1) identify how they feel or what they believe about something, (2) value that feeling or belief and, (3) if valued, act on it (Simon, Howe, & Kerschenbaum, 1995). The intention is for learners to become conscious of the values they hold, since those values influence their behavior. Then, they consider the legitimacy or goodness of that which they value. For example, learners could be asked to what extent they believe in gun control. After stating their preference, they are encouraged to share and explain their position and why they hold it. Once they have examined their value in relationship to the values others hold, learners are better able to prize their value or to modify or reject it. Once the value is prized, learners are expected to go the next step and act on the value. For example, learners might be asked, "All right, if you believe that strongly about gun control, what can *you* do?"

Moral Education   Moral education is akin to character education, values education (not value clarification), and citizenship education. All these techniques are designed to help learners develop more responsible behavior both in and out of school. According to Lickona (1988), teachers can do a number of things to enhance higher levels of students' morality and character, such as (1) serving as role models who are always respectful and caring of others and who intervene as necessary to get students to be respectful and caring, too, (2) creating a family or community atmosphere in the class so that all students feel worthwhile and care about one another, and (3) encouraging students to hold high academic and behavioral standards in order to teach the value of work as a way to develop oneself and contribute to a community (p.9).

4.13 Have you had experience with any of the humanistic approaches to education? Which ones?

Multiethnic Education   Multiethnic education refers to educational practices that encourage learners to revere their roots and culture—ideas, customs, skills, arts, and so forth—*and* to revere the culture and diversity of others. Proponents want learners to see the advantages of a pluralistic society. Related educational practices include helping learners become aware of the various contributions of ethnic and national groups to a nation's development and well-being, and encouraging learners to find out more about their own ethnic and cultural backgrounds.

Figure 4.7 illustrates key concepts associated with the humanistic approach to learning and teaching.

4.14 What is your reaction to humanistic approaches to learning?

Try Activity 4.2

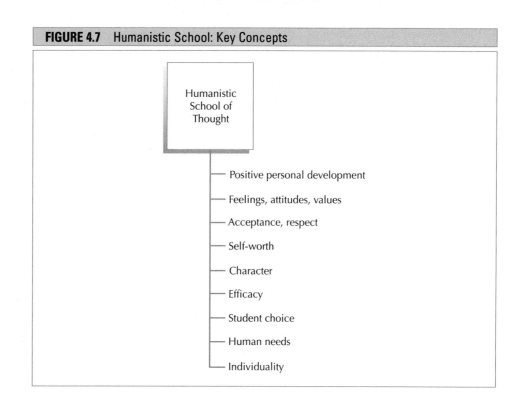

FIGURE 4.7 Humanistic School: Key Concepts

Humanistic School of Thought
- Positive personal development
- Feelings, attitudes, values
- Acceptance, respect
- Self-worth
- Character
- Efficacy
- Student choice
- Human needs
- Individuality

The Behavioral School of Thought

The third school of thought about learning, teaching, and education is behaviorism. **Behaviorists,** as the name implies, help us understand why we behave as we do. They are interested in finding out how external, environmental stimuli cause overt or observable learner behavior and how modifying a learner's environment can change behavior.

If you have studied psychology or educational psychology, you probably learned something about contiguity, classical conditioning, operant conditioning, and social learning—concepts of prime interest to behaviorists.

CONTIGUITY

Contiguity refers to simple stimulus-response (S-R) pairings, associations, or connections, such as lightning and thunder, which occur closely together. When one thing, a stimulus, is regularly associated with another, a response, an S-R connection is established. Like the combination of lightning and thunder, the S-R connection usually occurs within a very brief time span, thus, the *contiguity* label. We can learn by simple S-R pairing such facts as Columbus landed in America in 1492 and $9 \times 7 = 63$. A great many concepts and facts are learned through simple stimulus-response learning, for example:

STIMULUS	RESPONSE
Einstein	Theory of Relativity
Sodium chloride	Salt
Van Gogh	Artist
Andersonville	Infamous Civil War prison
Eiffel Tower	Paris
Gershwin	Composer

CLASSICAL CONDITIONING

Classical conditioning refers to learning that occurs when we already have an established connection (contiguity) between a primary or original stimulus and a response, and then we pair a new, secondary stimulus with the original stimulus long enough that it begins to evoke the original response even when the original stimulus is absent. Remember Pavlov's dogs? Pavlov, a Russian psychologist, found that his experimental dogs naturally salivated (responded) when his lab assistants fed them meat powder (a stimulus). Later, he found that the mere presence of his lab assistants (new stimulus) caused the dogs to anticipate being fed and to salivate. Let's consider a school example. Students and teachers alike associate a bell (stimulus) with the ending of a class period. Teachers often assign homework at or near the close of class. Thus, the mere assignment of homework (new stimulus) will elicit many behaviors or responses associated with the ringing of the bell—packing book bags and so forth. For this reason, some teachers assign homework at the beginning of class.

4.15 What kinds of S-R responses might you want from your learners? How can the responses be associated with something desirable so that they occur?

OPERANT CONDITIONING

Operant conditioning refers to learning facilitated through **reinforcement.** A learner does something correctly or appropriately and, consequently, receives a reward. Operant conditioning presumes that if we do something we are rewarded for or which is rewarding in itself, we will do it again. Conversely, if we do something that is not rewarded or rewarding, we will be less likely to repeat the behavior. Operant conditioning is based upon a pleasure-pain view of human behavior. To illustrate, consider Jason, a learner who has turned in a homework essay on gun control. The teacher has dutifully analyzed the essay and responded to it as follows: "This assignment is complete and well written. You have found and used many references. You have presented the major points on both sides, and you have drawn your own thoughtful conclusions. Obviously, you enjoy studying issues and responding to them. May I place your paper on our bulletin board?" Assuming Jason finds the teacher's comments and the display of his paper rewarding, he likely will want to write another essay. Chapters 12 and 13 will discuss more about reinforcement.

4.16 How is reinforcement used by your instructors?

SOCIAL LEARNING

Social learning is also called **observational learning.** Its main tenet is that you can learn a lot by watching others. According to its chief theorist, Bandura (1986), for observational learning to be effective, learners must attend to someone's behavior, retain what they observed the "model" doing, imitate or reproduce the behavior they saw, and experience reinforcement or satisfaction as a consequence. We know learners are most likely to model after persons who are somewhat like themselves and whom they perceive as competent, warm, or powerful. Thus, primary children frequently identify with parents or with television or movie characters, especially superheroes, and mimic what they do. A kindergarten teacher describes an example of social learning:

> The resurgence of Batman: Raymond brought in a "cape" and all the children were anxious to wear it and run around the room in it. During free play, children were busy making Batman equipment. Story time and singing time were always interrupted by children who were busy describing Batman antics. The entire morning was Batman-oriented and the children could not be interested in much else.

If an elementary school has a Halloween parade, characters such as Scooby-Doo, Snow White, Spiderman, or Harry Potter readily appear. On the other hand, if middle and secondary students have the occasion to wear costumes, they would more likely dress and act like rock or rap personalities or athletes.

"Of course I believe that a teacher should offer a positive role model; however . . .

Social learning also occurs when we see something good or bad happen to another person. For example, if we were to see a friend praised for her schoolwork, we might try to imitate what she does so we can be praised, too. Conversely, we might avoid doing what another student does if her behavior is not well received.

As a result of holding to classical conditioning, operant conditioning, and social learning, behaviorists suggest that you do the following:

4.17 To what extent do you believe you will model a former teacher(s)? In what ways?

- Make the classroom enjoyable intellectually, socially, and physically so that learners feel safe and secure.
- Be open and specific about what needs to be learned. Use specific behavior objectives when writing lesson plans (see Chapter 6) and share those objectives with learners.
- Be certain that learners have basic knowledge and skill that will enable them to learn new material.
- Show connection of new learning to previous learning.
- When new material is complex, introduce it gradually. Organize new material into sequential, short, easily learned parts.
- Associate what is to be learned with things learners like. For example, associate poetry with rap. Conversely, don't associate what is to be learned with things learners don't like. For example don't use schoolwork as punishment.
- Recognize and praise improvement. Don't expect students to learn at the same pace and in the same amounts.
- Find out what is rewarding to each student and use that to reinforce student learning. Some learners may be rewarded by receiving verbal public praise while others may find it embarrassing.
- When a task is new or difficult, provide more regular reinforcement. Once learners have mastered a new task, use only occasional reinforcement.
- Reinforce the learning behavior you expect from students: for example attending, engaging, trying, responding, improving, completing.
- Encourage shy or insecure learners' responses. Look for shy children who do not raise their hands and give them opportunity to participate. Caution all students to respect responses of others when they differ from their own, or even if they are incorrect.
- Create situations whereby each student has the opportunity to succeed.
- Demonstrate and model behavior that you want learners to imitate. For example, show enthusiasm for learning and respect for all.
- Draw attention to students who demonstrate desirable behavior or produce quality work but not to the point of causing them to be alienated from their peers.
- Ask parents to reinforce desired behaviors at home—to recognize enthusiasm for learning, effort, and growth.

4.18 What behavioristic beliefs do your teachers seem to use most and least?

Note that many of these beliefs are the same as those held by cognitivists.

BEHAVIORAL APPROACHES TO TEACHING

Behaviorists advocate certain educational practices they believe can be used to increase learning. These include programmed instruction, computer-assisted instruction, mastery learning, precision teaching, and applied behavioral analysis.

Programmed instruction (PI) involves organizing material to be learned or practiced into small parts called *frames* (see Highlight 4.2).

Learners respond to a question or problem (stimulus) in each frame; if their response is correct, they receive positive reinforcement and the next frame is pre-

An Illustration of Programmed Instruction That Follows an Operant Conditioning Pattern

Fill in the blank in each frame (1 to 5) and then check the answer against the correct answer "hidden" at the right, proceeding downward on the page.

1. The third prominent school of thought about learning is _____ .

   | Behaviorism |

2. This school of thought is interested in our _____ behavior.

   | Overt or observable |

3. When one stimulus is regularly associated with a response, a bond or _____ is formed.

   | Contiguity |

4. When a second stimulus has been associated with the original stimulus, that second stimulus may evoke the same response. This is called _____ conditioning.

   | Classical |

5. When we watch others and mimic their behavior, we call this _____ learning.

   | Social or observational |

sented. When learners respond incorrectly, they may be asked to repeat or be given more information to help them produce a correct response. Learners utilizing programmed instruction typically work at their own pace.

Computer-assisted instruction (CAI) refers to the use of computers to present programmed instruction or to otherwise assist learners with specific learning tasks. Many different kinds of CAI programs are available, and most require learners to engage in lots of drill and practice. Although most CAI programs follow an operant conditioning, stimuli-response-reinforcement pattern, CAI also can be used as a cognitivist approach; some CAI programs, like programmed instruction, teach new concepts, and others engage learners in creative tasks and problem solving. For example, some computer software programs encourage children to make up stories and to illustrate them.

Programmed instruction and CAI seem to be a little more effective than normal educational practices, probably because they make extensive use of practice and reinforcement. Classroom *use of reinforcement is highly related to student learning* (Ellson, 1986; Walberg, 1984).

Mastery learning is a third educational practice based upon behavioral theory. It, too, allows students to learn academic material at their own pace. In practice, all students in a class might be expected to reach a certain level of proficiency, for example, at least 80 percent correct responses on a geography test. Those who fail to reach that criterion level may receive additional time and corrective instruction until they obtain that score. The general intent is to give immediate, additional help to low or slow achievers so they stay even with higher or faster achievers. While low or slow achievers receive corrective instruction, high or fast achievers engage in enrichment work on the same or on a similar topic.

Advocates of mastery learning propose you (1) prepare a lesson with clear, specific objectives, (2) use learning material that allows students to accomplish those objectives, and (3) prepare not one, but two, tests. Following instruction, students take test 1. Those that meet some preestablished passing criterion, such as 80 percent, move on to supplementary enrichment activities, while those falling short receive corrective instruction based on a different instructional approach or using different instructional materials. After additional instruction, a second, similar test (test 2) is given to the lower achievers. When a large majority of all students (perhaps 80 percent) have passed either test 1 or test 2, the class moves on to new work. The cycle can be repeated until you, the teacher, feel that a large enough majority has reached mastery to permit going on.

According to Walberg (1984), use of mastery learning in science is highly related to student learning. Slavin (1999), concludes that its primary weakness is the amount of time needed to bring almost all students to mastery. That additional time must come from somewhere. He therefore concludes that mastery learning is most important when the material to be learned is critical or "high stakes" material, for example, the basic information or skills in any content field.

A useful reference on mastery learning is Guskey (1996).

Precision teaching occurs when learners master a fact or skill (such as correctly spelling a word or applying an arithmetic algorithm such as division), and then continue practicing these skills until they achieve a high level of precision or fluency. "Practice makes perfect." Precision teaching is reported to help children gain two years of academic growth in one (Sulzer-Azaroff, 1995). Its tenets derive from principles of information processing (see the section on short-term memory).

Applied behavioral analysis (ABA) also is based upon behavioral beliefs and findings and is informed by principles of operant conditioning. It is used mostly in clinical settings (hospitals, prisons, schools) to modify the behavior of clients toward more normal or acceptable patterns. ABA follows a prescribed procedure. First the practitioner—for example, you the teacher—identify a student (client) and the student's behavior that is to be changed. You then determine how often the student presently performs the desired behavior—for example, completing homework. This is called the **baseline.** Next, you introduce an **intervention.** An intervention is usually some reinforcement the student receives every time she performs the desirable behavior. Use of reinforcement encourages your student to behave appropriately more often, that is, more than the client did at the outset or baseline.

4.19 What do you think of the behavioral approach to learning?

Try Activity 4.3

Here is an illustration of ABA in a classroom. Jane produces very little when given a writing assignment, even one of her choice. In most cases, her text amounts to a few short sentences. Because she is fairly conversational, you decide you might encourage her to be more forthcoming by having her tell you what she would like to say. As she does, you prompt her to write down the ideas she is expressing. Each time Jane writes her ideas in a writing assignment, you praise her for any increase in the number and range of her ideas. When you evaluate her written work, you comment that, increasingly, Jane's compositions are more complete and interesting. You may even share one or more with the class.

Behavioral analysis always uses the principles of operant conditioning. A close cousin is **behavior modification,** which is also an attempt to change behavior but is a more general concept that includes use of hypnosis, drug therapy, and electroconvulsive shock treatment as well. Figure 4.8 presents key concepts associated with the behavioral approach to learning and teaching.

Is There a Single Best Approach to Student Learning?

We have identified three views of learning that influence the approaches teachers take to instruction. Figure 4.9 brings them together for comparison. Each approach has been defined, and its major beliefs and findings noted. Some have fostered the development and use of specific educational practices, which are briefly described. Table 4.1 compares the three approaches.

FIGURE 4.8 Behavioral School: Key Concepts

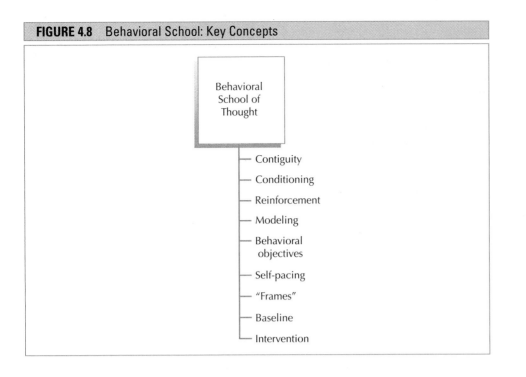

A great deal of controversy exists as to which of the approaches to learning is superior (Viadero, 1996). If you ask your university instructors, you may be surprised at the strength of their feelings. You may especially find that those who espouse cognitive or humanistic beliefs shun behaviorism, although the reverse is also true.

Teachers who work with exceptional individuals (see Chapter 3), especially those with learning and behavioral deficiencies, often have found that the behaviorist school of thought has been most helpful. There certainly is strong research support for applying its beliefs and findings. For example, Walberg (1986) reports that 98 percent of studies investigating the effects of behavioral learning on students have positive findings. At the same time, Walberg tells us good support also exists for cognitive and humanistic approaches to instruction (p. 222).

Dembo (1994) reminds us there are differences of opinion about learning not only among but also within the various schools of thought. He also points out what you have probably already concluded by now, that most educators draw from all three schools of thought. The secret, Dembo informs us, is to have a knack for knowing when to use ideas from the various perspectives since each has strengths and weaknesses, depending on the purpose you may have in mind. Anderson, Reder, and Simon (1996) agree. Speaking to the same point, Biehler and Snowman (2000) note that advocates of discovery learning, such as Bruner, do not suggest that students discover every fact or principle or formula they need to know but rather that certain types of learning outcomes can best be achieved through personal discovery.

4.20 Which features of which schools of thought about learning attracts you? Why?

Some Final Thoughts

Helping your students learn is the "bottom line." However, as you can recall from your own school experiences and from the teacher-reported problems that follow, doing so is not always simple. Therefore, you need to learn all you can about learning and teaching and to recognize that the two are inextricably bound together. You can be an excellent teacher *only* when you understand what is known about each

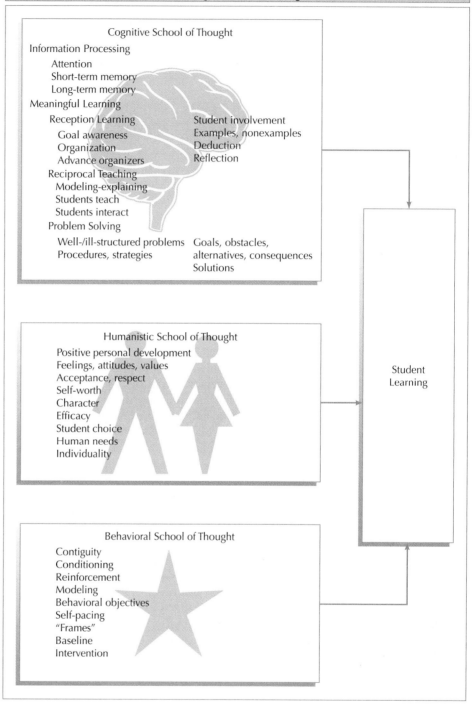

FIGURE 4.9 Three Schools of Thought about Learning

Cognitive School of Thought

Information Processing
 Attention
 Short-term memory
 Long-term memory
Meaningful Learning
 Reception Learning   Student involvement
  Goal awareness   Examples, nonexamples
  Organization   Deduction
  Advance organizers   Reflection
 Reciprocal Teaching
  Modeling-explaining
  Students teach
  Students interact
 Problem Solving
  Well-/ill-structured problems   Goals, obstacles,
  Procedures, strategies   alternatives, consequences
                                  Solutions

Humanistic School of Thought

Positive personal development
Feelings, attitudes, values
Acceptance, respect
Self-worth
Character
Efficacy
Student choice
Human needs
Individuality

Behavioral School of Thought

Contiguity
Conditioning
Reinforcement
Modeling
Behavioral objectives
Self-pacing
"Frames"
Baseline
Intervention

Student
Learning

and can put that knowledge to work every single time you arrange a learning experience. If your students experience difficulty or failure, you must "go back to the books" and analyze what may be interfering with learning. Never shrug your shoulders or give up on a single child. The knowledge needed to help each child learn is available; it is up to you to find and use it. Reflect on each incidence of failure to learn, and then regroup and try again and again. Remember, teachers are professionals with the opportunity, knowledge, and responsibility to make a difference.

TABLE 4.1 A Comparison of Cognitive, Humanistic, and Behavioral Views

	Cognitive	Humanistic	Behavioral
Focus	Understanding how we acquire knowledge	Understanding how we develop feelings, attitudes, and values	Understanding how our behavior is modified by our environment
Topics/Themes	Information processing Meaningful learning	Basic needs Affect (emotions, feelings, attitudes, values, predispositions, morals)	Contiguity Classical conditioning Operant conditioning Social, observational learning
Special concepts	Attention Short-, long-term memory Remember/Forgetting Advance organizers	Self-worth Efficacy	Reinforcement
Some instructional approaches that support . . .	Reception learning Reciprocal teaching Constructivism Problem solving	Inviting School Success Values clarification Moral/character education Multiethnic education	Programmed and computer assisted instruction Mastery learning Precision teaching Applied behavioral analysis

CHAPTER SUMMARY

- Three major perspectives, or schools of thought, on learning and teaching are the cognitive, humanistic, and behavioral perspectives.

- Cognitivists are interested in how knowledge is acquired. Their study centers around information processing and meaningful learning. Information processing looks at the phenomena of attention, short-term memory, long-term memory, remembering, and forgetting. Meaningful learning focuses on how learners can best learn to understand and use information.

- Humanistic proponents are interested in personal development, the self, and the way feelings, attitudes, and values are acquired. They are concerned that school learning focuses too much on academic learning to the detriment of learning about oneself. Therefore, humanists advocate educational and teaching practices that encourage self-knowledge and enhance self-concept. These practices include Inviting School Success (invitational learning), values clarification, moral and character education, and multiethnic education.

- Behaviorists are interested in how the environment can be changed or manipulated in order to change behavior in a desirable direction. They study contiguity, classical conditioning, operant conditioning, and social or observational learning as means to behavioral change. Educational practices that support the behaviorist school of thought include programmed instruction, computer-assisted instruction, mastery learning, precision teaching, and applied behavioral analysis.

- Most teaching draws from all three schools of thought according to the learning task at hand and the characteristics and needs of the students.

ISSUES AND PROBLEMS FOR DISCUSSION

ISSUES   Here are some related issues for you to debate.

1. Which school of thought—cognitive, humanistic, or behavioral—seems best under what learning circumstances?

2. What seem to be the most critical findings about learning that you should know and apply?

3. How should teachers be held personally accountable for using what is known about learning?

PROBLEMS   Following are some verbatim daily learning-related problems that teachers have shared with us. How does each relate to what we know about learning? How might you resolve them?

Problem 1: "Today, during a lesson on fractions, the class became rowdy. Since fractions seem especially difficult for them, they become frustrated. One of the girls blurted out, 'You can't make people learn who don't want to.'"

Problem 2: "The incident that caused me the greatest concern today happened during a reading class while working with a group of eight third-grade children. These children are unable to read or write above a first-grade level at best. The frustrating part is that they don't know words they have gone over and over before."

Problem 3: "Today I tried to teach the concepts of 'first, middle, and last' to the slow children in my kindergarten. Many approaches were used—three pictures placed on the chalkboard, three objects placed on the floor, three children standing behind each other in a line. Only a few got the concepts."

Problem 4: "The thing that bothered me today was brought to mind by something another middle school teacher said in the faculty lounge. She stated that nearly all her students can read and spell but do not understand what they are reading or the meaning of words they are spelling. During the next few days, I paid attention to the teacher's comment when working with my students. Yes, they can read and spell words, but half the time they have little or no understanding."

Problem 5: "A mother came to the door before 9 o'clock dragging her seventh-grade son. She had to hit him just to get him into the room. The boy is a truant and just sits in class without participating in work or activities. This upsets me because I have tried sincerely and affectionately to get him involved."

Problem 6: "I am concerned with the poor quality of handwriting. Only about a half-dozen students seem to be able to turn in readable work. Even though standards are set up for handwriting quality and handwriting is considered as part of the grade, it makes very little difference."

Problem 7: "Many of the students I teach have very low self-esteem. They don't think much of themselves and have little confidence in their ability to learn or do anything. Some are just waiting to drop out."

Problem 8: "Mary is such a shy girl who is very easily embarrassed. Consequently, she avoids performing publicly. That is very difficult in a foreign language class. Yet, she seems to enjoy learning and does all right in other ways."

THEORY INTO ACTION ACTIVITIES

ACTIVITY 4.1: Cognitive Approaches   How do teachers use the cognitive approach? If you are assigned to a classroom, observe your mentor teacher and describe how he or she uses either of the following cognitive approaches and related beliefs or findings.

1. Reception learning

_____

2. Reciprocal teaching

_____

3. Problem solving

_____

ACTIVITY 4.2: Humanistic Approaches   How do teachers use the humanistic approach? If you are assigned to a classroom, observe the mentor teacher and describe how he or she uses any of the following humanistic approaches and related beliefs and findings.

1. Inviting School Success

_____

2. Values clarification

_____

3. Moral education

_____

4. Multiethnic education

_____

ACTIVITY 4.3: Behavioral Approaches   How do teachers use the behavioral approach? If you are working in a school, observe your mentor teacher and describe how he or she uses any of the following or other behavioral approaches and related beliefs and findings.

1. Programmed instruction

_____

2. Computer-assisted instruction

_____

3. Mastery learning

_____

4. Precision teaching

_____

5. Applied behavioral analysis

_____

ACTIVITY 4.4: Which School of Learning Theory Most Appeals to You?   Are you mostly a cognitivist, humanist, or behaviorist, or are you about evenly some of each? Below are twenty-one statements related to learning. Although you may agree with most or even all of them, pick only seven by placing seven check marks on the corresponding blanks. Then go to the key that follows to find out which school of thought each statement you checked is most closely related to.

_____ 1. Students must make connections between new information and the information they already possess.

_____ 2. Anxious students should be given successful academic and social experiences.

_____ 3. Teachers should give greater attention to helping students learn more about themselves.

_____ 4. New information must be logically organized and presented to students.

_____ 5. Information presented to students should be associated with something they like or want.

_____ 6. Students' behavior is mostly the result of their feelings of confidence, self-worth, and personal dignity.

_____ 7. Students forget information unless they rehearse or think about it.

_____ 8. Students should be made aware of *specifically* what they must know and be able to do at the end of instruction.

_____ 9. Students should be encouraged to believe that they are academically and socially capable.

_____ 10. Students should interact with teachers and be encouraged to ask questions.

_____ 11. Reinforcement of appropriate student learning behavior is essential.

_____ 12. Students should be given a secure environment in which they are encouraged to make wise academic and social choices.

_____ 13. When students discover something on their own, they learn better.

_____ 14. Students need to see other students and/or the teacher demonstrating appropriate learning behavior.

_____ 15. Students should be accepted regardless of their school achievement, feelings, or other behavior.

_____ 16. Students need to learn how to learn.

_____ 17. Parents must reinforce their children's learning behavior.

_____ 18. Students should learn to respect themselves and others.

_____ 19. A most important goal of education is to help students become better problem solvers.

_____ 20. Material to be learned should be presented in small, sequential steps.

_____ 21. Students should be encouraged to pursue their own interests.

Key
Cognitively oriented statements are 1, 4, 7, 10, 13, 16, 19
Behaviorally oriented statements are 2, 5, 8, 11, 14, 17, 20
Humanistically oriented statements are 3, 6, 9, 12, 15, 18, 21

REFERENCES

Anderson, R., Reder, L. & Simon, H. (1996). Situated learning and education. *Educational Researcher, 25*(4), 5–11

Ausubel, D. P. (1977). Facilitation of meaningful verbal learning in the classroom. *Educational Psychologist, 12,* 162–178.

Bandura, A. (1986). *Social foundations of thought and action: A social cognitive theory.* Englewood Cliffs, NJ: Prentice Hall.

Biehler, R. F., & Snowman, J. (2000). *Psychology applied to teaching.* Ninth Edition. Boston: Houghton Mifflin.

Block, J. H., & Anderson, L. W. (1975). *Mastery learning in classroom instruction.* New York: Macmillan.

Combs, A. W. (1965). *The professional education of teachers.* Boston: Allyn and Bacon.

Cruickshank, D. R., & Associates (1980). *Teaching is tough*. Englewood Cliffs, NJ: Prentice Hall.

Danielson, C. (1996). *Enhancing professional practice*. Alexandria, VA: Association for Supervision and Curriculum Development.

Deci, E., & Ryan, R. (1990). In R. Dienstbier (Ed.), A motivational approach to self. *Nebraska symposium on motivation*. (pp. 240–250). Lincoln: University of Nebraska Press.

Dembo, M. H. (1994). *Applying educational psychology in the classroom*. New York: Addison-Wesley Longman.

Ellson, D. (1986, October). Improving productivity in teaching. *Phi Delta Kappan, 68*, 111–124.

Frederickson, N. (1984). Implications of cognitive theory for instruction in problem solving. *Review of Educational Research, 54*(3), 363–408.

Guskey, T. (1996). *Implementing mastery learning*. Belmont, CA: Wadsworth.

Leinhardt, G. (1992, April). What research on learning tells us about teaching. *Educational Leadership, 49*(7), 20–25.

Lickona, T. (1988). Educating the moral child. *Principal, 68*, 6–10.

Marzano, R., Pickering, D., & Pollock, J. (2001). *Classroom instruction that works*. Alexandria, VA: Association for Supervision and Curriculum Development.

Maslow, A. H. (1998). *Toward a psychology of being*. Second Edition. New York: John Wiley.

Neill, A. S. (1969). *Summerhill: A radical approach to child rearing*. New York: Hart.

Nuthall, G. (1995). Heuristic models of teaching. In L. Anderson (Ed.), *International encyclopedia of teaching and teacher education* (pp. 122–127). Oxford, UK: Elsevier Science.

Palincsar, A. (1986). The role of dialogue in providing scaffolding instruction. *Educational Psychologist, 21*, 73–98.

Palinscar, A., & Brown, A. (1989). Classroom dialogues to promote self-regulated comprehension. In J. Brophy (Ed.), *Advances in research on teaching*. Vol. 1: *Teaching for meaningful understanding and self-regulated learning*. Greenwich, CT: JAI.

Purkey, W. W., & Novak, N. (1996). *Inviting school success*. Belmont, CA: Wadsworth.

Rogers, C. R. (1983). *Freedom to learn in the 80's*. Columbus, OH: Merrill.

Schoenfeld, A. H. (1989). Teaching mathematical thinking and problem solving. In L. Resnick & L. Klopfer (Eds.), *Toward the thinking curriculum* (pp. 83–103). Alexandria, VA: Association for Supervision and Curriculum Development.

Simon, S. B., Howe, L. W., & Kerschenbaum, H. (1995). *Values clarification. Practical strategies for teachers and students*. New York: Warner Books.

Slavin, R. E. (1999). *Educational psychology: Theory into practice*. Boston: Allyn & Bacon.

Sulzer-Azaroff, B. (1995). Behaviorist theories of teaching. In L. Anderson (Ed.), *International encyclopedia of teaching and teacher education*. (pp. 96–100). Oxford, UK: Elsevier Science.

Sylwester, R. (1995). *A celebration of neurons*. Alexandria, VA: Association for Supervision and Curriculum Development.

Viadero, D. (1996, May 22). Debate over how children learn is reignited. *Education Week, 15* (35), p. 5.

Walberg, H. J. (1984, May). Improving the productivity of America's schools. *Educational Leadership, 41*, 19–27.

Walberg, H. J. (1986). Synthesis of research on teaching. In M. C. Wittrock (Ed.), *Handbook of research on teaching* (pp. 214–229). New York: Macmillan.

Watson, B., & Konicek, R. (1990, May). Teaching for conceptual change: Confronting children's experience. *Phi Delta Kappan, 71*, 680–685.

Wittrock, M. C. (1987). Models of heuristic teaching. In M. J. Dunkin (Ed.), *The international encyclopedia of teaching and teacher education* (pp. 69–76). Oxford: Pergamon Press.

Getting to Know Your Students and Motivating Them to Learn

Contents

Two of the most challenging tasks you face as a teacher are *getting to know your students* and *motivating them to learn*. With regard to the first challenge, this chapter will help you learn some of the many ways by which you can come to know your students. To assist you in meeting the second challenge, a review of research on motivating students to learn will be presented.

How You Can Get to Know Your Students

A major responsibility and delight for most teachers is getting to know their students. Scholars concur: Knowing your students is extremely important if you expect to become an expert teacher (Doyle, 1986; Emmer, 1987; Shulman, 1987; Wasley, 1999). One of the things that normally separates novice from more experienced teachers is that new teachers do not know much about their students (Berliner, 1986; Borko & Livingston, 1989; Carter et al., 1987; Zheng, 1992). Among other things, knowing your students enables you to organize them into a functional class, to interact with them more sensitively, and to teach them more effectively (Airasian, 2000). Wagner (2001) feels even more strongly: "Knowing students deeply, teachers are far more able to coach, nurture, and demand excellence from each one. No student remains anonymous or falls through the cracks" (p. 56).

There are two ways by which you can get to know your students. First, you can utilize existing information that has been collected by the school district about each of them since they began kindergarten. A second source of information about your students is that which you can unearth or discover yourself. Let's look closely at these two ways of getting to know your students so that you can use each effectively.

5.1 How important to you is getting to know students? What do you most need to know about them?

Using Existing Records

CUMULATIVE RECORDS

Chris Zajac had received her fifth-grade children's cumulative records, which were stuffed inside salmon-colored folders. . . . For now she only [looked at] her new students' names and addresses, and resisted looking [at other information contained in the records]. It was usually better at first to let her own opinions form. But she couldn't help noticing the thickness of some of the "cumes." "The thicker the cume, the more trouble," she told [another teacher]. (Kidder, 1989, pp. 8–9)

The major source of information about your students will be their cumulative or permanent school records. The **cumulative record** is a depository of information and documents that most school districts require for each child. That record begins when a student enters kindergarten and follows the learner until he or she leaves school or graduates. A student's cumulative record contains a variety of data: *personal information* (address, age, place of birth, special interests, hobbies); *home and family data* (names of parents or guardians, their occupation(s); names and ages of siblings, unusual home conditions); *school attendance records; scores on standardized tests* of aptitude and achievement; *year-end academic grades, teacher anecdotal comments* on students and comments written following parent conferences; and miscellaneous information such as health data, psychological reports, and written communications between school and home.

5.2 What might you want to know about students beyond the information usually contained in a cumulative record?

If you are now assigned to a school, chances are that cumulative records exist for the students you work with. Your mentor teacher may be willing and able to share them with you. If not, you will find five cumulative records in the appendix at the end of this chapter so that you can see what these records are like. The records have been minimally altered to protect the target students (for example, the photographs are not those of the student in the record). Two of the five students, Jack Brogan and Kathleen Glovak, are in fifth grade in a suburban school. The others, Benny Gamble, Julio Rivera, and Debbie Walker, are middle school sixth graders in an inner-city school. Take a moment to find the records and look them over, as we will refer to them later. For now, however, let's briefly consider two of the most important kinds of data contained in a "cume record"—scores on standardized tests and teacher anecdotal comments.

Standardized Test Scores A **standardized test** compares a student's score on that test with the scores of a very large number of similar students who have taken the same test. Thus, a standardized test score enables you to see how your students' scores compare to the scores of a much larger sample of similar students, such as other eighth graders locally or nationally. Standardized tests that measure potential, or aptitude, for learning are called aptitude tests, while those that measure how much students actually know are called achievement tests.

Aptitude Tests Aptitude tests that measure general potential to learn are referred to as general ability tests, or intelligence tests. These tests provide you with comparative information about such things as a student's ability to deal with abstractions and to solve problems. Look at Jack Brogan's cumulative record (at the end of this chapter). You will see he has taken two mental ability tests. His scores of 103 and 104 become meaningful only when compared against the national average of 100

"When my teachers told me that my records would follow me through life, I thought they were exaggerating."

on the same tests. All students whose records appear in the appendix score about average on their mental ability tests. Scores 20 or more points higher or lower than 100 are usually indicative of higher- or lower-than-average learning potential. Thus, Jack's scores are quite average.

For the past few decades, there has been increasing debate over the use of general ability tests. Some argue the tests are culturally biased favoring white, middle-class Americans—that the tests are written so that nonwhite and/or low SES students would be less likely to do well on them. Most school districts, however, continue to use aptitude tests, although they caution against placing too much confidence in such scores by themselves.

In Chapter 3, we learned about multiple kinds of intelligence (Highlight 3.2), including interpersonal insight, physical aptitudes, and the ability to learn in specific fields such as music. In this chapter's appendix, you may notice that the Madison School District students (Jack and Kathy) also took a musical aptitude test. Both scored at the 6th percentile, which means they did as well as or better on this test than only 6 percent of students who have taken it. Based on the test result alone, they would seem to have limited musical aptitude or potential.

Achievement Tests   Standardized tests are also used to measure achievement, that is, how much a student already knows compared to similar students. Again, turn to Jack Brogan's record (page 111). He has taken achievement tests in grades 1 through 4. In grade 1, he received a score of B (high normal) in readiness to read. In grade 2, Jack scored at the 40th percentile, which means his reading score was the same as or better than 40 percent of other students who have taken this test. In grades 3 and 4, Jack's standardized test scores are presented in another way. This form is called the grade level, or grade equivalent, score. A **grade equivalent score,** according to Airasian (2000), is one that represents the pupil's level of performance relative to pupils in his or her own grade. An example will make this definition clear. In fourth grade, Jack Brogan received a score of 4.2 on the "Middle Grades Achievement Test" (this name was substituted for the real test name). What does 4.2 mean? A grade level or grade equivalent score of 4.2 means that, compared to other fourth graders for whom the test was intended and on whom the test was "normed," Jack is average. Let's look at Benny Gamble's record (page 120). In grade 3, he took the "Metropolitan Achievement Test" in several subjects. In reading, his grade equivalency score was 5.3. This means that, compared to other third graders for whom the reading test was intended, Benny did very well; it does *not* mean that Benny necessarily is reading at a fifth-grade level, as the 5.3 might seem to indicate. Standardized tests will be discussed further in Chapter 9.

Teacher Anecdotal Comments   A second kind of information found in cumulative records and on report cards are teachers' **anecdotal comments,** or teachers' descriptions of their students.

Touliatos and Compton (1983) suggest you use the following guidelines for writing anecdotal comments:

- Cover only a single incident or event in the anecdote.
- Record it as soon as possible, with the date and time indicated.
- Begin with a description of the place where the situation occurred, the people who were involved, and the circumstances.
- Describe what transpired (events, reactions, responses—use direct quotes if possible). Try to write in a reportorial style; that is, describe, but do not interpret or editorialize, what you viewed. Be objective—avoid personal judgments.
- Describe how the episode concluded.
- If the episode is related to other episodes, state how and why.

5.3   Teacher Chris Zajac (p. 89) resisted looking at her students' cumulative files until she had formed her own opinions. What do you think are the advantages and disadvantages of learning about students from school records?

You will find out about students by reading anecdotal comments made by former or present teachers. After reviewing the literature on "teacher comments," Brualdi (1998) suggests that when you make comments about students keep the following in mind:

• Write specific rather than general comments. "Tabitha completes her work promptly, carefully and correctly" versus "Tabitha is a good student."

• When possible use words that promote a positive view of the student. "Josue is showing commitment to learning arithmetic and is steadily improving."

• When you must convey that a learner needs help, use words and phrases such as

"Trisha could profit by . . ."

"Trisha requires . . ."

"Trisha finds it difficult to . . ."

"Trisha needs help with . . ." These words and phrases give direction to the reader.

• Avoid or use the following words with caution: "unable, can't, won't, always."

Source: A. Birualdi (1998). *Teacher comments on report cards* (ERIC Document Reproduction Services ED 423 309). Washington, DC: ERIC Clearinghouse on Assessment and Evaluation.

When you look at the "teacher comments" and "personal comments" on the five appended cumulative record cards, it is clear that the teachers who wrote them did not provide all the information Touliatos and Compton suggest. Nevertheless, the comments tell us something about these teachers' perceptions of

• A student's learning characteristics (Jack Brogan has a "short attention span").

• A student's work habits (Jack is "not finishing his work").

• A student's social and personality characteristics (Jack "is quite immature, constantly talking, fools and daydreams," and so on).

• A student's achievement (Kathy Glovack "is doing strong average work, does very well in school").

• A student's problems ("Kathy doesn't like the student teacher").

• A student's maladies (Benny Gamble "complains of illness").

• A student's interests (Julio Rivera "likes science and music").

• A student's family (Debbie Walker's "stepfather has left home and is trying to get the baby daughter from the mother").

5.4 How might you be affected by reading the student folders in the chapter's appendix?

Try Activity 5.1

Individual Education Plans (IEPs)   In Chapter 3 you learned that, at times, detailed instructional plans are developed for children with special needs. Sometimes they become part of a learner's folder.

Unearthing New Information about Students

There may be occasions when you have no cumulative records or when they are inadequate for your needs. At such times, you may want to find out some things about students for yourself. There are several ways you can do so. Check with your principal beforehand to make sure your approach aligns with your school district's policy on student privacy.

OBSERVING STUDENTS

Observation, that is, looking and listening, is an excellent way to learn about students. You can observe them talking, reading, working independently and in groups, listening, and so forth. These observations can be either formal or informal.

Formal observation refers to carefully planned efforts to obtain specific information about a target student or students. The teacher, a teacher aide, another teacher, or a university student involved in a field experience could do formal observation. The use of a carefully designed observation instrument permits you to observe a student or students and then make subsequent observations in order to compare the results. Conversely, **informal observation** refers to casual, unplanned observations done incidentally. Such spontaneous observations, which are made under conditions that were not controlled and thus cannot be closely replicated, are nonetheless valuable to teachers.

Examples may make the distinction between formal and informal observation clearer. Suppose Jack Brogan is your target student. You note from comments in his cumulative record (pages 111–115) that he has difficulty interacting with other students ("minds other people's business, bothers people, has become sullen with other students"). To get a more complete profile of Jack, you decide to observe him. Now the choice of formal or informal observation comes into play.

If you observe Jack formally, you need to specify what you intend to look for. You must also decide how, when, and under what conditions you will make these observations. You might decide to observe his interactions with other students for one complete day: before he enters the building; when he enters and goes to his room; during the time before class begins; during class activities, recess, and lunch; and as he leaves the class and the building. You might even want to make up your own observation instrument or checklist (see Chapter 9 "Observational, Performance, and Authentic Assessment"). The following are questions you could use to focus your observation:

Try Activity 5.2

- With whom does Jack interact most and least?
- What circumstances surrounded positive interactions?
- What circumstances surrounded neutral interactions?
- What circumstances surrounded negative interactions?
- With whom were the positive, neutral, and negative interactions?
- Were the different kinds of interactions (positive, neutral, negative) related to different times of day, different activities, or other factors or circumstances?

On the other hand, if you observe Jack informally, your observations will not be systematic. You will only be describing spontaneous events and situations that you feel are interesting or important. Thus, informal observation is casual, impromptu, and general. Teacher comments made on cumulative record cards and on report cards (see, for example, page 118) are usually the result of informal observation.

Only from carefully structured, formal observation can you obtain the kind of information you need to address a true concern you may have about a student. Since formal observation is labor- and time-intensive, most teachers reserve it for special circumstances, such as when a student or students need academic or social help.

INTERVIEWING STUDENTS

Humans have an insatiable desire to find out about others. This assertion seems well supported by the number of radio and television talk shows in which persons of all kinds answer questions about what they are like and why. Certainly, one way to find out about persons is to talk with them directly.

Likewise, teachers can find out about their students both by talking casually with them and by formally interviewing them. Interviews may be particularly useful in uncovering personal information that cannot be obtained through observation. For example, you can observe Jack Brogan and try to deduce possible causes of his unsatisfactory interaction with his peers, or you can interview him in an attempt to uncover the cause.

Like observations, interviews can be formal or informal. A **formal interview** is a structured, face-to-face meeting to obtain specific information about the interviewee's

5.5 If you were Kathleen Glovack's student teacher, why might you want to interview her?

experiences, views, likes, and so forth. The key characteristics of a formal interview are *purpose* and *structure*. There are particular things you wish to find out, and in order to do so, you must frame your questions accordingly.

An **informal interview** is a face-to-face meeting that is more like casual conversation. The intention is to allow talk to flow naturally and spontaneously in more or less any direction. Perhaps you can categorize prominent interviewers such as Barbara Walters, Larry King, Oprah Winfrey, Sam Donaldson, Ed Bradley, and Jay Leno on a continuum between formal and informal.

What procedures are interviewers expected to follow? TenBrink (1974) offers the following guidelines; think about how you might follow them if you were interviewing Jack Brogan or Kathleen Glovack.

Try Activity 5.3

- *Be prepared.* Remember, if you are conducting the interview for a specific purpose, it must be carefully structured. In Kathy's case, you may want to find out how she feels about her student teacher and why. Have explicit, thoughtfully constructed questions ready.

- *Put the student at ease.* Begin by establishing a friendly, relaxed atmosphere. Use a warm-up period to talk for awhile about pleasant, nonthreatening things.

- *Guide the student.* Once you seem to be comfortable with each other, gently lead the child through your thoughtfully planned questions and probe for further, related information if that seems prudent. However, do not push too hard. You may recall times when teachers or parents "interviewed" you and perhaps met with resistance.

- *Know when to quit.* You may have to back off or stop if the interviewee feels threatened.

You can also obtain much useful information about a student through interviewing other teachers and through parent conferences. As with student interviews, the amount of useful information you obtain will be directly related to how well you prepare for the interview and how skillfully you follow good interviewing procedures.

In summary, if you are properly prepared and sensitive to others, the use of interviews can provide you with much-needed information that can help you understand and work more effectively with your students.

USING QUESTIONNAIRES

Thus far, we have suggested that you can obtain information beyond that contained in the school's cumulative record folders by watching, listening, and talking to your students. Another way you can acquire student information is to have students complete questionnaires. Questionnaires normally are given to an entire class rather than to an individual. However, individuals can be targeted.

Questionnaires range from asking open-ended questions to asking students to respond to very specific items. Some examples will make this distinction clearer. Open-ended questions, such as the following, allow students greater freedom of response. (Of course, questions would be modified according to the student's developmental characteristics, such as age.)

- What are you like?
- What is your favorite activity, hobby, sport, TV show, website, place, food, or subject? What are your least favorite things?
- How do you feel about yourself as a student?
- How would you describe your behavior in class?
- How do you get along with other students?
- What do you want teachers to be like?

5.6 Beyond the information usually found in a cumulative record, what else might you want to know that possibly could come out of an interview?

5.7 What might a teacher want to know that could be discovered through a questionnaire?

- What do you like most and least about school?
- When do you enjoy class most and least?
- What is it like for you at home?

Closed-ended items on a questionnaire are more specific. The respondent often is asked to read each item and then indicate to what extent he or she agrees with it. The respondent is forced to make a choice. The sample of items on the following mock questionnaire are all related to school attitude. They are adapted from Lewis (1986).

	Strongly Agree	Agree	Disagree	Strongly Disagree
1. I like school.				
2. My teachers care about me.				
3. School helps me feel good about myself.				
4. The things I learn in school are important to me.				
5. My teachers praise and reward me.				
6. I need more teacher help.				
7. School is boring.				

Following is another sample of closed-ended items. This time, yes or no answers are required. The items, adapted from Fraser and Fisher (1986), are intended to find out how students feel about the class they are in.

1. Pupils enjoy this class.	Yes	No
2. The difficulty of the classwork is about right.	Yes	No
3. Students get along with each other in this class.	Yes	No
4. This class is very competitive.	Yes	No

Try Activity 5.4

USING SOCIOMETRY

Sociometry is a technique used to obtain information about the social acceptability of individuals within a group. A **sociogram** is a diagrammatic representation of the social relationships that exist within a group at a *particular point in time* (see Figure 5.1).

Suppose you are the teacher of Jack Brogan and Kathleen Glovack, or the teacher of Benny Gamble, Julio Rivera, and Debbie Walker. Furthermore, assume you wish to know more about how their peers feel about each of these students, and how the students feel about their peers. If so, you might ask each class member to name three students they would like to sit near. As Figure 5.1 shows, the responses of the twenty-nine students in Jack and Kathleen's class reveal that

- No one chooses Jack.
- Four students would like to sit near Kathleen (three girls, one boy).

Ronald, the most nominated student in the class, was selected nine times. Five students other than Jack were not selected by anyone. Can you identify them?

Beyond frequency of nomination (popularity), teachers are also interested in attractions. Who nominated whom? Who chose each of the students? To what extent are the choices mutual? Are there cases of "unrequited love" or instances when students choose others who reject or spurn them?

Although sociometric nominations are one of the most dependable rating techniques (Anastasi, 1997), Touliatos and Compton (1983) urge caution when interpreting sociometric data. The information actually may indicate desired rather than

5.8 How might you put sociometric information to good use?

FIGURE 5.1 Sociogram

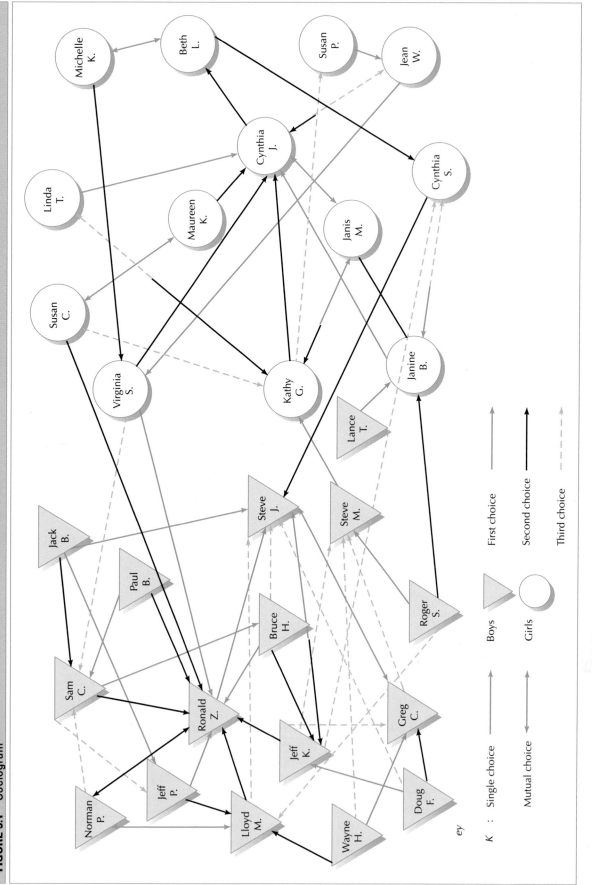

ey

K : Single choice

Boys

Girls

First choice

Mutual choice

Second choice

Third choice

Question: Name three children in your classroom whom you would most like to sit next to. (Note: Not all children made three choices.)

real associations among class members, and "too often high sociometric status is interpreted to mean leadership ability and good personality adjustment, while receiving no sociometric choices is commonly equated with maladjustment. Receiving many choices actually could . . . mean high conformity to the group, and [isolation] could be [a sign] of independence and creativity" (p. 201). Interested in sociometry? Visit the Sociometry Plus website at www.thesociometry.com/sociometry.html.

Try Activity 5.5 and 5.6

 Web Resource

USING AUTOBIOGRAPHY

Autobiography can provide a rich source of knowledge about its author. Thus, another way to obtain information about students is to ask them to write about some aspect of their lives. However, use of this technique is limited since it depends on students' verbal and writing ability. Additionally, it is time-consuming for the writers. Therefore, should you wish to obtain autobiographical information, limit the focus of the story. Ask students to recall and write about such topics as

- Who am I?
- The best day I ever had.
- My favorite year in school.
- My favorite teacher.
- My life at home.
- My life in the neighborhood.
- My life at school.
- My most memorable experience.
- My favorite things.

5.9 How would your teachers benefit from autobiographical information about you? What kinds of information would you want them to have?

Try Activity 5.7

USING PARENTS AND GUARDIANS AS SOURCES

Parents and care givers are important sources of information about students. Normally, parents know more about their children than anyone, and most teachers have opportunities to tap this supply of information. Formally, there are parent-teacher conferences. Some school districts mandate conferences and give teachers time to conduct them. For example, in the Madison School District where Jack Brogan and Kathy Glovack are students, yearly conferences are required. You probably noted the section titled "Parent-Teacher Conference Summaries" in the cumulative record folders. In the Urban School System where Benny, Julio, and Debbie are students, conferences are not required and the folders have no specific place to record them. Of course, Urban teachers do confer with parents. You will note in Debbie Walker's folder that there is a request from her third-grade teacher for a parent conference or a follow-up letter from the parent. Mrs. Walker indicated she had received the request, but there is no evidence that a conference took place or that she responded with a letter.

Unfortunately, most parent-teacher conferences are held only to provide information to parents and not also to obtain information from them. Certainly, it was important for Kathy Glovack's fourth-grade teacher to learn that Kathy didn't want to come to school because she didn't like the student teacher. Also, Kathy's third-grade teacher learned from Mrs. Glovack that there was a new baby in the home. This is potentially useful information. In Jack Brogan's case, parent conferences revealed that his father is strict, that his parents want him to behave and learn, and that they are cooperative and helpful.

What might teachers need to know about students that could be learned from parents and guardians? Parents can tell teachers about a student's behavior at home, about his or her likes and dislikes, habits, responsibilities, and so forth. While parents do not know everything about their children, they can aid you tremendously in getting to know your students needs' and abilities.

5.10 What do teachers absolutely *need* to know about a student's family background? What might they *want* to know that isn't absolutely necessary? What kinds of information are helpful? What family information is no one else's business?

"I said, 'Your son doesn't seem to listen very well'."

What might teachers need to know about parents and guardians that, in turn, would help them understand more about their students? Touliatos and Compton (1983) suggest the following: parental background and current family status, personal characteristics of parents ("the Brogans are strict"), parental perception of their relationship with each other and with the student, the roles of both parents and students in the home, and parental attitudes toward the student and any siblings. To find out about the personal characteristics of parents and other family members, teachers might ask them to tell what they are like as people and as parents, then ask how that may affect their son or daughter. To know how parents perceive their own and their children's roles and relationships in the home, teachers might ask them how family responsibilities and decisions are shared.

Try Activity 5.8

It is particularly useful to know how parents or guardians feel toward parenting and child rearing. You might consider asking them what it is like to be parents or guardians, how being a parent has affected their lives, what it is like to be the target student's parent or guardian, what they believe in as parents or guardians, and so on.

USING CASES

The **case approach** pieces together all existing information to form a comprehensive profile of the target student. Thus, a case pulls together information from cumulative records, observations, interviews, questionnaires, sociometric studies, autobiographies, parent conferences, and any other source and synthesizes it.

Normally, the best existing source of case history information is the cumulative record since it contains several kinds of information and is updated from time to time. When other data are available to fill in the blanks, teachers are able to complete the case. If other data are not available, they must collect the missing information.

Touliatos and Compton (1983) suggest that to have an overall picture of a student, you need the following data:

5.11 Would you like to have a complete profile of all the students you teach? What benefits would this offer?

- Identifying information (name, address, telephone, age in years and months, place of birth, gender, grade, race, nationality, religion).
- Family history (relationship of the parent, guardian, or caregiver to the student; parents' age, race, nationality, religion, cultural background, and language spoken in the home; family physical and health concerns; education; present work status; homeowner or renter; adequacy of housing; interests; pastimes).
- Student's medical history (general health, record of prominent illnesses and injuries).

- Student's school history (schools attended, level of performance in general and in specific subjects such as reading and math, aptitude test scores, achievement test scores, special interests, attitudes, relationships with others, friends).

A teacher-written case study of Debbie Walker is contained in Case 5.1. Her cumulative record folder is appended at the end of the chapter.

Try Activity 5.9

Evaluating and Using Information

It is one thing to need or want accurate student information to aid you in your teaching. It is another thing to understand and to use it wisely.

EVALUATING INFORMATION

Several questions should challenge you when you examine student data: Is this information suitable for my purpose? Just what is it that I want to know? Does this information supply the answers? Suppose you want to know about your students' aptitude for learning: To what extent are they likely to be able to deal with abstractions, solve problems, and learn? In this case you would need to have the results of a standardized test that measures learning aptitude. Because it has been constructed for the purpose of measuring learning potential, such a test is considered valid for that purpose. On the other hand, a standardized test that measures student achievement—what a student already knows—would not be suitable for that purpose. Although students' scores on achievement tests are often closely related to their scores on learning aptitude tests, these tests measure different things. A student may perform well on a learning aptitude test, thus revealing the potential to learn, yet may not do well on an achievement test. Conversely, another student may earn a high achievement test score but a low learning aptitude test score. Can you see how this could happen? Since standardized tests have been carefully developed to measure what they are supposed to measure, you need to make certain that you have the right test results for your needs.

A second question related to student data involves correctness. Here you need to ask: Is this information really accurate? Two major factors can contribute to inaccuracy. One relates to whether the information is biased, while the other relates to whether the information is stable. For decades, certain standardized tests have been criticized as biased, usually in terms of culture or gender considerations. As previously mentioned in the section on aptitude tests, some tests appear to be easier for students brought up in white, middle-class communities because they use Standard English and draw from typical middle-class experiences. Others supposedly exhibit gender bias, usually meaning they are easier for males than females. To the extent that such tests are biased, it is impossible to obtain truly accurate student scores. School districts are increasingly aware of the need to find objective tests that provide unbiased, culture- and gender-fair results.

Unfortunately, some degree of bias exists in everyone. Accordingly, be cautious about accepting any interpretation of student data provided by others, including teachers. Although most teachers have no intention of providing slanted information, they naturally become attracted to certain students and are put off by others. They tend to identify with and praise the "attractive students" and to reject and punish the "unattractive" ones. To some extent, the attraction teachers feel toward certain students is a function of their own background and personality. Generally, we tend to like those who are like us. We feel more comfortable around them (the "birds of a feather" syndrome).

Teacher bias is particularly evident when such things as race, nationality, gender, looks, and dress unfairly and incorrectly influence the teacher's perception of

5.12 How will you become aware of your personal biases? How will you deal with them?

Case 5.1

A Study of Debbie Walker, Written by Her Teacher

Debbie Walker, Grade 5, Edison School. One November morning, Debbie Walker, a transfer student from Baker Middle School, arrived hobbling on crutches and accompanied by her mother. Mrs. Walker explained that Debbie had broken her leg while helping carry furniture into the house from a moving truck. As a result of the accident, Debbie had missed almost two months of school. As soon as she entered our classroom, the children immediately accepted her. This was probably partially a result of her incapacitation. Lynette Overmire and several other children were anxious to help and made plans to escort Debbie to and from classrooms and to her home. This was the first indication that Debbie was able to exert a subtle yet profound effect on the behavior of her peers.

Debbie Walker was born in the city of Urban and has lived in inner-city ghetto areas all her life. During this time, she has attended eight different schools and has been a pupil in eighteen different classrooms. As a result of this continuous shifting, Debbie has never experienced any sense of security or permanency. Her home conditions (the family has fourteen children) are in a constant state of turmoil. In a fatherless home until recently, Debbie and her siblings have moved from one area of the inner-city ghetto to another. Often, the only concern of such families is to eke out a day-by-day existence.

Until recently, Debbie lived only with her mother and six of her twelve siblings. However, within the last two years she also had a "stepfather." More recently, the stepfather left the home and is seeking court action to obtain custody of his baby daughter. Debbie knows nothing of her biological father. She does not even remember one. She has grown up on public assistance. This family has packed up its belongings and criss-crossed the city almost as many times as Debbie has counted birthdays.

Physically, Debbie is relatively tall for her age. She is an African American and a member of the Baptist church. Her personal appearance varies from one day to the next. She does not seem to know how to be neat, clean, and well groomed.

Debbie's general attitude has been pleasant until recently. She has enjoyed helping in the classroom and about the school, and the children elected her to the position of class treasurer. Debbie has been assisting in the arts and crafts program in our after-school program at the Social Center. The arts and crafts teacher has praised Debbie's work.

Very recently, however, Debbie appears to be disturbed. Just last month, she was suspended from school for two days for encouraging two girls to fight each other outside the school building during lunch period. As a result of her suspension, she became sullen and would not complete her academic assignments. Now she has had her school and after-school responsibilities taken away from her.

Debbie had been relatively happy in school until these events occurred. This was reassuring, since she has been retained in the first, third, and fifth grades. She seems to enjoy art, music, and arithmetic the most. However, she claims she likes all her subjects.

Debbie uses fair Standard English. The mark of inner-city linguistic characteristics is evident in her speech pattern.

In a recent conversation with Mrs. Walker, we discussed Debbie's attitudes, general behavior, and failure to follow through with classwork. I indicated that this behavior was jeopardizing Debbie's school success. Her mother thinks that her friendship with Felicia Ault is the reason behind her change for the worse. It is true that Debbie and Felicia are close and have a somewhat negative influence upon each other and the other children. As mentioned earlier, Debbie is able to affect the behavior of her classmates through manipulation and subtle pressure.

Debbie's school achievement has been weak. She has taken three Kuhlman-Anderson IQ tests. The results reveal an IQ range from 86 to 103. Her achievement test scores are recorded on her cumulative record folder and should be interpreted according to her age and grade rather than just grade alone.

One hopes that Debbie's recent failure to complete her work and to behave in more appropriate ways in the school setting may pass. Now that she is encountering more homework, some provisions will have to be made for a quiet place at home for her to study. In a family as large as hers, this circumstance is improbable. Coming to school as she has recently with unfinished assignments may well have led to her frustration and antisocial behavior. Debbie must be continually encouraged to do her best to complete her work and to complete it on time. If she is able to develop this habit, she may soon be eligible to become a hall guard. This status, if attained, may ease her frustrations.

Source: D. R. Cruickshank. (1969). *Inner-city simulation laboratory.* Chicago: Science Research Associates.

students. Can you recall instances of possible teacher bias toward you or a friend based on one of these factors?

Teacher bias also can be positive but inaccurate. Each of us has a friend or relative whom we are attracted to for some particular reason. Sometimes we admire that person so much for one or two positive qualities that we overlook any negative qualities he or she may have. To us, that individual wears a halo. You will find certain students seem to wear halos, too. They can do no wrong. This bias phenomenon is aptly termed "the halo effect." Although it is difficult to detect and control, you must strive to observe and report the truth, the whole truth, and nothing but the truth about learners. This is a tall order.

Inconsistent information about students also presents a problem. Consider Benny Gamble's "general ability tests" (page 122). He took these aptitude tests in grades 1, 2, and 3 and received intelligence scores ranging from 97 (about average) to 116 (above average). Similarly, you might receive conflicting perceptions of a student from different teachers. One might report an eager hand-raiser as an aggressive attention seeker, while another might interpret the same behavior as that of a motivated learner. Which should you believe? Generally speaking, when information about a student is inconsistent, err on the positive side: Accept Benny's high score as indicative of what he can do under optimal conditions. And, for the same reason, believe the best about any learner with mixed credentials.

In summary, if teachers are to be effective, they must learn to obtain and use only the information about their students that suits their purpose, is unbiased, and is consistent or stable.

USING INFORMATION PROPERLY

The information we obtain affects the perceptions and expectations we have of students. Moreover, some types of information are more influential than others. Dusek and Joseph (1983) identified and compared the results of seventy-seven studies that were conducted to find out what most influences the academic and personal expectations teachers have for their students. The investigators looked for relationships between teachers' expectations and student gender, gender-role behaviors, physical attractiveness, race and social class, name stereotypes, conduct, and the teacher's previous experiences with a sibling. Five of these factors seem to significantly influence a teacher's judgment: student attractiveness, class conduct, race, social class, and cumulative record information, particularly test scores and teachers' anecdotal comments. To see how, turn to Spotlight 5.1.

In contrast, Dusek and Joseph note that it is unclear whether a student's name (desirable versus undesirable), gender-role behaviors (whether their behavior follows a gender-role stereotype), or a teacher's previous experiences with a student's sibling influence teacher expectations. The researchers conclude that teachers, on average, are not influenced by a student's gender. Although a student's gender does not seem to influence the teacher's academic and personal expectations of that student, we learned in Chapter 3 that teachers still treat boys and girls differently. To explain this seeming contradiction, consider two friends—one male, one female. Could you hold similar academic and personal expectations for them and still treat them differently?

Since certain information about students influences the perceptions and expectations of teachers, just how much should they read or hear about their students *before* classes begin? Airasian (2000) says that in the course of interviews with teachers, he found most of them wanted at least three kinds of information early on. They want to know about (1) any physical or emotional problem, (2) learners' special needs, learning problems, or disabilities, and (3) problematic or atypical parent custodial arrangements.

Factors That Influence Teachers' Perceptions and Expectations of Students

Variables	Type of Influence
Student attractiveness (physical)	Influences teachers' expectations for both academic achievement and social-personal relationships.
Student classroom conduct	Influences teachers' expectations of future conduct.
Race	Generally, white students are expected to outperform black students.
Social class	Generally, middle-class children are expected to perform better than lower-class students.
Cumulative record information	Teachers' expectations are influenced mainly by test scores and other teachers' comments.

Source: From J. B. Dusek & G. Joseph. (1983). The bases of teacher expectations: A meta-analysis. *Journal of Educational Psychology, 75* (3) 327–346.

5.13 Are you able to change your mind about people?

Fortunately, many teachers adjust their perceptions and expectations of students after working with them, after "getting to know them" (Good & Brophy, 1994). Yes, as teachers we tend to believe what we read, but we change those impressions in light of our experience.

Motivating Students to Learn

Try Activity 5.10

In addition to knowing your students, you must be able to motivate them to learn. Some teachers seem to come by this ability naturally. However, most of us have to learn how to motivate others. Fortunately for us, knowledge about motivation is abundant. Brophy (1998) has reviewed that knowledge and offers the following advice. The advice is applicable when we plan, teach, or evaluate students.

- Establish a classroom environment that is conducive to learning. How? *First,* make yourself "attractive" and engaging to your learners. It helps when students feel positively toward you. (See Chapter 11, "Effective Teachers: Personal Attributes and Characteristics".) *Second,* focus their attention on achieving goals—individual student goals and/or group goals. It helps when learners know what is to be done and, if possible, why. (See Chapter 4, Cognitive Approaches to Teaching and Learning). *Third,* teach what is worth learning, and teach it in ways that help students appreciate its value.

- Maximize the likelihood that learners will make an effort to learn. Students are more likely to make an effort to learn when (1) they believe they can perform a task successfully and will feel rewarded, (2) they believe they have the power to succeed (a sense of **efficacy**), and (3) they believe they will receive the support necessary to succeed.

5.14 How did your teachers maximize your interest in learning?

- Make special efforts on behalf of students who lack confidence and thus are reluctant to engage in learning. Make challenging but ability-related demands on them. Help them see that they can succeed with reasonable effort. Should they fall sort, help them understand why and show them how they can succeed.

Try Activity 5.11

- Make special efforts with students who have low expectations for themselves and readily accept failure. Provide them with continuous reassurance that they can succeed. Provide whatever support is needed. *Praise effort* and *accept progress. Individualize* as required. Collaborate with family and care givers.

- Make special efforts with apathetic and disengaged students. Help them appreciate how learning will empower them and make them more satisfied with themselves. Such students can benefit from use of incentives and by use of signed agreements or contracts (see Chapter 7 "individualized instruction")

There are students in almost every classroom who are academically unmotivated, referred to as *reluctant learners.* Perhaps, you can recall some. In fact, you may have been one yourself until someone or something turned you around. Hidi and Harackiewicz (2000) identified some tactics that have been found useful to "catch and hold" the attention of the academically unmotivated. Here are a few:

Make certain that what students are to read is easily comprehensible.

Additionally, try to find reading that contains novelty and surprise.

Give students choices. Even when seemingly trivial they seem to enhance student interest.

Consider single-gender groups or classes for some things that seem more difficult for either boys or girls. For example, it has been found that girls show higher levels of interest in physics when in a single-gender class.

Help students figure out how to make certain tasks less boring and more

interesting. For example, "How can we make this more fun?"

Make students socially responsible. For example, utilize cooperative learning (presented in Chapter 8) where, in some cases, each learner in a small group must become expert on a topic and share that expertise with peers.

Source: S. Hidi & Harackiewicz, J. (2000, Summer). Motivating the academically unmotivated. *Review of Educational Research, 70*(2), 151–179.

that spell out learning goals and rewards for success. Encourage learners by being patient yet determined for their success. Build on existing learner interests and make learning tasks as satisfying as possible.

- Use both *extrinsic* and *intrinsic* reward as suitable. However, it is better to have learners engage in activities for their own reasons and their own fulfillment (intrinsic), rather than do something to please others, to obtain a material reward, or to avoid a punishment (extrinsic). Always try to focus student attention on what they personally are accomplishing or will accomplish by learning. To increase intrinsic motivation: (1) encourage autonomy by giving learners frequent opportunities (within the boundaries of the curriculum) to make decisions about what they will learn and how, (2) match learning tasks to the ability of each student, (3) use as many activity-oriented projects as possible and provide learners with immediate knowledge of how well they are doing, (4) try to use *authentic* activities—those that have a relationship to and application in the real world, (5) adapt the activities, when logical, to meet the interests of students, (6) personalize learning and try to make it emotionally or affectively engaging, and (7) avoid boring and aversive tasks.

- Engage learners in tasks that permit them to accomplish curriculum goals and at the same time satisfy their own personal and social goals. Everyone wins.

- Encourage students to value learning. Do this by being an enthusiastic learner yourself, by treating students as eager learners, by avoiding classroom practices that cause student anxiety, by causing learners to think deeply, and by attaching learning to students' life experiences.

If you have these abilities or gain them, every day will be satisfying to you and your learners, and they will enjoy greater academic success.

5.15 When and why have you experienced a lack of motivation to learn?

Try Activity 5.12

Some Final Thoughts

As we have seen, sizing up students has its benefits and pitfalls. We have already alluded to the potential danger of relying exclusively or too heavily on certain kinds of information, such as standardized test scores and teachers' comments. Airasian (2001) offers suggestions on how teachers can overcome these and other possible problems. Our modifications of his suggestions follow:

- Be sensitive to the possibility that you will make poor initial judgments about students from biased, incomplete, or erroneous information or from having a poor first impression. Give each student a second chance to make a good impression.

- Do not rush to judgment about what any student is like. Over time, collect as much information as you can in order to find out who that person really is.

- Rather than relying on recorded information, how the student dresses or looks, and what others say, observe the student and try to get close enough to find out the truth for yourself. Looks can be deceiving!

A large number of formal instruments have been developed for assessing students. Using them can provide knowledge about your students' (1) cognition (intelligence, readiness to learn, maturation, language and number skills, cognitive style, and so on), (2) personality and emotional characteristics, (3) perceptions of the environment, (4) self-concept, (5) attitudes and interests, and (6) social behavior. These instruments are well described in a two-volume set edited by Johnson (1976).

On the other hand, the use of motivation has only benefits. Therefore, you should work toward improving your motivational prowess. The following quotations by famous motivators may provide additional ideas about how to be a skillful motivator yourself:

- The important thing is not so much that every child should be taught, as that every child should be given the wish to learn. (John Lubbock)

- A teacher who is attempting to teach without inspiring the pupil with a desire to learn is hammering on cold iron. (Horace Mann)

- Above all things we must take care that the child who is not yet old enough to love his studies, does not come to hate them and dread the bitterness which was once tasted, even when the years of infancy are left behind. (Marcus Fabius Quintilianus)

- That which anyone has been long learning unwillingly, he unlearns with proportional eagerness and haste. (William Hazlitt)

Web Resources

There are numerous Internet sites related to motivation. See http://ericir.syr.edu/cgi-bin/print.cgi/Resources/General_Education/Motivation.html. Two we particularly like are: "Motivating Today's Students: The Same Old Stuff Just Doesn't Work" http://eric.uoregon.edu/publications/text/portraits1.2.html (advice from teachers and a principal) and "Increasing Student Engagement and Motivation" http://www.nwrel.org/request/oct00/index.html (strategies).

CHAPTER SUMMARY

- Getting to know students is important to teachers. Expert teachers seem to know far more about their students than novice teachers do.

- While there are many ways to get to know students, the information they yield falls into two main categories: information obtained from existing student records and information teachers can obtain for themselves.

- The major source of existing information is the cumulative ("cume") records or folders (five examples are in the chapter appendix). Cumulative records normally contain personal information about a student, home-family information, school attendance data, academic grades, standardized test scores, teacher comments, and so forth. Generally, teachers seem most interested in obtaining standardized test scores and reading former teachers' comments.

- To interpret standardized test scores, it is necessary to know what the test attempts to measure and to understand terms such as *standardized test, percentile,* and *grade equivalent*. To judge teachers' comments, it is necessary to know something about the people who made them and how they reached their conclusions about the student. Teachers' comments are often brief, incomplete, and, at times, inaccurate.

- A second source of information about students is knowledge teachers obtain from observations, interviews, questionnaires, sociometrics, autobiographies, parents, and cases.

- Student observations can be formal (intentionally planned and carried out) or informal (spontaneous and unplanned). Formal observation requires the teacher to specify who will be observed and how the observation will take place. Informal observation requires only occasional and impromptu records of whatever catches the teacher's attention. Most teacher observations are informal.

- Interviews allow teachers to collect information that is difficult to gain through mere observation. Interviews also can be formal or informal. Following certain interviewing procedures increases both the amount and the quality of information obtained.

- Questionnaires are structured using either open- or closed-ended questions. Open-ended questions ask students to broadly describe their perceptions of themselves, their relationships with peers, and their school and home lives. Closed-ended questions force students to answer according to some preconstructed scale or by responding yes or no; they permit no elaboration.

- Sociometry is used to find out how students perceive their social and/or work relationships with peers. A sociogram is a visual representation of those relationships.

- Autobiographical writing provides students with the opportunity to tell about themselves. Use of autobiographical writing is somewhat limited because of the literacy demands it places on some students.

- Parents and care givers can tell teachers much about their charges, and the teacher should tap them for this information. Knowledge of parents and family also helps us understand students.

- The case approach is a technique used to bring together all information about a student in order to create a more complete picture. Thus, a good case contains a mixture of information obtained through all the techniques just mentioned.

- Teachers must be able to evaluate information about students. Of prime importance is how closely the available information relates to the decisions teachers must make. Information that fits the purpose is valid information. Also important is the accuracy and stability of information, which is referred to as its *reliability*. Being able to judge the validity and reliability of information is crucial to using it in decision making.

- Certain types of information influence teachers' perceptions and expectations of students more than other kinds. The most influential types of information seem to be class conduct, student attractiveness, social class, race, and cumulative records. All teachers seem to want to gain information about learners' physical, emotional, learning, or home problems early on. Fortunately, teachers adjust their early impressions of students based upon long-term, daily experience with them. Airasian (2001) offers suggestions for overcoming the tendency to think and act on first impressions.

- Teachers must be able to interest students in learning. Some of us are more able to do this than others.

- Student interest is increased when we establish an attractive learning environment by displaying personal characteristics students find engaging, letting students know what the lesson is trying to accomplish, and making the lesson worth learning.

- Students are more likely to undertake learning when they think the task is within their ability, they feel they can succeed, and they believe you will assist them as necessary.

- Students either lacking confidence or reluctant to learn are helped when you provide ability-related, yet challenging tasks on which they can succeed with reasonable effort.
- Students with low expectations for themselves should be given regular assurance that they can succeed and should be praised for effort and progress.
- Apathetic students are helped when they understand the personal value of learning, when they face tasks related to their interests, and when incentives are provided. Intrinsic incentives or rewards are preferable.
- Be enthusiastic about learning, and an enthusiastic learner yourself, and treat students as such.

ISSUES AND PROBLEMS FOR DISCUSSION

1. When should teachers receive cumulative record information?
2. What kinds of information about students *must* a teacher have? What kinds *shouldn't* a teacher have?
3. How much confidence should teachers place in standardized tests? How should teachers use test data?
4. What are the advantages and disadvantages of showing students and parents standardized test results?
5. How can a teacher reduce his or her bias toward certain students?
6. How can teachers find time to collect and use student information?
7. How much time should teachers devote to motivating students?
8. Are parents and caregivers or teachers more responsible for creating student interest in learning?
9. How can what is known about student diversity (Chapter 3) be applied to student motivation?
10. How does each school of thought about learning (Chapter 4) apply to student motivation?
11. How can what we know about our students be used when motivating them?
12. What do you think are the three most important principles of motivation?
13. How can we get better at motivation?

THEORY INTO ACTION ACTIVITIES

ACTIVITY 5.1: Review Some Cumulative Records If you are in a field experience, ask your mentor teacher if you can see the cumulative records for that class. If so, make a list of the kinds of information they contain. Make a second list of other kinds of information about students that might be helpful to you.

If you are not in a field experience, study the five cumulative records in the appendix and make the same two lists. What else do you need to know in order to understand or interpret specific information contained in the records? Be prepared to share your investigation with other students in this course.

ACTIVITY 5.2: Plan and Conduct a Formal Observation If you are in a field experience, ask your mentor teacher if you might formally observe a student. Ask your teacher to help you identify the target individual. Then, prepare for the observation by answering the following questions.

- Who is the target student, and why has he or she been targeted? What is the concern or problem?

1. Academic		
Easy to educate	vs.	Hard to educate
Interested in studies	vs.	Not interested in studies
Good study habits	vs.	Weak in study habits
Achieves well	vs.	Limited achievement

2. Citizenship		
Prideful of school, class	vs.	Little concern for school, class
Willingly performs class duties and assignments	vs.	Shirks responsibilities
Takes initiative, leads	vs.	Complacent

3. Social Interaction		
Popular	vs.	Unpopular
Friendly, likeable	vs.	Withdrawn, difficult to like
No conflicts	vs.	Many conflicts

4. Personal Traits		
Self-confident	vs.	Anxious
Understands self	vs.	Lacks self-understanding
Agreeable	vs.	Stubborn
Disciplined, respects authority	vs.	Undisciplined
Persevering	vs.	Distractible
Organized	vs.	Disorganized

5. Home Interaction		
Prideful of, identifies with family	vs.	Little concern for, identification with family
Good family relationships	vs.	Weak relationships
No conflicts	vs.	Many conflicts

Source: Suggested in part by D. R. Kadyrbaeva & I. L. Engels (1990).

- What useful information might be gained by watching and listening to the student?
- Specifically when will the student be observed?
- What will be recorded? A list of questions or a checklist is usually required.

ACTIVITY 5.3: Plan and Conduct an Interview If you are involved in a field experience, you may be able to plan and conduct an interview with a student. It can focus on gaining information on a number of things, including the student's qualities (depicted in Highlight 5.2). Beyond those, you can obtain knowledge of the learner's likes and interests, home environment, life outside of school, and personal aspirations.

Use these questions to guide you in preparing the interview:

- Who will the target student be?
- Specifically why was this student chosen? What is the interest or concern?
- What useful information might be gained by conversing with the student?
- When and where will the interview take place?
- What questions will you need to ask to obtain the critical information?

ACTIVITY 5.4: Develop and Use a Questionnaire You might enjoy constructing your own questionnaire in order to find out more about students. If you are in a school, begin by finding out what student information is already available. You can determine this with the help of your mentor teacher. If you are not in a school, use the five cumulative record cards in the chapter appendix.

Next, determine what else you wish to know. Again, Highlight 5.2 might provide ideas.

Third, construct the questionnaire items. These may be either open- or closed-ended. Keep the items few in number, short, clear, and as nonthreatening as possible. For example, if you wish to gain information about the student's attitude toward school or home, use open-ended questions like those on the left rather than closed-ended questions like those on the right:

"What are your most enjoyable moments at school?"	versus	"Do you enjoy school?"
"What are your most enjoyable moments at home?"	versus	"Do you enjoy being at home?"

After completing your questionnaire, have a few peers look it over and then share it with your mentor teacher and university instructor. Finally, decide if, or how, you or your mentor teacher should or could collect and use the new information.

ACTIVITY 5.5: Study a Sociogram   If you are in a field experience, ask your mentor teacher if he or she has made a sociogram of the present class. If so, ask if you could see it and find out how it was done. Ask your mentor teacher to discuss the results. Were they as expected? How were they used? You may wish to make a transparency of the sociogram to share with others in this course.

ACTIVITY 5.6: Develop and Administer a Sociogram   If you are in a field experience, see whether you may develop and administer a sociogram. If so, follow this procedure or one similar to it:

1. Select one student question from the following:
   a. "Which two persons in the class are your closest friends?"
   b. "If you were working on a group project that would receive a grade, with which two persons would you want to work?"
   c. If you were in some kind of difficulty, which two persons in the class would most likely help you?
2. Explain to the students that you are trying to find out more about the class in order to be a better teacher.
3. Ask the students to privately answer the question you have selected (a, b, or c).
4. Record the choices each student has made on a chart similar to this one:

RESPONDENT'S NAME	FIRST CHOICE	SECOND CHOICE
a. Julio		
b.		
c.		
d.		

5. Record who chose each student.
   a. Julio was chosen by Robert and Malcolm.
   b.
   c.
   d.
   e.
   f.

6. Select symbols to represent males and females (see Figure 5.1).

7. Place the symbols representing the most oft-chosen students toward the center of the page and those least chosen toward the outer edges. Since males often choose males and females choose females, it may be helpful to place boys on one half of the page and girls on the other (see Figure 5.1).

8. Draw different colored lines with arrows to represent first choices, second choices, and mutual choices (arrows go both ways—see Figure 5.1).

ACTIVITY 5.7: Obtain Autobiographical Information   If you are in a field experience, you may be able to gain some idea of how autobiographical information is obtained and used. Ask your mentor teacher if he or she obtains student information by way of autobiography. *If so,* find out what the teacher obtains and how. Also, ask how that information is most useful. *If not,* try to obtain permission to collect some. Then, decide what you most need to know and the subsequent topic or topics students should address. For example, assuming you want to know what their lives are like outside school, you might ask them to write about "My Afternoons and Evenings" or "My Weekends."

ACTIVITY 5.8: Use Parent-Supplied Information   If you are in a school assignment, ask your mentor teacher how he or she has used parent contacts to find out about students and their families. What has the teacher found out? Where is it recorded?

If such data are recorded in cumulative records, you may be able to read and reflect on them. What kinds of information have teachers obtained? What additional information could be useful?

ACTIVITY 5.9: Reading Cases   You may be able to obtain access to one or more cases. If you are involved in a field experience, ask your mentor teacher whether he or she has written any. Ask what caused the teacher to write the case and how he or she did it. Also, ask about the value of these cases. Perhaps you can share one of the cases with your peers in this course without revealing the student's identity.

ACTIVITY 5.10: Motivation in the Classroom   Perhaps you have an opportunity to observe a K–12 classroom teacher. If so, ask the teacher how he/she motivates students to learn, or observe and make a list of ways that the teacher uses motivation. Be prepared to share what you find out with your peers in this class.

ACTIVITY 5.11: Plan to Motivate   Select a topic that you might well teach. Describe specifically what you would do in order to motivate learners including those who lack confidence, have low expectations for themselves, and who are apathetic or reluctant to learn.

ACTIVITY 5.12: Motivational Techniques   Make a list of motivational techniques your teachers have used or create some of your own.

REFERENCES

Airasian, P. W. (2001). *Classroom assessment.* New York: McGraw-Hill.

Anastasi, A. (1997). *Psychological testing.* Sixth Edition. New York: Macmillan.

Berliner, D. C. (1986). In pursuit of expert pedagogy. *Educational Researcher, 15*(7), 5–13.

Borko, H., & Livingston, C. (1989). Cognition and improvisation: Differences in mathematics instruction by expert and novice teachers. In T. Russell & H. Munby (Eds.), *Teacher and teaching: From classroom to reflection* (pp. 49–70). London: Falmer Press.

Brophy, J. (1998). *Motivating students to learn.* New York: McGraw-Hill.

Brualdi, A. (1998). *Teacher comments on report cards.* (ERIC Reproduction Services ED 423 309). Washington, DC: ERIC Clearinghouse on Assessment and Evaluation.

Carter, K., Sabers, D., Cushing, K., Pinnegar, S., & Berliner, D. (1987). Processing and using information about students: A study of expert, novice and postulant teachers. *Teaching and Teacher Education, 3,* 147–157.

Cruickshank, D. R. (1969). *Inner-city simulation laboratory.* Chicago: Science Research Associates.

Doyle, W. (1986). Classroom organization and management. In M. C. Wittrock (Ed.), *Handbook of research on teaching* (pp. 392–431). New York: Macmillan.

Dusek, J. B., & Joseph, G. (1983). The bases of teacher expectations: A meta-analysis. *Journal of Educational Psychology, 75*(3), 327–346.

Emmer, E. (1987). Classroom management and discipline. In V. R. Koehler (Ed.), *Educators handbook: A research perspective.* New York: Longman.

Fraser, B. J., & Fisher, D. L. (1986). Using short forms of classroom climate instruments to assess and improve classroom psychosocial environment. *Journal of Research on Science Teaching, 23*(5), 387–413.

Good, T., & Brophy, J. (1994). *Contemporary educational psychology.* New York: Longman.

Hidi, S., & Harackiewicz, J. (2000, Summer). Motivating the academically unmotivated. *Review of Educational Research, 70*(2), 151–179.

Johnson, O. (1976). *Tests and measurements in child development: Handbook II. Volumes 1 and 2.* San Francisco: Jossey-Bass.

Kadyrbaeva, D. R., & Engels, I. L. (1990, December). Psychological-pedagogical characterizations of the school child. *Soviet Education, 32*(12), 32–44.

Kidder, T. (1989). *Among school children.* Boston: Houghton Mifflin.

Lewis, J. L. (1986). Failing students: Can we identify them in advance? Paper presented at the annual meeting of the American Educational Research Association in San Francisco (ERIC Document Reproduction Services ED 278 145).

Shulman, L. (1987). Knowledge and teaching: Foundations of a new reform. *Harvard Educational Review, 19*(2), 4–14.

TenBrink, T. D. (1974). *Evaluation: A practical guide to teachers.* New York: McGraw-Hill.

Touliatos, J., & Compton, N. H. (1983). *Approaches to child study.* Minneapolis: Burgess.

Wagner, T. (2001, December 5). The case for "New Village Schools": *Education Week, 21*(14), 42, 56.

Wasley, P. (1999, May). Teaching worth celebrating. *Educational Leadership, 56*(8), 8–13.

Zheng, J. (1992). An exploration of the pedagogical content knowledge of beginning and experienced ESL teachers. Master's thesis, Queens College of the City of New York (ERIC Document Reproduction Services ED 343 903).

FAMILY DATA

Father's Name __Maxwell__   Mother's Name __Helen__

Birthplace __Elton__   __Bloomington, IN__
Occupation __laboratory technician__   __retail sales__
Employer __Harley-Ryan__   __Talbot's__

OTHER CHILDREN

Name	Present age
1. Cheryl	8
2.	
3.	
4.	
5.	
6.	
7.	
8.	

SPECIAL HOME CONDITIONS

Grandmother (maternal) living in the home

PERSONAL DATA

Student's Name __BROGAN, Jack Robert__

Present Address __280 Falcrest Rd.__

Telephone __354-7520__

Present Age __9__ years __11__ mos.

Proof of Age __Birth certificate__

Place of Birth __Monroe__

Most Recent Picture

Special Activities, Interests, and Hobbies
__Enjoys mythology__

Special Health Conditions

TRANSFER RECORD

Transferred to M.S.D. from _____
Grade left M.S.D. __Lakeside for grade 2__
Transferred to _____
Reason _____
Reentered from __Lakeside__ in grade __4__

The name and data in this student record folder do not apply to the student's picture except for purposes of the teacher-training program.

All data pertaining to this student study are based on actual files; however, the names and dates, and locations have been changed and the person pictured is a child actor/model.

MADISON SCHOOL DISTRICT

Longacre _____ School

Student's Name _____ BROGAN, Jack Robert

ACHIEVEMENT

Primary
- V — Very good progress
- G — Good progress
- N — Needs to improve

Grades 2-8
- A — Excellent
- B — Above average
- C — Average
- D — Below average
- E — Failing

SUBJECT AREAS	1	2	3	4	5	6	7	8
English	G	B	C	C				
Social Studies		B	C	C				
Science		C	C	B				
Mathematics	G	B	C	C				
Reading	G	C	C	C				
Spelling		B	C	B				
Writing	V	B	C	C				
Teacher's initials	MC	HM	JH	FM				

PROMOTION
- F — Fast
- S — Slow
- A — Average
- U — Unearned

	1	2	3	4	5	6	7	8
	A	A	S	A				

ATTENDANCE RECORD

	Kdg.	1st	2nd	3rd	4th	5th	6th	7th	8th
Total days present	170	180	182	179	183				
Possible no. of days attendance	185	185	185	183	183				

TESTING PROGRAM

Ability Tests

Grade	Test Given	Age	IQ	Test Given	Age	IQ
1	Mental Ability	6	104			
3	Mental Ability	7	103			
4	Musical Aptitude (raw score 260/137 6 %ile)					

Reading Tests

Grade	Test Given	Score	Grade	Test Given	Score	Grade
1	Readiness Test	B (high normal)				
2	Primary Reading	40 %ile				

Other Achievement Tests

Grade	Test Given	Score	Grade	Test Given	Score	Grade
3	Upper Primary	2.8				
4	Middle Grades	4.2				

112

TEACHER COMMENTS

Needs to control his loud voice. Still immature. Attention span improving; good progress in reading and writing!

Maria Carrillo—grade 1

Sometimes fails to finish work because he fools and daydreams. Minds others' business more than his own. Too talkative. Forgets to wait his turn to speak.

Holly Maybee—grade 2

Jack shows little improvement in finishing his work. He still bothers other people. He does respond well when I ask him to take on a special responsibility or give him some extra attention. I would like to see him take more responsibility for his work and behavior.

Janice Hsieh—grade 3

Jack has shown slight improvement in completing assignments. He still needs an extra push most of the time. Is occasionally sullen with other students, but shows improvement in solving problems with his classmates.

Frances Markle—grade 4

PARENT-TEACHER CONFERENCE SUMMARIES

Grade

Grade

K Short attention span. Work is quite immature. Father is very strict. Sharon Wertz

1 Parents are disturbed because Jack is not finishing all his work and is a behavior problem because of constant talking. They want unfinished work sent home to do. They say they will follow through at home. Maria Carrillo

2 Parents very cooperative. Jack needs to be given responsibilities for jobs he can do for himself and needs discipline to follow up. Holly Maybee

3 I had a parent conference with Mr. and Mrs. Brogan. They were told Jack was not finishing enough work to keep up with his classmates or to be as successful as he should be in fourth grade. The difficulty seems to be immaturity, short attention span, and his tendency to daydream. He is too talkative and does not seem mature enough to follow directions and accept third-grade responsibility. I worked on giving Jack some responsibilities at school, and he picked up and improved the last month of school. His parents are encouraged. Janice Hsieh

4 Jack is still immature. Work not always completed without an extra "push." An assignment book is to be used so parents can check work not completed at night, and I will check it each morning. Both parents are very willing to help. Frances Markle

114

STUDENT'S NAME   Brogan, Jack

GRADE   3

SCHOOL   Lakeside

CLASSROOM TEACHER   _____

DISORDER   Interdental lisp - tongue thrust. Distorted sh sounds. No conference.

WORK DONE IN SPEECH CLASS   Jack was in a group of five third grade children who worked for correction of the s sound. The s in isolated words is now quite good. Jack can make the (below)

DISPOSITION OF CASE   Continue if fall reevaluation shows the need. There may be continued improvement over the summer.

Speech Therapist

correction nicely. In conversation he is using quite good carryover. However, some s sounds are now a distortion in place of a lisp.

Jack has five s words which he thinks he will use frequently this summer. He is to try to say them right always.

Student's Name ___ GLOVACK, Kathleen ___

PERSONAL DATA

Present Address ___ 142 Sellers Rd. ___

Telephone ___ 359-9874 ___

Present Age ___ 10 ___ years ___ 1 ___ mos.

Proof of Age ___ Birth certificate ___

Place of Birth ___ Elton ___

Most Recent Picture

Special Activities, Interests, and Hobbies _____

Special Health Conditions _____

TRANSFER RECORD

Transferred to M.S.D. from ___ Elton in grade 1 ___
Grade left M.S.D. _____
Transferred to _____
Reason _____
Reentered from _____ in grade _____

The name and data in this **student record** folder do not apply to the student's picture except for purposes of the teacher-training program.

FAMILY DATA

	Father's Name ___ Donald ___	Mother's Name ___ Virginia ___
Birthplace	Elton	Columbus, OH
Occupation	machinist	parapro
Employer	Elton Goods	M.S.D.

OTHER CHILDREN

	Name	Present age
1.	Roberta	14
2.	Todd	9
3.	Teresa	4
4.	Nicky	1
5.		
6.		
7.		
8.		

SPECIAL HOME CONDITIONS

_____

All data pertaining to this student study are based on actual files; however, the names and dates, and locations have been changed and the person pictured is a child actor/model.

MADISON SCHOOL DISTRICT

Student's Name _____ GLOVACK, Kathleen

Longacre _____ School

ATTENDANCE RECORD

	Kdg.	1st	2nd	3rd	4th	5th	6th	7th	8th
Total days present		168	175	176	172				
Possible no. of days attendance		185	185	183	183				

ACHIEVEMENT

Primary
V—Very good progress
G—Good progress
N—Needs to improve

Grades 2 - 8
A—Excellent
B—Above average
C—Average
D—Below average
E—Failing

SUBJECT AREAS	1	2	3	4	5	6	7	8
English	G	B	B	B				
Social Studies	G	C	B	B				
Science	G	C	B	B				
Mathematics	G	B	B	A				
Reading	G	C	A	B				
Spelling	G	C	B	A				
Writing	V	A	A	B				
Teacher's initials	RP	MG	DA	FM				
PROMOTION	A	A	A	A				

PROMOTION
F—Fast
S—Slow
A—Average
U—Unearned

TESTING PROGRAM

Ability Tests

Grade	Test Given	Age	IQ
1	Mental Ability	6/3	97
3	Mental Ability	8/2	99
4	Musical Aptitude (raw score 260/137 6 %ile)		

Reading Tests

Grade	Test Given	Score
1	Reading Readiness	B (high normal)
2	American Reading	2.4
2	American Reading	4.3

Other Achievement Tests

Grade	Test Given	Score
3	Middle Grades	5.5
4	Middle Grades	5.4

Kathy is a good average worker. Sometimes she is too

thorough and has trouble finishing the work. She is

quiet, but pleasant.

Ruth Parks--grade 1

Very quiet, dependable. Good worker. Always smiling!

Margarita Gascona--grade 2

Kathy is a quiet, but very good student. She is very

polite and pleasant.

Donna Amity--grade 3

Kathy is an excellent student. Very dependable; lovely

child. Beginning to overcome her shyness.

Frances Markle--grade 4

PARENT-TEACHER CONFERENCE SUMMARIES

Grade

1 With Mrs. Glovack. Progress report. Kathy doing strong
   average work. Ruth Parks

2 Conference with Mrs. Glovack. Kathy is doing well. Should
   speak up so she can be heard; rather shy. Mother is
   pleased with good work habits. Margarita Gascona

3 No conference—new baby in home—but discussed Kathy's
   good progress with mother at PTA. Donna Amity

4 Conference with mother. Kathy does very well in school.
   For a while, Kathy didn't want to come to school each
   morning. In speaking with her, we found she didn't like
   our student teacher. After our talk, she was fine. She
   has had some problems lately with her best friend, Janis
   Murdock, who has buddied up with Cynthia Jordan.
   Frances Markle

URBAN PUBLIC SCHOOL CUMULATIVE RECORD

(Elementary and Middle School Form)

Name <u>Gamble</u>   <u>Benny</u>
      (Last)   (First)   (Middle)

I.D.# <u>1092056</u>

Present age <u>11</u> yrs. <u>1</u> mos.

Place of Birth <u>Urban</u>

Pupil lives with   ☐ Both parents   ☒ Mother   ☐ Father

☒ Other (explain) <u>grandmother</u>

Father's name <u>Morris</u>   Employer <u>Post Office Department</u>

Mother's name <u>Lydia</u>   Employer _____

Address	Phone	Address	Phone
3526 Seneca Parkway	343-6580	5106 Hertel	266-4843
998 35th Street			
3526 Seneca Parkway	343-6580		
5245 College	266-4843		

Siblings   (List names of brothers and sisters in order of birth. Indicate sex by G for sister, B for brother. Express age differences as plus (+) or minus (−). Examples: +5 means five years older, −5 means five years younger.)

Sibling's Name	Sex	Age	Sibling's Name	Sex	Age	Sibling's Name	Sex	Age
None								

In case of emergency notify:

Name _____   Phone _____

Address _____   Relationship _____

All data pertaining to this student study are based on actual files; however, the names and dates, and locations have been changed and the person pictured is a child actor/model.

ELEMENTARY AND MIDDLE SCHOOL PROGRESS RECORD

Reporting Code

ACHIEVEMENT: The letter represents the degree to which the child has met the grade standards.

E = excellent
G = good
F = fair
U = unsatisfactory
GL = grade level
BL = below grade level

EFFORT: The numeral indicates the effort the child is making.

1 = doing his best
2 = could work harder
3 = making little effort

Progress Record, Grades K-2

Semester Beginning	Grade	Weeks in Grade	Days Present	Promoted to Grade	Reading	Oral Language	Composition	Spelling	Handwriting	Social Studies	Arithmetic	Science	Art	Music	Physical Education	Conduct	School	Room No.
FALL	Kg	20	85	Kg												F	COLERIDGE	108
SPRING	Kg	20	83	1			FAIR PROGRESS									F	CLLERIDGE	107
Fall	1	20	65	1A	E	F			E	G	G	E	F			G	Coleridge	205
Spring	1A	20	80	2	E	E			G	G	E	G	E	F		G	Coleridge	205
Fall	2	20	80	2	G	G	G	G	G	G	G	G	G	G	G	G	Coleridge	120
Spring	2	12	53	2	G	G	G	E	G	G	G	G	G	G	G	G	Coleridge	120
SPRING	2	8	34	3	E	G	G	E	G	G	E	E	G	G		E	COLERIDGE	209

Progress Record, Grades 3-6

Semester Beginning	Grade	Weeks in Grade	Days Absent	Promoted to Grade	Reading	Reading Level	Math	Math Level	Listening	Speaking	Writing	Spelling	Science	Social Studies	Art	Music	Physical Educ.	Conduct	School	Room No.
FALL	3	20	9	3	G	G	G	G	G	G	G	E	G	G	G	G	/	G	ALEXANDER	205
SPRING	3	12	7	3	G	G	G	H	G	G	G	E	G	G	G	G		G	"	"
Spr.	3	7	14	E	G	F	G	G	F	F	E	F	F	F	F	F		F	EDISON	204
Fall	4	20	7	4	E		F	GL	G	G	G	E	G	G	G	G		F	Edison	106
Spring	4	20	4	5	E		F	GL	F	F	G	E	G	G	GF			F	Edison	106
	5				attending school in the south (USA)													— — —		
	5	21	12	6	E	GL	F₂	GL	E₂	E₂	E₂	E₂	G₂	G₂	E₂	E₂	F₂	F	Edison	209

121

ELEMENTARY AND MIDDLE SCHOOL STANDARDIZED TEST DATA

General Ability Tests

Gr.	Name of Test	Form	C.A.	M.A.	I.Q.
1	KA		6.3	7.3	116
2	KA		7.1	7.8	110
3	KA		8.1	7.9	97

Achievement Test

Gr.	Name of Test	Subtest	Score
1	Metropolitan Readiness		82% ILE
3	Metropolitan Achieve.	Reading	5.3
		Spelling	5.1
		English	4.1
		Arithmetic	3.6

Bureau of Child Study Individual Exam Data

Gr.	

Personal Comments

Gr.	Remarks
2	Often complains of illnesses.
5	Claims pains in his back.

Special Activities, Abilities, Honors

Gr.	Remarks
5	Loves to read. Hall Guard Award.

Other Pertinent Information

Gr.	Examination	Evaluation	Gr.	Examination	Evaluation
1	Vision	Should wear glasses and be given front seat placement.			
1	Hearing	Pass			
4	Hearing	Pass			
5	Hearing	Pass			

Notes:

_____

_____

_____

_____

_____

_____

_____

_____

_____

_____

_____

_____

_____

_____

URBAN PUBLIC SCHOOL CUMULATIVE RECORD
(Elementary and Middle School Form)

Name _Rivera_____ _Julio_____ _Jesus_____   I.D.# _2783168_____
      (Last)   (First)   (Middle)

Present age ___11___ yrs. ___9___ mos.

Place of Birth _Puerto Rico_____

Pupil lives with [X] Both parents   [ ] Mother   [ ] Father

[ ] Other (explain) _____

Father's name _José_____   Employer _Lakeside Metals_____

Mother's name _Juanita_____   Employer _Barkley Fish Co._____

Address	Phone	Address	Phone
1241 Yale	273-7408		
12 Sword			
5142 Aldine	641-1059		

Siblings   (List names of brothers and sisters in order of birth. Indicate sex by G for sister, B for brother. Express age differences as plus (+) or minus (−). Examples: +5 means five years older, −5 means five years younger.)

Sibling's Name	Sex	Age	Sibling's Name	Sex	Age	Sibling's Name	Sex	Age
Maria	G	-2						
Luchina	G	-5						
Felice	G	-8						

In case of emergency notify:

Name _____   Phone _____

Address _____   Relationship _____

All data pertaining to this student study are based on actual files; however, the names and dates, and locations have been changed and the person pictured is a child actor/model.

ELEMENTARY AND MIDDLE SCHOOL PROGRESS RECORD

Reporting Code

ACHIEVEMENT: The letter represents the degree to which the child has met the grade standards.

EFFORT: The numeral indicates the effort the child is making.

E = excellent U = unsatisfactory
G = good GL = grade level
F = fair BL = below grade level

1 = doing his best
2 = could work harder
3 = making little effort

Progress Record, Grades K-2

Semester Beginning	Grade	Weeks in Grade	Days Present	Promoted to Grade	Reading	Oral Language	Composition	Spelling	Handwriting	Social Studies	Arithmetic	Science	Art	Music	Physical Education	Conduct	School	Room No.
FALL	K	20	92	K		— GOOD —										F	McNULTY	104
SPRING	K	20	94	Prim 1		— GOOD —										G	McNULTY	104
Fall	Pri 1	5	23	1B		-- Good --										G	McNULTY	106
Fall	1B	20	91	1	G	G				E	G	G		G	F	E	University	4
Spring	1	20	90	2	G	G				G	G	G		G	F	F	University	4
Fall	2	20	88	2	F3	F3			U3	F2	G2	G2	F1	F1	F2	F	University	10
Spring	2	20	95	3	G2	G			G	G	E	E1	E	E	GG	F	University	10

Progress Record, Grades 3-6

Semester Beginning	Grade	Weeks in Grade	Days Absent	Promoted to Grade	Reading	Reading Level	Math	Math Level	Listening	Speaking	Writing	Spelling	Science	Social Studies	Art	Music	Physical Educ.	Conduct	School	Room No.
Fall	3	20	2	3	G1	G	G1	G	G1	G	G2	G	G	G1	E	G	G1	G2	F	University	16
Sp.	3	20	1		G	E1	G	G2	G	G2	G2	G1	G	G1	G	G	G	G1	F	University	16
Fall	4	20	0	1	F2	BL	F3	GL	F2	F2	F2	F3	F3	U	G2	G2		F	Edison	202
Spring	4	20	2	5	G2	GL	F3	GL	F2	F2	F2	G1	F3	F3	E2	E2	G	F	Edison	202
	5	40	4	6	F1	BL	F3	BL	F2	G2	F2	G2	E1	F2	E2	E2	G1	F	Edison	209

ELEMENTARY AND MIDDLE SCHOOL STANDARDIZED TEST DATA

Name **Rivera, Julio Jesus**

All data pertaining to this student study are based on actual files; however, the names, dates, and locations have been changed and the person pictured is a child actor/model.

24

ID# _2783168_

General Ability Tests

Gr.	Name of Test	Form	C.A.	M.A.	I.Q.
1	KA		5-11	60	104
3	KA		9.4	8.6	91

Achievement Test

Gr.	Name of Test	Subtest	Score
1	Metropolitan Readiness		60%ile
3	METROPOLITAN ACHIEVEMENT	WORD KNOWL	3.6
		WORD DISCRIM	3.2
		READING	2.6
		SPELLING	4.0
		LANG.	3.2
		COMPUT.	3.0
		PROBLEM SOLVING	2.7

Bureau of Child Study Individual Exam Data

Gr.	

Personal Comments

Gr.	Remarks
5	Interested in science and music. Will need to watch carefully or else he will run around the room or the building or sneak out. Motivation hinges on praise and close supervision. Wants to please

Special Activities, Abilities, Honors

Gr.	Remarks
5	Winner of 5th grade Science Award

Other Pertinent Information

Gr.	Examination	Evaluation	Gr.	Examination	Evaluation
2	Teeth	Oral hygiene fair. Dental care needed.			
2	Hearing	Pass			
4	Hearing	Pass			

Notes:

REFERRAL FOR PUPIL HEALTH SERVICES

Pupil's name Julio Rivera   Date   10/16

Address 5142 Aldine

School Edison

Room 209

Reason for Referral:

Julio has trouble seeing the chalkboard assignments in the classroom. He complains of headaches.

Report: Eye referral given to pupil to take home for vision test.

Teacher Nurse **Mary Martin**

Vision Record on Child not Wearing Glasses

Urban Public Schools

Child's name Julio Rivera   Date 10/16

Address 5142 Aldine   Age 11

Parent's name Juanita   Grade five

School Edison

To the Doctor:

Please fill in the following for the guidance of the classroom teacher.

1. Should the child wear glasses?   Yes X   No ___
   If so, when   constantly

2. Should the child wear an occluder? Yes ___   No X
   If so, over which eye_____ when _____ duration _____

3. Should the child have front seat placement?
                                         Yes ___   No X

4. Should the amount of close work done by the child be
   limited?   Yes ___   No X
   If so, to what extent? _____

5. Vision test
   Uncorrected visual acuity   R 20/60   L 20/40
   Best corrected visual acuity R 20/25   L 20/25

Doctor's Signature

R J Manville

URBAN PUBLIC SCHOOL CUMULATIVE RECORD
(Elementary and Middle School Form)

Name Walker   Debbie   I.D.# 2585866
      (Last)   (First)   (Middle)

Present age 14 yrs. 1 mos.

Place of Birth Urban

Pupil lives with ☐ Both parents ☐ Mother ☐ Father

☒ Other (explain) Mother and stepfather

Father's name Gilliam   Employer _____

Mother's name Janice   Employer public assistance

Address	Phone	Address	Phone
5924 Brass	278-8113	3708 Park	
1343 New York	215-7788	1260 52nd Street	542-2275
702 31st Street			
947 33rd Street			

Siblings (List names of brothers and sisters in order of birth. Indicate sex by G for sister, B for brother. Express age differences as plus (+) or minus (−). Examples: +5 means five years older, −5 means five years younger.)

Sibling's Name	Sex	Age	Sibling's Name	Sex	Age	Sibling's Name	Sex	Age
Dewey	B	+10	Scott	B	+5	Melanie	G	−1
Carlton	B	+8	Gary	B	+4	Bishop	B	−4
Donald	B	+7	Louise	G	+3	Keith	B	−5
Douglas	B	+6	Todd	B	+2	Richard	B	−6
						Lori	G	−12

In case of emergency notify:

Name _____   Phone _____

Address _____   Relationship _____

All data pertaining to this student study are based on actual files; however, the names and dates, and locations have been changed and the person pictured is a child actor/model.

ELEMENTARY AND MIDDLE SCHOOL PROGRESS RECORD

Reporting Code

ACHIEVEMENT: The letter represents the degree to which the child has met the grade standards.

EFFORT: The numeral indicates the effort the child is making.

E = excellent	U = unsatisfactory
G = good	GL = grade level
F = fair	BL = below grade level

1 = doing his best
2 = could work harder
3 = making little effort

Progress Record, Grades K–2

Semester Beginning	Grade	Weeks in Grade	Days Present	Promoted to Grade	Reading	Oral Language	Composition	Spelling	Handwriting	Social Studies	Arithmetic	Science	Art	Music	Physical Education	Conduct	School	Room No.
Fall	K	13	48	/			Satisfactory									E	Edison	120
Fall		6	27				Satisfactory									G	Seward	107
Spring		9	90				Satisfactory									G	Seward	107
FALL	1B	17	31		U	F			F		U					G	SEWARD	117
FALL	1B	3	9	retain	U	F			F		U					G	LASALLE	215
Spring	1B	12	56	/	G	G			G		G					G	LaSalle	105
SPRING	1B	8	38	1A	G	G			G		G					F	LaSalle	103
FALL	1A	15	58	2B	E	G			G		E					U	LASALLE	109
Fall	1A	5	33	2B	G	G			G		G					G	Martin	101
Spring	2B	20	91	CDP		Promoted to Primary Continuous Development Program										F	Martin	101
Fall	2A	20	96	3B	G	G	F	F	G		U					F	Martin	203

Progress Record, Grades 3–6

Semester Beginning	Grade	Weeks in Grade	Days Absent	Promoted to Grade	Reading	Reading Level	Math	Math Level	Listening	Speaking	Writing	Spelling	Science	Social Studies	Art	Music	Physical Educ.	Conduct	School	Room No.
SPRING	3B	20	97	3A	F	BL	F	BL	F	G	U	U	F	F	F	F	X	F	Markum	212
Fall	3A	8	32	retain	F	BL	U	BL	F	F	F	F	F	F	F			F	Markum	302
Fall	3a	12	54	3a	4	BL	U	BL	7	7	7	U	7	U	7	E	U	7	Corcoran	309
Spg	3A	10	45	retain	7	BL	U	BL	7	7	7	U	U	7	7	E		7	Corcoran	208
SPRING	3a	9	44	4	U	BL	U	BL	7	7	U	7	7	U	G	G		G	Hess	205
Fall	4	20	3	4A	F	BL	F	BL	G	G	G	G	G	G	G	G	G	6	Hess	310
Spring	4A	20	4	5B	F	BL	F	BL	G	G	G	G	G	G	G	G	G	G	Hess	310
	5B	16	10		F	BL	F	BL	F	F	F	G	F	F	G	G	G	F	Hess	318
	5	4	3		No grades given due to late entrance.														Baker	316
	5	20	5		U	BL	U	BL	U	U	U	U	U	U				E	Baker	316
	5	29	11	6	G$_2$	U	G$_2$	G$_2$	E$_2$	G$_2$	G$_2$	E$_2$	G$_2$	G$_2$	E$_2$	E$_2$	E$_2$	F	EDISON	209

131

ELEMENTARY AND MIDDLE SCHOOL STANDARDIZED TEST DATA

Name — Walker, Debbie

All data pertaining to this student study are based on actual files; however, the names, dates, and locations have been changed and the person pictured is a child actor/model.

31

ID# 2585866

General Ability Tests

Gr.	Name of Test	Form	C.A.	M.A.	I.Q.
1	KA		6.0	5.8	94
1	KA		6.5	6.7	103
3	KH		9.2	7.11	86

Achievement Test

Gr.	Name of Test	Subtest	Score
3	Stanford Pri. "M"	Rdg	2.9
3	Metro Achievement	Reading	2.6
		Spelling	2.4
		Comp.	3.1
		Prob Solv.	2.8
4	METROPOLITAN ACHIEVEMENT	WORD KNOWL.	3.8
		WORD DISCRIM.	4.1
		READ'G	3.6
		SPELLING	4.6
		COMPUTE	4.1
		PROB. SOLVING	4.3

Bureau of Child Study Individual Exam Data

Gr.	

Personal Comments

Gr.	Remarks
5	FAILING TO COMPLETE ASSIGNMENTS. SUSPENSION FOR TWO DAYS. STEPFATHER HAS LEFT HOME AND IS TRYING TO GET BABY DAUGHTER FROM THE MOTHER. CASE IS PENDING IN COURT.

Special Activities, Abilities, Honors

Gr.	Remarks

Other Pertinent Information

Date __Jan. 14__

Dear Parent:

Your child __Debbie Walker__ is doing failing work __X__
          (grade 3)   poor work ___

in the following subjects:

Reading __X__   Social Studies _____

Arithmetic __X__   Spelling _____

Science _____   Penmanship _____

I believe this condition is caused by:

Inattention in class __X__

Poor conduct __X__

Poor study habits __X__

Health reasons _____

Absenteeism _____

I am available each school morning at 8:30 o'clock. You may come to see me if you wish or you may write me a letter telling me your plan to help your child.

Please sign this letter and return it to me.

Mrs Janice Walker   _Geraldine Phillips_
Parent's Signature   Teacher's Signature

               Lois Enright
                Principal

September 23

Dear Parents:

   Hess School is one of the schools in District 21 which has been
selected to provide after-school instruction in reading for pupils who need
such help. We are recommending that your child, __Debbie Walker__
take part in this program.

   These classes are to be held from 3:30 p.m. to 4:30 p.m. on Mondays,
Tuesdays, Wednesdays, and Thursdays, from September 27 to June 23. Will
you please remind your child that there will be no patrol boys on duty at
4:30 p.m. and that he/she should be especially careful when returning home.

   We sincerely hope that you will take advantage of this opportunity
for your child. Please sign the lower section of this letter immediately.

Very truly yours,

Geo. Mancuso

George Mancuso
Principal

.. ..

Date _____

   I hereby give my permission for my child, ___Debbie Walker___
to be enrolled in the after-school classes at Hess School on Mondays,
Tuesdays, Wednesdays, and Thursdays, from 3:30 to 4:30 p.m. beginning
September 27, to June 23. I will remind my child that there will be no
patrol boys on duty at 4:30 p.m. and that he/she should be especially
careful when returning home.

Present Room __318__   Grade ___5___   _____
Signature of Parent

After-school Room

I do not want Debbie to go because I an going to the hospital every day now. Mrs Janice Walker

---

*Dear Teacher,
Debbie has my permission to go to reading class.
Thank you
Her Mother Mrs Janice Walker*

31

Gr.	Examination	Evaluation	Gr.	Examination	Evaluation
1	Hearing	Pass			
1	Teeth	Carious			
2	Hearing	Pass			
3	Hearing	Pass			
4	Hearing	Pass			

Notes:

Needs to work on personal grooming and hygiene

The Act of Teaching

PART TWO

Teaching should be a conscious, deliberate act resulting from thoughtful decision making about what to teach and how students learn best. The five chapters in Part Two are intended to help you become an accomplished teacher. Chapter 6, Planning Instruction, will make you aware of factors that influence what is taught. Mostly, however, it concentrates on showing you how to make good decisions about planning *what* and *how* you will teach. Chapter 7, Four Instructional Alternatives, and Chapter 8, Four More Instructional Alternatives, contain readily usable information about eight prominent teaching strategies, as well as brief references to many others. Chapter 9, Evaluating Students' Learning, will inform you of the importance of assessing student learning and show you how you can do so effectively. Finally, Chapter 10, Reflecting on Teaching, addresses the importance of being a reflective practitioner, that is, a lifelong student of teaching.

Planning Instruction

Contents

You will be at an advantage as a teacher if you are a good planner. Why? Because teachers must plan lots of things. Among others, they plan the *organization and arrangement of the classroom* (placement of materials, equipment, furniture, displays), *classroom routines and rules* (transitions from one to another activity, how learners may move about and under what circumstances, how attendance will be taken), *how student records will be maintained*, and *parent conferences*. Mostly, however, teachers must plan *learning experiences* for students.

This chapter looks at instructional planning in order to help you meet this challenge. At the conclusion of the chapter, we hope you will see the benefits of good instructional planning and have the knowledge and skill necessary to develop learning experiences that you and your learners will enjoy and benefit from. Specifically, we hope that you will value planning, know that teachers differ in their approach to planning, know what factors determine what you will teach, be able to prepare suitable instructional objectives, and be able to construct instructional plans of varying duration. Finally, we hope you will be conversant with planning issues and problems teachers face.

Some Benefits of Instructional Planning

Instructional planning is the process by which teachers decide what to teach, how to teach it, and how they will determine the extent to which students have learned and are satisfied. These decisions are heavily influenced by a number of things, including what you learned in Chapters 1 through 5.

Planning Benefits Teachers

Let's start with the bad news and the good news. The *bad news* is that planning can be arduous and time consuming. The *good news* is that planning usually pays off. This is evident in our daily lives. If we plan for things they are more likely to happen. So, when you awaken in the morning and have a plan for the day you are more likely at nightfall to say, "What a good day." Or, when you are taking a course and you have a plan for succeeding in it you are more likely to do so. So it is with instructional planning: It is hard work but it pays off. It more likely gets you and your students to where you want to be.

Additionally, when teachers take time to think seriously about what their students should know and be able to do and how such learning should take place, the result is likely to be greater creativity and the elimination of "dry as dust" teaching. Such thoughtfulness can free teachers from long-time habits and personal prejudices and

"Are we that desperate for substitute teachers?"

enable them to use their full imaginative powers. Once they have developed a good instructional plan, teachers can enjoy greater confidence, security, and enthusiasm for putting the plan into action. Once they have thoughtfully planned, or *thought teaching through,* teachers should feel better and more excited about the teaching that will ensue.

PLANNING BENEFITS STUDENTS

Thoughtful planning promotes learning because it causes us to take into account the diverse backgrounds, interests, and abilities of students, as described in Chapters 2 and 3. Thus a thoughtful plan is more likely to attract and maintain students' attention and to facilitate learning and satisfaction given the instructional goals and available resources. Planning therefore increases the likelihood that students will be *interested,* will *learn,* and will be *satisfied.* Further, a thoughtfully planned lesson is more likely to maximize the use of time and, thereby, to minimize confusion and disruptions. If something goes wrong with your teaching, it probably can be traced to your ability to plan inviting lessons.

Instructional Planning May Be Mandated

As a new teacher, you will find that you are not only encouraged but sometimes required to develop instructional plans. Albert Shanker, late head of the American Federation of Teachers, underscores the need for and benefits of instructional planning. He wrote in *The New York Times* (September 28, 1980) that "no one quarrels with the idea that teachers must plan lessons in advance." Moreover, he notes that probably only a few teachers are so expert that they can teach effectively without overt planning. Among other things, Shanker urges teachers to (1) plan the sequence of their lessons, (2) provide for pupil motivation, (3) formulate clear and unambiguous questions, (4) present examples that move from the simple to the complex, (5) review, (6) provide for individual pupil differences, and (7) formulate worthwhile assignments.

Many principals and instructional supervisors require teachers to create and record written instructional plans. Sometimes teachers are required to submit "plan books" spelling out probable lessons one or two weeks in advance. These evidences

How would you like it if your school district provided all the lesson plans you would need? Some school districts are beginning to do so. For example, Chicago teachers can receive detailed daily lesson plans in each subject they teach. The plans, developed by a team of about 100 top Chicago teachers, are offered for several reasons: to help teachers see what needs to be taught for K–12 students to cover the information they are supposed to learn each day at each grade level; to help new teachers acclimate faster; and to guarantee a level of quality instruction systemwide. Teachers' reactions to lesson plans written by others vary. Opponents call it a "cookie cutter curriculum." Proponents say the plans are a boon for new teachers and teachers experiencing difficulties and a good guide and reference (Johnston 1999).

Source: R. Johnston. (1999, October 13). In Chicago, every day brings a new lesson plan. *Education Week, 19*(7), 1, 10–11.

of advance planning help principals, supervisors, and presumably teachers themselves in several ways. Most importantly, they provide assurance that teachers have thought about what they will do and how they will do it. Additionally, when observing beginning teachers, supervisors often follow the teacher's plan to see how well he or she carries it out. Finally, when teachers are absent, written plans are available for the substitute. This enables the substitute teacher to maintain instructional continuity.

Some school districts go so far as to provide lesson plans (see Highlight 6.1).

As you saw in Chapter 3, the federal government, as a consequence of the Individuals with Disabilities Education Act, requires detailed, written instructional plans for students with special needs. The resultant **Individual Education Plan** (IEP) is jointly prepared by the teacher, pupil, parent, someone who has recently evaluated the child (perhaps a psychologist), and usually the building principal or a special education teacher.

Since planning is so important to all students, it is essential that you learn to do it efficiently and effectively. Student teachers and beginning teachers, especially, are well advised to plan their teaching in considerable detail, leaving little to chance. Remember, plans are not mere window dressing or hoop jumping, they are a most vital part of the act of teaching.

Planning is so essential that many teacher educators, classroom teachers, school administrators, and state department of education officials have written about the need to plan. Here is an example:

The importance of planning—both long-range and daily—cannot be overemphasized. In each case, teacher candidates need to see how careful planning supports the learning process. Teacher candidates should observe how [their] clinical supervisors [cooperating or mentor teachers] choose effective teaching strategies to complement content and meet the needs of students.

6.4 What is your reaction to this advice about planning?

During any preservice teaching experience, the first several weeks of daily plans should result from the sharing of ideas by the teacher candidate and the clinical supervisor.

This procedure will set a pattern which can be altered as teacher candidates' plans improve and as they achieve greater independence in planning. Most beginners profit greatly from detailed lesson plans but they need help in making steady progress toward a type of planning they can carry on as beginning teachers. This may require planning for a self-contained classroom with eight or more preparations or with as many as six secondary classes and five preparations.

Each plan should be flexible to meet changes that inevitably occur during lessons. Teacher candidates should be encouraged to anticipate potential difficulties in the teaching strategy and be prepared to handle any difficulties which may occur. This rehearsal will reduce the need for a change in the lesson. (Baltimore Area Committee, 1991)

Different Approaches to Planning

Teachers approach instructional planning in different ways, just as people approach nearly everything, including taking vacations.

Picture it: You and a friend, Pat, decide to take a trip to the Eastern United States. As you discuss the trip, it becomes apparent the two of you are approaching this trip in very different ways. You have a carefully thought-out, detailed agenda with specific destinations in mind and a list of things you want to do once you arrive at each stop. You know how far you will need to drive each day, where you will stay each night, and approximately what your expenses will be. Although you will visit a few attractions along the way, you're careful not to let these brief excursions detract from the main purpose of the trip, to see the Eastern United States. You believe that if you pretty much follow the plan you've developed, you'll have a worry-free trip, you'll be able to visit most of the major attractions you want to see, and you'll stay within your budget.

Your friend Pat looks at you in sheer amazement! Pat's idea is to get in the car and go, stopping on the spur of the moment to see attractions along the way. Rather than be restricted by advance motel reservations, your friend wants to find a place to stay wherever you find yourselves at the end of each day. When you do get to the East Coast, your friend wants to "play it by ear," enjoying whatever you happen to do each day until your vacation time or money runs out. Pat prefers a less structured trip because "you never know what you'll find, and unplanned discovery is part of the adventure of a vacation."

You may chuckle at these different approaches to planning, but as a teacher, they will become familiar to you. That is because the different personal approaches to vacation planning parallel the different ways in which we teachers make instructional plans for our classrooms.

THE PROCESS APPROACH

There is no magic formula for approaching instructional planning. When we engage in planning, however, we locate ourselves somewhere along a continuum. One end of the continuum we'll call the "process approach." Remember your vacation mate who wanted to see the Eastern United States but who didn't want to do a lot of detailed planning? Pat said, "Let's go! The trip is worthwhile. We'll adjust along the way. Play it by ear."

Many teachers are like Pat. They see the value of certain learning experiences, but they plan these experiences only in a general way—a field trip to the historical society, a discussion of a major current problem or issue, a book to be read, an experiment to do. They believe such activities should be almost spontaneous, with little or no prearranged agenda. If not, the activity will be too teacher structured, too predictable, and thus downright boring to students. Beyond enjoying spontaneity, teachers who favor this process approach have a strong desire to be flexible and are confident and trusting that all will turn out well.

THE PRODUCT APPROACH

The other end of the continuum can be labeled the "product approach." For the sake of comparison, let's assume that's your approach. You want to go on an East Coast trip and you know precisely what you want to get out of the trip from beginning to end. You feel better and safer when you have a detailed plan. Similarly, as a teacher, you not only plan to generally engage your class in discussion of a topic such as "homelessness," but you also devise a set of questions to ensure depth and breadth of thought. Your questions include: What is homelessness? Who are the homeless? Why are some persons homeless? What are some consequences of homelessness?

"And then, of course, there's the possibility of being just the slightest bit too organized."

How do you feel toward homeless people? What are some ways the homeless might be treated? You are willing to sacrifice some flexibility and spontaneity for your feeling of security that your students will likely gain specific knowledge and insight. So, in contrast to the process-oriented teacher, your learning experience is structured to ensure that students will successfully reach what you see as important preconceived goals.

WHICH APPROACH TO USE?

Even though both the process and product approaches to planning have merit, as a novice instructor you should locate yourself on the product end of the continuum. As noted above, having thought through and constructed a detailed instructional plan you will be more at ease in the classroom since you will have given careful consideration to where you want your learners to go and how to get them there. Additionally, the greater attention you give to planning, the less likelihood things might go wrong.

On the other hand, there will be moments when teacher spontaneity is called for. We call these **teachable moments.** A teachable moment occurs when a classroom event happens that you or your learners want to immediately follow up on. For example, a significant national or world event has just occurred; a student brings to class materials from his grandparents who are vacationing in a country you are studying; a student is helping her father build shelves in the garage and wants to know how to calculate how many pieces of lumber are needed; or a child has just seen an historical movie and wants to know how accurate it is. At such times, rather than put these students off, temporarily postpone what was planned and assist, or have the class assist them in their inquiries. You think, "This is too important a potential learning experience to pass up." Teachable moments demand the process approach with all the spontaneity and ingenuity at your disposal.

6.5 Are you more attracted to the process or the product approach? Why might you have such a preference?

Therefore, as a novice we urge that you carefully plan as much as you can. Be particularly careful to plan instructional activities in areas where you feel less competent. At the same time be forewarned that there will be times when teachable moments happen and you must be quick on your feet.

As a seasoned teacher, depending upon your level of confidence, you can and probably will rely more on your experience and spontaneity. However, even then, you will need to carefully plan instructional activities that are either new or have been troublesome to you in the past.

Deciding What to Teach

One of the earliest decisions you must make is to determine the curriculum or *what is to be learned.*

FACTORS THAT INFLUENCE WHAT WE TEACH

Three things strongly influence curriculum content, or what is to be learned: society, the nature of learners, and the nature of the knowledge in a subject or discipline (see Figure 6.1).

Society At the societal level, all kinds of international and national events influence what is taught in schools. Some of the curriculum you have studied in school was shaped by scientific and political events. For example, in 1957, the world was stunned when the Soviets launched the first satellite, Sputnik. That event introduced the space age and the space race. It also prompted changes in American school curriculum. Because the Soviets beat the Americans into space, the American school curriculum was judged inferior, especially in science. As a result, since the late 1960s, tremendous efforts and federal monies have been devoted to teaching more science, making the science curriculum more rigorous and developing new ways of teaching that curriculum. For example, emphasis has moved away from

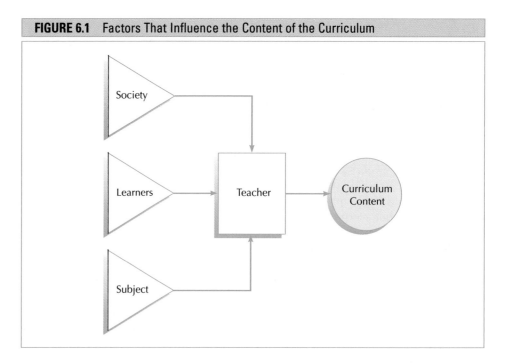

FIGURE 6.1 Factors That Influence the Content of the Curriculum

the memorization of scientific facts toward the use of laboratory experiences that encourage problem solving, the discovery of cause-and-effect relationships, and the application of scientific principles to practical purposes.

The rapidly developing technology associated with the space industry has also impacted the school curriculum. The availability of inexpensive, handheld calculators has brought about the demise of relatively inaccurate slide rules and led mathematics educators to reexamine the curriculum. Calculators offer a high degree of computational proficiency and can eliminate endless drudgery that many mathematics educators believe serves no practical purpose. Time formerly spent on computation can now be focused on other mathematical learning activities such as problem solving. Further, the widespread use of personal computers in classrooms and the instant accessibility of information via computers and satellites is changing America's curricular priorities.

More recently, dramatic political and economic changes in Eastern Europe, Asia, and Africa have required schools, teachers, and textbook publishers to alter the social science curriculum.

As a preservice teacher, you are experiencing some of this societal influence in your professional preparation. By the early 1980s, declining pupil test scores were blamed on, among other factors, poor teaching in elementary, middle, and secondary schools. The resulting national outcry for changes in the way teachers are educated has affected university education programs. Consequently, your teacher education program probably requires more general education prior to entering your professional course work; more study in the subject areas you plan to teach, such as mathematics, science, or English; more fieldwork in schools; and a thorough grounding in what is known about effective teachers and teaching (see Chapters 11 and 12). Relatedly, an increasing number of states require that teacher education students pass standardized proficiency tests to receive a teaching credential. These tests measure your general knowledge, knowledge of the subjects you will teach, and knowledge of how to teach, including planning.

While society expects schools and teachers to respond to timely events by altering the curriculum, it also expects them to preserve and pass along traditional information referred to as the "basics." Of course, not everyone in our society agrees on what knowledge, skills, or attitudes are basic and should be preserved in the curriculum. As a result, great arguments occur (Hirsch, 1989).

Nature of Learners   The second factor influencing what is taught is the nature of today's learners. Each generation of youth differs from the last. Part of this difference is attributable to changes in society. In Chapter 2, you learned that society is becoming more diverse and that today's children are emblematic of this diversity. Increasing numbers of students are minority children from low-income, single-parent homes where English is not spoken as a first language. In addition, today's youth are increasingly exposed to television violence and sexual intimacy, and they are exploited by advertising. The result is that children often are confused and victimized.

Another factor contributing to differences in youth today is earlier physical and social maturity. This phenomenon is traceable both to human evolution and to societal forces that encourage kids to grow up faster. Early maturity means that children are more likely to be independent, open and assertive, and better informed at an earlier age.

To be effective when planning and teaching, you must take into account your students' experiential and cultural backgrounds, developmental levels (intellectual, social, emotional, and physical), interests, and preferred ways of doing things. *Know thy students!* They need curriculum and learning experiences that are developmentally appropriate if you expect them to learn and to connect that learning to their personal lives and experiences (Willis, 1993).

6.6   What other recent international or national political, economic, social, or scientific events or discoveries are, or will likely be addressed in school curricula?

6.7   How could you modify the content you will teach for different kinds of learners described in Chapter 2 and 3?

6.8   Can you think of anyone (perhaps yourself) whose personality and experience needed to be more closely considered to help them learn?

Subject Field or Discipline The third factor influencing the curriculum is what knowledge experts consider essential in each field or discipline. For example, the American Association for the Advancement of Science (AAAS) has launched Project 2061. The report this learned society prepared represents the scientific community's effort to answer this question: What knowledge about science, mathematics, and technology should learners acquire by the time they graduate from high school? (See http://project2061.aaas.org/.) Similar reports outlining curriculum standards for specific disciplines have sprung up from the National Council of Teachers of Mathematics, the Music Educators National Conference, the National Council of Teachers of English, and several other professional organizations (see Table 6.1). These reports are very influential in shaping the school curriculum. Have you seen them?

TABLE 6.1 Source of Subject-Matter Curriculum Standards (http://www.mcrel.org/standards-benchmarks/)

Subject Field	Document
Arts	*National Standards for Arts Education* MENC Publications, 1806 Robert Fulton Drive, Reston, VA 22091
Civics	*National Standards for Civics and Government* Center for Civic Education, 5146 Douglas Fir Rd., Calabasas, CA 91302
Economics	*Voluntary National Content Standards in Economics* National Council on Economic Education, 1140 Avenue of the Americas, New York, NY 10036
English	*Standards for the Assessment of Reading and Writing* International Reading Association, 800 Barksdale Rd., P.O. Box 8139, Newark, DE 19714–8139
Foreign Languages	*Standards for Foreign Language Learning* National Standards for Foreign Language Education, Lawrence, KS
Geography	*Geography for Life* National Geographic, P.O. Box 1640, Washington, DC 20013–1640
Health	*National Health Education Standards* Association for Advancement of Health Education, Reston, VA
History	*U.S. History Standards* *World History; K–4 History* National Center for History in the Schools, 10880 Wilshire Blvd., Suite 761, Los Angeles, CA 90024–4108
Language Arts	*Incomplete Work of the Task Forces of the Standards Project for English Language Arts* University of Illinois
Mathematics	*Curriculum and Evaluation Standards for School Mathematics* *Professional Standards for Teaching Mathematics* NCTM, 1906 Association Drive, Reston, VA 22091–1593
Physical Education	*Content Standards and Assessment Guide for School Physical Education* NASPE, 1900 Association Drive, Reston, VA 22091
Science	*National Science Education Standards* National Research Council, e-mail scistand@nas.edu
Social Studies	*Expectations of Excellence: Curriculum Standards for Social Studies* Fulfillment House, Whitehurst & Clark, 100 Newfield Ave., Raritan Center, Edison, NJ 08837
Technology	*National Educational Technology Standards (NETS)* International Society for Technology in Education (ISTE) http://cnets.iste.org

The Formal and the Taught Curricula

THE FORMAL CURRICULUM

Eventually, all three factors affecting the curriculum trickle down into documents that teachers use when planning instruction. These documents mainly take the shape of state department publications, school district courses of study, and textbooks. State syllabi are often available for each field of study: reading, science and math, physical education, home economics, music, art, foreign language, health, and so forth. Larger school districts may have localized versions of these documents that are more responsive to the unique wants of individual communities. It is common for teachers of a particular subject and/or grade level to devote many hours of thoughtful committee work toward producing grade level courses of study.

Both state and local curriculum guides may focus on *philosophy* (what a field or subject of study is about and its importance), goals to be attained in that subject or field, the *scope and sequence* (what is to be taught and in what order), recommended *instructional activities,* recommended available print and nonprint *materials,* and ideas on how to examine learners and evaluate programs. These curriculum guides vary considerably in detail and specificity and, consequently, in length.

The most used (and sometimes overused) source for determining what students should learn is the textbook. This is so for several reasons. First, textbooks usually are readily available to teachers and learners alike. Second, textbooks are generally written by persons who have expertise both in the subject itself and in methods for teaching it. Third, teachers are often so overwhelmed by the demands of their jobs that they willingly accept the textbook's ready-made teaching materials and step-by-step instructions. Textbook packages are particularly attractive to beginning teachers who may receive little help on the job in learning how to create learning experiences using a variety of resources.

Some states engage in "statewide adoption" of texts. This means that a central committee selects one or more texts all school districts in the state must use. Other states allow local school districts or individual schools to make textbook adoption decisions. In these states, teachers are heavily involved in the process of textbook selection. Localized adoptions allow schools to compare the content of each textbook with both state and local curriculum guides and to take into consideration the nature of their learners and the demands of the community.

If you have access to a professional education library, it may have a curriculum library that contains copies of curriculum guides and textbooks in your area. It is a very good idea to begin to familiarize yourself with these materials.

 6.9 Do you have access to a curriculum library? What materials does it contain, and how could you use them?

THE TAUGHT CURRICULUM

Regardless of state and community efforts to standardize or guarantee a common curriculum, teachers can and do go off on their own. For example, in an alternative school in a large Northeastern city, the teacher and class in a course in American government might branch into a study of Native American government. Teachers have their own preferences and interests that affect what is or is not taught. Glatthorn (1987) and McNeil (1999) refer to what teachers actually teach as the "taught or operational curriculum." Said another way, the teacher, as shown in Figure 6.1, is the final curriculum filter.

In summary, we find that the curriculum, or what is to be learned, depends on societal needs, the subject to be learned, and the personal needs of learners. Although these three factors affect what appears in curriculum guides and textbooks, teachers unofficially decide what is ultimately taught based upon their own assessments of their students and their own teaching abilities and interests. You are the final filter.

 6.10 To what extent do you feel you should follow the formal curriculum? Why?

Writing Instructional Objectives

Once you have determined what is to be learned, you are ready to begin planning in earnest. However, as the Cheshire Cat explained to Alice, the plan you develop "depends a good deal on where you want to get to." Thus, the foundation of good planning is the preparation of good goals or objectives. An **instructional objective** or learning outcome is a statement of the concepts, attitudes, or skills that students are expected to accomplish by the end of some period of instruction. In other words, if you are to plan effectively, *you must first decide what your students need to know or be able to do as a result of the learning experience.* The question is, *why* are you going to teach or initiate the learning experience?

We cannot overemphasize the importance of writing and then sharing your instructional goals with your learners. You learned in Chapter 4 that telling students what they must know or what they should be able to do at the close of a learning activity increases learning. Research indicates that teachers who are able to identify the specific objectives of their lessons and take time to communicate them to their students are perceived as clearer, and teacher clarity relates both to student achievement and satisfaction (Cruickshank & Kennedy, 1986). Make certain your learners know precisely what is expected of them. As Confucius said, "Ignorance of purpose leads to mediocrity."

Writing good instructional objectives is really not difficult, but it does take understanding and practice. Three considerations are essential. First, you must decide the kinds of learning outcomes you want to express in the objective. Second, you must determine whether a general or specific objective is appropriate. Third, you must consider the information that needs to be included in the objective. Let's look at these three tasks more closely.

KINDS OF LEARNING OUTCOMES

As you begin to write your instructional objectives, your first consideration is to determine what kind of learning outcomes you seek. Do you want students to gain knowledge, skills, or attitudes?

Bloom (1956) developed a much-used formal classification system, or taxonomy, for learning outcomes. Bloom's *taxonomy of educational objectives* classifies learning outcomes into three types or domains: cognitive (knowledge), psychomotor (skill), and affective (attitude). A description of each follows.

Cognitive Domain   Educational objectives in the **cognitive domain** cause learners to engage in intellectual tasks. For example, learners given certain information might be called on to recall, understand, apply, break down, combine, or judge that information. Thus, a learner might be expected to recall the sum of the angles of a triangle, to analyze the events surrounding Columbus's voyage to America in 1492, or to identify and discuss the themes found in Jane Austen's novels.

Besides being classified according to type or domain (cognitive, affective, or psychomotor), instructional objectives are also classified *within* type according to the level or complexity of the learning outcome. Bloom's cognitive domain includes six levels, ranging from simple to complex, or, from lower- to higher-order types of thinking. Let's look at an example for each level:

1. *Knowledge.* Learners have knowledge of and the ability to *recall* or recognize information. Example: The learner can recite multiplication facts.
2. *Comprehension.* Learners *understand* and can explain knowledge in their own words. Example: The learner can explain why 6 sevens and 7 sixes are equivalent.
3. *Application.* Learners *apply* knowledge, that is they are able to use it in practical situations. Example: The learner can calculate the cost of purchasing six envelopes costing seven cents each.

4. *Analysis.* Learners are able to *break down* complex concepts or information into simpler, related parts. Example: The learner can break the numeric statement "6 × 7" into subparts or possible combinations (for example, 3 × 2 × 7).

5. *Synthesis.* Learners are able to *combine* elements to form a new, original entity. Example: The learner can hypothesize that if 6 sevens are 42, 7 sevens can be determined by adding another 7 to 42.

6. *Evaluation.* Learners are able to *make judgments.* Example: The learner can devise a strategy for evaluating the accuracy of solutions to multiplication problems with 7 as one integer.

Many educators believe that, unfortunately, teachers require mostly lower-order types of learning (knowledge and comprehension): When did Columbus reach America? Teachers much less frequently seem to prod students to develop higher-level, or higher-order, thinking (application, analysis, synthesis, and evaluation): Why did Europeans discover America in 1492? Although low-level knowledge is an essential foundation for higher levels of thinking, it is important that you develop objectives and prepare lessons that challenge students to reach all levels of cognitive ability (see Highlight 6.2 on page 150).

6.11 What do you think is the value of being able to develop a *cognitive* objective at each of Bloom's six levels?

6.12 Why do you think teachers tend to focus more on lower- rather than higher-order cognitive tasks?

Affective Domain   Bloom calls a second type or domain of learning outcomes affective. Bloom's **affective domain** deals with attitudinal, emotional, and valuing goals for learners. Although teachers most often associate their instructional outcomes with the cognitive domain, almost all teachers try to promote some change in student affect. For example, most teachers hope that their students come to enjoy and value the subject they teach, as well as learning in general.

Bloom organizes the affective domain into five levels, and again arranges them hierarchically. The five levels of the affective domain and examples of each follow:

1. *Receiving or attending.* Learners are willing *to attend to, concentrate on,* and *receive* information. Example: The learner listens attentively to Marjorie Kinnan Rawlings's story, *The Yearling.* (*The Yearling* is a novel about a young boy, Jody, who lives in the scrub and swamp of the hammock country of Florida. To survive, the family depends on a meager crop. Jody becomes attached to a tame fawn, Flag. However, to protect their crop from Flag, his parents are forced to kill the yearling.)

2. *Responding.* Learners *respond positively* to the information by *actively engaging* with it. Example: The learner participates in a discussion of *The Yearling.*

3. *Valuing.* Learners *express an attitude or belief* about the *value* of something. Example: After reading *The Yearling,* the learner may express the belief that life can be unfair and cruel and that life's worth is sometimes lessened by unkind circumstances.

4. *Organization.* Learners *compare* and *integrate* the attitude or value they have expressed with attitudes and beliefs they hold, thus internalizing the value. Example: The learner considers whether the attitudes or values they expressed after reading *The Yearling* are consistent with other values they or others hold.

5. *Characterization.* Learners *act out* their values. Example: The learner behaves in ways consistent with espoused values. If the learner believes that life is valuable but is often treated as a cheap commodity, he or she may join some group concerned with the preservation of life, such as the Society for the Prevention of Cruelty to Animals.

6.13 What do you think is the value of being able to develop an affective objective for each of Bloom's levels?

Psychomotor Domain   According to Bloom, objectives in the third, or psychomotor, domain relate to learning physical skills. Courses in child or adolescent psychology taught you that as children grow, they are able to accomplish successively more complex physical tasks. For example, early on, students learn how to hold a large

Teach to All Four Learner Abilities

All learners, to varying degrees, possess four intellectual abilities (Sternberg, 1997). They are the ability *to memorize* or remember information, *to analyze* it, to take information and *to create* something further from it, and *to apply* or put information to use. These four abilities equate to Bloom's knowledge, analysis, synthesis, and application. Sternberg believes that when we teach, unfortunately, we ask students to utilize only the first two—memory and analysis. For example, when teaching social studies, we may ask learners to "remember factors that have led to troubles in the Middle East" and we may

then ask them to "analyze how or why different countries chose sides in this conflict."

But what about creativity and application? Sternberg observes that we less often ask learners to use these abilities. In order to help learners reach full intellectual potential, there is a critical need to teach in ways that require them to use all four abilities. "By exposing students to instruction emphasizing each type of ability, we enable them to capitalize on their strengths while developing and improving new skills" (p. 23).

How might learners extend the use of knowledge about the post World War II Middle East into the realms of creativity and application? In the first instance, we might ask them to "consider how the troubles might be resolved." To engage learners in use of their ability to apply information, we might ask them "what lesson nations should learn from conflict."

Source: Robert J. Sternberg (March 1997). What does it mean to be smart? *Educational Leadership* (54)6, 20–24.

crayon, then to hold a thinner pencil. First, they learn to print, then how to write. Later, they learn to type and to use a word processor. Most subjects require some degree of psychomotor learning. In science, students learn how to organize and manipulate laboratory equipment. In music, they may learn how to use their voice or play an instrument.

Seven levels of the psychomotor domain have been identified (Simpson, 1972). Following are illustrations of possible objectives in this domain.

1. *Perception.* Learners *use sensory cues* (such as vision) to guide their later attempt to perform a skill. Example: The learner notices how to hold and move a brush to create a particular brushstroke.

2. *Set.* Learners are *ready to perform* a skill or an action. Example: The learner is mentally, physically, and emotionally prepared to perform the brushstroke.

3. *Guided response.* Learners *practice* the skill under the supervision of an expert. Example: The learner practices while the instructor coaches.

4. *Mechanism.* Learners *become more proficient* in the skill through practice. Example: The learner becomes more confident as the skill becomes second-nature or habitual.

5. *Complex or overt response.* Learners *perform* the skill with a high degree of proficiency. Example: The learner makes a great number of brushstrokes accurately and quickly.

6. *Adaptation.* Learners *modify* previously learned skills to perform related skills. Example: Building on previous skill, the learner creates different kinds of standard brushstrokes.

7. *Origination.* Learners create new, original performances based on previously learned skills. Example: The learner creates brushstrokes the teacher has not demonstrated or suggested.

6.14 What do you think is the value of being able to develop a *psychomotor* objective at each level Simpson suggests?

Try Activity 6.1

ANOTHER WAY OF CLASSIFYING LEARNING OUTCOMES

Gagné and Briggs (1992) provide another arrangement for thinking about and classifying learning outcomes, or objectives. Their system contains five groups of learning outcomes compared to Bloom's three:

1. *Verbal information.* This term is used to describe the vast amount of information obtained and stored in our memory. It is similar to the knowledge level in Bloom's cognitive domain. Example: Pupils learn factual information such as principles of physics or chemistry that they can retrieve as needed. Cognitive scientists refer to this as *declarative knowledge.*

2. *Intellectual skill.* This refers to learning how to do something mentally. It encompasses knowing how to do something rather than merely knowing about something. Example: Learners are able to create a balanced menu or devise a scale model based upon what they know about nutrition or about the object the model is based on. Cognitive scientists refer to this as *procedural knowledge.*

3. *Cognitive strategies.* This refers to learning ways of thinking and solving problems, including learning how to learn. Example: Learners learn to use an inductive approach to solve problems. Thus, knowledge of how to use induction would be a cognitive strategy. Problem solving usually combines the use of declarative and procedural knowledge.

4. *Motor skills.* Although Gagné and Briggs do not refer to the Bloom or Simpson designations of psychomotor skills, they seem to be the same type of learning outcome as Gagné and Briggs's motor skills.

5. *Attitudes.* Gagné and Briggs liken attitudes to Bloom's affective domain.

6.15 Which group of learning outcomes appeals more to you—Bloom's, or Gagné and Briggs's? Why? Could you make use of both?

GENERAL (BROAD) VERSUS SPECIFIC (NARROW) OBJECTIVES

For decades, educators have argued over exactly how precise objectives should be. Early in the twentieth century, teachers were required to write objectives with great detail and specificity. An example might be "Learners will know 6 sevens are 42." You can imagine the results—literally thousands of detailed objectives! By 1930, an overcorrection occurred and objectives were written so broadly that it became difficult for both teachers and test makers to choose between overly broad and overly narrow objectives. An example of an overly broad and unclear objective might be "Learners will be able to think independently."

Both general and specific objectives are valid and have their place. Since general objectives are more skeletal in nature, they make more sense when people are discussing the broad goals or aims of education or instruction. For example, general objectives are useful at the national and state levels, where the intention is to broadly define what schools should teach. Consider, for example, one of the six educational goals set by state governors and former President Bush in February 1990 for America to attain by the year 2000:

> By the year 2000, American students will leave grades 4, 8, and 12 having competency in English, math, science, history, and geography; they will learn to use their minds, will be prepared for responsible citizenship, further learning, and productive employment. (National Governors' Association, 1990)

Unfortunately, due to their skeletal nature, general objectives are written using terms that are open to interpretation. In the goal statement above, "having competency" and "being prepared" are examples of general objectives. How will the nation know whether American students are "competent"? Specifically what must they know and be able to do in each subject area? Moreover, how will we determine whether students can "use their minds" and are "prepared for responsible citizenship" and so on?

While such objectives indicate *what the learners will do,* they do not explicitly indicate *what pupils are to learn.* This is unfortunate since it focuses attention on the means of instruction (what the teacher or students will do), not on the ends (what learners will learn). Activities are not ends in themselves, but a means to an end. *The real purpose of instruction is to change pupils' behavior and enable them to do things they couldn't do before instruction occurred.* To help keep the real purpose of instruction in mind, teachers should write statements that describe the behaviors instructional activities are intended to help pupils learn (Airasian, 2001).

Again, general objectives are useful when making a skeletal outline of what students are to accomplish. Often teachers write them when engaged in long-range planning for the semester or year or when deciding what to accomplish during a month-long unit of instruction. Following are three examples of general objectives:

- Students will know what a verb is.
- Students will enjoy music.
- Students will be able to swim.

WRITING SPECIFIC OBJECTIVES

A third thing you must decide when you write instructional objectives is what information to include in them. Many educators believe that a good objective tells learners exactly what they are expected to know and be able to do. For example, *"Given a paragraph, the learner will identify every verb by circling it correctly."* This objective does just that: It tells the learners what they are expected to know (what is a verb) and what they are expected to do (find and circle each one correctly in a given paragraph).

A method has been developed to assist beginning teachers in writing such specific objectives. It goes like this:

Every objective should contain an A, B, C, and D where

- A stands for the audience the objective is written for. In the objective above, the audience, A, is *the learner.*
- B stands for the behavior expected of the learner. In the objective above, the behavior, B, is (the learner) *will identify every verb.* Table 6.2 contains a list of verbs that can be used to attain learning outcomes at various levels of each of Bloom's three instructional domains.
- C stands for the condition under which the learner identifies every verb. In the objective above, C, is *Given a paragraph.*
- D stands for the degree of proficiency or correctness that the learner must display. In the objective above the degree of proficiency, D, is *circling (each verb) correctly.*

Thus, if you want to be precise about your instructional objectives and want to write them as specifically as possible, you can follow this method. Here are examples, including the objective used above, of specific objectives coded with A, B, C, and D.

1. When given a paragraph, the learner will identify every verb by circling it correctly.
             C   A   B   D
2. Given ten sentences containing twenty misspelled words, the learner will
                          C   A
   underline at least sixteen of the misspellings.
      B   D
3. The learner will solve at least eight of ten binary addition problems.
      A   B   D   C
4. Given a 100-word speed test in class, the student will type at a rate of no
                  C   A   B
   less than thirty words per minute with fewer than four errors.
                          D
5. When presented flash cards of words containing the letter combination "ph,"
                          C
   the student will pronounce the words on at least eighteen of twenty cards correctly.
      A   B   D

TABLE 6.2	Verbs to Use When Writing Objectives at Various Levels of Bloom's Three Domains of Learning

1. **Cognitive domain**
   a. *Knowledge level*
      1. Objective: to know about
      2. Verbs to use: list, tell, define, identify, label, locate, recognize, describe, match, name, outline, reproduce, state
   b. *Comprehension level*
      1. Objective: to understand
      2. Verbs to use: explain, interpret, illustrate, describe, summarize, expand, convert, measure, defend, paraphrase, rewrite, apprehend, comprehend
   c. *Application level*
      1. Objective: to use knowledge and understanding
      2. Verbs to use: demonstrate, apply, use, solve, choose appropriate procedures, modify, operate, prepare, produce, construct
   d. *Analysis level*
      1. Objective: to break down
      2. Verbs to use: analyze, debate, differentiate, generalize, conclude, organize, break down, dissect, diagram, separate, subdivide, relate
   e. *Synthesis level*
      1. Objective: to combine, to create
      2. Verbs to use: create, combine, plan, design, produce, compile, develop, compose, devise, modify, organize, rearrange, reconstruct
   f. *Evaluation level*
      1. Objective: to judge
      2. Verbs to use: judge, evaluate, conclude, contrast, develop criteria, appraise, criticize, support, decide, compare

2. **Affective domain**
   a. *Receiving level*
      1. Objective: to be willing to attend to and to receive information
      2. Verbs to use: listen, be aware of, observe, be conscious of, recognize, realize, be tolerant
   b. *Responding level*
      1. Objective: to be willing to respond
      2. Verbs to use: respond, cooperate, appreciate, find pleasure in, comply, discuss
   c. *Valuing level*
      1. Objective: to develop attitudes and beliefs
      2. Verbs to use: value, opine, appraise, estimate, approve, appreciate, assess, believe, size up (See also "Evaluation level" under "Cognitive domain.")
   d. *Organizational level*
      1. Objective: to act out values
      2. Verbs to use: demonstrate, perform, act out, engage in, uphold

3. **Psychomotor domain**
   a. *Perception level*
      1. Objective: to notice, recognize, sense
      2. Verbs to use: notice, recognize, sense, perceive, detect
   b. *Set level*
      1. Objective: to be ready to try
      2. Verbs to use: be ready, be prepared, take steps, make preparation, desire
   c. *Guided response level*
      1. Objective: to try
      2. Verbs to use: try, perform, practice
   d. *Mechanism level*
      1. Objective: to improve
      2. Verbs to use: improve, become proficient, change, increase, decrease
   e. *Complex or overt response level*
      1. Objective: to be proficient
      2. Verbs to use: excel, master, perfect
   f. *Adaptation level*
      1. Objective: to adapt
      2. Verbs to use: adapt, adjust, accommodate, modify, modulate
   g. *Organization level*
      1. Objective: to create
      2. Verbs to use: create, originate, produce

Preparing specific instructional objectives, although time consuming, will cause you to be aware of and able to share with your learners *exactly* what you wish them to know and be able to do. Thus, there is little possibility that you and your learners are on "different pages." Additionally, such careful attention to detail will give you greater security, especially in your first teaching situations.

Try Activity 6.2

Counterpoint   Not all educators think teachers should use such specific instructional objectives. On the contrary, they believe their use may be counterproductive. Among potential negative consequences, they cite the following:

- Specific objectives, because they are so precise, are difficult to write. They are easiest to write when the learning outcome is at the lower levels of any of Bloom's three domains of learning. For example, it is easier to write a specific objective in the cognitive domain for "knowledge" than for "synthesis" or "evaluation." Look at the first objective above. You can see it is fairly simple to write an objective that calls for *identification* or *recall* of something. Try to write a specific objective that would call for learners to *analyze* the characteristics of verbs. That's not so easy. *The negative consequence of such objectives may be that students are challenged to learn mostly simple and factual information instead of engaging in higher-order thinking.*

6.16 As a novice, how specific do you believe your instructional objectives should be?

- Evidence exists that, in general, when teachers teach to set objectives learners are more likely to attain the specified knowledge, skills, or attitudes but fail to learn other, worthwhile related material. Marzano, Pickering, and Pollock (2001) note, "This phenomenon might occur because setting a goal focuses students' attention to such a degree that they ignore information not specifically related to the goal" (94). *The negative consequence of teaching to set, and especially specific objectives, is that learners may miss something of the bigger picture.*

- There are times when students should be given learning situations without predetermined, specific learning objectives. For example, taking a walk through the school neighborhood could be a very different experience for each learner. Why expect each one to concentrate on coming away with similar observations and impressions? Comparing uniquely individual observations and impressions after the walk might lead to knowledge and insights that could not possibly have been forecast. *The negative consequence of specific objectives here may be that spontaneity of learning can be lost.*

6.17 Can you think of ways to write specific learning outcomes yet still maintain a focus on higher-order thinking, spontaneity, and implementation of those outcomes?

- Experienced teachers seldom write specific instructional objectives. In fact, they seem to do much instructional planning by mentally making only brief notes of the procedures they will follow. *The negative consequence of specific objectives in this case may be that time devoted to writing specific objectives might not have much transfer to classroom teaching.*

WHEN ARE OBJECTIVES GOOD?

When developing any instructional plan, you prepare a sequence of related instructional objectives. However, it is essential that you also stop and reflect on those objectives to judge their appropriateness to the curriculum and your learners. You can judge instructional objectives by asking yourself the following questions:

- Are the objectives relevant to the curriculum for which students will be held accountable?

- Can this group of students achieve the objectives? Do the objectives correspond to the readiness and ability levels of students? Do the objectives take individual differences into account?

- Do the objectives promote learning outcomes across all learning domains (cognitive, affective, psychomotor)?

According to Biehler and Snowman (2000), the following conclusions can be drawn from the research on instructional objectives:

1. Objectives seem to work best when learners are aware of them, when learners treat the objectives as guides to learning specific sections of material, and when learners feel the objectives will aid learning.
2. Objectives seem to work best when they are clearly written and when the learning task is neither too difficult nor too easy.
3. Students of average ability seem to benefit more when they know what the objectives are than do those of higher or lower ability.
4. Objectives improve intentional learning but lead to a decline in unintentional or incidental learning of things that go unstressed. Incidental learning is more likely to occur when general rather than specific objectives are used.

Slavin (1999), who also reviewed research on instructional objectives, notes that communicating objectives to students has never been found to reduce student achievement and often has been found to increase it. He suggests that objectives communicated to students be general enough to encompass everything the lesson or course is supposed to teach in order to prevent students from focusing too narrowly, thus excluding much important information.

- Do the objectives promote a range of levels of understanding or performance (low or high) within each domain?
- Are the objectives written in terms of what learners are expected to know or do? Are they specific enough that students will be aware of exactly what they need to know and do?

Research findings related to instructional objectives are presented in Spotlight on Research 6.1.

Preparing Instructional Plans of Varying Duration

Once you have decided what to teach and have prepared good instructional objectives, you need to ask yourself, *How much* and *what kind* of instruction do students need to accomplish these objectives? This question could be asked in reverse order as well. For example, do you first decide how learning should take place and then allocate sufficient time as if the latter were variable? Or, conversely, do you decide how much time you have as if time were a constant and then decide how much or in what manner you can teach within that time span? Since the allocation of time to instruction or of instruction to time is often a burning issue, you may wish to discuss it in class. Perhaps you recall a course you were enrolled in, or a trip you took that ran out of time and was not completed. Let's turn our attention to the duration or scope of planning.

THE "LONG AND SHORT" OF PLANNING

As a teacher, you will regularly engage in long-, intermediate-, and short-range planning. Our vacation example can be used to illustrate this. You and your friend planned to take a vacation to the Eastern United States. This was your long-range plan. Then you determined the cities you would visit, the route you would take, and approximately how many days you would spend at various sites. This was the intermediate-range plan. Finally, for each day and site, you decided which specific things you wanted to do or see. Thus, you were also concerned with the daily and hourly routine. This was your short-term plan. Similarly, as a teacher, you will engage in long-range, intermediate-range, and short-term instructional planning for your students.

When teachers engage in long-range planning, they are deciding how generally to approach teaching either for an entire year or for a semester-long course. Teachers doing long-range planning first must choose a focus. The focus might be local

FIGURE 6.2 Plans of Different Duration

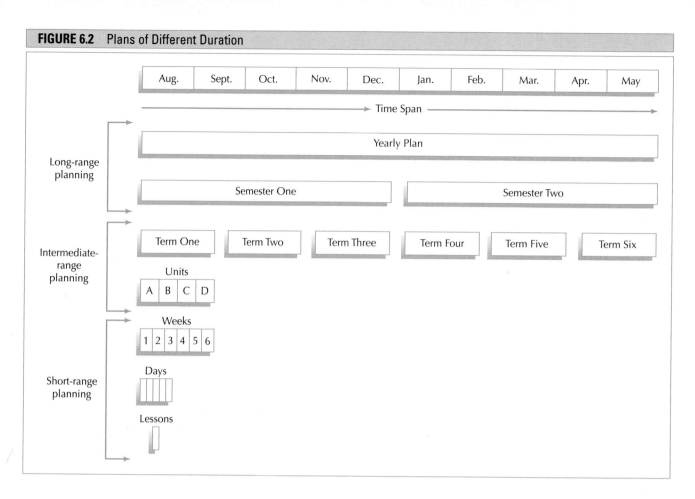

history, American or Canadian literature, or fourth-grade arithmetic. Second, the teacher needs to determine how many weeks, days, or hours are available for instruction. Interruptions such as holidays, vacations, or exam weeks are taken into account. Third, the teacher must select the content of instruction. For example, long-range planning for an American history course involves deciding which topics and information should be included in this course, given the time available.

Intermediate, middle-range, or unit planning involves decisions about how courses can be broken into chunks, parts, or units, each with a particular theme. In intermediate or unit planning, teachers arrange units or topics in a meaningful order, thus determining the sequence of the course. The history course could be broken into historical periods that students can examine chronologically. Arithmetic for fourth graders might be broken into a series of units on arithmetic processes that are sequenced from simple to complex. A university course outline or syllabus provides an example of long-range and intermediate-range planning.

Once intermediate planning is completed, teachers next plan for the short range; that is, for the week and for daily lessons. During short-range planning, you decide in detail what students must learn and how that can most effectively be accomplished. It is at this level of planning that specific instructional objectives are needed.

Figure 6.2 depicts plans of different duration (long-range, intermediate-range, and short-range), while Figure 6.3 shows the relationships among subjects, courses, units, and lessons.

PREPARING LONG-RANGE PLANS

As you have learned, teachers do long-range planning to determine what a year-long or semester-long course should include and how it may be taught. As mentioned,

6.18 How will you use long-, intermediate-, and short-range plans?

FIGURE 6.3   The Relationships among Subject, Course, Unit, and Lesson

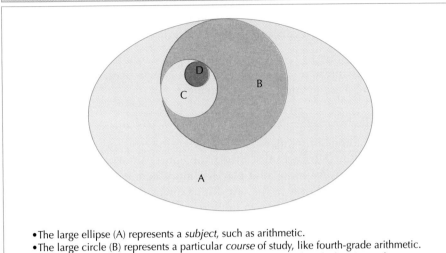

- The large ellipse (A) represents a *subject*, such as arithmetic.
- The large circle (B) represents a particular *course* of study, like fourth-grade arithmetic.
- The medium-sized circle (C) represents a segment or *unit* of study therein, such as multiplication of whole numbers.
- The smallest circle (D) represents an element or *lesson* within the unit on multiplication of whole numbers, such as multiplying by a one-digit number.

developing a long-range plan for teaching a course is similar to developing a vacation plan. Once you have a general vacation destination in mind, you start to collect ideas. Many will come from books and travel brochures. Other ideas may come from talking with people who have taken similar vacations. You use these ideas and materials as resources. You sit down with them and consider things such as

1. *Your objective.* Where specifically do you want to go and what do you want to accomplish? Is your aim to spend considerable time at a few sites, to see all the sites you can, or to experience the local culture?
2. *Your timeline.* How much time can you spend in each place you wish to visit? Where do you want to be by certain dates in order to get everything done?
3. *Needed resources.* What will you need to take along or secure along the way to ensure that the vacation is successful?

In other words, you take into account your goals, the order in which you think they can best be achieved, the time required, and the resources needed.

Similarly, when developing a course, you consider what it is your students are expected to know and to be able to do; what activities they might engage in and in what order; how much time is available (weeks, days, hours) to be divided among the various activities; and, finally, what resource materials are at hand. When engaged in long-range planning you should keep in mind that

- The course primarily should be derived from the established, formal curriculum; that is, it should fit into state and school district curriculum plans.
- The course should be developed to reflect what is known about the subject area. Thus, the content of the course should be up to date and reflect what experts in the field think is important.
- The course should be developed to take into account what you know about your learners. To some extent, then, each course you teach will be custom made. There is no one course that is good for all students because of the differences among learners noted in Chapter 3.
- Decisions regarding what to teach are value laden. Consequently, you must constantly guard against teaching only personal beliefs or biases about a

subject or issue. Likewise, guard against teaching what seems to be "politically correct," that is, presenting a position or information that presents only what special-interest groups regard as true or valid while ignoring or depreciating what others of different persuasions believe or know.

Try Activity 6.3

Glatthorn (1987) presents a model to follow when developing a course. At this point, you might try your hand at constructing a long-term plan. If you'd like to do so, turn to Activity 6.3 at the end of this chapter.

PREPARING UNIT PLANS

Once you have created a long-range plan for the course, the intermediate stage of planning begins. Ultimately you must divide the course into parts, or units; then you must plan the units. A unit or **unit plan** is a more detailed plan for teaching a major section or topic within a course. At the secondary level, units normally are taught over a period of weeks and are limited to one topic. For example, in an American history course, the content might be divided into topics based on chronological periods such as the colonial, federal, and early industrial eras. Several weeks would be allocated to learning about each period. Units developed for elementary grades are often shorter, only a few days or weeks long.

As a teacher, you will likely develop several types of units such as the following:

- *Resource units* are mostly prepared by and are available at minimal or no cost from state education departments, special interest groups, government agencies, and businesses. Consequently, they must be adapted to the particular classroom they are used in to ensure that the level of difficulty and the general appeal are appropriate. An example of a science resource unit is a package that might contain a set of lesson plans, slides, transparencies, student worksheets, and a teacher's guide on natural gas produced by the regional gas company. Of course, resource units are likely to favor the viewpoint of the governmental or commercial group that produced them. They may possess a subtle, "hidden" curriculum bias.

- *Teaching units* are prepared by a teacher or teachers for use with a particular group of learners. Ideas may come from resource units, but they primarily arise from the teachers and from learners who may help develop the unit. Although teaching units, like resource units, are prepared before teaching occurs, they are flexible and often modified in use.

- *Subject matter* units are a subtype of either a resource or teaching unit. They are developed and used for teaching academic subject matter that requires a sequential or linear approach. A course may consist of several subject matter units, each prerequisite to the next. Students must master the content of one unit before moving on to the next. Mathematics often involves subject matter units. A unit on square roots and radicals, for example, would be prerequisite to another unit.

- *Experience units* are more of a "happening" than a preplanned unit. No one defines in advance what students are to learn. Teachers and students merely decide what they will generally do from day to day and from lesson to lesson. The learning experiences evolve. An experience unit might revolve around the theme "Sound Surrounds Us." What the students are *experiencing* is of the greatest importance, so students keep journals of what they have learned as their adventure with sound unfolds. Experienced teachers and teachers who are process oriented probably are more comfortable and adept with experience units. Your friend and travel companion Pat may like to use these units.

- *Integrated units* are especially appropriate at the elementary level. Integrated units combine study from several fields such as social studies, language arts, science, and art around a central theme or topic. For example, an integrated unit on the Crusades might combine a historical and religious study of that period. Students might also read translated literature from that era, study life and customs during the Crusades, and depict them through art.

Parts of a Unit Plan   Although there are many types of units and unit plans, the typical unit plan includes the following parts or sections:

1. The *title* denotes the topic or theme under study, for example, "Sport in America or Canada." The topic usually is one the school district's curriculum or course of study requires. However, it may be one introduced for enrichment.

2. The *introduction* provides the rationale or reason why the unit is important to the course and in its own right. It should explain, in terms meaningful to students, why this unit is important, answering the ubiquitous student question: "Why do *we* have to know this?" The introduction also presents the parameters or scope (breadth) and sequence of the unit. By reading the introduction, one should be able to discern what main ideas or subtopics are addressed in roughly what order. The scope and sequence show how the main ideas build on each other and how the unit flows.

3. The *general objectives,* as noted earlier, broadly state the knowledge, skills, or attitudes students will acquire as a result of engaging in this unit. Before establishing the general objectives of a unit, you need to find out what your students know about the topic at hand so that the unit is neither too familiar nor unfamiliar, neither too easy nor difficult. Preassessment also enables you to remediate weaknesses or gaps in students' understanding of the topic and to increase the unit's appeal by building it around students' interests and perceived needs. You can preassess students in a number of ways, including informal observations, discussion, or questioning; formal pretesting of skills, knowledge, and attitudes; or examination of the curriculum previously studied by this group of students.

4. The *body* contains the unit's content, activities, and sequence of instruction. Included in the body are a topical outline, activities, resources, and a time frame.
   - The *topical outline* presents the main points and supporting points of the content. A detailed outline can become the wellspring for daily lessons.
   - The *activities* section denotes in general what the class or individuals can do in order to accomplish the unit objectives. What activities might they undertake to engage in learning the skills, knowledge, and attitudes the unit encompasses?
   - Also included in the body is the list of instructional *materials* and other *resources* that might be useful.
   - A *time frame* describes when the unit will begin and end and when students will undertake particular activities.

5. The *evaluation* section describes how learners will be evaluated in terms of achievement and satisfaction. To what extent do they know what they are expected to know? Can they do what they are expected to do?

6. A *bibliography* presents a list of resources useful to teachers in preparing and teaching this unit. A second list of references useful to students also should be prepared. If the unit will likely be revised and used again, it is a good idea to provide complete bibliographic references. In addition, it is helpful to make a note of where you obtained the resource (that is, your personal library, the school library, a friend's collection, or some other source) so that you can find it again.

Day One

Topic: Dinosaur Days

General Objectives

1. The student will define the term *dinosaur.*
2. The student will describe what the earth was like when dinosaurs lived.

Learning Activity

Discussion: What is a dinosaur? What do you know about them?

Independent study: Distribute resource materials on dinosaurs. Have students find out what life on earth was like when dinosaurs lived.

Evaluation

Independent activity: Make a drawing showing what the earth was like when dinosaurs lived.

Resources:

W. Lindsay. (1991). *The great dinosaur atlas.* London: Darling Kindersley.

T. Dewon. (1993). *Inside dinosaurs.* New York: Doubleday.

Crayons, paper for each student.

Day Two

Topic: Dinosaur Diets

General Objectives

1. The student will identify things dinosaurs probably ate.
2. The student will differentiate between meat-eating (carnivorous) and plant-eating (herbivorous) dinosaurs.
3. The student will cooperate and contribute while working on a small-group activity.

Learning Activity

Discussion: What do you suppose dinosaurs ate?

Cooperative groups: In groups of three, students classify characteristics of meat-eating versus plant-eating animals using animal pictures; then they decide if dinosaurs ate meat or plants by examining pictures of dinosaurs.

Evaluation

Sort dinosaur pictures into carnivorous and herbivorous dinosaurs and justify their grouping.

Resources:

H. Marsh. (1987). *Dinosaurs: Those terrible lizards.* Morristown, PA: Science Action Press (public library).

National Geographic. (1993, January). Twelve sets of animal pictures; twelve sets of dinosaur pictures (personal library at home).

Try Activity 6.4

Sometimes teachers break down the general information for a unit plan and present it in the form of **daily** or **block plans.** A block plan shows general objectives, learning activities, evaluation plans, and resources. Each block plan represents one class and serves as the outline or basis for one lesson plan. Highlight 6.3 shows a sequence of two block plans for a second-grade unit on dinosaurs.

Benefits of Unit Planning   Developing a unit or several unit plans, especially early in your teaching career, can be time consuming. However, it also tends to be an engaging and worthwhile exercise because of the flow of ideas and resources generated. Many benefits result from preparing and using units:

- Once completed, unit plans give clear direction for short-term planning—for a week, day, or lesson. An ounce of unit planning now may save a pound of work and classroom anxiety later.
- Good unit planning makes you more aware of your learners' unique qualities.
- Unit planning causes you to think imaginatively about how to get the job done using a variety of instructional materials and activities. It weans you away from mere textbook teaching.
- Unit planning asks you to consider how to help students study some topic or phenomenon in an *interdisciplinary,* or holistic, way. Through use of units, you can incorporate writing, reading, reporting, and so forth into learning activities.

TABLE 6.3   Selected Formats for Lesson Plans Listed by Author or Source

Eby (2000)	El-Tigi (2000)	Gagné & Briggs (1992)	Hunter (1985)	Jacobson et al. (1985) Moore (2000)
1. Title	1. Objectives	1. Objectives	1. Objectives	1. Determine content
2. Subject	2. Assess learner preparedness	2. Events, activities	2. Set induction	2. Objectives
3. Grade level	3. Resources needed	3. Resources needed	3. Input and modeling	3. Introduction
4. Description	4. Lesson description/ procedure	4. Notes and reminders	4. Checking for understanding and guided practice	4. Instructional method
5. Objectives	5. Closure		5. Independent practice	5. Lesson closure
6. Materials needed	6. Assessment/evaluation			6. Learner assessment
7. Procedures				
8. Evaluation				

TABLE 6.4   Parts of a Lesson Plan

1. Objectives—Indicates the lesson's objectives
2. Resources—Denotes resources and materials to be used
3. Set Induction—Describes how the lesson will be introduced
4. Methodology—Describes how teaching and learning will take place
5. Assessment—Makes clear how student learning will be determined
6. Closure—Provides for lesson ending

PREPARING LESSON PLANS

A **lesson plan** describes specifically what and how something will be learned within a brief period, usually one or a few class hours. Think back to the earlier analogy of vacation planning. The long-range plan is to tour the Eastern United States. The intermediate plan could be to visit Boston and would cover what you want to accomplish only within that part of the trip. The short-term plan is the day-to-day, hour-to-hour, minute-by-minute formulation of what you would do: for example, a daily plan could be to walk the Freedom Trail during the day Monday, attend a Boston Pops Concert Monday evening, shop Tuesday and see a Red Sox game, and so forth.

Lesson planning further defines a daily plan. It is even more detailed. It is an effort to ensure that on that day, every activity will go well.

Parts of a Lesson Plan   Many formats for lesson plans are used. A sampling is shown in Table 6.3. By comparing the formats, it is obvious that they have a lot in common. The lesson plan format we like appears in Table 6.4. Keep in mind that eventually you will need to choose your own lesson plan format unless your school district prescribes one.

Let's consider each part in our recommended lesson plan format:

1. *Objectives.* The challenge here is to write objectives at the lesson level that meet as many of the criteria for good objectives as possible. Remember, the objectives should be relevant to the curriculum; promote learning outcomes across the cognitive, psychomotor, and affective domains; promote a range of levels of understanding (low and high) within each domain; be written specifically enough that it is clear what each student must know and be able to do; and be achievable by your students.

Try Activity 6.5

2. *Resources.* What is available to assist learners? Assemble all the available human and material resources that might be used to help your learners gain the objectives. Many will be noted later in the section entitled Resources Useful When Planning. In practice, many teachers do this step first, before they write specific objectives. In any case, the lesson plan should specifically denote which resources you and the learners will use in order to accomplish the specific instructional objectives.

3. *Set induction.* How will learner interest be obtained? **Set induction** or **anticipatory set** are terms used to indicate the need to start the lesson by capturing learner attention and interest. During this part of lesson planning, we must think of ways to do so. One idea is to relate what is to be learned to what learners are interested in and/or have previous knowledge of (see *advance organizer* in Chapter 4). It has long been assumed and has now been confirmed that people work harder on tasks related to their knowledge and interests (Renninger, Hidi, & Krapp, 1992). Interest contributes to learning because, among other things, it stimulates a personal, emotional network of associations. By relating new learning to prior knowledge, associations, and connections also are more apparent. Chapter 12 details how to provide set induction, while Unit 1 (Microteaching Lesson Two) in part IV provides a practice exercise.

4. *Methodology.* How will teaching and learning proceed? Here you describe how learning will take place. Chapters 2 and 3 on student diversity and 4 on learning should be particularly useful in planning your methodology because they describe what is known about students and how they learn. Chapters 7 and 8 on instructional alternatives also are very relevant.

5. *Assessment.* How will learning be determined? This includes two things: how you plan to monitor students' learning during instruction and how you plan to evaluate learning at the lesson's conclusion. While instruction is ongoing, a teacher should "read" the students. To what extent does each one seem interested and engaged? Is the pace of the lesson appropriate? Are students learning? Your plan should include how you will determine such things. Informal indicators of interest and engagement might include facial expression, body language, and verbal responsiveness. Informal assessments can also be made by asking questions that check understanding and by observing how well and how frequently students apply what they have learned. Formal assessments, frequently used at a lesson's conclusion, include worksheets, homework, and quizzes. No matter which assessment technique you use, remember that it must provide evidence of the students' progress toward the lesson's objectives. See Chapter 9 for more help.

6. *Closure.* How will the lesson be concluded? All lessons need a good finish. But what is a good finish? Normally it takes the form of a review that gets students to summarize what they have learned and connect it to prior and future learning. In Chapter 4, you saw that when information is well-organized and connected to students' prior knowledge, it likely enters their long-term memory. You also learned that a review should require learners to think about the new information, to reflect on its application and its personal meaning. Many teachers conduct their review by asking students what they have learned or discovered.

Try Activity 6.6

Highlight 6.4 contains an abbreviated lesson plan designed to help learners discriminate between the terms *theme* and *variation*. How would you improve the lesson if you were teaching toward the same objective? Eight more lesson plans are in Chapters 7 and 8.

Try Activity 6.7

As mentioned earlier, you eventually need to develop your own style of lesson format unless the school district in which you teach mandates a particular one. Kagan and Tippins (1992) followed elementary and secondary student teachers into their classrooms to find out how they planned. Their study is reported in Spotlight on Research 6.2, on page 164.

Abbreviated Lesson Plan on the Topics of "Theme" and "Variation"

Objectives

1. Given several objects of a common kind or theme—for example, automobiles or sunglasses—the learner will see likenesses and differences among them.
2. The learner will demonstrate understanding of *theme* by drawing six objects with the same shape.
3. The learner will demonstrate understanding of *variation* by varying characteristics of the objects.

Resources

1. Pictures of a variety of automobiles
2. A variety of sunglasses
3. Paper, crayons, or markers

Set Induction (preparing learners to grasp the concepts *theme* and *variation* by causing them to think of themes and variations within their personal experience)

1. Show pictures of automobiles. "What is the same about each object in our pictures?" (all are automobiles) "What is different about the automobiles?" (color, shape, size)
2. Show sunglasses "What is the same about these objects?" (all are sunglasses) "What is different about them?" (color, shape, size)

3. "Can you think of other objects that have something in common yet are somewhat different?" (people, animals, toys)
4. "Today, we are going to learn two new words we can use to describe things that have something in common yet are somewhat different."

Methodology

1. "The two new words we want to explore are *theme* and *variation*. Print words on chalkboard.
2. "If I said that these pictures [hold up automobile pictures] have a common theme, what do you suppose I mean?" (They are alike in some way.) "What is the common theme?" (They are all automobiles.) Underneath the word theme on the chalkboard, write *automobiles.*
3. Repeat steps 1 and 2 with sunglasses.
4. "We know that things with something in common can also be different, or vary, in certain ways. As you said, automobiles and sunglasses have variations." Point to the word *variation* on the chalkboard. "How did you say they vary?" (They vary in size, shape, color.) Write *size, shape, color* underneath the term *variation* on the chalkboard.

5. "Do you think you can show that you understand the words *theme* and *variation?* Draw a group of objects that have a common theme but also show variation. Perhaps you could draw six leaves or six books or anything else that comes to mind."
6. "What ideas do you have for showing *theme* and *variation*, or what we call 'variations of a theme'?"
7. Pass out paper. Instruct students to fold paper into six sections and to draw one object in each section.
8. Circulate to guide, monitor, and assess understanding. Ask individuals, "What theme are you using?" and "What variation?"
9. Ask learners to share their themes and variations.

Assessment

1. See Methodology steps 8 and 9.

Closure

1. "What two new words did you learn today?"
2. "What does each word mean?"
3. "Why do you think these words are important? Why is it important to be able to notice likenesses and differences?"

EVALUATING LESSON PLANS

An Instrument for Use in Checking Your Lesson Plans Given all that has been said in this chapter, here is an instrument that might be useful should you be challenged to prepare a lesson plan and evaluate it.

Yes No 1. Does the lesson plan tie in with the curriculum?

Yes No 2. Are the objectives clear and measurable?

Yes No 3. Do the objectives promote learning across the cognitive, affective, and psychomotor domains when appropriate?

Yes No 4. Do the objectives promote the highest reasonable level of learning in a given domain?

Yes No 5. Are the objectives appropriate to the diversity of learner backgrounds and abilities?

Kagan and Tippins (1992) asked five elementary and seven secondary student teachers at the University of Georgia and the University of Alabama to assist them in answering this question. Because they wanted to see what would happen naturally, the researchers asked the cooperating teachers not to require their student teachers to use any particular lesson plan format. However, Kagan and Tippins gave the student teachers a format with six components: objectives, motivation, major activities, closure, student evaluation, and homework or follow-up. They then asked the student teachers to modify the format so that it worked for them.

As the semester went on, Kagan and Tippins found that (1) elementary teachers' plans became briefer and less detailed, while secondary teachers' plans became more detailed; (2) elementary teachers' plans focused more on learning activities, while secondary teachers focused more on incorporating an outline of a lecture into their plan, and (3) elementary teachers regarded written plans as ways of organizing for the lesson, but preferred to behave spontaneously rather than according to a "script."

The investigators cite the limitations of their study, particularly that only twelve student teachers were involved. However, they conclude that lesson plan formats probably differ not only between novice elementary and secondary teachers but also as a function of the lesson's academic content. Furthermore, Kagan and Tippins suggest that "it would probably be more productive to define lesson plans as lists of major instructional procedures" (p. 487) and that planners should not be required to list "objectives" and "materials" if they are self-evident in the instructional materials. They also suggest that requiring a section on "evaluation" may promote overuse of formal testing.

Yes	No	6. Is there provision in the lesson for informing learners of the objectives?
Yes	No	7. Are the instructional resources available, appropriate, rich, and varied?
Yes	No	8. Will technology resources be used as appropriate?
Yes	No	9. Is *set induction* provided?
Yes	No	10. Are the learning activities clear?
Yes	No	11. Do the learning activities take into account what we know about learning?
Yes	No	12. Are the learning activities appropriate for *your* learners?
Yes	No	13. Will the learning activities likely result in learners meeting the lesson objectives?
Yes	No	14. Is there a plan for ongoing monitoring of student learning?
Yes	No	15. Is there a plan for assessing learner accomplishments at the lesson's conclusion?
Yes	No	16. Is provision made for summarizing what has been learned, how it connects with past and future learning?
Yes	No	17. Is the lesson likely achievable in relationship to the time and space available?
Yes	No	18. Does the plan take into account what we know about good lessons? (Spotlight on Research 6.3)
Yes	No	19. Has thought been given to what might go wrong?
Yes	No	20. I think I will like teaching to my plan and learners should learn and be satisfied.
Yes	No	21. Other . . .

Internet Resources on Lesson Planning   For a list of online resources for lesson plans on a variety of topics, see Highlight 6.5 on page 166.

What Makes a Good Lesson?

Cooper and McIntyre (1994) wanted to find out what a good lesson was like in the eyes of teachers and their students. Thus, they interviewed 13 teachers and 325 students, the latter 11 or 12 years old. Teachers and students generally agreed on what constitutes a good lesson:

- Specific knowledge or skills are acquired.
- Students work on and complete the tasks.
- Students engage in deep reflection and produce new insights.
- Students are involved in and enjoy the learning activity.

- There is a low incidence of disruptive behavior.
- There is cooperation and harmony between teacher and student and among students.
- Teaching methods are considered effective.

REVIEW OF PLANS OF VARYING DURATION

Yinger (1980) outlines the levels of instructional planning. Table 6.5 incorporates his ideas with ours.

RESOURCES USEFUL WHEN PLANNING

As you make either long- or short-range plans, you will need to locate and use two kinds of resources, *curriculum guides* and *instructional material.*

Curriculum Guides   A *curriculum guide* will tell you what you are expected to teach. In a previous section The Formal Curriculum you learned that such guides prescribe what the state and your school district want students to know and be able to do. For example, the Chicago Public Schools have "academic standards" to guide teachers at each grade level K–12 (see http://intranet.cps.k12.il.us/Tutorial/Standards/standards.html).

Web Resource

Instructional Material   *Instructional materials* include those things that assist student learning of the curriculum. They include

- Resource units, which often are available from your state education department, federal agencies, professional associations, and special interest groups including business and industry. A resource unit is a plan for teaching something in the curriculum, for example, the Constitution.
- Textbooks and other print material.
- Nonprint material, for example illustrations, audio and videotapes, and computer-related material as instructional software.

Resources useful when planning instruction are available in your college or education libraries, at school district locations, and at state education departments. Another way to find instructional material is to search online using the Educational Resources Information Center (ERIC). ERIC is a national information network designed to provide you with ready access to educational literature such as curriculum guides, unit plans, lesson plans, ideas for innovative instruction, descriptions of promising practices and so forth.

For your use we have added selected websites for many subject areas in Highlight 6.6 on page 168.

Finally, don't forget that knowledgeable parents and community persons can be great resources for some areas of study.

Planning successful lessons is a challenging daily activity. Below are some sites that provide access to hundreds of lesson plans that might be useful to you. Remember, however, that any plan developed by another teacher for another group of students will need to be modified to meet your curriculum and your learners' needs.

- Lesson Plan Page: http://www.lessonplanspage.com/

- Lesson Planz.com: http://lessonplanz.com/
- K–12 Sources Curriculum and Lesson Plans: http://www.execpc.com/~dboals/k-12.html
- Ask ERIC Lesson Plans: http://ericir.syr.edu/Virtual/Lessons/
- Teachers' Page of Lesson Plans: http://www.library.ualberta.ca/subject/education/k12/lessonplans/index.cfm

- Yahoo: Education K–1: http://dir.yahoo.com/Education/K_12/Teaching/Lesson_Plans/
- Encarta Lesson Collection: http://encarta.msn.com/schoolhouse/default.asp
- Columbia Education Center: http://www.col-ed.org/cur/

COOPERATIVE OR TEAM PLANNING

Normally, you alone will plan what and how your students will learn. However, at some time when planning, you, like all teachers, will solicit the assistance of other teachers or your students. You will use either teacher-team or teacher-pupil planning.

Teacher-team planning often occurs when courses of study or units are being prepared. The principal benefit is that two or more teacher heads often are better than one. Team planning results in sharing purposes, materials, expectations, and instructional ideas. Since teachers tend to be social and gregarious, team planning also can satisfy the need for affiliation and interaction, discussed in Chapter 14.

Teacher-pupil planning is based on the notions that students should learn how to guide or direct their own learning and that they have the motivation and ability to do so. Teacher-pupil planning derives credibility from the fact that pupils are more likely to be responsive to events they helped plan than to events planned for them. Teacher-pupil planning provides the opportunity to plan activities that students perceive as more engaging and interesting. Last but not least, advocates note that the process can be an exercise in citizenship and responsibility.

A few cautions about teacher-pupil planning. Such planning should not stray too far from course, unit, or lesson objectives. Consequently, a secure teacher who can hold students to responsible, reasonable boundaries and standards should monitor and guide the planning process. Not all classes and students may be ready for this responsibility, and teacher-pupil planning must be tempered accordingly. While time consuming on the front end, advocates claim it results in greater student interest and time on task.

Overall, teacher-pupil planning requires skill and considerable forbearance. Teachers who use this technique must be able and willing to provide time, support, guidance, ideas, and resources. Time and effort aside, assisting students in planning what and how they may learn makes a great deal of sense if one of our goals as teachers is to help students become self-directed learners.

6.18 What advantages do you feel may result from collaborative planning?

Some Final Thoughts

At this point we have thought a good deal about planning. However, reading and talking about instructional planning, and even being skilled at planning does not make one a good teacher! *Planning is necessary but not sufficient for good teaching.* It is a means to an end, not an end in itself. On the positive side, planning helps keep

TABLE 6.5 Plans of Varying Duration

	Purposes	Sources of Helpful Information	Form of the Plan	Criteria for Judging Planning Effectiveness
Yearly planning	1. Establish yearlong general content (fairly general and framed by district curriculum objectives) 2. Establish basic curriculum sequence 3. Order and reserve resource materials	1. Students (general information about numbers and nature of returning students) 2. Curriculum guidelines (district objectives) 3. Resource availability 4. Personal experience with specific curricula and materials	General outline listing basic content and possible ideas in each subject matter area	1. Comprehensiveness of plans 2. Fit with own goals, district objectives, and learners
Term planning	1. Spell out details of content to be covered in next school term 2. Establish weekly schedules that conform to the goals and emphases for the term	1. Direct contact with students 2. Time constraints set by school schedule 3. Availability of resources	1. Elaboration of outline constructed for yearly planning 2. A weekly schedule outline specifying activities and times	1. Outlines: comprehensiveness, completeness, and specificity of elaborations 2. Schedule: comprehensiveness fit with goals for term balance 3. Fit with goals for term 4. Fit with learners
Unit planning	1. Develop a sequence of well-organized learning experiences built around a topic or theme 2. Present comprehensive, integrated and meaningful content at an appropriate level	1. Students' abilities, interests, etc. 2. Materials, length of lessons, setup time 3. Facilities available for activities 4. District objectives	1. Activity and content lists of outlines 2. Sequenced activity lists 3. Notes in plan book	1. Organization, sequence balance, and flow of outlines 2. Fit with yearly and term goals 3. Fit with anticipated student interest and involvement
Weekly planning	1. Lay out the week's activities within the framework of the weekly schedule 2. Adjust schedule for interruptions and special needs 3. Maintain continuity and regularity of activities	1. Student performance in preceding days and weeks 2. Scheduled school interruptions (for example, assemblies, holidays) 3. Continued availability of materials, aides, and other resources	1. Activity names and times entered into a plan book 2. Day divided into four instructional blocks punctuated by morning recess, lunch, and afternoon recess	1. Completeness of plans 2. Degree to which weekly schedule has been followed 3. Flexibility of plans to provide for special time constraints or interruptions 4. Fit with goals, learners
Daily planning	1. Set up and arrange classroom for next day 2. Specify activity components not yet decided upon 3. Fit daily schedule to last-minute intrusions 4. Prepare students for day's activities	1. Clarity of instructions in materials to be used 2. Setup time for activities 3. Assessment of class "disposition" at start of day 4. Continued interest, involvement, and enthusiasm	1. Schedule for day written on the chalkboard and discussed 2. Preparation and arrangement of materials and facilities in the room	1. Completion of last-minute preparations and decisions about content, materials, etc. 2. Involvement, enthusiasm, and interest communicated by students
Lesson planning	1. Relate to previous lesson 2. Progress to new, specifically designed task 3. Evaluate attainment (in individual terms) 4. Project to next lesson and relate to broader plan	1. Evaluation of previous lesson 2. The larger units of planning (daily, weekly, unit, etc.) 3. Feedback from class	See Table 6.3 and Highlight 6.3	1. Learner accomplishment of objectives 2. Evaluation during the lesson; at end of lesson; sometime later

ART TEACHING

ArtsEdNet
http://www.getty.edu/artsednet/
resources/

Art Education Resources K–12
http://falcon.jmu.edu/~ramseyil/
arteducation.htm

Art Education Web Guide
http://arts.searchbeat.com/learnart.htm

ENGLISH/LANGUAGE ARTS TEACHING

Awesome Library: English
http://www.awesomelibrary.org/
Classroom/English/English.html

Gumbo: Lesson Plans for English Teachers
http://www.geocities.com/SoHo/
Workshop/8405/

Teaching Ideas
www.ncte.org/teach/

FOREIGN LANGUAGE TEACHING

American Council on Teaching of Foreign Languages
www.actfl.org/

Internet Resources for Foreign Language Classes
http://www.memphis-schools.k12.tn.us/
admin/t/apages/flang.htm

Teaching Foreign Languages
www.eyesoftime.com/teacher/
FRNlang.htm

HEALTH TEACHING

Great Sites for Teaching About Health
http://www.education-world.com/
a_sites/sites058.shtml

MATH TEACHING

Center for Innovation in Mathematics Teaching
www.ex.ac.uk/cimt/

Arithmetic Classroom Materials
http://www.mathforum.com/arithmetic/
arith.lessons.html

This is MEGA Math
http://www.c3.lanl.gov/mega-math

MUSIC TEACHING

Children's Music Web
http://www.childrensmusic.org/

Children's Music Workshop
www.childrensmusicworkshop.com/

K–12 Resources for Music Educators
http://www.isd77.k12.mn.us/resources/
staffpages/shirk/k12.music.html

Music Is . . .
http://elwood.pionet.net/"hub7/
contents.html

PHYSICAL EDUCATION TEACHING

Physical Education Websites
http://www.geocities.com/sisso/
links.html

SCIENCE TEACHING

Science Spiders
http://www.sciencespiders.com/
TheScienceSpiders/

Science Websites
http://www.nsta.org/onlineresources/site/

SOCIAL STUDIES TEACHING

History/Social Studies Website for K–12 Teachers
www.execpc.com/"dboals/boals.html

Teacher Resources
www.hcss.org/resources/

objectives clear and decreases ad lib, off-the-cuff teaching. Although an impromptu approach may work for some teachers some of the time, it does not work for any teacher all of the time. On the negative side, the teacher with a plan must carry it out, and that requires more than planning knowledge. Teachers can plan extraordinary lessons, but they may not have thorough knowledge of what they will teach, or they may lack the instructional abilities to implement the plan. Chapters 7 and 8 will acquaint you with some of the best known and most powerful ways to teach.

CHAPTER SUMMARY

- Thoughtful instructional planning is extremely important for you and your learners. It will likely ensure that you will teach with greater confidence and more creativity. And, importantly, it should assure that you will accomplish your instructional purposes. Thoughtful planning is important to students because you will have taken into account their diversity, how they learn best and what interests and motivates them. Thoughtful planning is the prelude to good teaching.

- Instructional planning is often required by school districts so you may be required to keep a "plan book." The Individuals with Disabilities Education Act requires that you keep detailed plans for students with special needs.

- Teachers differ in their approach to planning. Some prefer very general plans to guide instruction. Others like a very detailed plan. Although both approaches have their advantages and disadvantages, newer teachers are advised to plan in detail until they have more professional experience and wisdom.

- The first task of planning is determining what it is that you are responsible for helping students to learn. That curriculum is found in state syllabi and school district curriculum guides. It results from what society at large deems to be important, what subject matter specialists suggest, and what is known about learners.

- The second task of planning is the preparation of instructional objectives that clearly indicate what students are expected to know and be able to do. There are three commonly used domains of instructional objectives: cognitive, affective, and psychomotor. When possible, effective instruction draws upon each. When possible, effective instruction encourages learners to function at the highest levels of each domain.

- Teachers are advised to prepare specific objectives as part of their instructional plans because they can be used to let learners know exactly what they are expected to know and be able to do. Such instructional objectives contain four kinds of information. They designate the "audience," the learning outcomes expected of the audience, the conditions under which the audience is to exhibit the learned abilities, and the degree or amount of proficiency expected.

- Instructional objectives are good when they are relevant to the curriculum for which learners are held accountable; achievable by your learners; promote learning in as many of the three domains as feasible; and pursue higher-order cognition, affect, or psychomotor skill.

- Research supports that learners benefit when they know what the instructional objectives are and when they result in learning experiences that are neither too easy nor too difficult.

- Instructional plans are of varying duration: long-range (semester, year), intermediate-range (monthly, weekly), short-range (daily, lesson). Since all are important and useful, you should be able to craft each.

- Lesson plans are critical. There are many formats for use in writing them and unless required to use one, you should find a model that you like. The format we like has six parts: objectives, resources, set induction, methodology, assessment, and closure. As teachers gain classroom experience and wisdom, plans are more brief and focus more on the learning activities (methodology).

- A number of Internet sites are devoted to the collection and sharing of lesson plans. Any lesson selected should be modified in ways that fit your curriculum and learners.

ISSUES AND PROBLEMS FOR DISCUSSION

ISSUES   Here are some questions worthy of debate in your class.

1. Which orientation to planning—process or product—is preferable?
2. Should written plans be mandated?
3. How specific should objectives be?
4. What must a teacher think about when planning instruction?
5. To what extent should planning be cooperative?
6. What kinds of persons under what circumstances might be able to teach off-the-cuff, that is, without a lesson plan?
7. Should lessons be standardized across teachers to ensure they are on target and well-formulated? (See Highlight 6.1).

PROBLEMS   Following are some planning problems teachers report. What would you do in each circumstance?

Problem 1:   "I planned a lesson in which the class would watch and discuss a televised program. My class was highly motivated to watch. Unfortunately, the TV didn't work."

Problem 2:   "I assigned seatwork to the students so that I could work with each reading group. It soon became apparent I had underestimated how long the independent work would take. Students finishing early became noisy and interruptive."

Problem 3:   "Today students were removed from the room in groups to take hearing tests. I could not continue with my plans because so many children were continually gone. Then, many of the children had to be retested because the tests were invalid. My daily plans were completely altered, and I accomplished very little teaching."

Problem 4:   "Today was a terribly rainy, wet day. Many of our students don't have proper raincoats and do not come to school on such days. Over one-third of my class was absent. I had planned to begin a new unit of work, and my entire day was disrupted."

Problem 5:   "There are times when regular teachers are absent and substitutes are not available. This means we have to break up and distribute the class of the absent teacher. Today I received three boys from another grade. They were unable to work with my children but obviously couldn't be expected to sit all day and do nothing. This meant that I had to devise and correct assignments for them and make out passes for the ones who eat in the school lunchroom."

Problem 6:   "Our lesson required use of the textbook and a state map. Many pupils arrived without one or the other, claiming they had forgotten them."

THEORY INTO ACTION ACTIVITIES

ACTIVITY 6.1: Recognizing Domains and Levels of Instructional Objectives   Given the following specific objectives, identify the level of each according to Bloom or Simpson by placing an X in the correct boxes.

1. Given a list of spelling words, each learner will use each word in a sentence and spell it correctly.
   Domain: ☐ cognitive   ☐ affective   ☐ psychomotor
   Level: ☐ knowledge   ☐ comprehension   ☐ application
   ☐ analysis   ☐ synthesis   ☐ evaluation

2. Given a reading assignment in Rawlings's novel *The Yearling*, each learner will make a judgment about the correctness of the Baxters' decision to kill Flag the fawn.
   Domain: ☐ cognitive   ☐ affective   ☐ psychomotor
   Level: ☐ receiving/attending   ☐ responding   ☐ valuing
   ☐ organization   ☐ characterization

3. At the conclusion of the typing course, each learner will demonstrate proficiency by typing 60 words a minute with five or fewer errors.
   Domain: ☐ cognitive   ☐ affective   ☐ psychomotor
   Level: ☐ perception   ☐ set   ☐ guided response   ☐ mechanism
   ☐ complex or overt response   ☐ adaptation
   ☐ origination

ACTIVITY 6.2: Recognizing Well-Written Specific Instructional Objectives   Read each of the following objectives and determine whether it is well-written. If it is, label the parts A, B, C, D. If it is unclearly written, rewrite it as a good-quality specific instructional objective and label the four parts.

- When dissecting a frog, the student will identify organs of the digestive system.
- Given a worksheet containing twenty addition examples requiring regrouping, the student will correctly complete seventeen.
- The class will know how to use a dictionary for an in-class oral quiz tomorrow.
- Students will be able to list and describe four types of soccer kicks or passes with 100 percent accuracy.

ACTIVITY 6.3: Developing a Long-Range Plan   Do the following to learn more about long-range planning.

- Talk with classroom teachers or your college instructors about how they plan for a year-long or semester-long course.
- Look through state or local school district courses of study, curriculum guides, and subject matter curriculum standards (Table 6.1) to see how they can help you in course planning.
- Develop a long-range plan for something you likely will teach during your field experiences or that you hope to teach as a beginning teacher. As part of that long-range plan, it might be helpful to
    a. Consult the state or school district course of study to learn the requirements for such a course.
    b. Talk with teachers who teach this course to determine what they include in the course and how and why they make those decisions.
    c. Collect and file as many related resources (print and nonprint) as you can.
    d. Determine the main topics the course will include and establish the order in which you will present them.
    e. Think about who the learners will be in the course and their interests, aptitudes, and past experiences.
    f. Write *general* objectives you want to accomplish in the course.
    g. Subdivide the course topics into parts or units and assign a time for each.
    h. Decide how you will be able to tell whether learners have accomplished the course goals and are satisfied with the course.

ACTIVITY 6.4: Developing a Unit Plan   Do the following activities to learn more about unit planning.

- If you are working in a school, talk with your mentor or cooperating teacher about unit planning. How does he or she organize various activities, experiences, and types of learning around topics, central problems, or areas of interest?
- Look over units your mentor teacher or university professor may have. Also, check to see if any are available through the professional education library or a materials resource center on campus.
- Develop a unit plan that contributes to the long-range plan you developed for Activity 6.3. If you didn't design a long-range plan, design a unit on some topic you probably will teach.

ACTIVITY 6.5: Recognizing Variations on the Theme of Lesson Planning   Look at different lesson plans that are available to you from your mentor teacher, education instructor, or other professional education students.

- What format similarities do they share?
- What is different about each lesson plan?
- Which format would be most useful to you when teaching?

ACTIVITY 6.6: Obtaining Classroom Teachers' Views of Lesson Planning If you are doing fieldwork, talk with your mentor teacher about how he or she plans a lesson. You might consider asking some of the following questions.

- When do you develop your lesson plans? How much time does it take each day or each week?
- What information do you write out in the lesson plan?
- Do you have the lesson plan in front of you when you teach?
- How do you know when to change or vary the lesson you have planned?
- What advice would you give a new teacher about planning?

ACTIVITY 6.7: Observing the Implementation of a Lesson Plan Observe a fellow student or teacher implementing a lesson. Did the teacher provide for each of the following? If so, describe briefly what the teacher did with regard to each:

- Set induction.
- Communication of objective(s).
- Methodology.
- Provision for diverse students.
- Closure or summary.
- Assessment.
- Practice.

ACTIVITY 6.8: Developing and Evaluating a Lesson Plan Develop a lesson plan for something you likely will, or hope to, teach. If you have developed a unit plan, as suggested in Activity 6.4, plan a lesson for use within that unit. Or you might develop a lesson plan for one of the Reflective Teaching Lessons contained in Unit 2 of the Practice Teaching Manual. Follow the format for lesson plans presented in this chapter. Be sure to include all the essential parts.

When you have completed the lesson plan, use the checklist on pages 163–164 to evaluate it.

REFERENCES

Airasian, P. W. (2001). Classroom assessment. New York: McGraw-Hill.

Baltimore Area Committee on Student Teaching. (1991, Spring). *Student teaching field experience handbook.* Baltimore, MD: The Committee.

Biehler, R., & Snowman, J. (2000). Psychology applied to education. Ninth edition. Boston: Houghton Mifflin.

Bloom, B., (Ed.). (1956). *Taxonomy of educational objectives. Handbook I: Cognitive domain.* London: Longman.

Cooper, P., & McIntyre, D. (1994). Patterns of interaction between teachers' and students' classroom thinking. *Teaching and Teacher Education, 10*(6), 633–646.

Cruickshank, D., & Kennedy, J. (1986). Teacher clarity. *Teaching and Teacher Education, 2*(1), 43–67.

Eby, J. W. (2000). *Reflective planning, teaching and evaluation for the elementary school.* New York: Macmillan.

El-Tigi, M. (2000). How to develop a lesson plan. An AskERIC write-a-lesson plan guide, http://eric.syr.edu/Virtual/Lessons/Guide.html.

Gagné, R., & Briggs, L. (1992). *Principles of instructional design.* Forth Worth, TX: Holt, Rinehart and Winston.

Glatthorn, A. (1987). *Curriculum renewal.* Alexandria, VA: Association for Supervision and Curriculum Development.

Hirsch, E. D. (1989). *A first dictionary of cultural literacy: What our children need to know.* Boston: Houghton Mifflin.

Hunter, M. (1985). Mastery teaching. El Segundo, CA: TIP Publications.

Jacobson, D., Eggen, P., Kauchak, D., & Delaney, C. (1985). *Methods for teaching.* Columbus, OH: Charles E. Merrill.

Johnston, R. (1999, October 13). In Chicago, every day brings a new lesson plan. *Education Week, 19*(7), 1, 10–11.

Kagan, D. M., & Tippins, D. J. (1992). The evolution of functional lesson plans among twelve elementary and secondary student teachers. *The Elementary School Journal, 92*(4), 477–490.

Marzano, R., Pickering, D., & Pollock, J. (2001). *Classroom instruction that works.* Alexandria, VA: Association for Supervision and Curriculum Development.

McNeil, J. (1999). *Curriculum: A comprehensive introduction.* New York: John Wiley & Sons.

Moore, K. (2000). *Classroom teaching skills.* New York: McGraw-Hill.

National Governors' Association. (1990, February). Report adopted by members of the National Governors' Association.

Renninger, K. A., Hidi, S., & Krapp, A. (1992). The role of interest in learning and development. Hillsdale, NJ: Erlbaum.

Simpson, E. (1972). *The classification of educational objectives: Psychomotor domain.* Urbana: University of Illinois Press.

Slavin, R. (1999). *Educational psychology: Theory into practice.* Boston: Allyn & Bacon.

Sternberg, Robert J. (1997, March). What does it mean to be smart? *Educational Leadership, 54*(6), 20–24.

Willis, S. (1993, November). Teaching young children: Educators seek developmental appropriateness. *ASCD Curriculum Update,* 1–8.

Yinger, R. (1980). A study of teacher planning. *The Elementary School Journal, 80,* 114–115.

Four Instructional Alternatives: Presentation, Discussion, Independent Study, and Individualized Instruction

Contents

Can you think of one or more of your teachers who helped you learn and even to enjoy learning? Now can you think of teachers who were not very effective? How did these teachers differ? One thing that characterizes effective teachers is their ability to use a variety of instructional alternatives or strategies. Like acclaimed actors and actresses who can play a large number of roles, *good teachers are multitalented*. On one day, they may have involved your class in a debate. On other days, you may have watched a demonstration, played an academic game, listened to an oral report, or used an individual learning module. The classroom always seemed varied and lively, and while this alone does not ensure effective teaching, it surely helps (see Spotlight on Research 7.1 on page 176).

In this chapter and the next, we hope to put you on the road to becoming a multitalented, versatile teacher. In this chapter you will take an in-depth look at four commonly known and used instructional alternatives, namely, *presentation, discussion, independent study,* and *individualized instruction*. Then, at the end of the chapter you will find a brief overview of thirty instructional alternatives, including these four. In Chapter 8, you will learn about four more of the thirty: *cooperative learning, discovery learning, constructivism, and direct instruction*. Being aware of the many possible ways to teach and gaining in-depth knowledge of eight will serve you well.

We first look in on presentation, discussion, independent study, and individualized instruction simply because they are the staples in almost all teachers' instructional repertoires and they persist over time. Accordingly, you need to be well-versed in each and skillful in its use.

Instructional Alternatives Defined

Just what is an instructional alternative? An **instructional alternative** is any teaching maneuver used to facilitate student learning and satisfaction. Over the centuries, a number have been developed, modified, and even combined (Broudy, 1963; Connell, 1987). As mentioned above, we identified thirty, four of which are now explored in depth.

Presentations: Teaching as Telling and Showing

In this information age, it is critical that students have more and more knowledge. Teacher presentation is one way through which knowledge can be obtained. Therefore, presentation of information is one of a teacher's most important instructional functions (Rosenshine, 1987; Henke et al., 1999). Presentation is synonymous with **reception learning,** which falls within the cognitive school of thought you learned about in Chapter 4.

WHAT IS A PRESENTATION?

By definition, a **presentation** is an informative talk a more knowledgeable person makes to less knowledgeable persons. You will present, or lecture, if you tell less informed students when to use a semicolon, what a peninsula is, why the seasons change, or how to multiply fractions.

Showing can enhance telling, so teachers often accompany their talks with demonstrations. For example, in addition to telling students why the seasons change, you might also use a film, videotape, computer graphic, or mechanical model to provide a visual demonstration.

PURPOSE AND CHARACTERISTICS OF TEACHER PRESENTATIONS

The purpose of a presentation is *to inform an audience of certain facts, ideas, concepts, and explanations.* However, talks can be very different in terms of length, formality, and who does the talking. In other words, teacher talks have a number of characteristics. Think of the many different kinds you have experienced.

In terms of length, some were long and some were short. At times, a teacher presented or talked for a whole class period, without interruptions or questions. Perhaps the teacher said he would answer your questions at the end, but by then you had forgotten what to ask. Other talks were of short duration.

Teacher presentations also vary according to degree of formality. Speeches are, of course, more formal than talks, and talks interspersed with teacher questions or student questions are even less formal. When teachers talk in order to force students to think or reflect, they are practicing a version of what is called the Socratic technique. Socrates taught by questioning his listeners about their views and opinions (What do you think?) and then interrogating them further about what they said (Why do you think that?). He talked in order to probe his listeners' minds and to force them to confront their thoughts and ideas.

A third dimension of teacher presentation has to do with the presenter. Is she the teacher, a guest, perhaps another teacher, or a parent or community figure? Teachers working together to share their expertise engage in what is called **team teaching** or collaborative teaching. Sometimes the collaborator isn't even present. An image and voice may reach us by television, computer, radio, or telephone. When prerecorded presentations are used as part of individualized, self-paced

7.1 Think of presentations you have experienced. What made some good and some bad?

instructional programs, they are referred to as audio, or audiovisual, tutorials. To illustrate, a student doing independent study in Spanish might watch a videotaped analysis of a classic novel such as Cervantes's *Don Quixote*.

Figure 7.1 depicts the purpose and key attributes of a presentation.

GOOD PRESENTERS

Before planning and embarking on a presentation, you must believe that your learners can best gain particular knowledge or skill by attending, looking, and listening to you or another presenter. There should be no better way by which the learner might learn. For example, say your students need to learn how to divide fractions. After looking at instructional resources on the topic that students might use to accomplish this goal, you conclude that you can teach the process better yourself and perhaps do it in less time.

In addition, you believe that when giving a whole-class presentation you can better monitor student learning: You can observe the extent to which the students seem to grasp what they need to learn. Finally, and importantly, you believe that you are a good presenter.

How can you become a good presenter? Let's pursue the answer by looking first at the related research literature. It seems that on a personal level, you should be friendly, humorous, enthusiastic, verbally fluent (in other words, talk effortlessly and smoothly), and clear (Kindsvatter, R., Wilen, W., & Ishler, M., 1988; Brown, 1987). Unfortunately, while such characteristics are helpful, they are not sufficient to make you a good presenter. You must also possess knowledge of your students (particularly with regard to their diversity) and, of course, have mastery of the subject you are presenting. In short, being a friendly, funny, dynamic, and talkative person will not do the job if you don't know your audience or what you are talking about. Don't be alarmed! Few people have all or even most of these desirable qualities. So everyone simply has to make the best of what they have and keep trying to improve. You cannot learn to teach overnight or even during your university preparation; it is a lifelong affair. You will find out how to be more humorous, enthusiastic, and clear in Chapters 11 and 12.

GOOD PRESENTATIONS

Persons who have thought about and studied the quality of teacher presentations tend to analyze them according to three primary factors: preparation, delivery, and closure (Brown, 1987; Gage & Berliner, 1976; Gilstrap & Martin, 1975; Rosenshine & Stevens, 1986). The following discussion centers on these three characteristics.

7.2 Given the characteristics of good presenters, which do you feel you have and which must you further develop? How might you do so?

7.3 To what extent do you think you are gaining knowledge about the things you will teach?

7.4 What to you are the most important characteristics of a good presentation?

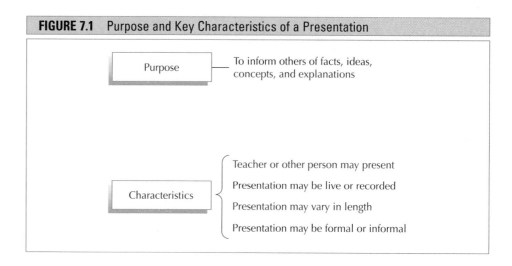

FIGURE 7.1 Purpose and Key Characteristics of a Presentation

Purpose — To inform others of facts, ideas, concepts, and explanations

Characteristics
- Teacher or other person may present
- Presentation may be live or recorded
- Presentation may vary in length
- Presentation may be formal or informal

Preparation   As with any form of instruction, you must first establish your topic and general purpose and then set the specific learning objectives you want learners to achieve. Once you have done that, and once you are satisfied that a presentation truly is your best instructional alternative, you should collect, review, and organize the available subject matter resources. Also consider the kinds of examples and illustrations you will need in order to make the information to be presented understandable to your diverse students.

Suppose your presentation topic is "Dinosaurs." What is the general purpose of your presentation? It could be to introduce the topic, to provide students with knowledge of dinosaurs, or to promote critical thinking. Let's say your presentation aims to provide knowledge of dinosaurs. If so, what information do you want to present? What should students know? Will they need to understand what a dinosaur was and the various kinds that existed, how they lived, why they became extinct, or perhaps how paleontologists study them? Once this question is answered, your teaching objectives should come into focus. Let's assume that your purpose is twofold: to tell what a dinosaur was and to talk about the kinds that existed. You must now decide what specific knowledge, skills, or attitudes you wish to foster in your learners. Suppose you decide that learners should be able to (1) define *dinosaur* as the name for two groups of reptiles that lived millions of years ago, (2) name the two groups, (3) describe the physical characteristics and living habits of the two groups and the species therein, and (4) locate where each group lived. Furthermore, you want students to compare how dinosaurs ruled the earth with how people rule the earth today. Once you have your purpose and learning objectives for the presentation in mind, you probably want to identify and collect instructional resources. What kinds? Look for computer software, books, articles, films, videotapes, models, exhibits, pictures. The use of visual aids can particularly increase students' interest and learning since we live in a visually oriented society. Sources of such instructional materials include the classroom, school library, public library, Internet, museums, and knowledgeable students. Students of all ages love dinosaurs. Tell students you are going to teach about dinosaurs, and you will be pleasantly surprised to see what they bring to class to share. Table 7.1 suggests how selected visual aids can improve your presentations.

With purpose and objectives in mind and resources collected, you are now ready to review your subject and create a plan for your talk. Keep in mind the diversity of your students—their interests, abilities, and background knowledge. *Be especially prepared to introduce concepts or ideas that are new to them.* Highlight 7.1 provides important information about how to teach a new concept.

TABLE 7.1 Improving Teachers' Presentations with Visual Aids

Visual Aids	Uses
Printed material that serves as advance organizers: handouts, outlines, "questions to think about"	Give these to your students before you begin your presentation to help students focus their attention and to guide their note taking during the presentation.
Overhead transparencies: outlines, drawings, charts, diagrams, maps, cartoons, quotes, key words and ideas	Use these at key times in your presentation to emphasize a point, to review, to organize and categorize information, to stimulate interest, to add a touch of humor, and to summarize.
Pictures and prints: photographs, paintings, posters, slides	Photographs or posters of important people, places, objects, and artwork can greatly aid student comprehension and stimulate interest.
"Clips" on videotape	Showing a segment of a newscast or some televised special can bring events and people to life.
Maps, wall charts, and globes	These can be especially useful if students have desk-size versions or their own small copies.
Concrete objects (manipulatives)	When possible, have examples for students to look at and handle. A lesson on trees could include different types of leaves and bark.

Source: The content of this table is attributed to Dr. Jeffrey Peck, Gardner-Webb University.

In summary, preparing a presentation includes (1) establishing the general purpose of the presentation and the specific learning objectives, (2) collecting and reviewing information to be presented, and (3) organizing or planning delivery.

Delivery Now we are talking about performance, about the presentation itself. Here you want to do many important things: get your students' attention, tell them what they are going to learn and what they are expected to know and be able to do, make the presentation clear, emphasize important points, monitor their understanding, and promote questions and comments. Do these things supportively, enthusiastically, and perhaps with a touch of humor and fun.

Do you remember the cartoon in Chapter 4, "First you have to get their attention"? Attention is where it all starts and, believe us, nothing good happens without it. In Chapter 4, you found that getting students' attention is easier when learners have had pleasant, rewarding school experiences (especially ones that relate somehow to your presentation) and when they have had some prior interest in your topic. As a learner, if I'm a "happy camper" and if I have a dinosaur model collection, I'm with you. If I'm an underachiever who thinks dinosaurs are like old teachers, watch out! That is why in Chapter 6, Planning Instruction, our lesson plan format contains a section on set induction. Winning coaches are great motivators. So are winning teachers.

As noted earlier, presentation fits the descriptions of expository teaching and reception learning from Chapter 4. Therefore, the rules given in Chapter 4 for good expository teaching apply here. They include: (1) present the learners with the learning objectives—tell them what they are expected to know and to be able to do, (2) use an advance organizer (relate new information to what they already know), (3) present information in an organized, step-by-step manner (don't overwhelm or underwhelm), (4) expect pupil interaction in the form of questions and comments, (5) move from general to specific ideas or information, (6) when teaching a new idea or concept, use both examples and nonexamples of it (Highlight 7.1), (7) use good explanations, and (8) encourage learners to reflect on and apply what they have learned ("Are there differences between the way dinosaurs and humans have ruled the earth?").

The term *concept* is used to refer to a group of ideas or objects that are alike and thus share a common name or label, such as tables, clouds, dogs, or dinosaurs. We learn many concepts through everyday experience rather than in school. Examples include hot, cold, wet, dry, loud, and quiet. However, a major function of formal education is to teach concepts. Remember when you were taught such concepts as "a meter," "carbon dioxide," "poetry," "the color wheel," "treble," and "long jump"? If your concepts were well taught, you learned and remembered them.

Teachers can present concepts in two ways, either through expository teaching or discovery learning. Since this section of the chapter is about presentations (expository teaching), the following classical concept-teaching procedure relates to the discussion. The concept *peninsula* is used in this example.

1. Begin with a clear definition that describes the attributes of the concept: "A peninsula is a *land area almost entirely surrounded by water* and *connected to the mainland* by a single strip of land or isthmus." (The attributes are in italics.)

2. Next, provide examples of the concept and relate the examples to the definition: "Look at the map. Arabia and Alaska are the largest peninsulas in the world. India is a peninsula with a very large mainland connection. The Baja Peninsula in lower California is a typical peninsula. Florida is a peninsula. Each is an area of land almost circled by water."

3. Now provide nonexamples or negative examples:
"Mexico is not a peninsula. It is connected to land on two sides. Australia is not a peninsula. It is completely surrounded by water."

4. Check for understanding:
"Which of the following are peninsulas? Korea, Turkey, Italy, Scandinavia, Newfoundland, Greenland, South America? Why?"

For an in-depth look at concept learning, see Hamilton and Ghatala, 1994, pp. 149–166.

Highlight 7.2 provides three simple rules to follow in order to make an explanation understandable. Spotlight on Research 7.2 presents research findings on effective presentations (see p. 183).

Handouts   You have undoubtedly attended presentations where the presenter distributed handouts containing some kind of related information and material. You probably found them helpful when they did any or all of the following: (1) made clear the purpose of the talk and what you were expected to know or to be able to do, (2) provided questions that helped you focus on important points, (3) contained an outline of the main points, or (4) included a quiz to check your understanding.

Closure   Everything has to end. So how should you conclude the dinosaur presentation? Several recommendations are consistent with what we know about short- and long-term memory and reception learning. Since you told learners what they *would learn* at the outset, now remind them of what they *have learned*. Review and summary are appropriate. Reiterate the major concepts, facts, and generalizations that you want learners to recall. Of course, you might consider drawing this information out of your students by way of questioning or recitation. Make them rummage around in their own minds.

Next, connect what students have learned about dinosaurs to what they knew prior to the presentation ("This is what you knew then. This is what you know now."). Help students see how their knowledge has grown with regard to what a dinosaur is, how dinosaurs are grouped, and so forth. Remember, this effort to tie new information to old enhances long-term memory and information retrieval.

Try Activities 7.1 & 7.2

Finally, check for understanding. Be especially sensitive to whether your students can use the information at the higher cognitive levels, demonstrating application, analysis, synthesis, and evaluation, as described in Chapter 6. For example, if it is

Making a Good Explanation

Teachers use explanation for at least two purposes. In one case, we explain a concept, idea, procedure, or rule so as to make it understandable. Thus, we explain a concept (global warming), a procedure (how to subtract), or a rule (we raise our hand to be recognized). In a second case, we explain something in order to account for its occurrence: why global warming occurs, how the subtraction algorithm works, or why the class must raise hands. Here explanation is akin to giving reasons.

A good explanation has three characteristics: It must be

- Complete
- Accurate
- Clear

When you give an explanation, remember C-A-C.

Of course, students should be called on to give explanations too. The quality of their explanations can also be judged according to C-A-C guidelines.

Source: D. Cruickshank & K. Metcalf. (1995). Explaining. In T. Husen & T. N. Postlewaite (Eds.), *International encyclopedia of education*. Second Edition. Oxford: Pergamon Press.

TABLE 7.2 Qualities of Good Presenters and Good Presentations

Good Presenters Are . . .	Good Presentations Include . . .
• Knowledgeable about the subject matter • Aware of learner diversity • Friendly • Humorous • Enthusiastic • Verbally fluent and audible	*When preparing:* • Choose the topic • Establish the general purpose • Set specific learner objectives • Collect, review subject matter and useful material • Plan the presentation • Prepare handouts *When delivering:* • Get students' attention • Tell students what they will learn and what they must be able to do • Relate new information to that in students' long-term memory • Present information step by step • Move from the general to the specific • Don't overwhelm or underwhelm • Emphasize important points • Use examples and illustrations to make things clearer • Use variety, such as visual aids, to maintain attention • Monitor understanding by promoting questions, comments • Avoid digressions *When closing:* • Review and summarize important points • Secure new learning to previous knowledge • Check for ability to use new knowledge at a higher cognitive level

---

your purpose, can learners generalize what they have learned about the lives of dinosaurs to other species? To what extent were the habits of dinosaurs similar to those of today's creatures?

A summary of the qualities of good presenters and good presentations is contained in Table 7.2. This is one of several tables contained in this and the next chapter that you will want to keep handy for future reference.

A sample presentation lesson plan appears as Lesson Plan 7.1.

LESSON PLAN 7.1

Abbreviated Presentation Lesson: Roman Numerals

Curriculum tie-in: This lesson may be linked to the study of Roman civilization or the study of numerical systems.

OBJECTIVES

1. Learners will recognize the basic Roman numerals (I, V, X, L, C, D, and M) and know their values. *Specific objective:* Given a list of Roman numerals, learners will correctly identify and circle all basic numerals.

2. Learners will understand two rules for creating other numerals. *Specific objective:* given a list of Arabic numerals, using the rules, learners will correctly translate all of them into Roman.

RESOURCES

1. Pictures of or documents containing Roman numerals (book preface pages, book chapter numbers, watch and clock faces, building cornerstones, inscriptions on statues, outlines).

2. Supplementary materials on Roman numerals contained in texts, encyclopedias, journals, and so forth.

3. Websites on Roman numerals.

4. Lesson plans on Roman numerals contained on the Web.

METHODOLOGY

1. *Set induction.* "I am going to show you a secret code. What is a code?" (Show resource objects and pictures containing Roman numerals). Ask, "What is this code called? Where did this code come from? Where have you seen it?"

2. Inform learners of what they will learn and be able to do as a result of the lesson (see Objectives).

3. Find out what learners know about Roman numerals. Ask, "What are some things you know about Roman numerals?"

4. Present/review the lesson information.

   a. There are only a few basic numerals (I, V, X, L, C, D, M).

   b. Other numbers are *mostly* created by either

      (1) Putting a number(s) of lesser value after one of greater value e.g.

      VI = 6, XII = 12, LXXVII = 77 or

      (2) Putting a number(s) of lesser value *before* one of greater value e.g.

      IV = 4, IX = 9,

      XL = 40.

ASSESSMENT

1. Given a list of fourteen Roman numerals, learners will circle only the seven basic ones.

2. Given a list of Arabic numerals, learners will convert them to Roman equivalents.

3. Reteach as necessary.

CLOSURE

1. Have students write summaries of what they know about Roman numerals and have them share their knowledge: e.g., Where are they found? What are the basic numerals? What are the rules for making others from them?

If more is to be learned about Roman numerals and their use:

2. Have interested students locate examples of uses of Roman numerals.

3. Have interested students locate additional information on Roman numerals.

WHEN TEACHER PRESENTATIONS SHOULD BE USED

Gage and Berliner (1976, 1998) tell us when to lecture. They believe that it is an appropriate instructional alternative when (1) information dissemination is the main goal, (2) the information to be disseminated is not readily available in another form, such as a book, (3) the information must be especially selected, organized, and presented for a specific group of learners, (4) it is important to arouse interest in the information, and (5) the material need not be remembered for a long time.

Although these factors define when presentations should be used, in actuality you will probably make use of them (1) if your former teachers frequently presented, and for the most part you liked and learned from them, (2) if you have prior knowledge about the topic or subject, (3) if you like to talk and have a knack for it, (4) if you believe your students will learn the material best this way, (5) if you have few related instructional resources, (6) if you lack time or competence to facilitate learning in another way, and (7) if presentations meet your personal and professional needs.

Studies of teacher presentations have been conducted mostly on university campuses. The following findings are reported by McLeish (1975). Whether the same findings hold true in elementary, middle, or secondary classrooms is unknown.

- The presenter's style increases retention. Presenters should be forceful and dynamic; they should use concrete objects and illustrations, simplify the complexity of what is to be learned, and present information slowly.

- For some students, attention falls off rapidly after the first 15 minutes of a presentation. At the 30- to 40-minute mark, the amount of information absorbed can be very low.

- Having students take notes during a presentation helps long-term but not short-term recall of information.

- Presentations are better than discussions for transmitting information but not as good for promoting student thought or reflection.

- Learners prefer small- to large-class presentations.

- Underachieving learners (students who should be performing at a higher level) are helped by being given supplementary assignments that engage them in some form of related activity and provide them with knowledge of how well they understand.

LIMITATIONS OF PRESENTATIONS

Of course, presentations have shortcomings. Among others, teachers may not know the area of study sufficiently to present it, presentations often do not involve learners enough, and they may be overwhelming, underwhelming, or boring. For these reasons they may trigger frustration in learners who do not have good attention, note-taking, or memory skills (Freiberg & Driscoll, 1996).

What if you don't have adequate knowledge to make a presentation in some area that you are responsible for teaching? What can you do? Good (1995) suggests some possible ways to overcome that shortcoming, including finding and using material to increase your knowledge, bringing in guest speakers including other teachers, and telling students that this is an area about which you are still learning. An obvious, other suggestion is to use a different instructional alternative that does not rest on the teacher knowing the material quite so extensively.

SUMMARY ON PRESENTATION

You have learned that informative teacher talks are common occurrences and that they differ in many respects. For example, they differ in degree of formality and length, with informal and shorter talks generally preferable. Presentations also differ according to whether they are live or recorded. To conduct a good presentation, the presenter should demonstrate certain qualities and follow certain procedures, as Table 7.2 noted. Like all instructional alternatives, teacher presentations have advantages and disadvantages for both teachers and learners. In general, when dissemination of information is the goal, they are efficient and economical. Like any instructional alternative, teacher presentations have their place and contribute to learner achievement and to teacher and learner satisfaction.

Try Activity 7.3

7.5 What factors in Chapter 1 may influence how you feel about using presentation?

Discussion: Learning through Informative Interaction

Lots of people, perhaps even you, think teachers talk too much. Scholars have provided evidence that teachers talk two-thirds of the time that class is in session. Do you get tired of constantly hearing what someone else has to say? Do you get squirmy if you have to sit and listen too long? To make matters worse, you may already have acquired from books or other teachers some of the information you are hearing. Listening can become boring, boring, boring! "Why doesn't the

CHAPTER 7
Four Instructional Alternatives:
Presentation, Discussion, Independent
Study, and Individualized Instruction

183

teacher let us talk about what we know and how we feel?" For this and other sound reasons, astute teachers include discussion as part of their repertoire.

WHAT IS A DISCUSSION?

7.6 How do you like discussions? What have been your experiences with them, good and bad?

A **discussion** is a situation wherein students, or students and a teacher, converse to share information, ideas, or opinions or work to resolve a problem. Conversely, a discussion is not a situation wherein a teacher asks a question, a student or students answer, and then the teacher asks another question. This question-answer-question format is called **recitation.** Its purpose is mainly to quiz students to determine what they know or understand. Some differences between a true discussion and a recitation are illustrated in Table 7.3.

PURPOSES AND CHARACTERISTICS OF DISCUSSION

According to a study by Parker and Hess (2001), students preparing to be teachers want to know the purposes, characteristics and procedures of discussion (see Spotlight on Research 7.3). Hopefully, what follows will serve your needs.

TABLE 7.3 Recitation and Discussion Compared

	Recitation	Discussion
Definition	When a teacher asks students a series of relatively short-answer questions	When a student or students and a teacher converse to share information, ideas, and so forth
Purpose	To determine what students remember or understand	To review what students have learned, encourage students to reflect on their ideas or opinions, explore an issue, resolve a problem, or improve face-to-face communication skills
Conceptual level	Questions are usually lower-level, cognitive domain. *Examples:* "When was America discovered?" "What is the sum of the angles of a triangle?" "What are the themes of Fitzgerald's novels?"	Discussion usually is at a higher cognitive level or may be in the affective domain. *Examples:* "What leads to exploration and discovery?" "Are exploration and discovery bad or good?" "If we find life on another planet, should we try to improve it?"
Role of the teacher	"Quizmaster"	Facilitator-moderator, participant, or observer-recorder

Purposes of Discussion   A discussion can serve a variety of purposes (Gall, 1987; Gall & Gall, 1990; Goldenberg, 1991; Roby, 1981). One purpose is to review and extend what students have learned in order to *ensure their mastery of a subject.* Hill (2000) presents us with a discussion model for subject matter mastery that follows certain steps. First, your students see, hear, or read something. Perhaps they view a documentary on using animals in medical research. Then they discuss what they have seen and heard. Among other things, they give attention to terms and concepts that need explanation, to the major ideas presented, and to the major message. Of course, the discussion could go well beyond merely processing (clarifying and rehearsing) the information received. You could, Hill advises, engage students in higher-order thinking by getting them to talk about the authenticity of the message or its effect if carried out. Such discussions primarily help us learn through rehearsal, that is, recalling and talking about things so they become more firmly fixed in our memories.

A discussion can also be held when the purpose is *to have students examine their ideas or opinions.* After studying about the use of animals in medical research, students could be asked to share their views about its appropriateness.

A third purpose a discussion might have is *to solve a problem.* Students are presented with political, economic, or social problems to discuss and resolve, such as these: How can better relationships be established with China? How can we reduce the national debt? How can violence by children be reduced? Closer to home, you and your classmates could address such questions as how to work with students at risk, how to locate instructional resources, or how we can become better classroom problem solvers.

Sometimes a discussion can help students *to improve their face-to-face or interpersonal communication skills.* The purpose is for learners to become better at being good contributors and active listeners, making a point, handling disagreements and conflicts, overcoming fear of speaking in public, and so forth.

Certainly, these are four good reasons for including discussion in your teaching repertoire. Can you think of others?

Characteristics of Discussions   We can consider discussions on the basis of a number of attributes or characteristics: the interaction pattern, group size and composition, and group arrangement.

Interaction Pattern   We have said that discussion differs from recitation, or the teacher question–student answer technique; interaction during discussions is less formal and more conversational. Moreover, the conversation can occur among students

CHAPTER 7
Four Instructional Alternatives:
Presentation, Discussion, Independent
Study, and Individualized Instruction

185

as well as between students and teacher. In the most lively discussions, everyone is an active participant. Simich-Dudgeon (1998) reviewed research on "collaborative talk" or discussion among students and tells us it contributes to student success.

Group Size and Composition   The whole class can engage in a common discussion, or it can be divided into groups. All other factors being equal, small groups are preferable since they allow more potential for participation. The composition of a group is also at issue. That is, should members be similar (homogeneous) or dissimilar (heterogeneous)? Arguments can be made for either position.

Group Arrangement   One rule seems to hold: To converse, participants should be face to face. Thus, arranging discussion participants in a circle is a common occurrence. On occasion, a panel discussion makes sense. A panel discussion is carried on when a preselected group of students discusses in front of others who observe. Students on the panel should be arranged face to face. Students who observe might surround the panel. This procedure and arrangement is referred to as a fishbowl—everyone is watching the panel or "fish."

Role of the Teacher   Of course, the interaction pattern suggests a number of different teacher roles and responsibilities. If the interaction is strictly among students, the teacher serves as observer, recorder, and perhaps arbitrator. At other times, you will want to be a member of the discussion group but not its official leader—you merely want to participate. Other occasions may call for you to be the facilitator-moderator. In this case, according to Van Ments (1990), the duty of the teacher is to "enable learners to reflect critically on their experiences . . . to explore different perspectives, to consider how their knowledge is rooted in personal experiences" (p.12). The role you choose to play—observer, participant, or facilitator—will vary according to circumstances such as the purpose of the discussion and the maturity and experience of the students.

For a visual summarization of the purposes and key characteristics of a discussion, see Figure 7.2.

GOOD DISCUSSION LEADERS

What does it take to be a good discussion leader? We believe you need to possess an assortment of beliefs and skills. First, let's look at four beliefs. Basically, discussion leaders should believe that students, like most persons, desire to communicate with others (Gall & Gall, 1976). We noted previously that teachers like to talk. Well, students like to talk, too, don't they? Persons who utilize discussion as an instructional alternative use it in part to legitimatize classroom conversation, that is, to make it acceptable and purposeful.

Teachers who use discussion also believe in the purposes of discussion: review and extension of what students have learned, examination of ideas and opinions, problem solving, and increased interpersonal communication skills. Democratic forms of government depend on persons so educated.

In addition to believing in the purposes of discussion, discussion users must have confidence in their students' capacities to think effectively. They have faith that, with guidance, students will employ higher-level cognitive skills such as application, analysis, synthesis, and evaluation. Discussion users also believe that by engaging students in discussion, they can accomplish many affective goals, such as encouraging students to respond and value. You may recall that these terms were introduced in the section entitled Writing Instructional Objectives in Chapter 6.

A fourth belief held by persons who favor discussion is that involving students in a well-conceived group experience will enhance their psychological and social growth. In such situations, they can learn to feel good about themselves and to

7.7   When, for the purpose of discussion, might it be preferable to form heterogeneous and homogeneous groups?

7.8   Which of the four beliefs of good discussion leaders do you hold?

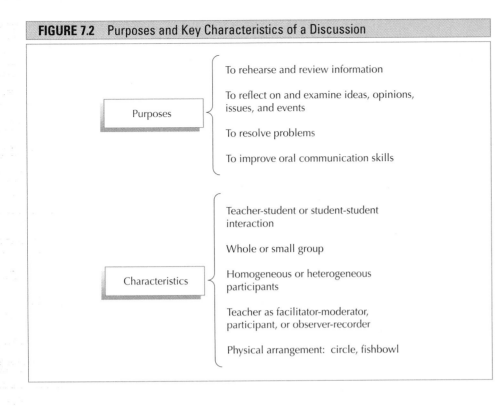

FIGURE 7.2 Purposes and Key Characteristics of a Discussion

Purposes
- To rehearse and review information
- To reflect on and examine ideas, opinions, issues, and events
- To resolve problems
- To improve oral communication skills

Characteristics
- Teacher-student or student-student interaction
- Whole or small group
- Homogeneous or heterogeneous participants
- Teacher as facilitator-moderator, participant, or observer-recorder
- Physical arrangement: circle, fishbowl

accept others. In addition, shy students can often be encouraged to participate, especially in smaller discussion groups. Good discussion leaders encourage and enhance student pride, dignity, sense of efficacy or personal power, and caring.

Beyond holding to these beliefs, you will be a better discussion leader if you have related skills. For example, can you limit your own talk? Remember, this is the students' conversational opportunity. Persons who have observed discussion remind us that frequently teachers talk too much even during discussions (Dillon, 1985, 1988). Could it be that many of us simply need to rein in our compulsion to talk? We must learn how to get *students* to ask more questions, explore and speculate more, make more references to *their* personal experiences, and so forth.

Additionally, you must be a facilitator, human relations expert, clarifier, and summarizer. As a *facilitator*, you are responsible for beginning the discussion, moving it briskly, and keeping the group on task and attentive. As a *human relations expert*, your job is to make everyone feel comfortable and important and to encourage full and equal participation. You must also moderate differences of opinion. As a *clarifier*, you must ensure that everyone's message is heard and understood. This might require that certain students' comments be limited, rephrased, or probed. Finally, as a *summarizer*, you need to be skillful in drawing the conversation together and ensuring that everyone sees the progress they have made toward the stated goal.

Bridges (1988) tells us that you also need skill in teaching three kinds of communication skills to your students. You must be able to help them know how to make remarks that are reasonable, to know when and for how long to speak, and to know how critical they should be of the remarks others make.

7.9 How do you feel about your abilities as a facilitator, human relations expert, clarifier, summarizer, and teacher of communication skills?

GOOD DISCUSSIONS

Can you recall thinking to yourself, Wow! That was a good discussion! What makes a discussion good? As is true of any instructional alternative, a discussion is good when it results in learning and satisfaction. Both of these outcomes depend on how the discussion was prepared, presented, and concluded (Bridges, 1988; Dillon, 1988, 1995; Gall, 1987; Gall & Gall, 1976; Goldenberg, 1991).

CHAPTER 7
Four Instructional Alternatives: Presentation, Discussion, Independent Study, and Individualized Instruction

187

Preparation   First, you need to decide whether you should use a discussion and why you want to use one. Do you remember the four purposes—to review and extend knowledge, examine ideas, solve problems, and improve communication skills? For illustration, let's say your purpose is to review what students have learned and to extend that knowledge. More specifically, let's say your goal is for students to review and extend what they have learned about dinosaurs from reading a hypothetical article called "The Age of Dinosaurs" in *National Geographic World*, a magazine written for students. From the article, the students ascertain how scientists have learned about dinosaurs and what they have learned. Consequently, students could discuss a number of things. Some are basic and factual. When did dinosaurs live? Where did they live? What kinds of dinosaurs existed when? How did dinosaurs live? What do scientists do to study dinosaurs?

At a higher level, you can ask participants to analyze, synthesize, and evaluate using the following ploy: "Dinosaurs haven't really become extinct—birds belong on the dinosaur family tree. So, you have a dinosaur bath in your backyard, you dine on roast dinosaur at Thanksgiving, and you munch on dinosaur nuggets at McDonalds. . . . What is a family tree? How do you suppose paleontologists decided birds and dinosaurs are related?" Another premise for discussion might be this: "Finding out about dinosaurs is both very time consuming and expensive. Why is it so important? Couldn't the time and money be spent on other things society needs more urgently?" The last questions move the discussion into the realm of reason seeking and addressing an issue.

Another early consideration when preparing for a discussion relates to student preparation. Are they ready? Perhaps you will need to remind the class or individuals about the need to listen, to take turns, and to be clear, reasonable, considerate, and so forth. Some older children may have watched *Firing Line, Meet the Press,* or *The McLaughlin Group* on television. As a result, they may believe a discussion is a verbal "knock-em-down" that stops just short of mental, if not physical, fisticuffs. Of course, if students have already been involved in discussions with good leaders, they should be more effective participants.

Try Activity 7.4

Next, you must think about your role, which raises questions about grouping, physical arrangements, and time management. If your students are not familiar with discussion, you will have to play the role of facilitator-moderator. Relatedly, you may want to hold a *whole-class* discussion with a less experienced group. That way you can exercise more control over such matters as staying on task, providing for equitable participation, and ensuring that everyone enjoys psychological safety. Students more experienced and mature in discussion enable you to take less dominant, directive roles.

Delivery   Once you have determined your purpose, students' readiness, your role, group arrangements, and time constraints, you are now ready to deliver. This means (1) making certain your students understand the purpose of the discussion ("Let's think further about the material on dinosaurs we have read"); (2) ensuring that you have related the discussion to something students previously learned or to something upcoming; (3) informing them of the discussion questions and potential information sources they can use in preparation ("Some discussion questions can be answered directly from the reading; for others, you will need to come up with your own answers or opinions"); reminding them of discussion rules (perhaps by handing out or posting a set of guidelines such as those in Table 7.4); and (4) organizing the participants. If several small groups will discuss, you may want to appoint or ask each group to select a facilitator and a recorder, and, of course, the students in these roles must know what is expected of them.

Throughout a discussion, effective performance of your role as either facilitator-moderator, participant, or observer-recorder is critical. You will especially need to

7.10   What factors from Chapter 1 may influence how you feel about using discussion?

TABLE 7.4 Discussion Guidelines for Students

- Everyone should have an equal opportunity to contribute.
- Encourage your classmates to join in.
- Ensure that everyone contributes by waiting your turn and taking part about as much as everyone else.
- Listen carefully to what others say and feel.
- Work to understand and, whenever possible, to support what others say and feel.
- Understand that your knowledge and ideas may not always be right.
- Stay on target and help others do the same.
- Be gracious with your peers.

remember that this is the students' time to talk: Your role is to encourage participation and elevate the cognitive or affective level of the discourse. *Give the discussants a purpose, a plan, and freedom to operate.*

Use of discussion as an instructional technique draws support and direction from various learning theories (described in Chapter 4), depending upon the purpose of the discussion. To illustrate, suppose the purpose of the discussion is to rehearse or practice. Such learning tasks are easier for students when teachers put to work beliefs and findings related to information processing and behaviorism. Or, suppose the purpose of the discussion is to reflect on events, ideas, or opinions. In such cases, we would want to apply the beliefs and findings from the humanistic school, particularly those relating to values clarification. If the purpose is to engage in problem solving, we might want to use what researchers know about meaningful learning.

Closure At the appropriate moment, the discussion should end. Sometimes it is fitting to close a discussion earlier than planned—for example, when the discussion has accomplished its purpose or when it is failing to do so. In any case, with the possible assistance of the participants, you need to pull the learning together. At this stage, review with students the extent to which they accomplished the purpose of the discussion. Point out where they need to go from here, that is, how the discussion will tie in with future work. A summary of the qualities of good discussion leaders and good discussions appears in Table 7.5 (see p. 190).

A sample discussion lesson plan appears as Lesson Plan 7.2 on page 191.

WHEN DISCUSSIONS SHOULD BE USED

A few guidelines will help you know when to select the discussion alternative from your teaching repertoire, dust it off, and put it to use. As a general rule, you should use discussion when any of its purposes coincide with your goal. Consequently, engage students in discussion when your goal is to review information, examine ideas and opinions, solve problems, or improve oral communication skills. You should also use discussion when you are more interested in long-term memory, higher-order thinking, motivation, attitude change, or moral reasoning. Finally, use discussion when it best meets your students' social and psychological needs. Discussion is effective when students have been mostly inactive listeners, when a more relaxed atmosphere is warranted, and when it would be beneficial to enhance student-to-student friendships and affiliation.

Since there is no research evidence on when or how teachers actually use discussions, our guess is that teachers initiate discussions mostly when pursuing the above goals. However, we are sure you will be guided by other things in your selection of discussion. One is your past experience. Have you been involved in many discussions, and are your remembrances of those experiences positive? Second, how adept are you as an interaction leader, facilitator, or participant? Are you pretty

Try Activity 7.5

TABLE 7.5   Qualities of Good Discussion Leaders and Good Discussions

Good Leaders	Good Discussions
• Believe students want and need to engage in purposeful talk • Believe students should be asked to review and use information, explore issues, and resolve problems • Believe students are capable of thinking and doing for themselves • Believe students can be helped to develop via discussion • Control their own talk • Get students thinking • Serve as skillful facilitators, human relations experts, clarifiers, and summarizers • Are skillful in teaching communication skills	*When preparing:* • Establish the general purpose • Set specific learner objectives • Consider the readiness of the class and individuals for discussion • Decide what role you will play, the class grouping, physical arrangements, and time allowance • Plan the discussion *When overseeing:* • Get students' attention • Ensure that participants understand and see the value in the purpose or goal • Relate the goal and task to previous knowledge and future work • Set out the specific questions or statements to be discussed • Remind participants of discussion rules • Monitor to ensure on-task behavior, balanced participation, and understanding • Encourage participants, elevate the level of discourse *When closing:* • Do so at the most appropriate time rather than at a specific time • Summarize progress toward the goal(s) • Tie new learning to previous knowledge • Establish what the participants might next want to know or be able to do

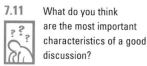

7.11   What do you think are the most important characteristics of a good discussion?

skillful with group interaction? Third, what is your willingness to give up or share the "chalk and talk"? Many teachers, and not just novices, are afraid to let students participate for fear of losing their intellectual or even managerial authority.

LIMITATIONS OF DISCUSSIONS

Although discussion has a goodly number of benefits, it also has shortcomings. Think and be prepared for these. What if the learners do not seem to know what they are supposed to do? What if learners do not know enough or are not mature enough to engage in the discussion? What if learners digress? What if the discussion is dominated by a few? What if some learners are reluctant to participate? As you learned from Table 7.5, you must follow good discussion procedures in order to avoid the above problems.

Discussions will be a disappointment if they are poorly conceptualized, conducted, or when learners are not ready to participate in them successfully (Van Ments, 1990, Battistich, Solomon, & Delucchi, 1993).

Spotlight on Research 7.4 (see p. 192) summarizes the research regarding what makes an effective discussion while Spotlight on Research 7.5 (see p. 193) reveals what students have to say about this instructional alternative.

SUMMARY ON DISCUSSION

Discussions serve at least four purposes: they can review and extend knowledge, examine ideas and opinions, solve problems, and improve oral communication skills. Most classroom discussions serve the first purpose; that is, students review

LESSON PLAN 7.2
Abbreviated Discussion Lesson Plan: Elephants

Curriculum tie-in: This lesson may be linked to the study of Africa, India, or Southeast Asia.

OBJECTIVE

1. Learners will find out, discuss, and organize what is known about elephants. *Specific objective:* Given material containing information about elephants, learners will create semantic maps that organize the knowledge into categories (see Methodology below).

2. They will also correct misconceptions they may hold about elephants, e.g., that male elephants rule the herd.

RESOURCES

1. Print and nonprint material on elephants.

2. Websites on elephants.

METHODOLOGY

1. *Set induction:* Ask learners, "What do you know about elephants?" Allow them to review that knowledge and list it on the chalkboard. DO NOT correct misconceptions at this point. See Closure below.

2. Inform learners of what they will learn and be able to do as a result of this lesson.

3. Inform learners that they (a) should locate knowledge about elephants, (b) list the knowledge on paper as you did at the chalkboard, (c) be prepared to share the knowledge with the class, and (d) be prepared to organize the knowledge in some way.

4. Following the independent work, learners discuss what they found and discuss how they think that knowledge can be organized.

5. The learners are guided as they discuss how the knowledge can be organized using semantic mapping. Put the term elephant on the chalkboard. Have students discuss what they have found out about elephants that can be categorized and into what categories the information seems to fit. Examples include

- Where elephants are found.
- An elephant's characteristics.
- What elephant families are like.
- Elephant food.
- Importance of elephants.
- Elephant enemies.

ASSESSMENT

1. Move around the room to monitor progress toward the following:
   Are learners knowledgeable about elephants?
   Are they able to construct semantic maps of the knowledge they have gained?
   Are they finding that certain things they believed true about elephants may not be so?

2. Reteach as necessary.

CLOSURE

1. Have learners discuss what they have learned and to what extent it is consistent with what they previously knew or thought they knew.

---

information they have previously learned from a presentation or from reading. Even then, however, students should review the material at the highest cognitive level. They should be prompted to analyze, synthesize, and evaluate information rather than merely be asked to respond to lower-level, factual questions as in a prototypical recitation.

In addition to their many purposes, discussions are characterized by multiple interactions with the teacher assuming the role of either facilitator-monitor, participant, or observer-recorder. Discussions may be whole-class or small-group in nature, and groups may vary in size and composition. For maximum effectiveness, participants must be arranged face to face.

Good discussion leaders need to hold certain beliefs and possess special abilities which are summarized in Table 7.5, column 1. Discussions can be improved by following the guidelines for preparation, delivery, and closure found in Table 7.5, column 2.

A number of advantages accrue from using discussion. Discussion provides personal and professional benefits for teachers and personal and educational benefits for participants. Research shows that discussions promote retention of knowledge and high-level thinking. They also contribute to learner motivation, attitude change, and somewhat enhanced moral reasoning.

Guidelines help teachers determine when to use discussions. Most likely, your actual use of discussion will be affected by past experiences, related abilities, and confidence in sharing teaching and learning with students.

Try Activity 7.6

Only a small number of studies of discussion have taken place in elementary and secondary classrooms. The rest have been conducted using university students, workers in business and industry, and adult volunteers for psychological studies. Gall (1987) provides us with the most recent summary of those findings. The interpretations and explanations, if any, are ours.

- Discussion generally is more effective than teacher presentation or lecture for promoting retention of knowledge and higher-level thinking (such as analysis, synthesis, and evaluation). This likely is true because the opportunity for rehearsing or using information is greater during discussion.
- Use of discussion generally results in increased motivation to learn. This probably is because engagement in discussion meets the personality needs of many students.
- Discussion is effective in changing attitudes and, to some extent, in advancing moral reasoning. Discussion can create a forum for ideas and idea changes.
- Discussion is less effective than lecture in helping students acquire factual knowledge. Presentations appear to be superior for sheer communication of information.
- After a discussion group reaches consensus, it tends to disregard any further, high-quality ideas that are presented. The group probably has struggled to reach a consensus and fears that new ideas would distract from it.
- Less capable but socially aggressive individuals may dominate discussions.
- Small group size results in more participation, increased satisfaction among members, and greater academic achievement.
- Groups in which members are more alike or homogeneous are more cohesive, communicate more, and experience greater self-esteem.

Heterogeneous groups may be more effective in performance. Birds of a feather may feel more comfortable together, but they may not challenge or assist one another sufficiently.

- Groups without a teacher leader or assertive members interact more often. They also achieve greater satisfaction from the discussion and are effective in handling complex tasks.

Watson's (1983) study is not among those that Gall reviewed. Watson observed ninety "discussion lessons" in English secondary school classrooms and concluded, somewhat negatively, that (1) students were mostly held accountable for knowing facts; (2) teachers did most of the higher-level thinking such as making generalizations, hypothesizing, and synthesizing; and (3) teachers did most of the talking. Watson concludes that most English teachers prefer whole-class discussion, which in this case amounted to a euphemism for teacher question—student answer, or recitation.

Independent Study: Teaching as Giving and Guiding Seat Work and Homework Assignments

A third commonly used instructional alternative is independent study or work, which, at times, is referred to as "seat work." We all can recall the countless hours we have spent, mostly alone, working on school assignments. Estimates are that students spend as much as 70 percent of their in-class time working independently. Add to that the time given to homework, and it's obvious that teachers rely heavily on independent study or practice (Dunkin, 1987).

WHAT IS INDEPENDENT STUDY?

7.12 What good and bad personal school experiences come to mind when you think of independent study?

We define **independent study** as any school-related assignment students do more or less alone. Examples include reading, writing a composition, rehearsing words for a spelling test, and preparing a report. When we think of students "working," we often envision them engaged in some kind of independent study or practice assignment.

PURPOSE AND CHARACTERISTICS OF INDEPENDENT STUDY

We can describe independent study on the basis of its purposes, types, teacher role, and the context in which it takes place.

When researchers at Stanford University (Phelan, Davidson, & Cao, 1992) asked high school students questions about their school experiences, they received many comments on both teachers and teaching. From these comments, the researchers concluded that "both high- and low-achieving students prefer teachers who draw them into the learning process by holding discussions in which ideas are explored and thoughts, feelings, and opinions are shared" (p. 700). Furthermore, the researchers concluded from students' remarks that during discussions, learners feel important and feel that what they think counts. Students are particularly complimentary of teachers who make the classroom a place where they feel comfortable in expressing themselves. As one student reported,

> [The teacher] makes the class feel comfortable talking about themselves and really expressing their feelings. Like if you read something and everyone interprets it differently, she wants to hear everyone's opinion. (p. 700)

Purposes of Independent Study   Teachers involve students in independent study for many reasons, some more justifiable than others. It is most justifiable *when students need to rehearse or practice something.* In Chapter 4, you saw how important it is for learners to rehearse what they are learning by thinking about it or repeating it. That is partly why we have interspersed questions and activities in the margins of this book. Rehearsal is part of information processing: It gets new information into our long-term memories.

As a teacher, you will probably use independent practice when you want to be certain that your learners gain specific knowledge or skills. Thus, if you are an elementary or middle school teacher, your students definitely will rehearse or practice reading comprehension skills, language arts skills such as writing paragraphs, and mathematics skills such as solving story problems and computation. Secondary teachers provide students with practice too, as do athletic coaches. If you have participated in sports, think of the innumerable times you have practiced shooting foul shots, dribbling a soccer ball, or flutter kicking until these acts became part of your motor memory.

There just is no way to avoid the need to provide students with opportunities to learn through rehearsal or practice. Obviously, students can also rehearse or practice information in a group discussion, but we cannot be sure students know something until they show they can use it independently.

The ultimate goal of formal education is to *help students learn how to learn* so that eventually they are not dependent upon schools or teachers. This is a second purpose served by independent study since it encourages students to acquire study skills

CHAPTER 7
Four Instructional Alternatives:
Presentation, Discussion, Independent
Study, and Individualized Instruction

193

"It's moments like this—when they're all so very, very quiet—that I get a strange, uneasy feeling."

that will serve them throughout life. These skills include how to locate, analyze, synthesize, and evaluate information. The more opportunities learners have to dig out, judge, and use information, the better equipped they will be to learn on their own. The curious child who was helped to learn about life in a pond at age 10 is more likely to want and be able to find out about our disappearing wetlands at age 20.

Independent study is also used, and occasionally misused, as a means to other ends. For example, teachers can use it for convenience. This would be the case *when learners are given work to keep them busy ("busywork") because their teachers must do something else.* The something else might be working with other students or simply taking a breather. Working with other students, of course, is necessary and therefore justifiable.

The worst misuse of independent study we have observed occurred in a school where one of the authors was principal. Stanley I., a teacher, loved to read. In fact, he often gave his middle school students independent work so that *he* could read. After giving his class the assignment, Stanley went to his desk, sat down, and opened the middle drawer where he always kept a novel. Students were not permitted to interrupt or to come to his desk. When someone came to his door, Stanley rose slowly and, with his upper legs, inconspicuously closed the drawer to conceal his covert activity.

It may take learners a while to catch on to the misuse of independent study or practice, but they can and do, as evidenced from the student's comment in Case 7.1.

Types of Independent Study By *type* of independent study, we refer to whether the teacher prescribes the work assignment or learners freely choose it. Teachers normally determine the material to be rehearsed. However, when the purpose is to provide opportunities to develop and practice independent study skills, students could select the work. For example, suppose you are teaching a unit on biography. Students could read a common biography you assign, or they could select one of personal interest.

Teacher's Role As with presentation and discussion, the objective of independent study is to facilitate students' learning and satisfaction. Clearly, learning and satisfaction during independent study are in jeopardy if you are not available to guide and monitor your students' work. Failure to monitor independent work is a tragic error. Students left entirely on their own may not only fail to learn but learn incorrectly. Of course, when independent study takes the form of homework, monitoring is not possible. Increasingly, however, parents are being asked to supervise and

I remember a history teacher in high school. I really liked her because her class was so organized and orderly. When we came in there were *x* number of questions on the chalkboard. We read a certain section of the book and wrote out the answers. When time ran out she would ask, "Do you have any questions?" As she said the word *questions*, the bell always rang. Now I've figured out she taught that way just to keep us busy. We didn't have time to do anything but write out answers. That wasn't really teaching!

There was no interaction of ideas and people. No real class.

Source: E. M. Bower. (1973). *Teachers talk about their feelings* (p. 17). Rockville, MD: National Institute of Mental Health, Center for Studies of Child and Family Health.

assist students with their homework. Unfortunately, parental availability, interest, and capacity to assist students vary. Some may be better teachers than we are; others might not have a clue about helping a child.

Context   We have already alluded to the fact that students can do independent work either in school or as homework. In-school assignments can be accomplished at a variety of times and in different places. Students reading biographies could work on them during class, during study or library periods, or after other class work has been completed. Some schools even have before- and after-school arrangements that give students an additional time and place to do independent work.

Figure 7.3 reviews the purposes and key characteristics of independent study.

GOOD INDEPENDENT STUDY LEADERS

If you are going to use independent study well, you must believe in its purposes and values, particularly as a way to provide rehearsal or practice and as a way to help students learn how to learn. Furthermore, you must have confidence in your students' ability to work alone.

7.13   Which beliefs about use of independent study do you hold?

Additionally, you must know how to get and keep learners involved in worthwhile independent activities. Kounin (1970) is most helpful here. He and his colleagues observed the behavior of teachers whose students stayed engaged in their seat-work assignments. The teachers had several things in common. They demonstrated valence and challenge arousal, variety and challenge, withitness, and overlapping. Since these terms are Kounin's inventions, they require definition.

Valence and challenge arousal is the ability to engender curiosity and enthusiasm in students and to get them involved in the independent work. Obviously, teachers who are enthusiastic themselves are more likely to beget enthusiasm in their learners. In Chapter 11, you will learn more about teacher enthusiasm.

Variety and challenge involves the ability to identify and assign independent study assignments that vary enough to be interesting and are challenging enough to maintain attention. Such assignments need to be demanding but not defeating. What we know from Chapter 4 about gaining and holding attention applies here.

Withitness is the ability to communicate to learners that we know what they are doing even when we are not nearby or looking at them. Perhaps you can recall teachers who seemed to have eyes in the back of their heads. Withitness is this kind of sixth sense.

Overlapping is the teacher's ability to attend to more than one thing at a time. In a sense it is akin to being a juggler. This ability is especially important when working with one or more students, such as when you are directing a group activity while the rest of the class works independently. In such cases, you work with one group while simultaneously monitoring the other students. You will learn more about overlapping and withitness in Chapter 13.

7.14   How do you feel about your ability to use *valence and challenge arousal, variety and challenge, withitness,* and *overlapping?*

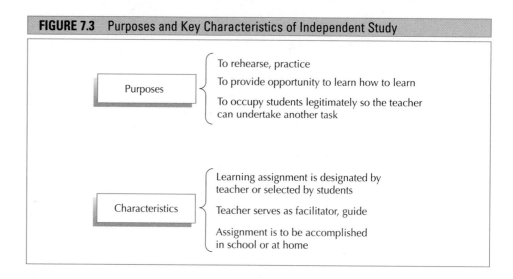

FIGURE 7.3 Purposes and Key Characteristics of Independent Study

Purposes
- To rehearse, practice
- To provide opportunity to learn how to learn
- To occupy students legitimately so the teacher can undertake another task

Characteristics
- Learning assignment is designated by teacher or selected by students
- Teacher serves as facilitator, guide
- Assignment is to be accomplished in school or at home

GOOD INDEPENDENT STUDY

Considerable agreement exists about what must be done to ensure good independent study (Anderson, Brubaker, Alleman-Brooks, & Duffy, 1984; Brophy & Good, 1986; Emmer et al., 1981; English, 1984; Gilstrap & Martin, 1975; Rosenshine, 1980; Rupley & Blair, 1987; Slavin, 1999). Let's review that opinion in terms of the preparation, delivery, and closure of independent study assignments.

Preparation   After determining a general purpose and specific instructional objectives, you must determine whether independent study is the instructional alternative of choice. As mentioned earlier, independent study seems preferable when the purpose is to have learners (1) practice or rehearse information, (2) acquire better self-study or learning skills, or (3) remain occupied in some legitimate way so you can undertake another teaching task, perhaps work with a reading group.

Try Activity 7.7   Next, determine the assignment type. Should all students receive a standard assignment, or should they be able to select one of their choice? In either case, we are advised to make sure their assignments are interesting, concise, and at the correct level of difficulty. Of course, older students can work independently for longer periods of time than younger ones, but it is wise to ensure that the assignment does not outlive the learner's interest in it. With regard to the assignment's level of difficulty, scholars suggest that the learner success rate should be somewhere between 80 and 100 percent. In other words, the assignment should be within the students' reach.

Whether the assignment is teacher-mandated or learner-selected, resources must be available so that students can undertake the task comfortably and successfully. If your assignment of choice is to have each student read a biography, a large assorted collection must be available so that the needs of diverse students are met.

Delivery   Delivery involves making the study assignment and guiding it to a satisfactory conclusion. When making the assignment, attention, valence and challenge arousal, and clarity are most important. Clarity is discussed in detail in Chapter 12. Clarity requires that you inform learners of the lesson's rationale, that is, why the assignment is important. To be clear, you must also ensure that students know specifically what they are to do and how to accomplish it. Instructions should also include time limits and indicate what students must or may do if they complete the assignment early. Learners should also be told precisely when and how they may get help. Can you remember times when you couldn't get help and how debilitating that was? This often happens when the independent work is to be done outside class.

"Omigosh! My science project is gone!"

What is your role during independent study? Foremost, it is to actively guide and facilitate learning. This cannot be done as novel-loving teacher Stanley I. did. Rather, you must be alert ("withit") and, whenever possible, be on your feet, moving, monitoring, interacting with individual learners, and diagnosing their progress. Even when you assign independent study in order to work on another teaching task, you cannot closet yourself from your students or shirk the responsibility of making sure they are doing all right. Thus, as Kounin (1970) notes, you need to have or to develop the capacity of overlapping—the ability to deal with more than one thing at a time. Finally, if your students are to be on task in their independent work, you must protect them from each other's needless, distracting interruptions. Properly delivered, independent study may require more of you than giving a presentation or guiding a discussion. Giving students something to do and ensuring their success is not that simple.

Like presentation and discussion, independent study draws support from learning theory. When its purpose is to rehearse or practice, follow the principles outlined in Chapter 4 for information processing and behaviorism. However, when the purpose is to help students learn how to learn, you will find assistance in the cognitive and humanistic or affective schools of thought. To illustrate, if you want students to independently learn something that is mostly cognitive, or knowledge-related, key principles from the cognitive school of thought should guide them. When they are to learn something mostly affective or relating to attitudes or values, the beliefs and findings of the humanistic school apply.

Closure   A major error many teachers make is to underestimate the importance of correctly closing a lesson. An independent study assignment is no exception. You cannot just create a worthwhile assignment, give it, and then forget it. You have to "close the deal." But what does that mean? Experts say you must collect the assignment, assess it, count it, and give learners feedback on how well it was done. Reteaching may also be in order. Reteaching is not done enough. Failure to do any of these things sends a message that independent work is not serious business—just busywork intended to occupy the learner's time. Remember the teacher (Case 7.1) who left no time at the end of class for students' questions? Perhaps you can recall teachers who gave you busywork. Without a doubt, students eventually catch on. When they sense that your assignment doesn't count, don't expect them to take it seriously. Would you?

7.15   Now that you are aware of what it takes to have good independent study, what would you suggest the teacher in the Case 7.1 scenario needs to do?

TABLE 7.6	Qualities of Good Independent Study Leaders and Good Independent Study

Good Leaders	Good Independent Study
• Believe independent study enhances learning through rehearsal • Believe independent study enhances learning how to learn • Believe students can work successfully independently • Exhibit clarity, valence and challenge arousal, variety and challenge, withitness, and overlapping	*When preparing:* • Establish the general purpose • Set specific instructional objectives • Consider the ability of individual learners to work independently • Plan the assignment so that it is interesting and at the optimal level of difficulty and length • Collect, prepare instructional resources *When delivering:* • Get students' attention • Inform learners of the rationale for the assignment and of the objectives • Relate assignment to previous and upcoming work • Make sure learners know what to do and how to do it before work begins • Make certain learners know when and how they may get help • Make sure learners know what to do if they finish early • Be alert, move about to monitor and interact with learners • Diagnose students' progress and provide assistance when needed *When closing:* • Collect assignments • Assess assignments • Provide feedback to students • Count assignments toward the grade

7.16 What do you think are the most important characteristics of independent study?

Try Activity 7.8

Expect and collect the assignment on time, holding the learner accountable. Assess the assignment, and go over it with students as soon as possible. Some whole-class, in-class assignments can be reviewed immediately. For example, if students take time for in-class practice in mathematics, go over the answers with them right away. Provide imediate feedback. And, don't forget to count independent study assignments as part of the grade. Walberg (1984) finds that when homework assignments are graded, student achievement improves.

A summary of the qualities of good independent study leaders and good independent study is contained in Table 7.6. Spotlight on Research 7.6 also explores what makes for good independent study. A sample independent study lesson plan is contained in Lesson Plan 7.3.

WHEN INDEPENDENT STUDY SHOULD BE USED

To reiterate, independent study should be used (1) when learners need to rehearse or practice information or a skill to get it into long-term memory, or (2) when learners need to learn how to learn independently. In the first case, we are saying that students need to practice: Remember the old adage "Practice makes perfect." In the second case, we are saying that a major, if not the ultimate, goal of education is to assist students in learning *how* to learn so that they no longer need schools and teachers. *They* are empowered!

Although we lack evidence to support our assumption, we believe independent study is used mostly in K–12 schools as a means to practice or rehearse. We think it

What Makes Independent Study Effective?

Fortunately, a little more research on this instructional alternative is available than is available for either discussion or presentation. The studies have taken place in K–12 schools, although mostly in elementary and middle grades. While Scott (1989) and Anderson (1995) provide the most recent general literature review, the individual studies of Emmer, Everston, Sanford, and Clements (1982), Fisher et al. (1980), Good & Grouws (1975), Gump (1967), Kounin (1970), Gartland (1986), and Rosenshine (1980) are most helpful. Most investigators have looked at independent study when its purpose is to rehearse or practice information just received through presentation or recitation.

Gump (1967) reports on the incidence of independent study, a strategy he finds commonly employed in elementary school classrooms. Rosenshine (1980) notes that independent assignments are usually both appropriate and at the correct level of difficulty. As we have already learned, Kounin (1970) finds that learners are more likely to be on task during independent study when teachers demonstrate valence and challenge arousal, variety and challenge, withitness, and overlapping. Several scholars found that the ingredients of good independent study are clarity of purpose, assignment, and procedures; good monitoring; and the provision of immediate feedback to learners (Emmer et al., 1982; Fisher et al., 1980). With regard to monitoring, Fisher et al. (1980) found that when teachers interact briefly but meaningfully with students during independent work, the students' on-task time increases by about 10 percent. Relatedly, Good and Grouws (1975) report that teachers whose students achieve more have more contacts with learners at work. Furthermore, these teachers take monitoring opportunities to give students relevant feedback and so help them be successful. Finally, Gartland (1986) finds that teachers should not provide student with more whole-class practice during a teacher presentation but instead should provide them with more monitored independent practice.

is used much less to prepare students for lifelong learning, although everyone recalls working on self-propelling independent reports. We also believe many teachers use this practice for a third purpose: to keep some students legitimately occupied so that teachers can work with other students in, say, a reading or math group. The key word is *legitimately*. Unfortunately, it is too easy to give students work that is nothing more than busywork; in other words, its sole intention is to keep students occupied.

One of the authors recalls visiting in a daughter's first-grade classroom on parents' night. The teacher was entertaining questions. One mother asked, "Why do the children spend day after day coloring dittoes and cutting them out?" The teacher, stymied for a moment and perhaps feeling found out, stammered a possibly suitable but unlikely answer: "To improve eye-hand coordination."

7.17 What factors in Chapter 1 may influence how you feel about independent study?

LIMITATIONS OF INDEPENDENT STUDY

Perhaps the greatest drawback to independent study is not with the technique itself but with its intentions, conduct, and assessment. If the intentions of such study are not clear and reasonable, students may resist the assignments or exert minimal effort. Said another way, when learners do not perceive the task as meeting some need or having value, they will not honor it.

In terms of the conduct of independent study, be forewarned that you must monitor the study, provide feedback, and help students see that the assignment is as valuable as other work (Anderson, 1981; Anderson, Brubaker, Alleman-Brooks, & Duffy, 1984; Dembo, 1994; Seifert & Beck, 1984).

7.18 How do you feel about the use of independent study?

MAKING GOOD HOMEWORK ASSIGNMENTS

Homework assignments are a form of independent study. Therefore, almost all the information in the section on independent study applies here. However, there are some additional tips that apply specifically when homework assignments are used (Paulu, 1998).

Abbreviated Independent Study Lesson: Writing a Brief Biography

Curriculum tie-in: This lesson may be linked to studies in almost any subject field.

OBJECTIVE

1. Learners will collect and synthesize biographical information, then prepare a brief, written biography. *Specific objectives:* Learners will

    a. Select a target person for whom a biography will be prepared.

    b. Establish what they want to learn about the person.

    c. Collect related information utilizing resources such as print material, electronic encyclopedias, the Internet, and the like.

    d. Organize found information into categories determined in *b* above.

    e. Synthesize the most interesting, useful information in each category.

    f. Prepare a written story of the target person's life that is organized, interesting, and follows the rules for spelling, grammar, and capitalization.

RESOURCES

1. Print and nonprint biographical resources: books, periodicals, electronic encyclopedias, and Internet sites on biography.

2. Activity sheet to be prepared that illustrates the categories of information that learners might seek about their target person.

METHODOLOGY

1. *Set induction:* "Have you ever seen the television show "Biography"? What is a biography? What biographies have you read or seen? Why do you suppose biographies are so interesting and helpful? How might learning about a person who is related to what we are studying be interesting and helpful?"

2. Inform learners of what they will learn and be able to do as a result of the lesson (see Objective above).

3. Get learners to consider the process of writing a biography: "How do you suppose a biography is written? What steps would need to be followed?" List steps on the board.

4. Have learners make a list of questions, the answers to which they think would provide the basis of an interesting (rather than boring) and informative biography.

5. Set parameters for the task: deadlines for selecting target person, for completing information collection and organization, for story length and completion.

6. Make certain learners know from whom and how they can get help.

7. Tell students that it is important that you monitor their progress and how you will do so.

ASSESSMENT

1. Learners will prepare a brief biography that targets a key person (one related to the study at hand) and that shows evidence of careful planning, organization, and good presentation as noted in the Objective.

CLOSURE

1. Have learners review the purpose of the task and how it will be accomplished.

2. Discuss ways by which the biographies will be used in class: oral presentations, classroom exhibits, placing them on the class or school website.

- Let learners, parents, and caregivers know when and how often assignments will be made and approximately how long they will be. Rules of thumb are as follows: for young children, no more than twenty minutes a *school day;* for fourth through sixth graders, twenty to forty minutes for most learners, for seventh through ninth graders, two hours a day, for older students two and a half hours per *school day.*

- Make sure that assignments serve a good purpose. They permit learners to review or practice what they are studying, allow learners to explore something in greater depth or breadth, get learners ready to learn something in the next day's class, or teach learners how to use learning resources such as libraries and reference materials. Never use homework for punishment (a bad purpose since it then is thought of in negative terms).

- Make certain that learners understand the good purpose and meaning of the assignment.

- Ensure that the assignment is clear and that learners know both what is to be accomplished and how.

"When do you get to start leaving your work at the office?"

- Make assignments that are neither too easy nor too difficult. Make absolutely certain that learners are capable of successfully accomplishing the work *before* they leave you.
- Vary assignments. Try to create assignments that provide for individual differences in how students learn (see Learning Style Diffrerences in Chapter 3). Take into account that your learners have different ability and attention differences (see Learning Ability Differences in Chapter 3).
- Teach school study habits that transfer to homework assignments (such as the need to eliminate distractions and the need to make certain materials necessary to complete the assignment are available).
- Provide learners with feedback on their work. Learners must have knowledge of results. What did they do well and not so well? Provide help (reteaching) as needed. Unexamined assignments are useless to the learner and convince students that they were just busywork. Worse yet, student errors go uncorrected, and thus are learned.
- Work with parents and caregivers to ensure that home assignments are meeting your expectations and theirs in terms of quality and length and find out what effects (positive and negative) they are having on a learner's home life.

Remember, good homework, like a good school assignment, encourages love of learning while bad homework is destructive.

Spotlight on Research 7.7 (see p. 202) presents what research tells us about homework.

SUMMARY ON INDEPENDENT STUDY

Try Activity 7.9

Independent study is an excellent instructional alternative that serves several important purposes. Mostly teachers use it for practice or rehearsal of information. However, it also helps students acquire study and inquiry skills that will serve them throughout life. During independent work, your role is to facilitate and guide learning. To do so, you must not only be available, but also must actively monitor. When you are not available or cannot monitor, as with home assignments, you must find someone else to fill this role.

Since considerable consensus exists regarding the benefits of independent study and how to conduct good independent study assignments, you should make use of this instructional alternative. Doing so will make you a better teacher and help your students achieve and be satisfied.

How much homework is done? A survey of 11 countries, the United States excluded, reports that the average range per week for 14 year olds is four and a half to nine hours. Another study comparing primary and secondary Japanese and American students reveals that the former spend four to five times as much time studying outside school.

How much homework should be done? More is usually better. However, the amount and kind depend on a number of variables: time available for the learner to accomplish the tasks and the teacher to provide feedback on it; learner ability and disposition; and material to be completed or mastered. It is important to have high expectations but also to be realistic.

What is the effect of doing homework on student achievement? Studies show that homework assignments have fairly consistent, positive effects on student learning. A study of students in Canada and the United States reveals that the achievement of a typical student at the 50th percentile of achievement doing no homework would move up to the 65th percentile if an average amount of homework was done. When homework is evaluated by the teacher in addition to merely being assigned, there is a substantial effect on achievement.

What are learner attitudes toward homework? Students aren't usually crazy about homework and rate it lower than all other major activities they engage in except work. As we would expect, students who fall behind academically find their classroom work and homework less satisfying and harder.

Source: Adapted from H. Walberg & R. Paschal. (1995). Homework. In L. Anderson (Ed.), *International encyclopedia of teaching and teacher education* (pp. 268–271). Oxford: Pergamon Press.

Individualized or Differentiated Instruction: Tailoring Teaching

7.19 How do you feel about individualism as opposed to conformity? To what extent should teachers tailor instructions to fit individuals?

If you want to get teachers upset, remark that classrooms in Japanese schools have many more students, as many as fifty. Why is the thought of large classes so distressing? Because American teachers, among others, believe that individual students cannot be well served when classes are large. After all, individuals and individualism is what America is all about. So we have striven to provide for individuals and individualism. How? Through individualized instruction.

WHAT IS INDIVIDUALIZED INSTRUCTION?

Individualized instruction is the term used to refer to any instructional maneuver that attempts to tailor teaching and learning to a learner's, or a group of like learners', unique strengths and needs. Said another way, individualized instruction means responding educationally to individuals. In Chapter 3, we found out that teachers must, according to the Individuals with Disabilities Education Act, develop an individualized educational program (IEP) for each student with educational challenges or handicaps. Of course, to a lesser extent, teachers try to meet the special needs of all children. You can probably recall some teachers who, more than others, took into account your strengths and needs.

As you will soon see, various types of individualized instruction exist. Each type more or less individualizes instruction. By "more or less," we mean some types do more, or go farther than others, in addressing learners' strengths or meeting learners' needs.

PURPOSE AND CHARACTERISTICS OF INDIVIDUALIZED INSTRUCTION

Individualized, personalized instruction has unique attributes. As the name implies, its most unique purpose is to tailor teaching to an individual's peculiar strengths and needs. No other instructional maneuver does just that.

The characteristics of individualized instruction also set it apart. Consider the role of the teacher. When individualizing instruction is the goal, the teacher's role is to know and care about individuals, about the diversity of students. The teacher can't teach the class as though everyone in it is alike any more than parents can treat their children as if they are all the same. It just won't do.

Another characteristic that sets individualized instruction apart is the unique way in which it deals with these five variables: the *goals of instruction, learning activities, resources, mastery level,* and *time.* When learners have a great deal of autonomy in regard to these five factors, we can say that instruction really has been *tailored, differentiated, customized,* or *personalized.* Let's consider each variable.

Goals of Instruction   As we learned in Chapter 6, the "formal curriculum" is set by the state and local school district. For the most part, teachers teach that curriculum. Perhaps all fourth grade classrooms study the history of Native Americans, while in the tenth grade everyone studies American government. However, what if one or more fourth graders is interested in learning about the discovery of gold in California and Alaska or some tenth graders want to study African-American history? To the extent that teachers allow students to choose the topic or subtopic of study, they are individualizing instruction, that is, meeting individual needs.

Learning Activities   In most classrooms, all students are asked to follow a similar learning procedure. For example, if the teacher's goal is to study the history of Native Americans, the teacher usually spells out how the class will do this. However, the teacher, after setting the goal, could permit a good deal of autonomy with regard to how individual students might attain the goal. In this case, the instructor could say, "We are going to study Native Americans. How would you like to do this? Would some of you prefer to read? To look at recorded documentaries? To interview Native Americans?" The greater the instructional autonomy teachers grant, the more they are individualizing and personalizing. Teacher Laurie Biser in Case 7.2 "How Teachers Individualize (see p. 204)," allows her learners this freedom of choice.

Resources   Even though students have individual preferences about how they want to learn, they need further individualization. For example, if several students want to learn about Native Americans through reading, a number of different kinds and levels of reading material must be made available. Teacher Rob Frescoln in Case 7.2, "How Teachers Individualize," makes such provision. Providing autonomy to choose how to learn carries individualization only so far. Providing a variety of resource materials for different ability levels takes it further.

Mastery Level   Another way you can individualize is to accept different levels of performance from different students. This is complicated because you also need to have high expectations for all. Perhaps the best way to put it is to have high expectations for all learners but even higher expectations for some. Thus, you might want all children to achieve at some agreed-upon level but want others to surpass that

CHAPTER 7
Four Instructional Alternatives:
Presentation, Discussion, Independent
Study, and Individualized Instruction

203

Willis and Mann (2000) provide illustrations of how teachers individualize instruction.

Pat Rutz, an East Hanover, New Jersey, primary teacher, differentiates learning activities for kids strong in math by allowing them to pursue higher-level math independently. For example, if some learners know the concept of place value, they are challenged by other related activities while she teaches the basic concept to the rest of the class.

When Ann Arbor, Michigan, fourth-grade teacher Laurie Biser teaches the multiplication facts, she is very aware that her students will learn them best when a variety of approaches are permitted. So, she expects them to learn using drawing, flash cards, or manipulatives (objects that may be arranged and rearranged such as coins and collector cards). Biser also uses contracts that permit students to choose from a variety of spelling activities worth different point values depending upon the level of difficulty. (See *contracts* in the section below, The Dalton and Winnetka Plans.)

Seventh-grade Chapel Hill, North Carolina, teacher Rob Frescoln accepts that his students differ greatly in their reading and writing skills. Thus, when they do research papers he provides a variety of texts at different reading levels. Furthermore, he has students work in mixed ability groups, each reading at his own level and then sharing what has been learned with the others. Frescoln believes that this approach helps all students to push themselves just a bit further.

Gaithersburg, Maryland, secondary social studies teacher Leon Bushe likes to engage students in mock trials. He divides his class of 30 into three groups of 10 and gives each group a court case involving a legal concept such as "beyond a reasonable doubt." Learners choose the role they wish to play (lawyers, witnesses, judge, etc.). To prepare for their roles in the trial and the trial itself, students must complete individualized reading and writing assignments.

Source: S. Willis & L. Mann. (2000, Winter). Differentiating Instruction. *Curriculum Update* (pp. 1–3, 6–7). Alexandria, VA: Association for Supervision and Curriculum Development.

---

level—to excel. In studying the history of Native Americans, children with little previous related knowledge could be expected to reach level X, while children who have had a keen interest in and prior knowledge of Native Americans could be expected to reach level Y. As Brophy and Evertson (1976) note, "The very idea of individualized instruction implies that there is a certain level of difficulty or content specificity that is optimal for each student" (p. 61). Teacher Pat Rutz in Case 7.2 provides different mastery levels.

7.20 In which ways are you most likely to individualize instruction?

Time The final variable that can be manipulated for individuals is time. You can, as is usually the case, expect all students to accomplish the goal in the same amount of time. Or time can be flexible, with some students taking more than others.

To repeat, individualized instruction has a unique purpose and characteristics. Its purpose is to serve the individual rather than the entire class. Consequently, the teacher is called upon to know and care about student diversity. The nature or character of individualized instruction is a function of several factors. It can differ according to the amount of autonomy given students to select what they will do and how they will do it. It can also differ according to the resources they have available, the level of mastery they are expected to achieve, and the time they are given to complete the task. Figure 7.4 depicts the key characteristics of individualized instruction.

7.21 Which of the various forms of individualized instruction have you experienced? What were they like for you?

TYPES OF INDIVIDUALIZED INSTRUCTION PROGRAMS

We have identified a number of procedures and programs that have been generated to individualize instruction. As you read about each, ask yourself, "To what extent does this idea really get at individual strengths and needs?"

The Dalton and Winnetka Plans Two of the earliest efforts toward individualization were the Dalton and Winnetka plans. The Dalton plan divided the school day into two instructional parts. In the morning, students had free time to work, often indepen-

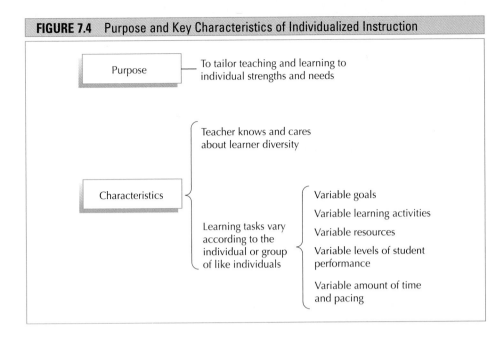

FIGURE 7.4 Purpose and Key Characteristics of Individualized Instruction

Purpose — To tailor teaching and learning to individual strengths and needs

Characteristics

- Teacher knows and cares about learner diversity
- Learning tasks vary according to the individual or group of like individuals
  - Variable goals
  - Variable learning activities
  - Variable resources
  - Variable levels of student performance
  - Variable amount of time and pacing

dently, without interruption, and at their own pace on contracted monthly assignments (Lawry, 1987a). In the afternoon, groups of learners engaged in social, vocational, and physical activity. The **contracts** were agreements students signed attesting that they would do certain prescribed academic work in mathematics, social studies, English, foreign language, or science. More recently, individual student contracts also prescribe, rather than leave open-ended, the time frame in which the work must be completed. Learners may also contract work at different levels of achievement and difficulty. Work contracted at a high level of achievement, when properly completed, would earn the learner a grade of A. Less demanding and difficult work would earn a lower grade. A format for a contract is shown in Highlight 7.3 (see p. 206). To learn more about what a Dalton type school is like, visit www.dalton.org.

The Winnetka plan also set aside the morning for the study of academic subjects such as arithmetic, reading, and language arts, which included handwriting, spelling, writing, and grammar. Students learned these subjects mostly through self-instruction. Consequently, many self-instructional textbooks and other materials were specially written, and students were periodically tested on their knowledge and skills (Lawry, 1987c). The Winnetka scheme of self-instruction using specially prepared materials was the forerunner of programmed and computer-assisted instruction and Individually Prescribed Instruction, described below.

Web Resource

Programmed and Computer-Assisted Instruction Programmed and computer-assisted instruction are outgrowths of the Winnetka plan (Lawry, 1987b). They were described in Chapter 4 as examples of instruction following the behavioral school of thought.

Both programmed instruction (PI) and computer-assisted instruction (CAI) use self-instructional formats. The material to be learned is broken down into small, easily learned segments. When students finish one segment correctly, they go to the next. If a student does not understand, he is redirected to try again or is provided additional information that facilitates understanding. Newer programs actually diagnose students' mistakes and provide them with highly individualized feedback. Some computer-assisted instruction has become very creative (see Case 7.3 on p. 207).

Individually Prescribed Instruction (IPI) IPI is described by Jeter (1980). At the beginning of a school year, IPI students are pretested in several subject areas to find out what they already know. According to the results, students are assigned work at

CHAPTER 7
Four Instructional Alternatives:
Presentation, Discussion, Independent
Study, and Individualized Instruction

205

Sixth-grade teacher John Swang (1993) has students use contracts in his middle school science classes. A modified form is shown here. Note that the student, parent, and teacher must all sign.

The National Student Research Center Scientific Research Contract

Date: _____

Student's signature: _____

Parent's signature: _____

Teacher's signature: _____

1. I would like to do a scientific research project on _____

2. I am interested in this topic because _____

3. Some of the questions I want to answer are _____

4. I will collect information from these sources: _____

   _____ Encyclopedia   _____ Journals

   _____ Trade books   _____ Atlas

   _____ Textbooks   _____ Almanac

   _____ Newspapers   _____ Other. Name: _____

   _____ Databases

5. My project will be ready by _____

appropriate academic levels. Students do not necessarily work alone; they may be given tasks to complete with other learners who are at the same level. At set intervals in the curriculum, learners take tests. If they are successful, they move on. If not, instruction is repeated.

Individually Guided Education (IGE)   IGE is another form of individualized instruction. A major difference between IGE and other systems is that IGE is done in a "nongraded" school. A **nongraded school** is one in which grade levels are blurred or nonexistent. In IGE schools, several teachers may be assigned to a unit of 100 to 150 students who would typically span several grade levels in achievement. The team of teachers develops and evaluates an instructional program for each child. "Ideally, each child's program is based on how and at what pace he learns best, and where he stands on mastering specific skills and concepts" (Rossmiller, 1976, p. 403). Pavin (1992) provides a review of the benefits of nongraded programs.

Tutoring   **Tutoring,** or coaching, is perhaps the oldest and best-known means of individualizing instruction. It is used either to give remedial instruction to a student or to provide supplementary information. In the first case, a child could be tutored if she or he couldn't count to 100 by an appropriate age or developmental level. In the second case, a child might be instructed as to how to create a crossword puzzle.

Many different persons serve as tutors, including teachers, teacher aides, students, and parents. Cross-grade tutoring occurs when older children work with younger ones. This is a fairly popular approach, although some question its academic value to

Ameritech is one of several companies trying to support computer instruction in America's classrooms. It has a traveling display that demonstrates newer ways computers can help students learn. Stratton (1993) describes three of them.

Jason, a high school freshman, opened a computer window and looked inside a storm cloud. The cloud was a model projected on the screen. Jason could rotate the image so he could see the column of heat in the cloud's center. Furthermore, he would vary the temperature or wind speed to see how the cloud would react.

Ten-year-olds Teruko and Sam talked to each other over speakerphones while viewing a world map on their separate computer screens. In this way, they could collaborate on a homework assignment on mapping.

Pupils in two Ohio cities were connected by a large-screen computer and telephone that enabled them to jointly study tissue and genetics. They could not only see and hear each other but also see and hear the teacher and see slides and other materials the teacher used.

the student tutor. Nixon-John (1994) describes how she effectively used peer tutoring to increase student enthusiasm about writing and improve their writing performance.

Distance Education   Another variation of individualized instruction is distance education (Feasley, 1982). As the name implies, the intention is to make education more accessible to persons not located near an instructional facility such as a public school. Distance education programs are used widely in Alaska and Australia where they serve rural or outback children. The means for providing instruction include telephone, radio, television, computer programs (CAI), and printed materials such as texts and guidebooks. Most of us are familiar with the concept of correspondence courses and correspondence study. This was, and is, the most popular form of distance education. When a student is ill or homebound, teachers often engage in distance education.

The Project Method   All six examples of individualized instruction described thus far have something in common: They intend to bridge the gap between what society expects students to know and what they actually know. In contrast, the Project Method allows students autonomy to pursue their own interests by engaging in an activity within the larger curriculum framework. A student or cluster of students decides what task they want to undertake. The task could be cognitive or knowledge seeking, affective or values related, or psychomotor skill building. Often it contains all three elements. The student or cluster then decides how they will undertake the task and even how it will be evaluated (Lawry, 1987b). Interest in the Project Method is on the rise, especially in science education where constructivist approaches to learning (see Chapter 8) are popular. Olson (1993) reports on project methods in Case 7.4 (see p. 208).

Individualization, then, is not any one kind of program. It eschews whole-class or mass teaching and embraces instead *group practices, adaptation of subject matter to the individual,* and, at its extreme, the *emancipation of students from the constraints of the curriculum planned by others.* Its tenets include self-direction, initiative, freedom, and responsibility and a preference for constructivist learning theory (Gibbons, 1971).

7.22   What values, knowledge, and abilities do you have that would help you implement individualized instruction?

GOOD USERS OF INDIVIDUALIZED INSTRUCTION

To be really good at individualizing instruction, we think you must have particular values, knowledge, and abilities. Foremost, you must prize diversity. Heck and Williams (1984) note, "you must comprehend, accept, value, and affirm respect for all people regardless of sexual, racial, cultural, ethnic, religious, and physical differences" (p. 53). Relatedly, you must value individualism by encouraging your students to think and do for themselves.

CHAPTER 7
Four Instructional Alternatives:
Presentation, Discussion, Independent
Study, and Individualized Instruction

207

Project-Based Learning

According to a report in *Education Week* (Olson, 1993), the project method is enjoying a renaissance. Olson notes that virtually all persons connected with the reform movement under the sponsorship of the New American Schools Development Corporation "have embraced some form of project-based learning" (p. 6). Project-based learning occurs when students plan and carry out the study of some topic or theme which causes them to investigate it using an interdisciplinary, cross-subject approach. The following examples are cited.

- Members of a class map the downtown area, interview store owners, and then write guidebooks for children's use
- Students who are working on a three-month unit of work entitled "Designing Spaces for People" design and build model structures for people living under peculiar climatic conditions

Olson informs readers that the project method was advocated and used by progressive educators in the 1930s and 1940s. She cites the Eight-Year Study done in 1942, which found that college students who had gone to progressive high schools outperformed their peers from more traditional schools in which they studied everything in separate subjects.

Gaining knowledge of your students is essential. The more you know about them, the better your potential to address their strengths and needs. Therefore, you must be inclined toward being a diagnostician and clinician. Chapter 5 provides suggestions for getting to know learners better.

You also need knowledge of and ability to use the various types of individualized instruction such as the Dalton and Winnetka plans, Individually Guided Education, the Project Method, and so forth. Finally, you will need interpersonal skills, including the ability to listen, to accept, and to encourage.

7.23 Which of the advantages of individualized instruction are most important in your eyes as a future teacher?

GOOD INDIVIDUALIZED EDUCATION PROGRAMS

Given the definition of individualized instruction and its purpose and characteristics, the following criteria should help you decide how good an individualized program really is.

- Is the program tailored to meet a learners' unique strengths and needs?
- How much autonomy do learners have with regard to the goals of instruction, the learning activities, resources, and time?
- Does it result in equity (academic, social, emotional) without hurting participants by stigmatizing, causing loss of self-esteem, or restricting friendships? (Corno & Snow, 1986)

Yes, individualized education, done well, has lots of potential advantages. Among other things, it can allow learners to pursue their interests, help them to take respon-

TABLE 7.7 Qualities of Good Users of Individualized Instruction and of Good Individualized Programs

Good Users . . .	Good Programs . . .
• Prize diversity	• Are tailored to meet individual learners' strengths and needs
• Value individualism	
• Know learners' strengths and needs	• Permit considerable learner autonomy with regard to goals, means, resources, time
• Have knowledge of and ability to implement such programs	• Result in greater equity
• Have strong interpersonal skills	• Have no damaging side effects

LESSON PLAN 7.4
Abbreviated Individualized Instruction Lesson: Favorite Book Club

Curriculum tie-in: This lesson may be linked to reading and literature.

OBJECTIVES

1. Learners will engage in reading books and periodically choose a favorite.
2. Learners will share the criteria used in selecting their periodic favorite. *Specific objective:* Learners will be consciously aware of their book reading and liking motives.
3. Learners will report on the book. *Specific objective:* Learners will determine what they think others would want to know about the book and subsequently prepare a report for class presentation and placement in a class "Favorite Books Folder." The report should include the reasons why the book was so appealing to the reader.

RESOURCES

1. Books on the Internet.
2. School and community libraries.
3. Bookstores.
4. Home.

METHODOLOGY

1. *Set induction:* "What is the most favorite book you have ever read? Why did you enjoy it so much? When you read a good book do you like to share the story with your friends, relatives, or parents? I thought you would and therefore I thought you might like to start a Favorite Book Club in our class."

2. Establish guidelines:
   - A folder will be kept containing what you want to tell others about your favorite new book. That might include the name and author of the book, the reasons why you chose to read it, what you think would interest others in reading the book, and anything else you might want to include. Perhaps you would want to include an illustration you make or the tape-recorded dialogue you make of some interesting passage you would like others to hear. What else you place in your book folder is up to you.
   - You may read the book(s) at home or in class—anytime your work is done.
   - You may choose a book of any length or on any topic that is in good taste.
   - You may submit a folder once a month, more than once a month, or less than once a month. How often you choose a favorite book will depend upon the books you choose (some you read may not be very favorite), the amount of time you have available to read, and other factors. The major goal is to locate and read material you truly enjoy and to share both our motives for reading and our discoveries.
   - Periodically, you will be asked to share your results in class.

ASSESSMENT

1. What have you found out about your reading interests? What kinds of books do you seem to like and why?
2. What do you believe your classmates most want to know about a book? How did you decide? Were you right?

CLOSURE

1. As a class, have students review what they have learned about how people chose books to read and how that is reflected in libraries.

---

sibility for learning, allow them to utilize their preferred learning style, expose them to a wide variety of educational resources geared to their ability level, challenge them to be as good as they can be, and permit them to work at their own best pace. Such advantages should make your class more attentive, enthusiastic, independent, and, of course, academically able.

A summary of what good users of individualized instruction and good programs are like appears in Table 7.7.

A brief individualized instruction lesson appears as Lesson Plan 7.4.

WHEN INDIVIDUALIZED INSTRUCTION SHOULD BE USED

Obviously, individualized instruction should be used whenever teachers hope to serve a student's unique strengths and needs. "OK," you say, "But isn't that all the time?" Of course, but human and material resources are not available to meet this ideal. Thus, you will need to compromise, using individualized, personalized instruction whenever a child is at risk of school failure and beyond that as often as possible.

From your experience, you know that, in almost all classrooms, teacher presentations and recitations prevail. In some instances, discussion is an occasional alternative

CHAPTER 7
Four Instructional Alternatives:
Presentation, Discussion, Independent
Study, and Individualized Instruction

209

There are so many variations on the theme of individualized instruction that it is difficult to generalize about its success. Walberg (1984) looked at the results of nearly 3,000 studies covering a variety of educational practices; included among them were studies of several forms of individualized instruction. In order of effectiveness, they include acceleration (that is, advancing students academically), science mastery learning, personalized instruction, adaptive instruction, tutoring, individualized science, diagnostic prescriptive methods, individualized instruction, and individualized mathematics. Obviously, some of these forms of individualized instruction are not well known. It will

suffice to say, however, that they all are arrangements that customize teaching and learning in some way to better serve students.

Ellson (1986) is another scholar who has studied educational practices to determine their effectiveness. Among those he reports as most beneficial are so-called nonconventional alternatives, including programmed instruction and performance-based instruction in which learning is constantly monitored and instruction regularly altered to help the learner succeed.

Slavin and Madden (1989) believe that good instruction for children at risk of school failure must entail individualization. They find support for and advocate

using one-on-one tutoring, individually adopted computer-assisted instruction, frequent monitoring of individual student progress, modification of instruction and grouping arrangements to meet individual needs, and having and using a wide range of instructional resources.

Finally, the U.S. Department of Education in a publication called *What Works* (1986, 1987) names several forms of individualized instruction among its findings on how best to teach and improve learning. The forms are having parents read to children, tutoring, and acceleration of gifted students.

Given these research findings, it would seem that individualizing instruction is well worth the extra effort required.

of choice. Most likely, individualized instruction is underutilized, even with children at risk. The only pervasive effort to compel its use is contained in the Individuals with Disabilities Act, which, as you know, requires that Individual Educational Programs (IEPs) be drawn up and followed for students with disabilities. That is not to say that teachers are unaware of the needs and strengths of individual students, nor that they totally ignore such information. Rather, for the most part, teachers do not in a regular and conscious fashion individualize. What they tend to do is ability-group children with similar needs or similar strengths. However, and sometimes unfortunately, the practice of homogeneous grouping is drawing fire from those who claim it has negative side effects such as stereotyping students in the less advanced groups.

Spotlight on Research 7.8 summarizes the research findings on individualized instruction.

LIMITATIONS OF INDIVIDUALIZED INSTRUCTION

The overwhelming disadvantage of individualization is, of course, that it is very time consuming when done properly. You cannot just give students any old thing to do, even on an attractive computer. Neither can you simply allow students to do whatever they please. Individualizing means responding responsibly to each individual as a person with unique educational needs.

SUMMARY OF INDIVIDUALIZED INSTRUCTION

We have learned what individualized instruction is, and we have seen that it takes many different forms. Most of the forms are fairly prescriptive and controlled. By this, we mean that students have little or nothing to say about what or how they will learn. The only part of individualized instruction that may be truly individualized is the time needed to learn. The forms are often tight programs that students move through as quickly as they can. However, in terms of student learning, these programs seem to work.

Few forms of individualized instruction allow students any real autonomy in deciding what they will learn and/or how. We mentioned one exception: the Project Method, a standby for generations, that seems to work for teachers and learners alike. You will see many classrooms, particularly in elementary and middle schools, where individuals or groups of children address themselves to topics they have an interest in and decide how they will learn about some aspect of the topic.

We have said that when teachers instruct students one on one, they must know the students and accept and prize their diversity. Furthermore, they have to value individualism and have good interpersonal skills, especially the ability to listen and encourage. If the individualized program you use is a good one, it will be tailored to each learner's strengths and needs, give students as much autonomy as possible, and help children achieve without causing personal embarrassment.

Good individualized instruction seems to be a standout approach. It can meet a great many personal, professional, and educational needs for teachers and students. This instructional alternative also has good support from research.

The "Best" Instructional Alternatives

What do teachers think are the best instructional alternatives for different kinds of students? Are certain alternatives better suited to high- or low-ability learners? Are some better suited to independent versus (as opposed to) conforming learners? Shuell and his colleagues undertook two studies in order to find answers (Shuell, Brown, Watson, & Ewing, 1988).

In the first study, ninety-one suburban elementary teachers received information about four different kinds of hypothetical students. The information portrayed each of the students as either (1) high ability–independent, (2) high ability–conforming, (3) low ability–independent, or (4) low ability–conforming. For example, the hypothetical high ability–independent learner was characterized as follows:

> Robby is an independent, productive worker. He is doing very well in all his subjects, and is usually ahead of [them] in tasks requiring complex verbal skills. His classmates look up to him for leadership. The teacher has assigned the class to read Black Beauty and asked them to be ready for a quiz. (p. 354, paraphrased)

After reading the four hypothetical student characterizations, the ninety-one teachers were asked to decide which of several instructional alternatives would be best suited for each student when engaged in a verbal learning task such as reading. The instructional alternatives teachers were to consider were lecture/explanation, seat work (supervised study), discussion, one-to-one teaching (individualized instruction), peer tutoring (individualized instruction), homogeneous grouping, or praise. We do not consider the last two areas to be instructional alternatives, and the investigators did not claim "praise" was one either. Still, it was included.

In the second Shuell study, twenty fourth- and fifth-grade teachers participated. First, they were asked to think about each of their present students with regard to five attributes: general academic ability, achievement orientation, classroom participation, motivation, and prior knowledge. Next, the teachers were asked to describe which instructional alternative was most appropriate for each student when engaged in a verbal learning task. The instructional alternatives teachers could choose among were the same as in the first study except that "homogeneous grouping" was replaced by "games," and "small-group work" displaced "discussion."

The investigators acknowledge that the two studies differ somewhat but believe the following conclusions are in order:

- Teachers believe different instructional alternatives work best for different learners.
- Teachers consider lecture/explanation and seat work most beneficial for high-ability students.

- Teachers consider one-to-one work, peer tutoring, and praise more appropriate for children of low ability.
- Teachers present mixed perceptions with regard to discussion. In study 1 (the hypothetical students), they felt it was equally inappropriate for either high- or low-ability learners. In study 2 (real students), they reported it appropriate for high-ability students.

Shuell and associates conclude that teachers do have definite ideas regarding how best to teach different learners and that, generally, these ideas are consistent with what we know about learning and teaching.

Overview of Thirty Instructional Alternatives

At the beginning of the chapter, we indicated that a brief overview of 30 instructional alternatives would follow the in-depth information on presentation, discussion, independent study and individualized instruction. Here they are, presented alphabetically. You will note that some have characteristics in common with others. For example, presentations and recitations are both normally led by the teacher.

- **Academic games or competitions**—Learners compete with each other one to one or team to team to determine which individual or group is superior at a given academic task such as in "spelldowns," anagrams, or project completion. Some well-known commercially available academic games include *Probe* (vocabulary and spelling) and *Rook* (mathematics). Cooperative learning, presented in the next chapter, may incorporate games and competition.
- **Brainstorming**—To generate creative ideas, learners are asked to withhold judgment or criticism and produce a very large number of ways to do something, such as resolve a particular problem. For example, learners may be asked to think of as many ideas as they can for eliminating world hunger. Once they have generated a large number of ideas, the ideas are subjected to inspection in respect to their feasibility.
- **Cases**—Students make detailed analysis of some specific, usually compelling, event or series of related events so that learners will better understand its nature and what might be done about it. For example, learners in a science class might investigate the occurrence of El Niño, or a disaster of human origin such as the infiltration of the zebra mussel in the Great Lakes.
- **Centers of interest and displays**—Collections and displays of materials are used to interest learners in themes or topics. For example, children may bring to school and display family belongings that reflect their ethnic heritage. The intention may be to interest the class in the notion of culture. Or, the teacher might arrange a display of different measurement devices to prompt interest in and exploration of that topic.
- **Colloquia**—A guest or guests are invited to class to be interviewed. Thus, a guest musician might serve as a stimulus for arousing interest in music and musical performance.
- **Contracts**—Written agreements students and teachers may enter into describe the academic work students plan to accomplish in a particular period of time such as over a week or month.
- **Cooperative learning**—See student-team learning.
- **Debates**—In this form of discussion, a few students present and contest varying points of view on an issue. For example, secondary students could debate the issue "Should public schools be financed by real estate tax, sales tax, or tax on personal income?"

"It was a very successful field trip. I managed to lose five of them."

- **Demonstrations**—In this form of presentation, the teacher or learners show how something works or operates, or how something is done. For example, a teacher could demonstrate how to use a thesaurus, how to operate a handheld calculator, or what happens when oil is spilled on water (as when an oil tanker leaks).

- **Direct instruction**—A teacher gives explicit, step-by-step instruction (Rosenshine, 1987). The advocated format or regimen is demonstration followed by guided practice and independent practice. Thus, the teacher might teach a reading, mathematics, or geography concept or skill; following that, students practice under teacher supervision; and finally, students practice independently to the point of mastery. (See Chapter 8.)

- **Discovery**—In discovery learning, students are encouraged to derive their own understandings or meanings. For example, students might be asked to find out what causes golf, tennis, basketball, and bowling balls to bounce differently on different surfaces. Experiments rather than teacher demonstrations are a part of discovery learning. (See Chapter 8.)

- **Discussion**—Described in this chapter, discussions occur when a group assembles to communicate with one another by speaking and listening about a topic or event of mutual interest. To illustrate, a group of learners convenes to discuss what it has learned about global warming.

- **Drill and practice**—In this form of independent study, the teacher explains a task and then learners practice it. After students learn how to use a thesaurus, for example, they could be asked to locate and use synonyms.

- **Field observation, fieldwork, field trips**—Students make observations or carry out work in an outside-the-school setting. Students might visit the local museum of natural history to see displays about dinosaurs, or they might begin and operate a small business to learn about production and marketing.

- **Independent study or supervised study**—Described in this chapter, independent study requires learners to complete a common task at their desks or as a home study assignment.

- **Individualized instruction**—Any of a number of teaching methods that tailor teaching and learning to meet a learner's unique characteristics.

- **Learning modules**—These are a form of individualized instruction that allow students to use a self-contained package of learning activities. The activities guide learners to know or to be able to do something. Students might be given a learning module that contains activities intended to help them understand good nutrition.

"Please feel free to call on me if any of you need individual attention."

- **Mastery learning**—As a class, students are presented with information to be learned at a predetermined level of mastery. The class is tested, and individuals who do not obtain adequate scores are retaught and retested. Those who pass undertake enrichment study while classmates catch up. (See Chapter 4.)

- **Oral reports**—Individuals or groups of learners are assigned or choose topics. For example, each may be asked to find out about one planet in our solar system. They share what they learn with other class members through oral presentations.

- **Presentations and lectures**—Students listen to a person who talks about a topic. The teacher, or a guest speaker, might tell the class all about the artist Dali, for example. Presentations are described in this chapter.

- **Problem solving**—Individuals or groups of learners are presented with a perplexing, difficult question or situation and are asked to think about and try to resolve it. (See Chapter 4.)

- **Programmed and computer-assisted instruction**—In this form of individualized instruction, students learn information in small, separate units either by reading programmed texts or by using computer-presented teaching programs. A correct answer to a question or problem enables the learner to advance, while an incorrect response requires repetition or relearning. (See Chapter 4.)

- **Project or activity method**—In this form of individualization, learners choose and work on projects and activities on related topics. Students might write on or present in graphic presentation "Life in the South" or "Life in the North during the Civil War." Learners not only choose topics but also the project that will show what they've learned. (See this chapter, Independent Study.)

- **Protocols**—Learners study an original record or records of some important event and then try to understand the event or its consequences. They might watch a film depicting actual instances of discrimination and then consider its causes and effects.

- **Reciprocal Teaching**—Teacher gradually shifts teaching responsibility to learners. (See Chapter 4, Learning Style Differences.)

- **Recitation**—Students are given information to study. They then recite what they have learned when the teacher questions them. For example, students might read about what causes different weather patterns, and the teacher might then question them to determine the extent and nature of their knowledge and understanding. (See Table 7.3.)

- **Role playing**—Learners take on the role of another person to see what it would be like to be that person. Thus, a student could play the role of an imaginary student no one likes or the role of an individual with handicaps.

- **Simulation games**—Students play a specially designed, competitive game that mirrors some aspect of life. For example, they might play the *Ghetto* (Toll, 1969) to find out about the problems and pressures ghetto dwellers face and, relatedly, to sense how difficult it is to improve one's lot in life. Another commercially available simulation game is *Gold Rush* (life and adventure in a frontier mining camp). Some simulation games are computerized, for example, *Oregon Trail* and *Amazon Trail*.

- **Simulations**—Learners engage with something intended to simulate—to give the appearance or have the effect of—something else. Thus, students may engage in a simulation of the United Nations General Assembly in order to have "firsthand" experience with how the Assembly works and what its delegates do.

- **Student-team, pupil-team, cooperative learning**—Learners are placed in groups or teams of four to six. Sometimes the groups are as diverse or heterogeneous as possible. In such cases, team members are often rewarded for the team's overall success. Under one type of cooperative learning, student teams might see a teacher presentation on division of fractions. They would then receive worksheets to complete. Team members would work together to find the answers. Finally, team members would take a quiz on division of fractions, and the team members' scores would be added to make up a team score. (See Cooperative Learning in Chapter 8.)

- **Tutoring**—In this form of individualization, either a teacher or a fellow student provides a learner or small group of learners with special help, usually because the student is not learning well enough with only conventional instruction (Medway, 1987).

7.24 Which instructional alternatives do you seem to prefer? Why?

The instructional alternatives we have briefly described are depicted on the Wheel of Instructional Choice in Figure 7.5.

A Special Note About Using Technology in Teaching

When you begin teaching you will likely find that your classroom or classrooms contain one or more computers (on average there is one for every 5.7 learners), that you will be connected to the Web, and that there will be plenty of computer-based learning resources available. To use these resources, your biggest tasks will be locating and selecting quality software and websites, deciding when and how such resources can be used, and meshing them with the curriculum (*Education Week*, 1999).

SELECTING QUALITY SOFTWARE AND WEBSITES

The good news is that the software available in your classroom likely will be satisfactory with regard to both its quality and ability to help learners develop a range of lower- and higher-level thinking skills (see Bloom's Taxonomy in Chapter 6). The bad news is that the software often does not match the state and school district curriculum requirements for your subjects and grade levels. In other words, you may have top-notch software, but it doesn't necessarily teach what students are expected to learn. Thus teachers must often search long and hard for instructional software to fill specific curriculum needs. This task is daunting—a majority of teachers report it is somewhat or very difficult to find the kinds of products they are looking for. The problem worsens in higher grades since less software is available.

Fortunately, some educational software is reviewed both by public and private content evaluators. Four states provide public, formal evaluations. They are the California Learning Resource Network at http://www.clrn.org/home/, the Florida

Web Resource

CHAPTER 7
Four Instructional Alternatives:
Presentation, Discussion, Independent
Study, and Individualized Instruction

215

FIGURE 7.5 Wheel of Instructional Choice

- Topics shaded in purple are discussed in detail in Chapter 6.
- Topics shaded in gray are discussed in detail in Chapter 7.

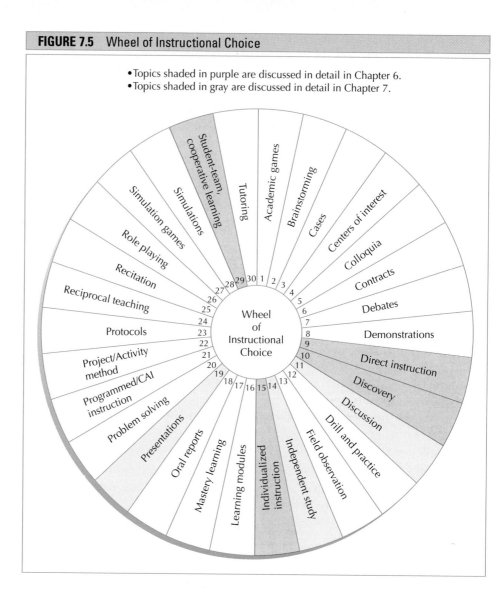

Web Resource

Educational Software Catalog at www.itrc.ucf.edu/doecat/, the North Carolina Department of Public Instruction at www.evalutech.sreb.org, and the Ohio School-Net Software Review Project at www.ohioschoolnet.k12.oh.us.

Many teachers are using the Web as well as, or instead of, software to provide learning experiences. Websites, as you may know, may have the advantage of being interactive, and they are more likely up-to-date and free. On the other hand, some teachers don't like the Web. They feel it is too difficult to find good sites and then find ways to tie them in to their normal lessons. They also worry that allowing students to explore the Web can result in their being distracted and that downloading website information can be a serious time constraint.

UTILIZING DIGITAL CONTENT

Even though you may want to use digital content to improve learning, it will be a challenge. Teachers cite problems with expense, time, and preparation. Overwhelmingly, teachers who use software cite expense as a major concern. Most teachers note that there is not enough time to find and to use digital content. Finally, nearly half of teachers are concerned about the amount of preparation time required to use software and websites.

Some teachers and students don't restrict themselves to using existing digital content. They develop their own software and websites. This is possible through use of "computer tools" that include the following:

- *Word processing* that allows learners to write and revise with the assistance of spelling and grammar checkers.
- *Spreadsheets* that permit adding up collected data, crunching statistics, and graphing.
- *Drawing/painting.*
- *Multimedia and presentation tools* that allow learners to create sophisticated class presentations.
- *Desktop publishing* that enables students to create materials for print or on the Web using scanning, design, and layout tools.

Teachers and learners who develop digital content are inclined toward discovery or inquiry-based learning (see Facilitating Discovery Learning Online in Chapter 8). Of course, in order to create digital content with your learners, you would need to be much more computer savvy than if you simply use already developed software. So, as your computer comfort level increases you will be more likely to try using some of the above tools with learners.

GET BETTER PREPARED FOR THE DIGITAL AGE

Obviously, you need all the preparation you can get in order to use digital technology. That preparation should include training on computers, in Internet basics, and in how to integrate technology into the classroom. It is the latter, integration, that presents the most problems. However, teachers who receive eleven or more hours of curriculum-integration training are five times more likely to feel much better prepared to integrate technology into their lessons than teachers who receive no such training. Presently, forty-two states require teacher technology training, yet teacher preparation programs are finding it difficult to fit training into an already packed preservice curriculum. It is likely that you and subsequent generations of teachers are and will be better prepared to use digital technology because of your exposure to it when growing up. So, the problem may partly take care of itself.

7.25 How prepared are you to utilize digital content in your classroom? What further preparation do you feel you need? How might it be obtained?

Some Final Thoughts

This chapter is intended to put you on the road to becoming a more multitalented, versatile teacher. Now you are generally aware of thirty ways to teach, and you have special knowledge about four that are considered teaching staples. For these four, you have learned their purposes and characteristics, what you must do to excel at each, and what benefits research tells us will accrue. We hope you have had the opportunity to try out each one and/or to observe a master teacher demonstrating each one. Furthermore, we hope you have reflected on how you feel about each. Consider yourself part way out on the diving platform leading to successful teaching. After Chapter 8, we think you will be ready to take the plunge.

CHAPTER SUMMARY

- An instructional alternative is a way of teaching intended to facilitate student learning and satisfaction. The most familiar alternatives are presentations, discussion, independent study, and individualized instruction. Other notable alternatives (presented in the next chapter) are direct instruction, cooperative learning, discovery learning, and constructivism. As many as thirty instructional alternatives exist and are depicted on the Wheel of Instructional Choice (Figure 7.5).

CHAPTER 7
Four Instructional Alternatives:
Presentation, Discussion, Independent
Study, and Individualized Instruction

217

- Presentations are informative talks a more knowledgeable person makes to less knowledgeable persons. These talks draw their strength from the cognitive school of thought, especially information processing and reception learning. They can be long or short, interrupted or uninterrupted, formal or informal, given by a teacher or by another person, and either live or recorded.

- Good presentations have three parts: preparation, delivery, and closure. Preparation requires the presenter to establish the general purpose and specific learning objectives, collect and review the information to be presented, and organize and plan delivery. Delivery requires the presenter to obtain students' attention, present the learning objectives and expectations, use an advance organizer, present the information in an organized, step-by-step manner, expect and promote pupil interaction, move from general to specific ideas, use examples and nonexamples when teaching new concepts, ask learners to reflect on what they have learned, and then ask them to use the information. Closure requires the presenter to review, summarize, relate the new learning to what students already knew, and check learners for understanding.

- Research indicates that the presenter's style is important, that good presenters are often friendly, humorous, enthusiastic, and verbally fluent, that attention falls off rapidly after fifteen minutes, that note taking aids long-term memory, that presentations are good for transmitting information and not as good for promoting students' thinking, and that underachievers need special consideration when using presentations.

- A discussion is a conversation wherein students, or students and teacher, interact to share information, ideas, or opinions, or work to resolve a problem. Discussions also are guided by learning theory. However, the theory the discussion leader draws from will vary according to the discussion's purpose, that is, whether it is mainly cognitive, affective, or some combination of the two. Discussions may take place between teacher and students or solely among students, and the teacher may be actively involved as leader or participant or merely serve as the observer. Finally, a discussion may involve the whole class, small group, or a panel.

- Good discussion leaders usually believe that students' participation in purposeful conversation is normal and healthy, that students must think aloud about information, ideas, issues, and problems, that students are able to think effectively, and that by thinking and interacting effectively, students experience psychological and social growth. Additionally, good discussion leaders control their own talk and are skillful facilitators, human relations experts, clarifiers, and summarizers.

- Good discussions include preparation, delivery, and closure. Preparation requires the leader to determine the purpose and specific objectives; determine students' readiness for discussion, particularly this discussion; decide what kind of interaction is best (teacher-student, or student-student) and, relatedly, what the teacher's role should be (leader, participant, or observer); and decide whether the discussion should involve the whole class or a small group and what the time parameters should be. Delivery requires that the leader ensure that students understand the purpose and objectives of the discussion, set the task, remind students of guidelines for behavior during discussion, organize the participants, and let them "have at it" as the leader fulfills his or her role. Closure requires the discussion leader to summarize and organize findings, conclusions, solutions, or whatever the objectives called for as well as assess students' learning and satisfaction.

- Research on discussions shows, among other things, that they generally are motivating, promote retention, foster higher-order thinking, and are effective in altering attitudes and advancing moral reasoning.

- Independent study includes any school-related assignment students do more or less alone. It is guided mostly by information-processing and behavioristic theories.

The purposes of independent study are to provide rehearsal and practice, opportunities to learn how to learn, and to occupy students legitimately so the teacher can perform other important tasks. Characteristics of independent study include the type (teacher-prescribed or student-chosen), the teacher role (the availability of the teacher to guide), and the context (in school or home).

- Good independent study leaders believe that the purposes of independent study are valuable. They have confidence in students' ability to work alone and are able to demonstrate valence and challenge arousal, variety and challenge, withitness, and overlapping.

- Good independent study includes preparation, delivery, and closure. Preparation requires the teacher to establish the general purpose and specific objectives, settle on the assignment's nature and type, and ensure that it is within learners' interest and ability. Delivery requires that the teacher be absolutely clear regarding the assignment's purpose, objectives, relationship to what has or will be learned, procedures, and time limit. Closure requires the teacher to collect, assess, and evaluate the work, giving learners specific feedback and reteaching when necessary.

- Research on independent study finds that it is commonly used, that it is more effective when teachers demonstrate certain leadership behaviors, and that its most important ingredients are (1) clarity of purpose, assignment, and procedures, and (2) monitoring, grading, and provision of immediate feedback.

- Research on well-conceived homework supports its use since it enhances learning.

- Individualized instruction refers to a number of instructional maneuvers that attempt to tailor teaching and learning to a learner's unique strengths and needs. There are many types of individualized instruction, including the Dalton and Winnetka plans, programmed and computer-assisted instruction, Individually Prescribed Instruction, Individually Guided Education, tutoring, and the Project Method. In some, individuals with like abilities are grouped.

- The teacher's role in individualized instruction is to know and care about the diversity of students and to see that the learning tasks are varied or modified for each individual. Good users of individualized instruction prize diversity, value individualism, know learners' strengths and needs, know about and have the ability to implement individualized instruction programs, and have good interpersonal skills.

- Good individualized instruction programs are tailored to meet individual learners' strengths and needs, permit considerable autonomy, result in greater equity, and have no damaging or harmful side effects on students.

- Research on individualized instruction makes it clear that its use is worth the extra time and effort. Its major limitation is that when it is properly conducted, it is very time consuming.

ISSUES AND PROBLEMS FOR DISCUSSION

ISSUES   Several issues and problems are related to instructional alternatives. Here are a few you might like to discuss in class.

1. Which instructional alternatives do you expect to handle most skillfully?
2. Which instructional alternatives work best for which purposes?
3. When deciding which alternative to use, what is the relative importance of teacher versus learner needs?
4. How can you become more competent in using a given instructional alternative?
5. Why do you suppose there is a dearth of useful research-based knowledge about instructional alternatives?

PROBLEMS   Teachers regularly report that they have difficulty "learning to use alternative methods of instruction" (Cruickshank et al., 1980). What would you have done in each of the following situations?

Problem 1:   "I spent the whole weekend reading about Geronimo and preparing to tell the class about him as part of Cultural Awareness Week. I chose Geronimo because there are no Native Americans in the class and I wanted to broaden the kids' perspectives. Well, I'll tell you, very few of the students had any interest whatsoever! Finally, I just cashed it in. So much for giving an 'interesting' talk."

Problem 2:   "No matter how many times we use group discussion, the same old problems crop up. Rashawn and Lawrence think they know everything and won't let others talk or respect what others say. Melody, Arnold, Diane, and Mary won't participate, and Barney sleeps."

Problem 3:   "Students really like to do individual study. They can't wait to get started. After that, some just sit, some carry on conversations with neighbors, some just copy word for word from a book. A few hurry through so they can fool around. Out of twenty-six, I'd say I can count on fourteen."

Problem 4:   "We have some pretty good software and audiovisual materials available. To add variety, I like to have the students use these resources instead of just listening to me. They waste so much time finding what they want and settling down that I usually wish I had done whole-class teaching."

THEORY INTO ACTION ACTIVITIES

ACTIVITY 7.1: Prepare a Presentation   Utilizing what you now know about learning (Chapter 4), good presenters, and good presentations, prepare a brief presentation for a group of peers on a topic chosen from group A or B below. The presentation should be no longer than ten minutes.

A. *Topics from this text*
   1. Attention
   2. Short-term memory
   3. Long-term memory
   4. Reception learning
   5. Bloom's taxonomy
   6. Writing a unit plan
   7. Writing a lesson plan
   8. (your choice)

B. *School curricula topics*
   1. Homophones
   2. Characteristics of Picasso's paintings
   3. The electoral college
   4. The musical scale
   5. Wilderness survival
   6. Peninsulas
   7. Triangles
   8. (your choice)

Assessment: Did you establish your general purpose, set specific learning objectives, collect and review related materials, and plan the presentation with student diversity in mind?

ACTIVITY 7.2: Deliver a Presentation   Deliver your Activity 7.1 presentation to a small group of your peers.

Assessment: To what extent did you

1. Obtain learners' attention and interest?
2. Inform learners of what they need to learn?
3. Relate new information to what they know?
4. Present information step by step?
5. Move from the general to the specific?
6. Provide just the right amount of information?
7. Emphasize important points?
8. Use examples and illustrations?
9. Use variety to maintain attention?
10. Ask questions and call for comments?

Were you

1. Friendly?
2. Humorous?
3. Enthusiastic?
4. Fluent and audible?
5. Able to take learners' differences into account?
6. Knowledgeable?

How well do your learners feel you did these things?

ACTIVITY 7.3: Observe a Teacher Presentation   Now that you have learned about presentations, it would be very helpful to observe one or more in a K–12 classroom. If you are enrolled in a field experience, find out when your mentor teacher will be giving a presentation. Talk with him or her about how it would help if you could see a presentation in action. If not so enrolled, perhaps you can obtain a videotape of a presentation made by a teacher or student teacher.

As you observe, record answers to these questions:

- What characteristics of a good presenter did the teacher demonstrate? (See Table 7.2, column 1.)
- What qualities of good presentations were evident in this one? (See Table 7.2, column 2.)
- Were any of the research findings on presentations borne out?

Additionally, talk with a student who was attentive and find out how he or she feels about presentations. Conversely, talk with another who was off-task or not attentive to determine his or her perceptions about this instructional alternative.

Finally, ask the teacher how well he or she felt the presentation facilitated learning and satisfaction.

ACTIVITY 7.4: Plan a Discussion   Plan a discussion for this class focusing on any one of the following topics. Plan it so that it has one of the following purposes: to review information; to examine ideas, opinions, or issues; to solve problems; or to improve communication skills. Reread the section Good Discussions for assistance.

Topics from this text

1. Factors influencing how we teach
2. The changing nature of childhood

CHAPTER 7
Four Instructional Alternatives:
Presentation, Discussion, Independent
Study, and Individualized Instruction

221

3. Student diversity
4. Three schools of thought about learning
5. Presentations or discussions
6. (your choice of topic)

Assessment: Did you have a clear purpose and outcomes in mind, take into account learners' differences, decide what role you would play, work out the physical arrangement, and establish the time frame?

ACTIVITY 7.5: Conduct a Discussion   Conduct the discussion you planned in Activity 7.4.

Assessment: Did you

1. Obtain learners' attention and interest?
2. Inform learners of the goal of the discussion and its value?
3. Relate what learners will discuss to their previous knowledge and experience and/or tie it to something they will learn?
4. Remind participants of the rules of (this) discussion?
5. Obtain a facilitator-moderator and recorder for each small group if small-group discussion was used?
6. Monitor understanding and participation?
7. Elevate the level of thinking and discourse?
8. Summarize?
9. Tie what was discussed to previous knowledge?
10. Connect the discussion to what will happen next?

Were you

1. Able to get learners thinking?
2. Able to keep your own talk under control?
3. A facilitator, human relations expert, clarifier, or summarizer as necessary?
4. Able to improve group communication skills?

ACTIVITY 7.6: Observe a Discussion   Try to observe a discussion involving K–12 students. If you do not have access to a K–12 classroom, perhaps your college instructor has a videotape of one. As you observe, record answers to these questions:

1. Which of the four purposes of a discussion seemed to be in play—to review, to examine ideas and opinions, to solve problems, or to improve oral communication skills?
2. What were the characteristics of the discussion? Was the interaction between teacher and students or among students only? Was the teacher a facilitator-moderator, participant, or observer-recorder? Was it a whole-class or small-group discussion? If small group, what was the composition of the group? What was the physical arrangement?
3. What beliefs and abilities related to good discussion did the teacher demonstrate?
4. To what extent did the discussion bear out any of the research findings on discussion?
5. To what extent did student learning and satisfaction occur?

ACTIVITY 7.7: Plan an Independent Study   Using what we know about learning and independent study, prepare an assignment for a group of peers on a topic chosen from purpose 1 or 2:

1. *Purpose:* To have peers independently rehearse or practice what you have learned about
   a. Presentation
   b. Discussion
   c. Independent study
2. *Purpose:* To have peers independently learn more about other instructional alternatives appearing on the Wheel of Instructional Choice (Figure 7.5).

In either case, did you establish your general purpose, set specific learning objectives, consider the diversity of the learners, and make the task interesting?

ACTIVITY 7.8: Conducting Independent Study   Conduct the independent study activity you planned in Activity 7.7.

Assessment: Did you

1. Get student attention?
2. Present the assignment's rationale and objectives?
3. Relate the assignment to previous or upcoming work?
4. Ensure that students knew what to do and how to do it?
5. Tell them how they could get assistance?
6. Ensure that they had something to do when they finished?
7. Monitor and interact with learners?
8. Diagnose individual progress and provide assistance?
9. Collect assignments?
10. Provide students with specific feedback?
11. Give credit for the work?

ACTIVITY 7.9: Observe Independent Study   If you are enrolled in a field experience, arrange to visit a classroom to see a scheduled independent study.

1. Which of the purposes for using independent study seemed to be in play (to provide rehearsal or practice of information, provide opportunities to learn independently, or keep students legitimately occupied so the teacher could do something else)?
2. Which of the behaviors of good independent study leaders did the teacher demonstrate?
3. Which of the qualities of good independent study were present?
4. Which of the research findings on independent study was the teacher able to apply?

Additionally, talk to two students, one who seemed to be very much on-task and another who was more off-task. Ask them how they feel about studying alone. Finally, get the teacher's reactions to the independent study. You might ask, "Do you feel the students accomplished what you wanted them to?"

ACTIVITY 7.10: Observe Individualized Instruction   If you are presently involved in a field experience, find out if your mentor teacher or another teacher is using some form of individualized instruction. Should you be able to observe, answer the following questions.

- How would you describe the setting, the class, and the lesson?
- Which of the following were altered to meet students' strengths and needs?

1. The goals and content of instruction.
2. Learning activities, or how students could choose to learn.
3. Materials and resources.
4. Mastery level, or how much students were expected to learn.
5. Pacing or time.
6. Other.

- To what extent did the lesson seem to accomplish the purpose of individualization, that is, to meet students' individual strengths and needs? Explain. Also, talk to the teacher and students. How do they feel about individualization of instruction?

REFERENCES

Anderson, L., Brubaker, N., Alleman-Brooks, J., & Duffy, G. (1984). *Making seat work work. Research Series 142.* East Lansing, MI: College of Education, Michigan State University.

Anderson, L. M. (1981). *Students respond to seat work: Implications for the study of students' cognitive processing.* East Lansing, MI: Institute for Research on Teaching, Michigan State University.

Anderson, L. M. (1995). Assignment and supervision of seatwork. In L. W. Anderson (Ed.), *International encyclopedia of teaching and teacher education* (pp. 264–268), Oxford: Pergamon Press.

Battistich, V., Solomon, D., & Delucchi, K. (1993, September). Interaction processes and student outcomes in cooperative learning groups. *The Elementary School Journal, 94*(1), 19–32.

Bower, E. M. (1973). *Teachers talk about their feelings.* Rockville, MD: National Institute of Mental Health, Center for Studies of Child and Family Health.

Bridges, D. (1988). *Education, democracy, and discussion.* Blue Ridge Summit, PA: University Press of America.

Brophy, J., & Evertson, C. M. (1976). *Learning from teaching.* Boston: Allyn & Bacon.

Brophy, J. E., & Good, T. L. (1986). Teacher behavior and student achievement. In M. C. Wittrock (Ed.), *Handbook of research on teaching.* Third Edition (pp. 328–375). New York: Macmillan.

Broudy, H. S. (1963). Historical exemplars of teaching method. In N. L. Gage (Ed.), *Handbook of research on teaching* (pp. 1–43). Chicago: Rand McNally.

Brown, G. A. (1987). Lectures and lecturing. In M. J. Dunkin (Ed.), *The international encyclopedia of teaching and teacher education* (pp. 284–287). Oxford: Pergamon Press.

Connell, W.F. (1987). History of teaching methods. In M. J. Dunkin (Ed.), *The international encyclopedia of teaching and teacher education* (pp. 201–214). Oxford: Pergamon Press.

Corno, L., & Snow, R. E. (1986). Adapting teaching to individual differences among learners. In M. C. Whittrock (Ed.), *Handbook of research on teaching* (pp. 605–629). New York: Macmillan.

Cruickshank, D., Applegate, J., Holton, J., Mager, G., Myers, B., Novak, C., & Tracey, K. (1980). *Teaching is tough.* Englewood Cliffs, NJ: Prentice Hall.

Cruickshank, D., & Metcalf, K. (1995). Explaining. In T. Husen & T. N. Postlewaite (Eds.), *International encyclopedia of education.* Second Edition. Oxford: Pergamon Press.

Dembo, M. H. (1994). *Applying educational psychology in the classroom.* New York: Dembo, Longman.

Dillon, J. T. (1985). Using questions to foil discussion. *Teaching and Teacher Education, 1*(2), 109–121.

Dillon, J. T. (1988). *Questioning and discussion: A multidisciplinary study.* Norwalk, NJ: Ablex.

Dillon, J. T. (1995). Discussion. In L. W. Anderson (Ed.), *International encyclopedia of teaching and teacher education* (pp. 251–254). Oxford: Pergamon Press.

Dunkin, M. (1987). Lesson formats. In L. W. Anderson (Ed.), *International encyclopedia of teaching and teacher education* (pp. 251–254). Oxford: Pergamon Press.

Education Week. (1999, September). *Technology Counts, 99* (19), 4.

Ellison, D. (1986, October). Improving productivity in teaching. *Phi Delta Kappan, 68,* 111–124.

Emmer, E., Everston, C., Sanford, J., & Clements, B. (1982). *Improving classroom management: An experimental study in junior high classrooms.* Austin: The University of Texas (ERIC Document Reproduction Services ED 261 053).

Emmer, E., Sanford, J., Evertson, C., Clements, B., & Martin, J. (1981). *The classroom management improvement study: An experiment in elementary school classrooms.* Austin: The University of Texas (ERIC Document Reproduction Services ED 226 452).

English, C. S. (1984). Measuring teacher effectiveness from the teacher's point of view. *Focus on Exceptional Children, 17,* 1–15.

Feasley, C. E. (1982). Distance education. In H. E. Mitzel (Ed.), *Encyclopedia of educational research.* Fifth Edition (pp. 450–458). New York: Free Press.

Fisher, C., Berliner, D., Filby, N., Marliave, R., Cahen, L., & Dishaw, M. (1980). Teaching behaviors, academic learning time, and student achievement: An overview. In C. Denham & A. Lieberman (Eds.), *Time to learn: A review of the beginning teacher evaluation study* (pp. 7–32). Washington, DC: National Institute of Education.

Freiberg, H., & Driscoll, A. (1996). *Universal teaching strategies.* Boston: Allyn and Bacon.

Gage, N. L., & Berliner, D.C. (1976). The psychology of teaching methods. In N. L. Gage (Ed.), *The psychology of teaching methods* (pp. 1–20). Chicago: University of Chicago Press.

Gage, N. L., & Berliner, D.C. (1998). *Educational Psychology.* Sixth Edition. Boston: Houghton Mifflin.

Gall, J., & Gall, M. (1990). Outcomes of the discussion method. In W. W. Wilen (Ed.), *Teaching and learning through discussion: The theory and practice of the discussion method* (pp. 25–44). Springfield, IL: Charles C. Thomas.

Gall, M. D. (1987). Discussion methods. In M. J. Dunkin (Ed.), *International encyclopedia of teaching and teacher education* (pp. 232–237). Oxford: Pergamon Press.

Gall, M. D., & Gall, J. P.(1976). The discussion method. In N. L. Gage (Ed.), *The psychology of teaching methods* (pp. 166–216). Chicago: University of Chicago Press.

Gardner, J. (1964). *Self-renewal: The individual and the innovative society.* New York: Harper.

Gartland, D. (1986). The effects of varying amounts of teacher-directed instruction and monitored independent seat work on the acquisition of syllabication rules by severely disabled readers. Unpublished doctoral dissertation. University Park: Pennsylvania State University.

Gibbons, M. (1971). *Individualized instruction: A descriptive analysis.* New York: Teachers College Press, Columbia University.

Gilstrap, R. L., & Martin, W. R. (1975). *Current strategies for teachers.* Pacific Palisades, CA: Goodyear.

Gold Rush. Post Office Box 997, Lakeside, CA: Interact.

Goldenberg, C. (1991). Instructional conversations. National Center for Research on Diversity and Second Language Learning. University of California, Los Angeles.

Good, T. (1995). Teachers' expectations. In L. W. Anderson (Ed.), *International encyclopedia of teaching and teacher education* (pp. 29–35). Oxford: Pergamon Press.

Good, T., & Grouws, L. (1975). *Process-product relationships in fourth grade mathematics classrooms.* Columbia: University of Missouri.

Goodlad, J. I. (1983). *A place called school.* New York: McGraw-Hill.

Gump, P. (1967). *The classroom behavior setting: Its nature and relation to student behavior.* Lawrence: University of Kansas (ERIC Document Reproduction Services ED 015 515).

Hamilton, R., & Ghatala, E. (1994). *Learning and instruction.* New York: McGraw-Hill.

Heck, S., & Williams, C. R. (1984). *The complex roles of the teacher.* New York: Teachers College, Columbia University.

Hill, W. F. (2000). *Learning through discussion: Guide for leaders and members of discussion groups.* Prospect Heights, IL: Waveland Press.

Jacobson, D., Eggen, P., Kauchuk, D., & Dulaney, C. (1985). *Methods for teaching.* Columbus, OH: Merrill.

Jeter, J. (1980). Individualized instruction programs. In J. Jeter (Ed.), *Approaches to individualized ecucation* (pp. 402–407). New York: Bowker.

Kindsvatter, R., Wilen, W., & Ishler, M. (1988). *Dynamics of effective teaching.* New York: Longman.

Kounin, J. (1970). *Discipline and group management in classrooms.* Chicago: Holt, Rinehart, and Winston.

Lawry, J. R. (1987a). The Dalton plan. In M. J. Dunkin (Ed.), *The international encyclopedia of teaching and teacher education* (pp. 214–215). Oxford: Pergamon Press.

CHAPTER 7

Four Instructional Alternatives:
Presentation, Discussion, Independent
Study, and Individualized Instruction

225

Lawry, J. R. (1987b). The project method. In M. J. Dunkin (Ed.), *The international encyclopedia of teaching and teacher education* (pp. 217–219). Oxford: Pergamon Press.

Lawry, J. R. (1987c). The Winnetka scheme. In M. J. Dunkin (Ed.), *The international encyclopedia of teaching and teacher education* (pp. 216–217). Oxford: Pergamon Press.

McLeish, J. (1975). The lecture method. In N.L. Gage (Ed.), *Psychology of teaching methods* (pp. 252–301). Chicago: University of Chicago Press.

Medway, F. J. (1987). Tutoring. In M.J. Dunkin (Ed.), *International encyclopedia of teaching and teacher education* (pp. 243–245). Oxford: Pergamon Press.

Nixon-John, G. D. (1994, Summer). The high school writing center: A room for one-on-one student tutoring. *Teaching and Change, 1*(4), 369–379.

Olson, L. (1993, February 17). Progressive-era conception breaks mold: NASDC schools explore "project learning." *Education Week, 12*(21), 6.

Parker, W., and Hess, D. (2001). Teaching *with* and *for* discussion. *Teaching and Teacher Education, 17,* 273–289.

Paulu, N. H. (1998). Helping your students with homework. Washington, DC: Office of Educational Research and Improvement, U.S. Department of Education.

Pavin, R. (1992, October). Benefits of nongraded schools. *Educational Leadership,* (2), 22–25.

Phelan, P., Davidson, A. L., & Cao, H. T. (1992, May). Speaking up: Student's perspectives on school. *Phi Delta Kappan, 73*(9), 695–704.

Roby, T. W. (1981, April). Bull sessions, quiz shows and discussions. Paper presented at the annual meeting of the American Educational Research Association, Los Angeles.

Rosenshine, B. (1980). How time is spent in elementary classrooms. In D. Denham & A. Lieberman (Eds.), *Time to learn: A review of the beginning teacher evaluation study* (pp. 107–126). Washington, DC: National Institute of Education.

Rosenshine, B. (1987). Direct instruction. In M. J. Dunkin (Ed.), *International encyclopedia of teaching and teacher education* (pp. 257–262). Oxford: Pergamon Press.

Rosenshine, B., & Stevens, R. (1986). Teaching functions. In M. C. Wittrock (Ed.), *Handbook of research on teaching* (pp. 376–391). New York: Macmillan.

Rossmiller, R. A. (1976). Individually guided education. In S. E. Goodman (Ed.), *Handbook on contemporary education* (pp. 402–407). New York: Bowker.

Rupley, W., & Blair, T. (1987, January). Assignment and supervision of reading seatwork: Looking in on 12 primary teachers. *The Reading Teacher, 40,* 391–393.

Schmuck, R., & Schmuck, P. (2001). *Group processes in the classroom.* New York: McGraw-Hill.

Scott, Rose Mary. (1989). The relationship between elementary teachers' use of theoretical knowledge about seat work during reading instruction and students' on-task behavior. Unpublished doctoral dissertation. Columbus: Ohio State University.

Seifert, E. H., & Beck, J. J. (1984, September–October). Relationship between task time and learning gains in secondary schools. *Journal of Educational Research, 78,* 5–10.

Shuell, T. J., Brown, S., Watson, D. G., & Ewing, J. A. (1988, March). Teachers' perceptions of the differential appropriateness of various teaching methods. *The Elementary School Journal, 88*(4), 339–356.

Simich-Dudgeon, C. (1998). Classroom strategies for encouraging collaborative discussion. In P. DiCerbo (Ed.), *Directions in language and education.* No. 12, Washington, DC: George Washington University.

Slavin, R. E. (1999). *Educational psychology.* Sixth Edition. Boston: Allyn & Bacon.

Slavin, R., & Madden, N. (1989, February). What works for students at risk: A research synthesis. *Educational Leadership, 46,* 4–13.

Stratton, (1993, February 19). Pupils see computer's classroom potential in action. *The Columbus Dispatch,* p. D1.

Swang, J. (1993, April/May). Ensuring Success in Science. *Learning, 93,* 24–27.

Toll, D. (1969). *Ghetto.* Indianapolis, IN: Bobbs-Merrill.

U.S. Department of Education. (1986, 1987). *What works: Research about teaching and learning.* Washington, DC: U.S. Department of Education.

Van Ments, M. (1990). *Active talk.* London: St. Martin's Press.

Walberg, H. (1984, May). Improving the productivity of America's schools. *Educational Leadership, 41,* 19–27.

Walberg, H., & Pascal, R. (1995). Homework. In L. Anderson (Ed.), *International encyclopedia of teaching and teacher education* (pp. 268–271). Oxford: Pergamon Press.

Wasley, P., Hampel, R., & Clark, R. (1997). *Kids and school reform.* San Francisco: Jossey-Bass.

Wasley, P. (1999, May). Teaching worth celebrating. *Educational Leadership, 56*(8), 8–13.

Watson, K. (1983). Some aspects of classroom discourse in English. Paper presented at the annual meeting of the Canadian Council of Teachers of English (ERIC Document Reproduction Services ED 233 365).

Willis, S., & Mann, L. (2000, Winter). Differentiating Instruction. *Curriculum Update* (pp. 1–3, 6–7). Alexandria, VA: Association for Supervision and Curriculum Development.

Wittrock, M. C. (1996). The learning by discovery hypothesis. In L. S. Shulman and E. R. Keislar (Eds.), *Learning by discovery: A critical appraisal.* Chicago: Rand McNally.

Four More Instructional Alternatives: Cooperative Learning, Discovery Learning, Constructivism and Direct Instruction

Contents

Chapter 7 introduced thirty instructional alternatives (illustrated in the Wheel of Instructional Choice) and elaborated on four commonly used choices: presentation, discussion, independent study, and individualized/differentiated instruction. Now let's turn our attention to four additional alternatives: cooperative learning, discovery learning, constructivism, and direct instruction.

Cooperative Learning: Teaching Learners to Like and Care for One Another

In a number of classrooms in which you have been a student, there has probably been a degree, perhaps a high degree, of competition among your peers. After all, nearly everyone in a class wants to get a good grade, and usually there are not enough to go around. Competition for good grades, however, may result in jealousy, even hostility, among learners. In an effort to reduce or eliminate competition and, relatedly, to build a sense of community, educators have searched for less competitive, nonconfrontational instructional alternatives. Mostly, they find some form of group work a suitable alternative. The group work of choice now is cooperative learning.

WHAT IS COOPERATIVE LEARNING?

Cooperative learning (formerly called student-team learning) is the term used to describe instructional procedures whereby learners work together in small groups and are rewarded for their *collective* accomplishments. Does that remind you of a team sport such as volleyball or soccer? The whole team does or doesn't do well depending on the contribution of each individual player and the extent to which they help one another. Cooperation is critical!

In cooperative learning, the groups or teams typically number from four to six. Their usual tasks are either to collectively learn or master content the teacher has previously presented, or to complete a teacher-assigned project as a team. In the first case, learners might work together to master spelling words the teacher has introduced. In the second, sometimes referred to as *group investigation* (Sharon & Sharon, 1989/1990), or *work groups* (Good, Reys, Grouws, & Mulryan, 1989/1990), they might work to learn about Native Americans of the Southwest or to solve a complex mathematical problem.

PURPOSE AND CHARACTERISTICS OF COOPERATIVE LEARNING

Instructional procedures bearing the title or resembling cooperative learning have something in common with all instructional alternatives—they encourage students to learn. However, in contrast to the others, cooperative learning encourages learners to work together for both the common and individual good. This purpose may remind you of the famous line d'Artagnon speaks in Alexandre Dumas's novel *The Three Musketeers*, "All for one, one for all, that is our device, is it not?"

8.1 How do you feel about classroom competition and cooperation?

8.2 Have you ever experienced cooperative learning? What was it like for you?

8.3 How important to you is the purpose of cooperative learning?

What are the key characteristics or attributes of cooperative learning systems? How is this "all for one, one for all" purpose achieved? Such systems are generally characterized by (1) the way the groups or teams are made up; (2) the kinds of tasks they do; (3) the groups' rules of behavior; and (4) their motivation and reward systems.

According to advocates, including Slavin (1995a, 1991a), groups must be heterogeneous in terms of gender, academic ability, race, and other traits. Heterogeneity is promoted for at least three reasons. First, cooperative learning is based partly on the humanistic school of thought about learning. That school of thought, as you recall from Chapter 4, focuses on the importance of personal and social development. One of its major objectives is to make students feel better about themselves and to be more accepting of others. Mixed groups offer a major means of achieving this goal.

A second reason to form heterogeneous teams is so that each member will have an equal opportunity to learn, since "talent" is about equally distributed to each group. Finally, heterogeneity is fostered because students with lower abilities are more likely to improve their achievement in mixed groups than in homogeneous groups (Fashalla & Slavin, 1997; Hoffer, 1992; Slavin, 1995a). Thus, heterogeneous teams would seem especially beneficial for students who are at risk of academic failure.

A second way cooperative learning can be characterized is by the kinds of tasks teachers typically assign to the teams. The most common assignment requires each team to master material the teacher presented previously. For example, Mrs. Braggins does a presentation on why the seasons change. She then asks the teams to review and learn the material in preparation for a quiz. Another common task is to ask teams to work on projects. Mr. Cruz asks his teams to read about the settling of California and then to collaboratively compose a letter as if a settler were writing to relatives in Spain describing the conditions of mission life.

Third, cooperative learning is characterized by rules of behavior required of team members: individual responsibility and accountability to oneself and the team, support and encouragement of team members, peer helping and tutoring, and, of course, cooperation. You can see how well the "all for one, one for all" analogy fits.

Finally, cooperative learning is characterized by a unique system of rewards. Rather than a mark based on personal effort, the individual receives a mark based on the team's achievement. If the students studied for and took a quiz on why the seasons change, the team's mark may be the average score for all team members. In the letter-writing assignment, all team members receive the score the letter earns. Again, we can liken such a situation to a sport where the team has a collective score and thereby wins or loses. Of course, this arrangement usually arouses peer pressure to do well and to help others do well. Thus, we think cooperative learning also derives some of its ideas from the behavioral school of thought, particularly operant conditioning and social learning.

FIGURE 8.1 Purpose and Key Characteristics of Cooperative Learning

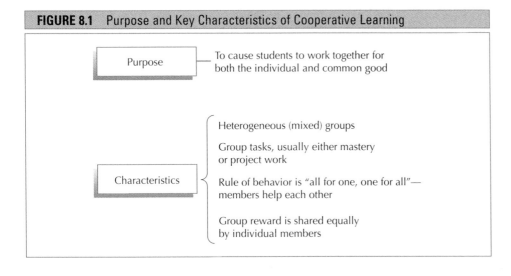

In some cases, as you will see, cooperative teams can compete against one another. In other cases, teams compete against themselves and get a better mark only when they surpass some earlier achievement. Figure 8.1 illustrates the purpose and key characteristics of cooperative learning.

8.4 How do you feel about cooperative learning's key characteristics?

VARIATIONS ON THE THEME OF COOPERATIVE LEARNING

There are many versions of cooperative learning. (Aronson, Blaney, Stephan, Sikes, & Snapp, 1978; Cohen, 1986; Johnson & Johnson, 1998; Johnson, Johnson, & Holubec, 1998; Sharon & Sharon, 1976; Slavin, 1995a; Solomon, Watson, Schaps, Battistich, & Solomon, 1990). We will briefly describe a few.

Student Teams, Achievement Divisions (STAD) Of the variations, the simplest to understand is STAD. In STAD, the student teams must master some content, usually presented by the teacher, perhaps new vocabulary. Students work in teams to ensure that all members can perform well on an upcoming vocabulary quiz. The STAD process involves teacher presentation, team study, individual quizzes, determination of team scores, and team reward or recognition. To arrive at a team score, an individual's score is often compared to past work she or he has done. If the work is better than comparable past work, the person earns "improvement points." The team score is the sum of the improvement points individual members earn. This kind of scoring is most easily done when students take quizzes in spelling, arithmetic, and other subjects with easily quantified scores.

Teams, Games, Tournaments (TGT) The procedure for TGT follows STAD except that, instead of an individual quiz being given, the teams compete against one another. Thus, the TGT procedure is teacher presentation, teamwork, team-versus-team competition, scoring, and team reward. In the team-versus-team competition phase, each member of a team is assigned to a table where he or she will compete against members from other teams. Top members from each team compete against one another in *equal competition;* the winner at each table is usually bumped up to the next higher level or table of competition. Think of this as comparable to the "ladders" used in sports competition—if you lose, you move down. Thus, competition always occurs among matched or somewhat like-achieving students. To some extent then, TGT loses the characteristic of heterogeneity, at least during academic competition.

Team-Assisted Individualization and Team-Accelerated Instruction (TAI) TAI combines the notions of cooperative learning and individually paced instruction. The latter means that students do not stay together academically, but instead learn or

CHAPTER 8
Four More Instructional Alternatives:
Cooperative Learning, Discovery
Learning, Constructivism,
and Direct Instruction

231

move through the material they are to master at their own pace. For instance, at the outset students take a proficiency test in arithmetic. Based on the results, they are placed on mixed-ability teams. However, instead of working together, each team member works on a different aspect or unit of arithmetic according to her or his needs. The unit usually contains some guide pages that provide information essential to completing the work. Thus, a unit on division of fractions would contain pages illustrating how to divide fractions. The unit also would contain practice exercises, a short test or tests, and an answer sheet. In TAI, team members check one another's work, and more advanced students serve as tutors. Rewards may be based upon the number of units each team has completed, the number of final tests they have passed, or other criteria. An important element of TAI is that while teams are at work, the teacher is free to pull together students working on similar units to diagnose their progress and further assist them.

8.5 Which form of cooperative learning appeals to you most? Why?

Cooperative Integrated Reading and Composition (CIRC)   CIRC is mainly used to teach reading and composition. In the typical CIRC procedure, the teacher sets a lesson in some specific area of reading or composition, for example, identifying the main characters and ideas in a piece of literature such as *Romeo and Juliet*. Student teams are then asked to read the story and to note the main characters and ideas. Team members, who may work in pairs, interact to check each other and gain consensus. They then may check their understanding with another pair on their team or against an answer sheet. While these paired and team activities are going on, the teacher convenes members from each team who are at a comparable proficiency or skill level in order to teach them a new reading skill, and the cycle continues. As with other forms of cooperative learning, points are given to teams based on individual members' performances on the activities and/or tests. The four forms of cooperative learning described are compared in Table 8.1.

GOOD LEADERS OF COOPERATIVE LEARNING

Cooperative learning procedures demand a lot from teachers. These approaches, depending on the type, require teachers to be responsible for presenting information, creating suitable group and possibly independent work assignments, establishing and maintaining cooperative groups, monitoring individual and group progress, convening and teaching small groups of learners, devising and maintaining progress records, and providing rewards.

Foremost, as the leader of any instructional alternative, you must believe in its purpose. You must have faith! In this case, you must subscribe to the "all for one, one for all" philosophy. Relatedly, you must be able to organize heterogenous teams

TABLE 8.1   Four Forms of Cooperative Learning and Their Individual Characteristics

STAD	TGT	TAI	CIRC
		Proficiency testing of students, team assignment	
Presentation of information	Presentation of information	Individual but team-assisted study	Pairs work and teams work
Individual student quizzes	Team-vs.-team competition	Individual student quizzes	Individual student quizzes
Team scoring	Team scoring	Team scoring	Team scoring
Recognition	Recognition	Recognition	Recognition

and ensure that team members also value cooperative, collaborative learning. Also, since STAD, TGT, and CIRC incorporate teacher whole-class or small-group presentation, you must be a good presenter (see Table 7.2). Finally, since all these variations of cooperative learning utilize some amount of independent study, you will also need to be good at facilitating this (see Table 7.6).

All forms of cooperative learning call for teachers who have the organizational skills to plan, monitor, facilitate, and track the work of disparate groups. Monitoring and facilitation are best accomplished when you have diagnostic and clinical skills, that is, when you are able to identify and help students and teams as they encounter problems. You must be a good juggler.

A subtle, yet very real, challenge teachers face when they use small-group instruction is the need to ensure that high-achieving students do not dominate the heterogeneous groups they are in. In a study of cooperative learning, King (1993) reports that "high-achieving students assumed dominant roles in the undertaking of group tasks, in group decision making, and in the frequency and quality of contributions" (p.399). To avoid passivity on the part of low achievers, King suggests that teachers must create positive expectations that low achievers "can do." As you can see, utilizing cooperative learning is not for the faint of heart.

8.6 What beliefs and abilities do you have that might help you implement cooperative learning? What might inhibit your use of it?

GOOD COOPERATIVE LEARNING

Since there are several forms of cooperative learning, each requires a somewhat different kind of teacher preparation, delivery, and closure. Therefore, we will restrict our comments to STAD since it is the simplest, best known, and most frequently used form. Furthermore, Slavin (1995) recommends it as "a good model to begin with for teachers who are new to the cooperative approach" (p. 54).

Preparation STAD, you may recall, is the form of cooperative learning in which the teacher presents information and then places students in heterogeneous groups to learn or master that information. Thus, two kinds of preparation are essential: (1) you must be prepared to provide information in the most effective way, and (2) students must be prepared to engage in group work so they can master the information.

Since a teacher presentation is called for, the information on good presentations in the previous chapter is useful. You may recall from Table 7.2 that as you prepare for a presentation, you must establish both its general purpose and its specific learner objectives (what learners should know and be able to do as a consequence of receiving the information). Johnson and Johnson (1998) offer a few questions useful in guiding teacher planning. They include: What do I want students to learn? What cognitive and affective outcomes should they achieve? What are some learning activities that can best accomplish these ends? What resources and assistance will learners need? In addition, you must collect and review materials that provide the knowledge you will present and, having taken these steps, plan the presentation. Finally, since a team assignment is to be undertaken following the presentation, you must organize that assignment and be ready to deliver it. You also must create a quiz.

Students must also be oriented to engage in STAD. Prior to its first use they must be told why it is being used, how it works, and, particularly, what is expected of them. Thereafter, each time STAD is used, learners need to be organized into heterogeneous groups and motivated to help one another learn. In some cases, students will need to be taught or reminded of the social skills they need to use. Highlight 8.1 lists some of these skills and discusses their importance.

Try Activity 8.1

Delivery Delivery of STAD involves two steps: (1) your presentation and (2) initiation and monitoring of the teamwork. Once more, the information on good presentations from Chapter 7 is applicable. To review, when delivering a good presentation you should get students' attention, tell them what they will learn and, as a result, what they should be able to do after learning; relate the new information to ideas

Johnson and Johnson (1989/1990) caution us that "people do not know instinctively how to interact effectively with others. Nor do interpersonal and group skills magically appear when needed. Students must be taught these skills and be motivated to use them. If group members lack interpersonal and small group skills . . . cooperative groups will not be productive" (p. 30).

The skills Johnson and Johnson feel are most necessary are to:

- Know and trust one another
- Communicate clearly and accurately
- Support one another through praise and encouragement
- Resolve conflicts constructively

learners already know; present the information in a step-by-step manner; don't overwhelm or underwhelm; emphasize the most important points students need to remember or use; use examples and illustrations to increase clarity; use variety to maintain attention; and make sure learners understand by asking them questions.

Following your presentation, teamwork begins. You must then accomplish the following:

1. *Set the team goals.* The major function of the team in STAD is to prepare its members to learn as much as possible in order to obtain a high team quiz score.

2. *Prepare students for teamwork.* In STAD, this requires forming them into heterogeneous groups, reminding them of the "all for one, one for all" philosophy of cooperative learning, communicating your expectations for individual and group behavior, and jogging their memories concerning the interactive or social skills they will need to use.

3. *Give the teams the assignment.* Depending upon the nature of the assignment, you may have prepared handouts, worksheets, or a practice quiz for the teams to work on collaboratively.

4. *Monitor the teams.* Although the intention is that students teach and help one another, you must be sure that this, in fact, is happening. Therefore, you must be up and about, observing and listening, and intervening when necessary. One of the biggest mistakes you can make is to assume students know what to do and to assume they are doing it correctly. An ounce of prevention is worth a pound of cure.

5. *Quiz the students.* At a previously designated time, individual team members take the quiz. Although students have worked together to get ready for the quiz, they must take it independently.

6. *Score the quizzes.* Students may score one another's papers, or you may want to collect and score them yourself. (There are advantages and disadvantages either way. Can you think of some of them?) Once you have scored individual quizzes, you need to calculate team scores. There are at least two ways to derive team scores. In one, you calculate an "improvement score" by comparing each learner's achievement on this quiz with her or his achievement on a similar, earlier quiz. If the score is better, the student receives one or more improvement points. Then you add all individual improvement scores to get the team improvement score. Another way to calculate a team score is simply to add the members' scores together. Most advocates of cooperative learning procedures favor the use of improvement scores.

7. *Recognize team accomplishment.* When improvement scores are used, teams that have improved performance receive some recognition. Thus, teams compete with themselves to improve, rather than against other teams to win. This is more gentle than rewarding teams that outperform other teams. Forms of recognition and reward can include printed certificates of achievement, recognition as

TABLE 8.2 Qualities of Good Cooperative Learning Leaders
and of Good Cooperative Learning (STAD)

Good Leaders of Cooperative Learning . . .	Good Cooperative Learning (STAD)
• Believe in the importance of getting learners to work together for the individual and common good	*When preparing:*
	• Prepare the presentation utilizing elements of a "good presentation" (Table 7.2)
• Are able to get diverse learners to work cooperatively	• Prepare the team assignment (Table 7.6)
• Are competent presenters and use independent study assignments effectively (see Tables 7.2 and 7.6)	• Prepare students for future engagement in cooperative learning by explaining effective interpersonal and interactive skills (see Highlight 8.1)
• Are especially effective organizers and coordinators of work	*When delivering:*
	• Make the presentation utilizing elements of a "good presentation" (Table 7.2)
• Are especially effective diagnosticians and clinicians, i.e., are able to identify and help students and teams having difficulty	• Set team goals
	• Prepare students for work with their team
	• Give the teams the assignment
	• Quiz the students
	• Recognize team accomplishments
	When closing:
	• Remind students of what they learned
	• Relate new learning to past or future learning
	• Provide opportunity for practical use of information

"super team" of the week, or special privileges. As mentioned earlier, cooperative learning draws from the behavioral school of thought and particularly from operant conditioning. If you do something well, you get rewarded.

Closure Little is said in the literature on cooperative learning about what, if anything, to do after you give grades and rewards. Considering what we know about short- and long-term memory (Chapter 4), we presume that students should be reminded of what they have just learned, the new information should be securely related and attached to what they already know or what they will learn next, and they should have the opportunity to apply the information in some way.

A summary of the qualities of good cooperative learning leaders and of the elements of good cooperative learning appears in Table 8.2. A sample cooperative learning lesson plan appears as Lesson Plan 8.1.

8.7 What factors in Chapter 1 may influence your use of cooperative learning?

Try Activity 8.2

When Cooperative Learning Should Be Used

Properly conducted, cooperative learning is an instructional alternative with strong support. It seems to reduce competition and increase cooperation and achievement. When should it be used? Our answer is, often—but not always. As indicated in Chapter 7, variety in instruction is extremely important. Teachers' comments interspersed throughout Slavin's book (1995) indicate that although students do not seem to tire of cooperative learning, the possibility of boredom exists. Consequently, teachers who use this instructional alternative make certain adjustments. For example, they vary team membership, tasks, and rewards.

A second reason to avoid putting all our eggs into the cooperative learning basket is that different kinds of educational objectives are best achieved using different instructional alternatives. Supporting this view, Stallings and Stipek (1986) note that TGT does not seem to produce as much achievement when used in social studies. Furthermore, they cite Sharon (1980), who questions whether the use of cooperative

CHAPTER 8

Four More Instructional Alternatives:
Cooperative Learning, Discovery
Learning, Constructivism,
and Direct Instruction

235

Abbreviated Cooperative Learning Lesson Plan: Applied Arithmetic

Curriculum tie-in: This lesson allows learners to see how arithmetic computation is used in everyday life. It also complements the social relationships curriculum.

OBJECTIVES

1. Each team of learners will cooperate to build the tallest free-standing structure at the lowest cost. *Specific objectives:* Given resources, teams of learners will build a free-standing structure that is as tall and as inexpensive as possible; teams will engage in arithmetic computations to determine its cost.

2. Teams will encourage arithmetic contributions from each member. *Specific objective:* Given the task, each team should strive to record at least one arithmetic contribution from each member.

3. Teams will employ good interpersonal skills. *Specific objective:* Learners will display respect for and consideration of others.

RESOURCES PER TEAM (others may be substituted)

1. 20 plastic straws (value $1 each), 10 small paper clips (value $.20 each), 20 straight pins (value $.10 each), roll of masking tape (value $.20 for each inch used).

2. Yard or meter stick.

3. Calculator (optional).

4. Encyclopedia material on building construction.

METHODOLOGY

1. *Set induction:* "What are some of the tallest buildings in the country? How do you think they can be built so tall?"

2. Inform learners of what they will learn and be able to do as a result of lesson.

3. Establish *heterogeneous* groups of four to six learners and provide each with space and building materials (see Resources above).

4. Establish roles: *builders, mathematicians, scientists* (who list principles of building used), *reporter* who observes and prepares a report for the class that includes such things as how tall the structure was, how much it cost, what principles of building were used, what arithmetic was most valuable.

5. Have students discuss how they can encourage and respect the ideas and skills of other team members.

6. Provide time for teams to read about buildings and to plan and build theirs.

7. Have each team reporter tell the class what rules of construction were used, what the successes and failures were, how each member contributed mathematically, what math was most useful, and what the height and cost of the building was.

ASSESSMENT: Monitor all groups to determine

1. How well learners are able to employ arithmetic properly and correctly.

2. To what extent team members employ good interpersonal skills.

3. To what extent all learners are involved as contributors.

CLOSURE

1. Ask learners to tell what they learned about building, the value of arithmetic, and helping all to contribute.

2. Ask them how arithmetic is used in other occupations and how their caregivers may use it.

---

learning, specifically STAD and TGT, can be as effective when the goal is to teach or use higher-level thinking skills such as analysis, synthesis, and evaluation.

Keeping these restrictions in mind, cooperative learning is probably best utilized when the class needs to develop a sense of harmony and community building (all for one, one for all), when students are at risk or generally suffer from low self-esteem, and when teachers want to help integrate mainstreamed students.

Teachers who select cooperative learning strategies probably believe in the "all for one, one for all" philosophy, feel they have good leadership and interpersonal skills, know that their organizational and monitoring abilities enable them to do more than one thing at a time (overlapping), and believe that this approach works.

Three kinds of students who seem to benefit from involvement in cooperative learning are described in Case 8.1.

Web Resource The Cooperative Learning Center maintains a website at http://www.clcrc.com/. It has several links, including one to "Cooperative Learning." Here, the following questions are addressed: What is cooperative learning? Why use it? What makes cooperative groups work?

Three teachers (Augustine, Gruber, & Hansen, 1989/1990) provide sketches of three kinds of students positively affected by cooperative learning.

Andy is a low-achieving elementary school student. He was failing several subjects and needed supervision to stay on task until cooperative learning was introduced. The changes are astonishing. His grades have improved to the point where he is passing all subjects. Additionally, Andy has become a "cheerful, confident child."

Susan, a child with handicaps mainstreamed in a regular classroom, was placed in a cooperative learning group. The group's task was to prepare for a chapter test. When the group's study time was over, Susan still was not ready. Instead of taking recess, her group colleagues stayed to work further with her. They also helped her the next day before the test was given. On the test, Susan and all her teammates received perfect scores.

Angela, a gifted student, excelled at school and also in piano, gymnastics, and dance. Her parents questioned how working in a group where she would be held to a group norm would be beneficial. After all, Angela did outstanding work on her own. After a conference, Angela's parents were convinced she might benefit from learning how to interact with less capable peers. Her group work has helped Angela become more tactful, respectful, and sharing.

LIMITATIONS OF COOPERATIVE LEARNING

The success of cooperative learning depends upon a number of conditions. First, research shows that for a cooperative learning activity to succeed, team members must not simply share answers but, more importantly, explain how they derived the answers and why they are correct (Slavin, 1995). Without this step, students are not able to apply or use the information later. Therefore, some students in each group must be "good teachers." Successful learning experiences also require that high achievers care for and help or nurture low achievers. The implicit assumption is that good students wish to help less able students.

A second important condition is that individual team members be accountable to the team. This "one for all" expectation is not what students have been accustomed to; what they are accustomed to is interpersonal competition.

Third, in order for cooperative learning to have a chance, team members must stay on task, since time on task is consistently related to students' learning (see Chapter 12). Students tend to get off task when the teacher is not present. Teachers must regularly monitor individual and small-group work during cooperative learning.

Fourth, in any team, individuals must get along with one another. In every classroom, certain students will find this difficult. There may also be students who will do less work or work less hard, thereby causing the team to suffer or cover up. Brophy and Good (1986) remind us that any form of small-group instruction is more difficult than teaching the class as a whole because these and other management problems are compounded (see Chapter 13).

Finally, teaching arrangements that encourage some children to provide assistance and others to receive it appear likely to increase dependency (Biemiller, 1993).

SUMMARY ON COOPERATIVE LEARNING

At the outset, we characterized cooperative learning as teaching learners to like and care for one another. We stated that the method is analogous to creating teams of musketeers who come to one another's assistance and who succeed together no matter what the circumstances. Cooperative learning seems to have a hint of romanticism about it when compared to its more common instructional cousins such as presentation, discussion, and independent study. In business jargon, it seems to have more "sizzle."

CHAPTER 8

Four More Instructional Alternatives:
Cooperative Learning, Discovery
Learning, Constructivism,
and Direct Instruction

237

We also learned that there are a number of different cooperative learning approaches but that most have four characteristics in common (see Figure 8.1): (1) they utilize teams that are mostly heterogeneous in composition; (2) the task the teams undertake usually involves either mastering material presented by a teacher, mastering written materials, or working on a project; (3) accountability is twofold—to oneself and to assisting the team and its members; and (4) rewards are generally tied to overall team improvement.

As with any instructional alternative, teachers who use this approach need certain attributes. They need to be good presenters, to be insightful in developing worthwhile team assignments, and to be able to monitor teamwork, diagnose problems, and prescribe remedies. Since the various forms of cooperative learning differ, each has a set of best procedures to follow. The qualities of good procedures for STAD appear in Table 8.2.

Like each instructional alternative on the Wheel of Instructional Choice (Figure 7.5), cooperative learning (student-team learning) has unique advantages and limitations. Its advantages mirror those offered by discussion, another student-centered alternative that meets a large number of students' needs. However, cooperative learning seems to be better than discussion at meeting students' needs to achieve academically and socially.

Try Activity 8.3

Certain cooperative learning processes have been subjected to controlled study, and most prove to contribute to student success, that is achievement and satisfaction (see Spotlight on Research 8.1). Little consensus exists concerning how frequently cooperative learning is used; estimates range from 7 to 20 percent of the time. However, we can assume from its repeated mention in the professional literature that cooperative learning is very much alive and well. One of its better known proponents sums it up, although perhaps a bit too optimistically: "Cooperative learning seems to be an extraordinary success. It has an excellent research base, many viable, successful forms, and hundreds of thousands of enthusiastic adherents" (Slavin, 1989/1995, p. 3).

Discovery Learning: Figuring Things Out for Yourself

You have probably heard of Sherlock Holmes, the famous detective created by Sir Arthur Conan Doyle. As you may recall, Holmes was regularly faced with baffling cases such as the sudden, mysterious death of Sir Charles Baskerville in the novel *The Hound of the Baskervilles* (Doyle, 1901). According to his great friend Dr. Watson, Holmes—as was his custom—demanded the facts. After gathering them, he would retreat into seclusion in order to "weigh every particle of evidence, construct alternative theories, balance one against the other, and make up his mind as to which points were essential and which immaterial" (p. 35) to solving the mystery. Holmes was the consummate inductive reasoner, always "putting two and two together" in order to reach some logical explanation or conclusion.

Many times we, too, face situations where we have to figure things out for ourselves. What is the meaning of a new word we find in a sentence? How can we get the word processor to double-space? Why did we get a C in the course instead of a B? How can we get a B next time?

Psychologists and educators (Bruner, 1977; Dewey, 1933; Joyce & Weil, 1999; Strike, 1975; Suchman, 1961; Taba, 1966) make the case that reasoning skills—Sherlock Holmes's, ours, or our students'—can be improved through use. They propose that we utilize discovery learning to give learners the opportunity to collect, organize, manipulate, and analyze data. Discovery learning is the instructional alternative many educators tout as the choice for teaching social studies, science, and mathematics. It falls within the cognitive school of thought under meaningful learning. See Chapter 4.

There are differences of opinion regarding the effectiveness of cooperative learning. Its founders and proponents give it very high marks (Fashala & Slavin, 1997).

Johnson and others (1981) reviewed 122 studies that compared the effectiveness of four instructional alternatives: cooperation, cooperation with intergroup competition, interpersonal competition, and independently done individual work. When cooperation and competition were compared, researchers found that the average student's achievement in a cooperative program equaled that of students at the 78th percentile who worked in either a competitive or individualistic arrangement. This means that a middle-achieving student in cooperative learning does as well as a higher-achieving student under the other two forms of instruction. Other findings indicate that the average student in the cooperative programs achieved at a level (1) equal to that of students at the 64th percentile in interpersonal competitive programs and (2) equal to that of students at the 69th percentile in individualistic programs. Johnson and associates did not find achievement differences between students in cooperative groups and students involved in intergroup competition. Nor have differences in

achievement been found between interpersonal competition and independent work (Runkel & Schmuck, 1982).

Similarly, Slavin's (1991) findings strongly support cooperative learning processes as facilitating student achievement. He found sixty-seven "high-quality studies" that compared achievement of elementary and high school students taught by cooperative processes to the achievement of similar students taught by traditional methods. In forty-one studies, or 61 percent of the research, the cooperatively taught students performed significantly better. In fact, in only one of the sixty-seven studies did traditionally taught students excel. Slavin notes, "In studies of methods such as STAD, TGT, TAI, and CIRC, effects on achievement have been consistently positive" (p. 76).

Slavin goes on to say that when students are rewarded according to the group's achievement, which depends on how much each learner learned, students learn even more. Achievement improves regardless of grade level, subject area, or geographic location of the school—urban, suburban, or rural.

In addition to the positive effects cooperative learning has on achievement, Slavin (1991, 1995) also notes that it produces many beneficial side-effects

including higher self-esteem, better intergroup relationships, greater acceptance of others, better attitudes toward school, and improved ability to work cooperatively.

After reviewing research on STAD, TGT, and Jigsaw (a form not presented here but described in Slavin, 1995a), Stallings and Stipek (1986) agree that these forms of cooperative learning seem to have positive effects on achievement. However, they warn us that many other variations on the theme of cooperative learning have not yet been investigated. Furthermore, Stallings and Stipek feel that the most important outcomes of cooperative learning may be in the affective domain of learning and include such things as greater mutual concern, more friendships with diverse students, a better feeling about school, and a sense of greater peer support.

Other caveats come from Webb (1982) and Battistich, Solomon, and Delucci (1993). Webb reminds us that, contrary to what Slavin and others have reported more recently, Michaels (1978) found individual competition promotes better achievement than group work does. Battistich and his colleagues, who are advocates of cooperative learning, note "that cooperative learning does not invariably lead to positive outcomes" (p. 20).

WHAT IS DISCOVERY LEARNING?

Discovery or **inquiry learning** refers to learning that takes place when students are asked to find out or figure out something for themselves as Sherlock Holmes does. Here are some classroom examples. Rather than telling students using water colors that if they want to use green they must mix blue and yellow, the teacher asks them to mix the two colors to find out the result. Rather than telling middle school students the value of *pi*, the teacher asks them to measure spherical objects to find it out. Rather than telling students the life cycle of a frog, the instructor has learners observe and record it. Do you see how discovery learning or figuring things out for yourself might result in greater understanding and better recollection?

8.8 Do you prefer having someone teach you something or figuring it out for yourself?

CHAPTER 8
Four More Instructional Alternatives:
Cooperative Learning, Discovery
Learning, Constructivism,
and Direct Instruction

239

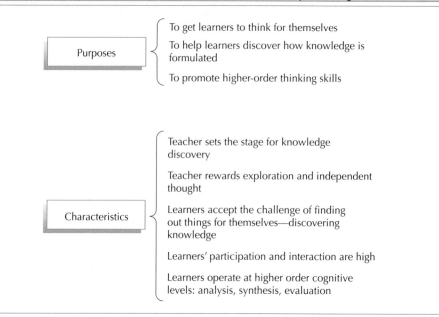

FIGURE 8.2   Purposes and Key Characteristics of Discovery Learning

Purposes
- To get learners to think for themselves
- To help learners discover how knowledge is formulated
- To promote higher-order thinking skills

Characteristics
- Teacher sets the stage for knowledge discovery
- Teacher rewards exploration and independent thought
- Learners accept the challenge of finding out things for themselves—discovering knowledge
- Learners' participation and interaction are high
- Learners operate at higher order cognitive levels: analysis, synthesis, evaluation

8.9   How important are the purposes of discovery learning?

8.10   How much do you value the key characteristics of discovery learning in Figure 8.2?

PURPOSES AND CHARACTERISTICS OF DISCOVERY LEARNING

Teachers use discovery learning to accomplish three educational purposes (see Figure 8.2). First, *they want learners to know how to think and find things out for themselves.* Conversely, they want them to be less dependent on receiving knowledge from teachers and accepting the conclusions of others. Secondly, users of discovery learning *want learners to see for themselves how knowledge is obtained.* This means such teachers want students to be able to learn by collecting, organizing, and analyzing information to reach their own conclusions. Third, *these teachers want learners to use their highest-order thinking skills.* Among other things, they want them to analyze, synthesize, and evaluate as described in Chapter 6, Planning Instruction.

The above purposes of discovery learning result in its having unique characteristics (see Figure 8.2). To begin with, the role of the teacher is not to impart knowledge but rather to create classroom experiences in which learners engage in order to discover knowledge. Read Case 8.2, in which teacher Deb O'Brien found an alternative to telling her learners that clothing does not produce heat. Instead she engaged learners in finding out for themselves that that is a misconception.

A second characteristic of discovery learning is that as learners engage in inquiry, the teacher encourages them to think deeply. Deb probably asked, "What could we try to find out if clothes make heat?" She helps learners think through their ideas and helps them formulate experiences that might be undertaken.

A third characteristic is that learners accept the challenge of finding something out for themselves rather than having the teacher give them an answer. They feel enabled.

As the process of inquiry goes on, it is characterized by a high degree of learner participation and interaction. There are lots of ideas and lots of give and take.

Finally, during the inquiry process, learners operate at high cognitive levels as the teacher asks questions such as, What do you think? How can we find out? How will we know? In teacher O'Brien's case the questions were "What is heat? How can we find out if it comes from clothing? Why do clothes make us feel warmer?"

Yes, the roles of teacher and learners change dramatically when you employ discovery learning. So does the process of learning.

A Teacher Uses Discovery Learning

Deb O'Brien introduced the new science unit on heat by asking her 9-year-olds, "What is heat?" She intended, through the question, to have them draw from their experiences, and this they did. They recalled that heat came from the sun and from fires, radiators, and assorted other sources. However, one boy posited that heat came from clothing such as coats and sweaters. His peers readily agreed. Deb recognized that to a 9-year-old, the observation seemed reasonable. After all, when they put "warm" clothing on, they were warmer. But how to currect this misconception? Should she tell them the truth? No. She felt it more appropriate that they learn it for themselves. So the class constructed an experiment. They wrapped thermometers in coats and sweaters and assumed the temperature thereon should rise. When it didn't, they sealed the clothing and thermometers in plastic bags. Still the thermometers recorded no heat change.

After numerous failed efforts to prove that clothes gave off heat, the learners were willing to entertain an alternative hypothesis—that clothing merely holds or contains the heat given off by those wearing it. These fourth-graders discovered for themselves knowledge about what causes and what contains or traps heat (Watson & Konicek, 1990).

GOOD FACILITATORS OF DISCOVERY LEARNING

To be effective with this instructional alternative, you must believe in its purposes. Do you think a major goal of education is to get students to think for themselves? Do you believe students have the ability to think for themselves? Even if you answer the first question affirmatively, you may be stymied by the second. After all, you have probably been in classrooms where some of your peers seemed less than able intellectually. However, keep in mind that the cause of their apparent ineptitude may stem from their never having the opportunity to build confidence in their own thinking ability. Belief in one's power to think must be planted and cultivated.

A second purpose of discovery learning is to get learners to find out how knowledge is constructed. Do you want them to know how concepts, facts, generalizations, rules, and laws are formulated? If you do, you have intellectual aspirations for your learners. You expect them to understand the very origin and nature of knowledge rather than just to memorize facts.

A third purpose of discovery learning is to get learners to develop their higher-order or critical thinking skills. Do you want them to know how to analyze, synthesize, evaluate, and solve problems? Can you persist in encouraging them to explore, investigate, search, observe, scrutinize, inspect, classify, measure, define, interpret, infer, predict, and hypothesize? If so, you will make an indelible mark on their minds and lives.

8.11 When your students don't understand, are you more likely to give them the answer or help them discover it?

8.12 What beliefs and abilities do you have that would help you to be a good practitioner of discovery learning?

CHAPTER 8
Four More Instructional Alternatives:
Cooperative Learning, Discovery
Learning, Constructivism,
and Direct Instruction

241

Aside from believing in the purpose of discovery learning, to be a good practitioner you need certain qualities. For example, you must enjoy inquiry yourself: You should be naturally curious and have "a strong interest in the discovery of truth by an empirical, critical, rational, 'intellectual' approach" (Anastasi, 1997, p. 488). Relatedly, you should believe that your learners are or can be curious, too. Moreover, you should be nurturing, thoughtful, patient, and accepting of learners' ideas while holding high expectations for them.

GOOD DISCOVERY LEARNING

Suppose you are sold on discovery learning and feel you have the ability to pull it off. What process or regimen would you follow? Persons either reviewing or advocating this instructional alternative suggest several stages and steps (Gilstrap & Martin, 1975; Harmin & Gregory, 1974; Joyce & Weil, 1999; Kauchak & Eggen, 1997; Orlich, 2000).

Preparation   When preparing any learning activity, you should have some broad purpose in mind. Perhaps it is to have students learn about pulse rate or rate of respiration. With that in mind, you decide *specifically* what students should know about either or both. Let's say you want them to know the meaning of pulse and respiration (concepts), how pulse and respiration are measured (procedures), the range of pulse and respiration rates (facts), normal rates (facts), and conditions that affect the rates (generalizations). To ensure your own knowledge of these areas and to have related resources available, you need to collect material on these topics.

Now you are ready to generate the discovery lesson. How can you create situations where students can find out these things for themselves? And, importantly, how can you create interest? What do you want students to notice or discover? How can they do so? Here we take into account all we have learned about lesson planning from Chapter 6, Planning Instruction.

Try Activity 8.4

Finally, in the preparation stage you need to be sure your students are ready to use scientific methods such as observation, recording, and analyzing. If they have not previously had experience with inductive and deductive reasoning, you will have to provide greater guidance and simplification.

Delivery   When you studied information processing in Chapter 4, you learned how essential it is to obtain and maintain students' attention. In Chapter 6, Planning Instruction, this message was reinforced by the concept of **set induction,** that is, doing something at the start of the lesson to grab the learners' attention. Can you think of something that would cause students to focus on learning about pulse and respiration? It could be a question such as, "What are some things our body must do to stay alive?"

Having gained your students' attention, you next might present a situation, real or hypothetical, that is challenging or baffling. Again, you can use questions such as "What do physicians do to find out if our systems are O.K.?" "How do they know?" "How do we know when our pulse rate and respiration are normal?" "What is normal? How can we find out?" "What might make our pulse and respiration rates change? How can we find out?" Depending on the specific objectives of your lesson, you would phrase questions that invite learners to discover answers. Getting them to phrase questions is even better. Table 8.3 reminds us of four forms of knowledge and provides examples of questions that promote each form.

Once you have presented students with a challenge, you need to ensure that they have a clear idea of how to investigate the question. "What can you do to discover the answers to these questions?" "Which ones might you be able to find out for yourselves without reading books?" "How could you do so?"

"How do you expect me to learn anything when you're the one who keeps asking all the questions?"

TABLE 8.3 Four Forms of Knowledge and Illustrative Questions That Could Be Used to Promote Discovery of Each

Form of Knowledge	Questions That Promote Discovery
1. *Concepts.* A concept is the name that describes a class of ideas or objects.	1.1 What is a mammal? 1.2 What is luck? 1.3 What is rap music? 1.4 What is a democrat?
2. *Facts.* A fact is a truth.	2.1 What is the average pulse rate? 2.2 What is the life history of the frog? 2.3 What is the sum of the angles of a triangle? 2.4 What happens when blue and red mix?
3. *Generalizations.* A generalization is an inference that may not be universally true but is widely supported.	3.1 How are families changing? 3.2 How should lessons be prepared? 3.3 What are the attributes of good teachers? 3.4 Why do students go south for spring break?
4. *Rules/laws.* A rule or law is an unchanging principle that governs a particular situation or set of conditions.	4.1 How are words divided into syllables? 4.2 How is table tennis played? 4.3 How are fractions divided? 4.4 Why do certain objects float?

8.13 How would you help learners come to know *any one* of these concepts, facts, generalizations, or rules/laws?

When students are ready to proceed with their observation, data collection, analysis, and so forth, your task is to monitor and display the qualities of a good discovery learning teacher. These include holding high expectations that students can learn on their own, nurturing them, being patient and accepting of their ideas, and causing them to be thoughtful and reflective. It is particularly urgent that you develop a secure environment that supports risk-free thinking. Fear of ridicule, failure, or criticism must be removed or your learners may be intellectually paralyzed. This does not mean that the environment is evaluation-free. Rather, it means that judgments result from thoughtful consideration and perhaps from the testing of all ideas.

Closure Following open and substantial consideration of the data they have unearthed, learners need to draw conclusions. "After your investigation, what can you conclude about pulse and respiration rates?" Here your task is to help learners organize and phrase the discoveries. To ensure that the discovery has become embedded in long-term memory, you next need to provide an opportunity to use it. In the case of pulse and respiration, perhaps students could assess family members' pulse rates.

Table 8.4 is a summary of the qualities of good discovery learning teachers and of good discovery learning procedures. An abbreviated discovery lesson appears as Lesson Plan 8.2.

FACILITATING DISCOVERY LEARNING ONLINE

You can accomplish the outcomes of discovery learning by utilizing certain computer software programs and by using the computer to search for information. The Dalton School in New York City exemplifies how (Wallis 1995).

A software program called *Archaeotype,* developed at Dalton, is a middle school level computer simulation of an archeological dig, complete with virtual excavation and shovel sounds. Groups of four or five students are assigned a "lot" to unearth at an ancient Syrian site. The purpose: to locate what is buried, analyze it, and create

Try Activity 8.5

8.14 What factors mentioned in Chapter 1 or Chapter 4 may influence your use of discovery learning?

TABLE 8.4 Qualities of Good Facilitators of Discovery Learning and of Good Discovery Learning

Good Facilitators . . .	Good Discovery Learning
• Believe in the purposes of discovery learning • Tend to be inquirers (curious) themselves • Are optimistic and confident in students' ability to inquire • Hold high expectations of students • Are nurturing • Are thoughtful • Are patient • Accept students' ideas • Are reflective	*When preparing:* • Determine the general purpose of the lesson • Determine the specific lesson objectives: identify the concepts, facts, generalizations, rules, or laws to be discovered • Collect useful resources and material • Plan the discovery lesson • Ensure that learners are ready to use inductive methods *When delivering:* • Obtain students' attention via set induction • Present the challenging or baffling situation • Utilize questions that will promote discovery (see examples in Table 8.3) • Ensure that learners know what they are supposed to do • Monitor and guide student activity and thinking • Encourage observation, collection and organization, manipulation, analysis of ideas and data, and so forth *When closing:* • Help learners to organize and phrase what they have concluded: the concepts, facts, generalizations, and so forth • Provide opportunity to use the new knowledge

and defend a thesis about the site and its inhabitants. To support the theories generated, the group has online access to libraries and art museums containing stores of related information. Thus, rather than receiving information about life in ancient Syria, students discover the knowledge for themselves. Quite literally, they construct it.

Another class at Dalton, after reading Shakespeare's *Macbeth,* is able to delve more deeply into the text and its characters by connecting online to various databases containing related information. For example, a group of students working on a paper on Lady Macbeth is able to access illustrations of the character, scenes in which she is portrayed in motion pictures, and dozens of essays about her. Obviously, the information obtained is far more extensive than would otherwise be available, and having it permits the group to formulate knowledge, to derive their own meaning about who this person was.

Web Resource To find out more about Dalton School curricular projects using discovery learning go to http://www.dalton.org/departments/nltl/nltl_projects/curricular_projects.html.

WHEN DISCOVERY LEARNING SHOULD BE USED

Given what we know, when should discovery learning be used? We believe it should be employed when your instructional goals coincide with its main purposes: (1) to get students to think for themselves, (2) to help them to discover how knowledge is created, and (3) to promote higher-order thinking. Additionally, discovery learning should be used when it best serves the personal and educational needs of you and your learners. Finally, it should be used only when you have developed the qualities of a good facilitator and you know and can follow the regimen for good discovery learning.

LESSON PLAN 8.2
Abbreviated Discovery Lesson: Secondary Colors

Curriculum tie-in: Art

OBJECTIVE

1. Learners will discover how to create secondary colors. *Specific objective:* Given the three primary colors (red, yellow, blue), learners will discover how they may be combined to form the secondary colors (orange, violet, green).

RESOURCES

1. Tempera paint: yellow, red, blue. One container of each per group of learners.
2. Water. One container of each per group of learners.
3. Paint brushes. One per learner.
4. Paper plates (glossy, nonabsorbent). One per learner.
5. Paper toweling. At least one sheet per learner.
6. Writing paper. One sheet per learner.

METHODOLOGY

1. *Set induction.* "Have you ever mixed things together? What have you mixed? What happened? Today you are going to discover what happens when certain colors are mixed."

2. "You will have three colors of paint: yellow, red, blue. How many combinations of these three colors can you make? (yellow with red, yellow with blue, red with blue) What colors do you think will result when you mix these three combinations? (orange, green, violet) Let's find out."

3. Place learners in groups of three to five around tables. On each place a container of yellow, red, and blue tempera paint, a container of water, paint brushes, paper plates, and paper toweling.

4. Provide directions such as the following:
"We are going to do two things—experiment by mixing paint and make a record of what we discover. Here is the order of things we will do. Mix yellow with red on the paper plate then write on your paper the color you got. Wash the new color out of the brush and dry it on the paper towel. Mix red with blue and do likewise, record the new color and wash the brush. Finally, mix blue with yellow . . ."
(You may want to have the groups stay together, mixing only one combination and discussing the results.)

5. Discuss the following:
What happened when you mixed combinations 1, 2, and 3?
Why do you suppose that some of your secondary colors look a little different? (Perhaps students mixed a little more of one primary color than the other.)
How can the primary colors we started with and the secondary colors we made be put on a chart, for example as a wheel or spectrum)?

ASSESSMENT

1. Learners are asked to take paper and create a picture containing grass, flowers, sun, and sky making sure they use the three primary and three secondary colors.

CLOSURE

1. Have students recall what they have learned: What are the primary and secondary colors? What happens when primary colors are combined? What happens when they are combined unevenly?

Of course, all the above is based on the premise that your learning objectives can be most effectively gained using this alternative. If that is not the case, you must be convinced that the time and energy it demands are worth it. Said another way, the ends of discovery learning should justify it as the means.

All teachers probably use some modified or abbreviated forms of discovery learning because of the influence of educational philosopher John Dewey (1933) and psychologist Jerome Bruner (1961, 1977). Both theorists admonished teachers to get students to think for themselves. Consequently, when you observe a reading class in an elementary school, you will often hear the teacher ask students to figure out the meaning of a new word from the sentence and paragraph the word is embedded in. In another classroom, you might see students investigating the leaves of different trees. Joyce and Weil (1999) note, "Probably nothing has been more consistently pursued yet remains more elusive than the teaching of thinking" (p. 42). However, even though discovery learning is widely recommended for this purpose, most teachers use it incidentally, as a part of recitation or discussion. For the most part, teachers persist in telling students what to think.

Try Activity 8.6

CHAPTER 8
Four More Instructional Alternatives:
Cooperative Learning, Discovery
Learning, Constructivism,
and Direct Instruction

245

What does research on discovery learning tell us? The results are mixed. Hofwolt (1984) reports that compared to more traditional teacher- and textbook-centered techniques, inquiry teaching produces significant learner achievement in science. Negatively, Wittrock (1966) strongly questions its use with slower learners. Slavin, Karweit, and Madden (1989) find more direct forms of instruction better for teaching concepts. (The last section of this chapter will introduce direct instruction.)

Nuthall and Snook (1973) conclude that "it is still necessary to find the experimental evidence which demonstrates convincingly that the discovery procedure is superior [to expository teaching or teacher presentations]" (p. 63). Merwin (1976) puts it all in perspective when he writes, "The research related to discovery learning is neither conclusive nor convincing enough to warrant its universal adoption. . . . However, one cannot ignore the successful learning outcomes as recorded in several [research studies]. For many students and teachers, discovery learning provides an exciting and rewarding [experience]; for others, it is fraught with frustration and failure" (p. 391).

Limitations of Discovery Learning   It is too bad that so promising an alternative also has formidable shortcomings. Most notably, not everything students must learn is amenable to classroom discovery. Students in most classrooms cannot be expected to discover chemical elements, the themes of famous writers and artists, or the way a computer works. Such knowledge is probably too complex for the minds of K–12 students. Even when they have the capacity to discover complex knowledge, there may not be sufficient time or appropriate resources to make the investigation. Perhaps that is why teacher presentations are still so common. They provide a fairly efficient way of getting complex knowledge to a large group of diverse learners.

8.15   How formidable do the limitations of discovery learning seem to you?

Another shortcoming is that some teachers simply do not have the experience or aptitude for this approach (Tamir 1995). Neither do all of their students—it may just not be your or their "style." In this case, perhaps teachers and students would like it more if they simply tried it more. Maybe it just needs getting used to.

Finally, discovery learning allows students to make errors. Unless these errors are corrected, serious confusion can result. Consequently, the teacher must closely monitor the results of discovery learning.

SUMMARY ON DISCOVERY LEARNING

As a student, if you have been exposed to discovery learning, you have been asked to take on the role of a detective. You were asked to investigate a situation in order to figure it out. Almost every day, you are faced with perplexing academic and nonacademic situations, and for the most part, you must cope with them on your own. Thus, any previous experience you have had with inductive thinking should be of help. If you have had teachers who mostly told you what to do and think, you are disadvantaged. Such teachers may have given you much knowledge but not taught you how to think.

Discovery learning holds promise in ensuring that your learners will be able to think for themselves. Its major purpose is to help students learn how to find out for themselves. To use this alternative effectively, you need to believe in its purposes; you must have certain qualities such as curiosity, optimism, and confidence in students' abilities to think and inquire; and you must have patience. Finally, you need to know and follow the discovery learning regimen or procedure illustrated in Table 8.4.

Discovery learning appears well-suited to certain teachers and students. It may be well-suited to others who have had little experience or bad prior experiences with the method. As teachers, one of our toughest jobs is to remediate bad past experiences students have had. Spotlight on Research 8.2 describes the negatives and positives of discovery learning.

Constructivist Teaching and Learning: Maximizing Learner Understanding

WHAT IS CONSTRUCTIVISM?

Constructivism is a way of teaching and learning that intends to maximize student understanding. As such, like discovery learning, it is situated within *meaningful learning* in the cognitive school of thought (see Chapter 4). Constructivism is defined as teaching that emphasizes the active role of the learner in building understanding and making sense of information (Woolfolk 2000); learners' construction of knowledge as they attempt to make sense of their environment (McCown, Driscoll, & Roop 1995), and learning that occurs when learners actively engage in a situation that involves collaboratively formulating questions, explaining phenomenon, addressing complex issues, or resolving problems (Gagnon & Collay 2001).

Constructivist ideas come from many persons including John Dewey, Jean Piaget, Maria Montessori and Liv Vygotsky and from educational movements such as progressive education, inquiry-discovery learning, open education, and whole language teaching (Gagnon, G. & Collay, M. 2001; Good & Brophy 1999).

As you will see it is one of the most challenging yet rewarding approaches to teaching.

PURPOSES AND CHARACTERISTICS OF CONSTRUCTIVISM

The purpose of constructivist teaching and learning is to enable students to acquire information in ways that make that information most readily understood and usable.

To make learning activities most understood and usable, constructivists have collected a number of ideas and brought them together to form a mosaic. The ideas, among others, include

- *Active learning* (when students are directly involved in finding something out for themselves) is preferable to passive learning (when students are recipients of information presented by a teacher).
- Learners should engage in *"authentic and situated"* activities, that is, the tasks they face should be concrete rather than abstract, real versus symbolic.
- Learning activities should be interesting and challenging.
- Learners should relate new information to that which they already have through *bridging*.
- Learners should reflect or think about what is being learned.
- Learning takes place best in *communities of learners*, that is, group or social situations.
- Rather than present information to learners, teachers facilitate its acquisition by ensuring the above.
- Teachers must provide learners with assistance or *scaffolding* that may be needed for them to progress.

Purposes and key characteristics are reviewed in Figure 8.3.

GOOD CONSTRUCTIVIST TEACHING AND LEARNING

Among suggestions about how to use constructivism as an instructional alternative are those of Brooks & Brooks (1993) and Gagnon & Collay (2001). We draw from both in the following discussion.

Try Activity 8.7

Preparation   Begin by identifying a relevant challenge for your learners—something that they should understand. Here we borrow from Gagnon & Collay's introduction and assume that the something to be understood is "the nature of fairy tales."

Rather than prepare a presentation on what constitutes fairy tales or have learners merely read about them, you decide that you want them to come to understand

CHAPTER 8

Four More Instructional Alternatives:
Cooperative Learning, Discovery
Learning, Constructivism,
and Direct Instruction

247

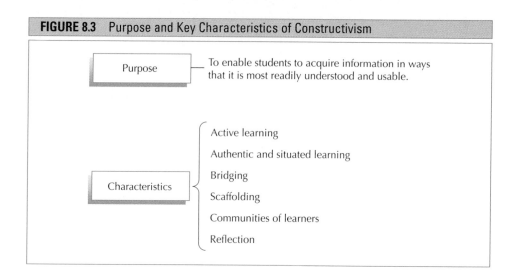

FIGURE 8.3 Purpose and Key Characteristics of Constructivism

Purpose — To enable students to acquire information in ways that it is most readily understood and usable.

Characteristics
- Active learning
- Authentic and situated learning
- Bridging
- Scaffolding
- Communities of learners
- Reflection

the concept as a result of examining personal experiences with them. With that goal in mind, you decide specifically what students should understand. You conclude learners should understand the core elements and characteristics of fairy tales (they contain one or more fairies or little people such as elves, goblins, leprechauns, poltergeists or trolls; fairies mostly do good deeds but often they play tricks).

Gagnon and Collay have established a nice framework for what they call a "constructivist learning design" or CLD. A CLD ensures that the key characteristics of constructivism are followed. Lesson Plan 8.3 is a modified version of their CLD for a lesson on fairy tales.

Try Activity 8.8

Delivery   Given the above CLD plan, its implementation is fairly straightforward. You have provided for set induction by sharing your experiences with fairy tales and asking learners to share theirs. The most important teacher tasks during the lesson are to ensure that groups are functional (pursuing the hoped-for results or objectives and interacting humanely) and that learners are all on the same page and contributing.

Closure   It seems wise at the lesson's end to determine the extent to which learners have constructed improved, more thoughtful understandings. Using the fairy tale CLD in Lesson Plan 8.3, you might ask, how, if at all, students' understanding of fairy tales increased or changed?

GOOD FACILITATORS OF CONSTRUCTIVIST LEARNING

To be good as a constructivist teacher you must strongly believe that your job is to ensure that learners acquire information in ways that make it readily understood and usable. Furthermore, you must believe that this can best be accomplished using constructivist principles including active learning, group learning, engaging learners in concrete rather than abstract tasks, helping them see the relationship between what they already know and new knowledge, helping them understand and make sense of new information (especially that which is discrepant), and considering the context, importance, and uses of newly acquired information. (See Table 8.5.)

WHEN CONSTRUCTIVISM SHOULD BE USED

Obviously, when you want to ensure that your students understand something well and can call upon it for later use, you need to use every possible approach. Many of the ideas about how learners come to understand best have been gathered by

LESSON PLAN 8.3
Constructivist Learning Design

Level: Middle school
Subject: Language arts
Title: Fairy tales
Designers: Ellen, Gail, and Sue

Describe the active learning *situation*—its purpose and how it will be accomplished:

- *Purpose of the lesson* is to have learners come to understand the concept and characteristics of fairy tales. *To accomplish this,* learners consider their personal experience with fairy tales, list their common characteristics, and define fairy tales. Then, learners compare what they think about fairy tales with information contained in resource material they are given.

Determine the *groups* and *group activities*:

- Learners form groups of three or four.

- Groups are provided with chart paper, marking pens, and tape for listing and posting the common characteristics of fairy tales and the group's definition of fairy tale.

Describe how new understanding will be connected or *bridged* to what learners already know:

- Briefly describe your experiences with fairy tales—perhaps with the *Tales of Mother Goose, Grimm's Fairy Tales,* or Barrie's *Peter Pan.*
- Have learners recollect their personal experiences with fairy tales in detail.

Provide questions to the groups:

- What experiences have you had with fairy tales?
- What are the common characteristics of fairy tales?
- How do you and your group define a fairy tale?

- How does your thinking about fairy tales compare with the material you just read?

Ensure that learners *exhibit* and share their understandings:

- Groups share their postings of common characteristics and definitions and try to reach agreement on the characteristics and definitions.

Reflection:

- Class was given print material about fairy tales and asked to compare what is written with their personally acquired understandings of fairy tales. Ask learners to describe how they felt and what they thought when their experiences and information differed from that of others—both peers and experts. How did they reconcile the differences? How has their knowledge been affected? What have they learned?

TABLE 8.5 Qualities of Good Facilitators of Constructivism and Good Constructivist Learning

Good Facilitators	Good Constructivist Learning
<ul><li>Believe in the purpose of constructivism</li><li>Tend to want learners to draw their own conclusions and form their own opinions</li><li>Have high respect for constructivist principles including active learning, concrete learning, group learning, and reflection</li><li>Are willing to help all students understand by intervening and providing support or scaffolding as needed</li></ul>	*When preparing:* • Determine the purpose of the lesson • Describe how the purpose will be attained • Decide how grouping will be used • Decide how to link new learning to old • Collect useful resource material • Decide how reflection will occur *When delivering:* • Ensure groups are pursuing lesson goals and interacting humanely with others • Ensure learners are together and contributing *When closing:* • Determine what learners now understand and the extent to which the understanding is new or different in some way.

constructivists in the hope that you can and will use them. I think most of us agree that our most memorable learning experiences were those in which we were immersed in a situation and learned from personal experience.

CHAPTER 8

Four More Instructional Alternatives:
Cooperative Learning, Discovery
Learning, Constructivism,
and Direct Instruction

249

SUMMARY ON CONSTRUCTIVISM

Understanding is the most important outcome of learning. Constructivists believe that to gain understanding requires students to engage in group experiences in which they learn through active involvement, by doing. In the process of learning by doing, the community of learners builds or creates new knowledge for themselves, connects that new knowledge to knowledge they already possess, and considers any discrepancies between the two. Learners also think about the new information they have come to understand and how it may be applied. Constructivists believe that the role of the teacher is to facilitate active involvement and to support groups and individuals to increase their likelihood for success.

Web Resource

Gagnon and Colloy maintain a website at www.prainbow.com/cld/cldn.html where additional information about constructivism is available.

Direct Instruction: Teaching in the Most Efficient Way

Recall that in Chapter 7 you learned about *presentations*, a teacher-dominated instructional alternative. A second variation on that theme is *direct instruction*. **Direct instruction** refers to instruction that is dominated by teachers but in addition adheres closely to what is known about effective teaching and how students learn (Rosenshine & Meister, 1995).

The purpose for using direct instruction is to help your students learn as effectively and efficiently as possible. There are two schools of thought about how to do this. The first proposes that the best way is to observe effective teachers (those regularly able to bring about a good amount of student learning) to find out what they do and then do the same kinds of things. This is a model-the-master or imitative approach and is somewhat like a novice athlete copying the behavior of a star sportsperson. The second school of thought feels that it is preferable to study what is known about how students learn and then apply that knowledge when teaching.

We call the first school of thought the *research-based school* and the second the *learning theory–based school.* Each of these kinds of direct instruction is important and each provides us with useful teaching models. The former includes the Basic Practice Model, Explicit Teaching, and Active Teaching. The latter includes the Mastery Teaching Program and the Direct Instructional System for Teaching and Learning (DISTAR). We present them both, treating them separately, although, as you will see, these schools are not mutually exclusive. Figure 8.4 on page 251 provides a graphic of the two kinds of direct instruction.

WHAT IS RESEARCH-BASED DIRECT INSTRUCTION?

At one time or another, we have all tasted something especially good and asked ourselves: "What's in this, and how was it made?" We ask because we appreciate the food and might like to prepare it ourselves.

Likewise, in schools, we see certain teachers who are especially good at helping students learn. We want to know how they do it—what is their "recipe"? We call these teachers "effective." What they do—their recipe—has been referred to as direct instruction, an overarching generic term (Rosenshine & Meister, 1995), and as Basic Practice (Murphy, Weil, & McGreal, 1986), Explicit Teaching (Rosenshine, 1986), and Active Teaching (Good, Grouws, & Ebmeier, 1983), its subtypes.

Research-based direct instruction is used to describe the practices of teachers who are more effective in bringing about student academic learning. You may ask, How do we know what effective teachers do? To find the answer, we must locate teachers who consistently produce greater learning gains than other teachers who teach comparable students. Next, investigators descend on these teachers' classrooms to observe, record, and analyze what they do. Chapter 12, Effective Teachers: Professional Skills

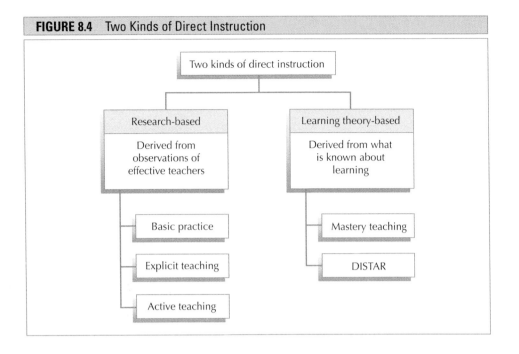

FIGURE 8.4 Two Kinds of Direct Instruction

Two kinds of direct instruction

Research-based — Derived from observations of effective teachers

Learning theory-based — Derived from what is known about learning

Basic practice

Explicit teaching

Active teaching

Mastery teaching

DISTAR

and Abilities, contains a description of many procedures effective teachers follow. Thus, that chapter ties in closely with this section. Here we will merely mention the attributes of effective teachers. You may wish to review Chapter 12 simultaneously.

PURPOSE AND CHARACTERISTICS OF RESEARCH-BASED DIRECT INSTRUCTION

What is the purpose of direct instruction, and what are its key attributes? Clearly, the purpose of direct instruction is to help students learn basic academic content such as reading, mathematics, and so forth in the most efficient, straightforward way.

The six key elements of research-based direct instruction have been compiled by Weil and Murphy (1982) and Murphy, Weil, and McGreal (1986), among others. Murphy, Weil, and McGreal (1986) call them teacher centrality, task orientation, positive expectations, student cooperation and accountability, nonnegative affect, and established structure.

Teacher centrality means that teachers exert strong instructional direction and control. The teacher decides what is to be learned and how, and is visibly in charge. **Task orientation** requires that the primary emphasis be on academic learning. Effective teachers engage learners in the pursuit of basic knowledge. **Positive expectations** indicate that effective teachers show concern for the academic progress of each student, and they expect each student to be successful. **Student cooperation and accountability** means that students are held accountable for their academic work and, furthermore, that they are expected to assist one another and to share materials. **Nonnegative affect** means these teachers ensure that learners feel psychologically safe and secure—that is, not threatened. Finally, **established structure** refers to the fact that effective teachers establish class rules and ensure that they are followed.

The purpose and key characteristics of research-based direct instruction are illustrated in Figure 8.5 on page 252.

VARIATIONS OF RESEARCH-BASED DIRECT INSTRUCTION

Previously, we noted that direct instruction goes by different subtypes and names, including Basic Practice, Explicit Teaching, and Active Teaching (see Figure 8.4). Let's take a look at each variation.

8.16 How important is the purpose of direct instruction?

8.17 What is your reaction to the key characteristics of direct instruction? How well do you believe you can implement each?

CHAPTER 8
Four More Instructional Alternatives:
Cooperative Learning, Discovery
Learning, Constructivism,
and Direct Instruction

251

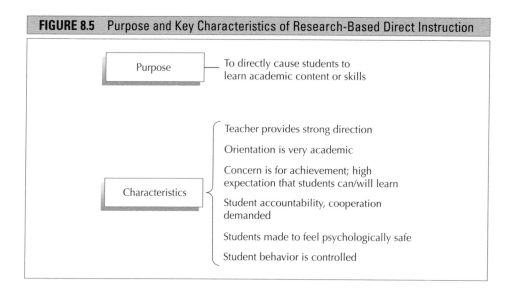

FIGURE 8.5 Purpose and Key Characteristics of Research-Based Direct Instruction

Purpose —— To directly cause students to learn academic content or skills

Characteristics
- Teacher provides strong direction
- Orientation is very academic
- Concern is for achievement; high expectation that students can/will learn
- Student accountability, cooperation demanded
- Students made to feel psychologically safe
- Student behavior is controlled

The Basic Practice Model (Murphy, Weil & McGreal, 1986) has four steps: lesson introduction, development, structured or guided practice, and independent practice.

In the introductory, or *orientation phase,* the teacher clearly establishes the content area to be studied, the instructional objectives, and the procedures to be followed. Additionally, the teacher communicates expectations to the students.

During the *development phase,* teachers present the information to be learned (concept, fact, generalization, skill, and so on). Regardless of the kind of research-based direct instruction, *teacher presentations are a constant.* Teachers provide clarity of presentation by demonstrating and by using examples. They also reinforce newly learned procedures and rules, and check students' understanding regularly to ensure progress.

Next, learners begin *structured, controlled practice.* Students try out or rehearse the information or skill the teacher has presented under the teacher's supervision. The teacher reinforces correct practice immediately and addresses incorrect practice, misunderstandings, and misconceptions as soon as they occur.

After teachers are satisfied that learners know or can do what is expected of them, the learners are set free to *practice independently.* However, even then, effective teachers move about the classroom, constantly monitoring and checking the work.

Explicit teaching is a second kind of direct instruction. It is described by Rosenshine (1987), Rosenshine and Meister (1995), and Rosenshine and Stevens (1986) as consisting of six phases of instructional activity: review and check homework, present new content/skills, guide student practice, provide feedback and correctives, move to independent practice, and conduct weekly and monthly reviews.

First, effective teachers *review* the previous day's work and homework, if assigned, and *reteach* when needed. This review of prior learning ensures that students are ready for the presentation of new information or skills. Such reviews often take the form of teacher questioning and recitation.

In the *presentation* stage, effective teachers inform their learners of the lesson's objectives, that is, what learners must come to know or be able to do. Good teachers provide an overview of what will happen during the lesson and how. Then the presentation proper begins with the teacher proceeding in small steps but at a rapid pace. A rapid pace is also referred to as gathering and maintaining *lesson momentum.* The teacher provides many detailed examples and illustrations, highlights or reinforces major points to notice and remember, and regularly raises questions to check for understanding. Most importantly, throughout the presentation, the teacher must be clear.

"Ms. Perkins certainly has a way with children."

Following the presentation and a quick check for understanding, *teacher-guided whole-class practice* begins. Guided practice often takes the form of a public recitation whereby the teacher asks a question, a student or students answer, and then the teacher asks another question (see Table 7.3). The teacher directs the questions to all students and provides them adequate time to think (see the discussion on wait time in Conducting Interpretive Instruction in Chapter 12). When students have difficulty, the teacher prompts or helps them think aloud. Guided practice continues until the class and individuals are responding correctly over 80 percent of the time.

Providing *feedback and correction* are part of the presentation. Investigators who observe effective teachers report that they use specific praise in moderation ("That is a good answer because . . ."). Correction of misconceptions may require review, reteaching, or more practice.

Having determined that their learners seem to know or be able to do whatever is needed, effective teachers provide opportunity for *independent practice.* Their intention is to have students rehearse the information or skill in order to get it into long-term memory. Independent practice should continue until learners' responses are rapid, confident, and highly accurate. Effective teachers hold students accountable for independent work, and they monitor it whenever possible.

Finally, effective teachers periodically engage their learners in *review* so that the information or skill is further embedded in long-term memory.

Active teaching is a third variation of research-based direct instruction (Good, Grouws, & Ebmeier, 1983). Constructed primarily from observations of effective mathematics teachers, it contains five instructional phases: the opening, development, independent work, homework, and continued review.

Opening refers to reviewing the concepts or skills recently taught and collecting homework. During lesson *development,* effective teachers do a number of things. They ensure that students have the knowledge needed to understand the new information to be presented. They develop the new concepts and skills using numerous lively illustrations and explanations. They make skillful use of questioning, examples, and problems. And, importantly, they repeat and elaborate as necessary. Good and Grouws (1977) found that when fourth-grade teachers spend about half of the mathematics class time on lesson development and increase students' participation in the lesson, learning gains are dramatic.

The *independent work* stage is characterized by uninterrupted practice. Students are forewarned that their work will be examined. The difficulty level of assigned work is intended to produce 80 percent or higher accuracy. During independent practice, effective teachers are careful to keep everyone involved and on task.

Effective elementary school teachers give about fifteen minutes of homework each night, Monday through Thursday. The assignment allows students to practice

CHAPTER 8

Four More Instructional Alternatives:
Cooperative Learning, Discovery
Learning, Constructivism,
and Direct Instruction

253

TABLE 8.6 Three Variations of Research-Based Direct Instruction

Basic Practice	Explicit Teaching	Active Teaching
• Introduce lesson	• Review previous work, check homework	• Review
• Develop lesson	• Introduce lesson	• Review, check homework
• Supervise practice	• Develop lesson	• Develop lesson
• Provide feedback, correction	• Check on understanding	• Check on understanding
• Provide independent practice	• Supervise practice	• Provide independent work in class
	• Provide feedback, correction	• Review
	• Provide independent practice	

newly acquired information and review the old. Finally, effective math teachers use *continued review.* They have students recall and use earlier learning by holding in-class weekly and monthly reviews.

As you can see, the three types or variations of the direct instruction approach—Basic Practice, Explicit Teaching, and Active Teaching—are nearly indistinguishable (see Table 8.6). This *should* be the case since the persons proposing the variations created them after having read essentially the same research studies on effective teaching.

GOOD DIRECT INSTRUCTORS

8.18 Which of the qualities of good direct instructors do you now have? Which qualities would you like to achieve or improve?

Good direct instructors are, by definition, effective teachers. So, what are effective teachers like? What are their personal attributes? As you shall see, we have devoted all of Chapter 11 to answering these questions. Briefly, effective teachers are enthusiastic, warm and accepting, and humorous. They hold high expectations that their students can learn. Furthermore, they are supportive and encouraging, businesslike, adaptable-flexible, and knowledgeable. If you want to find out more at this time, skip directly to Chapter 11.

GOOD RESEARCH-BASED DIRECT INSTRUCTION

Following are summaries of procedures that good direct instructors follow as they prepare, deliver, and close lessons.

Preparation   Authors of the various forms of research-based direct instruction give little specific attention to lesson planning or preparation. This probably is because the study of effective teachers focused on observing what they did in their classrooms when delivering instruction. However, it is probably true that effective teachers follow the preparation regimen good presenters use; that is, they establish the general purpose of the lesson, set specific learning objectives, collect and review subject matter and useful, related materials, and plan the presentation.

Delivery   Effective teachers know and use many delivery techniques. Direct instruction usually seems to begin with a review of homework or of an independent assignment. The review helps to determine the level of learners' understanding and accuracy. When either are low, reteaching is appropriate.

Following homework review and collection, the effective teacher ensures that learners are ready for the new material. That readiness may result from the homework review. If not, it is necessary to go over earlier related information or skills. When readiness is evident, the specific objectives of the lesson are communicated in terms of what the students are to know and to be able to do. The students are oriented to the lesson and its parts and to the way it will be conducted.

Now that the students are ready and aware of what is to be accomplished and how, the presentation is given. Instructional clarity is critical. The notion of clarity is fully developed in Chapter 12, and the behaviors characterizing clear teachers appear in Table 12.6. These behaviors include a step-by-step presentation, use of examples and illustrations, cuing learners to important elements to notice and remember, and using numerous questions directed to all students in order to encourage participation and check understanding.

After the learners have achieved a good level of understanding, guided whole-class practice of the information or skill begins. The teacher provides exercises, and students respond to them aloud so that everyone is on the same page, so to speak, and the teacher is able to hear what students are thinking. The teacher acknowledges correct responses and reminds students specifically why their responses are right. Should misunderstandings and errors occur, the teacher reteaches, often using a different approach.

As soon as the teacher feels that learners are able to work on their own with a high level of accuracy, independent practice starts. At the outset, learners are informed that their work will be examined and that a high level of accuracy—for example, above 80 percent—is expected. After the work is assigned, the teacher monitors to help students stay on task and reduce errors. Practice continues until responses are both rapid and accurate and learners are confident.

Closure In the closure stage, a research-based direct instruction lesson fulfills two requirements. One is the assignment of related homework. Assignments should be short, but regular. Secondly, the teacher reminds students of the importance of the lesson's objectives and the need to be able to recall and use the newly acquired information or skill. The teacher plans dates and times of weekly and monthly reviews.

Slavin (1999) notes that the regimen and principles of research-based direct instruction fit closest to reception learning, described in Chapter 4. Rosenshine and Stevens (1986) agree, pointing out the correspondence between the results of research on direct instruction and what we know about information processing, including the limits of short-term memory, the importance of elaboration and practice, and the need for continued practice. That research confirms the need to review previously learned information and skills, the need to limit the amount of new, difficult information presented, the need to proceed in small steps, the need to rehearse, elaborate, and summarize in student words and language, and the importance of overlearning.

A summary of the qualities of good research-based direct instructors and direct instruction appears in Table 8.7. A sample lesson plan appears as Lesson Plan 8.4.

8.19 What is your reaction to the approaches good direct instructors use?

WHEN RESEARCH-BASED DIRECT INSTRUCTION SHOULD BE USED

Peterson (1979a) and others address the question of when direct instruction should be used. She concludes that it is superior when the goal is to improve achievement in basic skills as measured on tests. Rosenshine (1986) agrees, and specifies that it is most valuable when teaching knowledge and explicit concepts and procedures. He provides examples such as teaching factual historical information (such as the chronology of the colonization of Africa), teaching grammatical concepts (what a sentence is), and teaching mathematical processes or procedures (how to solve an algebraic equation). *In other words, use direct instruction when the content to be learned is well-structured, clear, and unambiguous.* Berliner (1982) feels that direct instruction is more suitable when the material is arranged in a hierarchical or sequential manner. He also feels it is most useful during the first stages of instruction with unfamiliar material.

CHAPTER 8

Four More Instructional Alternatives:
Cooperative Learning, Discovery
Learning, Constructivism,
and Direct Instruction

255

TABLE 8.7 Qualities of Good Leaders of Research-Based Direct Instruction and of Good Direct Instruction

Good Leaders of Research-Based Direct Instruction Are . . .	Good Research-Based Direct Instruction
• Enthusiastic • Warm, accepting • Humorous • Supportive • Encouraging • Businesslike • Adaptable-flexible • Knowledgeable • Holders of high expectations for student success • See also Table 6.2, Qualities of Good Presenters and Good Presentations	*When preparing:* • Research on effective teaching hardly addresses what teachers do to prepare. We might assume they do the same things they would do when preparing a good presentation. (See Table 6.2.) *When delivering:* • Collect, review homework • Review earlier, related information • Communicate to learners what they are to know and be able to do • Present an overview or orientation of how the lesson will be conducted • Present information/skill to be learned • Proceed in small steps • Maintain a quick pace • Use many illustrations, examples • Encourage involvement of all students • Ask many questions to check for understanding • Repeat and elaborate on major points to notice, remember • Provide teacher-guided whole-class practice • Provide feedback and reteach to eliminate misunderstandings • Ensure that students can practice with at least 80 percent accuracy • Provide independent practice • Let students know the work will be examined • Monitor the work to keep students involved and to eliminate errors • Continue practice until learners are confident and their responses are both rapid and accurate *When closing:* • Assign short, regular, related, homework • Establish when this information or skill will next be reviewed

8.20 What to you are this instructional alternative's strengths & weaknesses?

Peterson (1979a, 1982) also addresses the related question, with whom should direct instruction be used? In response, she notes that this approach has been shown to be very effective for teaching younger, less able learners. She also suggests that it may be the instructional alternative of choice when teaching children who need direction from others.

Peterson (1979a) suggests that direct instruction is similar to "traditional teaching." To some extent, this is true. Generally speaking, traditional teaching is directed toward learning academic content. It is also characterized by a teacher-centered and teacher-dominated classroom. However, if traditional teaching equaled direct instruction, all "traditional" teachers would be effective, and we know that is not the case. Only a few traditional teachers are able to outperform the rest when teaching comparable students. So we can only say that traditional teaching is like direct instruction in kind but falls short of it in implementation. Specifically, direct instruction demands not only teacher direction but *strong* teacher direction, not only an academic orientation but *strong* academic orientation, and so forth. Consequently, it is probably safe to say that traditional teaching

LESSON PLAN 8.4
Abbreviated Direct Instruction Lesson: Roman Numerals

Curriculum tie-in: This lesson can be linked to the study of Roman civilization or the study of numerical systems.

OBJECTIVES

1. Learners will recognize the Roman numeral V and the rules used to create 4 and 6 from it. *Specific objective:* Learners will recognize that V = 5 and that placing I before V decreases its value by one while placing I after V increases its value by 1.

2. *Specific objective:* Learners will know and be able to use the Roman numerals for 1–6.

RESOURCES

1. Homework assignment: to locate objects containing Roman numerals that are on an assignment sheet (I, V, X, L, C, D, M).

METHODOLOGY

1. *Set induction.* "We will continue to think about the number system developed by the Romans. Yesterday I gave you an assignment sheet containing seven Roman numerals and asked you to find objects displaying some or all of them. What examples did you find?"

2. Inform learners of what they will learn and be able to do as a result of the lesson. "Today we will learn the Roman symbol for 5 and how the Romans used it to create the numbers 4 and 6. At the end of the lesson you will know the Roman numerals representing our numerals 1–6."

3. Begin the presentation proceeding in small steps, utilizing a quick pace, using as many examples as possible, involving all learners, checking for understanding, providing practice and reteaching as necessary. An example follows.

4. "V represents our Arabic numeral 5. What does V stand for? Placing the Roman I (1) *after* V represents V + I. V + I then equals 6. What does VI represent? On your paper write the Roman numerals for 1, 5, 6. Placing the Roman I *before* V represents V – I. What does IV represent? Write that numeral on your paper. Now you know the Roman numerals for 1, 4, 5, and 6. What numerals don't you know from 1 through 6? Romans simply used two Is for II and three Is for 3. Write the Roman numerals for 1–6 on your paper. You have learned two rules Romans used when creating numerals: When a second numeral is placed after another it *increases* its value by that amount: when a second numeral is placed before another it *decreases* its value by that amount.

(Student) go to the board and write the Roman numerals I–VI one under the other. (Student) go to the board and write the Arabic equivalents beside each Roman numeral.

Which of the following are incorrect? IIII = 4, VI = 3, IV = 6? Go to the board and correct each."

ASSIGNMENT

1. Complete this test with 100 percent accuracy.
   1 written in Roman is _____
   5 written in Roman is _____
   IV written in Arabic is _____
   6 written in Roman is _____

2. Reteach as necessary.

CLOSURE

Review:
What is V?
How is V used to make 6?
How is V used to make 4?
What is the rule?
How are the following made: 2, 3, 7, 8?

---

would have to be ratcheted up to have characteristics identical to those of research-based direct instruction. This kind of direct instruction probably is used only by teachers determined to help their students achieve academically.

LIMITATIONS OF RESEARCH-BASED DIRECT INSTRUCTION

Of course, research-based direct instruction has its critics. Slavin (1991a, b) points out that it deemphasizes students' autonomy. Gersten and Keating (1987), advocates themselves, acknowledge critics who say the tight structure may stifle children. Peterson (1979b) informs us that this approach does not promote achievement in creativity, abstract thinking, and problem solving or higher-level cognitive skills. Stallings and Kaskowitz (1975) feel it is not as good as other instructional alternatives for improving cooperation, attitude toward school, and, relatedly, school attendance. Spotlight on Research 8.3 reviews the findings on research-based direct instruction.

CHAPTER 8

Four More Instructional Alternatives:
Cooperative Learning, Discovery
Learning, Constructivism,
and Direct Instruction

257

Do students taught via direct instruction learn more? Since the variations are all based upon research on teaching—the effective teaching model—we would expect that teachers following Basic Practice, Explicit Teaching, and Active Teaching would be successful in bringing about students' academic achievement. Research seems to mostly support that expectation.

Orlich (2000) reports that research-based direct instruction "has been readily adapted for teaching the basics and for special education" (pp. 164–165).

Relatedly, they note that it has been demonstrated to be effective. For example, they refer to Peterson (1979a, 1979b) who reviewed a great number of studies that compare the use of traditional, direct teaching with more open, indirect, student-centered instruction. Peterson found students receiving direct instruction tended to perform better on achievement tests and slightly worse on tests of higher-order, abstract thinking involving creativity and problem solving.

Rosenshine (1987) reports similarly that on the basis of classroom studies, students taught with structured curricula using teacher-centered instruction generally do better than those taught by way of discovery learning, individualized instruction, or independent study approaches.

Slavin (1991) summarized research on Active Teaching as exemplified in the Missouri Mathematics Program (MMP). He notes that in several studies, MMP students gained somewhat more in mathematics than did comparable students taught in other ways.

Perhaps the most damning criticism points to the fact that the promising practices of effective teachers, on which direct instruction is built, mostly derive from observations of effective elementary teachers teaching reading and mathematics. These content areas are more structured; that is, they follow a more sequential, step-by-step learning process than other content areas such as social studies, art, and science.

WHAT IS LEARNING THEORY-BASED DIRECT INSTRUCTION?

The second school of thought about direct instruction is based on learning theory. By that, we mean its advocates have constructed instructional procedures that are based upon and mimic what we know about human learning.

Theory-based direct instruction describes how teachers put into use what is known about learning. Sponsors of this school of thought are less interested in what teachers do than in what they ought to do. What they ought to do, advocates say, is to use the beliefs and findings of one or more schools of thought about learning described in Chapter 4.

PURPOSE AND CHARACTERISTICS OF LEARNING THEORY-BASED DIRECT INSTRUCTION

The purpose of both types of direct instruction is identical: to help students learn academic content in the most straightforward way. The two types also seem to share the same overall characteristics (see Figure 8.5).

VARIATIONS OF LEARNING THEORY-BASED INSTRUCTION

The two best known and most widely used forms of learning theory-based direct instruction, as depicted in Figure 8.4, are the Mastery Teaching Program (Hunter, 1982, 1984, 1995) and the Direct Instruction System in Arithmetic and Reading, or DISTAR (Becker, 1986).

The Mastery Teaching Program Hunter seems to have based her teaching model mainly on learning theory, particularly instructional theory as proposed by Gagné

A second-year Baltimore teacher, Matthew Carpenter, was observed and interviewed to see what the DISTAR program was like and how he felt about it.

As a result of one of the observations, the observer notes, "Mr. Carpenter's sixth graders . . . were working on their *reasoning* and *writing skills*. Their task: Take two sentences and make a new sentence from them that begins with the word 'No' and use the word 'only'. Mr. Carpenter then reads the two sentences. 'The wolves howled and ate at night' and 'The wolves did not eat.'

While his students are bent over their paper writing answers, he checks their work. (DISTAR theorists believe it's important to catch errors quickly before they are imprinted in learners' brains.)

Soon, Mr. Carpenter says, "The answer is . . .?" Students shout in unison. "No, the wolves only howled at night."

Similar unison chanting of answers is audible from classrooms up and down the hall.

During an interview, Mr. Carpenter notes, "I like the structure (DISTAR provides). I think it's good for this group of kids. (Ninety-six percent of Arundel School's students are considered poor in that they come from families qualifying for free school lunches.)

Source: D. Viadero. (1999, March 17). A direct challenge. *Education Week, 18*(27), 41–43.

(Rosenshine & Stevens, 1986). Her program has the same purpose (to foster academic learning) and shares most of the key characteristics of research-based direct instruction programs (teacher centrality, task orientation, and so forth; Figure 8.5). *A major difference is that Hunter suggests that instructional alternatives other than teacher presentation may be just as effective, depending on the lesson objectives.*

Slavin (1999) notes the stages or steps in Hunter's (1982) version: getting students set to learn, input and modeling, checking understanding, and guided practice. Do they sound familiar? Obviously, they are quite similar to those advocated by educators who take the research-based road.

The Direct Instruction System for Teaching and Learning (DISTAR) The developers of DISTAR believe your task is to find out what children need to know to succeed in school and then to teach it to them following principles of learning theory that come mostly from the behavioral school of thought (Chapter 4). The program was developed mainly for use with low SES children.

A major difference between DISTAR and all other forms of learning theory–based direct instruction is that it is very heavily scripted. Teachers are told precisely what to say and do from lesson beginning to end. Benjamin (1981) describes DISTAR as leaving nothing to chance. "Every action by the teacher—verbal and nonverbal—is specifically outlined; every student response is similarly choreographed" (p. 72). Consequently, DISTAR is said to be teacher-proof. Any instructor can use it and obtain the same result (see Case 8.3).

Stallings and Stipek (1986) refer to Bereiter-Englemann DISTAR programs as "carefully structured, highly verbal, patterned drill and practice" (p. 734). These authors provide an extensive description of the background, development, and use of DISTAR.

It seems that regardless of whether we generalize from the observation of what effective teachers do in their classrooms, or whether we speculate what teachers should do from learning theory, when academic learning is the goal, we end up with many of the same principles and ideas.

GOOD LEARNING THEORY-BASED DIRECT INSTRUCTORS

The qualities of teachers who use direct instruction based on learning theory are not documented. However, we can presume they are like the qualities of effective teachers, so Table 8.7 and Chapter 11 should be helpful.

CHAPTER 8
Four More Instructional Alternatives:
Cooperative Learning, Discovery
Learning, Constructivism,
and Direct Instruction

259

Findings on Learning Theory-Based Direct Instruction

Do students of teachers who use learning theory-based direct instruction learn more? We would presume so, but let's look at the research.

Research on the Mastery Teaching Program has not generally shown "that the students of teachers especially trained in this variation have learned more than other students" (Slavin 1991, p. 253). Slavin suggests this may be because at some time *all* teachers have been exposed to and use learning theory and associated instructional maneuvers. Therefore, when it comes to learning theory, all teachers teach about the same way, anyway. However, Hunter, the developer of the Mastery Teaching Program, feels that the reason her program has had limited success is that it has not been properly implemented.

What does research on DISTAR reveal? Much to the alarm of its critics, DISTAR has mostly been very effective in its purpose. Stallings and Stipek (1986) tell us that when low SES students spend four years (kindergarten through grade 3) in the Direct Instruction Follow-Through Model, they achieve close to national norms on achievement tests, performing much better than similar students who received other kinds of instruction. Meyer (1984) reports that students from an inner-city Brooklyn, New York, school that used DISTAR in grades 1 through 3 were more likely to complete secondary school. Gersten and Keating (1987) also found positive long-term effects such as lowered dropout rates and increased proportions of students applying for college. Stallings and Stipek conclude, "One implication for elementary [teachers] is that a structured, carefully sequenced program for low-achieving children in the lower grades helps them to succeed academically" (p. 741).

GOOD LEARNING THEORY-BASED DIRECT INSTRUCTION

Good direct instruction, according to the Mastery Teaching Program (Hunter 1982, 1984), requires following a specific procedure: getting students ready to learn, providing input, modeling, checking for understanding, and providing and guiding practice. Inasmuch as these steps are very similar to those which effective teachers use, the information in Table 8.7 can again be our guide.

WHEN LEARNING THEORY-BASED DIRECT INSTRUCTION SHOULD BE USED

Studies of DISTAR (Gersten & Keating, 1987) seem to support its use in much the same ways we would use direct instruction based on effective teaching. It seems mostly to benefit students at risk of school failure. The American Federation of Teachers considers it one of the most promising approaches to raising student achievement.

Studies of the Mastery Teaching Program offer less clear direction. The Mastery Teaching Program is more likely to be utilized with children of different SES, while DISTAR is used almost exclusively with low SES students. Perhaps for this reason, DISTAR seems very popular in large metropolitan districts. The related research findings are contained in Spotlight on Research 8.4.

LIMITATIONS OF LEARNING THEORY-BASED DIRECT INSTRUCTION

Much of the criticism aimed at research-based direct instruction applies here as well. Additionally, DISTAR largely is scripted and repetitive—teachers are told exactly what to say and do—and therefore it can become tiring and stifling to teachers and students. One study found that by age 15, 46 percent of the students receiving direct instruction had been identified as having emotional problems—a significantly higher percentage than children not in the program (Viadero, 1999).

SUMMARY ON DIRECT INSTRUCTION

Rather than being one precise instructional alternative, direct instruction is a label given to related efforts to improve the *academic learning* of K–12 students.

There are two major kinds of direct instruction. The first kind, research-based, derives from observing effective teachers to see what they do to bring about consistently higher levels of student learning. There are three variations on this kind of direct instruction: Basic Practice, Explicit Teaching, and Active Teaching. Advocates who developed these variations believe that you should be educated and trained in direct instruction according to their particular model. Doing so, they say, should increase your ability to bring about student learning.

The second kind of direct instruction derives from learning theory—what we know and believe about how people learn. There are two popular variations of this kind: the Mastery Teaching Program and the Direct Instruction System for Teaching and Learning (DISTAR). Scholars who developed these forms believe that you should be educated and trained according to their model. Furthermore, they believe that after education and training, you will know how to use what is known about learning and, consequently, your students will benefit academically.

Both kinds of direct instruction have the same purpose, which is to help students learn academic content. They also share common characteristics, including strong teacher direction, an academic orientation, high expectations for student achievement, student accountability and cooperation, a psychologically safe classroom atmosphere, and strict classroom rules and regulations.

Within the first kind of direct instruction, good instructors must have the qualities of effective teachers, which are elaborated in Chapter 11. These include enthusiasm, warmth, and humor. They must also be supportive and encouraging, businesslike, adaptable, and knowledgeable in their teaching area. Within the second kind of direct instruction, the requisite teacher qualities are not as clear.

Both kinds of direct instruction require teachers to follow regimens mostly characterized by three words—practice, practice, practice. Effective teachers use many and varied kinds of practice, which is one of the major elements of learning.

For the most part, research findings support direct instruction, especially for low SES students in highly structured subjects such as reading and mathematics. DISTAR has been extended for use in many subjects. Over forty DISTAR programs are available commercially from Science Research Associates, a subsidiary of McGraw-Hill.

8.21 What factors mentioned in Chapter 1 may affect your use of Direct Instruction?

Try Activity 8.9

Is There a Single-Best Instructional Alternative?

In Chapters 7 and 8 you have learned about eight instructional alternatives: presentation, discussion, independent study, individualized instruction, cooperative learning, discovery learning, constructivism, and direct instruction. However, which is better?

According to experts, it all depends upon your purpose (National Academy of Sciences, 1999). "Sometimes a lecture is needed to propel students to the next level of understanding. The trick is 'sometimes'." Experiential or hands-on learning is appropriate at other times. Experiential learning can be as ineffective as a dull presentation if it doesn't have a clearly defined purpose. "It's knowing when to use which [instructional alternative] based on the principles of learning." (Bransford 1999).

Does this conclusion sound similar to the one reached in the section at the end of Chapter 4 on learning, Is there a single best approach to student learning?

Some Final Thoughts

At the outset of Chapter 7, you were asked to think of a teacher who helped you learn and enjoy learning. We assumed that those teachers that you targeted would have a number of admirable personal and professional qualities and, further, that one of those qualities would be the ability to use a wide repertoire of instructional alternatives.

CHAPTER 8

Four More Instructional Alternatives:
Cooperative Learning, Discovery
Learning, Constructivism,
and Direct Instruction

261

8.22 How would you rank the eight instructional alternatives presented in Chapters 7 and 8? What accounts for your attraction to your top two choices? How does your ranking compare with your classmates'?

So that you may someday be thought of as an exceptional teacher, too, you have learned about eight teaching strategies, namely: presentation, discussion, independent study, individualized instruction, cooperative learning, discovery learning, constructivism, direct instruction. If you have had the opportunity to reflect on these practices and especially to try the end-of-chapter activities related to each method, then you have reached some degree of competence with them. Of course, practice makes perfect, and knowledge does not always equate with skill. To truly be skillful with any instructional alternative, you must work with it over time. In the months and years ahead, we hope you will find these two chapters particularly useful desk references as you strive to be the best teacher you can be.

CHAPTER SUMMARY

- Cooperative learning describes instructional procedures that place learners in small work teams that are rewarded for what they collectively accomplish. The purpose of cooperative learning is to engender in students a collective caring, an "all for one, one for all" philosophy. Principal characteristics include small, heterogeneous teams and tasks that revolve around either mastering some knowledge or skill or participating in a group academic project. Cooperative learning draws on the cognitive, behavioral, and humanistic schools of thought, and its variations include STAD, TGT, TAI, and CIRC.

- Good leaders of cooperative learning believe in its purpose; they are able to get students to work together, are competent presenters, effective organizers, and good work coordinators; and they are able to identify and help students and teams having difficulty.

- Good cooperative learning includes preparation, delivery, and closure. In STAD, preparation requires planning a good presentation, preparing the teams' assignments, and getting students ready to engage in teamwork. Delivery requires making a good presentation, setting team goals, preparing for teamwork, giving teams their assignment, quizzing students, and recognizing team accomplishments. Closure requires that students be reminded of what they have learned, that they relate new learning to earlier learning and that students have the opportunity to use new learning.

- Cooperative learning has certain limitations. It requires higher-achieving students to assist low achievers and presumes high achievers are willing to do so. Additionally, since cooperative learning is a group activity, substantial teacher monitoring is necessary to keep teams on task.

- Discovery learning takes place when students are presented with experiences and are asked to derive their own meaning and understanding from them. Its purposes are (1) to provide students with the opportunity to think for themselves in order to figure something out, (2) to help students discover how knowledge is gained, and (3) to promote higher-order thinking skills such as analysis, synthesis, and evaluation.

- In discovery learning, the teacher is a catalyst who causes students to discover knowledge rather than spoon-feeding it to them. Teachers ask many, mostly higher-order questions: "Why?" "How come?" "What would happen?" and so forth. Good discovery learning teachers believe in its purposes, tend to enjoy inquiry, are optimistic that students are inquiry oriented and capable of learning in this fashion, and hold high expectations of students; they are nurturing, thoughtful, patient, reflective, and accepting of students' ideas.

- Good discovery learning includes attention to preparation, delivery, and closure. Preparation includes determining the general purpose and specific objectives students are to accomplish, collecting useful materials, and planning lessons around inductive procedures. Delivery includes obtaining students' attention; presenting the baffling situation that requires investigation; promoting inquiry through use of observation, manipulation, analysis, and so forth; ensuring that learners know what to do; setting them free to inquire; monitoring; and, when necessary, guiding their inquiry and encouraging positive student interaction. Closure includes helping learners organize and define what they have found out and draw conclusions from it.

- Among the limitations of discovery learning are that not all things are amenable to classroom discovery, some discovery is too complex for K–12 student minds, and time constraints often limit the ability to explore.

- Research results on discovery learning are mixed and inconclusive. It seems a viable alternative that will enhance learning for some children while frustrating others.

- Constructivists want to maximize the likelihood that learners will understand and be able to use information. To do so, students must engage in active social or group learning (learning by doing and sharing); learning should be situated or occur in as realistic settings as possible; learners must bridge or relate new learning to what they already know or think they know; learners must interact with others and reflect on what they encounter; and teachers must provide scaffolding or help that enables students to learn successfully.

- A constructivist lesson has identifiable parts: purpose of the lesson (a challenge), establishing groups and group activities, bridging, question posing, exhibits, and reflection.

- Good leaders of constructivist lessons believe in teaching for understanding, engage students in active learning, want learners to draw their own conclusions and opinions, and are willing to provide all necessary assistance.

- Direct instruction is one of several terms used to descrube the sequence of instructional events (1) that "effective" teachers have been observed to follow or (2) that teachers should follow if they want to utilize what is known about learning. Two major kinds of direct instruction are consistent with this definition. The first derives from observing effective teachers and includes three major subtypes: Basic Practice, Explicit Teaching, and Active Teaching. The second kind derives from analyzing and applying learning theory and has two major subtypes: the Mastery Teaching Program and DISTAR. The primary purpose of all these variations is to maximize learning of academic content or skills.

- Direct instruction teachers provide strong academic direction, have high expectations that students can and will learn, make students feel psychologically safe, urge them to cooperate, hold them accountable for their work, and closely monitor and control students' behavior. Good leaders of direct instruction are enthusiastic, warm and accepting, humorous, supportive, encouraging, businesslike, adaptable or flexible, and knowledgeable.

- Good direct instruction has three phases: preparation, delivery, and closure. The preparation that direct instruction teachers engage in is not clear. We can only assume it equates to preparing a good presentation. In DISTAR, preparation requires being well acquainted with the teacher's instructional manuals. Delivery requires some very major tasks including (for most variations) collection and review of previous work, reteaching when necessary, presentation of new material, teacher-guided practice and, finally, independent practice until 80 percent or higher proficiency is achieved.

- Generally, research on direct instruction is encouraging. All of its variations have been investigated; with the possible exception of the Mastery Teaching Program, they have proven to be more or less successful in increasing academic achievement in the basic skill areas such as reading and mathematics.

CHAPTER 8

Four More Instructional Alternatives:
Cooperative Learning, Discovery
Learning, Constructivism,
and Direct Instruction

263

ISSUES AND PROBLEMS FOR DISCUSSION

1. Some instructional alternatives foster competition, others cooperation. Which is preferable?

2. Some instructional alternatives depend upon whole-class instruction. Others depend upon the use of groups or independent work. Which is preferable?

3. Some instructional alternatives require teachers to teach directly (see Chapter 1). Others, more indirect, require teachers to draw things out of their students. Which is preferable?

4. Some instructional alternatives are more suitable to our personality and professional, job-related needs. Which alternatives are most attractive to you?

5. Some instructional alternatives meet different learners' needs. Which learner needs are the most important to you? To your classmates?

6. Given your responses to these questions, which instructional alternatives appeal most to you?

THEORY INTO ACTION ACTIVITIES

ACTIVITY 8.1: Prepare a Cooperative Learning Lesson   Although a cooperative learning activity generally spans several class periods, one can be developed to fit a short period of time. Following the STAD procedure, plan a cooperative learning activity for use in this class. Explain how you plan to briefly present information, establish teams and charge them to master the material, give team members a quiz, determine scores, and provide recognition and reward.

Assessment: Did you follow the planning procedures for good presentations and good cooperative learning? (See Tables 7.2 and 8.2.)

ACTIVITY 8.2: Conduct a Cooperative Learning Activity   Deliver the lesson you prepared in Activity 8.1.

Assessment: To what extent did you actually follow the procedures for good presentations and good cooperative learning? (See Tables 7.2 and 8.2.) To what extent did you model the personal qualities of good facilitators of cooperative learning? (See Table 8.2.) How well do your peers feel you succeeded?

ACTIVITY 8.3: Observe Cooperative Learning   It would be advantageous for you to see cooperative learning used in K–12 classrooms. Such observations would serve to confirm or deny what you have read and also help fix the concept in your long-term memory.

If you are assigned to a K–12 classroom, find out if and when your mentor teacher plans to use cooperative learning. If your mentor does not plan to do so, try to arrange a visit to a class where some sort of cooperative learning activities are in effect. If you cannot arrange to see this instructional alternative, perhaps your university instructor has a videotape on it. Videotapes are available from the Johns Hopkins Team Learning Project, Johns Hopkins University, 3505 N. Charles Street, Baltimore, MD 21218–7570, and from Teaching Inc., P.O. Box 788, Edmunds, WA 98020.

As you observe, record answers to these questions:

- Did the cooperative learning session have these identifying characteristics: heterogeneous groups, group cooperation, and group reward? How effective were these characteristics—did they work?

- What qualities of good cooperative learning were most obvious? (See Table 8.2 for ideas if STAD was the process used.)

- Did certain students seem to benefit more and others less? Why?
- What teacher and student needs seem to have been most fully met?

Additionally, talk with students about how they feel about cooperative learning and ask the teacher his or her perceptions of it.

ACTIVITY 8.4: Prepare a Discovery Lesson   Using what you have learned about meaningful learning in general and about discovery learning in particular, prepare a discovery lesson that might be used with a group of your classmates. The lesson should be as brief as possible and should require your learners to discover some form of knowledge, either a concept, a fact, a generalization, a rule, or a law. (See Table 8.3 for ideas.)
Assessment: Did you follow the procedures for good discovery learning?

ACTIVITY 8.5: Deliver a Discovery Lesson   Deliver your discovery lesson to a small group of your peers.
Assessment: Following the lesson, have your learners respond to these questions. To what extent did you

- Challenge learners by presenting them with the need to find something out for themselves?
- Ensure that learners knew what they were to do?
- Provide them with useful resources if needed?
- Monitor and guide their activity and thinking?
- Encourage inductive processes: observation, organization, manipulation, and analysis?
- Encourage supportive peer interaction?
- Assist learners in phrasing their conclusions?
- Provide opportunities for learners to use their new knowledge?

ACTIVITY 8.6: Observe Discovery Learning   Hopefully, you will be able to observe a discovery lesson. If you are assigned to a field experience, ask your mentor teacher if one is scheduled. Perhaps the teacher would conduct one just for you. Don't be afraid to ask. If a live discovery lesson is not available, perhaps your university instructor has captured one on videotape. In making your observation, whether real or recorded, answer the following questions:

- To what extent did the lesson possess the characteristics of discovery learning: the teacher acting as catalyst, students constructing their own knowledge, and the discovery revolving around mostly higher-order thought-provoking questions?
- What did the teacher do to prepare the lesson?
- What qualities of good discovery teaching were displayed by the teacher?
- What qualities of good discovery learning were most evident?
- In your opinion, what teacher and student needs did discovery learning seem to meet?
- Why do you believe that some students seemed to benefit more than others?

Interview students who seemed to benefit most and least. Ask them how they feel about discovery learning. Finally, ask the teachers how they like this instructional alternative and what they think are its advantages and disadvantages.

ACTIVITY 8.7: Prepare a Constructivist Lesson   Using what you have learned about meaningful learning in general and constructivism in particular, prepare a lesson

CHAPTER 8
Four More Instructional Alternatives:
Cooperative Learning, Discovery
Learning, Constructivism,
and Direct Instruction
265

that you can lead in this class. The lesson should be as brief as possible and require learners to maximize understanding of something using constructivist ideas. Ideas might include

- A lesson in which learners think about and discuss the meanings or implications of good teaching.
- A lesson in which learners are asked to think about and discuss their understanding of constructivism or the relationship of constructivism and discovery learning.

Assessment: Did you follow the procedures for good constructivist teaching?

ACTIVITY 8.8: Deliver a Constructivist Lesson   Engage your peers in the constructivist lesson.

Assessment: Following the lesson have learners respond to these questions: To what extent

- Was the objective of the lesson to increase learner understanding?
- Was the lesson set or situated in reality or a close approximation of it?
- Were groups expected to think and share thinking?
- Were the learners expected to begin from what they already know or think they know?
- Were groups provided with questions that focus on improving understanding?
- Were learners expected and given opportunity to exhibit their understandings?
- Were learners expected to consider discrepancies between what they knew or thought they knew and changes in their perceptions and knowledge?

ACTIVITY 8.9: Observe Direct Instruction   A number of schools are attempting to put into practice what is known about effective schools, educational practices, and teaching (Cruickshank, 1990). Many of those schools are the ones most likely to be implementing one or more of the direct instruction approaches you read about in this chapter.

If you are involved in a field experience, you may have the opportunity to observe one or more teachers using Basic Practice, Explicit Teaching, Active Teaching, the Mastery Teaching Program, or DISTAR. If not, perhaps your instructor has a videotape.

As you observe, record answers to these questions:

- To what extent were the characteristics of direct instruction evident: the teacher providing strong academic direction, the teacher holding high expectations for student achievement, the students being held accountable for their work, the students expected to be cooperative, the students feeling psychologically safe, and the teacher controlling behavior?
- What qualities of a good leader of direct instruction were evident? (See Table 8.7.)
- To what extent was the teacher able to follow the regimen for good direct instruction? (See Table 8.7.)
- What teacher personality and professional needs did the instruction seem to meet?
- What student personality and educational needs did the instruction seem to meet?

Talk with the teacher about his or her feelings about direct instruction. Finally, ask a few diverse students whether they like to be taught this way.

Anastasi, A. (1997). *Psychological testing*. Sixth Edition. Englewood Cliffs, NJ: Prentice Hall.

Aronson, E., Blaney, N., Stephan, C., Sikes, J., & Snapp, M. (1978). *The jigsaw classroom*. Beverly Hills, CA: Sage.

Augustine, D. K., Gruber, K. D., & Hansen, L. R. (1989/1990, December–January). Cooperation works. *Educational Leadership, 47*(4), 4–7.

Battistich, V., Solomon, D., & Delucci, K. (1993, September). Interaction processes and student outcomes in cooperative learning groups. *The Elementary School Journal, 94*(1), 19–32.

Becker, W. C. (1986). *Applied psychology for teachers*. Chicago: Science Research Associates.

Benjamin, R. (1981). *Making schools work*. New York: Continuum.

Berliner, D. (1982). Issue: Should teachers be expected to learn and use direct instruction? *ASCD Update, 24,* 5.

Biemiller, A. (1993) Lake Wobegon revisited: On diversity and education. *Educational Researcher, 22*(9), 7–12.

Bransford, J. D. Cited in Hoff, D. J. (1999, January 13). NAS hoping to bridge divide on learning methods. *Education Week 18*(18), 9.

Brooks, J., & Brooks, M. (1993). *The case for constructivist classrooms*. Alexandria, VA: Association for Supervision and Curriculum Development.

Brophy, J., & Good, T. L. (1986). Teacher behavior and student achievement. In M. C. Wittrock (Ed.), *Handbook of research on teaching* (pp. 328–375). New York: Macmillan.

Bruner, J. S. (1977). *The process of education*. Cambridge, MA: Harvard University Press.

Bruner, J. S. (1961). The act of discovery. *Harvard Educational Review, 32,* 21–32.

Cohen, E. G. (1986). *Designing group work: Strategies for the heterogeneous classroom*. New York: Teachers College Press.

Cruickshank, D., Tracey, K., Novak, C., Mager, G., Holton, J., Applegate, J., & Myers, B. (1980). *Teaching is tough*. Englewood Cliffs, NJ: Prentice-Hall.

Cruickshank, D. R. (1990). *Research that informs teachers and teacher educators*. Bloomington, IN: Phi Delta Kappa.

Dewey, J. (1933). *How we think*. Boston: Heath.

Doyle, A. C. (1901). *The hound of the Baskervilles*. New York: Grosset & Dunlap.

Ellson, D. (1986, October). Improving productivity in teaching. *Phi Delta Kappan, 68,* 111–124.

Fashella, O., & Slavin, R. (1997). Effective and replicable programs for students placed at-risk in elementary and middle schools. Paper prepared for the Office of Research and Development (Grant No. R1170-40005) Washington, DC: U.S. Department of Education.

Gagnon, G., & Collay, M. (2001). *Design for learning: Six elements in constructivist classrooms*. Thousand Oaks, CA: Corwin Press.

Gersten, R., & Keating, T. (1987, March). Long-term benefits from direct instruction. *Educational Leadership, 44*(6), 28–31.

Gilstrap, R. L., & Martin, W.R. (1975). *Current strategies for teachers*. Pacific Palisades, CA: Goodyear.

Good, T., & Brophy, J. (1999). *Looking into classrooms*. Boston: Addison-Wesley/Longman.

Good, T., & Grouws, D. (1977). Teaching effects: A process-product study in fourth grade classrooms. *Journal of Teacher Education, 28,* 49–54.

Good, T. L., Grouws, D., & Ebmeier, H. (1983). *Active mathematics teaching*. White Plains, NY: Longman.

Good, T. L., Reys, B. J., Grouws, D. A., & Mulryan, C. M. (1989, December; 1990, January). Using work groups in mathematics instruction. *Educational Leadership, 47*(4), 56–62.

Harmin, M., & Gregory, T. (1974). *Teaching is. . . .* Chicago: Science Research Associates.

Hoffer, T. B. (1992, Fall). Middle school ability grouping and student achievement in science and mathematics. *Educational Evaluation and Policy Analysis, 14*(3), 205–227.

Hofwolt, C. A. (1984). Instructional strategies in the science classroom. In D. Holdzkom & P. Lutz (Eds.), *Research within reach: Science education* (pp. 41–58). Washington, DC: National Science Teachers Association.

Holloway, J. (1999, November). Caution, constructivism ahead. *Educational Leadership, 57*(3), 85–86.

Hunter, M. (1982). *Mastery teaching*. El Segundo, CA: TIP Publications.

Hunter, M. (1984). Knowing, teaching, and supervising. In P. Hosford (Ed.), *Using what we know about teaching*. Alexandria, VA: Association for Supervision and Curriculum Development.

Hunter, M. (1995). Mastery teaching. In J. Block, S. Everson, & T. Guskey (Eds.). *School improvement programs* (pp. 181–204). New York: Scholastic Press.

Johnson, D. W., & Johnson, R. T. (1998). *Learning together and alone: Cooperation, competition, and individualization*. Boston: Allyn & Bacon.

Johnson, D. W., & Johnson, R. T. (1989/1990, December/January). Social skills for successful group work. *Educational Leadership, 47*(4), 29–33.

Johnson, D. W., Johnson, R. T., & Holubec, E. J. (1998). *Cooperation in the classroom*. Revised Edition. Edina, MN: Interaction.

Johnson, D. W., Maruyama, G., Johnson, R., & Nelson, D. (1981). Effects of cooperative, competitive, and individualistic goal structures on achievement: A meta-analysis. *Psychological Bulletin, 89*(1), 47–62.

Joyce, B., & Weil, M. (1999). *Models of teaching*. Boston: Allyn & Bacon.

Kauchak, D. P., & Eggen, P. D. (2003). *Learning and teaching: Research-based methods*. Boston: Allyn & Bacon.

King, L. H. (1993). High and low achievers' perceptions of cooperative learning in two small groups. *Elementary School Journal, 93*(4), 399–416.

McCown, R., Driscoll, M., & Roop, P. (1995). *Educational psychology: A learning centered approach*. Boston: Allyn & Bacon.

Merwin, W. C. (1976). The inquiry method. In S.E. Goodman (Ed.), *Handbook on contemporary education*. New York: Bowker.

Meyer, L. A. (1984). Long-term academic effects of the Direct Instruction Project Follow-Through. *Elementary School Journal, 84*, 380–394.

Michaels, J. W. (1978). Classroom reward structures and academic performance. *Review of Educational Research, 47*, 87–98.

Murphy, J., Weil, M., & McGreal, T. (1986). The basic practice model of instruction. *The Elementary School Journal, 87*, 83–95.

Murray, H. A. (1963). *Explorations in personality*. New York: Oxford.

National Academy of Sciences. (1999). *How people learn: Brain, mind, experience, and school*. Washington, DC: National Academy Press.

Nuthall, G., & Snook, I. (1973). Contemporary models of teaching. In R.M. Travers (Ed.), *Second handbook of research on teaching* (pp. 47–76). Chicago: Rand McNally.

Orlich, D. C. (2000). *Teaching strategies: A guide to better instruction*. Boston: Houghton Mifflin.

Pavin, R. (1992, October). Benefits of nongraded schools. *Educational Leadership*, (2), 22–25.

Perkins, D. (1999, November). The many faces of constructivism. *Educational Leadership, 57*(3), 6–11.

Peterson, P. (1979a, October). Direct instruction: Effective for what and for whom? *Educational Leadership, 37*, 46–48.

Peterson, P. (1979b). Direct instruction reconsidered. In P. Peterson & H. Walberg (Eds.), *Research on teaching: Concepts, findings, and implications*. Berkeley, CA: McCutchan.

Peterson, P. (1982). Issue: Should teachers be expected to learn and use direct instruction? *ASCD Update, 24*, 5.

Rosenshine, B. (1986). Synthesis of research on explicit teaching. *Educational Leadership, 43*(7), 60–69.

Rosenshine, B. (1987). Direct instruction. In M.J. Dunkin (Ed.), *The international encyclopedia of teaching and teacher education* (pp. 257–263). Oxford: Pergamon.

Rosenshine, B., & Meister, C. (1995). Direct instruction. In L. Anderson (Ed.), *International encyclopedia of teaching and teacher education*. Second Edition (pp. 143–148). Oxford: Elsevier Science Ltd.

Rosenshine, B., & Stevens, R. (1986). Teaching functions. In M. Wittrock (Ed.), *Handbook of research on teaching*. Third Edition (pp. 376–391). New York: Macmillan.

Rossmiller, R. A. (1976). Individually guided education. In S.E. Goodman (Ed.), *Handbook on contemporary education* (pp. 402–407). New York: Bowker.

Runkel, P. J., & Schmuck, R. A. (1982). Group processes. In H. E. Mitzel (Ed.), *Encyclopedia of educational research*. Fifth Edition (pp. 743–755). New York: Free Press.

Sharon, S. (1980). Cooperative learning in small groups: Recent methods and effects on achievement, attitudes, and ethnic relations. *Review of Educational Research, 50*, 241–271.

Sharon, S., & Sharon, Y. (1976). *Small group teaching*. Englewood Cliffs, NJ: Educational Technology Publications.

Sharon, Y., & Sharon, S. (1989, December; 1990, January). Group investigation expands cooperative learning. *Educational Leadership, 47*(4), 17–21.

Slavin, R. E. (December 1989/January 1990). Here to stay or gone tomorrow: Guest editorial. *Educational Leadership, 47*(4), 3.

Slavin, R. E. (1995a). *Cooperative learning: Theory, research, and practice*. Boston: Allyn & Bacon.

Slavin, R. E. (1991, February). Synthesis of research on cooperative learning. *Educational Leadership, 48*(5), 71–82.

Slavin, R. E. (1999). *Educational psychology*. Fourth Edition. Boston: Allyn & Bacon

Slavin, R. E. (1995b). Cooperative learning. In L. Anderson (Ed.), *International encyclopedia of teaching and teacher education*. Second Edition (pp. 139–143). Oxford: Elsevier Science Ltd.

Slavin, R., & Madden, N. (1989, February). What works for students at risk: A research synthesis. *Educational Leadership, 46*, 4–13.

Slavin, R. E., Karweit, N. L., & Madden, N. A. (1989). *Effective programs for students at risk*. Boston: Allyn & Bacon.

Solomon, D., Watson, M., Schaps, E., Battistich, V., & Solomon, J. (1990). Cooperative learning as part of a comprehensive classroom program designed to promote prosocial development. In S. Sharon (Ed.), *Cooperative learning: Theory and research* (pp. 231–260). New York: Praeger.

Stallings, J., & Kaskowitz, D. H. (1975, April). A study of follow-through implementation. Paper presented at the annual meeting of the American Education Research Association, Washington.

Stallings, J. A., & Stipek, D. (1986). Research on early childhood and elementary school teaching programs. In M. D. Wittrock (Ed.), *Handbook of research on teaching*. Third Edition (pp. 727–753). New York: Macmillan.

Stratton, L. (1993, February 19). Pupils see computer's classroom potential in action. *The Columbus Dispatch*, p. D1.

Strike, K. A. (1975). The logic of learning by discovery. *Review of Educational Research, 45*, 461–483.

Struthers, D. B. (1990, October). Cooperative learning: Fad or foundation for learning? *Phi Delta Kappan, 72*(2), 158–162.

Suchman, R. J. (1961). Inquiry training: Builds skills for autonomous discovery. *Merrill Palmer Quarterly, 7*, 147–171.

Swang, J. (1993, April/May). Ensuring success in science. *Learning, 93*, 24–27.

Taba, H. (1966). *Teaching strategies and cognitive functioning in elementary school children*. Cooperative Research Project 2404. San Francisco: San Francisco State University.

Tamir, P. (1995). Discovery learning and teaching. In L. Anderson (Ed.), *International encyclopedia of teaching and teacher education*. Second Edition (pp. 149–155). Oxford: Elsevier Science Ltd.

Viadero, D. (1999, March 17). A direct challenge. *Education Week, 18*(27), 41–43.

Walberg, H. (1984, May). Improving the productivity of America's schools. *Educational Leadership, 41*, 19–27.

Wallis, C. (1995, Spring). The learning revolution. *Time, 145* (12), 49–51.

Watson, B., & Konicek, R. (1990, May). Teaching for conceptual change: Confronting children's experience. *Phi Delta Kappan, 71*, 680–685.

Webb, N. M. (1982). Student interaction and learning in small groups. *Review of Educational Research, 52*(3), 421–445.

Weil, M. L., & Murphy, J. (1982). Instruction processes. In H. Mitzel (Ed.), *Encyclopedia of educational research* (pp. 890–917). New York: Free Press.

Willis, S., & Mann, L. (2000, Winter). Differentiating instruction. *Curriculum update*. Alexandria, VA: Association for Supervision and Curriculum Development, pp. 1–3, 6–7.

Woolfolk, A. (2000). *Educational psychology*. Eighth Edition. Boston: Allyn & Bacon.

CHAPTER 8
Four More Instructional Alternatives:
Cooperative Learning, Discovery
Learning, Constructivism,
and Direct Instruction

269

Evaluating Students' Learning

Contents

At many points during the instructional process, teachers make decisions about how well their students are learning and how effective their instruction has been. These assessment decisions, while often difficult, are important in helping teachers improve their performance and their students' learning (Cross & Frary, 1999; Mac-Donald, 1992; McMillan, 2001). They require teachers to measure student learning in one or more of several ways and to use that information to make judgments about the effectiveness of their instruction.

In this chapter, we examine ways teachers can more accurately assess student learning and thereby make judgments about the effectiveness of their own instruction. We begin by defining instructional assessment and underscoring its importance in effective teaching. Next, we examine several factors that influence the quality of assessments, and then we look at the principal types of assessment. The next sections then deal respectively with standardized tests and testing and with teacher-made assessments and test construction. In the final section, we discuss systems for grading student performance and ways to effectively and fairly assign grades.

Defining Classroom Assessment, Measurement, and Evaluation

When teachers think of instructional assessment, they most often think of tests or projects administered to students at the end of instruction. However, good classroom assessment requires more than that. It requires teachers to continually gather information about their students' progress from a variety of sources, to synthesize that information, and then to make a judgment or evaluation about how well or how much each student has learned.

Classroom assessment serves at least two important purposes for effective teachers. First, it provides information about the effectiveness of instruction. By gathering information before, during, and after instruction, teachers are able to plan and adapt instruction to better meet students' needs. Second, the information gained through assessment helps them make more accurate determinations about what an individual student has or has not learned and why. Thus, they can reteach when necessary, avoid unnecessary repetition, and help the student correct or modify misconceptions, errors, and inaccurate strategies.

The process of gathering objective information or data about students' performance is referred to as **measurement.** Measurement merely describes, usually in the form of a number or score, how much students have learned or how well they have performed. For example, students' scores on a twenty-item quiz represent a measurement of how well the students understand the material. In themselves, these numbers do not represent good, bad, acceptable, or unacceptable performance. The "goodness" of a student's score is determined by making a judgment about the measured score, that is, by comparing the score obtained through

9.1 What personal biases or opinions do you have that might influence your judgments of student performance?

measurement to some standard or to other students' scores. This judgment is referred to as an **evaluation.**

The process of collecting, synthesizing, and interpreting information to aid in decision making is called **assessment.** While measurement is generally considered objective and nonjudgmental, assessment is always subjective to some degree. As the teacher, you must decide what your students' scores indicate. For example, does a numerical test score of 85 represent good, average, or poor performance? In making this decision, you must consider each student's score either in relation to how well other students did or in relation to some minimum score you have established. You may also consider other factors, not directly measured, that affect a student's score. For example, was the child feeling ill at the time of measurement? Did the child's performance improve from the last measurement, even if it did not meet the minimum acceptable score? Did you feel that the measurement was somehow unfair to the student?

While assessment of student performance often involves more than measurement, you must remember that the more you allow personal opinions or biases to influence how you interpret the results of measurement and make judgments, the less accurate your assessments will be. Further, even if you attempt to be objective in interpreting information, both the methods you use to gather your information and the sources you use influence the accuracy of your assessment. Let us now examine the factors more closely and then turn our attention to the various types of assessment.

Factors Influencing Assessment Quality

To use assessment effectively, teachers must consider several factors that influence the accuracy and usefulness of their assessments. First they must select appropriate sources of information, then they must ensure that their measurements and judgments are accurate, and finally they must determine how and why they will use the assessment.

SOURCES OF INFORMATION

In Chapter 5, we discussed several sources of information, such as cumulative records, observations, and interviews, that allow teachers to get to know their students better. These and other information sources help teachers find out about students' strengths and weaknesses, likes and dislikes, and problems and successes. Teachers use this information to organize their classrooms and plan their curricula. In this chapter, we are most interested in sources of information that help determine what a student has learned and in what areas or ways the student may need more instruction. Although some of the more informal sources discussed in Chapter 5 can be used to assess academic achievement, teachers mostly gain this kind of information by analyzing students' work or through testing.

Analysis of Students' Work   Obviously, a great deal of useful information about academic achievement is gained through analyzing students' work. In contrast to merely examining the score a student obtains on a given piece of work, such as a homework assignment, teachers often want to know how a student arrived at an answer. For example, what process or method did the child employ, and how accurately did he or she employ it? By looking closely at the process the student used, the teacher can identify errors that prevent the student from completing the work accurately. Homework assignments, projects, worksheets, and even tests or quizzes can be designed so that teachers can observe and analyze students' work. When teachers do this, it is important that they give students feedback about their performance (see Chapter 12).

"I see many of you anticipated a sneak quiz today."

Testing   Testing is the most recognized source of assessment information. Tests require students to demonstrate how well they have learned targeted content and allow teachers to describe their students' performance. Tests, like other instructional activities, can also be structured so that students are forced to demonstrate how they solve problems or arrive at conclusions. Thus, tests are a rich source of information. As with information from any source, however, the information tests provide is useful only when it is accurate and unbiased. Further, tests provide only one measure of students' progress.

Effective assessment requires that teachers collect and synthesize as much accurate information from as many sources as possible. They must integrate the data they gain from informal observations and interactions with students with the more formal measurements they obtain through testing, student projects or performances, and other available sources. However, the value of these teacher judgments depends largely on the accuracy of the information they obtain.

ACCURACY OF INFORMATION

The data that teachers obtain about students and their progress is never completely accurate. For a variety of reasons, no measure is ever totally free of bias or error. In fact, some of the information sources just noted are easily identified as subject to inaccuracy. For example, opinions from teachers or parents are likely to be somewhat inaccurate because they are highly subjective. Likewise, teachers' observations of their students are inevitably selective and incomplete; they are influenced by personal values and, consequently, are open to error and bias. Thus, teachers must take care to identify potential biases or errors when gathering and using information from these and other sources.

Tests are also subject to error. No test precisely measures a given student's knowledge or achievement in a subject area. First of all, tests are selective. They normally measure only part of what a teacher attempts to teach. Also, they do not test for knowledge that a student may have acquired from other sources such as books, friends, or other teachers. They may also omit some incidental things that a student has learned from the test-giving teacher. Furthermore, the student's internal condition at the time of testing can influence results. Perhaps the student was tired or ill when taking the test. Or perhaps the test emphasizes material that the student happened to review just before taking the test. In each case, the score obtained is not a full or accurate measure of the student's total knowledge on the subject.

A teacher's primary considerations when determining the accuracy of information gained from tests, projects, or other sources used to gauge student performance are (1) does the information provided by the assessment reflect what it was intended to measure *(validity)*, and (2) does the assessment provide consistent measurements *(reliability)?* These two factors are often discussed as they relate to tests, but they are equally important in judging information collected from any other assessment (Wiggins, 1998).

Validity   **Validity** is the term used to describe the *degree* to which a test or other assessment measures what it was intended to measure. Validity is based upon the extent to which our assessment meets three criteria. First, a valid assessment measures understanding or mastery of what was actually taught and nothing more. In other words, the knowledge or tasks the assessment addresses should include as much of the content covered during instruction as possible, but it should not include content the students were not exposed to. Specifically, a valid assessment measures students' mastery of *each* of the teacher's major instructional objectives.

Second, a valid assessment measures performance in whatever *domains* (cognitive, affective, psychomotor) and at whatever *levels* (see Bloom's taxonomy in Chapter 6) the teacher's instructional objectives targeted. For example, if a history teacher reviews lessons that focused on knowledge (facts) about the American Revolution and then spends considerable time getting her or his students to analyze, synthesize, and make evaluations based on these facts, then the assessments, to be valid, should emphasize these three higher cognitive levels.

Third, just as a valid assessment reflects the balance between the various domains and levels of instruction, it should also reflect the emphasis the teacher places on various content areas. For example, if social and economic conditions in the American colonies receive roughly equal instructional time as prevailing ideologies of the period, then a valid assessment should cover both bodies of content in roughly equal proportions.

Perhaps an extended example would be useful. Let's suppose that you teach a three-week unit on slavery and that you base your instruction on four cognitive objectives—one at the knowledge level, two at the synthesis level, and one at the evaluation level. During instruction, you spend one day on the reasons for slavery in the United States, three days on the practice of slavery, three days on causes of the demise of slavery, and two days on the impact of the Emancipation Proclamation on slaves and the Southern economy. A valid assessment would require your students to demonstrate understanding of each of these topics: reasons, practices, causes of demise, and impact. Further, the assessment would ask students to use their knowledge to (1) recall some information (the knowledge-level objective), (2) synthesize some information, and (3) evaluate one or more situations. The assessment should place the greatest emphasis on the topics of the practice and demise of slavery (three days on each of these), somewhat less emphasis on the impact of the Emancipation Proclamation (two days), and the least emphasis on reasons for slavery (one day). Students would not be asked to demonstrate understanding of other topics, for example, the impact of slavery on African cultures, even though there might have been incidental learning in this area.

To summarize, validity is the accuracy with which an assessment measures what you want it to measure. It thus gives you information about your students' learning and the success of your instruction. You have probably noticed from our discussion that a single assessment cannot perfectly meet every criterion for validity. Validity is not either-or, but rather a matter of degree, so you must decide whether a given assessment is *sufficiently* valid for your purposes. In later sections, we discuss the ways you can make your assessments more valid.

Reliability   In addition to measuring what you want it to measure, you probably hope that your assessment provides you with *consistent* measures of your students' learning. This consistency is referred to as *reliability.* Specifically, reliability means that an assessment will yield nearly the same scores if the individuals were to engage in it repeatedly. As with validity, no assessment can be expected to provide exactly the same measurements every time, so reliability, like validity, must be thought of as a matter of degree.

An assessment that lacks reliability produces results that do not accurately reflect students' understanding or ability due to some error in the assessment itself. An analogy might help clarify. Let's assume you want to measure the dimensions of the bookshelves in your classroom. You locate a thin metal yardstick that was left lying in the bright sun on the windowsill and begin to measure the shelves. You record the dimensions of four shelves, but then you are interrupted by a call from the office. You lay the yardstick on the air-conditioning duct and go to the office. When you return, you realize that you left the paper you were recording the measurements on in the office. Rather than return to get it, you pick up the yardstick from the air-conditioning duct and remeasure the first four shelves. Sometime later in the day, you find the original paper and notice that the two sets of measurements for the shelves are not the same: The shelves are slightly smaller in the earlier measurements than in the later ones. You might conclude that the shelves changed length during that time. However, the real explanation is that the metal yardstick did not give you reliable measures because it expanded from lying in the sun (thus making the shelves appear smaller) and contracted from lying on the air-conditioning duct (thus making the shelves appear larger).

This same problem can occur when an assessment is not reliable. Unreliable assessments lead us to draw inaccurate conclusions about student learning. If they have engaged in a flawed assessment that produces unreliable results, students may appear to have made little academic progress when, in fact, they may have learned quite a lot. Reliability is difficult to assess. Manufacturers of commercially available tests usually provide statistical indications of the reliability of their tests called **reliability coefficients.** These coefficients range from .00 to 1.00, with zero representing no reliability and 1.00 indicating perfect reliability. Generally, reliability coefficients above .85 are considered acceptable. Although you may be unable to compute the reliability coefficient of your own assessments, you can improve their reliability by formalizing and structuring your assessments and by being certain to score objectively and consistently. Guidelines for constructing reliable tests and other assessments appear in a later section.

9.2 Did you ever feel that a teacher had made an inaccurate assessment of your performance? Why do you feel the assessment was inaccurate?

TYPES OF ASSESSMENT: FORMATIVE VERSUS SUMMATIVE

We have seen that instructional assessments use information from a variety of sources and that this information can have various degrees of accuracy. Instructional assessments also vary in terms of their use. Typically, we think of assessment as occurring after instruction with the results used to determine students' grades. However, Scriven (1967) pointed out that assessment conducted *after* instruction is completed is not very useful in improving instruction or learning. Although necessary to assign grades, postinstructional assessment does not help the teacher or the student correct deficiencies. More important, according to Scriven, is assessment conducted *during* instruction. This type of assessment can be used to adapt instruction to meet the needs of the student while learning is taking place.

Scriven introduced two terms to describe these different types of assessment. **Formative assessment** refers to assessment conducted during the course of instruction. Such assessment provides feedback while it is still possible to influence the instructional and learning process. Although student performance may be graded during formative assessment, the primary purpose is to provide feedback that can be used to plan or alter instruction. Formative assessment enables the teacher to form effective instruction and thereby improve students' performance. Formative assessment consists of both informal teacher observations and examples of student

TABLE 9.1 Characteristics of Formative and Summative Assessments

	Formative	Summative
Purpose	To monitor and guide a learning process while it is still in progress	To judge the success of a learning process at its completion
Time of assessment	During the process	At the end of the process
Type of assessment technique	Informal observation, quizzes, homework, pupils' questions, worksheets	Formal tests, projects, term papers
Use of assessment information	Improve and change a process while it is still going on	Judge the overall success of a process; grade, place, and promote

Source: From P. Airasian. (1994). *Classroom assessment.* Fourth Edition. New York: McGraw-Hill.

work, including responses to teachers' questions or any work students might complete within a larger unit of instruction. The feedback provided through formative assessment allows the teacher to adjust instruction and improve students' performance before a final assessment of learning is conducted.

Summative assessment is the term used to describe assessment conducted *after* instruction is completed. This type of assessment is used to make final judgments about a student's learning. Its primary purpose is not to adapt instruction or to remedy learning deficiencies; rather, it attempts to *summarize* a student's achievement or progress, generally in the form of a grade or score. Summative assessment generally involves information gathered from examinations or other projects due at the end of the term. In many cases, formative assessment of similar but less encompassing student work has taken place prior to this final assessment.

Effective teachers use both formative and summative assessments. However, formative assessments conducted and then communicated to students through a variety of formal and informal methods is most closely related to improved learning (Brophy, 1981; Guskey & Bailey, 2001). Table 9.1 provides a brief comparison of formative and summative evaluation.

Standardized Testing and Standard Scores

You may remember from Chapter 5 that a common type of assessment in schools is **standardized testing.** We all remember the days we spent in classrooms, our No. 2 pencils sharpened and ready on our desktops, waiting with trepidation for the teacher to finish reading the directions and to tell us to "open your test booklets and begin." Perhaps more recently, you remember taking the Scholastic Aptitude Test (SAT) or the American College Test (ACT) before entering college. In each case, you were taking a standardized test. The results were to be used to help others make judgments about how much or how well you had learned. They made these judgments by comparing your scores with those of similar students who also had taken the test.

Standardized testing has become increasingly common in U.S. public schools in recent years. The results of these tests represent the most common method of evaluating teachers and schools (Eisner, 1999; Worthen, Sanders, & Fitzpatrick, 1997). Calls for greater accountability for students' learning and more rigorous standards have prompted many states to require students to pass standardized tests at several grade levels. Ten years ago it was estimated that 127 million standardized tests were administered to students in the United States each year. Nearly $900 million per year was spent on developing, administering, and scoring these tests, and this figure has increased (Willis, 1990). Because teachers are routinely expected to administer and interpret the results of standardized tests, we now turn our attention to this form of assessment. We will examine the standardized testing process and discuss how the scores from such tests are reported and used.

THE STANDARDIZED TESTING PROCESS

Standardized tests get their name because they are administered and scored in consistent, uniform ways. Any student taking a nationally standardized test will take the test under roughly the same conditions as any other student, no matter where or when the test is administered. This uniformity includes all controllable factors that might influence a student's performance on the test: the materials used, the time limits, oral instructions, preliminary demonstrations, policies for handling questions from students, and any other detail believed to affect test performance (Anastasi & Urbina, 1997; Gregory, 1996).

For example, when you took the SAT or ACT, you completed the test under the same conditions as all other students who took the exam. You were given the same instructions, the test booklet and scoring sheets or computer interface were the same, the questions you answered were of equivalent difficulty and type, the equipment you were allowed to use was the same (pencils, calculators, and so on), you had the same amount of time to complete each section, and your scores were reported in the same ways. As a result, you are able to compare your performance with that of all other students who took the exam, even if they took it at another time or in another place. This ability to make comparisons across large groups of pupils is the greatest benefit of standardized tests.

Standardized tests offer several benefits in addition to allowing comparisons of students. They are efficient in measuring a wide range of student learning relatively quickly and inexpensively. They are fairly and objectively scored. They tend to be more reliable than teacher-made tests, and they can be developed to assess higher-order thinking. In spite of these benefits, standardized tests are often criticized for emphasizing low-level basic skills and for cultural, racial, and gender bias (e.g., Isaac & Michael, 1997; Linn, 1991; Wiggins, 1998). Often, the harshest criticisms of standardized tests arise when the tests are misused or their results misinterpreted (Popham, 1997).

Each standardized test has been developed for use with targeted groups of students and is appropriately used only with similar students. For example, some standardized tests, like the Iowa Test of Basic Skills (ITBS) or the California Aptitude Test (CAT), are meant to assess broad learning outcomes for students of particular grade levels across the United States. Because every student taking the ITBS takes it under the same conditions, and because scores are always reported in standard ways, it is possible to compare the achievement of students from all across the country.

As a classroom teacher, you will probably be expected to administer standardized tests and to interpret their scores to students and their parents. When administering a standardized test, it is important that you exactly follow the directions provided. Failure to do so makes the results of the test less accurate and may put your students at a disadvantage. A major responsibility when administering the test is to allow all students an equal opportunity to do well. Thus, you must ensure that each student has the necessary materials, desk space, and time. Further, you should carefully read the instructions using a calm, clear, relatively slow speaking voice that all students in the room can hear. Voice inflection, tone, and facial expression should reinforce the instructions. You must also monitor students as they complete the examination, making sure that students begin and end at the appropriate times and do not cheat. Each standardized test will provide instructions for administering the exam, and you are well advised to follow them.

9.3 What standardized tests have you taken?

Try Activity 9.3

"It's exam week, and they're not in a good mood. Let's be careful out there."

9.4

Do you get anxious or nervous about taking standardized tests? Why or why not?

You can help your students improve their performance on standardized tests even if you do not know the exact content to be tested. By helping them develop good test-taking skills, you enable them to better convey what they do know. Students who are knowledgeable about how to efficiently complete standardized tests can be expected to achieve higher scores than students who are not (Anastasi & Urbina, 1997; McMillan, 2001; Walker-Wilson, 2002). While this level of **test sophistication** does not change how much your students know about the content, it gives them a better opportunity to demonstrate their knowledge. That's why you should prepare your students for upcoming standardized testing by providing them with opportunities to respond to questions of similar types and under similar conditions. You may also wish to give students suggestions about when or if to guess at the correct answer and how to manage their time. Such guidance helps students feel more comfortable and confident when taking the test and—especially for disadvantaged students—can substantially improve their test performance (McMillan, 2001).

INTERPRETING STANDARDIZED TEST RESULTS

The use of standardized tests has increased greatly in recent years and so has the responsibility of the teacher to convey the meaning of the results to students and parents. While most of you are familiar with the standardized testing process, few of you have ever had to interpret the results of a standardized test to anyone. In this section, we examine the various ways of reporting standard scores. Knowing this, you can then use this information to evaluate your students' progress and improve your own teaching.

Criterion- versus Norm-Referenced Scores   To interpret test scores, you must compare a particular score to some standard. The two most widely used standards are (1) the scores of other students or (2) an established, fixed criterion. When you compare students' scores to one another, you are using a **norm-referenced** approach. In this approach, the number of items a student answered correctly or incorrectly (called *raw score*) is less important than how the child's performance compares to other students who took the test. Norm-referenced test scores provide little information about what specific learning a student has gained or in what areas the student may need remediation. What they do show is how well the student's achievement compares with other students in the class, school, district, state, or nation who have taken the test. Because comparisons of all students who took the

TABLE 9.2 Comparison of Norm-Referenced and Criterion-Referenced Tests	
Norm-Referenced Test	**Criterion-Referenced Test**
Reports the student's performance in relation to other students who took the test	Reports the student's performance in relation to a fixed, usually predetermined standard
Provides information about general learning and achievement	Provides information about specific learning and mastery of particular objectives
Is useful in making policy decisions at the national, state, and local levels	Is useful in designing the most appropriate instruction for individual students

test are possible, even if the students were in different schools or different parts of the country, schools or state agencies often use the results of norm-referenced testing to make policy decisions.

When you compare students' raw scores to an established standard or criterion, you are using a **criterion-referenced** approach. In this approach, the number of items answered correctly or incorrectly is used to determine whether a student has mastered specific learning objectives. When a student's score is lower than the established criterion, the testers believe that the student has not sufficiently mastered the objectives. The results of criterion-referenced testing provide very detailed information about the specific learning the student has gained and the particular areas in which the student needs more work. Thus, criterion-referenced test results can be of tremendous benefit in evaluating, planning, or adapting classroom instruction. However, they give little information about how well your students' performance compares with that of other students. A comparison of norm-referenced and criterion-referenced tests appears in Table 9.2.

TYPES OF SCORES FROM STANDARDIZED TESTS

The results of standardized tests are reported in a variety of ways, including as both criterion-referenced and norm-referenced scores. In fact, most test reports provide several types of scores for each student on the same section or sections of the test. Because these scores are often confusing and because teachers are increasingly expected both to understand and communicate them to parents, it is critical that we devote some of this chapter to explaining the most common types of scores from standardized tests.

In order to understand, communicate, and use the information provided by standardized tests, we must first understand (1) the various types of scores that can be reported and (2) what they mean in terms of student performance. Students' performance on tests may be reported as *standard scores* like z-scores and T scores, which are often discussed in education textbooks. However, most standardized tests now report students' performance in terms of raw score, percentile ranks (PR), Normal Curve Equivalent scores (NCE), stanine scores, and grade equivalent scores. In the sections that follow, we will discuss what these scores mean using the example test report presented in Figure 9.1.

Raw score is the number of test items or points that a student obtained on a particular section of the test. Just like the raw score that a student may obtain on a classroom quiz or paper, for example 8 out of a possible 10, this number can only be interpreted if we have additional information. In the example in Figure 9.1, raw score is reported in the first column (RS). As you can see, two numbers are presented for each portion of the test and are separated by a slash. The first number tells us how many items the student completed successfully and the second number indicates the total number of items possible. In this example, our student accurately completed 11 of 17 items in the area of Reading Comprehension, 9 of 15 items in

FIGURE 9.1. Individual Student Test Report

Test Date: 5/12/00
Norms Date: 1998

School: Metropolitan Community
District: Metropolis County

Form: A Level: 14

Student Record Sheet
Student Name: BERTRAND, Adrian L.
Birthdate: 05/20/90
Grade: 4.7
Teacher: Smith, T.

						SCORES		
	RS	**MCL**	**DP**	**SP**	**NP**	**NCE**	**GE**	**ST**
Reading Comprehension	11/17		70	63	52	61	4.5	5
Vocabulary	9/15		63	51	50	50	4.5	5
Mathematics	12/18		89	81	77	66	4.7	6
COMPOSITE	32/50		74	65	60	55	4.4	5
Science	15/18	*	92	85	79	67	4.8	7
Social Studies	11/15	*	79	74	72	62	4.7	6

Vocabulary, and 12 out of 18 in Mathematics. The next column (MCL) uses this information to indicate whether the student met the established minimum competency level of 75 percent. As such, this column represents a criterion-referenced method of interpreting the student's performance on each section of the test.

Another common form of standard score is **percentile rank (PR).** When you received the results of your ACT or SAT, they were likely reported as percentile rank scores. Percentile rank makes use of some known characteristics of the normal curve. A percentile rank score indicates what percentage of people taking the test scored at or below a given score. Thus, a percentile rank of 50 indicates that a student's raw score was the same as the mean, that her score was equal to or better than 50 percent of the people in the original norming sample. Test reports often include percentile rank scores based upon multiple norming groups (e.g., all students in the school, in the district, in the state, or in the nation). As a result, interpretation of these scores requires that we know and understand the comparison or norming group on which they are based.

Our example above may help make this clearer. The third, fourth, and fifth columns report our student's performance in terms of percentile rank. The third column (DP meaning District Percentile) uses other students in our district as the norming group, the fourth column (SP for State Percentile) uses students in our state, and the fifth column (NP) uses a national norming group. Remember, however, that each of these percentile rank scores is a way to interpret our student's raw score on each section of the test. In the example test report above, DP reports a percentile rank of 70 in Reading Comprehension based on other students in our district, SP indicates that a raw score of 11 is a percentile rank of 63 when compared with other students in our state, and NP reports that this same raw score reflects a percentile rank of 52 based on the national norming group. While each of these scores is based on the student's raw score of 11 in Reading Comprehension, they differ because this raw score is compared to the performance of three different groups. A raw score of 11 in Reading Comprehension is as good as or better than 70 percent of the students in our district, as good as or better than 63 percent of students in our state, and as good as or better than 52 percent of students nationwide. Which of these percentile rank scores is most useful? It depends on what the information is to be used for, a question that we will leave for another time. For now, it is enough to understand what PR scores mean.

Normal Curve Equivalent (NCE) scores look very much like percentile rank scores, but they are easier to use when doing calculations with students' test scores. As a result, many district personnel (like school counselors or administrators) prefer to rely on these scores. Like percentile rank, NCE scores have a mean of 50. However, NCE scores use an equal interval scale of 21.06 percentile points for each standard deviation. Thus, as a student's score moves farther from the mean, NCE and PR scores begin to vary considerably. In the example above, our student's performance in Reading Comprehension is reported as an NCE of 61 (based upon the national norming group).

Stanine scores are commonly used to report the results of standardized tests in education. Stanine gets its name from the scale it applies to standard scores. In this scale, 5 is the midpoint, or mean, and the entire scale contains nine values. Hence, it is a "standard nine," or "stanine" scale. Using our example, our student's raw score of 12 in mathematics represents a stanine score of 6. In this example, the stanine score is based upon the national norming group.

Grade equivalent (GE) scores are easily interpretable and particularly common in education. Grade equivalent scores compare a student's performance with the scores of other students of varying grade levels who took the same test. For example, if a student's raw score is similar to that obtained by seventh graders who took the test, the grade equivalent score would be 7. Decimal places are used to indicate months of the academic year, with 1 referring to the first month of the academic year and 10 typically referring to the summer. Thus, our student's GE score of 4.8 on the science portion of the test means that the raw score of 15 was roughly equal to that of fourth-grade students in the eighth month of the school year (approximately April). The scale for grade equivalent scores is created by administering the test to large numbers of students at various grade levels and computing the distribution of scores for students at each month of each grade.

It is important to note that the students at various grade levels all take the *same* test. If the test is intended for students in the fourth grade, all students in the norming sample take this fourth-grade test, *not* a more or less advanced version. In this example, if our fourth-grade student had achieved a GE score of 9.1, his score on this fourth-grade test was roughly equal to that of students in the first month of ninth grade. This score would indicate only that our fourth grader had mastered the fourth-grade material as well as the typical ninth-grader. It does *not* mean that the fourth-grade student is capable of doing ninth-grade work.

Remember that no test is completely accurate in measuring a student's knowledge or ability. Some error is always present. Because of this, many test manufacturers now report student performance not as a single score, but as a range of scores that the student would likely obtain if he or she took the test several times. This **score band** includes the student's actual score (usually at the middle of the band) and indicates how much above and below that score the student might have performed. Although less precise than other types of scores, score bands are a useful way to use the results of standardized tests. They prevent us from attempting to make very fine judgments between students whose scores did not differ much.

Try Activity 9.1

SUMMARY OF STANDARDIZED TESTING

Teachers are commonly required to administer standardized tests, interpret the results to students and parents, and utilize the results to improve instruction. It is important that you be aware of the appropriate uses of such tests in order to avoid misusing their results. Elementary teachers, especially, are expected to present and interpret the results of standardized tests to parents on a regular basis. You must know what standard test scores mean and do not mean, and you must be able to convey this information to parents.

Teacher-Made Assessments

Standardized tests are increasingly important in determining educational policy at the national, state, and district levels. However, the most common form of classroom assessment remains the teacher-developed assessment (Burke, 1994). It has been estimated that students spend well over 10 percent of classroom time in teacher-developed evaluation activities (Crooks, 1988). Well-made teacher-constructed assessments have several advantages over standardized tests. First, since the classroom teacher develops them, they can be keyed to the specific content and objectives that teacher has taught rather than to general content "most" teachers teach at that grade level. Second, teacher-made assessments are far less expensive than commercially produced tests. Third, when they are well-constructed around the instructional objectives, teacher-developed assessments provide more detailed and specific information on how well students have mastered the course content. However, in spite of these advantages, teacher-made assessments are often poorly constructed and thus often provide inaccurate information. Even advocates of teacher-developed assessments concede that many teacher-made assessments are much worse than the standardized tests students take (Brandt, 1992).

Because teacher-made assessments are so common and potentially valuable, we now engage in an extended discussion of how best to develop and use the two primary types of teacher-made tests: pencil-and-paper tests and observational or performance assessment. After defining and describing each type of assessment, we will discuss the specific strengths and weaknesses, note considerations in selecting or developing appropriate instruments, and suggest methods of scoring.

PENCIL-AND-PAPER TESTS

The most recognizable and traditional type of teacher-made assessment is the pencil-and-paper test. Each of us has spent countless hours frantically writing our responses to essay questions or using our pencils to fill in the dots on a scoring sheet. And, perhaps just as often, we have spent time after the exam thinking about how unclear some of the questions were or wondering why the instructor asked so many questions about one aspect of the content while totally neglecting other aspects. In each case, we were prevented from giving a true account of how much we had learned because of a poorly developed test. It is your ethical responsibility as a teacher to make sure that your students have the opportunity to make a valid showing of how much they have learned.

Pencil-and-paper tests most often use items of two types. One type requires students to select a correct response from a list of possible answers called **selected response items.** Multiple-choice, true-false, matching, and completion items are all selected response types. The other type of item requires students to develop or create a response in their own words. These are called **created response items.** Essay or short-answer questions are examples of created response items.

Each item type possesses advantages and disadvantages depending on the ease or difficulty of construction and scoring. In other words, one type of item is easier to write but more difficult to score, while the other is just the opposite. Many people believe that one item type is inherently better than another, for example, that essay items are more valuable than multiple choice. However, this is not necessarily true. Moore (1992) writes

A common misconception is that selected response items test only for facts or knowledge-level behaviors. In truth, any type of test item can be used to measure any instructional outcomes at any level. Although it is often difficult to write selected response items at the higher levels, it is also difficult to write high-level items of any kind. (p. 123)

Thus, we should know about and be able to use items of each type when appropriate.

Created Response Items   Created response items require students to compose an answer, generally in their own words, rather than select the appropriate answer from a list. Created response items can require students to generate anything from a short sentence to a multiple-page essay. Well-written created response items can allow students to demonstrate learning at all cognitive levels—from recall through evaluation. They can push students to organize or reorganize ideas and concepts, apply content in unique ways, and solve problems. Poorly written created response items may discourage creativity, confuse and frustrate students, and result in unfair and inaccurate judgments about students' progress.

Created response items possess several advantages. First, they are easy to write—much easier, in fact, than selected response items. This is especially true when the teacher is attempting to assess higher-level cognitive processes. Thus, created response items require less time to construct. Second, because students must organize and express their answers in their own words, created response items allow teachers to assess students' ability to communicate ideas. Third, they reduce the likelihood that students will simply guess the correct answer.

Created response items also have disadvantages. Although they can be constructed rather easily and quickly, they are extremely time-consuming to score. Imagine, for instance, the high school teacher who administers a five-item essay exam to four classes, each with thirty students. If the response to each item was only one-half page, this teacher would have to read 300 pages of students' responses! Providing prompt and detailed feedback to students about their performance on this exam would be a daunting prospect.

Another disadvantage of created response items is that they limit the amount of content the test can cover. Because students must be allowed sufficient time to think about the item, compose an answer, and put it on paper, the test can include only a few items. Thus, a test consisting entirely of created response items cannot possibly assess all that has been taught or learned. In essence, the validity of the test is reduced because it does not cover all important aspects of the content.

The final and most troubling disadvantage of created response tests is that they are difficult to score reliably. Created response items require teachers to make judgments about the quality of students' responses. Several factors can bias these judgments and result in unfair scoring. For example, the quality or legibility of the students' handwriting, grammar, writing style, or length of response have long been known to influence the score that teachers assign to created responses (Stanley, 1958). This may be a particular problem for young students or for students with limited English proficiency. In addition, teachers' opinions and expectations of students can lead them to score responses unfairly. For instance, a student who has contributed to class discussions and seems motivated and interested is likely to receive a higher score than another student who is perceived as uninterested and unmotivated but makes the same response.

Created response items can be written as **restricted response** or **extended response items.** Restricted response items set explicit parameters within which students are to respond. Such items may restrict the topic or topics to be included or the length or space devoted to the response, and they often make specific suggestions about aspects of the content the response should address. Restricted response items do not allow students as much flexibility or creativity in responding. However, because they reduce variability in the style, length, and topics of students' responses, they are generally more reliable and fair than extended response items.

Restricted Response

List, describe, and present an example of each of three literary devices Poe uses to set the mood in the introductory paragraph of "The Fall of the House of Usher." Use no more than five complete sentences.

Extended Response

Discuss and provide examples of the literary devices Poe uses to set the mood in the introductory paragraph of "The Fall of the House of Usher."

Extended response items often do not place any restrictions on students' responses. As a result, they allow much greater creativity and flexibility in creating the response. Students can write as much or as little as they wish and can include all aspects of the content they deem necessary. Extended response items give us a better picture of how well students can communicate and approach problems creatively, but they are more open to biased and unfair scoring. As a result, you should use restricted response items in most situations. Examples of restricted and extended items are shown in Figure 9.2.

Once you have decided that your instructional objectives can best be assessed through created response items, you can do several things to improve the validity, reliability, and thus the accuracy of your test. First, key the test to your instructional objectives. Your goal should be to create assessment instruments that provide accurate measures of how well each student has mastered all the objectives. The test should be representative of the breadth, depth, and emphases of the objectives and should require students to perform or respond at cognitive levels matching your objectives. If you have written clear and complete instructional objectives, constructing a created response test is a relatively easy procedure. Just follow these guidelines.

- First, consider which objectives are most important to your assessment. As noted earlier, created response items take students longer to complete, so you may be unable to assess all objectives. In that event, you should select those most critical to students' mastery of the material, those that were most emphasized in instruction, or those that are broad enough to encompass other objectives. However, you must be realistic in determining how many created response items students can handle. All students should be able to answer all questions in the time allowed.

- Second, write restricted response items for each objective. Always begin these items with the verb from your objective (compare, contrast, list, and so on), and provide specific information about the length, components, and style to be used. It is also a good idea to indicate whether spelling or grammar will be considered, whether an outline is acceptable, and how much weight you will apply to each element of the response.

- Third, after writing the item, it is a good idea to immediately compose a complete model response that can serve as your guide in scoring students' responses. Make a note about the time it took you to construct your answer, and use this to determine how much time students will need to answer the item. (Remember, it will take students much longer to think about, create, and write their answers.) Then, after making sure that your response provides a satisfactory answer, identify and list the characteristics or components that make it exemplary.

- Fourth, try to use several items requiring relatively short answers rather than a few questions requiring extensive answers. This allows you to assess more of your objectives (improving the validity of the test) and gives students a better

"I didn't understand half of what you wrote—I like that in a thesis."

opportunity to accurately demonstrate what they know (better reliability). It is also wise to construct the test in such a way that all students are expected to answer all items.

Before duplicating the test, write instructions for completing the test that include guidelines for composing and writing each response, information about how you will score the items, and the weight you will give each item. When appropriate, suggest the amount of time students should spend on each item as well. Then carefully proofread the test, perhaps asking a colleague to read through it for clarity and to ensure that your time frame is reasonable.

As noted earlier, a major weakness of created response tests is that they are difficult to score reliably and objectively. Using restricted rather than extended response items helps by more clearly defining the range of information and detail that students should include in their responses. In addition, judging each student's response against the components and characteristics you identified in your model response makes scoring more consistent and objective. Guidelines for improving your scoring of created response items follow.

- First, attempt to score the tests without knowing which student made the response you are reading. You might have students put their names only on the last page of the test, assign each student a code to use in place of their name, or cover the students' names until you have scored all items.

- Second, score only one item at a time for all papers. This allows you to more consistently apply the same criteria to all students' responses. It also reduces the likelihood that you will allow your opinion of an early answer to influence your scoring of one you read later.

- Third, don't score all papers at once. Scoring essay examinations takes a great deal of time and energy. If you become fatigued, you are less likely to be objective and accurate in your scoring. It is best to score all students' responses to one particular item, then move to another item, and so on until you begin to feel tired. Do not attempt a marathon session in which you sit for hours in order to "get through" a stack of papers.

- Fourth, after scoring all responses, reread all or a random sample of the papers to ensure that you have scored them accurately. It is often a good idea to organize the papers into high, moderate, and low scores and then to reread some papers in each category to check your scoring.

- Fifth, when necessary, adjust your scoring to reflect poor teaching. When no student is able to respond to an item with reasonable accuracy, you may wish to eliminate the item or reconsider the criteria you used to score it.

Try Activity 9.2

Created response items serve a useful purpose in classroom assessment. Because they are easy to construct, they are less time-intensive up front. They are also easier to adapt to higher-order cognitive processes. However, they are extremely time-intensive to score, and highly susceptible to scoring bias. These characteristics have led some to suggest that created response items, in spite of their intuitive appeal, are appropriate only when selected response items *cannot* be used (e.g., Borich, 1992; Isaac & Michael, 1997). Table 9.3 briefly summarizes the guidelines for writing and scoring created response items.

Selected Response Items Selected response items require students to select the most appropriate answer from a list of alternatives or to complete the item with a single, short answer (usually a word or short phrase). Students are not asked to compose a new or unique response, as in created response items. As noted earlier, many people believe that selected response items are not effective in assessing students' higher-order cognitive skills. However, such items, when written carefully, can be as effective as any other item in encouraging students to use high-level thinking skills.

TABLE 9.3 Guidelines for Writing and Scoring Created Response Items

Writing Items	Scoring Items
1. Key all test items to your instructional objectives.	1. Compose a model response immediately after writing each item.
2. Select the most important objectives, and write at least one item for each.	2. Identify components that make your response exemplary.
3. Begin each item with the verb from your objective.	3. Score all student responses against the model.
4. Write restricted rather than extended response items.	4. Score items without knowing which student constructed them.
5. Include as many items as students can reasonably complete.	5. Score only one item at a time for all papers.
6. Indicate whether spelling and grammar will be considered in scoring.	6. Avoid becoming fatigued.
7. Proofread carefully before duplicating.	7. Review a sample of the tests to check the accuracy of your scoring.

One way to do this is to write items that require students to identify metaphors or to answer questions about an extended, detailed scenario or problem.

Selected response items possess many advantages. Probably the most important is that they are less subject to scoring bias—the student either does or does not select the appropriate alternative. Reliability and fairness are increased because scores are not based upon the judgment of the scorer. Also, since selected response items take less time for students to complete, they allow the teacher to assess more content and objectives. As a result, tests that use these items tend to be more valid. Scoring is easy, quick, and less subject to bias. Because they do not require students to compose an answer, selected response items measure students' mastery of the content rather than their ability to write or communicate effectively.

On the other hand, selected response items are difficult and time-consuming to write. They are much more time-intensive up front than created response items are. A major weakness of selected response items is the difficulty of constructing items that encourage students to apply higher-order cognitive skills. While such items can be written, they usually take considerable thought. As a result, selected response items often emphasize lower-order thinking.

There are four types of selected response items: multiple-choice, matching, true-false, and completion. In the following sections we will examine the construction, uses, and scoring of selected response items.

Most of us have taken innumerable **multiple-choice** tests during our schooling. Nearly all standardized tests use them, as do many teacher-made tests. Multiple-choice items consist of two parts: a **stem** which presents a problem or asks a question, and several **alternative responses.** Students are expected to select the alternative that offers the best solution to the problem or that best answers the question the stem presents.

Multiple-choice items possess several strengths. They are probably the most versatile selected response item in that they can be used to evaluate learning in any content area and at all cognitive levels. Because each item takes relatively little time for students to complete, multiple-choice questions allow teachers to evaluate more instructional objectives than created response items. Similarly, multiple-choice items allow teachers to make fine discriminations in the depth and breadth of students' understanding. In contrast to created response items, multiple-choice items can be easily and reliably scored.

There are two primary disadvantages in using multiple-choice items. The greatest disadvantage is that they are difficult and time-consuming to construct, particularly when writing items to assess learning at the higher levels of thinking. High-level items require teachers to process the information at the more advanced levels, then create a problem or question that is likely to elicit similar processing in students, and finally to generate several *realistic* alternative responses, each requiring high-level thinking. A second disadvantage is that, unlike created response tests, multiple-choice tests do not allow us to evaluate how well students are able to communicate their understanding. Students merely select a response.

There are several things you can do to improve the validity and reliability of your multiple-choice tests. As with any test, you should write your multiple-choice items during the planning process to match your instructional objectives. Using your objectives or instructional plan as your guide, you then determine roughly the number of items to devote to each part of the content. You now have a rough test plan and are ready to begin writing or selecting individual test items.

The process of writing multiple-choice items begins with the stem. It must be clearly written in simple language, and it should ask a question or present a problem—not just make an incomplete statement. The stem should be clear enough that the respondent could generate the most appropriate answer even if the alternative responses were not presented. Be certain that each stem presents a new problem and that neither the stem nor alternative responses provide clues to other items. It is also wise to avoid using negative questions or statements in the stem or alternative responses.

For example, the stem, "The American Revolution could not have been won if the British military had not . . ." is confusing. It includes too many negatives and does not ask a question. A better way to write this stem would be, "Which of the following errors the British military made was critical to the outcome of the American Revolution?" This stem avoids negatives, presents a complete question, and uses clearer wording.

After writing the stem, you construct three to five reasonable alternative responses, writing the correct response first and then the others. It is not necessary to include an equal number of alternatives for every item. To reduce the likelihood that students can guess the correct answer, each alternative should present a reasonable answer to the problem presented in the stem, but only one should be most defensible. Avoid responses that are unreasonable and avoid using "none of the above" or "all of the above" since they encourage guessing. Be certain that neither the stem nor the responses provide grammatical clues to the correct response or to other items. This is most often a problem when the stem is an incomplete statement. For example, the stem might be, "George Washington was a . . .". In this example, the correct response must begin with a consonant to be grammatically correct. The response, "affluent land owner" would probably not be the correct answer because it doesn't complete the statement grammatically.

Finally, each alternative should be roughly the same length (in poorly constructed items the longest response is often the most appropriate). Figure 9.3 summarizes the guidelines for writing effective multiple-choice items.

Matching items can be thought of as a series of multiple-choice items with all stems using the same list of alternative responses. Matching items present a list of stems, often called *descriptors,* in the left column, and a slightly longer list of alternatives in the right column. Students are to select for each stem the most closely related or appropriate alternative. Matching items are effective in assessing students' ability to identify relationships between words, terms, or factors. Thus, they are most useful in measuring learning at the knowledge and comprehension levels. Matching items can require students to match terms or words with definitions, short questions with answers, symbols with proper names, descriptive phrases with other phrases, causes with effects, principles with situations in which they apply, and parts or pictorial units with names.

Matching items are less versatile than multiple-choice, but more effective than true-false or short-answer items. They are easy to construct and score. Because

1. Write the stem so that it presents a complete question or problem. Avoid stems that are incomplete statements.

2. The stem should be sufficiently clear that the learner could generate the correct answer even if it were not provided.

3. Avoid using negative questions or statements in the stem or responses.

4. Avoid placing grammatical cues that suggest the correct alternative in the stem.

5. Write the correct response first, then generate between two and four reasonable alternatives.

6. Write alternative responses of roughly equal length.

7. Avoid using "none of the above" or "all of the above."

8. To assess higher-order thinking, write items that require students to identify metaphors or to answer questions about an extended, detailed scenario or problem.

9. Avoid establishing a pattern of responses.

10. Proofread all items carefully.

11. Place the entire item (stem and all alternatives) on the same page.

students can complete them quickly, a large number of items can be used and, thus, more of the objectives assessed. The most significant disadvantages of matching items are related to the low level of thinking they require. Matching items encourage memorization and recall rather than understanding, and they tend to focus on trivial material.

As with other types of items, it is best to write matching items during the planning stage. As a general rule, a series of matching items should include between ten and twelve stems dealing with a clearly related set of ideas or concepts. When items deal with obviously different topics, students can more easily guess the correct answer to any one stem because some alternatives could not apply. The stem should be the longer of the two-item parts, it should be numbered, and it should appear in the left column. Alternative responses should be shorter in length, lettered, and appear in the right column. The list of alternatives should contain about 25 percent (two or three) more items than the list of stems, and the instructions should specify whether alternatives can be used more than once. As with multiple-choice items, each alternative in the list should present a plausible answer to the stem. The entire series of matching items, including the stems and alternatives, should appear on a single page so that students need not go back and forth between pages. Lastly, clear instructions should be given about how to record answers. Generally, space should be provided so that students can record their answers in blanks to the left of each numbered stem. Figure 9.4 depicts an abbreviated series of both good and poor matching items.

True-false items ask students to indicate whether a statement is true or false. Because the response options are limited to one of two choices, these items are sometimes called *alternative choice*.

Alternative-choice items appear often in teacher-made tests. They are easy to construct and score, but they are not very reliable or versatile. They allow the teacher to assess whether students have learned large amounts of material, but they encourage guessing and memorization rather than understanding. Most items of this type are written at the knowledge level, in part because few high-level statements are definitively true or false.

When alternative-choice items are deemed the most effective way to evaluate students' knowledge- (recall-) level learning, the guidelines in Figure 9.5 can improve their quality.

Alternative-choice items are efficient only when assessing student recall of large amounts of content. However, to make true-false items more versatile, some have

FIGURE 9.4   Examples of Poor and Good Matching Items

Poor Matching Series

For each numbered item on the left, write the letter of the most appropriate description from the column on the right.

____ 1. Abraham Lincoln

____ 2. Jefferson Davis

____ 3. Gettysburg

____ 4. John Wilkes Booth

____ 5. Slave auction

a. A cemetery in Pennsylvania

b. Where slaves were traded

c. President of the Confederacy

d. President of the U.S.

e. Assassinated Lincoln

Good Matching Series

For each numbered description in the left column, write the letter that corresponds to the most appropriately described individual from the right column. Each individual may be described more than once.

____ 1. President of the Confederacy

____ 2. Assassinated Lincoln

____ 3. Confederate General

____ 4. Killed at Bull Run

____ 5. Union General

a. Abraham Lincoln

b. John Wilkes Booth

c. Ulysses S. Grant

d. Robert E. Lee

e. Jefferson Davis

f. James Madison

FIGURE 9.5   Guidelines for Writing Alternative-Choice Test Items

1. Write each item as a true statement, and then change some to make them false.

2. False statements should be false because of substantive information rather than trivialities.

3. Keep all items the same length (false items are often shorter than true).

4. Avoid direct quotes from the textbook or lecture notes. Quotation items are nearly always recall level.

5. Avoid using negative statements. Negative statements are more difficult to write clearly.

6. Be careful of specific determiners ("always," "never," and so on). Since few things are "always" or "never" true, a testwise student will guess "false." Likewise, avoid indefinites ("sometimes," "often," and so forth). Since most things happen only some or most of the time, testwise students will guess "true."

7. Limit each statement to one main idea or point. Including too much information in one item will only confuse students.

8. When possible, include the crucial information near the end of the statement to help make the stem clearer.

9. Be certain that each statement is genuinely true or false.

10. Include approximately an equal number of true and false items.

11. Avoid a pattern of responses (for example, alternating true and false).

---

suggested requiring students to correct false statements or to explain their answers. When these tasks are required, the item more closely resembles a completion or created response item and may push students beyond mere recall.

Completion items require students to supply missing words from a statement or write a short phrase that answers a question posed in a stem. These items may present statements with critical words or phrases deleted and symbolized by blanks, or they may ask simple questions. Although they do not present a list of alternative responses as other selected response items do, neither do they require students to create unique responses.

FIGURE 9.6 Guidelines for Writing Completion Items

1. Provide clear instructions regarding the use of synonyms, spelling, and so on.
2. Be certain that only one correct answer is possible.
3. Avoid using direct quotes from the textbook or class notes.
4. When including blanks, try to use no more than one. Multiple blanks in a statement make it less clear.
5. Require only a single word or brief, definitive phrase rather than an extended response.
6. Direct questions generally are clearer than incomplete statements.
7. Be certain each statement is factually correct.
8. Omit only key words or phrases, not trivial information.
9. When using blanks, place the blank at or near the end of the statement to make the statement clearer.
10. When the response is to be numeric, include in the statement the units in which the student is to express the response.

Completion items are particularly useful with young children who may be able to write but cannot easily create extended responses. Completion items are easier to construct than other forms of selected response items because they do not require you to develop plausible alternative responses. Like other selected response items, they require little response time and thus can be used to assess a large amount of content. Further, because responses are not provided, students don't guess as much. On the other hand, these items typically focus only on recall of specific names or facts. They are also difficult to score objectively. For example, a student may not have provided the expected response because she could not remember the specific term or name, but she did provide a description of the person whose name she could not remember. Is this a correct or an incorrect response?

Completion items are most appropriate for assessing young learners or knowledge-level instructional objectives. Figure 9.6 provides guidelines for writing effective completion items.

Packaging the Test As noted earlier, the most effective assessments are planned early in the instructional process. Regardless of the type of test items used, it is wise to develop your test items either while planning (shortly after developing instructional objectives) or as you conduct instruction (to match the instructional methods and emphases). In developing a pencil-and-paper test, validity and reliability are primary considerations. You want to ensure that the test accurately measures the breadth, depth, and levels of students' learning. Thus, you should attempt to ensure validity—the closest possible match between your objectives or topical coverage and the assessment.

One way to improve validity is through the use of a **test blueprint.** A test blueprint is a matrix that depicts the relationship between instructional objectives or topics covered, cognitive levels, and items on a test. An example of a test blueprint appears in Table 9.4. As you can see, the topics of instruction are listed in the left column. Across the top are each of the six levels of Bloom's taxonomy of cognitive objectives. The far-right column indicates the total number of test items for each objective, and the bottom row indicates the total number of test items at each cognitive level.

When building a test, you first determine the total number of items you wish to include and put this number in the bottom row of the far-right column. Then you determine how many items will address each topic and indicate this in the right column. This judgment should be based on the importance of the topic and on the emphasis you placed on it during instruction. For each topic, you then decide how many questions to ask at each cognitive level and indicate this in the appropriate columns. You can include some test items at cognitive levels *lower* than the instruc-

TABLE 9.4 Test Blueprint for Unit on Dinosaurs

Topic	Recall	Comprehension	Application	Analysis	Synthesis	Evaluation	Totals
Names of dinosaurs	10 (40%)						10 (40%)
Physical characteristics		3 (12%)					3 (12%)
Carnivores	1 (4%)		2 (8%)				3 (12%)
Herbivores	1 (4%)		2 (8%)				3 (12%)
Extinction	2 (8%)	3 (12%)	1 (4%)				6 (24%)
Totals	14 (56%)	6 (24%)	5 (20%)				25 (100%)

tional objective (because the higher levels require students to use lower-order skills), but it is not appropriate to include items that require higher levels of thinking than your instruction directly promoted. After completing the test blueprint, you "build" the test to include the number and types of items identified in the blueprint. If you have developed a number of potential test items as you planned or conducted instruction, you construct the test simply by selecting the best of these items.

In the example provided (Table 9.4), the teacher wishes to construct a twenty-five-item test that assesses students' learning in five topical areas of a unit on dinosaurs. The blueprint indicates that the greatest instructional emphasis was placed on helping students learn the names of dinosaurs, because ten items, or 40 percent, of the test, relate to this topic. Slightly less emphasis is placed on the causes of extinction (six items), while roughly equal emphasis is placed on physical characteristics, herbivores, and carnivores (three items each). The blueprint also suggests that students will be expected only to recall the names of dinosaurs, perhaps through true-false or completion items. But some higher-level thinking will be required of students on the other topics, probably through multiple-choice or matching items.

In addition to using the test blueprint, you can do several other things to improve the quality of your tests. Figure 9.7 lists all the suggestions.

Administering the Test   After constructing the test, you can improve the accuracy of your assessment by providing students with as much information as possible about the nature of the test and by following preset testing procedures. Students should know well in advance when a test will be administered, what material will be covered, what types of items will be included, and how the test will be scored. This allows them to better prepare. In addition, it is a good idea to establish a set of procedures for test taking and then to follow them consistently. These procedures would include information about what materials are required for tests, whether the teacher will answer questions during the test, what students are to do when they have completed the test, and so on. Establishing these procedures provides continuity for students and allows them to concentrate on the test rather than to have to remember a new set of expectations each time. Figure 9.8 lists several suggestions for administering classroom tests.

OBSERVATIONAL, PERFORMANCE, AND AUTHENTIC ASSESSMENT

Sometimes students' learning is not easily measured by pencil-and-paper tests. When the instructional objectives require students to produce a product, follow a set of procedures, or perform a physical task, the most effective form of assessment involves *observing* and *evaluating* the quality of their product, procedure, or performance. For example, an art teacher might evaluate the quality of students' projects, a speech teacher might assess students' ability to make speeches of various

9.5   Do you prefer to take created response or selected response tests? Why? How might this influence the way you test your own students?

FIGURE 9.7 General Suggestions for Test Construction

1. Use a test blueprint to improve the validity of the test.

2. Write several more items than you will use. Then select the items that best fit your test blueprint.

3. Include some questions that all students can answer correctly.

4. Use only two or three item types in each test. Use only one type for young learners. Using several types of questions in a single test can be confusing to students.

5. Be certain to include clear and thorough instructions on the test. These should inform students about recording their answers, scoring, weighting of items, and so forth.

6. Organize all test items of similar type together. For example, keep multiple-choice items separate from completion items.

7. Properly space items to improve clarity. More space should be provided between items than between stems and responses. Created response items must allow sufficient space for students' answers.

8. Include as many items as possible to enhance reliability, but be realistic about the number of items students can complete. Remember that created response items take much longer to complete than selected response items.

9. Keep all parts of each item on the same page. In other words, ensure that each stem and its alternative responses appear on the same page.

10. Check to ensure that there is no predictable pattern of correct responses.

11. Provide space for pertinent information (name, date, course or course number, and so on).

12. *Proofread the test!* Check for clarity of directions, grammatical accuracy (especially among distractor alternatives), typographical errors, spelling, and format.

FIGURE 9.8 Guidelines for Administering Classroom Tests

1. Establish test-taking procedures, teach them to students, and then follow them consistently. For example, students should know whether questions will be answered after they begin the test, what to do when they are finished with the test, and so on.

2. Allow sufficient time for all students to complete all parts of the test. Don't let time keep some students from doing as well as they could.

3. Organize the physical setting before students enter the room to begin the test.

4. Before handing out the test, be certain that all students have the necessary equipment or materials to complete the test.

5. Explain or review test procedures or rules (for example, what to do when finished with the test) before handing out the test.

6. Control distribution of the test so that no student receives the test much sooner than others. It is wise to have students wait to begin reading or working on the test until your signal.

7. Note corrections before students begin.

8. Avoid discussion of the test or items after students have begun. If you must provide additional information or guidance about the test or an item to any student, announce this information to all students.

9. Monitor test behavior throughout the testing period.

kinds, a physical education teacher might assess how well students demonstrate proper technique in throwing a ball, a science teacher might evaluate how well students follow a set of procedures for conducting an experiment, or a language arts teacher might evaluate students' ability to write creatively.

Pencil-and-paper tests require learners to perform a *cognitive* task and then to record an answer that indicates the result. Performance assessments require students to demonstrate learning by *performing tasks* or *producing products* that the teacher can observe and evaluate. As a result, performance assessments are often

"Dad, I got an A+ on my science project!"

believed to be more authentic or realistic than traditional forms of testing. In addition, such authentic assessment is often more formative in nature and, as a result, is more conducive to changes in instruction (Bol & Stephenson, 1998; Burke, 1994). Thus, many educators believe that such *authentic assessment* should replace most if not all pencil-and-paper assessments (Haertel, 1999; Wiggins, 1998).

As with all forms of assessment, a primary concern in authentic assessment is the accuracy of the information gathered. Although teachers observe students' performances or products in informal ways throughout the learning process, such informal observations occur spontaneously. By contrast, to make authentic assessment or performance assessment most fair and useful, teachers carefully plan formal observation and evaluation based upon well-defined criteria, permitting the teacher to make accurate judgments about performances or products (Arter & McTighe, 2001; Wiggins, 1998). This provides greater validity and reliability. Conducting formal evaluation of student performances or products using written checklists, rating scales, or rubrics is a common way to increase the validity and reliability of performance assessment.

Checklists   A checklist is a written instrument that lists the specific elements deemed necessary for desirable performance. The teacher observes students' performance or products and then marks whether or not each element was present. The overall performance is judged according to the extent to which it included all necessary elements. For example, a music teacher might assess students on their ability to play three scales. An example of the checklist for this performance appears in Figure 9.9.

An advantage of checklists is that they can help the teacher and student focus on the most important aspects of a performance. Although the total task may be complex, the checklist can help the student see what things must be done to perform the task. Similarly, the checklist provides specific feedback about elements of the student's performance that are or are not present. Thus, the student and teacher know precisely what the student needs to improve.

The primary disadvantage of checklists is that the quality of each specific element is not evaluated. The checklist allows the teacher to record only whether the element was present, not how well the element was performed. For instance, in Figure 9.9, the teacher records whether the student used proper instrument position while playing each scale. However, although some students may have better instrument position than others, the checklist does not provide for differentiation or assessment of quality. Another difficulty in using checklists lies in making a judgment about the

FIGURE 9.9   Checklist for Scale Performance

Criterion	B♭	F	G
1. Correct notes	_____	_____	_____
2. Good tone quality	_____	_____	_____
3. Consistent rhythm and tempo	_____	_____	_____
4. Proper instrument position	_____	_____	_____
5. Proper posture	_____	_____	_____
6. Good breath control	_____	_____	_____

overall performance. Is each element on the checklist absolutely necessary for effective performance? If so, students must be expected to demonstrate every checklist element in the performance. In some cases, however, there are likely to be some elements that are desirable but not absolutely necessary. In these cases, how many of the elements must be demonstrated for a student's performance to be acceptable? These questions are difficult to address.

Rating Scales   A rating scale is much like a checklist in that it lists the specific elements of desirable performance. However, rating scales allow the teacher to make a judgment about the quality of each element. Rating scales assess not just whether an element was present, but also how well or accurately it was performed. As a result, rating scales possess the strengths of checklists with fewer of the disadvantages.

Three types of rating scales are commonly used in the classroom (see Figure 9.10). In *numeric* rating scales, a number indicates the quality of performance. A higher number generally reflects greater quality. *Graphic* scales require the observer to place a mark along a continuum indicating performance quality. *Descriptive* scales rate performance on a continuum that includes terms that describe various levels of quality.

Arriving at a grade or overall judgment about a student's performance is somewhat easier using rating scales than using checklists. The teacher makes such judgments by summarizing across the ratings of the specific elements. Typically, summarization produces a single number representing a measure of the overall quality of the performance. Numeric scales are particularly easy to summarize either by adding the item ratings or by computing the mean rating. Graphic and descriptive scales can be summarized numerically by assigning a number to each graphic or descriptive item rating and then proceeding as you would with numeric scale data. It is sometimes useful to summarize the student's performance more descriptively, particularly when graphic or descriptive scales are used. In such cases, the descriptors for each performance element can be combined into a single global scale and an overall rating assigned based upon total performance.

Rubrics   A rubric is a matrix or table that expands on the detail included in descriptive rating scales, the specificity of checklists, and the ease of synthesis of numeric rating scales. In most rubrics, each column represents a particular aspect of performance to be evaluated (for example, grammar, writing style, spelling, and punctuation) and each row conveys descriptions of the characteristics of each element at varying levels of mastery. Usually, the rubric presents a numeric scale or score associated with performance at each level for each element (Wiggins, 1998).

Figure 9.11 (see page 296) depicts a rubric for evaluating students' writing. The four columns indicate the four aspects of students' writing we wish to evaluate (grammar, spelling, punctuation, and capitalization). For each of these aspects of writing there are four rows, each describing a level of performance. Also, notice the

FIGURE 9.10 Rating Scales for Scale Performance

Numeric Rating Scale

Circle the number representing the quality of the student's performance (1 = unsatisfactory, 2 = poor, 3 = average, 4 = good, 5 = excellent).

Criterion			Rating		
1. Student plays correct notes.	1	2	3	4	5
2. Student uses good tone quality.	1	2	3	4	5
3. Rhythm and tempo are consistent.	1	2	3	4	5
4. Proper instrument position is used.	1	2	3	4	5
5. Proper posture is evident.	1	2	3	4	5
6. Student uses good breath control.	1	2	3	4	5

Graphic Rating Scale

Place a check on each scale to represent the quality of the student's performance.

Criterion — **Rating**

1. Student plays correct notes.
   Poor — Fair — Good — Superior

2. Student uses good tone quality.
   Poor — Fair — Good — Superior

3. Rhythm and tempo are consistent.
   Poor — Fair — Good — Superior

4. Proper instrument position is used.
   Poor — Fair — Good — Superior

5. Proper posture is evident.
   Poor — Fair — Good — Superior

6. Student uses good breath control.
   Poor — Fair — Good — Superior

Descriptive Rating Scale

Criterion — **Rating**

1. Student plays correct notes.
   Some notes; some in tune — All notes; most in tune — All notes; all in tune

2. Good tone quality is used.
   Unclear, fuzzy, soft — Clear, but soft and weak — Clear, strong, and loud

numbers that appear at the top of the columns and to the left of the rows, indicating the total possible score for each aspect and the range of scores associated with varying performance levels within each row. On the basis of these numbers, we can see that the writing assignment is worth a total of 40 points and that each of the four elements is of equal value (that is, they each contribute one-fourth of a student's total score on this assignment). While this rubric allows for some teacher flexibility within each row by applying a range (for example, 8–10 for exemplary) at each level, these ranges are not necessary in a rubric.

Using this rubric, the teacher can more easily and more consistently assign scores to students' work. Importantly, students can also use the rubric to evaluate their own or others' work and to provide more meaningful feedback. The rubric helps both the teacher and the student focus attention on the aspects of the writing considered most important. For these reasons, rubrics are often used in combination with portfolios.

Rating scales, checklists, and rubrics are effective ways to improve the accuracy of your assessment when judging students' performances, products, or projects (Linn & Burton, 1994). They are most accurate when they meet four conditions. First, the specific elements that constitute effective performance or an acceptable product must be identified, delineated, and made known to the learners. Second, each specific element must be observable and described thoroughly in clear terms. Third, the setting or context in which the performance or product will be judged must be specified. And fourth, performance is evaluated using predetermined scoring or rating procedures.

FIGURE 9.11 Rubric for Evaluating Students' Writing

	Grammar 10 points	Spelling 10 points	Punctuation 10 points	Capitalization 10 points
Exemplary 8–10 points	• All sentences are complete thoughts. • All verbs match their subjects. • All pronouns are used appropriately. • No conjunctions are used at the beginnings of sentences.	• Every word is spelled correctly. • Every word is written legibly.	• Each sentence ends with appropriate punctuation. • Commas are used appropriately throughout. • Apostrophes are used correctly to represent plural and singular possessives.	• Each sentence begins with a capital letter. • All proper nouns are capitalized.
Good 5–7 points	• All sentences are complete thoughts. • Most verbs match their subjects. • All pronouns are used appropriately. • Few conjunctions are used at the beginning of sentences.	• Most words are spelled correctly. • Every word is written legibly.	• Most sentences end with appropriate punctuation. • Commas are used appropriately throughout. • Apostrophes are used to represent most possessives.	• Most sentences begin with a capital letter. • Most proper nouns are capitalized.
Fair 2–4 points	• Some sentences are complete thoughts. • Some verbs match their subjects. • Some pronouns are used appropriately. • Some conjunctions are used at the beginnings of sentences.	• Most words are spelled correctly. • Most words are written legibly.	• Some sentences end with appropriate punctuation. • Some commas are used appropriately. • Few apostrophes are used to represent possessives.	• Some sentences begin with a capital letter. • Some proper nouns are capitalized.
Poor 0–1 points	• Few or no sentences are complete thoughts. • Few or no verbs match their subjects. OR • No attempt was made.	• Few words are spelled correctly. • Few words are written legibly. OR • No attempt was made.	• Few sentences end with appropriate punctuation. • Few commas are used appropriately. OR • No attempt was made.	• Few sentences begin with a capital letter. • No proper nouns are capitalized. OR • No attempt was made.

Portfolio Assessment   Portfolio assessment is a particular type of performance assessment and is among the most popular alternatives to traditional testing (Burke, Fogarty & Belgrad, 1994; Daniels, 1999; Wiggins, 1998). Even advocates of alternative assessment acknowledge that the validity and reliability of portfolios can be problematic, but they claim well-designed portfolios offer an excellent and supportive approach to student assessment (Elliot, 1994; Isaac and Michael, 1997; Wiggins, 1998).

A *portfolio* is a collection of student work that is intended to demonstrate accomplishment. The individual pieces that are included can be selected to reflect a student's growth or development over time, competence level or ability in academic performances, or ability to analyze or evaluate one's own work (Burke, 1994; Eby, 1992; Wiggins, 1998; Worthen, Sanders & Fitzpatrick, 1997). In portfolio assessment, the student and teacher identify several samples of work based upon the purpose of the portfolio. These samples can include a variety of products, including papers, projects, quizzes, homework, journals, and even tests. You might also choose to include video- or audiotapes of student performances. In addition to these samples of students' work, the portfolio might also include evaluations of the work by the student, by other students, and by the teacher. Thus, the portfolio is a collection of student work that provides detailed and descriptive information about how well the student is doing or how much she or he has improved.

Portfolio assessment goes beyond merely collecting students' work. As an assessment tool, portfolio assessment uses the collection of student work (the portfolio) as the medium for evaluating student performance. Like any performance assessment, it is critical that we clearly understand what the portfolio is intended to do, what kinds of work are most likely to help us evaluate the students' performance in meaningful ways and thus should be included, and on what basis we will make judgments about quality. For example, if we want to use portfolio assessment to help us make judgments about our students' ability to write effectively, we must be certain that the types of written work students include give each student the opportunity to demonstrate the range of skills we are expecting, that we have clearly established criteria with which to make our judgments fairly and consistently, and that students understand how and why the portfolio is to be used.

Grading and Assigning Grades

In most cases, the final step in our classroom assessment is assigning each student a grade. Grades represent a simple way to summarize students' performance or learning over time and across a variety of experiences. Thus, while assessment involves both summative and formative techniques, grading is typically a summative process. Ultimately, you must synthesize the information you have about a student's learning or progress, make a judgment about the quality of the progress, and assign a grade that you believe accurately and fairly represents this judgment.

Grading is an important, though often intimidating, part of teaching. Many teachers report anxiety and dread about determining and reporting students' grades (Airasian, 2001; Burke, 1994; Guskey & Bailey, 2001). Some of this anxiety is due to the importance parents, students, and school officials place on grades as the primary source of information about the student's progress. Assigning grades is also difficult because it forces teachers to move from the role of facilitator of learning to that of objective observer and judge (Marzano, 2000). Finally, grading is often intimidating to teachers because many teachers do not feel sufficiently prepared to meet this challenge (Mertler, 1999).

9.6 Why do you suppose some teachers dislike assigning grades? How do you feel about this aspect of your professional responsibilities?

In spite of the difficulty and anxiety associated with grading, grades are used for several reasons (Airasian, 2001; Marzano, 2000). *Administratively,* grades are used to make decisions about which classes students should take, how well they are progressing, and whether they should be advanced to the next grade or graduated. *Informationally,* grades tell parents, students, and school officials how well students are learning and progressing. For some students, grades serve a *motivational* purpose, pushing them to work harder. For all these reasons, it is a teacher's responsibility to select and implement a grading system that is accurate, fair, consistent, and supportable.

In selecting and implementing a grading system, three factors must be considered. First, what assignments, performances, or projects should you consider in the grade? Second, what standard will you use to make judgments about the quality of the students' performance? And, third, how will you synthesize information from several assignments or sources into a single grade? Let's look at each of these factors.

WHAT SHOULD YOU CONSIDER WHEN ASSIGNING A GRADE?

The grade that you assign represents a summary of how well the student performed in several tasks or situations. The goal is to assign a grade that accurately reflects both the depth and breadth of the student's learning, which, in turn, should match the teacher's instructional emphases.

"I don't know why you're so surprised by his poor grades. Every day you asked him what he did at school, and every day he answered, 'Nothing.'"

Generally your grades should include information from as many sources as possible. The more sources of information, the more accurate your "picture" of the student's progress will be. Common information sources include tests, quizzes, homework, performances, portfolios, and projects. By including information from several of these sources, you are better able to judge the quality or extent of a student's progress.

Some teachers also consider attendance records or informal observations of a student's behavior, attitude, participation, motivation, or effort. However, it is generally best to include in the grade only factors that directly reflect a student's achievement (Airasian, 2001; Marzano, 2000; Stiggins, 1997). When the grading system combines achievement with other less clearly defined factors, such as motivation or attitude, grades become inconsistent and less informative. To address this problem, some elementary school grading systems assign each student two grades: One reflects achievement, while the second is a judgment about motivational or behavioral factors. When only one grade can be assigned, it should indicate only the student's achievement. Information about other factors can be conveyed through written notes or conferences with the student or the student's parents.

While it is desirable to include information from as many sources as possible, teachers must be realistic about the number of assignments they can evaluate and record. Certainly it is realistic to include all test scores in the grade as well as scores from all major products, projects, or performances the students completed during the grading term. However, you may need to be selective about how many other assignments to include. For example, if you have daily quizzes or daily homework assignments, it may be unreasonable to include every quiz or homework score in the final grade. Each teacher must decide how many of these factors to consider in the students' final grades.

WHAT STANDARD SHOULD YOU USE?

As noted earlier, grading requires that you make judgments about the quality of students' progress or learning. The information obtained from the sources we have discussed does not tell you whether a student has performed well. You make that determination by comparing students' performance to some standard or criterion. The three most commonly used standards are (1) the performance of other students, (2) a predetermined fixed standard of performance, or (3) each student's earlier performances.

FIGURE 9.12   Sample Raw Scores on a 100-Point Test

Student	Score
Bill	85
Mary	83
Joan	83
Karen	82
Kevin	82
Pam	81
Paul	78
Elizabeth	76
Kaya	76
Kip	75

Comparison with Other Students   You may recall from our explanation of test scores that when a given score is reported as a comparison with other students' scores, it is a *norm-referenced assessment.* We use the same term to describe grades that compare a student's performance with that of other students. When we talk of teachers who "grade on the curve," we mean that the teacher is using a norm-referenced grading system. In this system, the grade a particular student receives depends upon how well the other students in the class performed. If the student did better than most other students, the grade will be high; if the student did more poorly than most other students, the grade will be low.

Norm-referenced grading systems typically take one of two forms. In a *fixed percentage system,* the grading scale defines what percentages of the class will get particular grades. Generally, the scale is constructed so that most students get Cs, somewhat fewer get Bs and Ds, and the fewest number of students get As and Fs. For example, in the fixed percentage scale that follows, 10 percent of the students would receive an A, 10 percent an F, 20 percent a B, 20 percent a D, and 40 percent a C. Thus, using the sample test scores depicted in Figure 9.12, Bill would get an A; Mary and Joan a B; Karen, Kevin, Pam, and Paul would get Cs; Elizabeth and Kaya Ds; and Kip an F. This is true even though the difference between Bill and Kip is only 10 points and in spite of the fact that the highest score was only 85 out of 100.

GRADE	PERCENTAGE
A	10%
B	20%
C	40%
D	20%
F	10%

As you can see, in this type of grading system, grades are only an indication of how well the student performed *compared with other students,* not of how high or low they scored. If all students performed well, those who performed even slightly less well would receive lower grades. Thus, an A on one assignment does not equal an A on another.

More common is a *flexible distribution system.* In this system, students' grades are still based upon comparison with other students, but the percentages of students who will receive each grade are not predetermined. Instead, the percentages are adjusted to reflect situations where all students do well or all students do poorly. Unlike the fixed percentage scale, the flexible scale can be adjusted so that no students receive any particular grade. In the set of scores depicted in Figure 9.12, all the students performed at roughly the same level. None of them appears to have done particularly well, and none particularly poorly. You might elect to adjust the scale so that no students receive an A, D, or F. Thus, you might award Bs to students with scores from 81 to 85, and Cs to students with scores from 76 to 78.

Norm-referenced grading systems are commonly used. However, the effects of this form of grading are predominately negative, particularly for less able students. Norm-referenced grading reduces students' motivation, increases anxiety, promotes negative interactions among students, diminishes students' study habits, and reduces learning (Marzano, 2000). Additionally, grades based upon this system are difficult to interpret because they do not provide an accurate indication of subject mastery (Airasian, 2001). For these reasons, it is wise to avoid using this system.

Comparison with a Predetermined Standard   Students' grades can also be determined by comparing performance with a predetermined standard. These grading systems are *criterion-referenced* assessments. In this type of system, a student's grade in no way depends upon the performance of other students. Instead, the grade is based upon the extent to which the performance demonstrates mastery. Usually, this means the proportion of points earned (for example, on a test) out of the total number possible. If a student gets most of the possible points, the grade is high; if the student gets fewer of the possible points, the grade is lower. The teacher determines the proportions associated with particular grades in advance and compares each student's performance with this scale. A common criterion-referenced grading scale follows:

PERCENTAGE	GRADE
92–100	A
84–91	B
76–83	C
65–75	D
00–64	F

Let's use the test scores in Figure 9.12 to see what grades we would assign using this criterion-referenced system. In this example, no students would receive an A, Bill would receive a B, most students would receive a C, and Kip would receive a D. As you can see, using a criterion-referenced scale, any student could receive *any* grade.

The criterion-referenced system is intended to measure students' learning against an objective standard rather than against the performances of other students. Thus, grades assigned using this system are more likely to be accurate indicators of students' achievement (Airasian, 2001). A primary advantage of this system is that the meaning of particular grades is clearer. An A represents a given level of performance regardless of the situation or the ability of other students in the class. Although determinations about the scale are subjective, grades assigned using a criterion-referenced system are considered less subject to bias. For these reasons, the criterion-referenced system is generally the most appropriate system for assigning grades.

Comparison with the Student's Earlier Performances   Norm-referenced and criterion-referenced grading systems assign grades by comparing a student's performance with an external standard. However, these systems do not account for differences in students' abilities or background knowledge. A student who has little aptitude in a subject is graded using the same standard as a student who finds the subject very easy. Thus, some teachers believe that a **self-referenced grading system** is more student centered and more desirable. In a self-referenced system, grades are determined by comparing a student's current performance with past performance. In other words, the grade is based upon individual improvement. A student who improves a great deal will receive a high grade; a student who improves only slightly will receive a lower grade. This approach is commonly used with portfolios to assess students' growth or development over time.

Self-referenced systems predetermine how much improvement is necessary for a student to receive a particular grade. As with criterion-referenced scales, differing amounts of improvement are associated with different grades. The scale below depicts a self-referenced scale for assigning grades based on improvement.

POINTS IMPROVED	GRADES
Perfect score	A
12 or more	A
9–11	B
4–8	C
1–3	D
No improvement or decline	F

Self-referenced scales typically include allowances for students who are already performing at high rates. This is done to avoid penalizing students for doing well. For example, a student who received 98 out of 100 on the previous performance could improve no more than 2 points, earning a D on the scale. However, in the scale, a student could still earn an A if he or she receives a perfect score on the current performance. In spite of this allowance, self-referenced scales are biased against students who do very well in early performances. It is more difficult to improve or maintain performance that is already nearly perfect than to improve very weak performance. Although self-referenced grading systems avoid the competition or rigidity of norm- and criterion-referenced systems, the grades assigned in self-referenced systems do not reflect the level of a student's mastery or ability in the subject. An A may mean near-perfect mastery or only limited mastery from a student who performed very poorly at first. In spite of its intuitive appeal, self-referenced grading systems probably should be avoided. Table 9.5 on page 302 compares the three types of grading systems.

9.7 Which grading system do you prefer as a student? Why? Which do you as a teacher believe is most desirable?

Try Activity 9.4

HOW WILL ASSESSMENT INFORMATION BE SYNTHESIZED?

In assigning grades that represent an overall judgment about a student's performance, several types of performance (tests, quizzes, homework, projects, and so on) must eventually be combined into a single letter, number, or symbol. After determining which performances to grade, you must then determine how to grade each one. Finally, you must combine the grades from the selected performances and arrive at a single grade that reflects overall learning. A variety of computer programs are available that use information provided by the teacher to store and then synthesize individual student performances. However, because these programs require the teacher to determine how selected performances should be included in the final grade, it is important to understand the factors that must be considered.

As you prepare to synthesize selected performance scores, remember that the scores reflect different content, objectives, and levels of importance. Not all scores or grades are of equal value. For example, Figure 9.13 presents performance grades for five students. As you can see, the teacher recorded information about students' performance on two tests, two homework assignments, a quiz, and a project. If we were to look only at the grades, each would be considered of equal importance or weight. Bill's grade of A on the first test receives no more weight than Karen's A on the quiz. However, you probably want the test scores and project to carry more weight than the homework or quiz scores.

TABLE 9.5 Comparison of Norm-Referenced, Criterion-Referenced, and Self-Referenced Grading Systems

	Norm-Referenced System	Criterion-Referenced System	Self-Referenced System
What comparison is made?	Pupil to other pupils	Pupil to predefined criteria	Pupil to pupil's earlier performance
Method of comparison	Grading curve; percent of pupils who can get each grade	Standard of performance; scores pupils must achieve to get a given grade	Standard of improvement; amount of improvement pupils must exhibit to get a given grade
What the grade describes	Pupil's performance compared to others in the class	Pupil's percentage of mastery of course objectives	Pupil's improvement from earlier performance(s)
Availability of a particular grade	Limited by grading curve	No limit on grade availability	No limit on grade availability

FIGURE 9.13 Sample Term Grades (Numeric Conversion)

Student's Name	HMK 1	HMK 2	Quiz	Test 1	Test 2	Project
Adams, Bill	✓ (3)	+ (5)	B (4)	A (5)	A (5)	A (5)
Darby, Joan	✓ (3)	✓ (3)	B (4)	C (3)	B (4)	A (5)
Evans, Karen	+ (5)	✓ (3)	A (5)	B (4)	B (4)	B (4)
Stone, Elizabeth	+ (5)	✓ (3)	A (5)	B (4)	B (4)	A (5)
Thompson, Kaya	– (1)	✓ (3)	D (2)	C (3)	B (4)	C (3)

Synthesizing grades is easier if you establish a grading system that reports all grades in the same fashion, for example, as letters, scores, checks, or pluses. However, some teachers elect to use different symbols for different types of assignments. In Figure 9.13 homework grades are reported as checks, pluses, or minuses; while tests, quizzes, and projects are reported as letter grades. In this case, you must convert each of these different symbols to a single scale. You could do this by converting all symbols to numbers. Using the information in Figure 9.13, you could convert the homework grades to numbers by awarding 5 points for a plus, 3 for a check, and 1 for a minus. Similarly, you could convert letter grades by assigning 5 points for an A, 4 for a B, 3 for a C, 2 for a D, and 1 for an F. Now, all the information is in numeric form and can be synthesized mathematically, typically by computing the average of the scores. However, before doing so, you must decide how important each number or grade is in the overall summary. For example, the project is probably most important, the tests next, and the homework and quizzes less so.

Most teachers weight individual performance grades just prior to synthesizing them. To do this, they multiply each individual performance score by a weight that reflects its importance. Using the converted (numeric) information in Figure 9.13, each individual test score could be multiplied by 2 and the project score by 3. The resulting weighted numeric scores appear in Figure 9.14. You could now use these weighted or adjusted scores in your synthesis.

FIGURE 9.14 Sample Term Grades as Weighted Numeric Scores

Student's Name	HMK 1	HMK 2	Quiz	Test 1	Test 2	Project	Average Grade
Adams, Bill	3	5	4	10	10	15	4.7 (A)
Darby, Joan	3	3	4	6	8	15	3.9 (B)
Evans, Karen	5	3	5	8	8	12	4.1 (B)
Stone, Elizabeth	5	3	5	8	8	15	4.4 (B)
Thompson, Kaya	1	3	2	6	8	9	2.9 (C)

When all scores have been converted to the same, usually numeric, scale and weighted to reflect differing levels of importance, you are ready to synthesize them into a single grade.

To do this, add the weighted individual performance scores. Then divide this total by the *weighted* number of performances. In our example, the original number of performances was 5, but we multiplied some of these in order to weight them. The *weighted* number of performances is 10 because the tests each count as 2 performances and the project counts as 3.

Try Activity 9.5

Homework 1	= 1
Homework 2	= 1
Quiz	= 1
Test 1 ($\times$ 2)	= 2
Test 2 ($\times$ 2)	= 2
Project ($\times$ 3)	= 3
Weighted total	= 10

Student's grades are determined by comparing their weighted averages to the 5-point scale we originally used to convert symbols and letters to numbers. Figure 9.14 depicts the weighted averages and grade for each of the five students.

Grading is an anxiety-producing but important part of teaching. It is often the final result of your overall assessment program. When well planned and accurately implemented, grading is a fair, accurate, and supportable process that can provide valid information about students' learning and performance.

Some Final Thoughts

An important part of effective teaching is assessing students' learning. Doing so helps teachers determine not only how well or how much students have learned, but also how effective their own instruction has been. Accurate evaluation requires that teachers gather valid, reliable information from diverse sources and then make judgments based on that information. Tests, both standardized and teacher-made, are the most recognized source of assessment information, but most teachers use a variety of other sources, both formal and informal. Their ultimate goal is to make fair, consistent, and valid judgments which give valuable feedback to students, parents, themselves, and other education professionals.

CHAPTER SUMMARY

- The process of collecting, synthesizing, and interpreting information to aid in decision making is called *assessment*. The process of gathering objective information that describes students' performance, usually in numeric terms, is referred to as *measurement*. *Tests* are the most commonly used measurement instruments. The process of making a qualitative judgment (good or bad performance) based on assessment information is referred to as *evaluation*.

- The effectiveness of an assessment depends upon the sources used to gain information and the accuracy of the information. Formal sources of information such as tests, quizzes, homework, projects, or performances are more teacher controlled and can be repeated as needed. Informal sources such as teacher observations of spontaneous student behavior; conversations with students, parents, or other teachers; or access to students' logs and diaries can also be valuable but are more prone to subjective bias and error.

- The accuracy of assessment information depends upon its validity and reliability. *Validity* is the term used to describe the degree to which a test or other data source measures what it is supposed to measure. A valid assessment of student learning (1) measures understanding or mastery of all the important content or skills that were taught and nothing more; (2) assesses them in the same ways and at the same levels as they were taught; and (3) maintains the same content emphasis as the instruction.

- *Reliability* refers to the consistency with which an assessment source, such as a test, yields nearly the same scores for anyone who might take the test repeatedly. The primary way to improve reliability is to obtain information from as many valid sources as possible. Although reliability is often difficult to assess, test manufacturers typically provide information about the reliability of their tests.

- Assessment can be conducted either during instruction or at the conclusion of instruction. Formative assessment is conducted during the instructional process and is used primarily to help improve student and teacher performance. Summative assessment is conducted at the conclusion of instruction and is used primarily to make final judgments about a student's learning. Effective teachers make use of both types of assessment to improve their teaching and make good instructional decisions.

- Standardized testing has become increasingly common in U.S. public schools in recent years, and the results of these tests are often used to make policy decisions at the national, state, and local levels. Standardized tests get their name because they are administered and scored in consistent, uniform ways. They typically control the materials students may use, limit the time they can take, provide the instructions, and control any other details believed to affect test performance. Although standardized tests are effective in measuring a wide range of learning, are scored objectively and fairly, and can be designed to assess higher-level thinking, their results are often misinterpreted and misused. Teachers can help their students perform better on standardized tests by giving them experience in taking similar kinds of tests and by offering suggestions about when to guess and how to manage time.

- The results of standardized tests are commonly reported in one or more of the following ways.
  1. Students' test scores can be reported as a raw score, in relation to the scores of other students, or in relation to some predetermined criterion or standard.
  2. Raw score is the number of items answered correctly. It tells us little about what or how much the student has learned.

3. A criterion-referenced score compares the student's raw score with an established standard of mastery and provides detailed information about the specific objectives a student has mastered.

4. A norm-referenced score compares the student's raw score with the performances of other students who took the test (usually reported as standard scores).

- Standardized test scores are reported in a variety of forms. Some test reports include students' raw or obtained scores. However, nearly all standardized tests report normal curve equivalent (NCE), percentile rank, stanine, and grade equivalent scores for students. In addition, many test publishers also provide score bands, ranges within which the most accurate measure of a student's performance would likely fall.

- The most common form of classroom assessment is developed by the teacher. When properly constructed, such assessments can be more cost-effective and valid than standardized or commercially produced tests because they reflect the instruction a teacher actually provided to a specific group of students rather than some national norm. Teacher-made pencil-and-paper tests use two types of test items: created response items and selected response items. Created response test items, which require students to compose an answer in their own words, are relatively easy to write. These items not only assess students' understanding but their ability to communicate. However, they are also time-consuming to score and are difficult to score reliably and objectively. Restricted response items make the parameters (expected length and coverage) of students' answers explicit. Extended response items do not impose parameters and thus allow students to be more creative.

- Selected response items, which require students to select the most appropriate answer from a list of alternatives, are easier to score objectively and typically allow the tester to assess a greater range of content. However, these items require more time to write and often elicit only lower-level thinking. Selected response items include multiple-choice, matching, true-false, and completion items.

- Observational, performance, and authentic assessments require students to apply learning by performing physical tasks or producing concrete products for observation and evaluation. Because students are actually applying their learning to solving real problems, the term *authentic assessment* is often used to refer to this type of assessment.

- Formal observation and performance evaluation are most accurate when they are based upon well-defined criteria. Checklists, rating scales, and rubrics are the most common instruments teachers use to guide observational assessment. They each list the specific elements deemed necessary to desirable performance. While checklists allow the observer only to indicate whether or not an element was present, rating scales allow the observer to make a judgment about the quality of each element presented. Rubrics tend to expand and improve upon these by providing greater detail and description of performance levels.

- In portfolio assessment, samples of each student's work are collected to see progress or development over time. Portfolios might include tests, quizzes, papers, and other student projects, as well as evaluation of the products and portfolio by the teacher, the student, or the students' peers. A critical feature of portfolio assessment is the learner's involvement in collecting and evaluating the work samples.

- Grading is an attempt to summarize students' performance or learning across a variety of experiences and over an extended time period. In spite of the anxiety many teachers experience in assigning grades, the grades serve several important administrative, informational, and motivational purposes. Although grades should be based on as many different sources of information as possible, teachers should not become unrealistic about how many student performances they can include in their grading system.

- Although factors such as behavior or attitude can be considered when assigning grades, it is best to limit grades to students' academic achievement. When grades are based upon factors other than achievement, they are less informative. To overcome this limitation, some elementary school grading systems allow the teacher to assign each student a grade for achievement and a grade for behavior or attitude.

- Teachers can also assign grades by comparing students' performances to one another, to a fixed standard, or to themselves. Norm-referenced grading systems compare each student's performance to the scores of other students.

    1. In a fixed percentage system, the percentage of students who will receive each grade is predetermined. Most students in this system get Cs.

    2. In a flexible distribution scale, the percentage of students who will receive each grade is adjusted to reflect situations where all students do well or all students do poorly.

    3. Research has shown that norm-referenced grading systems promote several negative consequences, including competition, anxiety, and reduced learning.

- Criterion-referenced grading systems assign grades by comparing students' performance with a predetermined standard that shows how well each student has mastered the targeted objectives or content.

- Self-referenced grading systems compare each student's current performance with his or her previous performance. Many believe this system is more equitable for students of lower ability who fare poorly when compared to other students. However, a problem with self-referenced grading is that the grades assigned do not provide information about how much a given student knows, only how much she or he has improved.

- Ultimately, teachers must synthesize several sources of information in order to assign a single grade that reflects students' overall performance. The process of synthesizing is easier if all grades are recorded in a similar fashion, for example, as letters or numbers. However, when different types of grades have been used, all must be converted to the same, usually numeric, scale.

- To develop an overall course grade, each assignment grade must be weighted to reflect its relative importance within the course.

- The most common way to synthesize assignment grades is to (1) convert them all to numbers, (2) compute the arithmetic mean or average, and (3) convert this numeric average into a letter grade.

ISSUES AND PROBLEMS FOR DISCUSSION

PROBLEMS   Teachers made the following comments or described the following incidents. What do you think about each, or how would you deal with it?

Problem 1:   "About three weeks into the second grading period I received a telephone call from a parent who was angry about the grade I had given her daughter. She had spoken with another parent whose child had been receiving similar marks throughout the grading period, but who ended up with a higher grade. When I checked my grade book, I remembered that I had given the other student a slightly higher grade than she had earned through points because I felt she had worked very hard. Tomorrow I am to meet with the principal and this parent to explain the discrepancy. I'm a little nervous about what may happen."

Problem 2: "I told my students at the beginning of the year that each grading period they could drop their two lowest scores before I assigned period grades. Now, with two more units remaining in the grading period, several students realize that they can earn a good grade without doing anything for these last three weeks. I'm not sure what to do. These units are important, and I want them to be responsible for the material."

Problem 3: "Our state administers a required standardized test at the end of each school year. The test results are published by school and district in local newspapers. I *hate* giving standardized tests, and *this* one is *awful!* There are so many things that I want students to know and think about that this test just doesn't cover. My principal had been applying a lot of pressure to improve our school's scores, but I don't want to focus on the test."

THEORY INTO ACTION ACTIVITIES

ACTIVITY 9.1: Interpreting Standard Test Scores   Explain what each of the following scores would tell us about the student's performance.

1. A raw score of 21/25
2. A percentile rank of 32
3. A score band ranging from the 55th to 63rd percentiles
4. An NCE score of 37
5. A stanine score of 8
6. A grade equivalent score of 6.3

ACTIVITY 9.2: Writing Created Response Items   Write a broad instructional objective from your subject area. Develop an extended response item that assesses students' mastery of the objective, and write a model response. Next, rewrite the item as a restricted response item using your model response as a guide.

ACTIVITY 9.3: Writing Selected Response Items   Using the instructional objective you developed in Activity 9.2, write at least three selected response items that you could use to assess students' mastery of all or part of the objective. Now, write a single multiple-choice item that requires students to at least synthesize information related to the objective in order to answer.

ACTIVITY 9.4: Developing a Scoring Rubric   Identify a performance task that would allow you to assess students' mastery of some aspect of your subject area. Next, develop a set of procedures or guidelines that help students understand what they are to do, under what circumstances they will do it, and how they will be evaluated. Finally, develop a detailed rubric by which students' performance of the task could be scored. Have a classmate read through your task guidelines and rubric to make sure they are clear.

ACTIVITY 9.5: Developing a Grading System   Develop a reasonable grading system for a course you are likely to teach. Include and justify a variety of sources of information, the way each source will be graded or scored, the weight you will apply to each, and the standard you will use to assign grades.

ACTIVITY 9.6: Synthesizing Assessment Information   Using the grading system you developed in Activity 9.4, randomly assign grades or scores for each assignment to ten imaginary students. Based upon the system you have chosen, synthesize this information and assign a letter grade to each student. You should be able to clearly explain how and why each student is receiving the assigned grade.

REFERENCES

Airasian, P. (2001). *Classroom assessment.* Fourth Edition. New York: McGraw-Hill.

Anastasi, A. (1981). Coaching, test sophistication, and developed abilities. *American Psychologist, 36,* 1086–1093.

Anastasi, A., and Urbina, S. (1997). *Psychological testing.* Seventh Edition. Upper Saddle River, NJ: Prentice-Hall.

Arter, J., and McTighe, J. (2001). *Scoring rubrics in the classroom: Using performance criteria for assessing and improving student performance.* London: Corwin Press.

Bol, L., and Stephenson, P. (1998). Influence of experience, grade level, and subject area on teachers' assessment practices. *Journal of educational research, 91*(6), 323–331.

Borich, G. (1992). *Effective teaching methods.* Second Edition. New York: Merrill.

Brandt, R. (1992, May). Overview: A fresh focus for curriculum. *Educational leadership, 7.*

Brophy, J. (1981). Teacher praise: A functional analysis. *Review of Educational Research, 51*(1), 5–32.

Burke, K. (1994). *How to assess authentic learning.* Arlington Heights, IL: Skylight.

Burke, K., Fogarty, R., and Belgrad, S. (1994). *The portfolio connection.* Arlington Heights, IL: IRI/Skylight Training and Publishing.

Choate, J., Enright, B., Miller, L., Poteet, J., & Rakes, T. (1995). *Curriculum-based assessment and programming.* Boston: Allyn and Bacon.

Crooks, T. (1988). The impact of classroom evaluation practices on students. *Review of Educational Research, 58*(4), 438–481.

Cross, L., and Frary, R. (1999). Hodgepodge grading: Endorsed by students and teachers alike. *Applied Measurement in Education, 12*(1), 53–72.

Daniels, V. (1999). The assessment maze: Making instructional decisions about alternative assessment for students. *Preventing school failure, 43*(4), 171–178.

Eby, J. (1992). *Reflective planning, teaching and evaluation for the elementary school.* New York: Merrill.

Eisner, E. (1999). The uses and limits of performance assessment. *Phi Delta Kappan, 80*(9), 658–660.

Elliot, S. (1994). *Creating meaningful performance assessments: Fundamental concepts.* Reston, VA: Council for Exceptional Children.

Fuchs, L. (1994). *Connecting performance to instruction.* Reston, VA: Council for Exceptional Children.

Guskey, T., and Bailey, J. (2001). *Developing grading and reporting systems for student learning.* London: Corwin Press.

Haertel, E. (1999). Performance assessment and education reform. *Phi Delta Kappan, 80*(9), 662–667.

Haertel, E. (1986, April). Choosing and using classroom tests: Teachers' perspectives on assessment. Paper presented at the annual meeting of the American Educational Research Association, San Francisco.

Hills, J. (1981). *Measurement and evaluation in the classroom.* Columbus, OH: Merrill.

Isaac, S., and Michael, W. (1997). *Handbook in research and evaluation.* Third Edition. San Diego, CA: Educational and Industrial Testing Services.

Gregory, R. (1996). *Psychological testing: History, principles, and applications.* Second Edition. Needham Heights, MA: Allyn and Bacon.

Linn, R. (1991). Dimensions of thinking: Implications for testing. In B. Jones & L. Idol (Eds.), *Educational values and cognitive instruction: Implications for reform* (pp. 179–208). Hillsdale, NJ: Erlbaum.

Linn, R., and Burton, L. (1994). Performance-based assessment: Implications of task specificity. *Educational measurement: Issues and practice, 13,* 3–8, 15.

MacDonald, R. (1992). *A handbook of basic skills and strategies for beginning teachers.* New York: Longman.

Marzano, R. (2000). *Transforming classroom grading.* Alexandria, VA: Association for Supervision and Curriculum Development.

McMillan, J. (2001). *Essential assessment concepts for teachers and administrators.* London: Corwin Press.

Mertler, C. (1999). Assessing student performance: A descriptive study of the classroom assessment practices of Ohio teachers. *Education, 120*(2), 285–297.

Moore, K. (1992). *Classroom teaching skills.* Second Edition. New York: McGraw-Hill.

Popham, w. (1997). Assessment apathy. *Education Week, 18*(35), 32,

Scriven, M. (1967). The methodology of evaluation. In R. W. Stake (Ed.), *Perspectives on curriculum evaluation. AERA Monograph Series on Curriculum Evaluation, no. 1* (pp. 39–83). Chicago: Rand McNally.

Stanley, J. (1958, April). ABCs of test construction. *NEA Journal,* pp. 224–229.

Stiggins, R. (1997). *Student-centered assessment.* Columbus, OH: Merrill.

Walker-Wilson, L. (2002). *Better instruction through assessment: What your students are trying to tell you.* Larchmont, NY: Eye on Education.

Wiggins, G, (1998). *Educative assessment: Developing assessments to inform and improve student performance.* San Francisco, CA: Jossey-Bass.

Wiggins, G. (1989). Toward more authentic and equitable assessment. *Phi Delta Kappan, 70,* 703–713.

Willis, S. (September, 1990). Transforming the test: Experts press for new forms of student assessment. *ASCD Update,* 3–6.

Worthen, B., Sanders, J., and Fitzpatrick, J. (1997). *Program evaluation: Alternative approaches and practical guidelines.* Second Edition. New York: Longman.

Reflecting on Teaching

Contents

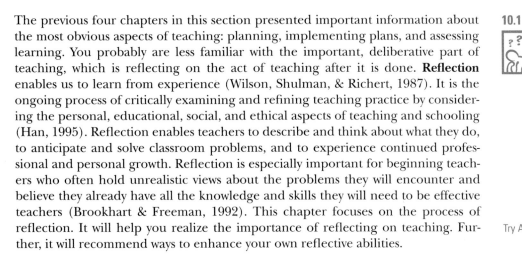

The previous four chapters in this section presented important information about the most obvious aspects of teaching: planning, implementing plans, and assessing learning. You probably are less familiar with the important, deliberative part of teaching, which is reflecting on the act of teaching after it is done. **Reflection** enables us to learn from experience (Wilson, Shulman, & Richert, 1987). It is the ongoing process of critically examining and refining teaching practice by considering the personal, educational, social, and ethical aspects of teaching and schooling (Han, 1995). Reflection enables teachers to describe and think about what they do, to anticipate and solve classroom problems, and to experience continued professional and personal growth. Reflection is especially important for beginning teachers who often hold unrealistic views about the problems they will encounter and believe they already have all the knowledge and skills they will need to be effective teachers (Brookhart & Freeman, 1992). This chapter focuses on the process of reflection. It will help you realize the importance of reflecting on teaching. Further, it will recommend ways to enhance your own reflective abilities.

10.1 Give an example of how you reflect every day.

Try Activity 10.1

A Tale of Two Student Teachers

Let's look into two classrooms to see how two different student teachers deliberate on identical mathematics lessons. In each lesson, the student teacher assigns students to work in groups of three. Using plastic blocks in a variety of shapes and colors, each group of students is to sort the cubes into piles or sets that are alike in some way, describe the characteristics of each set, and determine the number of possible combinations of sets they can make from their assortment of blocks. Throughout the lesson, the students are active and excited. Too quickly, time runs out, and both student teachers dismiss their respective students for lunch.

After the math lesson, Student Teacher A feels proud of the lesson. "That was a great lesson because the students enjoyed it. I wish my supervisor had observed it! I used manipulatives and small groups, just like we were told to do in our education courses."

But the classroom is a mess! Plastic blocks are piled on desks and scattered on the floor. "Now I have to clean this up. There are cubes everywhere!"

As she picks up, she thinks of the students. "I sure hope they got the idea of sets. They have to be ready for a test next Tuesday, and they didn't do very well on the last test." She is concerned about how prepared they are for more difficult math concepts later in the year.

She sighs as she walks to the teachers' lunchroom fifteen minutes late. "Another lesson done. This semester is sure going fast! It's almost the end of the grading period and of my student teaching experience. And I'm surviving!"

After an identical kind of lesson, Student Teacher B responds quite differently. She, too, is pleased with how the lesson progressed and with the enthusiasm the students displayed. This raises questions in her mind. "Why did the lesson go so well? What worked? I guess it was the use of manipulatives. That made math more fun for students. And working in groups—they always seem to enjoy that. Or at least most of them enjoy working in groups. I noticed today that some students seemed quiet or confused, as though they were withdrawing from the group. They weren't involved in dividing the blocks into sets, either. I wonder if they were learning by just watching, or if they were learning at all."

This leads her to question whether she chose the right instructional approach for the lesson. "I wonder if it would have been better to have students work individually with manipulatives instead of in groups. That way I could have circulated around and prevented some students from withdrawing from the lesson. I could have held them all accountable for learning. Why did I decide to put them into small groups? Was it because that's what I was told to do in my college courses, or is it really a better approach for this class of students? No, I think that the students came up with more combinations and sets because they were working in groups. I think I made the right decision."

Her classroom, too, is in disarray. "Look at this mess!" As she collects the blocks, she thinks, "Where could I have saved time so that the students would have had time to clean up? Next time, I think I'll assign one person in each group to gather the supplies. I'll give them a five-minute warning before the end of class, too."

Student Teacher B also thinks about her students' learning. "I wonder what they really learned about sets from this lesson. Tyler seemed to understand; his eyes just lit up! Andre seemed to have problems. He'll need more practice; I can work with him tomorrow. From what I observed, most of them got the idea of sets and the relationships among sets."

Teacher B sighs as she walks to the teachers' lunchroom fifteen minutes late. "I feel good about the lesson, though," her thoughts continue. "Their enthusiasm makes my job a lot easier! Next time, though, I have to make time for cleanup. And I will monitor students in the groups more closely to be sure that everyone is involved. With more difficult math concepts ahead, the students can't slack off now!"

How are the reactions of the two student teachers similar? How do their reactions differ? Both teachers gave good lessons, motivated students, and experienced relatively few problems. Student Teacher A was upbeat about the lesson, and justifiably so. She thought she was doing what good teachers do and that her teaching was effective. As a result, she will probably use precisely the same approach in future lessons.

In contrast, Student Teacher B had deeper afterthoughts about the teaching and learning during the lesson. She pondered: "Am I doing the right things in the right ways? Why am I doing things this way?" By asking herself many self-challenging questions, she was reflecting on teaching. She analyzed her decisions related to the lesson and assessed her personal satisfaction with the lesson. Further, she used her responses to those questions to plan changes in her teaching behavior. As a result of this reflection, it is likely that her future lessons will be even better than this one.

While both of these student teachers are good teachers, Student Teacher B is better. She is a reflective practitioner; she is already developing habits of thought that will make her a wiser teacher and ensure her consistent professional growth in increasingly complex classroom settings.

Characteristics of Reflective Practitioners

10.2 Think of a situation when you questioned a classroom event or theory. How did you respond?

Reflective practitioners, like Student Teacher B, share certain characteristics. They are deliberative, open-minded, responsible, and sincere; they have a spirit of inquiry. Let us examine these qualities more closely.

First, reflective practitioners routinely and purposefully *deliberate* or reflect on teaching. You recall that Teacher B reflected about many aspects of her lesson. Reflection helps you make rational decisions about teaching and learning and helps you assume responsibility for the results of those choices in the classroom (Ross, 1987).

Reflective practitioners are *open-minded* (Dewey, 1933). They are willing to question their own views of and reactions to their teaching practices and the school culture. Student Teacher B showed open-mindedness when she questioned the wisdom of dividing her students into groups for the math lesson. She openly explored, rather than defended, her decision. Open-minded teachers view situations from multiple perspectives, search for alternative explanations for classroom events, and use evidence to support or evaluate a decision or position.

Reflective practitioners take *responsibility* (Dewey, 1933). Student Teacher B assumed responsibility for her teaching decisions. She decided to use group work to teach her students about sets. The result was that some students withdrew from the group and were not engaged in the learning activity. Rather than ignore the struggling students, Student Teacher B accepted responsibility for her decision and resolved to help Andre in class the next day. Further, she took responsibility for running out of time and resolved to work more effectively within the time allotted for math lessons. Thus, reflective practitioners consider and accept the consequences of their decisions and the changes they make in teaching style, in the learning environment, or in the school culture.

Furthermore, reflective teachers are *sincere* as they closely investigate their teaching (Dewey, 1933). They take reflection seriously. Their reflection is purposeful and exciting because it helps them better understand who they are as teachers. Their reflection is not "idle meandering or daydreaming"; rather, it focuses on the goal of improving their effectiveness as teachers (Boud, Keogh, & Walker, 1985). This difference in thinking was evident between the two student teachers. While Student Teacher A's thoughts after the lesson were random and unfocused, Student Teacher B's reflection eagerly probed various aspects of the learning experience her lesson provided. She did not merely accept the fact that students enjoyed the instructional method she selected. She wanted to know why it was successful. Further, she thought sincerely about the individual learning that resulted from the lesson. Goodman (1984) points out that this sincerity enables you to work through any fears or insecurities you may have about questioning your teaching, your beliefs, and the educational values you see in the school environment and in society.

Generally, then, we could say that a *spirit of inquiry* characterizes reflective teachers. Reflective teachers are interested in the subtleties of the art and science of teaching. They want to learn all they can about teaching from both theory and practice. They think deeply about their course work and about how it should impact their teaching. For example, Student Teacher B drew on a theory she learned in her college courses when she decided students would learn more about sets by working in small groups. Inquiring teachers learn by studying teaching, by observing other teachers, and by analyzing and reflecting on the practice of others (Schön, 1987). They continue to learn when they practice and subsequently analyze their own teaching skills (Cruickshank, 1987).

Because of the individual nature of reflective thinking and the uniqueness of each teacher's reflection, reflective practice has been referred to as **inquiry-oriented teaching** (Wellington, 1991). This process of inquiry leads teachers to become "students of teaching" (Dewey, 1904). Dewey contends that it is more important for you as a future teacher to learn to think about your work than it is to master specific techniques of teaching and classroom management.

What distinguishes teachers who are students of teaching from those who are not? To summarize, they inquire into and analyze their own teaching behavior and the teaching of others. They are sincerely interested in the fine points of the art

10.3 Are you a student of teaching? Why or why not?

Try Activity 10.2

and science of teaching, and they want to learn all they can about teaching. They are open-minded and willing to consider why they teach as they do. They take responsibility for the consequences of their teaching. They deliberate on their teaching, and as a result of this reflection they change or modify their patterns of teaching behavior.

Benefits of Reflecting on Teaching

Reflection may sound like a lot of work, but preservice teachers like you report that they value and benefit from reflecting on teaching (Richert, 1990). Reflection holds both immediate and long-term benefits for you as a teacher. Even now, reflection can enhance your learning about teaching and increase your ability to analyze classroom events. Later, when you are teaching, reflective thinking can improve your classroom life, enable you to monitor yourself, and stimulate your personal and professional growth.

Perhaps the most important benefit of reflection as you prepare to teach is that it *enhances your learning about teaching.* According to learning psychologists, reflectivity plays a central role in learning from your course work and from your field or school experiences (Han, 1995; Jadallah, 1996). To learn the most from these experiences, you need four things. First, you must have a concrete learning experience, such as grading homework papers for your cooperating teacher. Second, you must have an opportunity to reflect on the experience by recapturing and evaluating it. So, after grading the assignments, you might think back on the distribution of grades, consider the nature of the homework assignment and how students benefited from it, and even challenge why teachers assign homework to students. You might conclude that while good students did well on their homework, less able students did poorly. As a result, you might decide that homework assignments must be individualized to provide a meaningful learning experience for all students.

The next step in the learning process is to integrate your reflections with what you already know and believe about teaching and learning. This leads you to recognize new ways of doing things, resolving problems, or clarifying issues. Finally, you must engage in active experimentation, applying the insights you have gained to make decisions and solve problems (Boud et al., 1985; Kolb, 1981). The experience of grading and reflecting on homework assignments may have led you to clarify your beliefs about homework. As a result, you may begin to consider evaluating students' learning using an authentic strategy discussed in Chapter 9, such as portfolios.

This scenario suggests that one of the best ways to increase your learning about teaching is to strengthen the link between the learning experience and the reflection that follows; that is, by taking time to reflect on the experiences and ideas you have been exposed to in your teacher preparation program (Boud et al., 1985; Emery, 1996).

A second benefit of reflecting on teaching that you can begin to take advantage of now is that reflection *increases your ability to analyze and understand classroom events.* That is, reflection makes you more thoughtful and wise (Cruickshank, 1987; Fien, 1996). Liston and Zeichner (1987) observed that preservice teachers tend to look at classrooms with a wide rather than narrow lens. Perhaps you have experienced this yourself, sitting in the corner of a classroom, observing everything superficially but focusing on nothing closely or critically. The students may appear to be naturally well behaved because you are not concentrating on analyzing and understanding the cues and nonverbal desists the teacher uses to prevent students from drifting off task (see Chapter 13).

Because preservice teachers do not always understand the teaching they observe, Ross (1987) found that most still use whim or emotion as much as logic or evidence in making decisions about how they will teach. Further, most preservice teachers see no logical way to differentiate among conflicting positions or different teaching approaches, such as between direct instruction and discovery learning. They tend to hold tightly to one teaching approach they have observed to be effective, such as discovery learning, rather than to analyze when and how this approach would work best with different groups of students and different instructional tasks.

Reflection enables you to examine and analyze classroom events rather than simply observe them. Reflective teachers such as Student Teacher B are better able to ask themselves basic questions about teaching. They are more analytical and less judgmental when they consider their teaching and that of others. Reflection leads teachers to consider the underlying assumptions about, beliefs about, and implications of the practices they are using and how these practices affect students as they learn (Cruickshank, 1987; Han, 1995). In short, reflective teachers understand what teaching and learning are all about. Preservice teachers who practice analyzing classroom events by reflecting on them are less anxious about student teaching than are their peers who observe classrooms through a wide, unfocused lens (Cruickshank, Kennedy, Williams, Holton, & Fay, 1981).

A third benefit of reflection is that reflecting on teaching will *enhance your classroom life* as a teacher by helping you establish an inviting, predictable, and thoughtful environment. This is because reflective teachers are better able to apply what they have learned from course work to their classroom practice (Cruickshank, 1987). This will benefit both you and your students. Hundreds of teachers and administrators who were asked to consider the personal and professional benefits of higher-level thinking, including reflection, support this. They suggest that teachers with good thinking abilities and habits are usually more sensitive, accepting and empathic, tolerant and open-minded, flexible, wise, reasoning, resourceful, creative, informed, objective, observant, aware, and self-understanding (Cruickshank, 1986). In Chapter 13, we will discuss why the attitudes and approaches of such teachers are essential to establishing an inviting, predictable classroom environment in which students feel secure, respected, and free to explore and learn.

Unfortunately, many teachers rely on trial and error rather than reflective thinking when establishing their classroom environments. Dewey (1916) distinguished between trial-and-error activity and reflective activity as two approaches teachers use. With trial and error, he commented,

> We simply do something, and when it fails, we do something else, and keep on trying till we hit upon something which works, and then we adopt that method as a rule-of-thumb measure in subsequent procedure (p. 169).

Using trial and error sets up a random, unpredictable classroom environment that students find upsetting and threatening. In contrast, when teachers consistently use reflective activity to make decisions, their students experience a predictable, inviting classroom environment that makes them eager to learn. Further, when a reflective teacher models thinking and problem-solving skills, students begin to think and to use those skills to resolve their own problems (Martin, 1984). As a teacher, you will indeed enhance your classroom life as students respond to the predictable, thoughtful environment!

A fourth benefit of engaging in reflection is that teachers who use reflective skills become *self-monitoring*. It is impossible for you to be prepared for every situation you may encounter during your teaching career. And, unfortunately, during most of your teaching career you will not receive feedback on your teaching performance, strengths, and weaknesses. By analyzing and reflecting on your teaching, however, you can assess your needs and monitor your teaching performance and

10.4 Have you seen examples of teachers using trial and error? In what ways, and how did it work?

FIGURE 10.1   Immediate and Future Benefits of Reflection

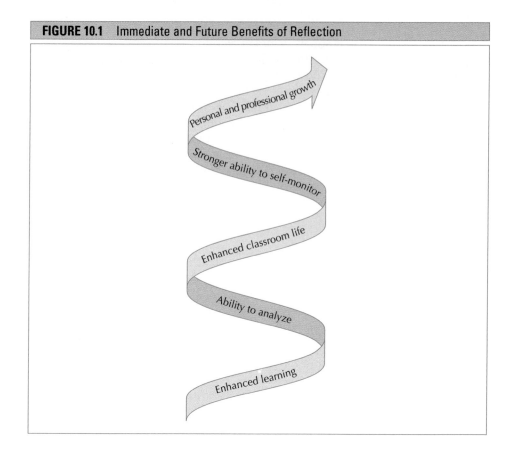

satisfaction (Valverde, 1982). During reflection, teachers learn by studying themselves, and this helps them grow in self-understanding (Boyd & Fales, 1983; Cruickshank, 1987). Reflective thinking helps teachers create and clarify meaning in terms of who they are *per se* and who they are in relation to the world of teaching and education (Boyd & Fales, 1983; Schön, 1983). By extracting personal meaning from their teaching and learning experiences, they direct themselves toward their teaching and professional goals (Cruickshank, 1987).

Teachers who are not introspective and self-monitoring tend to be governed by routine, tradition, and authority (Dewey, 1916). They miss out on *personal and professional transformation,* a fifth benefit of reflective thinking (Figure 10.1). Smyth (1989) considers the "spiral of empowerment" resulting from reflective practice as its greatest benefit and as a necessity for teachers. Because a person's preconceptions of teaching, learning, and the purposes of the school will greatly influence how he or she interprets teaching experiences, these beliefs and values must be examined rather than merely accepted. Questioning personal and societal beliefs and values is intended "to raise consciousness, to challenge complacency, and to engender a higher order of professional practice" (Wellington, 1991). As teachers reflect on the factors that affect their teaching behavior, such as those discussed in Chapter 1, they can rid themselves of unfounded beliefs about teaching and learning. They are then able to develop new or revised beliefs more likely to lead to effective teaching and student learning (Cruickshank, 1987).

This sort of reflective practice provides teachers with a better way of understanding the role teachers and schools play in addressing or perpetuating social problems. By examining even deeper issues of ethics, morals, and justice in education, reflective thinking engages teachers in the redesign and reconstruction of their world.

10.5   What values and beliefs about teaching and learning will influence your reflective thinking?

10.6   Which benefit of reflection is most important to you?

Try Activity 10.3

Developing Reflective Abilities

To meet the demands of today's classrooms, you must be willing and able to reflect on classroom events. Your professional growth and satisfaction as a teacher will, in part, be linked to this ability.

How can you develop your reflective abilities? Many methods have been suggested and tried. Five of the most promising are presented here.

DIALOGUE JOURNALS

Writing about a classroom experience can help you develop reflective abilities because it enables you to play back and recreate classroom events and to gain a new perspective on those experiences (Tremmel, 1993; Wallace, 1996). A **dialogue journal** goes a step further by providing you with feedback on the experience and on your thinking. In a dialogue journal, you carry on a running conversation that expresses thoughts, questions, and problems related to your roles, responsibilities, and practices as a teacher. A colleague, cooperating teacher, or university instructor regularly responds to your entries by sharing thoughts, reactions, and questions that come to mind. Krol (1996) found that comments that stimulate you to reexamine or think more deeply about the topic are the most helpful. Electronic dialogue journals, where the discussion takes place online in a secure chat room or bulletin board, are even easier and often more timely than paper journals.

Try Activity 10.4

A dialogue journal can help you internalize various ideas about teaching and become more flexible and mature in your thinking (Bolin, 1988). It can also help you see alternative ways of dealing with classroom events and recognize the connection between teachers' actions and students' outcomes (Krol, 1996). Figure 10.2 on page 318 shows what entries in a dialogue journal might have looked like for Student Teacher B following her mathematics lesson on sets.

DISCUSSIONS

Another way you can construct meaning from your teacher preparation experiences is by talking about them. If your discussion is focused and purposeful rather than random, it can help you engage in higher-level thinking and even in attitude change (Cruickshank, 1986, 1991; Jadallah, 1996).

Some researchers have found that talking about experiences is a better reflective tool than writing about them, partly because of the feedback you receive from your peers (Emery, 1996; Jadallah, 1996; Pultorak, 1996). Electronic discussions, which provide immediate feedback without the social constraints that sometimes limit discussion in a regular classroom, may be even more powerful. Schön (1983) and Emery (1996) say that it is most effective to discuss your classroom experiences, especially the methods and strategies you have tried while teaching. To be truly reflective, however, the discussion should be geared toward critical self-reflection and should involve four steps, which we have modified from Smyth (1989):

10.7 Rate your natural ability to reflect. Are you a reflective person?

1. *Describe* what you did by elaborating on one specific lesson or classroom event.
2. *Inform* yourself and others of what is behind this classroom event. What did the event mean? What principles or theories did the event or teaching behavior illustrate?
3. *Confront* the knowledge of teaching, learning, and social theories you identified in the previous step. Ask yourself: Why did I choose this teaching strategy? What causes me to draw from this theory? What interests and objectives does my classroom practice serve?
4. *Reconstruct* the classroom event or lesson by asking how you might have done things differently. It is important that in this step you reconceptualize or refine your understanding of teaching and learning theories as they apply to this

FIGURE 10.2 Sample Dialogue Journal Entries for Student Teacher B

Student Teacher B Entry

Today's math lesson on sets went well, but a few things bothered me about it. I broke the students down into groups of three and had them sort the blocks with similar characteristics into groups, then count and describe those sets. I'm glad I had them working in groups because they identified a lot of sets . . . more than we would have as a whole class, I think. The thing that bothered me, though, was that some students weren't involved in the group work. About five students seemed to withdraw . . . and how are they supposed to learn if they don't participate? I thought students were supposed to participate more in small groups, not less!

Cooperating Teacher Entry

Your lesson went really well! You had a clear objective and communicated it well to the students so that they knew exactly what they were supposed to do in their small groups.

I think you are being a little bit hard on yourself about the level of student involvement in the small groups. Because I was observing, I could see perhaps more closely what students in each group were actually doing. Some of the students who seemed to not participate looked to me like they were just participating more sporadically than the more outgoing students in the group. Simon, for example, may have looked uninvolved, but remember that he is a very reflective learner. He just thinks before he acts! If you are concerned about small groups, try to think through how you assigned the students to groups. Are the personalities compatible? Are the ability levels mixed? Are there gender or ethnic considerations? Also, think about what you can do to hold all students accountable for participating in the group in some way. Don't give up . . . small groups are challenging, but also effective!

Student Teacher B Entry

I never thought about how complicated it is to assign students to groups, and how that could impact the lesson! I just assigned them randomly for this lesson. They all seem to get along so well together that it never occurred to me that some of them might not work well together in a small-group situation. Can you provide me with any "inside information" you have about potential mismatches so that I can assign the groups more carefully next time?

Cooperating Teacher Entry

I have a committee meeting tomorrow at 3:30, but we could meet for about fifteen minutes right after school to discuss my "insights." Also, I have some notes from a cooperative learning workshop that you might be interested in reading. Keep up the good work!

---

specific classroom or school context, and that you bring your teaching practices more in line with those theories.

Perhaps you can identify each of these steps in Student Teacher B's reflections on her math lesson. Which steps is Student Teacher A missing?

PORTFOLIOS

While teaching portfolios can be used to collect teaching **artifacts** or to help with job interviews, increasingly they are being used to promote reflection. A **portfolio** provides a structured opportunity for you to document and describe your teaching, to connect this to what you know about teaching and learning, and to reflect on how and why you teach the way you do (Loughran & Corrigan, 1995; Wolf, Whinery, & Hagerty, 1995; Zubizarreta, 1994). Preservice students describe portfolios as a different yet complementary way to reflect on their teaching. While journals and discussions help them to reflect on daily classroom occurrences, portfolios enable them to view theory, field experience, and the challenges of teaching in a broader perspective (Borko, Michalec, Timmons, & Siddle, 1997).

Assembling a portfolio involves three processes: collecting, selecting, and reflecting. Your instructors, for example, might require a portfolio entry to demonstrate that you are aware of and address the special needs of students in your classroom. You think immediately of Amber, a visually impaired student. You *collect* artifacts such as student records documenting her medical condition, a seating chart showing where you placed Amber during whole-class instruction, and sample lesson plans, worksheets, and activities that show modifications for Amber. Next, you *select* two or three of the artifacts that best illustrate how you address Amber's learning needs. Finally, you *reflect* on Amber's situation, on what you know about teaching and learning that can help you effectively teach students with special challenges, and on what the artifacts show about how you work with Amber. This written reflection, in which you analyze your own teaching, is the most important part of the portfolio.

ACTION RESEARCH

Action research is the process of conducting classroom research to answer questions or solve problems about teaching and learning involving a specific group of students in a particular setting (McKay, 1992). Unlike traditional research, which requires you to pore over books and journals in search of information and solutions, action research occurs in schools. Classroom teachers engage in action research to help them better understand their teaching and to solve problems related to learning. In action research, a teacher identifies a classroom-related question, plans classroom-based methods of gathering information related to the question, and then collects information about the phenomenon under study (Eisner, 1985). By reflecting on the information gained, the teacher increases his or her understanding of the event and is able to suggest a course of action. Increasingly, action research is seen as a major form of professional development for teachers and as central to school reform (Holly, 1991).

You can conduct action research during your field experiences by following the action research cycle: planning, acting, observing, and reflecting (Kemmis & McTaggart, 1982). For example, you could plan to focus on one student, whom we'll call Jennifer, who seems to be underachieving. You wonder why Jennifer doesn't work up to her potential. To find out, you and your cooperating teacher develop a plan of action: make Jennifer the leader of her reading group. To see if she becomes more motivated, you observe her during reading lessons and, every few minutes, record whether she is paying attention and engaged in the learning task. You might also interview Jennifer, querying her about her attitudes toward school, the teacher, and other subjects. Through conversation and by investigating her permanent record, you can gain insights into her home life: how supportive her parents are toward education, whether she has a quiet place in which to study, and what cultural factors may explain her motivation. Taken together, these resources should enable you to analyze Jennifer's learning and behavior. After careful reflection, you can make inferences about why Jennifer performs as she does in school and suggest ways to help her.

Used in this way, action research can contribute to your professional growth by making your field experiences more meaningful and sharpening your reflective abilities. Later, when you have your own classroom, action research can help you solve some of the "mysteries" of teaching and learning unique to your school situation.

ON-CAMPUS LABORATORY EXPERIENCES

Laboratory experiences are contrived teaching experiences carried out on campus, often with a small group of peers, rather than in an actual classroom setting. Some on-campus laboratory experiences such as microteaching, discussed in Part Four, Unit 1 of the Practice Teaching Manual, are intended to help you practice and build basic teaching skills. Simulations, discussed in Unit 3, provide you with practice in solving vexing classroom problems.

Reflective Teaching, a program provided in part in Unit 2, was specifically developed to help preservice and in-service teachers become more thoughtful teachers (Cruickshank, 1991). Reflective Teaching provides you with a teaching experience in a supportive environment that serves as the basis for subsequent reflection. In

Patricia J. Dixon of Tallahassee, Florida, thought she was encouraging her middle school science students to participate. But they were not reacting as she expected. They were reluctant to ask questions, make assumptions, or join in discussions. She wondered if her nonverbal communication was the reason, and decided to use action research to find out.

Using one class with 23 students, Ms. Dixon videotaped the class for five days. She asked the group five questions to get their perception of her nonverbal behavior and recorded their responses. When she analyzed the tapes and student responses, she found out some startling things! This action research helped her become more aware of what she was saying to students and, more importantly, how she was saying it.

- Students most openly and willingly answered questions when she stood with her hands or palms up.
- Participation was discouraged when she placed her hands on her hips, but hands in her pockets or behind her back created a casual atmosphere and encouraged responses.
- Mismatched verbal and nonverbal behaviors confused students.
- Head nodding, especially combined with a smile or laughter, encouraged students to respond.

- Being close to students encouraged them to respond. More important than proximity, however, was showing that she was listening to their response rather than distracted by grading papers, watching the clock, or reading ahead.
- Eye contact showed students that she was listening to them.
- Students preferred an even, uniform tone of voice because it made them feel safe.

Source: P. J. Dixon. *Encouraging participation in a middle school classroom*. [Online]. Available: http://www.enc.org/professional/research/journal/science.

Reflective Teaching, you engage in all aspects of the teaching cycle (planning, implementing, assessing, and reflecting) by presenting a short, content-neutral lesson based on specific objectives to a group of peers. The Reflective Teaching experience is structured to promote analysis and reflection about the teaching and learning processes through small-group and whole-class discussions.

Research on the effectiveness of Reflective Teaching shows that preservice teachers find it enjoyable and that they benefit greatly from the immediate, nonthreatening feedback (Bainer & Cantrell, 1992; Peters, 1980). More importantly, research suggests that the Reflective Teaching program can make you a more reflective teacher. Preservice teachers who engaged in Reflective Teaching were better able to think and talk critically about teaching (Cruickshank et al., 1981). Troyer (1988) found that if preservice teachers are informed about the nature and importance of reflective thinking, as you have been by reading this chapter, they are even more reflective in analyzing classroom teaching situations.

Some Final Thoughts

Yes, teaching is a complex activity. But in spite of this, you can increase the likelihood that you will be an effective teacher if you develop the ability to reflect on your teaching and the teaching practices of others. Hopefully, your teacher preparation program and cooperating teachers are helping you to reflect on your own teaching and the teaching you observe. You will surely benefit if, in addition, you take specific steps to develop attitudes essential to reflective thinking. You will enhance your learning and teaching as you make reflection a careful, consistent part of your life.

CHAPTER SUMMARY

- Teaching is a complex activity that requires teachers to think about or reflect on what they do.

- Good teachers can become even more effective by reflecting on teaching.
- Reflective practitioners share certain characteristics.
  1. They routinely and purposefully deliberate or reflect on teaching.
  2. They are open-minded, freely questioning their own views and reactions to their teaching practices.
  3. They consider and accept responsibility for the consequences of the decisions they make in the learning environment.
  4. They are enthusiastic and eagerly focus on ways to improve their teaching.
  5. They become "students of teaching" by inquiring into theory and practices related to teaching and learning.
- Reflective thinking offers immediate and future benefits for preservice teachers.
  1. Reflecting on learning experiences enhances learning.
  2. Reflective thinking increases the ability to analyze and understand classroom events.
  3. Reflection enhances the teacher's classroom life by helping him or her establish an inviting, predictable, and thoughtful learning environment.
  4. Reflective teachers are self-monitoring, which means they can direct their own personal growth.
  5. Reflection leads to personal and professional growth and empowers teachers to redesign teaching and the school culture.
- Teachers can develop reflective thinking skills in many ways.
  1. The interaction provided through a dialogue journal can help you internalize ideas and build flexible, mature thinking about teaching.
  2. Focused and purposeful discussions can build higher-order thinking skills and attitude changes.
  3. Teaching portfolios complement other reflection experiences and help you reflect on teaching more broadly.
  4. Action research, a field-based approach to reflecting on teaching and solving problems related to learning, can contribute to the development of reflective thinking skills.
  5. Clinical experiences, such as Reflective Teaching, conducted on campus in a supportive environment can enhance reflective thinking skills.

ISSUES AND PROBLEMS FOR DISCUSSION

1. Do teachers need to be reflective to be effective at bringing about students' learning and satisfaction? Why or why not?
2. What should teachers reflect about? Should they be compelled to think about some aspects of education more than others?
3. Do you agree with Dewey that it is more important to learn to reflect than to master teaching skills? Why or why not?
4. What prevents teachers from reflecting? What could a building principal do to encourage teachers to become more reflective?

THEORY INTO ACTION ACTIVITIES

ACTIVITY 10.1: Ask your cooperating teachers what it means to reflect on teaching. Ask if they reflect on their teaching. If so, when do they reflect? What do they reflect about? What is the result of that reflection?

ACTIVITY 10.2: Identify and interview a teacher you consider a "student of teaching." Compare the interview results with those your classmates obtain. What commonalities do you find among teachers who are students of teaching?

ACTIVITY 10.3: Design a weekly schedule for a teacher that would be conducive to reflective thinking. Share it with a teacher or principal for their reaction.

ACTIVITY 10.4: For two weeks, keep a dialogue journal by carrying on a written or electronic conversation with a friend about your preservice teacher education. Reflect back on the experience. What did you learn? How did the exchange help you? What problems existed?

REFERENCES

Bainer, D. L., & Cantrell, D. (1992). Nine dominant reflection themes identified for preservice teachers by a content analysis of essays. *Education, 112*(4), 571–578.

Bolin, F. S. (1988). Helping student teachers think about teaching. *Journal of Teacher Education, 39*(2), 48–54.

Borko, H., Michalec, P., Timmons, M., & Siddle, J. (1997). Student teaching portfolios: A tool for promoting reflective practice. *Journal of Teacher Education, 48,* 345–357.

Boud, D., Keogh, R., & Walker, D. (Eds.). (1985). *Reflection: Turning experiences into learning.* New York: Nichols.

Boyd, E. M., & Fales, A. W. (1983). Reflective learning: Key to learning from experience. *Journal of Humanistic Psychology, 23*(2), 99–117.

Brookhart, S. M., & Freeman, D. J. (1992). Characteristics of entering teacher candidates. *Review of Educational Research, 62,* 26–60.

Cruickshank, D. R. (1986). Critical thinking skills for teachers. *Teacher Education Quarterly, 13*(1), 82–89.

Cruickshank, D. R. (1987). *Reflective teaching: The preparation of students of teaching.* Reston, VA: Association of Teacher Educators.

Cruickshank, D. R. (1991). *Reflective teaching.* Revised Edition. Bloomington, IN: Phi Delta Kappa.

Cruickshank, D. R., Kennedy, J. J., Williams, E. J., Holton, J., & Fay, D. E. (1981). Evaluation of reflective teaching outcomes. *Journal of Educational Research, 75*(1), 26–32.

Dewey, J. (1904). The relation of theory to practice in education. In C. A. McMurry (Ed.), *The relation of theory to practice in the education of teachers.* Third yearbook of the National Society for the Scientific Study of Education, Part I (pp. 9–30). Chicago: University of Chicago Press.

Dewey, J. (1916). *Democracy and education: An introduction to the philosophy of education.* New York: Macmillan.

Dewey, J. (1933). *How we think.* Boston: Heath.

Dixon, P. J. *Encouraging participation in a middle school classroom.* [On-line]. Available: http://www.enc.org/professional/research/journal/science.

Eisner, J. (1985). Facilitating action research in school: Some dilemmas. In R. Burgess (Ed.), *Field methods in the study of education.* Lewes: Falmer Press.

Emery, W.G. (1996). Teachers' critical reflection through expert talk. *Journal of Teacher Education, 47,* 110–119.

Fien, J. (1996). Reflective practice: A case study of professional development for environmental education. *Journal of Environmental Education, 27,* 11–20.

Goodman, J. (1984). Reflection and teacher education: A case study and theoretical analysis. *Interchange, 15*(3), 9–26.

Han, E. P. (1995). Reflection is essential in teacher education. *Childhood Education, 71,* 228–230.

Holly, P. (1991). Action research: The missing link in the creation of schools as centers of inquiry. In A. Lieberman & L. Miller (Eds.), *Staff development for education in the '90s: New demands, new realities, new perspectives.* New York: Teachers College Press.

Jadallah, E. (1996). Reflective theory and practice: A constructivist process for curriculum and instructional decisions. *Action in Teacher Education, 18,* 73–85.

Kemmis, S., & McTaggart, R. (1982). *The action research planner.* Victoria, Australia: Deakin University Press.

Kolb, D. A. (1981). Learning styles and disciplinary differences. In A. W. Chickering & Associates (Eds.), *The modern American college.* San Francisco: Jossey-Bass.

Krol, C. A. (1996). *Preservice teacher education students' dialogue journals: What characterizes students' reflective writing and a teacher's comments.* Paper presented at the meeting of the Association of Teacher Educators, St. Louis, MO. (ERIC Document Reproduction Services ED 395 911).

Liston, D. P., & Zeichner, K. M. (1987). Reflective teacher education and moral deliberation. *Journal of Teacher Education, 38*(6), 2–8.

Loughran, J., & Corrigan, D. (1995). Teaching portfolios: A strategy for developing learning and teaching in pre-service teacher education. *Teacher and Teacher Education, 1,* 565–577.

Martin, D. (1984). Infusing cognitive strategies into teacher preparation programs. *Educational Leadership, 42*(3), 68–72.

McKay, J. A. (1992). Professional development through action research. *Journal of Staff Development, 13*(1), 18–21.

Peters, J. L. (1980). The effects of laboratory teaching experience (Microteaching and Reflective Teaching) in an introductory teacher education course on students' views of themselves as teachers and their perceptions of teaching. Doctoral dissertation, The Ohio State University, Columbus.

Pultorak, E. G. (1996). Following the development process of reflection in novice teachers: Three years of investigation. *Journal of Teacher Education, 47,* 283–291.

Richert, A. (1990). Teaching teachers to reflect: A consideration of programme structure. *Journal of Curriculum Studies, 22,* 509–527.

Ross, D. D. (1987). Reflective teaching: Meaning and implications for preservice teacher educators. Paper presented at the Reflective Inquiry Conference, Houston.

Schön, D. A. (1983). *The reflective practitioner: How professionals think in action.* San Francisco: Jossey-Bass.

Schön, D. A. (1987). *Educating the reflective practitioner.* San Francisco: Jossey-Bass.

Smyth, J. (1989). Developing and sustaining critical reflection in teacher education. *Journal of Teacher Education, 40*(2), 2–9.

Tremmel, R. (1993). Zen and the art of reflective practice in teacher education. *Harvard Education Review, 63,* 434–458.

Troyer, M. B. (1988). The effects of reflective teaching and a supplemental theoretical component on preservice teachers' reflectivity in analyzing classroom teaching situations. Doctoral dissertation, The Ohio State University, Columbus.

Valverde, L. (1982). The self-evolving supervisor. In R. Sergiovanni (Ed.), *Supervision of teaching* (pp. 81–89). Alexandria, VA: Association for Supervision and Curriculum Development.

Wallace, J. (1996). Words, words, words . . . *Science and Children, 33*(5), 16–19.

Wellington, B. (1991). The promise of reflective practice. *Educational Leadership, 48*(6), 4–5.

Wilson, S. M., Shulman, L. S., & Richert, A. E. (1987). 150 different ways of knowing: Representations of knowledge in teaching. In J. Calderhead, (Ed.), *Exploring teachers' thinking* (pp. 104–124). London: Cassell.

Wolf, K., Whinery, B., & Hagerty, P. (1995). Teaching portfolios and portfolio conversations for teacher educators and teachers. *Action in Teacher Education, 17*(1), 30–39.

Zubizarreta, J. (1994). Teaching portfolios and the beginning teachers. *Phi Delta Kappan, 76,* 323–326.

The Effective Teacher

PART THREE

The role of the classroom teacher is critical. The teacher is, after all, the point of contact between the educational system and the pupil: the impact of any educational program or innovation on the pupil operates through the pupil's teachers. Thus, maximizing teacher effectiveness is a major goal of education (Medley, 1986, p. 4).

Most people enter teaching because they want to make a difference in the lives of young people. They are concerned about the emotional and social welfare of the child, with developing children's ability to think carefully and to make decisions, and about helping their students gain an understanding of topics and subjects that are important.

In fact, Cruickshank and Haefele (2001) have described at least ten kinds of good teachers (see Table P3–1). Every teacher draws upon each of these areas, though we are all better in some than in others. As you progress in your teaching career you will develop qualities across the ten kinds of good teaching. However, while all teachers make some difference in their students' lives, some teachers consistently have a greater and more positive influence than others. They seem to relate to students better and to be more successful in helping their students gain meaningfully from their instruction.

In *The Act of Teaching*, we have chosen to focus our attention on what Cruickshank calls the *effective teacher*. What exactly is an "effective" teacher? What makes one teacher more effective than another, and what can be done to improve effectiveness? The next four chapters are devoted to answering these questions. In Chapter 10, Effective Teachers: Personal Attributes and Characteristics, we describe research on teaching and then examine the personal attributes or characteristics associated with effective teachers. In Chapter 11, Effective Teachers: Professional

TABLE P3–1 Good Teachers, Plural

Ideal teachers meet subjective standards set by school principals, supervisors, and education professors.

Analytic teachers use observation techniques (e.g., Flanders Interaction Analysis) to record the extent to which they are meeting their instructional intentions.

Effective teachers bring about higher student achievement.

Dutiful teachers perform their assigned teaching duties well.

Competent teachers pass tests (e.g., NBPTS, Praxis) that indicate they possess requisite teacher attributes.

Expert teachers have extensive and accessible professional knowledge and can do more in less time.

Reflective teachers examine the art and science of teaching to become more thoughtful and skillful practitioners.

Satisfying teachers please students, parents-caregivers, colleagues, and/or supervisors.

Diversity-responsive teachers are sensitive to the needs of learners who are different.

Respected teachers possess and demonstrate qualities regarded as virtues.

Skills and Abilities, we focus on the professional skills effective teachers use to maximize their students' learning. In Chapter 12, How the Effective Teacher Manages the Classroom, we discuss the organizational and managerial strategies effective teachers use to maintain a positive learning environment. Finally, Chapter 13, The Teacher as a Problem Solver, explains how effective teachers solve classroom problems.

Effective Teachers: Personal Attributes and Characteristics

Contents

In this chapter we examine the personal attributes or characteristics of teachers whose instruction seems most successful. Our emphasis is on an examination of those personal attributes of a teacher that seem most closely connected to students' learning. Before discussing specific personal attributes, we will examine how researchers have studied effective teachers and defined effective teaching. Then, we will look at eight attributes characteristic of effective teachers; they are

1. Enthusiastic.
2. Warm and humorous.
3. Credible.
4. Holding high expectations for success.
5. Encouraging and supportive.
6. Businesslike.
7. Adaptable/flexible.
8. Knowledgeable.

Research on Teaching

To understand the importance of teachers' characteristics and the behaviors associated with effective teaching, it will be helpful if we first determine what the term *effective teaching* means and how effective teachers can be identified.

DEFINING EFFECTIVE TEACHING

There are many ways to define effective teaching. Most people would agree that good teachers are caring, supportive, concerned about the welfare of students, knowledgeable about their subject matter, able to get along with parents, administrators, and colleagues, and genuinely excited about the work that they do (Raspberry, 1993). Certainly, these characteristics are valuable. But they overlook an important aspect of effective teaching—the fact that effective teachers are able to help students learn.

For over a century, educational researchers have attempted to identify effective teachers. Early research defined effective teachers as those who received high ratings from their superiors. This research attempted to link administrative ratings with such traits as teachers' buoyancy, cooperativeness, dependability, emotional stability, expressiveness, forcefulness, judgment, mental alertness, personal magnetism, physical drive, and ethical behavior.

Although this type of research continued until the mid-1960s, the results were discouraging. None of these personality traits were consistently tied to the rating

11.1 Why do you think each of us has unique ideas about what good teaching is? What clues does Chapter 7, on instructional alternatives, offer?

levels teachers received. Many scholars concluded at that point that little could be determined about what made teachers effective.

Fortunately, several events occurred during the 1960s that prompted valuable and productive research into the definition and nature of effective teaching. Among the most powerful catalysts for more productive research was the *Equality of Educational Opportunity* study (Coleman, Campbell, Wood, Weinfeld, & York, 1966). This study was commissioned by the United States Department of Health, Education, and Welfare to examine the differences between schooling opportunities and resultant learning outcomes for white and black children.

Coleman, the major investigator, and his colleagues found that students attending some schools did indeed achieve more than students attending others. However, when he investigated why this was true, he found that differences in pupils' achievement among schools was associated largely with one factor—the socioeconomic status (SES) of the pupils and community the school was located in. What was even more surprising and disappointing to many educators was Coleman's finding that the usual factors thought to contribute to school achievement, such as class size, textbook quality, the school facility, and teachers' experience, had little impact on student learning.

Reanalysis of Coleman's findings and numerous studies since (e.g., Walberg and Fowler, 1987; Chall, 2000) continue to suggest that SES overshadows all other variables in its relationship to students' achievement. Perhaps as much as 75 percent of a student's success in school seems to be a result of that student's socioeconomic, family, and cultural background—factors teachers have little or no control over. This finding is increasingly important in light of the current demographic trends noted in Chapters 2 and 3, such as reduced parental involvement and more children living in poverty. However, Coleman and others did find a few school, teacher, and pupil characteristics that also contributed to differences in students' learning. These factors included the qualities of the teacher and the educational aspirations or motivation of the students.

Needless to say, educators were extremely disturbed by the news that most of students' school achievement was determined by their SES rather than the school they attended or the teachers they experienced. These reports prompted renewed interest in defining and describing effective teaching. Many educators reasoned that since schools and teachers seemed to have limited influence, it was important to learn how to make the most of that influence. Thus, educational researchers sought to identify the characteristics of teachers and schools that seemed to be making the most difference for their students. Thus was born a second and highly productive era of research on effective teaching. In this second era of research, researchers identified effective teachers not according to supervisor ratings but according to their ability to help students gain the most from instruction.

THE SEARCH FOR EFFECTIVE TEACHERS

11.2 How would you feel if you were told that you would be hired, fired, promoted, or receive salary increases based on your students' performance on a standardized test? Would it change your approach to teaching? If so, how?

Shortly after publication of the Coleman report, educators began to investigate teachers' behaviors and attributes that seemed linked to greater learning. Guided by the notion that students' learning was, in part, the result of these attributes and behaviors, educational investigators began identifying teachers who were consistently able to produce high levels of learning. Often, though not always, the researchers measured learning by performance on standardized achievement tests. Then the investigators observed these teachers to determine whether they possessed common characteristics or teaching behaviors that might explain their students' success. Thus, in this era, research considered a teacher who produced more learning than others teaching similar students to be an effective teacher.

Over the past four decades, educational research has identified a number of teacher behaviors and attributes associated with greater learning. These behaviors also seem linked to other desirable outcomes for students, such as increased satisfaction and better attitudes toward school, better self-concept, and higher graduation rates (Needels & Gage, 1991; Wenglinski, 2000). One of the most exciting things about these findings is that they describe real teachers in real classrooms with real pupils. They are not just theory; they are what living, breathing teachers do. By being aware of what these effective teachers are like and aware of what they do, you can learn to incorporate these characteristics and behaviors into your own teaching.

Effective Teachers: Personal Attributes and Characteristics

Although *teachers' personal attributes* are expressed through behavior, they are primarily inherent personality traits that all teachers possess and exhibit to varying degrees. For example, some teachers naturally display greater enthusiasm than others through their speech and actions. This may be the result of greater enthusiasm for their work or simply differences in personality that limit or enhance their ability to express enthusiasm. Some personal attributes, like enthusiasm or warmth, are difficult to acquire or to enhance because they are so firmly rooted in our personalities. Others, such as professional, businesslike demeanor, are somewhat easier to acquire and modify. By becoming more aware of personal attributes that research shows are common among successful teachers and by matching them against your own natural tendencies, you will be able to begin building your own unique teaching persona—one that will maximize your ability to make positive connections with your students.

The remainder of this chapter will deal with eight personal attributes identified by research as common among effective teachers. To guide our discussion, we have organized these attributes under three broad headings: motivating personality, orientation toward success, and professional demeanor. *Motivating personality* includes the attributes enthusiasm, variety, and warmth and humor. These attributes help get and keep students involved and interested in learning. *Orientation toward success* means teachers believe in their own and their students' abilities to be successful. Attributes like expecting success and being encouraging and supportive of students convey this orientation. *Professional demeanor* means that the teacher is focused on helping students learn. Effective teachers are professionally knowledgeable and businesslike; students see them as credible and worthy of trust. As you will see, these three groups of attributes are highly interrelated. For example, being prepared for class conveys confidence, builds credibility, makes the atmosphere of the classroom more businesslike, and enables teachers to more easily adapt their instruction to students' needs.

The following pages will examine these attributes in some depth. First, we will present a definition or description of each, followed by an examination of the research that supports its importance. Finally, we will discuss the specific behaviors that characterize each attribute. As you read these sections, remember that these attributes have been linked to increased student learning. Consider the extent to which you naturally possess and demonstrate each one, and ways in which you might employ them more effectively with your students.

Motivating Personality

Effective teachers possess a motivating, stimulating personality. They seem to enjoy what they are doing, they are supportive of students, and they are believable and easy to trust (Peart & Campbell, 1999; Young, Whitley, & Helton, 1993). In this section, we discuss three particular attributes that are characteristic of teachers with motivating personalities: enthusiasm, warmth and humor, and credibility.

ENTHUSIASM

One of the teacher attributes most closely linked to desirable student outcomes is enthusiasm. Enthusiastic teachers convey to students that they are confident and enjoy what they are doing, that they trust and respect students, and that the subject they teach is valuable and enjoyable (Carusso, 1982; Ellis, 2001). Enthusiastic teaching helps students persist at tasks, motivates them, and leads to increased learning and satisfaction (Denight & Gall, 1989; Gallagher, 1994; Patrick, Hisley, & Kempler, 2000; Wang, Haertel, & Walberg, 1993).

Although enthusiasm is difficult to define, Good and Brophy (2000) suggest that a teacher's enthusiasm has two important dimensions: interest and involvement with the subject matter, and vigor and physical dynamism. Enthusiastic teachers often are described as dynamic, stimulating, energetic, and expressive. Their behavior suggests they are committed to students and to their subject.

People convey enthusiasm through variety in speech, gestures, and facial expressions. As they teach, enthusiastic teachers move around the room, front to back as well as side to side. They are animated and gesture with their hands, arms, head, and shoulders to reinforce or emphasize their points. They maintain eye contact with all students, encourage all students to participate, and solicit and use input from all students. Enthusiastic teachers maintain a brisk lesson pace while allowing and adjusting for students' understanding. They promote interest by varying the speed, pitch, and inflection of their voices, and they use pauses to reinforce points and add variety. Their changes in facial expression (for example, eyes widening or narrowing, smiling or frowning) are frequent and positive and further reinforce what they say.

Maintaining such a dramatic, animated presence from 8:15 A.M. until 3:00 P.M. is a difficult, perhaps impossible task. Fortunately, constant enthusiasm is not necessary. In fact, like other factors, levels of animation are most effective when they vary. A teacher who never ceased moving, always using broad gestures and smiling, would soon become routine or even annoying. Nonetheless, remember Denight and Gall's (1989) advice: While teachers often expect students to be interested in *what* they say, students more often react to *how enthusiastically* it is said.

Remember, you are only enthusiastic if your students perceive you to be. In other words, just feeling enthusiastic about your students and your subject does not ensure that your students will see you as enthusiastic. What behaviors do students perceive as teachers' enthusiasm? Table 11.1 presents teacher behaviors that students use to differentiate between enthusiastic and unenthusiastic teachers. Note that none of these behaviors alone conveys enthusiasm. Rather, they collectively lead students to perceive the teacher as enthusiastic.

WARMTH AND HUMOR

Whether you realize it or not, as the adult authority in the classroom, you will set the tone, define roles, establish parameters, and promote patterns of interpersonal relationship among your students. Teacher warmth and humor are important factors in promoting a supportive, relaxed, satisfying, and educationally productive environment for your students (Brown, Tomlin, & Fortson, 1996; McDermott & Rothenberg, 2000; Soar & Soar, 1979). By contributing to a safe and productive environment, warmth and humor indirectly promote learning. In Chapter 13 we will also see that a supportive classroom climate reduces students' misbehavior.

While most people watching various teachers could probably agree on whether they conveyed warmth and humor, it is difficult to explain precisely what constitutes warm behavior or a good sense of humor. However, the two attributes are related.

Warmth   A teacher manifests warmth through positive, supportive interpersonal relationships with students (Goleman, 1998; Peart & Campbell, 1999). It is important that you allow students to get a sense of your personality. Students often say that

11.3   Do you think it would be better to feel enthusiastic but be unable to convey it to students, or to lack enthusiasm but be able to act enthusiastic? Why?

11.4   Are you an enthusiastic person? Do you easily convey enthusiasm? How is your enthusiasm conveyed?

11.5   Is there something you may have to teach that you feel unenthusiastic about? How will you deal with it?

Try Activity 11.1

TABLE 11.1 Teachers' Enthusiasm

Enthusiastic Teachers . . .	Unenthusiastic Teachers . . .
• Appear confident and friendly	• Appear anxious or defensive
• Establish and convey the relevance of the subject to their students	• Are mechanistic, go through the motions without relating the lesson to the students' interests or needs
• Use broad, animated gestures to emphasize or reinforce points	• Often stand or sit in one spot throughout the lesson
• Are creative and varied in their instructional approach	• Use only one or two instructional alternatives
• Are engaged and dramatic when they teach	• Are disinterested and disengaged
• Maintain eye contact with all students	• Avoid eye contact with students
• Use varied pitch, volume, inflection, and pauses to make vocal delivery more interesting	• Speak in a monotone
• Are patient	• Are impatient
• Are insistent that students successfully complete tasks	• Give up quickly when students do not easily arrive at the correct response
• Are aware of and quickly deal with off-task behavior	• Ignore students' off-task behavior
• Maintain a quick lesson pace	• Use time inefficiently; stall
• Have a sense of humor; can laugh at themselves	• Are frequently critical
• Use movement to maintain interest and attention	• Seldom move from the front of the room

Source: Adapted from V. Carusso. (1982). Teacher enthusiasm: Behaviors reported by teachers and students. Paper presented at the annual meeting of the American Educational Research Association, New York.

good teachers "are real people." Positive classroom relationships are fostered when you are friendly, maintain a positive attitude, demonstrate interest in your students as individuals, appear to be open and willing to "work things out" with students, and work hard to help them succeed academically. On the other hand, you reduce warmth and injure classroom relationships when students perceive you as unfair, when you are overly judgmental or inflexible, or when you discourage student-teacher interactions.

Specifically, then, what can you do to convey warmth to your students? Many of the teacher behaviors that convey enthusiasm also convey warmth. Figure 11.1 lists suggestions to help you promote a sense of warmth with your students.

FIGURE 11.1 Conveying Warmth

1. Greet students by name at the door. Comment on their personal achievements outside your classroom or other aspects of their personal lives.

2. Smile frequently.

3. Be yourself. Convey your personality, likes, dislikes, even opinions.

4. Use nonthreatening physical proximity to students. Moving closer to students can be used to convey a sense of trust and openness.

5. Encourage students to approach you and to be open with you. Keep most in-class interactions on academic topics, but express interest and willingness to talk with students about nonacademic concerns outside of class.

6. Draw out students' opinions, feelings, and ideas, and actively incorporate these into your instruction.

7. Provide remediation and time for all students to master the material and to be successful.

8. While conveying genuine interest, concern, and acceptance of all students, avoid becoming "one of the students" by lowering expectations or joining them socially. This is especially true for new teachers who may be close in age to their students.

Humor   An appropriate sense of humor is one of the characteristics students frequently note in the teachers they enjoy (McDermott & Rothenberg, 2000). These teachers make learning fun. Humor can defuse tension, communicate the teacher's security and confidence, promote trust, and reduce discipline problems.

Effective use of humor has both a spontaneous and a deliberate, or planned, dimension. We convey a sense of humor through our ability to laugh when something funny occurs. During the course of a typical school day, any number of humorous events or accidents occur. Don't be afraid to laugh at these things. You must especially learn to laugh at yourself. All teachers make mistakes. They trip over the cord to the computer and drop stacks of papers as they rush to hand them back. Laugh at these events! Keep them in perspective, and don't take yourself too seriously. On the other hand, avoid sarcasm or cynicism, and be extremely careful about teasing students. Sarcasm and cynicism often send a message of indifference, disinterest, or dislike. And, although some students may respond positively to teasing by the teacher, many may respond negatively by assuming the role of "class clown" or, perhaps more serious, by feeling hurt or embarrassed. Be yourself, be a real person, but remain aware that you set an example for acceptable classroom behavior that students will tend to follow.

While much classroom humor is spontaneous, effective use of humor in the classroom also has a deliberate dimension. Plan lessons that incorporate or point out amusing aspects of the topic. This should go beyond using cartoons and jokes to more substantive aspects of the lesson. For example, a middle school English teacher might use humor to initiate a unit on Edgar Allen Poe's work by humorously drawing attention to his eccentric life and work. The teacher could appear in dark, drab clothes like those Poe might have worn, perhaps with a black plastic bird (a raven) on his shoulder. He could play the role of Poe, exaggerating demented or paranoid speech and mannerisms, to introduce Poe's work in the context of his life. The teacher might talk as Poe would have about the difficulties of his life and writing, introducing the works to be studied in class. The intentional, structured combination of humor and content would make the lesson more memorable and the teaching more effective.

Warmth and humor are means to desirable ends, not ends in themselves. Used in moderation, they help create a relaxed, comfortable environment in which students can learn. However, teachers who place too much emphasis on warmth and humor actually reduce learning (Chall, 2000). Thus, warmth and humor are best used naturally and sparingly.

"If I smile for the yearbook picture, no one will recognize me."

CREDIBILITY

Effective teachers appear to students to be credible and worthy of trust (Thweatt & McCroskey, 1998). Once again, it is important to point out that your credibility exists in the eyes of the beholders, your students. Regardless of a teacher's knowledge, experience, education level, or position—all elements that might be expected to ensure your credibility—you are credible only when your students believe you are. In the early grades, teachers, as adult authority figures, have some degree of built-in believability with students. However, as students become more mature, they are less likely to assume that teachers are automatically credible. As university students, you continually make judgments about the credibility and trustworthiness of your instructors. These judgments determine, at least in part, the perceived effectiveness of each instructor.

What can you do to establish yourself as credible and trustworthy? Three elements seem important: your credentials, the messages you send to students, and your behavior (Beatty & Zahn, 1990; Frymier & Thompson, 1992; Thweatt & McCroskey, 1998). Your credentials are most likely to influence the perceptions of young students who are relatively knowledgeable about the subject or who are highly motivated to succeed. However, even under these conditions, your credentials are only helpful if students are aware of them. The content of the messages you deliver also impacts your credibility. When you are able to demonstrate to students how the topics you present are related to their interests and needs, they view you as more credible. Most important, however, is your behavior. Credibility and trust are the result of being open, honest, and equitable in your dealings with students, and of openly soliciting and accepting students' comments or criticisms, of defining your expectations and the relevance of the subject, of communicating clearly, and of demonstrating interest and concern for your students' success. As you can see, credibility and trust must be earned.

11.7 What factors do you use to determine the credibility of your teachers?

11.8 Have you ever had a teacher who betrayed your trust? What happened? How did it make you feel toward the teacher?

Orientation Toward Success

Effective teachers are positive people. They generally believe in their students' abilities to learn and in their own ability to help students be successful. Importantly, they seem able to communicate a positive attitude and to develop this in their students. Specifically, effective teachers have high expectations of success and are encouraging and supportive of students.

HIGH EXPECTATIONS FOR SUCCESS

Effective teachers hold high expectations of success for themselves and their students. They genuinely believe all students can master the content and that they themselves have the ability to help all students learn. It would appear that teachers' expectations *cause* differences in learning. Research indicates that when teachers' expectations of students rise, students learn more (Gill & Reynolds, 1999; Saracho, 1991).

It is unclear exactly how teachers' expectations contribute to learning. However, research suggests that the expectations teachers have for both themselves and their students affect teachers' behavior, which in turn affects students' learning (Coleman, 1998; Kolb & Jossim, 1994). For example, if you believe that Joanna is incapable of learning certain material, you are likely to spend less time working with her, focusing instead on other students you believe are more likely to benefit from your help. Thus, Joanna receives less academic guidance and is more likely to fail.

Students are quite adept at sensing cues that subtly communicate your expectations for them. If you hold low expectations for a particular student, not only that student but other students are likely to sense this and to adapt their perceptions and expectations accordingly. In short, students are constantly monitoring teachers' behavior and are likely to sense the attitudes and expectations behind that behavior. As a result, a student is likely to pick up and internalize any teacher behavior that signals low expectations for that particular student and to lower his or her self-expectations (Gill & Reynolds, 1999; Walberg, 1991). This, of course, increases the likelihood that the student *will not* learn the material.

Most students enter school confident and expecting to be successful, but they quickly learn to adapt their self-perceptions to the expectations of the teacher (Raspberry, 1993; Kaufman & Aloma, 1997). Brophy (1982) and others have found that the students most susceptible to the positive and negative effects of teachers' expectations are young, low achievers, students in transition (from elementary to middle school, for example), or students particularly fond of the teacher. Thus, unfortunately, some of the very students who most need their teacher's help and support are those for whom many teachers normally hold low expectations (Brophy, 1982).

Discussions of teachers' expectations and students' success often focus on the idea of **self-fulfilling prophecy**—that you get what you expect. Cooper and Tom (1984) and Kolb & Jussim (1994) indicate that self-fulfilling prophecy is only one of two ways in which teachers' expectations affect learning and that it is, at most, a minor contributor.

More important are what Cooper and Tom call **sustained expectations.** Initial teachers' expectations may be more or less accurate and thus affect teachers' initial behavior and students' learning. However, expectations can and should be continually modified to more accurately reflect students' ability. The tendency some teachers have to stubbornly refuse to adjust their initially inaccurate (normally low) expectations of certain students can seriously impede learning. Whereas the effects of initial expectations are limited, sustained expectations have a cumulative effect. That is, they continually and repeatedly influence unsuccessful student performance over extended periods of time. The result is a vicious downward spiral— teachers expect certain students to fail, those students fail, the teachers lower their expectations still further, the students again fail, and so on.

You should try to convey to your students that you expect them to be successful and that you will help them be so. You should set realistic goals, convey them clearly, and work to provide each student the opportunity to succeed. A good rule of thumb is to ensure that every student is successful most of the time. This is particularly true for students who are not academically oriented or whose academic self-concept is low (Gill & Reynolds, 1999; Obiakor, 1999). For students who find school difficult and who may not believe they can be successful, you should attempt to structure assignments and activities they can complete successfully 80 to 95 percent of the time. This helps build students' confidence in their own abilities, and motivates them to try other, more difficult academic tasks. Even academically oriented students who may be confident of their abilities need to be successful most of the time. A success rate of 70 to 85 percent seems to lead to improved motivation and learning for these students.

Thus far we have discussed students' success in terms of only two types of students—successful and unsuccessful—each needing a specific level of success. You may have noted that academic confidence and optimal levels of success are inversely related. That is, as students' confidence and ability increase, the need for very high levels of success diminishes. To put it another way, less academically able or less confident students need to experience success more often. However, as the unsuccessful student becomes more academically competent and confident, you should structure tasks that take this into consideration. To keep the student challenged and motivated you should gradually make assignments more difficult so that the student is still successful most of the time, but not as often.

You must also be careful to avoid prejudging students or failing to adapt your expectations when necessary. All students have more ability in some areas than in

11.9   In what ways did your teachers convey their expectations for you? How did it make you feel? How did it affect your learning?

"Ms. Krenshaw, please send in someone who laughed at me in high school."

others, even within the same subject. In classes where they feel confident of their ability, students are likely to participate actively and freely. An effective teacher will tune in to a student's strengths and weaknesses and provide opportunities for more success in problem areas and somewhat less success in areas the student is already proficient in. Effective teaching requires the teacher to constantly match students' ability levels with task difficulty.

Teachers also convey high expectations for success when they provide *remediation* for students who fail to master material the first time. Your instructional plans should include time for remediation using a variety of alternative instructional sources and materials (old textbooks, magazines, videotapes, computer programs, and so on). You should also be sure to give these students the attention they need in order to succeed. This attention should include both your own time and opportunities for group work and peer tutoring. When you devote time to helping students understand the material, you convey a positive message both about your expectations and about the importance of the material.

When most teachers think about expectations for success, they generally think of teachers' expectations for students. However, the most effective teachers also maintain high expectations for themselves as well. Their own high personal standards motivate them to be well-prepared for class, use class time efficiently, and provide substantive feedback to students. They exhibit thorough knowledge of their subject, convey confidence and calm, dress, act, and speak professionally, and work to correct deficiencies in their own professional ability.

Try Activity 11.2

As we have discussed, you will most often convey your expectations indirectly, through your actions rather than your words. How, then, can you convey high expectations to students? Table 11.2 contrasts the behaviors of teachers who hold high expectations of students with those of teachers who hold low expectations.

ENCOURAGING AND SUPPORTIVE

Effective teachers are encouraging and supportive of students, addressing students' needs to belong, to be liked, and to be successful (Wang, Haertel, & Walberg, 1993). Ornstein and Lasley (2000) define teachers who are encouraging as those who respect and genuinely believe in students' abilities. They help students feel accepted as individuals, and they recognize effort and potential, not merely correct answers. Thus, encouragement relates to other important attributes like warmth, enthusiasm, and expectations for success. Through encouragement and support, you can help students meet your expectations for success even when they experience some difficulty along the way.

11.10 Do you believe you can help *all* students learn? Explain.

TABLE 11.2 Teachers' Behaviors That Convey High or Low Expectations of Students and Themselves

Teachers with High Expectations . . .	Teachers with Low Expectations . . .
• Clearly inform students of the lesson objectives	• Do not convey the objectives or convey unclear objectives
• Provide extended, organized, well-paced explanations	• Provide explanations that are incomplete and often unclear
• Clearly relate lesson content to student interests	• Make few attempts to relate lesson content to student interests
• Set reasonable standards and modify them frequently	• Set standards that are too high or low and are too rigid
• Plan for and provide remediation when necessary	• Do not provide remediation
• Maintain consistent discipline and task direction	• Do not maintain consistent discipline or task direction
• Solicit and incorporate input from students they instruct	• Discourage or ignore student input
• Frequently smile, nod, and maintain eye contact	• Convey less attention in academic situations
• Call upon all students frequently and equitably to respond	• Seldom and inequitably call on students to respond
• Use wait time to allow students to consider before responding	• Allow students little or no wait time as they attempt to respond
• Help students modify incorrect or inadequate responses	• Frequently provide praise for incorrect or inadequate responses
• Use criticism infrequently	• Frequently criticize students' performance
• Provide extensive, frequent, and specific feedback	• Provide infrequent and vague feedback
• Seldom interrupt students while they are working	• Often interrupt students while they are working

Encouragement is particularly important when students are most likely to experience reluctance and difficulty. This occurs in the early stages of learning a new task or concept, in low-achieving students, and for minority and female students (Campbell, 1986; O'Halloran, 1995). Encouragement can motivate students to attempt tasks they may be reluctant to start and to continue working when they are struggling or becoming frustrated.

How can you encourage students without being condescending? First, a classroom environment that is supportive, safe, and open will promote students' willingness to begin new or unfamiliar tasks. Students must feel that the tasks you assign are realistic and important, that you will help them succeed, and that they can approach you for assistance if needed. Figure 11.2 lists some ways to demonstrate your encouragement and support.

FIGURE 11.2 How to Demonstrate Encouragement and Support for Your Students

1. Use positive comments about students' abilities rather than negative comments about their performance.
2. Be aware of and note improvement, not just perfection.
3. Help students learn to work through their own problems and evaluate their own work.
4. Be optimistic, positive, and cheerful.
5. Demonstrate good, active listening when students are speaking (focus your attention on the student, nod, and so on).
6. Provide several alternative routes to task completion and allow students some degree of choice.

When students have begun a task but are becoming frustrated and are ready to give up, it is important to help them continue. Words of encouragement such as, "You can do it," "What you've done so far is good. What *could* we do next?" "I understand how frustrating this is, but I know that you can do it," "Let's try the next step together," "Don't give up, you're getting there," or "I *know* you can do it" indicate to students that you are aware of and sympathetic to their struggles but that you are confident they can work through the task successfully. It is important in this situation that you help the students accurately complete the next step in the process with as little direction as possible. Ask questions or point out factors that help the students discover what they need to do next rather than simply give the students the right answer. By helping students work through problems mostly on their own, you build their confidence.

11.11 Do you believe *all* students can be academically successful in your classroom? Why or why not?

Professional Demeanor

Attributes under this heading may be the easiest for you to modify. Effective teachers, while being motivating and positive, also establish and maintain a professional demeanor. They are businesslike and task-oriented, yet flexible and adaptable when necessary to help students be successful. They are knowledgeable not just of the subjects they teach, but also of **pedagogy** and students.

Businesslike

A common characteristic of effective teachers is a task-oriented, businesslike classroom demeanor (Cruickshank, 1990; McDermott & Rothenberg, 2000). When you first hear effective teachers described in this way, you may imagine a cold-hearted, unsmiling taskmaster who uses an "iron hand" to force students to do nothing but work seriously on boring, quiet tasks. However, this is not the case at all. In fact, students often perceive businesslike teachers to exhibit greater warmth and concern than other teachers (Chall, 2000; Hoffman, 2001).

The business of the classroom is learning. A businesslike teacher is one who emphasizes and focuses classroom activities on tasks most likely to help students learn. He directs his own behavior and his students' behavior toward the successful and efficient attainment of meaningful, clearly defined learning outcomes. If the teacher does this, learning is likely to improve and the teacher can be considered successful—that is, effective. If the teacher spends too much energy and time on tasks or activities not likely to improve students' learning, the teacher will be unsuccessful.

An analogy may help demonstrate this idea. Imagine for a moment a young boy who has suffered life-threatening injuries in a serious automobile accident. His family accompanies him to the hospital. The physician meets the patient and his distraught family at the emergency room door. She acknowledges the family and immediately begins to determine the nature of the boy's condition. The family is directed to wait in the emergency room lobby, feeling anxious and alone. When the little boy's condition is stabilized, the physician briefly speaks to the child's family. She then instructs a nurse to stay with the family for a few minutes, excuses herself, and immediately begins treating another emergency admission. The physician's behavior toward the family seems somewhat cold, but she has saved the little boy's life.

Now let us assume for a moment that rather than beginning immediately to treat the young boy, the doctor, feeling tremendous sympathy for his family, spends several minutes consoling them. The physician instructs an aide to prepare the little boy for treatment while she remains to talk with the boy's family, build rapport with them, and console them. After several minutes they feel somewhat better, and the physician leaves them to attend to the child. Unfortunately, during this time the little boy's condition has worsened. Although we might consider the physician a caring person, we would probably not consider her an effective physician.

Exaggerated though the analogy may be, it makes the point that the effective physician is the one who most effectively conducts the "business" of medicine. The best doctor would save lives *and* exhibit warmth and caring. However, we would expect a physician to focus on the primary business of the profession. Thus, sympathy and caring are important but not sufficient for effective doctoring . . . *or* for effective teaching.

There appear to be four aspects of businesslike teacher behavior. A businesslike teacher is goal-oriented, serious, deliberate, and organized.

GOAL-ORIENTED

Businesslike teachers focus their efforts on helping students achieve learning goals. In the chapter on planning instruction, we discussed the importance of establishing the desired outcomes of instruction and of basing our instruction on these objectives. Businesslike teachers establish clear, realistic, specific objectives and communicate these to students. They plan and conduct instruction in ways that efficiently and systematically move students toward the objectives. They actively seek input from students about the reasonableness of the objectives and about problems the students may be having, and they use this information to modify their instruction when necessary. They optimize activities and time devoted directly to helping students reach the established goals and minimize approaches, comments, questions, or behaviors that are not directed toward the goals.

SERIOUS

Businesslike teachers value learning and model this to students through their words and actions. This does not mean that they do not use humor, but their humor is natural and without cynicism or sarcasm. These teachers convey seriousness of purpose through earnest and genuine expressions indicating the value of the tasks at hand, reasonable expectations, guidance in task execution, and efficient use of time. The teacher treats the subject seriously, maintains a professional and confident image, and uses appropriate verbal and nonverbal behaviors.

DELIBERATE

Also important is a businesslike teacher's ability to establish and maintain a sense of purpose throughout each lesson. Careful planning of instruction allows such teachers to be concise, thorough, and exact in conducting instruction. Businesslike teachers organize instructional activities or tasks in a logical sequence including a clear introduction, presentation, and closure. This type of teacher deliberately conducts instruction in ways that devote equal attention to all students.

Although deliberateness requires systematic planning and implementation of instruction directed toward specific goals, it does not mean that the teacher is inflexible. When the teacher becomes aware that students do not understand or that the planned instructional activities are not working effectively, they adapt the activities. Teachers must adapt as quickly as possible, but not without careful consideration of the learning objectives. In other words, they might ask why the planned activity is not helping students reach the goals, what alternative activities might help, and which alternative can immediately be implemented? Even when teachers deviate from planned instruction, they should remain focused on the original learning goals.

ORGANIZED

Businesslike teachers organize the classroom and instruction based upon the established goals. Furniture, resources, materials, equipment, and activities are organized

TABLE 11.3 Teachers' Businesslike and Nonbusinesslike Behavior

Businesslike Teachers . . .	Nonbusinesslike Teachers . . .
• Establish clear academic goals and objectives	• Fail to establish academic learning goals
• Communicate the goals and objectives to students	• Do not communicate the goals and objectives to students
• Plan lessons directed at helping students reach the objectives	• Do not plan sufficiently or direct instruction toward objectives
• Seek input from students about the reasonableness of goals	• Disregard or fail to solicit students' input about the reasonableness of goals
• Emphasize activities and time devoted to academics	• Emphasize nonacademic activities and use time inefficiently
• Treat the subject seriously and respectfully	• Are sarcastic or make light of the subject
• Maintain a professional image	• Seem to be "one of the kids"
• Involve all students in the instructional activities	• Neglect some students while focusing mainly on good students
• Organize the room and equipment to minimize disruptions	• Fail to carefully organize the physical setting
• Use aides or volunteers to provide additional academic attention for students	• Use aides or volunteers primarily to deal with administrative tasks

to minimize disruptions. Teachers use available personnel, such as aides or parent volunteers, to promote desirable learning outcomes rather than to reduce their workload. Even classroom management and discipline procedures are intended to promote the established goals.

Generally, then, a businesslike teacher is openly focused upon the business of promoting students' learning. Guided by clearly established goals and objectives, the teacher plans for, implements, and adapts whatever instruction will most efficiently help students reach learning objectives. Although many distractions may arise, the teacher minimizes activities or time not directed toward reaching the objectives. Remember that this businesslike focus can be maintained without sacrificing genuine warmth and caring for students. Table 11.3 contrasts the behaviors of teachers who are businesslike with those of teachers who are not.

Adaptable/Flexible

A supervising teacher once told her student teacher, "No matter what you plan for, something else will happen." Teaching may not be quite that unpredictable, but certainly the most effective teachers are prepared for and able to adapt to a variety of circumstances (McDermott & Rothenberg, 2000; Walberg, 1990). As you have probably noticed from your years of experience as a student, an effective teacher must be flexible and adaptable.

In the next chapter, we will discuss the importance of systematically building variety into your instruction and instructional activities. However, for now, let us focus on the ability to react appropriately and relatively quickly to changing classroom circumstances.

Flexibility and adaptability in this sense requires that you be *aware* of the need for change and be *able* to adapt to those changes. As you work with students, you must consciously monitor the effectiveness of the activities you and your students are engaged in. Through a variety of verbal and nonverbal cues, you can ascertain, or "read," the need for adapting or flexing. Nonverbally, students may appear puzzled, confused, frustrated, or bored. Verbally, they may appear unable or unwilling to respond accurately to your questions, to complete assigned tasks, or to ask meaningful questions. In each case, you must first be aware that a problem exists and

11.12 Do you feel you can be flexible and adaptable when you teach? How could thorough planning help make you *more* flexible during the lesson?

FIGURE 11.3 Enhancing Flexibility and Adaptability

1. Clearly define goals, objectives, or intentions and make them known to students.

2. When planning instruction, consider students' characteristics, attributes, preferences, and interests.

3. Plan instruction that is interesting to the students and is directed toward the intended learning outcomes.

4. While implementing the planned instruction, systematically and continually monitor students' verbal and nonverbal behavior to determine the appropriateness of your instruction (for example, puzzled or frustrated looks, inability to answer questions or to complete tasks, and student questions or comments that indicate a lack of understanding).

5. When the planned instruction appears to be inappropriate, attempt to determine why and to identify alternatives.

6. When necessary, implement an alternative and again monitor its effectiveness.

then be willing to adapt your goals and instruction as needed. In short, you should avoid a tendency to stick with your lesson plan if it is not working. Next, you must determine potential alternatives that will help you reach the established objectives, select an alternative, and implement it, often in a matter of a few seconds. Chapter 12 will present specific skills that will help you read and adapt your instruction.

Figure 11.3, based upon the work of Csikzentmihalyi (1990) and others, notes characteristics of the flexible, adaptable teacher. Notice that some of these suggestions are directed at planning developmentally appropriate instruction to reduce the need for subsequent changes. Still, as noted in Chapter 6 on planning, even the best plans often need some adjustments to fit individual students and classes.

The ability to recognize the need for change and to adapt instruction accordingly is probably the most difficult task for beginning teachers. However, with time and a conscious attempt to develop a varied teaching repertoire, you can improve your ability to adapt your instructional approach, even during the lesson!

Knowledgeable

Brief mention should be made of the role of subject matter knowledge in effective teaching. Knowledge of the subjects they teach seems intuitively to be an important attribute of effective teachers. Certainly it is reasonable to believe that good teachers know their subjects well. However, there is little agreement regarding *how much* knowledge a teacher must have to teach well (Cruickshank, 1990; Glass, 2002). We have all experienced teachers who were obviously quite knowledgeable about the subject they taught but unable to help students learn it, as well as teachers who effectively facilitate learning with substantial but not overly extensive knowledge of the subject.

Research findings are mixed on the direct importance of teachers' subject knowledge in promoting students' learning (e.g., Druva & Anderson, 1983; Evertson, Hawley, & Zlotnick, 1984; General Accounting Office, 1984; Wenglinsky, 2000). However, research seems consistently to indicate that knowledge of the subject is important but not sufficient for effective teaching (Chen & Ennis, 1995; Graeber, 1999; Peart & Campbell, 1999; Porter & Brophy, 1988). The most effective teachers combine subject knowledge with knowledge of teaching (that is, pedagogy) and knowledge of students. Collectively, this unique professional wisdom is sometimes referred to as pedagogical content knowledge (Shulman, 1986). Knowledge of the subject and of learners helps make the teacher more aware of the misconceptions students are likely to have or to develop about the subject. Knowledge

11.13 Which of the three types of knowledge Porter and Brophy (1988) defined do you feel you most possess? Which do you feel you least possess?

"For that *you went to college?"*

of pedagogy and of learners allows the teacher to select and implement instructional alternatives that can best address students' misconceptions. Thus, effective teachers are knowledgeable about their subject and how best to help the individual students in their classes come to understand it appropriately.

Some Final Thoughts

In this chapter we have discussed eight teacher attributes or characteristics that help students learn more effectively. We learned that effective teachers are positive and confident about their own and their students' success, are supportive and encouraging of students, and are professional in their demeanor. We also saw that these teachers primarily convey these attributes through behavior and that speech is sometimes at odds with how a teacher really feels. It is important to remember that these attributes and the specific behaviors that seem to communicate them to students are interrelated. When one is modified, the other also changes. Though teachers' attributes are difficult to change, teachers should be aware of how various attributes impact on students and should work to enhance those that have positive effects.

CHAPTER SUMMARY

- There are many types of good teaching, each of which has particular strengths or advantages. As a result, it is difficult to define exactly what constitutes the most effective type of teaching. In fact, while research on effective teaching has been conducted for over a century, until the last half of the twentieth century, many believed that effective teaching could not be described or taught.

- Civil rights developments during the 1960s prompted an era of research on effective teaching. The *Equality of Educational Opportunity* study, by Coleman and his associates, spurred increased interest in identifying and describing effective teaching. Coleman found that teaching and schools made little difference in students' achievement. The greatest single contributor to academic success was the student's SES and family background.

- Researchers in this era began to define effective teachers as those who helped their students learn more than other teachers with similar students. These researchers observed the classrooms and classroom behaviors of effective teachers and found that they shared several common attributes and abilities that tended to increase students' learning and satisfaction with teaching and to enhance students' self-concept.

- Personal attributes are primarily inherent personality traits that everyone possesses and exhibits to varying degrees. Attributes are expressed through verbal and nonverbal behavior, and some, like warmth, are difficult to change because they are so much a part of our personalities. Other attributes, such as businesslike demeanor or flexibility, can be modified through awareness.

- Effective teachers' personal attributes can be organized around three broad characteristics: motivating personality, orientation toward success, and professional demeanor.

- At least three specific attributes are associated with teachers who possess a motivating personality: enthusiasm for their students and their subject matter, warmth and humor, and credibility and trustworthiness.

- Teachers' enthusiasm promotes learning by helping to motivate students, by keeping them persistent at tasks, and by helping them feel more satisfied with the teaching. Enthusiastic teachers vary their voices, gestures, and expressions; they move around the room from front to back and side to side; and they maintain a quick lesson pace involving high levels of interaction with students.

- Warmth and humor seem mostly to influence students' learning indirectly by promoting an environment that makes students feel free and motivated to participate. Teachers convey warmth by being "real" people, by demonstrating concern for students' success, and by being open. Humor can be spontaneous or planned. Teachers should be able to laugh at themselves and their mistakes; they should avoid using sarcasm or teasing students. However, warmth and humor, if overemphasized, actually reduce classroom learning, so they are best used naturally and sparingly.

- Credibility and trustworthiness create a relaxed, supportive environment where students trust the teacher to help them succeed. Teachers develop credibility and trust through open, honest teacher-student interaction, not through a teacher's position or credentials; and these qualities exist only if students perceive them.

- Effective teachers are positive people, oriented toward and optimistic about their own and their students' success. Specifically, effective teachers have high expectations for success and are encouraging and supportive of students. They believe in their own ability to help every student learn successfully. Expectations appear to influence teachers' behavior toward students, which in turn affects learning. When teachers expect certain students to fail, they tend to reduce the amount of time and attention devoted to those students, thus increasing the likelihood the students will be unsuccessful. Even more critical than inaccurate initial expectations is the failure to modify those expectations when necessary.

- A good rule of thumb for teachers is to ensure that every student is successful most of the time. Students with low academic self-concepts should be successful almost every time, until their confidence improves. Students with strong academic self-concepts should also be successful most of the time, but not quite so often. Remediation, that is, providing reteaching when a student doesn't master the content, is a good way to convey high expectations and to promote success.

- Effective teachers are encouraging and supportive of students and convey a sense of genuine respect for them and for their individual abilities. Encouragement and support are most important when students are reluctant to begin new tasks or when they experience difficulty and frustration. Teachers demonstrate encouragement and support by avoiding negative comments, by noting improvement—not just perfection, and by helping students reach realistic goals.

- Effective teachers exhibit a professional but flexible demeanor in the classroom. Businesslike behavior, the ability to be flexible and adaptable when necessary, and thorough understanding of subject, pedagogy, and learners all enhance professional demeanor.

- Businesslike teachers focus on promoting learning in a variety of ways. They direct classroom activities toward helping students reach the established goals and objectives. They establish the importance and seriousness of the subject and of the goals and convey this importance to students. Instruction and instructional activities are deliberate and carefully planned to allow the teacher to be concise, thorough, and efficient. The classroom and classroom activities are organized to help students reach the desired goals.

- A professional demeanor also includes the ability to calmly and effectively adapt to changing classroom circumstances. This includes the ability to "read" what is happening in the classroom: the level of students' understanding and motivation, changes in the classroom environment, and problems with instruction. When problems arise, teachers must "flex" or adapt their instruction to more effectively reach the established goals.

- Teachers who exhibit a professional demeanor are also knowledgeable of their subject, pedagogy, and students. Knowledge of the subject is most useful when it is integrated with knowledge of pedagogy and knowledge of learners. Only then can teachers select, plan, and implement the most effective instruction.

ISSUES AND PROBLEMS FOR DISCUSSION

PROBLEMS   Teachers commented on the following incidents or problems. Would you have anticipated these situations? What would you do in each situation?

Problem 1:   "Funny incident! I was on playground duty last week with kindergarten, first, second, and third graders. A little kindergarten child got stuck on top of the jungle gym crying his heart out! *Naturally* I climbed in and rescued him. Then the bell rang for kids to come in, and guess what 49-year-old teacher was stuck inside the jungle gym? Yours truly!!! One of the third graders had to tell the teacher how to put her head out first and then the rest of me! Hazardous duty? Nope. Just a funny happening."

Problem 2:   "A student returned with a cast on his lower left arm. Giving him the usual sympathy and understanding was not enough. During class he did many things to draw attention to himself. I was quite irritated at the end of class and had to struggle with myself to keep my temper and irritation under control. He is a very immature student and this demonstrated his immaturity again."

Problem 3:   "I have one little boy who copies even when he knows the correct answer. I'm trying to build his self-confidence; but, he continues to look on others' papers. When I move him away from the rest of the class, his work is very good. He seems to need reassurance by looking at others' work."

Problem 4:   "My greatest concern today was having a change in the regular schedule and having to decide which lessons my class would have to omit. The school nurse wanted to show a filmstrip and talk with the class. To reinforce this, I had the children do a work paper and make a paper puzzle. So, we had a long health class. But, because of this, the decision had to be made to have only one of the regular classes of writing, language, or social studies."

THEORY INTO ACTION ACTIVITIES

ACTIVITY 11.1: Observing Enthusiasm in the Classroom   During your next visit to a classroom, take the time to observe the teacher's level of enthusiasm. Use the behaviors in Table 11.1 as a guide. Did the teacher demonstrate these behaviors? How enthusiastic did the teacher appear to you? If you have an opportunity, ask students how enthusiastic they believe their teacher to be. Do their perceptions match your own? Why or why not?

ACTIVITY 11.2: Maintaining Positive Expectations   If you have friends who are currently student teaching or are in their first year of teaching, arrange to speak with them about maintaining positive expectations. What do they find most difficult? Do they feel they have high expectations for all students? Do they seem to hold high expectations for themselves? What do they do to avoid becoming pessimistic or lowering their expectations too far? What advice might they offer to help you maintain positive expectations?

REFERENCES

Beatty, M., & Zahn, C. (1990). Are student ratings of communication instructors due to "easy" grading practices? An analysis of teacher credibility and student-reported performance levels. *Communication Education, 39,* 275–282.

Brophy, J. (1982). Successful teaching strategies for the inner-city child. *Phi Delta Kappan, 63*(8), 5–32

Brown, W., Tomlin, J., & Fortson, S. (1996). Best and worst university teachers: The opinions of undergraduate students. *College Student Journal, 30,* 431–434.

Campbell, P. (1986). What's a nice girl like you doing in a math class? *Phi Delta Kappan, 67,* 516–520.

Carusso, V. (1982). Teacher enthusiasm: Behaviors reported by teachers and students. Paper presented at the annual meeting of the American Educational Research Association, New York.

Chall, J. (2000). *The academic achievement challenge: What really works in the classroom?* New York: Guilford Press.

Chen, A., & Ennis, C. (1995). Content knowledge transformation: An examination of the relationship between content knowledge and curricula. *Teaching and Teacher Education, 11,* 389–401.

Coleman, J., Campbell, J., Wood, A., Weinfeld, F., & York, R. (1966). *Equality of educational opportunity.* Washington, DC: U.S. Department of Health, Education, and Welfare, Office of Education.

Cooper, H., & Tom, D. (1984). Teacher expectation research: A review with implications for classroom instruction. *Journal of Educational Psychology 70*(1), 77–89.

Cruickshank, D. (1990). *Research that informs teachers and teacher educators.* Bloomington, IN: Phi Delta Kappa.

Cruickshank, D., & Haefele, D. (2001). Good teachers, plural. *Educational Leadership, 58*(5), 26–30.

Denight, J., & Gall, M. (1989). Effects of enthusiasm training on teachers and students at the high school level. Paper presented at the annual meeting of the American Educational Research Association, San Francisco.

Druva, C., & Anderson, R. (1983). Science teacher characteristics by teacher behavior and student outcome: A meta-analysis of research. *Journal of Research in Science Teaching, 20,* 467–479.

Ellis, A. (2001). *Teaching, learning, and assessment together: The reflective classroom.* Larchmont, NY: Eye on Education.

Evertson, C., Hawley, W., & Zlotnick, M. (1984). *The characteristics of effective teacher preparation programs: A review of research.* Nashville, TN: Peabody College, Vanderbilt University.

Frymier, A., & Thompson, C. (1992). Perceived teacher affinity-seeking in relation to perceived teacher credibility. *Communication Education, 41,* 388–399.

Gallagher, S. (1994). Middle school classroom predictors of science persistence. *Journal of Research in Science Teaching, 31,* 721–734.

General Accounting Office. (1984). *New directions for federal programs to aid mathematics and science teaching* (GAO/PEMO-84-5). Washington, DC: General Accounting Office.

Gill, S., & Reynolds, A. (1999). Educational expectations and school achievement of urban African American children. *Journal of School Psychology, 37,* 403–424.

Glass, G. (2002). Teacher characteristics. In A. Molnar (Ed.), *School reform proposals: The research evidence* (EPSL–0201–101–EPRU). Tempe: Arizona State University, Education Policy Research Unit.

Goleman, D. (1998). *Working with emotional intelligence.* London: Bloomsbury.

Good, T., & Brophy, J. (2000). *Looking in classrooms. Eighth Edition.* New York: Addison-Wesley Longman.

Graeber, A. (1999). Forms of knowing mathematics: What preservice teachers should learn. *Educational Studies in Mathematics, 38,* 189–208.

Hoffman, N. (2001, March 28). Toughness and caring. *Education Week, 20*(28), 40, 42.

Kaufman, K., & Aloma, R. (1997). Orchestrating classroom complexity: Interviews with inner city educators. *The High School Journal, 80,* 218–226.

Kolb, K., & Jussim, L. (1994). Teacher expectations and underachieving gifted students. *Roper Review, 17,* 26–30.

McDermott, P., & Rothenberg, J. (2000). *The characteristics of effective teachers in high poverty schools: Triangulating our data.* Paper presented at the annual meeting of the American Educational Research Association, New Orleans. (ERIC Document Reproduction Service No. ED442887). Educational Research Association, New Orleans.

Medley, D. (1986). Teacher effectiveness. In H. Mitzel (Ed.), *The encyclopedia of educational research* (pp. 1894–1903). New York: Macmillan.

Needels, M., & Gage, N. (1991). Essence and accident in process-product research. In H. Waxman & H. Walberg (Eds.), *Effective teaching: Current research.* Berkeley, CA: McCutchan.

Obiakor, F. (1999). Teacher expectations of minority exceptional learners: Impact on "accuracy" of self-concepts. *Exceptional Children, 66*(1), 39–53.

O'Halloran, C. (1995). Mexican American female students who were successful in high school science courses. *Equity and Excellence in Education, 28,* 57–64

Ornstein, A. & Lasley, T. (2000). *Strategies for effective teaching.* New York: McGraw-Hill.

Patrick, B., Hisley, J., & Kempler, T. (2000). "What's everyone so excited about?" The effects of teacher enthusiasm on student intrinsic motivation and vitality. *The Journal of Experimental Education, 68,* 217–36.

Peart, N., & Campbell, F. (1999). At-risk students' perceptions of teacher effectiveness. *Journal for a Just and Caring Education, 5,* 269–283.

Porter, A., & Brophy, J. (1988). Synthesis of research on good teaching. *Educational Leadership, 45*(8), 74–85.

Raspberry, W. (1993, September 27). Children will learn if they're properly taught. *The Columbus Dispatch,* 9.

Saracho, O. (1991). Teacher expectations of students' performance: A review of the research. *Early Child Development and Care, 76,* 27–41.

Shulman, L. (1986). Those who understand: A conception of teacher knowledge. *American Educator, 10,* 9–15, 43–44.

Thweatt, K., & McCroskey, J. (1998). The impact of teacher immediacy and misbehaviors on teacher credibility. *Communication Education, 47,* 348–358.

Walberg, H. (1991). Productive teaching and instruction: Assessing the knowledge base. *Phi Delta Kappan, 71*(6), 470–478.

Walberg, H., & Fowler, W. (1987). Expenditure and size efficiency for public school districts. *Educational Researcher, 16,* 5–13.

Wang, M., Haertel, G., & Walberg, H. (1993). What helps students learn? *Educational Leadership, 51*(4), 74–79.

Wenglinsky, H. (2000). *How teaching matters: Bringing the classroom back into discussion of teacher quality.* Princeton, NJ: Educational Testing Service.

Young, B., Whitley, M., & Helton, C. (1998). Students' perceptions of characteristics of effective teachers. Paper presented at the annual meeting of the American Educational Research Association, New Orleans. (ERIC Document Reproduction Services ED 426 962).

Effective Teachers: Professional Skills and Abilities

Contents

The *personal* attributes of teachers discussed in Chapter 11 are vital in establishing an environment that supports students and encourages them to learn. Although teachers can modify these attributes through awareness and determination, they are often difficult to change substantially. In contrast, teachers can acquire and use a variety of *professional* skills that research shows can have a profound impact on students' learning. In fact, these skills may be among the most critical factors in determining a teacher's effectiveness (Metcalf, 1992; Rosenshine, 2002; Wang, Haertel, & Walberg, 1993–94; Wenglinsky, 2000). This chapter focuses on the following seven teaching skills, all important in helping students learn (from Cruickshank, 1990):

1. Establishing set.
2. Using variety.
3. Optimizing instructional time.
4. Using questions.
5. Providing clear instruction.
6. Monitoring students' progress.
7. Providing feedback and reinforcement.

To guide our discussion of these teaching skills, we will organize them into four broad areas of classroom instruction. First, we will discuss how teachers engage and maintain students' attention; second, how teachers optimize instructional time; third, how teachers go about interactive instruction; and fourth, how teachers use feedback and reinforcement.

As you read this chapter, remember that these are skills that effective teachers use consistently and proficiently. The better you are at incorporating them into your teaching style, the more your students will gain from instruction since research has linked them to students' learning. Further, it has been shown that any teacher can learn to use these skills more effectively to increase learning in his or her classroom (Cruickshank, 1990; Feden, 1994; Gage, 1989; Joyce & Weil, 1996; Walberg, 1990). Consequently, we have incorporated practice exercises that will help you acquire these behaviors into Units 1, 2, and 3 of the Practice Teaching Manual.

Focusing and Engaging Students' Attention

Effective teachers are able to get students' attention at the beginning of a lesson and to hold their attention throughout the lesson. (Feden, 1994; Lunenburg, 1998; Wang, Haertel, & Walberg, 1993–94). To accomplish this, teachers must be skilled in establishing set (providing a context for the lesson and instruction) and in using variety.

ESTABLISHING SET

Students learn more when teachers begin their lessons by **establishing set,** that is, by providing a context for the lesson and the instruction. This is variously referred to as **set induction,** providing advance organizers, or lesson entry. Whatever the label, you may recall from Chapter 6 that a teacher uses this skill at the beginning of an instructional segment and generally intends it to do one or more of the following:

1. Capture students' attention or provide them with a framework for the lesson.
2. Help students relate new material or information to what they have previously learned.
3. Determine students' entry-level knowledge prior to introducing new content.

When our purpose is to engage students' attention in a new instructional activity, we are establishing **orientation set.** This type of set may vary from a few minutes at the beginning of a single lesson to a full class period at the beginning of a new unit of study. When the primary goal of a set is to help students understand how the new material relates to what they learned previously, we are using **transition set.** This might include a brief review of previous lessons, a discussion to focus students on what they already know about a topic, or a single sentence that shows the relationship to previous material (that is, "Yesterday we learned two causes of the Civil War. Would someone name them for me?" . . . "Today we'll learn two more reasons . . ."). We use **evaluative set** to establish what students already know about a topic. The teacher might ask students questions about the topic or give a short quiz or pretest to make judgments about how best to teach the lesson.

The notion of establishing set before introducing students to new material relates closely to cognitivist approaches to learning (Perkins, 1993), particularly reception learning (see Chapter 4). Brophy and Good (1986), Feden (1994), and others note that learning increases and becomes more efficient when new material is related to previously learned material. Schuck (1985) and Waxman (1987–88) both report that students' achievement and long-term retention is greater when teachers deliberately establish set. Generally, establishing set seems to help students learn more by focusing their attention, improving their ability to self-monitor their understanding, and increasing the likelihood that new information is linked to existing knowledge or schema (Eby, 2001; Feden, 1994).

To be effective, information or activities used to establish set must be (1) at a higher level of abstraction or broader in scope than the content to be learned in order to encompass the specific concepts of the lesson and (2) related directly to students' prior knowledge (Camp, 1993; Rosenshine, 2002). Thus, the early minutes of a lesson may be used to promote several goals and are critical to establishing a tone and instructional pattern that allow students to learn.

The beginning of the lesson should accomplish four goals. First, it should be more than a simple, dry introduction, an overview of the material, or a statement like "Open your math books to page 79." Establishing an effective set requires a configuration of several general characteristics (Arends, 2001). First, the topic should be introduced in a way that makes it novel, interesting, or relevant to students. Often teachers begin a lesson by performing a demonstration with a surprising or unexpected outcome in order to stimulate curiosity about the topic of the lesson. For example, at the beginning of a lesson on chemical reactions and their by-products, a teacher might drop a small piece of potassium into a beaker of water and allow students to see the reaction (the potassium will spark, sputter, and eventually burn up).

A second goal of the beginning of the lesson is to establish an interactive climate and tone. It is important that teachers immediately involve students in responding to questions or in thinking and talking about the topic. In the previous example,

12.1 What is the most memorable lesson entry you've ever experienced? Did it help you learn more?

FIGURE 12.1 Establishing Set

1. Review previous material.
2. Ask a curiosity-provoking question or pique students' interest by using a unique problem or scenario.
3. Provide an overview of the major points or topics of the lesson.
4. Demonstrate the concept or ideas of the lesson.
5. Provide a visual schema that depicts the relationship of various aspects or concepts of the lesson.
6. Provide a problem (orally, visually, or by some other means) to engage students in processing the concepts to be learned.
7. Convey interest, enthusiasm, and curiosity about the topic.
8. Inform students of the objectives or goals of the lesson, and point out its relevance to their lives.

---

the science teacher might ask students what they think will happen before the potassium is dropped into the water. After students have observed the reaction, the teacher could ask them what they observed and what might explain it, and gradually guide them toward the major topic of the lesson.

A third objective of the lesson introduction is to direct students' attention to important aspects of the content or communicate the lesson objectives. Sometimes teachers will put a topical outline on the board to highlight important aspects of the lesson. Sometimes they use a demonstration, note the major reasons behind the events in the demonstration, and explain how the lesson will focus on these reasons. For example, after asking students to explain what they observed, the science teacher in our example might use students' responses to note that the chemical reaction produced new compounds, that it is possible to write an equation that depicts this reaction, and that by the end of the day's class they will be able to write equations for reactions like this.

Fourth, the entry should link today's lesson with what students already know. "Remember yesterday we talked about . . . ? How might that explain what we saw in the demonstration? . . . Well, today we're going to talk about . . ." Figure 12.1 presents some specific ways of establishing an effective set for your lessons.

Try Activities 12.1 and 12.2

USING VARIETY

Educators have long believed that variety increases students' motivation and learning, and researchers have supported this belief. Effective teachers use variety in virtually every aspect of their classroom behavior including nonverbal behavior, instructional approaches, classroom organization, questioning, types of assessment, and gestures. We have all experienced teachers who taught every lesson for the entire year in the same way, with the same activities arranged in the same order, using the same, monotonous voice patterns and few gestures. This lack of variety in instructional patterns can negatively affect learning. Imagine a teacher (perhaps you can even remember one) who responded to every student's answer or contribution with, "Exactly!" The first few times you witness a student receiving this response, it seems enthusiastic and encouraging. However, eventually, even if every student's answer is correct, "Exactly!" is no longer effective and may, in fact, become annoying. The same holds true for many other teacher behaviors (Henson, 1980).

Rosenshine and Furst (1971) identified variety as the second strongest predictor of teachers' effectiveness. However, variety probably does not directly improve learning. Instead, it has a positive effect on students' attention and involvement, thus making students more receptive to learning. Teachers who use variety not only prevent students from becoming bored, they keep them interested and actively involved in the lesson. A teacher's knack for variety fosters interest and engagement on the part of students; this in turn leads to increased learning (Doyle, 1986).

"Go to kindergarten, finger-paint, have quiet time, play with building blocks, eat lunch, listen to a story, take a nap, color, go home from kindergarten—day after day, week after week. I'm 5, and I'm in a rut."

Several researchers have identified specific ways teachers can introduce variety into their classrooms (Brophy & Good, 1986; Ellis, 2001; Rohrkemper & Corno, 1988). Their suggestions can be organized into two major categories: variation in instructional activities and materials, and variation in teacher-student interaction.

Instructional Activities and Materials   As we discussed earlier, one way of establishing effective set in your lessons is to pique students' interest by presenting novel situations or problems. In addition, teachers can vary their instruction by using a variety of instructional alternatives: cooperative learning, discussion, seat work, direct instruction, inquiry learning, and so on (see Chapters 7 and 8). Ideally, every lesson should allow students to experience the content through several senses. You might tell students about certain ideas or have them read about them; ask them to conduct an experiment or activity in which they manipulate materials and can see, feel, hear, taste, or even smell the results of their manipulations; then organize them into small groups to write a summary of their observations.

Interacting with Students   In addition to introducing students to content in a variety of ways, Brophy and Good (1986) emphasize the importance of varying the ways teachers interact with students. Even having students work independently in small groups can become monotonous if used without variation. Ensuring that there are multiple and different steps to the groups' tasks, interjecting questions or encouraging comments, and breaking up the task with some whole class conversation or discussion of groups' progress will help keep students involved.

Teachers should also vary the ways in which they reinforce or praise students for desirable performance or inform them about their progress. Smiling at students, maintaining eye contact, moving closer, laughing, and gesturing toward students often can be reinforcing and convey support and interest. More explicitly, you can give students rewards for desirable performance. Verbal praise, recognition of outstanding work, free time, or tokens are examples. Brophy and Good note that, just as a single instructional alternative eventually becomes monotonous and ineffective, so too does a single form of reward. Likewise, teachers can and should provide students with information about their performance in a variety of forms—not just in written comments or grades on students' papers. Verbal information from the teacher, peers, and group are important ways of accomplishing this. We will discuss reinforcement and feedback in detail later in this chapter.

12.2 Why do you think it is so easy for teachers to "get in a rut" rather than use variety? What will you do to make sure that you continually incorporate variety?

Try Activity 12.3

Using Instructional Time Efficiently

The most effective teachers learn to optimize the time available for instruction. It's only reasonable that students learn more when they spend more time engaged in learning activities. Three factors contribute to more efficient use of instructional time: (1) time on task, (2) maintaining momentum, and (3) smooth transitions.

OPTIMIZING TIME

Research has shown that **time on task** is consistently related to increased learning. When teachers and students spend more time actively engaged in academic tasks, students learn more (Brophy & Good, 1986; Brush, 1997; Doyle, 1986; Karweit, 1984; Walberg, 1988; Yair, 2000). Interestingly, however, only a small percentage of available instructional time is actually used for meaningful instruction (Bracey, 2001; Glass, 2002). An examination of the reasons for this can show where time is lost and how to maximize the use of available time.

It is useful to think of instructional time in terms of four levels, somewhat like the target in Figure 12.2. At each level, less time is used for instruction than is available. For example, at the broadest level is **mandated time;** that is, the formal time scheduled for school or academic activities. The length of the school year, day, and periods determine the maximum time available for instructional activities. Teachers are compelled to work within the constraints and schedules established by their state, school district, and school. Schools in most states schedule approximately 185 school days; the typical school day is about 7½ hours in length; and the typical high school period is about 50 minutes. It should be noted, however, that there is much disparity even in amounts of mandated time (Doyle, 1986; Harnischfeger & Wiley, 1978; Karweit, 1984; Rosenshine, 1980). In fact, Harnischfeger and Wiley found a difference of 45 minutes in the length of the school day for second graders *within the same school district!* In this school district, as in many others, the maximum available time for school-related activities is much greater for some students than for others.

Obviously, not every minute of mandated time is used for instruction. Some time is scheduled for lunch, moving from class to class, recess, homeroom, and other

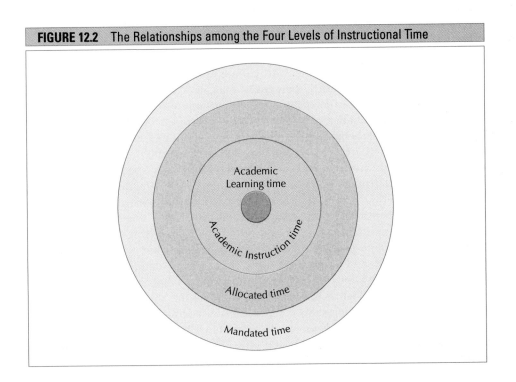

FIGURE 12.2   The Relationships among the Four Levels of Instructional Time

"They never quit, do they?"

noninstructional activities. Thus, only a portion of mandated time is actually allocated to instruction.

Allocated time is the amount of mandated time intended or scheduled for academic activities. Research indicates that less than 75 percent of mandated time is allocated to academic tasks. Nonacademic activities (that is, convocations, field trips, pep rallies, special programs or speakers, and so on) and formal transitions (that is, passing periods, restroom breaks) take over 25 percent of mandated time. Based upon Rosenshine's data, it would appear that only about seven of every ten mandated days is actually available for academic or instructional purposes. The remaining three days are consumed by the nonacademic activities cited above (Bracey, 2001; Glass, 2002; Smith, 2000).

The next circle in Figure 12.2 represents the amount of allocated time during which the teacher is actually conducting instructional activities. This is called **academic instruction time.** Just as allocated time is always less than mandated time, the amount of time spent in academic instruction is always less than is allocated. Doyle (1986) reports that less than 60 percent of allocated time in elementary schools and less than 45 percent of allocated time in high schools is spent in academic instruction. While allocated and mandated time are often beyond the control of teachers, maximizing the amount of allocated time spent in academic instruction *is* their responsibility (Clare, Jenson, & Kehle, 2000; Smith, 2000).

Most teachers do not realize how much class time they spend in noninstructional tasks and activities. For example, although a seventh-grade social studies teacher may have 50 minutes of allocated time five days a week, not all of the 250 minutes allocated to instruction will be devoted to it. Some time will be spent socializing, organizing or preparing instructional materials, giving directions, or intervening in discipline problems. Additional time will be lost to absenteeism, administrative requests, and other disruptions. Using Doyle's data, of the 250 minutes allocated over five days, fewer than 145 minutes will be spent in academic activities.

Returning again to Figure 12.2, let's now examine the smallest but most critical circle. This inner circle represents the amount of academic instruction time during which students are *actively* and *successfully* engaged in learning and is referred to as **academic learning time (ALT),** or engaged time. Two factors are considered in determining academic learning time. First is the amount of time a given student is actively engaged in the instruction/learning process. Rather than daydreaming, doodling, or misbehaving, the student is attentive to the learning activity. This attention may be overt, such as answering a question, participating in a discussion, solving pencil-and-paper problems, manipulating concrete materials in an experiment, or talking to another student about the instructional task. It may also be less obvious, as when students are actively thinking about the academic task even if they do not exhibit any outward signs of engagement.

The second factor considered in ALT is a student's success at the activity. If a student is actively engaged in completing an academic activity incorrectly, she may actually be practicing and learning an incorrect process. For academic instruction time to be considered "engaged," or academic learning time, *given learners must be actively engaged in meaningful academic tasks at which they are mostly successful.*

This suggests that, even though teachers may be conducting instruction, it is unlikely that every student will be engaged in the activity at any given time. In fact, no individual student is likely to be engaged 100 percent of the time. Thus, more time is lost. Borich (2000) suggests that an effective teacher probably maintains an academic engagement rate of 80 to 95 percent. However, Yair (2000) indicates that in most classrooms, students spend about 30 percent of instructional time engaged in academic activity under the supervision of a teacher or aide. If we consider these data in terms of our middle school social studies example, of the 145 minutes per week when the teacher was providing instruction, the typical student would be *engaged* for only about 50 minutes.

An examination of the tremendous loss of time between mandated and engaged time shows how critical it is for teachers to take full advantage of the time they have. As previously noted, while state and school officials generally set mandated or allocated time, teachers can increase their students' academic learning time through the skillful application of professional teaching skills.

Try Activity 12.4

One way to guard against loss of academic learning time is to be aware of potential detractors (Hargreaves, 1994). At the district level, time is frequently lost to snow days, weather delays, and teachers' strikes. At the school level, fire drills, convocations, trips, passing periods, lunch, recess, and homeroom periods reduce time. At the classroom level, time is lost by starting class late or ending early, by providing unmonitored study time, by spending too much time on administrative tasks, by using films, computers, or games excessively, by spending too much time on discipline problems, by failing to monitor or making too many transitions, or by straying from the lesson at hand.

How, then, can teachers improve their use of time? First, they should deliberately attempt to use most of the available time for instruction rather than other tasks. Begin and end each lesson on time. Have materials, equipment, and activities planned and ready so that you can begin as soon as the period begins. Establish and enforce rules requiring students to be on time and to be prepared for class. To avoid wasting time at the end of the lesson, plan more instruction than you think you will need. If you finish early, spend the remaining time reviewing with students rather than having them do individual seat work or giving them "free time." If individual seat work is assigned, monitor students to be sure they are engaged in the learning task. It is also helpful to use and enforce a signal that indicates to students that they may begin putting away their materials at the end of the lesson or period. This allows you to keep students involved for the maximum amount of time and prevents the problem created when students close their books or stand to leave while you are attempting to finish the lesson. Make sure, however, that you allow students sufficient time to put away materials before leaving the room or moving to another activity.

Establishing and maintaining rules and procedures for routine activities can also provide more time for instruction by reducing the amount of time needed for giving directions. Chapter 12 provides detailed information about rules and

12.3 Are you good at managing your time? Do you think you will be better or worse at managing classroom time? How will you know?

procedures. Briefly, though, you should teach and enforce procedures for obtaining or returning materials and equipment, checking homework, making up missed work, and completing group or individual seat work. Similarly, when you must give directions, explain the tasks and procedures clearly and completely. Check for understanding of these procedures, answer students' questions, and give them feedback *before* telling them to begin.

Another important factor in increasing students' engagement is to create and maintain a highly interactive instructional pattern. Use a variety of instructional behaviors and alternatives. Make assignments interesting, relevant, and at a level that allows most students to complete them successfully without your guidance. Spend the majority of your classroom time in teacher-directed activities where you can more carefully monitor students' engagement. Randomly circulate around the room, especially when students are working in small groups or at individual seat work. Reinforce students verbally and nonverbally for remaining on task, and quickly redirect off-task behavior.

Maintaining Momentum   The concept of momentum is related to the effective use of time. Momentum refers to the flow of activities and to the pace of teaching and learning maintained in the classroom. The most effective teachers maintain a smooth, relatively rapid instructional pace. Their classroom activities are orderly, and changes occur easily without disrupting the instructional flow since these teachers have established effective routines and follow them. The speed at which they conduct instructional activities, while brisk, matches the difficulty of the content and the students' abilities.

Your skill in maintaining momentum is important when considered in light of the research on time. Your goal should be to maximize your students' engagement, to help them work through relevant materials and activities as quickly and as successfully as they can. By adapting the pace of your instruction to students' abilities and success and by working to maintain a smooth flow of classroom activities with few disruptions and little "down time," you help students learn more.

It is easier to maintain momentum in teacher-directed instructional activities than during seat work or small-group work (Brush, 1997; Leather, 2000; Walberg, 1991). Teacher-directed instruction allows the teacher greater control of the pace and flow of the lesson, whereas small-group or individual seat work relies heavily on students' motivation to maintain momentum.

You must consider how best to maintain momentum when planning and implementing instruction. The pace of instruction must be adapted to the difficulty or complexity of required tasks. For example, you must plan for and use a slower pace early in the learning process or when the task requires higher-order thinking skills. For lower-order tasks such as drill and practice or recitation, a quicker pace is more appropriate. Further, the pace should vary in your long-term plans, including your weekly and monthly reviews.

Effective teachers must learn to monitor and deal with concurrent classroom activities. While working with a small reading group in the back of the room, they must also be aware of and keep students working at their desks in the front of the room, at learning centers, or on projects. Momentum is enhanced when teachers organize their classrooms to minimize disruptions and time lost to giving directions or reexplaining. Rules and procedures that enable students to complete tasks on their own help reduce disruptions. Teachers must also be careful to avoid getting "bogged down" in unimportant or minor aspects of the topic, digressing from the topic at hand, or spending too much time with a single student or group of students.

Making Smooth Transitions   Instructional transitions are "points in instructional interactions when contexts change" (Doyle, 1986, p. 406). Instructional transitions require that teachers refocus students' attention on changes in the direction of a discussion or lesson. Transitions occur when you change the topic, its focus, or the activity at hand. Major transitions take place between class meetings or lessons (the time from the end of one class to the beginning of the next class), between lessons in the same room (particularly in elementary classrooms), and between different instructional activities within the same lesson (changing from lecture to lab work). Because major transitions often involve changes in equipment or location, they take more time, and when poorly planned, they are a major contributor to classroom disruption. We will discuss major transitions and how to deal with them more fully in Chapter 13.

 12.4 How might you monitor your use of instructional time?

Minor transitions occur within a lesson when the speaker moves from one aspect of the topic to another, when the speaker pauses, or when the speaker changes (a new speaker begins). These minor transitions are necessary and desirable because they help learners organize their thinking by signaling the move from one topic or aspect of the topic to another. They also allow more people to contribute to the discussion or lesson.

Transitions, particularly minor transitions, are frequent occurrences in classrooms and largely determine the smoothness and momentum of the lesson. Poor transitions can greatly detract from effective use of instructional time. As a result, teachers should work to ensure that their transitions are few in number and that they are as well-organized and as brief as possible. Problems result when transitions are not well-structured, when students do not want to stop what they are doing or have not had sufficient time to complete the assigned task, or when the next instructional segment is delayed for some reason (Brown & Brown, 1999).

To make your instructional transitions smoother, you should practice the following routine. First, plan for the transitions. When preparing your lessons, you can predict points where changes in focus or activity will occur or when waiting is inevitable. You should determine what materials and procedures you will need to begin the next segment as quickly as possible and what both you and your students should do during the transition. An important part of planning for transitions is having all materials and equipment prepared, readily available, and in working order. Also, you can routinize daily or frequent transitions through patterns or procedures. For example, students can be taught what they are to do when they finish a test early, while you take roll, or when they move from one area of the room to another. Establishing these patterns saves time that might otherwise be spent giving directions and allows students to engage in constructive activities rather than just sit and wait. Figure 12.3 lists specific steps you can take to optimize your use of time.

FIGURE 12.3 Optimizing Instructional Time

1. Have materials and equipment ready prior to class.
2. Begin on time.
3. Establish and enforce rules for entering the classroom and beginning class.
4. Establish and enforce procedures for routine tasks and transitions, like turning in work and obtaining or putting away equipment, so that students can do these chores without your direction.
5. Plan more instructional material than you think you will need.
6. Maintain a relatively brisk instructional pace, varying the pace as needed to accommodate learners and match the difficulty of the content.
7. If you finish your planned lesson early, use the remaining time to review with students. Avoid giving students "free time" or individual seat work.
8. Establish a signal that informs students when they are to begin putting away their materials or when they are dismissed.
9. Maintain a highly interactive instructional pattern. Question all students, move frequently, use variety, and convey enthusiasm to help keep students actively engaged.

Conducting Interactive Instruction

Effective teachers are able to conduct instruction that keeps students actively involved in the lesson. In addition to establishing set and using variety to keep students motivated, the best teachers are skilled in questioning, in helping students come to a clear understanding of the content, and in monitoring understanding.

USING QUESTIONS

The most effective teachers establish and maintain highly interactive classrooms—classrooms characterized by student-student and teacher-student dialogue rather than simply teacher talk (Feden, 1994). Integral to this type of classroom is the teacher's ability to use questions effectively. Bellon, Bellon, and Blank (1992) state, "Questioning is the instructional process that is central to verbal interaction in the classroom. The questions teachers ask serve as the interface between teacher expectations and student responses" (p. 308). This interface in interactive teaching is critical because it shifts the focus from the teacher to the students.

Effective questions require students *to actively process information and compose an answer.* Good questions increase students' engagement, raise the level of thought, help students organize their thoughts, guide students more successfully through academic tasks, and allow the teacher to monitor understanding and provide feedback. In spite of the obvious value of good questions, it appears that teachers seldom use questions as effectively as they could (Alexander, Jetton, & Kulikowich, 1994; Orstein & Lasley, 2000). Most teachers' questioning patterns include giving information that is unnecessary or confusing, posing more than one question at a time, or failing to specify the nature of the expected answer (Sigel, 1990; Traver, 1998). What, then, do we know about good questions and questioning patterns?

Questions comprise about one-third of the classroom interactions between teachers and students (Fisher, et al., 1984), and educational research has shown that effective questioning directly and indirectly influences the amount, level, and type of learning. Good and Brophy (2000) reviewed research on questioning and concluded that students learn more when teachers ask frequent questions and include a variety of questions in their lessons. Wilen and Clegg (1986) also reported that teacher questioning is related to increased achievement among students. Further, research on questioning suggests that teachers' use of higher-order questions promotes students' higher-order thinking (LeNoir, 1993). Morine-Dershimer and Beyerbach (1987) and Good and Brophy (2000) conclude that questions are important because the more frequently students interact with the teacher and their peers about the subject, the more they learn. The following discussion organizes what researchers know about questioning into three areas: asking questions, obtaining answers, and following up questions or reacting to student responses.

How to Ask Questions   If teachers want their questioning to be effective, they must be sure to phrase questions clearly and concisely. Too often, teachers ask questions that are almost impossible for students to answer accurately. They fail to make clear what it is they want to know of students or how they want them to answer. Clear questions use natural, unambiguous language appropriate to the level of the students. They are also concise, including only the words, terms, and information students need in order to answer the questions. They describe the specific points students should attend to, but they do not include unnecessary words or parenthetical expressions. Finally, they are directed toward academic content or the objectives of the lesson.

To be effective, questions should require students to *process* or think about what they are learning and to *compose* an answer. This means teachers should avoid asking rhetorical questions or questions that have only one answer. Closed-response questions, which can be answered with a simple yes-no or true-false response, allow stu-

12.5   When you teach, do you ask lots of questions? Do you ever get nervous about asking questions when you're in front of a group? Why?

dents to guess at the answer without processing the content. Even when students do process what they have learned in order to answer a closed-response question, they can still *select* a response rather than *compose* one. It is easy to reword closed-response questions to require students to create more thoughtful, detailed responses.

Rhetorical questions, that is, questions asked for effect rather than to generate students' responses, are problematic because they can, over time, inhibit students' responses. Students become unsure whether a question is merely rhetorical or whether they are supposed to respond. For similar reasons, teachers should avoid including the answer within the question or answering a question themselves.

In addition, teachers should take care to ask only one question at a time. Many times teachers ask multiple questions without realizing it. While asking a question, they think of another aspect of the content they also want to address. As a result, it may not be clear whether one answer is expected for all the questions or whether a different answer is expected to each question. Similarly, students probably are confused when their teacher asks a question and then immediately rephrases it. This creates two problems. First, students' thinking about the original question is interrupted and, second, the rephrasing is often sufficiently different from the original to make the students wonder if it is a separate question.

An additional consideration in formulating and asking questions is the *type of question* or level of thought required of the students. Questions can be of several types or levels and are intended for a variety of purposes (Barden, 1995). Questions may be lower- or higher-order, convergent or divergent, narrow or broad, and content or process.

The lower- and higher-order delineations refer to the level of thought required in order to answer the question. Bloom's taxonomy, discussed in Chapter 6, is the most frequently used system for organizing questions along this hierarchy. Lower-order questions require students to respond at the knowledge, comprehension, and sometimes application levels of the taxonomy. Students can generally answer these questions using existing knowledge, either by recalling and then restating them, by rephrasing them, or by performing a task. Higher-order questions require the cognitive skills of analysis, synthesis, or evaluation and thus require more complex and original thinking.

Questions can also be categorized as convergent or divergent—labels that refer to the direction of thought required to reach an answer. In answering convergent questions, students' thought processes proceed from broad or general to narrow or specific. These questions require one or a small number of correct responses. Factual questions asking who, what, when, or where as well as closed-response (yes-no) questions are examples of convergent questions. These questions are most appropriate for helping to reinforce specific, important aspects of the content.

Divergent questions require thinking that moves from the narrow or specific to the broad or general. They require students to identify or generate several potential answers—any of which might be accurate. The difference between convergent and divergent questions is easy to see in mathematics instruction. Suppose students are presented with the numeric statement 7×9. A convergent question might be "What is seven times nine?" Students are expected to arrive at the one correct answer. This example is also a lower-order question. However, the same numeric statement (7×9) might also serve as the basis for a divergent question like "How many different ways could you determine what seven times nine is?" To answer this question, students might use simple addition, commutative property, combinations of mathematical principles, manipulative solutions, or other creative methods to generate answers to the question. Rather than focus on the single correct answer, as in the convergent question, students must expand on or diverge from the initial facts to generate the answer.

Questions may also emphasize *content* or *process*. Content questions deal directly with the information being learned and make up about 80 percent of the questions

Try Activity 12.5

teachers ask (Borich, 2000). The question and the expected answer are drawn directly from the content of instruction, and the teacher generally has a "correct" answer in mind. Content questions are often associated with lower-order cognitive processes. However, because they focus students' attention on important aspects of the content, they have been found to improve students' achievement (Borich, 2000). On the other hand, teachers use process questions to stimulate students' thinking. Although these questions deal with content, they place less emphasis on the "correctness" of answers and more on pushing students to think about the content in different, creative, or complex ways (Mencke & Pressley, 1994). Thus, process questions are generally higher-order and divergent. These questions are used much less often than content questions and are less closely related to achievement. However, they do appear to promote students' abilities to think at higher levels and to solve problems (Blythe, Allen, & Powell, 1999; LeNoir, 1993).

Several common recommendations for improvement apply to each of these types of questions. First, just as in other aspects of instruction, you should use a variety of question types. Although most teachers rely heavily on lower-order, convergent questions, the importance of developing students' thinking and problem-solving abilities requires that you deliberately incorporate process, higher-order, and divergent questions into your lessons. Second, you should match the type and level of questions you ask to your objectives and your students. When teaching toward lower-order objectives, lower-order questions make sense. When your objectives include higher-order processes or when you want to promote students' critical thinking, you must integrate higher-order, divergent, and process questions into your lessons.

To ensure good phrasing and appropriate types of questions, you should consider your questions and questioning patterns when planning your lessons. After all, good class discussion and interaction don't just happen. Some questions emerge spontaneously from the lesson as a result of students' comments or questions. These you cannot plan in advance. However, you can write many of the critical questions into your lesson plan. There are at least four important reasons for doing this.

First, integrating planned questions into your lessons increases the likelihood that you will conduct an interactive lesson. Second, when you prepare questions in advance, you are more likely to focus them on the major objectives of the lesson. If you rely totally on spontaneous questions, you can easily get side-tracked and ask too many questions on one aspect of the lesson while neglecting others. Third, including some pivotal questions in the lesson plan makes it more likely that you will ask a variety of questions at a variety of levels. Divergent, higher-order, and process questions are more difficult to develop than are convergent, lower-order, and content questions. That may partly explain why teachers use them less often (Dillon, 1988; Gall, 1984; Glickman, 2002; Sigel, 1990). Preparing some of these questions in advance, even if you don't use them all, directs your attention toward more advanced levels of thinking. Fourth, writing pivotal questions in advance makes it more likely that you will phrase the questions clearly and concisely.

Obtaining Good Answers   After teachers have developed and phrased their questions, they must get students to respond to them. As mentioned, asking clear and varied types of questions at a variety of levels promotes students' participation. Research also suggests that soliciting answers in certain ways can enhance the effectiveness of questions and the quality and quantity of students' responses. It is particularly important that teachers use wait time and that all students participate.

Wait time refers to the pauses that effective teachers use when they solicit and react to students' responses. Rowe's (1974) work has served as the basis for most subsequent research on wait time. The early research of Rowe and others focused on the importance of asking a question, pausing, and then calling on a student to

FIGURE 12.4 Sequence of Teachers' Questioning

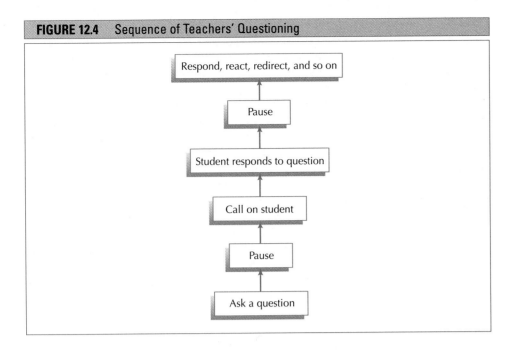

respond. More recently, investigators have determined that in addition to pausing after the question is asked, it is also important to pause before reacting to the student's answer or calling on a second student to respond (Tobin, 1987). Thus, wait time includes (1) the pause between the teacher's question and the student's response and (2) the pause between a student's response and the teacher's reaction. Figure 12.4 depicts this sequence.

Most teachers pause for less than one second before calling on a student to respond. In contrast, the most effective teachers include pauses of from three to five seconds after asking a question and before reacting to a student's response. Research on wait time has found that those three- to five-second pauses produce the following desirable and important outcomes: students' responses are longer and more thorough, the cognitive level of students' responses is higher (for example, they display more analysis, synthesis, and evaluation), students volunteer more information to support their responses, and students' confidence in their responses is greater. In addition, more students respond to questions, particularly those labeled as "slow." Finally, positive interactions among students and between students and the teacher increase, as do the number of relevant questions students ask (Berliner, 1987; Rowe, 1974; Tobin, 1987; Traver, 1998; Wang, Haertel, & Walberg, 1993–94).

Increasing wait time seems a simple thing to do, but, especially for beginning teachers, it often proves difficult. A pause of five seconds can seem like an eternity when you are insecure about the effectiveness of your instruction or unsure whether anyone will answer your questions! Still, as you learn to incorporate these pauses, they become easier, and they give all students increased time to think and participate.

You can do several things to make your use of wait time more effective. First, you should adopt a policy restraining students from shouting out their answers. Allowing callouts prevents you from controlling the length of the pause after your question and reduces wait time. After asking a question, count to five in your head while scanning the room, then call on a student to answer. Do not repeat, rephrase, or add to the question until at least several seconds have passed. Doing so interrupts students' thinking and may interfere with their ability to respond. When students

12.6 Why might you feel that the pause you use after a question is longer than it really is?

respond, it is important you do not interrupt before they have completed their answers, even if they are absolutely correct. When they are finished answering, pause, use a few seconds to think about their answers, allow other students to think about the answer, and consider how best to react or follow up.

The use of wait time must be balanced against the brisk pace needed to maintain the momentum of a lesson. Specifically, teachers should match wait time with the level or difficulty of the question asked. Lower-order, convergent questions generally require shorter pauses than higher-order, divergent, and process questions. Vary wait time to accommodate the students' need to process the question, generate an answer, or consider the response of another student.

The second factor to consider during the response phase of questioning is how to maximize student participation. Morine-Dershimer and Beyerbach (1987) found that students' learning and affect were related to the number of opportunities students had to participate in the lesson and to respond to questions. Thus, a goal of your questioning should be to ensure that all students have an equal opportunity to respond successfully. Questioning can help you monitor understanding, keep students engaged, and serve as a measure of the success of your instruction, but it is imperative that you ask *all* students to respond to your questions. This is especially difficult but important in a class with diverse abilities or cultural backgrounds.

Mastering the effective use of wait time will increase participation in your questioning. However, most teachers still call primarily on volunteers to respond to questions. This practice results in an unfair distribution of questions and unequal opportunities to respond (Coladarci & Gage, 1984). Effective questioning requires that you call on all students, especially nonvolunteers. A good practice is to ask a question, pause to allow all students to think about the question and develop a response, and then select a student to respond. To ensure an equitable distribution of questions, it can be helpful to use a pattern in selecting students to answer. For example, you might write each student's name on a note card and then randomly select from the students' cards for participation. Using a pattern enables you to know which students have already been asked to respond. To keep all students alert, even when they have already answered a question, it is a good idea to vary your pattern and to call randomly on students to make follow-up responses.

Incorporating wait time and equitably distributing the opportunity to respond work together to improve the effectiveness of your questioning. Wait time allows more students the opportunity to process an answer. While some students can do this relatively quickly (usually those who volunteer most frequently), others require more time to arrive at an answer. Thus, wait time increases the number of students who can respond accurately to the question. Calling on all students, even when they do not volunteer, maintains students' engagement. It allows all students some opportunity to interact with you and to be successful, and provides you with a more complete assessment of how well students understand the material.

Following Up Students' Responses   After a student has responded to your question, you must respond or react to the reply. This phase of the questioning process is called follow-up. Your follow-up behavior will either encourage or discourage thoughtful, successful participation in your lessons and, thus, the long-term success of your instruction (Latham, 1997).

The most frequent though ineffective teacher's reaction is "OK" or "uh-huh" (Sadker & Sadker, 2001). Instead of such routinized and meaningless responses, you should attempt to clarify, synthesize, expand, modify, raise the level of, or evaluate students' responses. The effective use of follow-up is based upon the accuracy and confidence of the students' responses (Good, 1988; Rosenshine & Stevens, 1986; Sternberg, 1994). They can range from correct and confident to wrong and careless. Rosenshine and Stevens (1986) suggest the following responses and reactions:

12.7   Does it make you feel uncomfortable when a teacher calls on you to respond when you haven't volunteered? Why or why not? Could the teacher help you feel better about it?

"Say your car gets 23 miles per gallon at 55 miles per hour and your fuel tank holds 16 gallons. If gas costs 86¢ per gallon and you know the capitals of all 50 states, how much will it cost to drive to the capital of Nebraska?"

1. When a student responds correctly and confidently, accept and acknowledge the response and move on. Do not overpraise.

2. When a student responds correctly but hesitantly, provide feedback to the student or use additional questions that encourage the student to determine why the response is correct. Before moving on, be certain the student understands why the answer was correct.

3. When a student responds confidently but incorrectly, reinforce the initial effort, then use additional questions to help the student arrive at the correct answer. Avoid giving the student the answer or calling on another student to respond. You may give reinforcement for participation and effort, but there should be no confusion regarding the fact that you are reinforcing participation, not accuracy.

4. When a student responds incorrectly and carelessly, provide the correct response and move on. You should never avoid following up or correcting an incorrect answer.

Generally then, follow-up is used any time the student fails to respond accurately and/or confidently. These follow-ups can be divided into four types: providing the correct answer, probing, redirecting, or rephrasing. Providing the correct answer is advisable only when a student has responded carelessly and incorrectly. The remaining three follow-up methods deserve discussion.

Probing means asking additional questions of the responding student to help expand or raise the level of the response (Danielson, 1996). Probing questions are often intended to focus attention on important aspects of the question that enable the student to improve the response (see Figure 12.5). In this case, probing should include convergent questions phrased in simple but not condescending terms. Frequently, more than one question is needed to address particular aspects of the original question or response and to guide the student toward a more correct or complete answer.

Probing can also be used to raise the level of a student's response. As noted earlier, teachers generally ask convergent, content questions at the lower cognitive levels. Further, most students respond with lower-order, convergent answers, even when the teacher has asked a higher-order or divergent question (Cazden, 1986; Sternburg, 1994). Probing can be used after such a response to prompt the student to use higher-order processes. Simple ways of doing this include asking students to

FIGURE 12.5   Examples of Follow-up Questioning Techniques

Probing (to raise the level of a student's response)

Teacher:	"Why might President Ford have pardoned former President Nixon?" (Pause) "David?"
David:	"To prevent embarrassment of the Republican party."
Teacher:	"Can you explain how the pardon might prevent embarrassment?"
David:	"Well, if the investigation had continued, they might have found that there were a lot of other people, mostly Republicans, who were involved."
Teacher:	"Why do you think that might be true?"
David:	"Hmmm. Well, because since then some others have admitted being involved or named people who were."
Teacher:	"OK, so let's say President Ford doesn't pardon Nixon and all of this is revealed, what do you think would be the result?"

Probing (to help a student answer correctly)

Teacher:	"Ball, bed, bug, baby. These are all words that begin with the *b* sound. What are some other words that begin with the *b* sound?" (Pause) "Danielle?"
Danielle:	(Silence)
Teacher:	"Okay, does Danielle start with a *b* sound?"
Danielle:	"No, it's a *d*."
Teacher:	"Right. What about Brittany? Does Brittany start with a *b* sound?"
Danielle:	"Yeah!"
Teacher:	"Okay, Danielle. Think of the sound. What words do you know that start with that sound?"
Danielle:	(Pause) "Bunny!"
Teacher:	"Right! Bunny!"

Redirecting (after an incorrect response)

Teacher:	"What was the name of the Watergate special prosecutor?" (Pause) "Trevor?"
Trevor:	"Strom Thurmond?"
Teacher:	"No. Thurmond is a senator. What was the name of the special prosecutor?" (Pause) "Steve?"
Steve:	"Archibald Cox."
Teacher:	"Yes."

Rephrasing (to clarify a question)

Teacher:	"Why did Gerald Ford pardon Richard Nixon?" (Pause) (No student responses) "What was the reason Ford gave for the pardon in the speech we just watched?" (Pause) "Kassandra?"
Kassandra:	"He said he thought the country needed to put the issue behind us and move on."

explain why they responded as they did, to provide an example that supports their answer, or to describe how their response would change if a particular aspect of the original question had been different.

Redirecting is another way of following up an incorrect response. When redirecting, the teacher asks another student to answer the same question (see Figure 12.5). This method of follow-up is highly effective with students whose academic self-concepts are strong. It appears that students who are academically confident are challenged by this technique and motivated to work harder. However, redirecting is not effective with students whose academic self-concepts are weak. In fact, redirecting following an insecure student's incorrect response is likely to result in reduced self-concept, motivation, participation, and learning (Coladarci & Gage, 1984).

Rephrasing simply means restating the same question in different terms. When students fail to respond to a teacher's question, it is often due to poor phrasing of the initial question. Thus, rewording the question can make it clearer, simpler, or focus students' attention on critical aspects (see Figure 12.5). Rephrasing generally is not an effective follow-up technique and should be avoided. A better technique is to elicit some type of response, then use probing questions to help the student arrive at a correct response. While all teachers occasionally ask poorly stated ques-

TABLE 12.1   The Do's and Don'ts of Effective Questioning

Do	Don't
1. Match questions to the objectives and use a variety of question levels and types.	1. Emphasize only lower-order or convergent questions.
2. Ask lots of questions throughout the lesson.	2. Use questions mainly to review at the end of the lesson.
3. Ask a question, pause, and then call on a student by name to respond.	3. Allow callouts or fail to include pauses after your questions.
4. Ensure that all students get equal opportunities to successfully answer questions.	4. Rely on volunteers.
5. Follow up lower-order, inaccurate, and incomplete answers.	5. Overlook or allow to go uncorrected inappropriate or incomplete answers.
6. Write questions, especially critical questions, into your lesson plan.	6. Rely solely on your ability to generate spontaneous questions during interaction.
7. Keep questions clear, brief, and to the point.	7. Use long questions or ask multiple questions simultaneously.
8. Ask questions to keep students engaged.	8. Ask questions as a punitive, disciplinary tool.
9. Write the objectives and summary of the lesson as questions.	9. Devise questions only on major points.
10. Match nonverbal behavior with the questions you ask.	10. Convey disinterest in asking questions or in students' responses.

tions, careful consideration of questions during planning, monitoring their effectiveness during instruction, and questioning with confidence will eventually reduce the need for rephrasing.

Try Activity 12.6

To summarize, questioning is a vital aspect of effective, interactive teaching. It promotes a number of desirable outcomes and can be used for several purposes. Table 12.1 provides an overview of correct and incorrect questioning techniques.

PROVIDING CLEAR INSTRUCTION

Throughout this chapter we have focused on teachers' attributes and behaviors that appear to directly or indirectly promote greater learning, achievement, and motivation. Each characteristic or behavior is grounded in research. We now turn our attention to a complex teaching skill that may contribute more to teacher effectiveness than any other.

Instructional clarity has been the focus of much research ever since Rosenshine and Furst (1971) identified it as the "most promising teacher variable related to student achievement" (p.107). **Instructional clarity** refers to the teacher's ability to provide instruction that helps *students come to a clear understanding of the material.* Thus, clarity is something students achieve, not something the teacher does. However, research has identified specific teacher behaviors that students say help them achieve this clarity of understanding (e.g., Hines, 1981; Hines, Kennedy, & Cruickshank, 1985).

According to students, clear teachers emphasize important points by repeating them, writing them on the board, pausing after stating them, and reviewing them. They monitor students' clarity of understanding by asking questions and providing students with activities and experiences that allow them to apply their knowledge. When students do not understand, clear teachers repeat, review, or rephrase important points. Not surprisingly, teachers who most often and most proficiently use these behaviors to help students understand are associated with significantly greater student learning and satisfaction than teachers who do not (Chesebro &

McCroskey, 2001; Gliessman, Pugh, Brown, & Archer, 1989; Halprin, Easterday, & Elrod, 1994; Hativa, 1998; Metcalf, 1992; Metcalf & Cruickshank, 1991).

The teachers' behaviors that make instruction clear apply not only to the ability to explain content clearly, but also to the ability to structure presentations. Importantly, this lesson-structuring problem applies to both teacher-directed and student-directed instruction (Feden, 1994; Metcalf, 1991; Rosenshine, 2002). These specific behaviors involve (1) preparing and entering the lesson, (2) introducing and emphasizing content, (3) elaborating on important ideas or concepts, and (4) monitoring students' understanding and remediating when students fail to understand. The following discussion of teacher clarity will be organized around these four topics.

Preparing and Entering the Lesson Clear instruction is logically organized and is conducted in a way that helps students see the relationships between major concepts or ideas. Accordingly, clear teachers organize their lesson content and activities logically, inform students of the objectives of the lesson, and introduce the content or activities step by step. During planning, these teachers determine the most logical way to introduce content based upon their students' abilities, previous learning, and the natural structure of the content. Chapter 6 explained some of the ways this can be done (for example, chronologically). For logical organization to make instruction clearer, the organization must be obvious and logical *to students*.

At the beginning of the lesson, teachers should inform students of the lesson objectives. As noted in our discussion of establishing set, teachers should provide an overview of the lesson to help students establish a mental framework for the concepts or activities and to enable them to monitor their own understanding. Students find instruction clearer when the teacher gives it step by step. In other words, teachers should provide instruction and instructional activities in a way that makes the relationship between the concepts obvious to students. Doing so helps students incorporate the new learning with previous learning more accurately.

12.8 Have you ever had a teacher who was obviously knowledgeable, but not clear in helping you understand? How did you feel? Did the teacher realize the problem?

Introducing and Emphasizing Important Points Beyond planning and organizing, clear instruction focuses students' attention on important aspects of the instruction. A common way to do this is to write the major points on the board and/or have students record them. It is important, however, that you monitor your use of the board to ensure that you do not overuse it for minor or unimportant points. Students will perceive things you write on the board as important. Consequently, if you fill the board with minor points or fail to put some or all of the major points on the board, the effectiveness of this technique is reduced.

Another way to reinforce important aspects of the lesson is to point them out through verbal structuring or cuing. Enumerating important points helps structure them. For example, "The first point we will discuss is . . ." "Second, . . ." and "Finally, . . ." enables students to organize their thoughts and the content. Likewise, comments such as, "It is important for you to remember this" or "Listen carefully because this is an important point" alert students to pay close attention to what you are about to say. Repeating important points also cues students. You might combine these reinforcers into a pattern in which you state a point, pause or write it on the board, and then repeat it. To provide even more reinforcement, you could note that this is an important point, state it, write it on the board, and then repeat it.

Finally, you reinforce major points when you review or summarize them. In Chapter 6 we applied the term *closure* to this element of the lesson. Upon completing the lesson or important segments of the lesson (immediately preceding a transition), you should summarize or have students summarize the major ideas of the lesson segment. This serves to repeat major points, further identify them as important, help achieve closure, and prepare students for a smooth transition to the next segment.

Elaborating on Important Ideas or Concepts   In addition to identifying and reinforcing major points for students, you can deepen their understanding of the content by providing examples, explanations, and elaborations. Examples and nonexamples (items that do *not* fit the concept) that illustrate the major points can be vital to students' understanding. Examples can be verbal, written, pictorial, or concrete depending upon the content and the level of the learners. For instance, if learners are familiar with ants, merely noting that ants are an example of an insect may be sufficient. They do not need to see an ant for the example to be useful. However, if you were to use a potentially unfamiliar example of an insect, such as a walking stick, a concrete or pictorial example might be necessary. Further, you would need to make clear how or why the example relates to the concept—in this case, what characteristics classify a creature as an insect. Adding nonexamples, such as a scorpion, would further clarify the concept.

Relatedly, clear instruction helps students see how things are similar or different. You can describe, demonstrate, explain, or show students how two ideas, concepts, examples, or ways of doing things are alike and how they differ. Again, this type of instructional behavior helps students assimilate new information more accurately. When the lesson involves learning a task or skill, it is important that you demonstrate the task and, while doing so, explain what you are doing and why. For example, if you were helping students learn to draw circles with a compass, you might place the pointer and explain why you put it there; explain that the pointer must be kept securely in place with one hand, and show them how to do so; place the marker end of the compass solidly on the paper; and then demonstrate and explain how to turn the compass, ensuring that the mark is complete.

Students also note that clear teachers explain unfamiliar words, whereas unclear teachers often fail to do so. A good rule of thumb is to assume that all new terms are unfamiliar to students and explain or define them *before* using them in the lesson. Finally, students' understanding is enhanced when you briefly pause after introducing something important. Just as wait time allows students to think about a question, pausing after introducing an important point allows students to think about it. It also signals the importance of the ideas.

Ensuring Students' Understanding   The final aspect of instructional clarity involves monitoring and correcting students' understanding by providing opportunities for students to apply the concepts or ideas. Critical to this is your ability to use frequent questions at a variety of levels. In addition to asking questions that assess students' understanding, you should build time for student-generated questions into the lesson. Often, if you have established an open and interactive climate, simply including a long pause after a lesson segment will prompt students who do not understand to ask for clarification. You may also call for students' questions by asking "Are there any questions?" However, in such a general call for questions, extended wait time is critical. Many students will have to think through the content to determine whether they need to ask questions, some will need time to formulate the question they want to ask, and some will need time to work up the courage to ask. Thus, after inviting questions, it would not be inappropriate to pause for as long as five to ten seconds while scanning the room. A better alternative would be to ask for specific questions, such as "What questions do you have about the three points we just discussed?" and then follow up to see how well students understand.

In addition to allowing time for questions, you should include activities that ask your students to demonstrate examples, then closely monitor their performance and provide corrective feedback as needed. In Chapter 6 this was described as providing guided practice. You can have students work individually at their seats, in small groups, or at the board with the entire class contributing. When a student cannot answer a question, cannot accurately apply the content to the examples, or asks a question indicating misunderstanding, it is important that you correct the

Try Activity 12.7

FIGURE 12.6   Behaviors That Characterize Clear Teachers

1. The lesson is planned and implemented in an organized manner.

2. Students are informed of the lesson objectives in advance.

3. The lesson is conducted step by step.

4. The teacher draws students' attention to new or important points by writing them on the board, by repeating them, by reviewing them at appropriate points in the lesson, and by incorporating deliberate pauses that allow time for processing and reflection.

5. The teacher presents and works examples that explain and support the concept or ideas being taught.

6. The teacher explains unfamiliar words before using them in the lesson and points out similarities and differences between ideas.

7. The teacher asks students lots of questions and gives application exercises to find out if students understand the content.

8. The teacher carefully monitors students' work for understanding.

9. The teacher encourages and allows time for students to ask questions.

10. When students do not understand, the teacher repeats main points, presents additional examples or explanation, or elaborates until the students achieve clear understanding.

misunderstanding. Several of the earlier mentioned behaviors, like repeating things, rephrasing, probing, or providing additional examples and further explanation may help clear up confusion.

To summarize, instructional clarity refers to a broad and important set of teachers' behaviors. The major focus of clarity is on helping students understand what you have taught. Remember, clarity is something the student, not the teacher, achieves. However, by learning to use behaviors that make instruction clearer to students, you can greatly improve the effectiveness of your teaching. Figure 12.6 summarizes ten specific behaviors related to clear instruction.

MONITORING STUDENTS' PROGRESS

Effective teachers are adept at monitoring students' understanding, not just their behavior. They carefully and continually assess students' performance and progress and check for understanding in a variety of ways. If students seem to lack understanding, it cues effective teachers to review and possibly adapt their instruction. Monitoring also conveys teachers' interest in their students' progress and task orientation. If the teacher has established an interactive environment in which students participate freely by asking and answering questions, many opportunities will be available for monitoring understanding.

Research has not directly related monitoring student understanding to improved learning. As noted, however, monitoring is an important element of instructional clarity. It is also closely tied to the effective use of instructional time and to effective feedback, each of which has been found to influence students' learning.

Monitoring is especially critical in the early stages of learning when misunderstandings or lack of background knowledge are most likely to affect students. Monitoring during this time allows teachers to correct students before they learn and habituate improper patterns of thinking or behavior. As we will discuss in detail later, it also allows teachers to provide feedback to help students understand why their performance is correct.

You can monitor student understanding in numerous formal and informal ways. Tests, quizzes, homework, and projects are examples of formal monitoring. Although formal monitoring is important, particularly in determining grades, informal monitoring is more frequent and immediate, and it can impact more directly on instructional behavior and learning. Good teachers are constantly aware, or "withit" (Kounin, 1970). They ask many questions of all students, provide a supportive, open environment in which students feel free to ask questions or clarify misunderstandings, and watch for verbal and nonverbal indications that students do not understand.

Specifically, you can improve your ability to monitor students' understanding in several ways. Establish set and use advance organizers at the beginnings of lessons to help students understand the task and monitor their own progress. Get to know students and call on them by name. Move around the room to monitor attention and stay in closer proximity to all students. Maximize interactive, whole-group instruction and minimize small-group or individual work, especially when no additional adult help is available. Use good questioning techniques: Call on all students—not just those who raise their hands; ask questions at a variety of cognitive levels; and allow wait time. Maintain eye contact with all students by scanning the room for both understanding and misbehavior. Convey openness and availability for help. Spend very little time sitting at your desk, even when students are engaged in individual seat work. Instead, move around, scan, avoid turning your back to the class, and be careful not to spend too much time with any one student or group of students. As you will see in Chapter 13, these behaviors are also characteristics of teachers who are effective classroom managers.

12.9 Did you ever feel as if a teacher were "clueless" about your lack of understanding? How did it make you feel? Why did the teacher seem to remain unaware?

PROVIDING FEEDBACK AND REINFORCEMENT

During the instructional process, effective teachers frequently provide students with information about their academic performance. They most commonly do this through feedback and reinforcement. Although similar, feedback and reinforcement are not the same. Reinforcement is meant to improve students' motivation, while feedback is intended to inform students about the accuracy of their performance. In order to use these skills effectively, teachers must understand each of them and how to apply them.

Both reinforcement and feedback are ways of responding to students' performance. They are skills that teachers employ after a student has done something—for example, answered a question, contributed to a discussion, turned in homework, or completed a project. In a classroom where the teacher has established an interactive tone, opportunities for teachers to provide feedback and reinforcement arise naturally and almost constantly. Zahorik (1987) indicates that about one-third of classroom interactions are teachers' responding behaviors. Thus, a teacher's ability to respond appropriately can greatly influence students' performance and motivation.

Feedback   **Feedback** (sometimes called *knowledge of results,* or *KR*) is primarily intended to (1) inform students about the quality and accuracy of their performance and (2) help them learn how to monitor and improve their own learning. For example, teachers use feedback on students' papers to inform them of how well they did in comparison to some standard, what could be improved, and how to improve. The information teachers provide through feedback relates directly to the quality or accuracy of the student's academic performance (Glickman, 2002; Walberg, 1991).

For some students, feedback can also provide reinforcement by helping them feel more secure in their ability to complete the task successfully. However, feedback is not always reinforcing, nor is it intended to be.

Teachers must be able to use both feedback and reinforcement effectively. However, skill in providing feedback is more important in helping students learn than ability to provide reinforcement, particularly praise (Chall, 2000; Wittrock, 1986). While feedback helps the learner to accurately understand and successfully complete necessary tasks, it does not necessarily reinforce or reward the student's performance.

Effective feedback includes information about (1) the *criteria* used to evaluate performance, (2) how the *student's performance relates* to the standard, and (3) specifically how the performance can or should be *improved* (Behets, 1997; Chesebro & McCroskey, 2001; Wittrock, 1986). Most people think of feedback as verbal or written comments from the teacher. However, students often learn about the adequacy of their performance simply by observing or comparing their own performance with some standard. Thus, while students can learn from feedback provided by the teacher or peers, they can also learn by watching or listening to their performance through video- or audiotaping. The immediate goal of feedback is to improve students' understanding and performance. A long-range goal is to enable learners to judge for themselves the adequacy of their own work or performance.

Several principles can make teachers' feedback more effective:

1. Provide feedback as frequently as possible—every day for every student, if possible. It is important that you plan and maintain a highly interactive environment providing a variety of opportunities for students to practice or perform, and that you monitor and provide feedback on these performances.

2. Provide feedback as soon after performance as possible. For example, return papers quickly, try to grade immediately following performance, and provide verbal feedback while monitoring students' practice.

3. Make your feedback specific rather than general. For example, use students' names and comment specifically on their performance instead of simply saying "good job" or writing "weak here."

4. Focus feedback on the *quality* of the student's performance, not on his or her intentions or motivations. Good feedback can convey confidence in a student's ability without giving the impression that incomplete or inaccurate work is acceptable and without appearing cold and impersonal. One way to do this is to include feedback on the process (how to do it better) along with the adequacy of the performance.

5. Design and use feedback that teaches students how to gauge their own progress and performance. Gradually allow students to assume more and more responsibility for assessing their progress. Allow them to score their own or each other's papers and provide mutual feedback, to engage in peer editing as a part of the writing process, to watch or listen to recordings of their performances, and so on.

Reinforcement Reinforcement is intended to strengthen and increase the frequency of a desirable behavior or response, usually by providing some type of reward. Reinforcement lets students know when they have done something well in the hope that they will do it again or with greater frequency. When a normally quiet student voluntarily responds to a question, you might attempt to reinforce him, perhaps through a smile or gesture, in the hope that he will contribute more often in the future. Your focus should be on rewarding the student for his participation (that is, his behavior), not necessarily on the accuracy of his response. Chapter 13 will discuss this type of reinforcement further.

In contrast to feedback, which is directed toward improving the quality of students' performance, reinforcement is directed toward increasing motivation. Often reinforcement is provided through verbal praise, but it can take many forms. Repeating or paraphrasing a student's comment or answer or including it in your discussion can be reinforcing. Nonverbal expressions like nods or smiles, eye contact, gestures, or proximity may also reinforce students. More tangibly, reinforcement can take the form of free time, candy, tokens, or other rewards.

Reinforcement, particularly in the form of praise or rewards, is only marginally effective in increasing learning (Chall, 2000; Walberg, 1991). In fact, the relationship between learning and the use of praise seems to be curvilinear. That is, increasing the use of praise will help students learn more only up to a point. After that, increased praise will probably diminish learning. One reason for this may be that praise and other rewards are reinforcing only if the student perceives them to be. If the reward is embarrassing or of no interest to the student, the reward is likely to diminish rather than increase learning (Kennedy, 1997; Wittrock, 1986). A second problem with praise and reinforcement is that teachers often unknowingly reinforce the wrong behavior (Callahan, Clark, & Kellough, 2002). For example, to get an unsuccessful student to contribute more often to class discussions, teachers may praise an incorrect or inappropriate contribution rather than the behavior of participating. The result may be that the student does contribute more often, but also learns inaccurate content.

Because reinforcement focuses on students' motivation and self-concept, it is most important early in the learning process and with low-achieving students. However, teachers seldom use it in these situations (Kennedy, 1997). Reinforcement is most likely to be successful (1) when it specifically identifies the behavior or performance being rewarded, (2) when it is contingent upon desired behavior or performance (it is not offered when students respond or behave incorrectly), and (3) when it is believable. Criticism (the opposite of praise) can be effective with high-achieving students when used in moderation. Generally, however, it is not effective in promoting learning, and it often is counterproductive, diminishing students' self-concept and motivation (Chall, 2000).

Although a powerful tool, reinforcement should be used sparingly and with caution. Brophy (1981) notes that teachers should try "structuring the classroom in order to elicit good student performances in the first place rather than on reinforcing good performance after it has been elicited" (p.16). Teachers should provide heavy reinforcement and feedback to all students early in the learning process and to low-achieving students throughout. Especially with older students, reinforcement and praise should be low-key, private, and specific to the student's performance.

Reinforcement can and should focus on both motivation and outcome. However, it should be keyed to desirable performance, and the teacher should make clear the specific behavior being reinforced. Although some students should be rewarded for participation even if the response is incorrect, make clear that the reward is for *participation*, not incorrect *performance*. When offering reinforcement or praise, be certain to match verbal and nonverbal behavior. That is, don't tell a student she did a nice job with a scowl on your face! Closely monitor the effectiveness of your reinforcement of each student. Remember, although you may intend your actions to be reinforcing, the student may not perceive them that way. Finally, allow yourself to be somewhat spontaneous with your use of praise; it is more sincere.

12.10 Do you agree that feedback is more important in promoting student learning than reinforcement? Why or why not?

12.11 Why do you think teachers emphasize reinforcement and neglect adequate feedback?

Some Final Thoughts

Running through all the specific behaviors discussed in Chapters 11 and 12 is the notion of providing students with instruction that will maximize their learning and their motivation to learn. Establishing set helps students focus. Momentum, variety, and enthusiasm maintain students' interest and engagement. Questions, when used well, help students process the lesson content in order to better understand it. Thus, although we have emphasized teachers' personal attributes and professional behavior, we must always remember that these are merely efficient means to desirable ends. They are not ends in themselves. For example, questions are not used for their own sake, but to help students learn more and better. However, much evidence indicates that these attributes and behaviors are critical in maximizing learning and motivation. They are the foundation upon which instructional alternatives and classroom management strategies are built. The better you are able to use them, the more effective your use of any instructional method, alternative, or strategy will be.

CHAPTER SUMMARY

12.12 What can you do now to help ensure that you will make use of what is known about effective teaching in your own classroom?

- Effective teachers possess a repertoire of professional skills that enable them to help students learn more. These professional skills are more open to improvement than personal attributes are. They can be organized around four aspects of instruction: engaging and maintaining students' attention, optimizing the use of instructional time, promoting meaningful teacher-student interaction, and providing effective feedback and reinforcement.

- Skilled teachers engage students' attention and maintain their interest and motivation by establishing set at the beginning of the lesson and incorporating variety in their lessons.

- There are three major types of set. Orientation set engages students in a new instructional activity. Transition set helps students see the relationship between past and present learning. Evaluative set establishes what students may already know about a topic.

- The beginning of a lesson is critical because it establishes a climate or tone for the lesson. The beginning of the lesson should engage students' interest through an interesting or provocative problem; should establish an interactive climate that encourages students to participate; should make students aware early in the lesson of the major topics, objectives, or tasks for the lesson; and should make clear the relationship between the current lesson and previous lessons.

- An effective teacher uses variety in nonverbal behavior, instructional approaches, types of assessment, and a host of other areas. Variability, which Rosenshine and Furst (1971) found to be closely related to students' learning, probably increases learning by helping students remain more interested and engaged.

- The most effective teachers maximize the time available for instruction. The three factors most closely related to the efficient use of instructional time are time on task, momentum, and smooth transitions.

- *Time on task* is a broad term that refers to the amount of time students are actively engaged in academic tasks. Generally, the more time students spend actively engaged in academic tasks, the more they learn. However, only a small percentage of available time is actually used for academic tasks.

- Instructional time can be organized around four levels. Mandated time is the formal time scheduled for school or academic activities: for example, the length of the school year, day, or period. Allocated time is the amount of mandated time intended solely for academic activities. It excludes such things as passing or lunch periods. Academic instruction time is the amount of allocated time during which the teacher is conducting instructional activities. This is time left after taking attendance, giving directions, and so on. Academic learning time is the amount of time a given student spends actively engaged in academic tasks she is mostly successful at doing. This eliminates the part of academic learning time when the student may not be paying attention or may be inaccurately learning the content.

- From mandated to academic learning time, much opportunity for learning is lost. Effective teachers maximize students' engagement by beginning and ending on time, minimizing time spent giving directions, establishing rules and procedures that minimize disruptions, and actively monitoring students' engagement. They also create a highly interactive and varied environment that gets students' attention and holds it throughout the lesson.

- Momentum refers to the flow and pace of classroom activities. Maintaining momentum helps maximize academic learning time by maintaining a brisk instructional pace that still allows students to be successful. Momentum must be adapted to students' needs and to the difficulty or complexity of the required tasks. Generally, teacher-directed instruction allows greater control of momentum and instructional time.

- Instructional time is enhanced when teachers plan for and implement smooth transitions. Transitions are points where students' attention is refocused to new topics or activities.

- Teachers should work to minimize the number and length of transitions and to make them as organized as possible. They should develop routines and procedures for frequently occurring transitions, should inform students about what they are to do ahead of time, and should monitor the transition.

- Effective teachers keep students involved in their lessons through questioning, instructional clarity, and monitoring of understanding.

- Questioning involves not only asking good questions but knowing how to obtain answers and how to react to students' responses. The most effective questions require students to process information and formulate a correct answer. Closed-response questions should be avoided or minimized. Questions should be phrased clearly and concisely in direct, natural, unambiguous language and should vary in form and in cognitive level depending upon the objectives of the lesson. Teachers ask more and better questions when they include them in their lesson planning. Teachers can enhance the effectiveness of their questioning by using wait time and maximizing student participation. Wait time refers to the pauses teachers place between the question and a student's response and between a student's response and the teacher's reaction. Ideal wait time appears to be between three and five seconds, and allows students to think about the question or response.

- We should address questions to all students, not just volunteers. This keeps the class alert, allows everyone to participate, and permits the teacher to better monitor the success of instruction.

- After a student responds to a question, the teacher's reaction is critical. Possible responses include probing, redirecting, rephrasing, or giving the student the answer. Probing means asking the student additional questions to expand or raise the level or accuracy of the response. Redirecting involves asking another student to answer the same question. This should generally be avoided. Rephrasing means rewording the original question to make it clearer. Generally, this should be done only after the student has unsuccessfully attempted to respond.

- Teachers whom students find most enjoyable and helpful provide instruction that leads them to a clear understanding of the material. Instructional clarity is achieved through logical organization, identifying and reinforcing main points, using good examples to elaborate, and monitoring and correcting.

- Clear teachers use logical organization by informing students of the lesson objectives early in the lesson and presenting the content so that students can see the relationships between concepts or ideas.

- Clear teachers help students identify and reinforce important aspects of the lesson by noting and repeating major points and writing them on the board. Reviews and summaries are included throughout the lesson to help reinforce major points and draw broader conclusions.

- Clear teachers elaborate on important ideas and concepts using concrete, verbal, or written examples and by explicitly showing how ideas, concepts, and tasks are similar to and different from one another.
- Clear teachers monitor and quickly correct students' misunderstandings by asking questions and assigning application exercises throughout the lesson to monitor understanding and to allow students to clarify their own misconceptions.
- Effective teachers carefully and continually assess students' understanding through good questioning and by establishing an open, interactive classroom climate in which students are more likely to ask for help.
- Effective teachers provide students with frequent feedback and reinforcement for their academic performance. Although reinforcement and feedback are both means of responding to student performance, they are designed to achieve different ends.
- Feedback is primarily informational and is intended to help students improve their performance. It is probably more important than reinforcement in promoting learning.
- The most useful feedback includes the standard performance was judged against, how the student's performance compares with that standard, and specifically how the performance can be improved. Feedback should be provided frequently, as soon after performance as possible, and should focus on the quality of performance rather than the student's intentions or effort.
- Reinforcement is intended to strengthen or promote desirable behavior by providing some type of reward. Reinforcement is directed toward motivating students. Thus, it is most useful at points where students are most likely to become frustrated and give up (for example, early in the process of learning a task or at any time with less able students).
- Reinforcement in the form of verbal praise is only marginally effective. The most effective reinforcement is specific to the behavior being rewarded, contingent upon the desired behavior or performance, and believable or genuine.

ISSUES AND PROBLEMS FOR DISCUSSION

PROBLEMS   The following are problems and concerns teachers have expressed. How do you feel about them? What would you do in each teacher's place?

Problem 1:   "Today I spent all afternoon on one lesson. I spent from 12:30 to 1:15 and again from 1:30 to 2:15 on math. They were all 'higher than kites' and it was probably due to Halloween. I caught about five kids writing notes instead of paying attention. When I checked to see if they knew what they were doing, they didn't!"

Problem 2:   "We have a good program called 'Book It' to encourage reading. My main concern today is providing my first-grade 'Book It' students with adequate time for oral book reports without neglecting the rest of the class."

Problem 3:   "What concerns me is the way so many of my students won't listen to directions. I gave a math assignment and had about ten kids that didn't know what to do. The lack of inner discipline I see in many students worries me."

Problem 4:   "Today's class was disrupted by constant talking. Every time the group was given a new direction or activity, they began talking. I had to remind them more than once to remain quiet."

Problem 5: "I find it difficult to meet with three reading groups all working at different levels in the 60 minutes allotted to reading. I find myself neglecting the top group. Also, I don't like giving the groups busywork since it is wasted time for everyone, including the grader. How do others deal with this?"

THEORY INTO ACTION ACTIVITIES

You have learned about the importance of developing several professional skills to improve your instruction. The following exercises will help you apply your understanding.

ACTIVITY 12.1: Planning to Establish Set   Develop a lesson plan for a ten-minute lesson segment in which you will establish at least one of the three types of set. Then, ask a classmate to evaluate the plan using the guidelines in Figure 12.1.

ACTIVITY 12.2: Establishing Set in the Classroom   Conduct an observation of a teacher, focusing on the teacher's use of set induction. Did the teacher establish set? How long did the set take? Which type or types were used? To what extent did the teacher include the four general aspects of effective set? What, if anything, could be done to establish set more effectively?

ACTIVITY 12.3: Variety in College Instruction   Think about one of your current courses. Keep a running list or journal of the forms of variety the instructor uses over a two-week period. Then, label each type of variation as "variety of instructional materials" or "techniques" or "interaction." Which type of variety is used most often? How effective is the instructor's use of variety? List some specific ways in which the teacher could enhance variety.

ACTIVITY 12.4: Observing and Recording Instructional Time   Make two detailed observations of the use of time during teacher-directed lessons. You will need a stopwatch or watch with a second hand. In the first observation, record the amount of time the teacher devotes to academic tasks (for example, providing instruction, answering content questions, and so forth) and the amount of time devoted to noninstructional tasks (taking attendance, correcting behavior, giving directions). What proportion of the time was devoted to instructional tasks? To noninstructional tasks? What might the teacher do to increase the amount of instructional time?

In a second lesson, use this same procedure to assess the academic learning time of one student. At the beginning of the lesson, select a student to observe. Record the amount of time the student appears to be engaged in academic tasks and compare this with the total length of the lesson. What percentage of the time was the student engaged? Were there particular activities that seemed more or less engaging to the student? What did the student do when not engaged? Do you believe this student is typical of the other students in the classroom?

ACTIVITY 12.5: Asking Clear Questions   Rewrite each of the following questions to make them more effective.

1. "What did we say was the capital of Russia?"
2. "True or false? 6×8 is the same as 8×6."
3. "What is the importance of the Eighteenth Amendment to the Constitution? Today we're going to talk about that."
4. "David, you weren't paying attention. What did Aaron just say?"

5. "What could possibly justify the enormous loss of human life during the Vietnam War?"

6. "Can anyone tell me who wrote *A Christmas Carol?*"

ACTIVITY 12.6: Planning for Effective Questioning   Generate a list of questions you might use if you were teaching a lesson on American holidays. Attempt to include questions of each type and level. For example, generate lower- and higher-order questions, convergent and divergent questions, process and content questions, and so on.

ACTIVITY 12.7: Planning for Giving Clear Instructions   Develop a plan for a short lesson following the suggestions for instructional planning in Chapter 6. Then make notations to help you improve the clarity of the lesson. For example, underline or highlight specific information you will write on the board, indicate points where you will review and summarize, and include questions you will ask to monitor students' understanding.

REFERENCES

Alexander, P., Jetton, T., & Kulikowich, J. (1994). Contrasting instructional and structural importance: The seductive effect of teacher questions. *Journal of Reading Behavior, 26*(1), 19–45.

Anderson, L., Evertson, C., & Brophy, J. (1979). An experimental study of effective teaching in first-grade reading groups. *The Elementary School Journal, 79,* 193–223.

Arends, R. (2001). *Learning to teach.* Fifth Edition. New York: McGraw-Hill.

Arlin, M. (1979). Teacher transitions can disrupt time flow in classrooms. *American Educational Research Journal, 16,* 42–56.

Barden, L. (1995). Effective questioning and the ever-elusive higher-order question. *American Biology Teacher, 57*(7), 423–426.

Behets, D. (1997). Comparison of more and less effective teaching behaviors in secondary physical education. *Teacher and Teacher Education, 13,* 215–224.

Bellon, J., Bellon, E., & Blank, M. (1992). *Teaching from a research knowledge base: A development and renewal process.* New York: Macmillan.

Berliner, D. (1987). But do they understand? In V. Richardson-Koehler (Ed.), *Educators' handbook: A research perspective* (pp. 259–293). New York: Longman.

Bloom, R., & Bourbon, L. (1980). Types and frequencies of teachers' written instructional feedback. *Journal of Educational Research, 74,* 13–15.

Blythe, T., Allen, D., and Powell, B. (1999). *Looking together at student work: A window into the classroom* (videotape). New York: Teachers College Press.

Borich, G. (2000). *Effective teaching methods.* Fourth Edition. New York: Prentice Hall.

Bracey, G. (2001). At the beep, pay attention. *Phi Delta Kappan, 82,* 555–556.

Brophy, J. (1981). Teacher praise: A functional analysis. *Review of Educational Research, 51*(1), 5–32.

Brophy, J., & Evertson, C. (1976). *Process-product correlations in the Texas Teacher Effectiveness Study* (Final report) (Research Report 74–4). Austin: University of Texas Research and Development Center for Teacher Education. (ERIC Document Reproduction Service ED 091 094)

Brophy, J., & Good, T. (1986). Teacher behavior and student achievement. In M. Wittrock (Ed.), *The handbook of research on teaching* (pp. 328–375). New York: Macmillan.

Brown, S., & Brown, D. (1999). Making the most of a 30-minute class. *Strategies, 13*(2), 33–36.

Brush, T. (1997). The effects of group composition on achievement and time on task for students completing ILS activities in cooperative pairs. *Journal of Research on Computing in Education, 30,* 2–17.

Callahan, J., Clark, L., & Kellough, R. (2002). *Teaching in the middle and secondary schools.* Seventh Edition. New York: Prentice Hall.

Camp, W. (1993). Improving your teaching: Set induction. *The Agricultural Education Magazine, 66,* 20–21.

Cazden, C. (1986). Classroom discourse. In M. Wittrock (Ed.), *The handbook of research on teaching* (pp. 432–469). New York: Macmillan.

Chall, J. (2002). *The academic achievement challenge: What really works in the classroom?* New York: Guilford Press.

Chesebro, J., & McCroskey, J. (2001). The relationship of teacher clarity and immediacy with student state receiver apprehension, affect, and cognitive learning. *Communication Education, 50*(1), 59–68.

Clare, S., Jenson, W., & Kehle, T. (2000). Self-modeling as a treatment for increasing on-task behavior. *Psychology in the Schools, 37,* 517–522.

Coladarci, T., & Gage, N. (1984). Effects of a minimal intervention on teacher behavior and student achievement. *American Educational Research Journal, 21,* 539–555.

Cruickshank, D. (1990). *Research that informs teachers and teacher educators.* Bloomington, IN: Phi Delta Kappa.

Danielson, C. (1996). *Enhancing professional practice: A framework for teaching.* Alexandria, VA: ASCD.

Dillon, J. (1988). *Questioning and teaching.* New York: Teachers College Press.

Doyle, W. (1986). Classroom organization and management. In M. C. Wittrock (Ed.), *The handbook of research on teaching* (pp. 392–431). New York: Macmillan.

Eby, J. (2001). *Reflective planning, teaching, and evaluation for the elementary school.* New York: Prentice Hall.

Ellis, A. (2001). *Teaching, learning, and assessment together: The reflective classroom.* Larchmont, NY: Eye on Education.

Feden, P. (1994). About instruction: Powerful new strategies worth knowing. *Educational Horizons, 74,* 18–24.

Fisher, C., Berliner, D., Filby, N., Marliave, R., Cohen, L., & Dishaw, M. (1984). Teaching behaviors, academic learning time, and student achievement: An overview. In D. Strother (Ed.), *Time and learning* (pp. 97–122). Bloomington, IN: Phi Delta Kappa.

Gage, N. (1989). Process-product research on teaching: A review of criticisms. *The Elementary School Journal, 89*(3), 253–300.

Gall, M. (1984). Synthesis of research on teachers' questioning. *Educational Leadership, 42,* 40–47.

Glass, G. (2002). Time for school: Its duration and allocation. In A. Molnar (Ed.), *School reform proposals: The research evidence* (EPSL–0201–101–EPRU). Tempe: Arizona State University, Education Policy Research Unit.

Glickman, C. (2002). *Leadership for learning: How to help teachers succeed.* Alexandria, VA: Association for Supervision and Curriculum Development.

Gliessman, D., Pugh, R., Brown, L., & Archer, A. (1989). Research-based teacher training: Applying a concept teaching model to the development and transfer of a learning-related teaching skill. Paper presented at the annual meeting of the American Educational Research Association, San Francisco.

Good, T. (1988). Research on teacher effects: Uses and abuses. *Elementary School Journal, 89*(1), 3–21.

Good, T., & Brophy, J. (2000). *Looking in classrooms.* Eighth Edition. New York: Addison-Wesley Longman.

Halpin, R., Easterday, K., & Elrod, J. (1994). A study of teachers' usage of vague terms in the geometry classroom. *International Journal of Mathematical Education in Science and Technology, 25,* 649–654.

Hativa, N. (1998). Lack of clarity in university teaching: A case study. *Higher Education, 36,* 353–381.

Hargreaves, A. (1994). Time and teachers' work: An analysis of the intensification thesis. *Teachers College Record, 94*(1), 87–107.

Henson, K. (1980). What's the use of lecturing? *The High School Journal, 64,* 115–119.

Hines, C. (1981). A further investigation of teacher clarity: The relationship between observed and perceived teacher clarity and student achievement and satisfaction. Doctoral dissertation, The Ohio State University. *Dissertation Abstracts International, 42,* 3122A.

Hines, C., Kennedy, J., & Cruickshank, D. (1985). Teacher clarity and its relationship to student achievement and satisfaction. *American Educational Research Journal, 22,* 87–99.

Joyce, B., & Weil, M. (2000). *Models of teaching*. Sixth Edition. Needham Heights, MA: Allyn & Bacon.

Karweit, N. (1984). Time-on-task reconsidered: Synthesis of research on time-on-task. *Educational Leadership,* 32–35.

Kennedy E. (1997). A study of students' fears of seeking academic help from teachers. *Journal of Classroom Interaction, 32,* 11–17.

Latham, A. (1997). Asking students the right questions. *Educational Leadership, 54,* 84–85.

Leather, R. (2000). Concentration skills. *Child Education, 77*(12), 40–41.

LeNoir, W. (1993). Teacher questions and schema activation. *The Clearinghouse, 66,* 349–352.

Luiten, J., Ames, W., & Aerson, G. (1980). A meta-analysis of advance organizers on learning and retention. *American Educational Research Journal, 17,* 211–218.

Lunenborg, F. (1998). Techniques in the supervision of teachers: Preservice and inservice applications. *Education, 118,* 521–525.

Mencke, D. and Pressley, M. (1994). Elaborative interrogation: Using 'why' questions to enhance the learning from text. *Journal of Reading. 37*(8), 642–645.

Metcalf, K. (1991). Improving problem-solving instruction using research of instructional clarity. *Issues and Trends in Education, 1,* 6–12.

Metcalf, K. (1992). The effects of a guided laboratory experience on the instructional clarity of preservice teachers. *Teaching and Teacher Education, 8*(3), 275–286.

Metcalf, K., & Cruickshank, D. (1991). Can teachers be trained to be more clear? *Journal of Educational Research, 85,* 107–116.

Moore, K. (2001), *Classroom teaching skills*. Fifth Edition. New York: McGraw-Hill.

Morine-Dershimer, G., & Beyerbach, B. (1987). Moving right along. . . . In V. Richardson-Koehler (Ed.), *Educators' handbook: A research perspective* (pp. 207–232). New York: Longman.

Ornstein, A., Lasley, T. (2000). *Strategies for effective teaching*. New York: McGraw-Hill.

Pate, R., & Bremer, N. (1967). Guiding learning through skillful questioning. *Elementary School Journal, 67,* 417–422.

Perkins, D. (1993). Teaching for understanding. *American Educator, 17,* 28–35.

Rohrkemper, M., & Corno, L. (1988). Success and failure on classroom tasks: Adaptive learning and classroom teaching. *The Elementary School Journal, 88*(3), 298–312.

Rosenshine, B. (2002). Converging findings on classroom instruction. In A. Molnar (Ed.), *School reform proposals: The research evidence* (EPSL–0201–101–EPRU). Tempe: Arizona State University, Education Policy Research Unit.

Rosenshine, B., & Furst, N. (1971). Research on teacher performance criteria. In B. Smith (Ed.), *Research in teacher education* (pp. 37–72). Englewood Cliffs, NJ: Prentice Hall.

Rosenshine, B., & Stevens, R. (1986). Teaching functions. In M. Wittrock (Ed.), *The handbook of research on teaching* (pp. 376–391). New York: Macmillan.

Sadker, M., & Sadker, D. (2001). Questioning skills. In J. Cooper (Ed.), *Classroom teaching skills* (pp. 143–180). Boston: Houghton Mifflin.

Schuck, R. (1985). An empirical analysis of the power of set induction and systematic questioning as instructional strategies. *Journal of Teacher Education, 36,* 38–43.

Sigel, I. (1990). What teachers need to know about human development. In D. Dill and associates (Eds.), *What teachers need to know: The knowledge, skills, and values essential to good teaching*. San Francisco: Jossey-Bass.

Smith, B. (2000). Quantity matters: Annual instructional time in an urban school system. *Educational Administration Quarterly, 36,* 652–682.

Sternberg, R. (1994). Answering questions and questioning answers: Guiding children to intellectual excellence. *Phi Delta Kappan, 76,* 136–135.

Tobin, K. (1987). The role of wait time in higher cognitive learning. *Review of Educational Research, 56,* 69–95.

Traver, R. (1998). What is a good guiding question? *Educational Leadership, 55*(6), 70–73.

Walberg, H. (1988). Synthesis of research on time and learning. *Educational Leadership, 45*(2), 143–178.

Walberg, H. (1990). Productive teaching and instruction: Assessing the knowledge base. *Phi Delta Kappan, 71*(6), 470–478.

Walberg, H. (1991). Productive teaching and instruction: Assessing the knowledge base. In H. Waxman and H. Walberg (Eds.), *Effective teaching: Current research* (pp. 33–62). Berkeley, CA: McCutchan.

Wang, M., Haertel, G., & Walberg, H. (1993–94). What helps students learn? *Educational Leadership 51*(4), 74–79.

Waxman, H. (1987–88). Effective lesson introductions and pre-instructional activities: A review of recent research. *Journal of Classroom Interaction, 23*(1), 5–7.

Wenglinsky, H. (2000). *How teaching matters: Bringing the classroom back into discussions of teacher quality.* Princeton, NJ: Educational Testing Service.

Wilen, W., & Clegg, A. (1986). Effective questions and questioning: A research review. *Theory and Research in Social Education, 14,* 153–161.

Wittrock, M. (1986). Students' thought processes. In M. Wittrock (Ed.), *The handbook of research on teaching* (pp. 297–314). New York: MacMillan.

Yair, G. (2000). Not just about time: Instructional practices and productive time in school. *Educational Administration Quarterly, 36,* 485–512.

Zahorik, J. (1987). The effects of planning on teaching. *The Elementary School Journal, 71,* 143–151.

How the Effective Teacher Manages the Classroom

Contents

"I feel ready to teach, but what do I do if some student tells me to shut up?"

The fear and confusion this student teacher expresses reminds us that a common, persistent problem among teachers, and perhaps the greatest fear of new teachers, is student misbehavior.

Feelings of inadequacy are compounded by the realization that teachers are *expected* to be good classroom managers. Administrators expect teachers to effectively manage their classrooms and students, and often equate control of students with good teaching. Likewise, members of the community expect teachers to control students both at school and at extracurricular events and to teach students self-control. Even students expect teachers to exert classroom control in order to establish a good learning environment. Finally, teachers themselves expect their students to be controlled. In poorly managed classrooms, teachers feel that their goals are thwarted because management takes so much time, energy, and patience that there is little opportunity for instruction. These teachers report feeling frustrated and dissatisfied with teaching (Cruickshank & Associates, 1980).

Because well-managed classrooms are so important to everyone, you should begin developing a classroom management plan at once. Your plan should include four parts. First, you must anticipate and decide *how to prevent management problems* from occurring. Second, you should decide how to *monitor your students' behavior* in order to maintain a good learning environment. Third, you should plan *how to react when students misbehave* in your classroom. Finally, you need to decide *how to reestablish a positive classroom environment* after correcting misbehavior. This chapter is organized to help you develop specific management strategies in each of these four areas.

13.1 What expectations do you hold for yourself and your students regarding classroom management?

What Is Classroom Management?

Traditionally, classroom management has been focused on how teachers react *after* students misbehave. The emphasis was on **discipline,** or the specific actions teachers or others take in response to a student who disobeys a reasonable classroom or school rule (Wolfgang & Kelsay, 1995). Some teachers spend as much as 80 percent of their time and effort trying to control student behavior (Englander, 1986).

Surprisingly, this approach does not seem to work. Teachers who are obsessed with disciplining students or who neglect instructional preparation in favor of total control tend to end up with *more* control problems than teachers who are well prepared and who focus their efforts on helping students achieve academically (Brophy & Evertson, 1976). This may be because teachers, especially novices, frequently believe learning cannot take place until the classroom is organized and the students are under control. They focus their time and energy on controlling students rather than on teaching-learning processes (Anderson 1991; Dollard, 1996).

Research suggests that these control-oriented teachers may be trying too hard and teaching too little. That is, they are not presenting the clear, uninterrupted, brisk-paced lessons essential to students' involvement and learning. Every research study attempting to link learning with some classroom influence shows that effective management skills are positively related to students' achievement. That is, when students spend more time engaged in learning tasks and correspondingly less time engaged in nonacademic behaviors, they learn more. In short, academic engagement is inversely related to students' misbehavior (Hawley & Rosenholtz, 1984).

In the 1970s, research by Kounin shifted attention from reactive disciplinary strategies to **proactive,** or preventive, views of classroom management. Effective proactive management includes establishing clear rules and predictable routines, monitoring behavior, consistently enforcing rules, and anticipating behavior problems and responding immediately (McGinnis, Frederick, & Edwards, 1995). It is clear that the most effective classroom managers are those who prevent problems from arising in the first place (Brophy, 1983; DiGiulio, 2000; Kounin, 1970). Kounin's work reminds teachers that although they must be able to discipline students when necessary, effective instruction must be the first priority. Indeed, proactive techniques reduce disruptive behavior by at least 75 percent (Freiberg, 1996; Jones & Jones, 2000). Doyle (1983) found that the curriculum and daily academic work are an integral part of classroom management because they can motivate students, engage them in challenging activities and thinking, and prevent them from drifting into misbehavior. Effective classroom managers, then, strive to elicit students' cooperation and involve them in high-interest activities, thus preventing potential discipline problems.

For today's classrooms, a comprehensive management plan should include both proactive (preventive) and reactive (disciplinary) management strategies. **Classroom management,** then, can be defined as the provisions and procedures necessary to create and maintain an environment in which teaching and learning can occur (Duke, 1987). This means that when you plan your classroom management strategies you need to consider the sort of classroom environment you want and the rules and routines you need to establish this environment. Further, you must learn how to hold students accountable for following classroom procedures and how to reinforce and reward students for doing so. Finally, you need to plan how you will intervene when misbehavior does occur.

13.2 What are your greatest fears about classroom management?

13.3 How, if at all, have you changed your mind about classroom control?

Preventing Management Problems

Evertson (1989) describes the transition from the world of preservice education to the real world of teaching as problematic and traumatic. Why? Because preservice teachers like yourselves rarely see practicing teachers take an empty classroom, multitudes of raw materials, a designated group of students, and school goals and organize them into a dynamic, safe, cooperative learning environment. Think about the classroom observation experiences you have had thus far. Most education students observe and practice in classrooms that are already well-established. As a result, the issue of how to set up a classroom with a positive learning environment in which students learn prosocial behaviors is generally overlooked in teacher preparation programs.

Fortunately, even if you have not observed a teacher establishing a positive learning environment, you do not have to depend on your intuition or on trial and error when you attempt to set up your own classroom. Research over the past two decades tells us exactly what effective classroom managers do to prevent management problems and to establish classrooms where teaching and learning occur. Effective teachers begin early in the school year to systematically implement a carefully developed plan. They thoughtfully establish the physical and psychological environments in their classrooms. Further, they plan and implement classroom routines to make the classroom a more predictable place. Let's focus in more detail on these aspects of preventive management.

ESTABLISHING THE PHYSICAL AND PSYCHOLOGICAL ENVIRONMENT

The classroom environment has a powerful impact on students' behavior, learning, and motivation. Years ago, Lewin and his associates showed that the interaction between one's needs and the surrounding environmental conditions is a key factor in explaining an individual's behavior (Lewin, Lippitt, & White, 1939).

Teachers can manipulate two elements of the classroom environment to increase learning and improve behavior (Anderson, 1991). The **physical environment** consists of those aspects of the classroom that are independent of the people who inhabit it. The shape and size of the room, the seating arrangement, and the location and availability of equipment and materials are major aspects of the physical environment. Because these are concrete and observable, most of the students in a classroom would describe the physical environment in the same way.

In contrast, the **psychological environment** exists only in the minds of those who occupy the classroom. As a result, the students and teacher may experience and describe the psychological environment in different ways. The psychological environment is sometimes referred to as the classroom **climate.** It includes the emotional tone of the classroom and the comfort level students feel with the teacher, learning tasks, and one another as a social group (Eggen & Kauchak, 2000; Walberg, 1987).

Planning the Physical Environment Effective classroom management starts with decisions about the physical environment in the classroom. While there is little evidence that classroom materials and equipment strongly influence students' achievement (Wang, Haertel, & Walberg, 1993–94), there is substantial evidence that other factors such as room arrangement and seating patterns can affect the behavior of students and their attitudes toward school and learning (Ainley, 1987; Gunter, Shores, Jack, Rasmussen, & Flowers, 1995). How you arrange your classroom and your students' places within it, then, are important management considerations.

The fact that the classroom environment influences students' behavior and learning makes sense when we recall the ideas of Maslow (Maslow & Laury, 1998). As mentioned in Chapter 4, Maslow identified a hierarchy of the needs that motivate human behavior. Maslow's work suggests that everyone, students and teachers alike, has a basic need to feel safe and secure in their surroundings. Further, they need to feel valued as members of the social group and to be challenged by new and varied experiences. Savage (1991) suggests that students often misbehave as they try to meet these basic needs. For example, a student seated near the pencil sharpener may feel threatened when other students congregate there, leaning on her desk and talking while they await their turn. She may verbally or physically lash out at the students to keep them out of "her" space. Thoughtful management of the physical environment can minimize or eliminate this and many other classroom problems.

Seating Patterns One of the most obvious aspects of the physical environment that teachers can manipulate is the seating arrangement. Students need to know that the classroom is a safe, comfortable place for positive social and academic experiences. They need enough space to move freely and to work at their desks without distractions.

As you plan, remember that seating arrangement affects peer interaction. How do students interact when they are seated in rows? They tend to be focused on instruction and to persist at independent learning tasks since it is difficult for them to

13.4 Where do you prefer to sit in a classroom? Why?

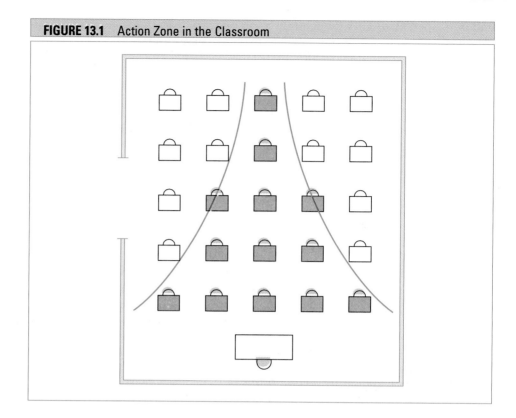

FIGURE 13.1   Action Zone in the Classroom

interact with each other (Wheldall, Morris, Vaughan, & Ng, 1981). In contrast, students seated face to face around tables interact more frequently with their peers. Sitting around a table seems to influence the development of student leadership abilities. Weinstein (1987) found that when students are assigned to sit at tables with two on one side and three on the other, twice as many leaders emerge from the side where only two students sit, perhaps because these students can influence more people. In a circular seating arrangement, students are most likely to speak to those seated directly across from them. They rarely speak to persons seated beside them. This suggests that teachers can influence the flow of discussion by purposefully seating students. For example, when a quiet student sits opposite the leader, chances are that the quiet student will participate more than usual. Conversely, placing an overly vocal student next to the leader should prevent that student from dominating the discussion.

Seating arrangement also affects the interactions between students and the teacher. Students seated in the front and down the middle of the classroom define a triangular area in which most interaction occurs called the *action zone* (Figure 13.1). Teachers are physically closer to and interact more frequently and more positively with students seated in the action zone. These students tend to participate more, work more persistently, and hold more positive attitudes toward the class. Students seated outside of this zone and farther from the teacher attain lower levels of achievement and hold less positive attitudes toward learning (Adams & Biddle, 1970). Research suggests that students who choose seats outside the action zone tend to have lower self-esteem, to doubt their academic ability, and to feel threatened by the classroom environment or the teacher. Seated along the periphery of the classroom, these students are less engaged with the teacher and the lesson and are more easily distracted. This leads to increased failure, which reinforces their self-doubt and low self-esteem (Dykman & Reis, 1979).

In Chapter 12, we discussed the importance of an interactive classroom to learning. When students are involved and interacting in the classroom, they feel a sense

FIGURE 13.2   Impact of Teacher's Movements on Action Zone

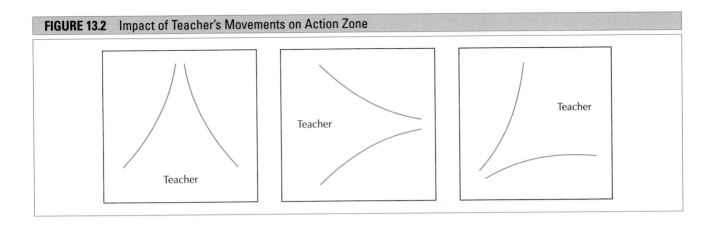

of belonging and, because they are occupied, they are less likely to misbehave. This suggests that teachers should consider the student-teacher action zone when arranging students. While allowing students to select their own seats, especially at the secondary level, has some psychological benefits, it may be advisable to gradually move students with academic or behavioral problems into the action zone to increase their academic engagement. Relatedly, teachers should be sure to call on students, especially nonvolunteers, seated on the edges of the classroom. The location of the action zone can be changed by the way a teacher instructs and monitors students. Because the action zone is defined in terms of the teacher's position in the classroom, it can be redefined by relocating the teacher's desk or teaching station, or by circulating to all parts of the room while monitoring students (Figure 13.2).

No single seating arrangement is ideal for all classes, learning situations, or individuals. Dunn (2001) found that the best arrangement has wide walkways so that the teacher can easily move among students (Figure 13.3). Moving around the classroom during instruction makes it possible to monitor all students more closely

FIGURE 13.3   Seating Arrangement for Teacher Mobility

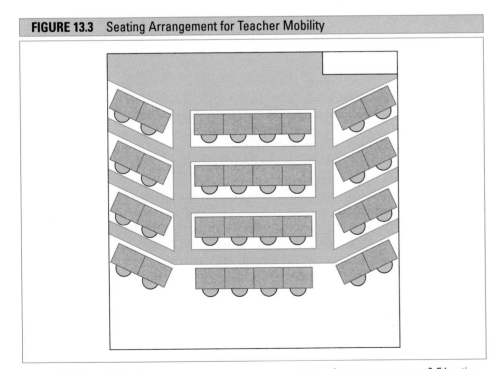

Source: D. W. Dunn (2001). Do seating arrangements and arrangements = classroom management? *Education World.* [Online]. http://www.educationworld.com/a_curr/curr330.shtml

Try Activity 13.1

and to interact with them more equitably. Many teachers prefer to cluster students around tables to encourage cooperation, interaction, and support.

Rather than constantly changing the arrangement of student seats, some teachers use a "home base formation" that serves as a semipermanent arrangement. This formation should be suitable for many teaching situations and easily moved into alternative formations as needed. Borich (2000) suggests traditional rows as the home base formation because this arrangement conveys a businesslike appearance, is easily monitored, and can be reorganized quickly into small groups, circles, or other formations for increased interaction among students. Weinstein and Mignano (2002) agree that novice teachers should seat students in rows until they feel confident in their management abilities. However, the arrangement may be modified later based on students' characteristics as well as the level of interaction the teacher expects.

Equipment and Materials   Where and how you store supplies and equipment will affect their accessibility. Providing students ready access to reference books and supplies will reduce the number of times you need to handle supplies or give instructions about their location and distribution. Students should have access to resources and supplies without reaching across other students' desks or crowding their chairs. Equipment should also accommodate the physical needs of students. For example, provide appropriate scissors and desks for left-handed students and wheelchair accessible laboratory equipment when needed. Organize your classroom to prevent lines and bottlenecks around storage areas, reference shelves, and supply tables. When several students are waiting or pushing to get supplies, inappropriate behavior is bound to erupt. Putting the wastebasket and the pencil sharpener near the door, for example, creates congestion in that area and increases the likelihood of behavior problems.

Room Arrangement   Research attests to the impact of room arrangement on students' behavior and learning. It suggests that an attractive, well-organized environment leads to more positive attitudes, better grades, and more receptive students. Further, students persist longer at tasks, participate more in discussions, and feel closer to the group in pleasantly arranged classrooms. Conversely, unattractive classrooms have been linked to frequent absenteeism, discomfort, fatigue, and complaints from both parents and students (Santrock, 1976; Sommer & Olsen, 1980; Wang et al., 1993–94). A pleasant and comfortable physical environment is especially important to students with low self-esteem or with a history of school failure; that is, students who are at risk of failing or leaving school (Raviv, Raviv, & Reisel, 1990).

Today, teachers have more physical space to arrange and manage. In 1970, an average elementary school provided 62 square feet for each student. By 1995, each pupil had 111 square feet—a 79 percent increase (White, 1996)! This is due to new teaching methods, increased use of technology, and greater community demands on school space. Middle and high schools have grown similarly. Regardless of whether your actual classroom space is larger, it will be more complex. Regular classrooms are being outfitted to accommodate disabled students and rewired to incorporate new technology into everyday instruction. Distractions and congestion can be minimized in these complex classrooms by arranging furniture in a way that orients students toward the primary sources of information yet also gives them access to resources and activities without disturbing others (Anderson, 1991). For example, if you do choose to seat students in groups or around tables, be sure all students can see the teaching center of the room without looking around other students, turning their chairs, or uncomfortably twisting their bodies. The teacher should also have an unrestricted view of all students.

When arranging the physical environment, it is also important to consider the types of instructional activities that will occur in the classroom. Use open space or

13.5   Recall a classroom that you think had a good physical environment. What was it like?

FIGURE 13.4   Floor Plan of Good Classroom Arrangement

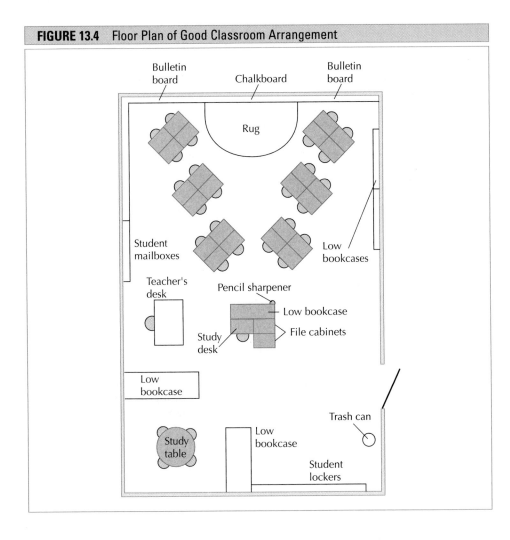

furniture to establish activity boundaries or to separate incompatible activities. For example, you might use low bookcases to separate group work or activity centers from seat work areas. Dividers like these should be high enough to provide an undisturbed work space for students in that area, but low enough for you to see students in all parts of the room. Also, be sure to provide open lanes for movement between frequently used activity areas, such as between students' desks and learning centers or the pencil sharpener. You will also need to determine where to direct student traffic to avoid distractions and congestion where students are working. Figures 13.4 and 13.5 contrast good and poor classroom arrangements. What advantages and problems do you see with each arrangement?

Planning the Psychological Environment   We can think of the psychological environment as the climate or atmosphere of the class that potentially influences what students learn. A positive learning environment promotes cooperative working relationships and helps prevent discipline problems (Bellon, Bellon, & Blank, 1996). Three aspects of the psychological environment are consistently linked with students' learning: emotional affect, or tone; task orientation; and organization (Wang et al., 1993–94).

Tone   An **inviting classroom** is an appealing, positive place that provides a sense of physical and emotional safety for students and the teacher. That is, it has a positive tone. Maslow's hierarchy of needs (Maslow & Laury, 1998) outlines what motivates

13.6   What classroom characteristics make you feel energized and ready to learn?

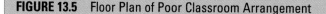

FIGURE 13.5 Floor Plan of Poor Classroom Arrangement

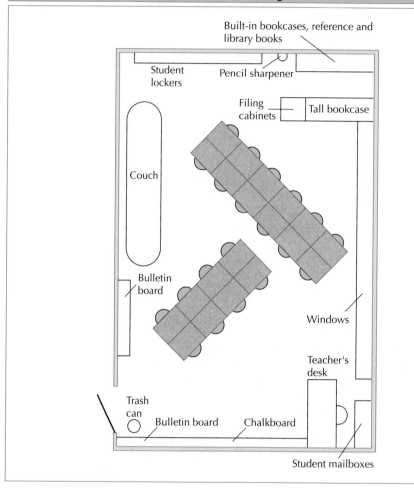

and influences human behavior and helps us understand why an inviting classroom is so important (Figure 13.6). Maslow described the most basic human need as that for safety and security, followed by a need for acceptance or esteem and recognition. Only when these needs have been met is it possible to fulfill the human need for aesthetic pleasure and mental challenges. This suggests that students are most able to learn and to behave appropriately when they feel safe, secure, and accepted.

How can you create a classroom where students feel psychologically and emotionally safe? Such a classroom is characterized by three qualities: it is attractive, it encourages prosocial development, and it exhibits ownership.

Effective teachers use color, light, temperature, and displays to create an attractive classroom tone where students feel safe and comfortable (Anderson, 1991). For example, to offset the cold impression that wood or linoleum floors, Formica desks, fluorescent lights, and plaster or concrete walls convey, you could use soft, textured bulletin board coverings, plants, family photographs, a rocking chair with a seat cushion, and posters. Conveying a sense of softness and safety is especially important for young children. Use light, texture, and color in a coherent, orderly way and in moderation. Overuse may overstimulate students, tiring them emotionally and distracting them from learning.

Even if you share a classroom with other teachers you can create a sense of softness and psychological safety. One teacher carried a small vase of flowers from room to room to soften the mood in any classroom in which she taught her English

13.7 Do the needs of today's students differ from those of students when you were in school? How could this influence your classroom environment?

The Effective Teacher

388

FIGURE 13.6   Hierarchy of Human Needs

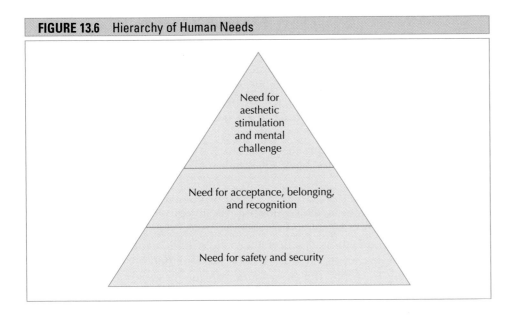

classes. Carrying a colorful, textured book bag or a personalized coffee mug or wearing colorful neckties or accessories conveys a sense of softness to students. Your worksheets and handouts add to the positive tone if they are duplicated on colored paper, contain pictures or cartoons, and are neat and uncluttered.

Traditional classrooms are often described as lonely, isolated, silent, competitive, and lacking in spontaneity and interaction (Lyman & Foyle, 1990). In contrast, inviting classrooms are communities of learners that demonstrate trust and mutual respect between teacher and students, cooperative relationships among students, and a sense of student satisfaction (Anderson, 1991; Canter, 1996). This psychological environment encourages prosocial development in students.

You can create such an environment by modeling the trust and respect you want from students. Canter (1996) stresses that you should listen to your students, look them in the eye, and give them your complete attention during interactions. You should speak respectfully with students and be aware of words and actions that students, especially those from different cultural and ethnic groups, consider disrespectful. Because depersonalization among students and teachers is a major cause of discipline problems in some schools, Canter suggests getting to know your students as individuals. Greet them at the door by name and with a hello and a smile. Acknowledge their birthdays and other events in their lives and attend their sports events, recitals, and concerts. This shows students that you care about and support them both in and out of the classroom. When students feel that their teachers care about them, they are more intrinsically motivated to learn and to assume responsibilities in the classroom (Grolnick, Ryan, & Deci, 1991).

Freiberg (1996) observed that too often classroom environments based on trust and support in the elementary grades are replaced by classrooms that emphasize compliance and obedience in later grades, especially in urban schools. Without a cooperative, supportive psychological environment, students tend to pass through school without active involvement, commitment, or a sense of belonging (Rogers & Freiberg, 1994) and tend to achieve little. In contrast, inviting classrooms exhibit ownership. Recall that Maslow suggested that a feeling of belonging and recognition of achievement are basic human needs. Students sense ownership when they participate in activities that increase status, visibility, recognition, and group cohesiveness. Cover classroom walls with students' work. Let students create signs and exhibits. Feature student information and newspaper clippings.

13.8   How can a teacher show respect for students?

The teacher is an obvious member of an inviting classroom, too. Research suggests that when students perceive their teacher as a "real" human being, they are more receptive to teaching and learning. This is especially true when the teacher and students come from different cultural, ethnic, or socioeconomic backgrounds (Scollon, 1981). By giving students insights into your hobbies, family, pets, and priorities, you contribute to an inviting psychological environment in which it is safe to share and express oneself. The objects on your desk, your personal reaction to the books being read in class, and casual discussion about weekend events, school sports activities, or current events all contribute to your humanness in the students' eyes. Sharing your personality, however, should not interrupt or impinge on instructional time.

13.10 What qualities do you have that will enable you to establish an inviting classroom? What skills do you need to acquire?

Task Orientation A classroom with a positive psychological environment is a busy, task-oriented place. In task-oriented classrooms, students perceive there are definite learning goals to pursue and believe they will be held accountable for reaching those goals. Relatedly, they spend most of the classroom time working toward those goals. Even during free time, the classroom environment should encourage intellectual exploration. For example, learning centers displaying enrichment books and motivational posters add to a task-oriented environment. Simply by placing an unusual object on your desk or on a table, perhaps something from your travels or a trophy you won, you can stimulate such inquiries as "Where did you get this?" and foster interaction and cognitive growth.

Try Activity 13.2

Organization A classroom with a positive psychological environment is also organized in a predictable way. Clear, concise, concrete limits define appropriate behavior and learning. Routines provide structure by establishing where to find supplies, how to turn in papers for grading, when to sharpen pencils, and how to gain the teacher's attention. Teachers who are effective managers organize their classrooms with appropriate rules and routines. This is the focus of our next section.

ESTABLISHING CLASSROOM RULES AND ROUTINES

13.11 Think about a typical day. What routines do you follow to organize your life and make it less complex?

Effective classroom management is proactive. As we have seen, by thoughtfully establishing the physical and psychological environments in your classroom, you can prevent much misbehavior. A second way to prevent misbehavior is to organize the procedures and movement in the classroom. In a well-organized classroom, students clearly understand how to behave responsibly and are guided toward prosocial behaviors by the predictable structure of the classroom. You can prevent misbehavior in your classroom and establish a learning environment, then, by developing rules and implementing routines that create order and structure. Classroom **rules** are directions that teach prosocial behaviors and create an environment conducive to learning. Classroom **routines** are established procedures that direct and coordinate how students move and how events occur.

13.12 What problems have you had because teachers haven't developed or communicated routines?

Jackson (1990) characterizes classrooms as unpredictable and complex. This is especially true of today's classrooms because of increased student diversity, more pressure on teachers to ensure that learning takes place, and shifting societal norms (see Chapter 2). This complex, unpredictable environment complicates learning for many students because they feel insecure or unsafe. Specifically, Jackson contends that many students fail at school, both behaviorally and academically, not because they lack intelligence or needed personality traits, but because they are unsuccessful in deciphering or understanding classroom procedures. According to Evertson and Harris (1992), new activities are especially problematic because they require students to "read" the required behaviors correctly or else risk negative reactions from the teacher and other students. This suggests the need for explicit classroom rules and routines that are thoroughly communicated to students and that make the classroom less complex.

Teachers also benefit from the rules and routines that create a less complex, more predictable room. A predictable classroom is less stressful for the teacher. Certain routines, such as taking attendance and collecting papers, become automatic, predictable classroom events and enable teachers to use class time more effectively. Routines help ensure that needed materials are available and that students know how to go about their learning activities. Routines make lessons smoother and more effective by reducing interruptions for questions such as, "Where is the glue?" or "Where should I put my homework?"

Given the benefits of classroom rules and routines for both students and teachers, it seems wise to consider how to establish them. Indeed, in well-organized and managed classrooms, teachers spend at least as much time early in the year planning and establishing classroom rules and routines as they do on content instruction (Emmer, Evertson, & Anderson, 1980).

Developing Classroom Rules   Too often, teachers develop rules and assume that appropriate student behavior will follow. But rules alone, without a management plan that includes classroom routines, individual responsibilities, and a discipline strategy, have a marginal effect on behavior (McGinnis, Frederick, & Edwards, 1995). Research shows that children and teenagers do not see the connection between rules and good behavior. DiGiulio (2000) contends that rules that threaten and punish are harmful because they relieve the student of the responsibility of making decisions about fairness and appropriate behavior. Successful teachers have rules and consequences, but do not depend on the rules alone to teach prosocial behavior. They create a classroom community with rules based on understandings about how students should treat each other and engage in learning (see Table 13.1), and they discuss behavior with students and use those discussions to set limits. Most important, they actively and concretely *teach* and model appropriate prosocial behavior rather than merely telling or explaining rules to students. As we have seen, in an effective, inviting classroom, the management plan is built on a foundation of trust and respect and involves learning prosocial behaviors.

Try Activity 13.3

Researchers provide guidelines for establishing effective classroom rules (McGinnis et al., 1995). The general consensus is that five rules is the maximum number that students can easily recall, although this number may need to be expanded or reduced based on grade level. Rules should convey exactly what type of behavior is expected in observable, measurable terms. The wording of the rules should be simple and specific enough to avoid alternative interpretations. It is also best to state rules positively and to explain the desired behavior. For example, "keep your eyes on the teacher" is better than "no looking around." Finally, rules should be posted in a prominent place for all to see. Using pictures to illustrate rules helps young children, those with visual learning styles, and students with reading or language difficulties.

Should students have a voice in developing classroom rules? McGinnis et al. (1995) note that student input is generally beneficial, and Wolfgang and Kelsay (1995) point out that it is key in establishing a democratic classroom. You need to

---

TABLE 13.1   Basic Understandings of Prosocial Behavior

1. Respect is nonnegotiable—Every person in the classroom shall give and receive respect.

2. Cooperation over competition—Cooperation is the norm, although there are learning situations in which individual work is required.

3. Achievement is valued—All types of students achievement are expected and welcome.

4. Full inclusion is practiced—Every person in the classroom sees and is inclined toward what is good for others as well as their own individual good.

Source: R. DiGuilio (2000). *Positive classroom management.* Thousand Oaks, CA: Corwin.

be aware, however, that students tend to be more strict, to set behavioral standards too high, to suggest too many rules, and to impose harsher punishments. It is best if the teacher has a basic framework of rules in mind, then incorporates students' input into the list of rules that emerges from the discussion and that all parties agree to. Keep in mind that the focus of rules is to teach prosocial behavior and to create a learning community, not to threaten or intimidate.

Developing Classroom Routines   Several researchers have observed effectively managed classrooms to better understand the types of routines that are in place. Their findings suggest that effective managers establish four types of routines in their classrooms: management, activity, instructional, and executive planning routines (Leinhardt, Weldman, & Hammond, 1987; Yinger, 1979). For each one, the teacher must predetermine to whom the routine applies, when it applies, and what procedures or steps are involved.

Management Routines   **Management routines** involve nonacademic matters such as distributing and collecting materials and papers, leaving and entering the room, making transitions between activities and classes, starting and ending the school day, cleaning the room, and taking attendance. They are the nuts and bolts of a smoothly functioning classroom.

Many management routines are related to classroom transitions. Transitions are frequent classroom events. Doyle (1986) observed about 31 major transitions each day in most elementary classrooms, and Steele (1988) found that transitions in secondary classrooms occur three or four times per hour. While effective classroom managers conduct transitions in approximately 30 seconds, less effective teachers require up to nine minutes (Steele, 1988). As we learned in Chapter 12, poorly conducted transitions are disruptive, waste instructional time, and encourage misbehavior.

Which procedures lead to quick and easy transitions in your classroom? *First, you must signal the students that a transition is about to begin.* The signal may be verbal or nonverbal. Some teachers, for example, use a phrase such as "Attention, please" to attract students' attention before beginning the transition. Elementary teachers often use nonverbal cues such as dimming the lights or raising their hand. Songs or clapping sequences are especially effective with primary students. A clapping sequence requires students to stop what they are doing, put all supplies down, and clap their hands while they focus their attention on the teacher. The nature of the signal is less important than what it does. That is, students must be taught to respond with full attention to the teacher as soon as the signal is given. Never proceed with the transition until all students have responded to the cue and are attending to you.

Second, give clear directions about what students are to do. When students are first learning the transition routine, it is a good idea to reinforce understanding by writing directions on the chalkboard or by asking students to repeat them. With younger students or students with limited English proficiency, it is especially important to demonstrate each step of the directions and to check for understanding. You might, for example, ask everyone to point to where they are to put the glue when they clean up and then to point to where they are to put their finished projects. If you are breaking the class into small groups, ask the students to point to where their group will meet. Never allow students to begin moving until all students have convinced you that they know exactly what they are to do next.

Third, signal students to make the transition. Perhaps the most difficult aspect of classroom transitions is monitoring students who are in different stages of carrying out the directions. Monitoring is much easier if all students make the transition at once. That is, part of the class should not be finishing the last step of a laboratory experiment while others are cleaning up and still others are assembled in the front

Most predictions about education and schools in the next decades directly or indirectly involve technology. Experts agree that technology will be a determining factor in how and what teachers will use for instruction. As a result, routines must be developed so that technology enhances rather than interrupts the learning environment.

Tomorrow's Predictions: Predictions of what we might see in 21st century schools include

- Classrooms like studios.
- Individual workstation and research space for each student.
- Computers integrated into the desktops of students and teachers.
- Notebook or backpack computers assigned to all students in place of textbooks.
- Teachers seen as managers of information and complex environments rather than authoritative sources of information. Teachers' main roles as coaches and facilitators of learning.
- More individual and group projects, promoting a multidimensional classroom approach.
- Personal learning plans and contracts instead of whole-group content delivery.

- Learning centers providing instruction in areas of focus whether in a traditional discipline area or in a cross-discipline thematic area such as pollution.
- Tutoring by peers, parents, senior citizens and other volunteers to reduce the labor costs of education (Zenger & Zenger, 1999).

Today's Routines: In reality, few of today's classrooms are close to these predictions. Instead, the number of computers and time to use them is often limited, and many teachers lack essential training and experience with technology use and integration. As a result, one challenge is developing routines for using technology. Below are the routines established by two teachers to promote learning using technology and to prevent management problems.

- "I have one computer for 26 students in my fourth-grade class. One thing I have found successful is to provide a question of the day about the particular history topic that I am teaching. I bookmark a website in the morning. I leave a small notepad and pencil near the computer. I also put a Popsicle stick on each student's desk with his or her number. When they have answered the question at the computer, they leave their stick by the computer. This way I can tell who still needs to go back to the computer. At the end of the day, we pull names to find out who answered the question correctly."
- "Many of my learning centers in my eighth-grade classroom require research. Not all of the students have access to a computer at home. I have found it very useful to have sites ready for them to use for their research. I have bookmarked them in the past, but the students did not know the best sites to go to for their particular research needs. I also ended up with so many sites bookmarked that it became difficult to find the one you wanted. I have now created a notebook with the first page from the sites I have found useful. This allows the students to preview the material that will be found on the site. This cuts down on the amount of time the students need to be at the computer randomly surfing, and they go directly to a useful site and conduct their research. We update the notebook as we discover useful sites."

of the room awaiting the class discussion. This requires that you manage *three* different groups of students at one time. Some students will inevitably make the transition more quickly than others; therefore, it is important that you monitor all stages of the transition. Circulate around the room, encouraging the slower students and letting everyone know that you are aware of what is going on throughout the room. Use statements like, "Thanks for doing such a thorough job of cleaning up, Sam. Now you're ready to move to the front of the room," or "I see that four people are already cleaned up and waiting quietly in their seats for the discussion to begin."

Once students learn the directions and your expectations during transitions, these become management routines that save instructional time and reduce the stress on both you and your students. Because students know what they are to do, they are less likely to misbehave.

Activity Routines Generally, when teachers think about a school day or a class period, they think of it as made up of many different kinds of activities. For example, an elementary teacher may conceptualize the morning as including attendance and announcements, sharing time, silent reading, whole-class reading time, and then recess. These activities are the basic structural units of the classroom. Effective teachers establish **activity routines** that spell out how each kind of activity will be conducted. This includes its location, duration, and participants. Further, activity routines specify the content, structure, and sequence of the activity and let students know what materials are needed. Activity routines also provide important guidelines for appropriate student behavior and interactions. They establish acceptable ways for the students and teacher to gain each others' attention and apprise students of when it is acceptable to interact with one another.

One primary grade teacher, for example, sits in a rocking chair with her students seated around her on a rug while she reads to them. This "rug time" is an established activity with routines. When the teacher announces that it is rug time, students know to get up from their desks, push in their chairs, and quietly walk to the rug area, taking nothing with them. At the rug area, students know they are free to choose where they will sit but must avoid crowding other students or sitting near someone who might distract them. Although they do not need to raise their hands to talk, students may not interrupt the teacher or their classmates while they are talking. At the end of the story, students know that rug time is over and they return to their desks in an orderly fashion. The students in this class follow the rug time routines automatically without being reminded of how to behave, where to sit, and so forth. This teacher has a well-established activity routine!

One secondary English teacher has activity routines to hold students accountable for their assignments and seatwork. She posts a weekly chart listing the daily assignments and how many points each is worth. Students keep a copy of the chart in their notebooks and record the number of points they earn. The chart also tells students what materials and books to bring to class each day. When students are absent, they are responsible for consulting the list to find out about missed assignments, talking with the teacher the first day they return to class, and completing the assignments and placing them in a special folder within two days. Any papers returned during their absence can be picked up in another folder.

Instructional Routines **Instructional routines** establish what the teacher will do while teaching. For example, when one mathematics teacher is about to begin teaching a new concept, he sets up the teaching station by pulling down the projection screen and focusing the overhead projector. His overhead transparencies are in a three-ring binder, so he turns to the appropriate lesson and pulls out the sequenced transparencies for that lesson. Immediately following the lesson, he washes and returns the transparencies to the notebook. Routine use of the overhead projector and transparencies is the backbone of this teacher's instruction and signals students that he is about to introduce new information.

Instructional routines such as this correlate with the teacher's strategies or style, making the teaching more predictable and efficient. As a teacher, you should establish routine ways of giving directions, demonstrating, instructing, monitoring, reviewing, and questioning students. Such routines are especially helpful for young students and for those with limited English proficiency or limited attention spans. In these situations, directions must be clearly presented, reinforced, and checked.

Let's examine the instructional routine one kindergarten teacher uses for giving directions in a bilingual classroom. When giving directions for completing one activity, the teacher clearly outlines the three things the students need to do: color the picture of the astronaut, cut it out, and paste it somewhere on the class moonscape mural. As she describes what to color, she prints the key word "color" on the chalkboard and draws a crayon after the word. She then quickly models how to color the astronaut. The teacher repeats this procedure for the next two directions in the sequence, cutting and pasting. After she has told and shown the students what they are expected to do, she checks their understanding of the directions by asking individual students to remind the class of the first, second, and third things they are to do. By the time the children begin the activity, the teacher is certain that they all heard, saw, and understood the tasks. Her predictable approach to giving directions is especially important for her students with limited English skills.

Executive Planning Routines   **Executive planning routines** include establishing how, when, and where you will complete your teaching tasks—for example, how and when you will plan for instruction, correct papers, use your preparation time at school, and fulfill clerical responsibilities such as filling out attendance reports and grade cards. Establishing these routines helps you manage time more effectively so that you can balance your professional and personal life.

Some teachers involve students in executive planning routines. A secondary math teacher, for example, has students check their own homework with red pen or pencil. Another teacher has students trade papers to check. Both teachers collect papers afterward to record grades and are careful to return all papers by the end of class on Friday. While involving students in various routines saves time, you will need to consider the merits versus the risks of these systems.

Because these are such personal routines, they vary tremendously from teacher to teacher. Some teachers stay after school one hour each day to correct papers and to handle clerical chores; others arrive an hour early in the morning or relegate these tasks to preparation periods. Some teachers work in teams one evening each week to plan for instruction, others develop their weekly plans on Saturday morning, while still others plan each evening for the next day's activities. In establishing your own executive planning routines, talk with expert teachers about how they manage their time and balance their many roles. In this way, you can benefit from their years of experience.

STARTING THE SCHOOL YEAR

Establishing a positive learning environment and developing rules and routines are important ways to prevent management problems. Teachers must implement these proactive measures and gain student cooperation early in the school year, and then maintain them throughout the year. Following are guidelines for preventing classroom problems based on researchers' observations of well-managed elementary and secondary classrooms (Evertson, Emmer, & Worsham, 2000; Emmer, Evertson, & Worsham, 2000).

Begin to Establish Routines on the First Day of Class   The first time they meet with students, effective classroom managers clearly demonstrate that they have thought about routines and procedures, and they begin to implement them immediately. As previously discussed, you should plan the way you will arrange your classroom space, furniture, and equipment and procedures for their use. To prevent overburdening the students, your first meetings with the class should focus on routines that address students' concerns: guidelines for interacting with others; procedures for meeting basic needs such as using the pencil sharpener, restroom, and drinking fountain; your expectations as their teacher.

Clearly Communicate and Model Classroom Routines   Simply announcing or posting classroom routines and rules will not establish a well-managed classroom. Researchers found that effective managers devote a large amount of time during the first days of school to *teaching* the routines. In fact, effective elementary teachers

13.13   What personal responsibilities will affect your professional life as a teacher? What executive planning routines will you need to implement to balance these demands on your time?

Try Activity 13.4

spend more time during the first days of school teaching about management issues than academics (Leinhardt, Weldman, & Hammond, 1987). They follow up this initial instruction with about three weeks of reviewing and remediating the routines (Emmer, et al., 1980). Of course, secondary students more familiar with school routines would not need such a prolonged emphasis on routines, but they do need to learn what you expect.

How do you teach routines and rules? First, you must clearly communicate and model them. Further, you should help students understand *why* the routines are necessary. Especially with secondary students, a discussion developing rules and routines that benefit the students, teacher, and the class as a whole is important. Finally, provide situations in which the students can practice the routines and give immediate, specific feedback on their performance and cooperation.

Be Sure Students Feel Good about the Classroom Arrangement and Routines If students feel comfortable with the classroom arrangement and the availability of supplies, they are more likely to use them carefully and quietly. Similarly, if they feel that the rules and routines are realistic and attainable, they are more likely to follow them.

You can help ensure that students feel comfortable and successful in their new classroom by providing situations in which they can practice using classroom resources and following routines. Then observe. If an arrangement or routine seems awkward or unnatural for students or if it just doesn't work, discuss with students more appropriate ways of doing things. Once you and the students have agreed upon a set of rules and routines, it is a good idea to limit instruction to whole-class teaching rather than breaking down into small groups. This will give you time to observe how well the routines fit the class. It will also ensure that all students have mastered the routines before they are placed in small-group or individualized situations that are more difficult for you to manage.

Communicate That You Are Prepared and Competent Your teaching behaviors should always communicate to students that you are well-prepared and capable of instructing and managing. This doesn't mean that you will be a perfect teacher and classroom manager, but it does mean that you will be predictable. That is, students will know what is expected of them as members of a learning community, and the consequences of disrupting that community. This predictability establishes an environment in which you are able to teach, students are able to learn, and misbehavior is less likely to occur.

Hold Students Responsible for Following Routines and Rules Early in the year, effective classroom managers remind students of appropriate procedures prior to an activity and correct them if they follow routines improperly. Such frequent feedback is essential to learning both the classroom routines and expectations for students' behavior.

Monitoring Students' Behavior

Even when students have settled into the classroom and have learned the routines and procedures, your management work is still not done! Observations of effective classroom managers show us that such teachers monitor students' behavior throughout the year. Evertson (1987) points out that even the best learning environment can deteriorate if it is not maintained. Monitoring enables you to signal students when they are drifting into inappropriate behavior and to redirect their attention to instruction, thus preventing more serious misbehavior.

FIGURE 13.7 Teachers' Behaviors That Hold Students Accountable

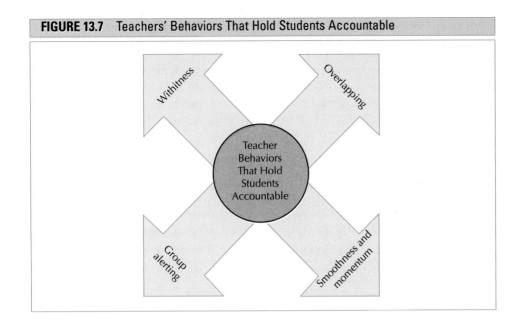

HOLDING STUDENTS ACCOUNTABLE

Unfortunately, students are sometimes reluctant to take responsibility for their behavior and learning. As a result, teachers must be alert to follow through and reinforce the classroom norms and responsibilities established early in the year. Teachers need to develop creative and constructive procedures not only to hold students accountable for their learning and behavior, but also to help them take responsibility for maintaining a learning environment.

In a classic study involving years of classroom observations, Kounin (1970) described strategies effective classroom managers use to monitor students and to hold them accountable for their behavior and learning throughout the school year (Figure 13.7).

Withitness Effective managers monitor classrooms using **withitness;** that is, they are aware of students' behavior in all corners of the classroom at all times. Such teachers seem to have eyes in the backs of their heads! How can you communicate to your class that you are "withit"? For one thing, try not to turn your back to the class when you are writing on the chalkboard. Instead, stand at an angle to the chalkboard so that you can easily glance over your shoulder to observe students' behavior. Similarly, when working with individual students, remain standing and periodically scan the entire classroom. Establish eye contact with students who seem to have questions or who you sense may begin to act inappropriately. Withit teachers detect inappropriate behavior early and deal with it quickly. They know who started the problem and do not depend on students to tell them what happened. Nor do they scold the wrong student. Withit teachers not only prevent classroom problems, they also produce greater student achievement (Anderson, Evertson, & Brophy, 1979; Brophy & Evertson, 1976).

Overlapping Effective classroom managers are also able to monitor more than one classroom activity at a time, an ability called **overlapping.** Overlapping is especially important when students are involved in collaborative work. Teachers who overlap can, for example, instruct a small group of students while keeping the remaining students on task. Suppose that you are working with a group of five students on math problems while the rest of the class is working on a review exercise. As you scan the classroom, you notice that a group in the back corner has stopped working and started talking. Using overlapping, you could ask your group to try the next problem on their own. You then establish eye contact with the misbehaving students to signal them to get back to work. Or you could walk back to them to determine whether they have a question and to redirect their attention to the review exercise. By the time the students in your group finish working the next problem, you would be back to continue your instruction.

Smoothness and Momentum   Overlapping is closely related to two other strategies, **smoothness** and **momentum.** These suggest that you should move the class through the lesson at a brisk pace without interruptions. In well-paced lessons, students are less likely to misbehave. In Chapter 12, we discussed how effective teachers use cues—for example, verbally identifying the first, second, and third points in the lesson—to help students focus and proceed smoothly and quickly through the lesson. In addition, effective teachers who demonstrate smoothness focus on the subject at hand rather than attending to irrelevant or intrusive details; they do not interrupt children engaged in learning activities; and they follow through rather than leaving activities "hanging in mid-air." Have you ever been interrupted when taking a test by a teacher announcing a correction of a typographical error? That teacher was not demonstrating smoothness.

Momentum concerns a teacher's ability to avoid behaviors that slow down the pace of the lesson. Such behaviors include overdwelling on students' behavior or on a minor point in the lesson and dealing with students individually rather than as a group. A teacher exhibiting good momentum, for example, gives clear directions regarding an assignment to the entire class, then checks for understanding of those directions. A teacher lacking momentum fails to give clear directions and so must respond to students individually when they question the details or directions of the assignment. While students are waiting for the teacher to answer their questions, they can easily drift into misbehavior.

Group Alerting   You can also monitor students' behavior by using group alerting. **Group alerting** is the process of gaining and maintaining students' attention and holding them accountable for their behavior and learning. As discussed in Chapter 12, you can keep everyone's attention by calling on nonvolunteers as well as volunteers and by using various questioning strategies to keep students in suspense about who will be called on to recite.

You can also keep students alert by asking or reminding them of what they should be doing, by having them repeat rules and routines they should be following, and by calling attention to appropriate behavior. Further, general comments such as "I'm still waiting for everyone to put their pencils down and look up here" or "I see that two people need to stop whispering and turn to page 572 and follow along" will alert students regarding their behavior.

Controlling the time available for a task also keeps students engaged in learning activities. When allocating time to group activities and independent work, be sure to give students just enough time to complete the task. Too little time will cause concern, stress, frustration, and perhaps inappropriate behavior. Too much time may allow students to drift into casual conversation or other interfering behaviors. Cuing or reminding students about the time helps them to be accountable for their behavior. Statements such as "We'll begin cleaning up in five minutes, so you should be finishing the last step of your experiment" should prod students who are off task toward more appropriate behavior.

Likewise, using **proximity** or adjusting the amount of space between you and your students can influence their behavior and keep them alert. Moving toward off-task students raises their awareness of your presence and helps them refocus attention on the learning activity. If the inappropriate behavior persists, it may be necessary to pause next to the students until they adjust their behavior and reenter the lesson (Gunter, Shores, Jack, Rasmussen, & Flowers, 1995). Think about how you feel when a teacher stands near your desk. Your level of concern can become so elevated that your palms sweat, you are distracted, and learning is actually inhibited. So use proximity for monitoring behavior rather than for intimidation.

Finally, the visibility of the teacher and availability of materials in the classroom also hold students accountable and alerts them to behave appropriately. Circulate randomly around the classroom during independent seat work or small-group projects. Students need to see you are available to answer questions and to redirect their attention. Similarly, supplies and materials that students need should be visible and accessible. This removes one excuse for not engaging in the appropriate activity.

Try Activity 13.5

REWARDING AND REINFORCING STUDENTS

A second key to maintaining a learning environment is to use reinforcement and rewards. Incentives and rewards add interest and excitement to classroom routines while directing attention to prosocial behaviors (Emmer et al., 2000). According to **reinforcement theory,** which is based on operant conditioning (discussed in Chapter 4), behavior that is rewarded is strengthened and therefore likely to be repeated. Conversely, behavior that is not somehow reinforced will eventually diminish. Early psychologists like Thorndike and Skinner recognized the importance of **positive reinforcement;** that is, providing something that an individual needs, values, or desires, as perhaps the most effective means of encouraging prosocial behaviors (Goetz, Alexander, & Ash, 1996). The use of reinforcement theory has evolved over the past two decades. Whereas reward systems once emphasized controlling students, they now focus on helping students to take responsibility and to control themselves. Reward systems have also shifted their focus from inhibiting misbehavior to rewarding positive academic performance and social choices (Brophy, 1983; Evertson & Harris, 1992). Correctly implemented, reinforcements and rewards provide a systematic and humanistic approach to guiding students away from misbehavior and toward independent self-control, which is essential for a learning environment.

Unfortunately, because teachers are consumed with other classroom events, many appropriate things students do go unnoticed or at least unrewarded in today's busy classrooms. By monitoring behavior and acknowledging students who behave responsibly, teachers reinforce the importance of such behavior (Cruickshank & Associates, 1980). Similarly, many teachers unintentionally reinforce and thus encourage undesirable behaviors. For example, researchers who studied student out-of-seat behavior observed that the more frequently teachers corrected students by using the command "sit down," the more students got out of their seats! Inadvertently, the teachers were giving students the attention they were seeking only when they got out of their seats, thus encouraging the unwanted behavior.

Applying Reinforcement Theory   Although using reinforcement to maintain a learning environment sounds easy, it can be difficult. First, the teacher's delivery is vital in determining a reinforcement's effectiveness. As we learned in Chapter 12, reinforcers must be given immediately after the desirable behavior, not hours, days, or weeks later. Otherwise, the effect of the reinforcer is dramatically reduced. Further, in order to effectively influence students' behavior, the reinforcement must be specific rather than general. At the elementary level, the most powerful reinforcers identify both the individual who is behaving appropriately and the appropriate behavior. For example, it is relatively ineffective to tell Cindy, an impulsive student, that you appreciated how good she was in class today. She does not know what she did right, so she cannot repeat that behavior tomorrow. Further, the reinforcement was too far removed from her appropriate behavior. Instead, tell her five times during the day that you notice she is raising her hand before speaking in class, a real improvement. Point out how this appropriate behavior helps both her and her classmates to learn. This specific, immediate feedback encourages her to control herself and to take responsibility for raising her hand in the future.

Second, it is essential to remember that students respond differently to different kinds of reinforcers. In other words, what is rewarding to one student may not be rewarding to others. For example, some students thrive on praise, while others cringe upon receiving public recognition. At least in part, this varied response is linked to cultural and socioeconomic differences among students. Shade's research (1982) found that many minority students value group identity over individual recognition. Individual public recognition is considered disrespectful and inappropriate (Garner, 1989). In these situations, it is appropriate to reinforce group efforts rather than to single out one individual for praise. Similarly, some adolescents who are embarrassed at being singled out for attention appreciate it when public recognition is given to several students at the same time.

Sometimes what is reinforcing to students surprises teachers. For example, in one kindergarten class the teachers used stickers to reward students for following the class routines. To the students, however, the stickers themselves were not sufficient reinforcement. The real reward was in being allowed to wear the stickers on their faces throughout the day! In another situation, a middle school awarded points to students for appropriate behavior. Students could redeem 1,000 points for lunch with the principal at a fast-food restaurant nearby. Teachers soon found that this was not an appropriate reinforcer; while the students wanted the principal to take them to lunch, they wanted to keep it short. They wanted to get back to school early enough to play basketball with their friends during the lunch break!

A wise teacher is aware of the types of reinforcers learners need and want. Four types of reinforcers are commonly used in classrooms: social, activity, tangible, and negative reinforcers (Goetz, Alexander, & Ash, 1996; Hunter, 1990; Kazdin, 2000). **Social reinforcers** send a positive message to the student from the teacher. Verbal praise, smiles, time spent with students, and appropriate physical contact are social reinforcers that are easy to give, cost nothing, and are seldom overused. These are often the most powerful reinforcers. However, while these are effective in monitoring students' behavior and maintaining a learning environment, they may not be strong enough to eliminate misbehavior in some situations.

When dealing with older students, verbal reinforcers should focus on benefits for the student rather than on the teacher's approval (Hunter, 1990). Whereas primary grade students are usually delighted that their behavior pleases the teacher, some older students may not care about the teacher's approval or about maintaining a learning environment. Some may even prefer to annoy the teacher and disrupt the classroom! While a statement such as "I like the way Max is getting right to work on his math problems" may effectively encourage a primary student, it is important to show the benefit of that appropriate behavior to Max if he is an older student. Try saying, "Max you've gotten right to work on your math problems! That means you'll have them finished before the end of the period so you won't have any homework." At the secondary level, it is often preferable to reinforce students quietly or privately rather than aloud in front of the entire class.

Activity reinforcers are privileges not routinely accorded to everyone. Access to the gym or computer, extra free or recess time, working with a friend, and class responsibilities such as taking messages to the office or helping to decorate a bulletin board are examples of activity reinforcers that many students prefer. The weakness with using such activity reinforcers is that they may not be immediately available. This makes immediate reinforcement impossible and weakens their effectiveness.

Tangible reinforcers are concrete objects that a student needs or wants. Often referred to as external or extrinsic rewards, they include stickers, food, award cer-

Teachers can and should help students feel good about themselves, but how should they go about this? Praise is a powerful tool, but used inappropriately it becomes a negative force. Carol S. Dweck and Claudia Mueller conducted a series of studies to examine the link between praise and self-esteem.

Impact of Praise for Intelligence The researchers gave 400 fifth-graders a puzzle task that was challenging but easy enough for them to complete successfully. After the task, they praised one group for their *intelligence* ("Wow! You got so many correct! You must be really smart!") and the other group for their *effort* ("You must have worked really hard"). The groups were equally successful, enjoyed the task equally, were eager to take the problems home to practice, and were equally confident about their performance on future tasks.

Next, students chose if they wanted to try a challenging task from which they'd learn a lot or an easier task. Most of the students who had received praise for being intelligent following the first task chose the easy task, which would allow them to keep looking smart. Most of the students who received praise for their effort selected the challenging learning task. This suggests that if we praise students for being intelligent, we send a message that looking smart is what is important. But, when we praise students for effort and hard work that leads to achievement, they want to keep engaging in learning. They aren't distracted from learning by a concern about how smart they might or might not look.

The Impact of Difficulty Next, the researchers gave all the students a set of difficult problems on which they didn't do well. They found that the students who were praised earlier for being intelligent did not like this second task, were no longer interested in taking the problems home to practice, and began to question their intelligence. While they felt smart when they were succeeding, they now felt dumb because of the setback. They depended on outside praise to maintain their confidence.

The students who had been praised for effort, however, liked the difficult task as much as the earlier easy task even though they missed some of the problems. Many of them liked the difficult task better and were eager to take the problems home so they could practice. These students didn't feel that their lack of success reflected their intelligence—only that they had to work harder in order to get them all correct. These students were able to keep their self-esteem intact in spite of the setback. They still thought they were smart, and they still enjoyed the challenge.

Finally, the researchers gave the students a third set of problems as easy as the initial set. Incredibly, students who had been praised for intelligence performed poorly; significantly worse than they had on the first set of problems. In contrast, students who were praised for working hard had the highest scores; significantly better than they had on the first set. This suggests that the different kinds of praise affected not only what students thought and felt about themselves, but also how well they were able to perform academic tasks.

The researchers were amazed at the power of one sentence of praise. Students very quickly pick up on messages about their personal qualities and actions. Comments from teachers and parents tell them how they should think about themselves. No matter how objective we try to be, our feedback sends messages about what we think is important, what we think of students, and what should be important to them. This research suggests that these messages have powerful effects on self-esteem and performance.

Source: C. M. Mueller & C. S. Dweck. (1998). Intelligence praise can undermine motivation and performance. *Journal of Personality and Social Psychology, 75,* 33–52.

tificates, and points or tokens redeemable for larger rewards or special events. Hunter (1990) suggests that tangible reinforcers be used sparingly and with caution, usually as a last resort when students do not respond to social or activity reinforcers. Because these extrinsic reinforcers are seldom related to the desired behavior, they can divert the student's attention away from being a responsible, productive, self-directed learner. Lepper (1983) found, for example, that to motivate students toward more appropriate behavior it is sometimes necessary to initially use external rewards but to gradually phase them out as the behavior changes. In contrast, if students are already motivated to behave appropriately, Lepper found that using tangible rewards was harmful because it undermined students' motivation to learn and to behave appropriately.

A less positive but often effective reward for shaping appropriate behavior is by using **negative reinforcement.** Negative reinforcement is important in helping students to develop self-control in the classroom because the student is in charge of what happens (Hunter, 1990). With negative reinforcement, something unpleasant is removed from the student's life when he or she makes good choices about how to behave. This reinforces the desirable behavior. For example, if a student who has been giggling with a neighbor reforms her behavior because of the teacher's glare, the student has removed the negative reinforcer (teacher's glare).

As a teacher, how will you know what kinds of reinforcers will work with your students? One way is to observe the students, especially during free time when they display their interests. Also, especially with older students, you can simply ask them. Many teachers use this information to develop a **reinforcement menu** that lists the various reinforcers available to them as they help students learn to be responsible for their behavior.

Scheduling Reinforcement   Most teachers are aware of the need to reinforce appropriate behavior, especially when students are learning to take responsibility such as at the beginning of the school year. When students begin to behave prosocially and to demonstrate self-control, teachers begin omitting the reinforcement. They expect the students to behave automatically thereafter (Hunter, 1990). Remember, though, that many students have had a lot of practice and reinforcement for behaving inappropriately. They may not realize the impact of their behavior and choices on the learning environment. As a result, change doesn't happen overnight. Shaping behavior through reinforcement takes time, persistence, and planning. Students need to be reinforced more than once or twice to help them learn appropriate behavior. They need to recognize their responsibility to themselves and to their classmates. The more frequently behaviors are reinforced, even for small amounts of progress, the more thoughtful students will become and the faster their behavior will change.

Teachers who are effective managers are aware of the importance of scheduling reinforcement. **Scheduling** means changing the frequency of reinforcement in response to students' behavior. As students become more comfortable with the classroom rules and routines, teachers should reinforce behavior intermittently rather than regularly. In most situations, teachers can gradually eliminate external rewards as students increasingly experience academic and social success and become intrinsically motivated (Woolfolk, 2001). McCaslin and Good (1992) suggest that unless the reinforcement schedule and rewards are adjusted as students progressively assume more responsibility and self-control, conflict and tension will erupt in the classroom.

When teachers persist with frequent, regular reinforcement long after students have mastered the desired behaviors, two things generally result. First, the students begin to ignore the teacher and the rewards; then they become bored with what they perceive as manipulation, and their behavior deteriorates. Morgan (1984) pointed out that rewards should not be ends in themselves but rather symbols of how much the student is learning and progressing. In other words, although you need to reinforce students for raising their hands in September, you certainly shouldn't still reward that behavior in May!

Many times during the school year, life becomes hectic for teachers and students alike. Holidays, report cards, inclement weather, and sports events are a few examples of events that raise stress levels in the classroom. Teachers often resign themselves to the fact that students are going to forget the rules and routines at such times and behave much as they did at the beginning of the year. While many teachers unconsciously return to a "catch 'em and punish 'em" mode, scheduling suggests a return to a schedule of regular, frequent reinforcement like that used at the beginning of the year. Returning to a frequent reinforcement schedule and re-

13.14   What reinforcers worked for you in elementary school? In secondary school?

Try Activity 13.6

minding students of their responsibilities enables a teacher to maintain the learning environment during periods of classroom stress.

Criticisms of Reinforcement Theory   Teachers who apply reinforcement theory in the classroom have a powerful tool to establish a positive learning climate by teaching students to make good decisions about their behavior. Nevertheless, classroom use of reinforcement and rewards has drawn criticism. Critics and advocates of reinforcement theory alike are quick to point out that there is a danger of teachers misapplying these strategies. Unfortunately, when rewards are misused, they do not produce lasting changes in attitudes or behavior. Further, they are ineffective in helping students become caring, responsible people or self-directed learners (Kohn, 1999). Criticisms and dangers of applying reinforcement theory follow.

1. Some people object to the application of reinforcement theory because they think it is "bribing" students to do what they should do anyway: follow the classroom rules.

2. Some critics state that teachers frequently use rewards to overcontrol students. This amounts to doing things *to* students rather than working *with* them, and ultimately frays relationships. Others emphasize that rewards should focus on academic achievement rather than social behavior. After all, a quiet class is not necessarily a learning class.

3. Some charge that reinforcement theory is impractical for classroom use. The expense and time associated with implementing a system of rewards and tokens makes this approach unacceptable to many teachers. Further, it is unlikely that teachers can monitor or systematically reinforce more than a fraction of the desirable behaviors occurring in their classrooms.

4. Others suggest it is questionable whether praise and social reinforcement have powerful effects on most students after first or second grade.

5. Critics warn that emphasizing rewards causes students who are already intrinsically motivated to lose interest in whatever they are rewarded for doing, and in learning for its own sake. Further rewards tend to encourage underachievement and to stifle creativity and risk taking.

Reacting to Misbehavior

The findings of Kounin and others help us understand how to manage the classroom as a whole. They tell us how to establish a management system that involves students in learning and reduces deviancy. While this is an essential aspect of classroom management, it can only reduce instances of misbehavior, not eliminate them entirely. Effective managers couple skills in preventing and monitoring inappropriate behavior with skills in quickly stopping misbehavior. Let us now turn our attention to the skills and techniques that effective teachers use in responding to misbehavior that disrupts the learning environment.

Student misbehavior is any action that the teacher perceives as disruptive to the order of the classroom (Bellon et al., 1996). Misbehavior ranges from very subtle actions to physically aggressive behavior. Cangelosi (2000) classifies the most commonly exhibited misbehaviors in elementary and secondary schools as inappropriate talking (that is, excessive talking, talking out of turn, unnecessary talking) and inappropriate movement, such as clowning and out-of-seat behavior. Other common misbehaviors include tardiness, cutting class, not bringing supplies and books, inattentiveness, daydreaming, and mild verbal and aggressive acts. Less frequently, teachers encounter misbehavior such as crying, arguing, fighting, stealing, and cheating. Increasingly, teachers must also react to students' use of narcotics, alcohol, and weapons. Albert (1996) encourages teachers to think of misbehaving

13.15   What type of misbehavior troubles you the most?

students as students with a "choosing disability"—an underdeveloped ability to choose appropriate behavior. Responding to misbehavior, then, is the process of helping students decide to control themselves so that they can function productively in group settings such as the classroom (Bellon et al., 1996).

It is important to keep in mind that there is no foolproof method for correcting misbehavior. No single discipline technique will solve the variety of behavior problems exhibited in today's classrooms. To respond to misbehavior in an effective, professional way, teachers must carefully consider the context of the misbehavior and the student's motivation before choosing how to react. That is, they must be good classroom problem solvers (see Chapter 14).

WHY STUDENTS MISBEHAVE

Teachers can respond more appropriately to misbehavior if they understand why students misbehave. Dreikers, Pepper, Grunwald (1998) propose that, whether they are aware of it or not, students misbehave in order to meet four basic needs. Most misbehavior, at least at the elementary level, is due to students *seeking attention* (Albert, 1995; Glasser, 1998; Savage, 1991). These students need extra attention and want to be center stage. They distract teachers and classmates by making noises, using foul language, and causing interruptions during class. Second, some students misbehave because they are *seeking power.* These students want to be the boss and want things done their way. To show the teacher and classmates that "you can't push me around," they refuse to comply with rules or requests and are likely to challenge and argue with others. Third, misbehavior may be caused by a student's *seeking revenge.* The misbehavior often occurs in response to an earlier power struggle in which the student felt embarrassed, humiliated, or treated with disrespect in front of peers. Students seeking revenge may threaten physical harm or get indirect physical revenge by breaking, damaging, or stealing. A fourth reason students misbehave is that they are *seeking isolation.* These students are trying to avoid failure. They feel inadequate and believe they can't live up to their own, their family's, or the teacher's expectations. They procrastinate, pretend to have disabilities, and turn in incomplete work hoping everyone will leave them alone so they won't have to face the fact they aren't working up to their potential. Unfortunately, being left alone further erodes their sense of adequacy.

While much misbehavior is due to students' attempts to meet their needs, Sylwester (1971) points out that some misbehavior is actually caused by teachers. Sylwester identified four teacher behaviors that cause misbehavior in the classroom. *Inadequate preparation* is perhaps the most common. Failure to plan, structure, and supervise the pace of learning activities causes students to become restless and misbehave. For example, one study found that elementary students working directly with teachers were on task 97 percent of the time. Students working independently were on task only 57 percent of the time (Frick, 1990). Teacher planning and supervision make a difference! Second, *differential treatment* of students often causes misbehavior because students think the teacher has certain favorites or enemies. *Verbal abuse,* especially "friendly" sarcasm, also causes student reactions and misbehavior. Finally, if students feel that a teacher *responds unfairly* to misbehavior, further misbehavior often results.

In order to manage misbehavior, teachers need to be aware of what motivates students to misbehave and how their own behavior influences the behavior of the students. This suggests that teachers must develop sensitivity and a broad range of skills and techniques to draw upon when reacting to misbehavior in the classroom.

DECIDING HOW TO REACT TO MISBEHAVIOR

Teachers who are good classroom managers are also good decision makers (Bellon et al., 1996). When misbehavior erupts, teachers must decide *when* and *how* to in-

13.16 What caused you to misbehave in school?

13.17 How will you determine the cause of a students' misbehavior?

*"How come when you say we have a problem,
I'm always the one who has the problem?"*

tervene. Effective teachers deal with misbehavior as quickly as possible (Albert, 1995; Evertson, 1989). But how do they decide how to intervene? At least four concerns should shape the decision: whether intervention will interrupt the lesson, the nature and severity of the misbehavior, the student involved, and the time the misbehavior occurred.

First and foremost, teachers must decide to what extent the intervention will interrupt or interfere with the instructional activity (Bellon et al., 1996). Doyle (1986) warns that, while most teachers intervene about sixteen times per hour, interrupting the lesson to deal with misbehavior is "inherently risky" since it distracts from ongoing instruction. For example, the most successful teachers that Kounin (1983) observed kept students on task 98.7 percent of the time. The least successful teachers intervened 986 times a day, which meant the students were engaged in learning only 25 percent of the time.

Further, decisions on how to intervene should be based on the nature and severity of the misbehavior, the student involved, and the time the misbehavior occurred (Doyle, 1986; Wolfgang & Kelsay, 1995). Beginning teachers are often told they must be consistent in how they deal with misbehavior, or students will become confused and the misbehavior will increase. Many teachers find this expectation confining and frustrating, especially at the secondary level where students may challenge the teachers' fairness. Dreikers and colleagues (1998) suggest that, since the same teacher-imposed consequences are not equally effective on all students, it is better to develop a range of intervention strategies. A normally responsible student who neglects to turn in one assignment, for example, should not require the same punishment as a student who repeatedly misses assignments. It is essential, though, that the intervention seems logical and fair to the students and their parents. Ideally, the intervention will educate students about how their actions affect their lives and the lives of those who must share classroom space and experiences with them (Wolfgang & Kelsay, 1995). Further, Curwin and Mendler (1999) encourage teachers to discuss with their students the fact that "fair is not always equal." They should point out that just as students require individualized academic plans to meet their different learning needs, they also have varying social needs that require a range of alternative consequences. This enables teachers to be both consistent and flexible when intervening in students' behavior, especially in diverse, inclusive classrooms.

13.18 Describe a classroom incident you observed in which the teachers' intervention distracted from the lesson.

TYPES OF INTERVENTION

Unfortunately, little research is available to suggest how effective teachers respond to repeated student misconduct (Reynolds, 1992). Effective classroom managers, however, have a repertoire of intervention strategies that range from subtle, unobtrusive actions to radical strategies such as expulsion. To be effective, intervention strategies must be delivered calmly, firmly, and with intensity immediately after the misbehavior, and must be confined to the offending students (Erickson & Mohatt, 1992). Negative responses to misbehavior, such as criticism, shouting, scolding, ridicule, and sarcasm, are not effective (Canter, 1996; Swick, 1985). Further, while public reprimands, corporal punishment, and other punitive actions may stop misbehavior temporarily, they are ineffective in the long run because they fail to teach constructive substitute behaviors and to emphasize student responsibility and choices (Goldstein, 1989; Wolfgang & Kelsey, 1995). Teachers using these negative and punitive approaches generally find that their students become more aggressive and unsettled and less concerned with learning than do effective classroom managers (Swick, 1985).

How, then, should we react when students misbehave? The following list of strategies is appropriate for classroom intervention. They are arranged from the most subtle, nonintrusive measures to stronger corrective interventions.

Extinction   Effective teachers generally ignore minor distractions and instances of inattention. For example, if a student misbehaves to gain the teacher's attention and that attention is withheld, it is likely the behavior will disappear. This intervention strategy is called **extinction.** It suggests that a teacher should ignore minor attention-seeking misbehavior the first time it happens as long as it is not dangerous or distracting to other students (Hunter, 1990).

It is important to understand that extinction is a nondirective response. That is, while students may cease the distracting behavior, they still don't know how they should behave. The key, then, is not how you react to the misbehaving student, but how you respond to the other students in the class who are behaving appropriately. While you ignore the misbehavior, you praise or give attention to the appropriate behavior of another student near the offender. This communicates to offenders what they should be doing (Albert, 1996; Hunter, 1990; Martin, 1981).

Let's look at an example. As you begin a lesson, Keyla begins to tap her pencil on the desk in an effort to distract you and gain your attention. In applying extinction, you would ignore Keyla's pencil tapping but turn to Ricardo, who sits nearby, and praise him for listening closely to the directions. This suggests to Keyla that in order to gain the teacher's attention, she too must listen closely to the directions.

Although extinction has been used effectively to eliminate disruptive behavior, off-task behavior, tantrums, and aggression (Goetz et al., 1996), it is quite difficult to practice. One reason is that it basically requires you to do something unnatural. You have been trained to be aware of everything going on in your classroom and, upon recognizing misbehavior, to "nip it in the bud." Recall that Kounin's research (1970) shows that effective classroom managers are "withit," or aware of everything that is happening in the classroom, and that they communicate their awareness to students. The principle of extinction suggests that you *not* communicate directly with students if your response provides them with the attention they are inappropriately seeking. Instead you provide attention or positive reinforcement only when a student chooses to act appropriately.

Another problem with the use of extinction is that it takes time to change behavior. Worse yet, ignoring attention-seeking behavior may, at first, actually increase incidents of misbehavior (Cruickshank & Associates, 1980; Kounin, 1970). In some cases, ignoring students' behavior leads to aggression, presumably in reaction to increasing frustration. If Sam, for example, gained the teacher's attention in fourth grade by getting out of his seat, it is likely he will try the same method in your fifth-grade class. If you do not respond the way the fourth-grade teacher did, he may assume that you simply don't see him and get out of his seat even more frequently. After all, if he gained attention from teachers in the past by behaving in

Students abusing other students is a problem in today's schools. Students are emotionally abusive to each other when they heckle or "put down" others. This behavior often escalates into intimidation and physical aggression. Bullies affect the academic achievement and the welfare of others. Because they create an insecure, unsafe classroom climate, bullies must be dealt with—immediately.

Bullying behavior stems from a need for attention, power, and self-confidence. These students enjoy the attention they get from heckling and ridiculing others. The need to achieve a feeling of power by dominating others is evident when they put down, intimidate, and hurt others. Although bullies may realize that hurting others is wrong, this behavior meets their basic need to feel important. Bullies also need to belong to a group.

Because their behavior is unacceptable to most classmates, they may become leaders through intimidation. The power exerted through verbal and physical force usually makes bullies feel more independent and more in control of their lives, thus enhancing their self-confidence (DeBruyn, 2001).

What should you do about bullies? Firm rules against bullying, closer supervision in areas where bullying usually takes place, and reinforcement of good behavior are often recommended (Noll, 2000).

On an individual basis, however, being gentle rather than tough is effective (DeBruyn, 2001). Although bullies appear tough, they may, in fact, be weak and using antics to cover up insecurity and social ineptness. Because they are generally unable to express their feel-

ings appropriately, they use aggression to keep others away and to hide their insecurities (Noll, 2000). Try establishing one-on-one relationships with bullies to help them achieve classroom, school, and social success. These students often accept responsibilities well and will cooperate with you if they realize that you like them for a talent other than bullying. Bullies often lack a strong and successful adult role model and think that "strength" always wins. Their aggression meets some psychological need, so help them find healthier and more acceptable ways to meet these needs. You'll find that bullies are often extremely loyal if they realize that you care about, respect, and even trust them for who they are, in spite of their inappropriate behavior.

---

this way, why should he expect a different reaction now? However, if you consistently ignore the misbehavior and redirect attention toward the appropriate behavior, the misbehavior should eventually disappear. More importantly, you will have prevented interruptions to your lessons.

Mild Desists Effective managers deal with potentially serious disruptions early by using nonverbal intervention and mild desists. Nonverbal strategies such as establishing eye contact, shaking the head, using facial expressions, moving closer, touching or gesturing, and redirecting attention are highly effective, yet they do not interrupt the flow of the lesson or distract other students in the class. Indeed, a study of middle school teachers found that nonverbal strategies stopped misbehavior 79 percent of the time. Teachers in the study identified as the "more effective managers" had an even higher success rate, stopping misbehavior with nonverbal strategies 95 percent of the time (Lasley, Lasley, & Ward, 1989)!

Subtle verbal desists are also effective. Slowing your speaking rate, pronouncing things more distinctly, speaking more softly, or (even more powerful) pausing briefly and looking around are all nonobtrusive, more private ways of conveying to students that they need to adjust their behavior. Likewise, using the misbehaving student's name, directing short questions or comments to the disruptive student, calling the name and pausing briefly, or redirecting the student back to the lesson ("Open to page 271 and follow along") are effective yet largely nonintrusive verbal interventions. Brophy (1982, 1983) points out that such subtle but direct public interventions are often more effective than ignoring misbehavior or praising appropriate behavior. This is particularly true for older students who misbehave because they are seeking attention or are bored.

13.19 How do you feel when a teacher uses mild desists to correct your behavior?

Reprimands   Verbal reprimands are widely used in classrooms. White (1975) found that teachers in all grades reprimand students once every two minutes. Sadly, the number of reprimands exceeds the amount of praise given in every grade after second grade. Further, it seriously interrupts instructional time (see Chapter 12).

Teachers often reprimand students for not listening, breaking school rules, or creating noise others can hear outside the classroom. The use of reprimands tends to be highly situational. Teachers seem to be more tolerant, or at least to deliver fewer reprimands, immediately following a lesson and during the last few minutes of the period. Teachers also appear more tolerant when the misbehavior is minor, brief, and not likely to escalate or when it is caused by a usually well-behaved student (Bellon et al., 1996).

Reynolds (1992) outlines the way effective managers deliver reprimands. They talk with misbehaving students in private rather than in front of the class, thus minimizing power struggles and face-saving gestures. They question the students to determine whether they understood why the way they chose to behave was inappropriate, and they ask for explanations. Also, effective managers make sure that students understand why the behavior is unacceptable; they try to get the students to accept responsibility for the behavior and to make a commitment to change. They instruct or model more acceptable ways for the students to behave. Finally, effective managers warn students about the consequences of continuing the misbehavior, help them understand how the consequences of disruptive behavior are detrimental to them and to the learning environment, and ask the students to make a choice about their behavior. They follow through with the consequences if the misbehavior does not change.

Time-Out   For more serious misbehavior, using a time-out strategy may be effective (Figure 13.8). **Time-out** reduces unwanted behavior by removing the offending student from the situation and, therefore, from the attention and rewards the situation provides. During time-out, the student may be excluded from an activity, asked to put her hands or head on her desk, removed to a desk in the back of the room, removed from the classroom, or sent to a time-out room.

Time-out is especially effective for students who misbehave to draw attention from their peers or who are overly active. If, for example, a student kicks the volleyball across the gymnasium during a physical education class to show off to his classmates, the teacher would ask the student to sit on the bleachers for ten minutes to think about what he has done. If the student enjoys playing volleyball with his teammates, being removed from the situation is punishment. He is likely to consider what he did wrong and resolve to behave appropriately if he wants to reenter the game.

It is important to remember certain guidelines when using time-out. First, the time-out period must be brief, usually from five to twelve minutes, depending on the age of the student. A rule of thumb is that the time-out should be one minute long for each year of the child's age. Longer periods of time do not make the treatment more effective (Kazdin, 1982). An extended time-out period could increase

FIGURE 13.8   Types of Intervention

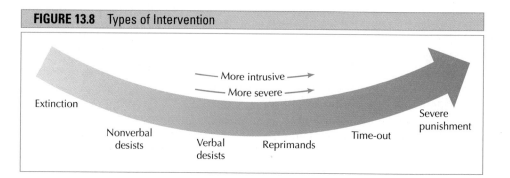

the student's resentment if he or she considers the time-out unfair, or it may cause the student to fall behind in class work.

Second, during time-out, the student must be isolated. It is best to isolate the student in the classroom to retain opportunities for learning (Kazdin, 1982). Asking a disruptive student to leave a math lesson for time-out in the hallway where he gets attention from every passerby may be more of a reward than a punishment, especially if he doesn't like math! However, if the misbehavior is so severe that the student's continued presence is likely to disrupt instruction, the isolation may need to occur outside the classroom. It is important that classmates or other school personnel not talk with the student during isolation. If a student is sent to another classroom or to the office for time-out, school personnel should be asked not to interact with the offending student.

Third, the offending student should be allowed to return to the regular classroom activity after the designated time has elapsed or when she decides to behave appropriately, for example, sitting quietly and attending to the lesson. Some teachers ask students to identify what they did wrong and how they should have acted as a condition for returning to the activity.

Finally, students should be held accountable for the work they miss during a time-out. The work should be completed on the students' own time or at home rather than during recess or a special activity, which would serve as a second punishment.

Time-out can be an effective way to influence student behavior if you correctly apply and monitor it. Above all, don't forget about the student! Too many teachers remove distracting students from the situation, return to the lesson, and promptly forget about the student in time-out. The extended, unfocused time in isolation negates the impact of the time-out procedure for the misbehaving student.

USING PUNISHMENT IN THE CLASSROOM

Punishment is something undesirable, painful, or discomforting that is applied to the student in response to misbehavior. It is intended to weaken the probability that the inappropriate behavior will recur (Savage, 1991). Punishments include interventions such as verbal reprimands, time-out, detentions, or more severe verbal or physical reactions. The most effective punishments are brief and mild; they involve restitution and allow students to quickly regain normal status (Bellon et al., 1996). Punishment should also provide students with information about how to change their behavior (Brophy & Evertson, 1976; Wolfgang & Kelsay, 1995).

13.20 As a student, were you ever punished? How did you feel?

Criticisms of Punishment   Teachers can easily misuse punishment, especially if they respond spontaneously or emotionally to inappropriate behavior. For legal and ethical reasons, severe punishment is discouraged in today's schools. Some of the more common criticisms are summarized below.

1. Critics contend that while punishment may temporarily restore a student's appropriate behavior, in the long run it has undesirable side effects on both the offending students and the entire class (Steele, 1988). This is because punishment causes a negative emotional tone in the classroom. Some students become resentful of the teacher and vow to avenge the punishment, especially if they consider the punishment unfair or too harsh. Also, by experiencing punishment or seeing others being punished, some students become so anxious and fearful that their academic performance suffers.

2. Another criticism of punishment is that it often strengthens bad behavior, especially if the punishment is administered publicly. This is especially true for students who receive little or no attention at home or who are behaviorally disadvantaged. Punishment may be the only type of attention they know how to gain. To such children, anything, even punishment, is better than being ignored.

3. Others point out that punishment fails to model appropriate behavior and actually models aggressive behavior. Punishment also breeds avoidance behavior, which may be counterproductive to learning and socialization (Stipek, 1997). Becker (1986) contends that most of the undesirable behaviors observed in school and society (cheating, truancy, sneaking, hiding, lying) are really escape and avoidance behaviors that children learn in order to avoid punishment at school or at home.

4. Punishment does not remove the underlying causes of the misbehavior. Students still do not know how to resolve conflicts, deal with frustrations, or follow classroom rules and routines after punishment. It is important, then, that discipline focus on educating students to make appropriate choices about their behavior and social responsibility (Wolfgang & Kelsay, 1995).

Guidelines for Using Punishment   Advocates of the appropriate use of punishment point out that, when carefully used, intervention or punishment can be effective. For example, softly delivered, firm reprimands for misbehaviors are much more effective than shouting. The following guidelines apply to using punishment in the classroom.

1. *Use punishment sparingly.* Punishment should be reserved for serious misbehavior and generally used as a last resort. Further, a teacher should never punish out of anger or frustration. Effective classroom managers take responsibility for dealing with problem students rather than referring them to others such as the guidance counselor or principal (Brophy & Rohrkemper, 1981). In short, effective classroom managers take responsibility for managing their students' behavior and do so in a professional manner.

2. *Use punishment quickly.* Effective classroom managers react to students' misbehavior quickly—usually when the behavior starts. Effective managers don't threaten students or issue warnings unless they follow up on those reminders. Further, Emmer et al. (1980) found that effective managers plan their penalties ahead of time and discuss those consequences with students.

13.21 What logical consequences would you use for the common misbehaviors discussed in this chapter?

3. *Use punishments related to the misbehavior.* In selecting consequences for possible use in your classroom, it is important to make sure they logically relate to the misbehavior. For example, if a student turns in a poorly prepared paper, the logical consequence is to have him rewrite it, rather than to keep him after school or assign him additional math problems for homework. Punishments that are not related to the offense may be seen as arbitrary to students, and the teacher may appear dictatorial. Illogical punishment may also hinder learning. For example, assigning regular schoolwork as punishment is inversely related to gains in students' learning (Brophy & Evertson, 1976).

13.22 What qualities do you have that will help you deal with misbehavior?

4. *Use punishment after careful consideration.* Since punishment is complex and situational, teachers should be aware of the context; they should know how the students will interpret the punishment and what the punishment will require of them. It is possible, for example, for teachers to administer a "punishment" that the student does not perceive as punishment. For some students, being forced to sit out of a physical education class or to stay inside during recess may be a blessing in disguise. Can you see why? Further, the effectiveness of some forms of punishment differs according to the emotional needs of the student.

Try Activity 13.7

5. *Avoid complex, time-consuming punishment systems.* Some teachers try to implement complex intervention systems that require extensive record keeping or time-consuming conferencing. Even if these systems are effective, they may be too complicated to be practical (Bellon et al., 1996). Further, they generally do not provide the immediate reinforcement vital to changing students' behavior (Evertson & Harris, 1992).

Reestablishing the Learning Environment

No matter what intervention you choose to employ in a given classroom situation, you will need to reestablish a positive classroom climate and a positive relationship with the offending student as soon as possible. After all, the message you want to convey is that while the behavior is unacceptable, the student is an acceptable person and an important part of the class. You can use the strategies listed earlier in the chapter to reestablish a positive, cooperative relationship among students and between you and the offending student.

Sometimes the management system established at the beginning of the year just don't seem to work, and sometimes the reinforcement and intervention strategies you employ are not effective. Don't panic or resign yourself to putting up with a disorganized or unruly class for the remainder of the year. Evertson (1989) recommends reexamining your management system periodically, discussing it with students, and repairing and restoring the system as needed. These "second beginnings" are best introduced after natural breaks in the school year, such as after a weekend or holiday. They should be implemented using clear communication, student cooperation, careful monitoring, and consistent accountability, just as you would introduce a management plan at the beginning of the school year. There is nothing wrong with making a mistake and starting over, as long as the repaired management system contributes to a more effective learning environment.

Some Final Thoughts

Good classroom management is essential to classroom learning. Effective managers plan how to prevent behavior problems, how to monitor student behavior, how to react when students misbehave, and how to reestablish a positive classroom environment after correcting misbehavior. They know how to review and adjust their management plans. By developing and following proactive behavior management plans, you will help establish an effective learning environment for your students and minimize stress in the classroom.

CHAPTER SUMMARY

- Nearly everyone expects teachers to be good classroom managers. Administrators often consider teachers who exert strong control to be their best teachers, while parents and the community expect teachers to teach students self-control. Likewise, students expect teachers to exert control and to establish a positive learning environment. Finally, teachers who are poor classroom managers feel frustrated and dissatisfied with teaching.

- Classroom management consists of all the provisions and procedures a teacher uses to create and maintain a classroom environment in which teaching and learning can occur. Traditionally classroom management focused on reactive management, that is, how teachers reacted to (or disciplined) students who misbehaved. This approach neglected the close relationship between instruction and classroom management. Today's classrooms stress proactive management, or preventing control problems from erupting in the first place.

- Effective classroom managers prevent control problems by organizing and establishing a classroom environment that is safe and predictable, both physically and psychologically.

- The physical environment consists of those concrete elements that are independent of the people who inhabit the classroom. The psychological environment is intangible and exists only in the minds of teachers and students.

- Seating patterns influence peer interactions, teacher-student interactions, and student attitudes or affect. Students seated at tables interact more than students seated in rows and, consequently, tend to develop better leadership skills. Students seated in a circle speak more to those across from them and less to those seated next to them. An action zone of teacher-student interaction is composed of students seated toward the front and middle of the class. These students enjoy the teacher more and feel more involved in the class. Because no single seating arrangement is ideal, experts recommend a flexible arrangement that the teacher can modify for various activities.

- Although teachers cannot control the number of students in their classes, they should ensure that all students have comfortable desks and lockers and that materials and equipment are readily available without crowding students or making them wait. Likewise, they should arrange their rooms to produce a safe, stimulating environment for students. This includes arranging furniture to (1) minimize distractions and congestion; (2) establish activity boundaries between incompatible activities; (3) allow the teacher to monitor in all parts of the room; and (4) provide open lanes for movement, especially between desks and around supply areas.

- In a classroom with a positive tone, students feel safe, comfortable, respected, and responsible. In such classrooms, (1) students' basic needs are met; (2) color, light, temperature, and displays are used to create softness, stimulation, and emotional safety; (3) mutual respect, cooperation, and student responsibility are present; (4) student and teacher ownership are evident; (5) the environment is busy and task-oriented; and (6) teachers' expectations are clear, and structure is provided.

- Classroom routines that control and coordinate movement and events help prevent classroom management problems. These routines fall into four categories: management routines, activity routines, instructional routines, and executive planning routines.

- Management problems can be minimized by arranging the classroom environment and establishing routines early in the school year. The task of establishing classroom rules and routines begins on the first day of class and routines, like instructional lessons, should be clearly communicated, modeled, and taught to students. Teachers should also provide opportunities to practice. Finally, teachers should communicate that they are prepared and competent to manage the classroom and should hold students responsible for following the classroom routines.

- Monitoring students' behavior throughout the year by signaling students who are beginning to misbehave and redirecting their attention to the lesson prevents serious misbehavior. Effective monitoring involves the use of withitness, overlapping, smoothness and momentum, and group alerting techniques.

- Teachers can monitor and maintain students' behavior by using rewards and reinforcement. Reinforcement theory posits that behavior that is rewarded is strengthened and likely to be repeated; behavior that is not rewarded is likely to diminish. To be effective, targeted behaviors must be clearly communicated and must be reinforced immediately after the behavior.

- Since different students respond to different types of reinforcement, teachers should develop a reinforcement menu that meets the needs and wants of individual students. Such a menu should include (1) social reinforcers such as praise, smiles, and physical contact; (2) activity reinforcers such as free time or class responsibilities; (3) tangible reinforcers such as redeemable tokens; and (4) negative reinforcers such as removal from detention.

- As students' behavior improves, teachers must change the reinforcement schedule. Desirable behaviors should be reinforced less frequently following mastery, and more complex behaviors should be reinforced after students have learned simple behaviors.

- Many critics disparage the use of reinforcement in classrooms. Some view reinforcement as bribing students, others as overcontrolling them. Some feel that praise and social rewards are ineffective after the primary grades and that extrinsic rewards may actually reduce internal motivation. Finally, some critics say reinforcement theory is impractical for classroom use because of the time, expense, and complexity involved.

- Even with a well-planned and monitored management system, misbehavior will occur. Such misbehavior can result from a need for attention, power, revenge, or isolation. Also, teachers sometimes cause the misbehavior by failing to prepare, by treating students differently, by verbally abusing them, or reacting in ways that students perceive as unfair.

- Teachers must decide when and how to intervene when students misbehave and must respond quickly. When deciding how to intervene, they should consider the extent to which intervention will interrupt instruction, the nature and severity of the misbehavior, the student involved, and when the misbehavior occurred.

- Effective classroom managers have a repertoire of intervention strategies they can use to respond to students' misbehavior. These include extinction, mild desists, reprimands, overcorrection, time-out, and other forms of punishment.

- Critics charge that punishment has undesirable long-term side effects, that it sometimes strengthens bad behavior, that it teaches aggressive and avoidance behavior, and that it does not remove the underlying cause of the behavior problem. However, punishment may be effective in reducing repeated, serious misbehavior. When using punishment, the teacher should administer it quickly and thoughtfully, should make sure it is logically related to the misbehavior, and should choose the intervention after careful consideration of the context, the way students will respond to the punishment, and the complexity of the intervention system.

- Periodically, it may be necessary to evaluate and reestablish the learning environment in the classroom. For example, after intervening in misbehavior, the teacher needs to reestablish a positive climate of mutual respect and cooperation. It is a good idea to periodically review the effectiveness of the management plan and to adopt new routines when needed.

ISSUES AND PROBLEMS FOR DISCUSSION

1. What should the goal of classroom management be?
2. Should teachers share their personal lives and interests in the classroom? Why or why not?
3. Do students have rights in the classroom? Do teachers?
4. Is it ethical for teachers to influence or control student behavior? Explain your answer.
5. Should teachers be responsible for the behavior of students outside the classroom? Give reasons for your position.
6. Should students' behavior be factored into their grades? Why or why not?
7. Should teachers send misbehaving students to the principal's office? Give examples to support your position.
8. Should principals be expected to support teachers' classroom management practices and decisions? Why or why not?

9. Should states outlaw some forms of punishment, such as paddling, even if parents advocate them? Explain.

10. How should teachers respond to the increased violence in today's schools?

THEORY INTO ACTION ACTIVITIES

ACTIVITY 13.1: Observing Seating Arrangements

1. Ask your cooperating teacher what he or she thinks are the most important things to take into account when deciding how to seat students in a classroom.

2. Observe in several classrooms that have different seating arrangements for students. Draw a diagram of the way the desks are arranged. Then make a sociogram by drawing arrows to indicate the conversational flow among students. Keep track of these student interactions for ten minutes. When you compare the student interactions across different seating arrangements, what do you notice?

3. Figure 13.9 is a diagram of a music classroom. The fifty students were seated in two rows of folding chairs. The teacher was very frustrated because the students talked and misbehaved so much she could hardly teach. Analyze the seating arrangement and make suggestions about changes that might prevent students from misbehaving. Also suggest instructional behaviors the teacher should adopt to monitor students and hold their attention.

4. Visit a classroom. Observe students and the seats they are assigned to. Do the students seem to "fit" comfortably in their seats? Are left-handed and special-needs students accommodated? Try sitting in a student seat yourself. How does it feel? Could you sit there comfortably for a morning or a day?

ACTIVITY 13.2: Organizing the Physical and Psychological Environments of the Classroom

1. As you enter the classroom, what are your feelings and first impressions? What messages about learning and the teacher does the classroom send? How would

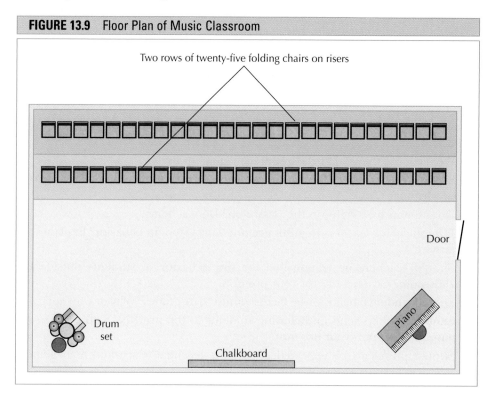

FIGURE 13.9 Floor Plan of Music Classroom

you feel about spending many hours each day in this classroom as a student? As a teacher?

2. Draw a floor plan for the classroom. Be sure to include all furniture and workstations in the classroom on your drawing. Now observe the flow of students around the classroom for thirty minutes. Draw those patterns on your floor plan. Identify areas of heavy traffic flow and bottlenecks that may threaten the students' sense of psychological safety in the classroom.

3. Softness in the room helps students to feel safe and meets aesthetic needs. Look around the room for examples of softness and list them.

4. What do you see that communicates something about the people who occupy this room? How is student ownership of the classroom expressed?

5. Now observe the teacher-student interactions in the room, especially during instruction or discussion. Construct a sociogram showing the patterns of interaction. Try to identify the action zone in the classroom. Does the teacher make any efforts to accommodate students sitting outside the action zone?

6. Does the classroom provide an enriched environment? Identify and describe ways the teacher uses the physical environment to stimulate students' growth and learning.

7. Evaluate the physical and psychological environments you have observed. What are the strengths? From your point of view, how could the classroom setting be changed to make it a more accessible and inviting environment?

ACTIVITY 13.3: Developing Classroom Rules

1. Ask your cooperating teacher about classroom rules.
   a. What are they? Are they posted? Why or why not?
   b. How does the teacher develop the rules?
   c. How does the teacher introduce the rules at the beginning of the year?
   d. Analyze the rules for clarity, simplicity, positive tone, and practicality.
2. Ask a student about classroom rules.
   a. What are they?
   b. How were the rules developed?
   c. How did the students learn the rules?
   d. Are the rules enforced? If so, how and when?
3. Compare responses from the teacher and student with your own observations.

ACTIVITY 13.4: Developing Classroom Routines

1. Ask your cooperating teacher what he or she thinks about routines and which are the most critical.
2. Observe and describe the following management routines in an elementary or secondary classroom.
   a. How does the teacher pass out and distribute student papers and work?
   b. What routines are established for student transitions: entering the room, leaving the room, and moving from one instructional activity to another?
   c. How does the teacher begin and end the school day or class period?
   d. What routines are in place for students to sharpen pencils, use the restroom, dispose of trash, or meet other individual needs?
   e. Are students given responsibilities in the classroom? What evidence do you see of this? How are student responsibilities assigned?
3. Observe and describe the following activity routines in an elementary or secondary classroom.
   a. When and how do students gain the teacher's attention? Does this routine change throughout the day based on the type of activity or other factors?
   b. Identify and describe one activity routine in the classroom.

4. Observe and describe the following instructional routines in an elementary or secondary classroom.
   a. What routine or procedure does the teacher use to give directions or assignments?
   b. Listen closely to how the teacher asks questions or leads a discussion. What routines does the teacher follow?
5. Observe or discuss the following executive planning routines your cooperating teacher utilizes.
   a. When does the teacher plan for instruction?
   b. What executive routines does the teacher have in place for grading papers, running dittos, typing tests, and performing clerical tasks?
   c. What advice would the teacher give you about balancing your personal and professional lives as a new teacher?
6. From what you have observed and heard, how important do you think routines will be in your classroom? Cite three specific routines you are now aware of that you plan to adopt in your own classroom someday.

ACTIVITY 13.5: Holding Students Accountable

1. Ask your cooperating teacher what he or she does during the first day and week of school.
2. Observe your cooperating teacher. Describe behaviors the teacher uses to communicate to students that he or she is "withit."
3. Describe how your cooperating teacher exhibited the ability to overlap.
4. When observing in your cooperating teacher's classroom, look for things that threaten the smoothness and momentum of the lesson. How does the teacher deal with each of these?
5. Observe as your cooperating teacher monitors students by using nonverbal behaviors. Describe the nonverbal behaviors you observe.

ACTIVITY 13.6: Reinforcement in the Classroom

1. Observe your cooperating teacher for thirty minutes, focusing on teacher-student interactions. List specific examples of social reinforcers the teacher used. How did students respond?
2. What is the teacher reinforcing? Is it behavior or academic performance? (You may need to keep a tally to answer the question accurately.)
3. List specific examples of activity reinforcers you observed. How did students respond to them?
4. List examples of tangible reinforcers or rewards the teacher used. How did students respond?
5. From your observations, which types of reinforcement seemed to be most effective in bringing about desired behavior? How can you explain this?

ACTIVITY 13.7: Types of Intervention

1. Interview three teachers to determine what they think about using extinction in the classroom. Have they tried to extinguish inappropriate behavior? Do they think the approach works?
2. Observe a classroom for examples of extinction. How does the misbehaving student respond?
3. Observe a teacher interacting with students for thirty minutes. Keep a tally of the nonverbal and verbal mild desists the teacher uses to intervene in misbehavior. Which approach does the teacher use most frequently? Which approach seems most effective with the students in that classroom?

4. Talk with a variety of teachers and ask them what types of intervention they use. Make a list. Does the type of intervention used vary according to grade level? Years of teacher experience? Other classroom variables?

5. Survey several students, parents, and teachers to see if they agree or disagree with the use of punishment in the classroom. What kinds of punishment do they deem appropriate? What do they think is inappropriate?

6. Use the Internet to find the discipline policy of a local school district. Evaluate it based on what you learned from this chapter and teacher interviews.

REFERENCES

Adams, R. S., & Biddle, B. J. (1970). *Realities of teaching: Exploration with videotape.* New York: Holt, Rinehart, and Winston.

Ainley, J. G. (1987). Equipment and materials. In M. J. Dunkin (Ed.), *The international encyclopedia of teaching and teacher education.* New York: Pergamon.

Albert, L. (1996). *Cooperative discipline.* Circle Pines, MN: American Guidance Service.

Albert, L. (1995). Discipline: Is it a dirty word? *Learning. 24*(2), 43–46.

Anderson, L. M., Evertson, C. M., & Brophy, J. (1979). An experimental study of effective teaching in first-grade reading groups. *Elementary School Journal, 79,* 193–223.

Anderson, L. W. (1991). Classroom environment and climate. *Increasing teacher effectiveness* (pp. 36–53). Paris: UNESCO.

Becker, W. C. (1986). *Applied psychology for teachers: A behavioral cognitive approach.* Chicago: Science Research Associates.

Bellon, J. J., Bellon, E. C., & Blank, M. A. (1996). *Teaching from a research knowledge base.* Englewood Cliffs, NJ: Prentice Hall.

Borich, G. D. (2000). *Effective teaching methods.* Fourth Edition. Boston: Pearson.

Brophy, J. E. (1982). Supplemental group management techniques. In D. Duke (Ed.), *Helping teachers manage classrooms* (pp. 32–51). Alexandria, VA: Association for Supervision and Curriculum Development.

Brophy, J. E. (1983). Classroom organization and management. In D. C. Smith (Ed.), *Essential knowledge for beginning educators* (pp. 23–37). Washington DC: American Association of Colleges for Teacher Education.

Brophy, J. E., & Evertson, C. M. (1976). *Learning from teaching: A developmental perspective.* Boston: Allyn & Bacon.

Brophy, J. E., & Rohrkemper, M. M. (1981). The influence of problem ownership on teachers' perceptions of and strategies for coping with student problems. *Journal of Educational Psychology, 73,* 295–311.

Cangelosi, J. S. (2000). *Classroom management strategies: Gaining and maintaining students' cooperation.* Somerset, NJ: John Wiley & Sons.

Canter, L. (1996). First, the rapport—then, the rules. *Learning, 24*(5), 12–14.

Cruickshank, D. R., & Associates. (1980). *Teaching is tough.* Englewood Cliffs, NJ: Prentice Hall.

Curwin, R. L., & Mendler, A. N. (1999). *Discipline with dignity.* Alexandria, VA: Association for Supervision and Curriculum Development.

DeBruyn, R. L. (2001, March 12). Handling the bully. *The Master Teacher, 12*(26), 1–2.

DiGiulio, R. (2000). *Positive classroom management.* Thousand Oaks, CA: Corwin.

Dollard, N. (1996). Constructive classroom management. *Focus on Exceptional Children, 29*(2), 1–12.

Doyle, W. (1983). Academic work. *Review of Educational Research, 53,* 159–199.

Doyle, W. (1986). Classroom organization and management. In M. C. Wittrock (Ed.), *Handbook of research on teaching,* Third Edition (pp. 392–431). New York: Macmillan.

Dreikers, R., Pepper, F., & Grunwald, B. (1998). *Maintaining sanity in the classroom: Classroom management techniques.* Second Edition. Florence, KY: Taylor Francis.

Duke, D. L. (1987). Environmental influences. In M. J. Dunkin (Ed.), *The international encyclopedia of teaching and teacher education* (pp. 548–553). New York: Pergamon.

Dunn, D. W. (2001). Do seating arrangements and assignments = classroom management? *Education World.* [Online]. http://www.educationaworld.com/a_curr/curr330.shtml.

Dykman, B., & Reis, H. (1979). Personality correlates of classroom seating position. *Journal of Educational Psychology, 71,* 346–354.

Eggen, P. D., & Kauchak, D. (2001). *Educational psychology: Windows on classrooms.* Englewood Cliffs, NJ: Prentice Hall.

Emmer, E. T. (1987). Classroom management. In M. J. Dunkin (Ed.), *The international encyclopedia of teaching and teacher education* (pp. 437–445). New York: Pergamon.

Emmer, E. T., & Evertson, C. M. (1981). Synthesis of research on classroom management. *Educational Leadership, 38,* 342–347.

Emmer, E. T., Evertson, C. M., & Anderson, L. M. (1980). Effective classroom management at the beginning of the school year. *The Elementary School Journal, 80,* 219–231.

Emmer, E. T., Evertson, C. M., & Worsham, M. E. (2000). *Classroom management for secondary teachers.* Fifth Edition. Boston: Allyn & Bacon.

Englander, M. E. (1986). *Strategies for classroom discipline.* New York: Praeger.

Erickson, F., & Mohatt, G. (1992). Cultural organization of participant structures in two classrooms of Indian students. In G. Spindler (Ed.), *Doing the ethnography of schooling: Educational anthropology in action* (pp. 132–174). New York: Holt, Rinehart, and Winston.

Evertson, C. M. (1987). Creating conditions for learning: From research to practice. *Theory into Practice, 26,* 44–50.

Evertson, C. M. (1989). Classroom organization and management. In M. C. Reynolds, (Ed.), *Knowledge base for the beginning teacher* (pp. 59–70). New York: Pergamon.

Evertson, C. M., Emmer, E. T., & Worsham, M. E. (2000). *Classroom management for elementary teachers.* Fifth Edition. Boston: Allyn & Bacon.

Evertson, C. M., & Harris, A. H. (1992). What we know about managing classrooms. *Educational Leadership 49*(7), pp. 74–78.

Freiberg, H. J. (1996) From tourists to citizens in the classroom. *Educational Leadership, 54*(1), 32–36.

Frick, T. W. (1990). Analysis of patterns in time: A method of recording and quantifying temporal relations in education. *American Educational Research Journal, 27,* 180–204.

Garner, B. (1989). Southeast Asian cultural and classroom culture. *College Teaching, 37,* 127–130.

Glasser, W. (1998). *The quality school.* New York: Harper Trade.

Goetz, E., Alexander, P. A., & Ash, M. J. (1996). *Education psychology.* Englewood Cliffs, NJ: Allyn & Bacon.

Goldstein, A. P. (1989). Teaching alternatives to aggression. In D. Biklen, D. Ferguson, & A. Ford (Eds.), *Schooling and disability.* (The Eighty-eighth Yearbook of the National Society for the Study of Education, pt. 1, pp. 168–194). Chicago: University of Chicago Press.

Good, T. L. (1983). Recent classroom research: Implications for teacher education. In D. C. Smith (Ed.), *Essential knowledge for beginning educators* (pp. 55–64). Washington, DC: American Association of Colleges for Teacher Education.

Grolnick, W. S., Ryan, R. M., & Deci, E. L. (1991). Inner resources for school achievement: Motivational mediators of children's perceptions of their parents. *Journal of Educational Psychology, 83,* 508–517.

Gunter, P. L., Shores, R. E., Jack, S. L., Rasmussen, S. K., & Flowers, J. (1995). On the move: Using teacher/student proximity to improve students' behavior. *Teaching Exceptional Children, 28*(1), 12–14.

Hawley, W. D., & Rosenholtz, S. J. (1984). Good schools: What research says about improving student achievement. *Peabody Journal of Education, 61*(4), 15–52.

Hunter, M. (1990). *Discipline that develops self-discipline.* Thousand Oaks, CA: Corwin.

Jackson, P. (1990). *Life in classrooms.* New York: Teachers' College Press.

Jones, V. F., & Jones, L. S. (2000). Comprehensive classroom management: Creating communities of support and problem solving. Sixth Edition. Needham Heights, MA: Allyn & Bacon.

Kazdin, A. E. (2000). *Behavior modification in applied settings.* Florence, KY: Brooks and Cole.

Kazdin, A. E. (1982). The token economy: A decade later. *Journal of Applied Behavior Analysis, 15,* 431–455.

Kohn, A. (1999). *Punished by rewards: The trouble with gold stars, incentive plans, A's, praise, and other bribes.* Boston: Houghton Mifflin.

Kounin, J. S. (1970). *Discipline and group management in classrooms.* New York: Holt, Rinehart, and Winston.

Kounin, J. S. (1983). *Classrooms: Individuals or behavior settings?* (Monographs in Teaching & Learning, no. 1). Bloomington, IN: Indiana University, School of Education. (ERIC Document Reproduction Service ED 240 070).

Lasley, T. J., Lasley, J. O., & Ward, S. H. (1989, April). Activities and desists used by more and less effective classroom managers. Paper presented at the annual meeting of the American Educational Research Association, San Francisco.

Leinhardt, G., Weldman, C., & Hammond, K. M. (1987). Introduction and integration of classroom routines by expert teachers. *Curriculum Inquiry, 17,* 135–175.

Lepper, M. (1983). Extrinsic reward and intrinsic motivation: Implications for the classroom. In J. Levine & M. Wang (Eds.), *Teacher and student perceptions: Implications for learning.* Hillsdale, NJ: Erlbaum.

Lewin, K., Lippitt, R., & White, R. (1939). Patterns of aggressive behavior in experimentally created social climates. *Journal of Social Psychology, 10,* 271–299.

Lyman, L., & Foyle, H. C. (1990). *Cooperative grouping for interactive learning: Students, teachers and administrators.* Washington, DC: National Education Association.

Martin, J. R. (1981). A new paradigm for liberal education. In J. F. Soltis (Ed.), *Philosophy and education.* Chicago: University of Chicago Press.

Maslow, A., & Laury, K. (Ed.). (1998). *Toward a psychology of being.* Somerset, NJ: John Wiley & Sons.

McCaslin, M., & Good, T. L. (1992). Compliant cognition: The misalliance of management and instructional goals in current school reform. *Educational Researcher, 21*(3), 4–17.

McGinnis, J. C., Frederick, B. P., & Edwards, R. (1995). Enhancing classroom management through proactive rules and procedures. *Psychology in the Schools, 32,* 220–224.

Morgan, M. (1984). Reward-induced decrements and increments in intrinsic motivation. *Review of Educational Research, 54*(1), 5–30.

Mueller, C. M., & Dweck, C. S. (1998). Intelligence praise can undermine motivation and performance. *Journal of Personality and Social Psychology, 75,* 33–52.

Noll, K. (2000). Taking the bully by the horns. [Online]. http://www.mondovista.com/bully.html.

Raviv, A., Raviv, A., & Reisel, E. (1990). Teachers and students: Two different perspectives?! Measuring social climate in the classroom. *American Educational Research Journal, 27,* 141–157.

Reynolds, A. (1992). What is competent beginning teaching? A review of the literature. *Review of Educational Research, 62*(1), 1–35.

Rogers, C. R., & Freiberg, H. J. (1994). *Freedom to learn,* Third Edition. Columbus, OH: Merrill.

Santrock, J. W. (1976). Affect and facilitative self-control: Influence of ecological setting, cognition, and social agent. *Journal of Educational Psychology, 68*(5), 529–535.

Savage, T. V. (1991). *Discipline for self-control.* Englewood Cliffs, NJ: Prentice Hall.

Scollon, R. (1981). *Teachers' questions about Alaska Native education.* Fairbanks, AK: University of Alaska Center for Cross Cultural Studies. (ERIC Document Reproduction Service ED 238 661).

Shade, B. J. (1982). Afro-American cognitive style: A variable in school success? *Review of Educational Research, 52,* 219–244.

Sommer, R., & Olsen, J. (1980). The soft classroom. *Environment & Behavior, 12*(1), 3–16.

Steele, B. F. (1988). *Becoming an effective classroom manager: A resource for teachers.* Albany: State University of New York.

Stipek, D. J. (1997). *Motivation to learn: From theory to practice.* Boston: Pearson.

Swick, K. J. (1985). *Disruptive student behavior in the classroom.* Washington, DC: National Education Association.

Sylwester, R. (1971). *The elementary teacher and pupil behavior.* West Nyack, NY: Parker.

Walberg, H. J. (1987). Psychological environment. In M. J. Dunkin (Ed.), *The international encyclopedia of teaching and teacher education.* (pp. 553–558). New York: Pergamon.

Wang, M. C., Haertel, G. D., & Walberg, H. J. (1993–94). What helps students learn? *Educational Leadership, 51*(4), 74–79.

Weinstein, C. S. (1987). Seating patterns. In M. J. Dunkin (Ed.), *The international encyclopedia of teaching and teacher education* (pp. 544–548). New York: Pergamon.

Weinstein, C. S., & Mignano, A. J., Jr. (2003). *Elementary classroom management: Lessons from research and practice.* Third Edition. New York: McGraw-Hill.

Wheldall, K., Morris, M., Vaughan, P., & Ng, Y. Y. (1981). Rows vs. tables: An example of the use of behavioral ecology in two classes of eleven-year-old children. *Journal of Educational Psychology, 1,* 171–184.

White, K. A. (1996, October 2). New teaching methods, technology add to space crunch. *Educational Week, 16,* p. 12.

White, M. A. (1975). Natural rates of teacher approach and disapproval in the classroom. *Journal of Applied Behavior Analysis, 8,* 367–372.

Wolfgang, C. H., & Kelsay, K. L. (1995). Discipline and the social studies classroom, grades K–12. *Social Studies, 86,* 175–182.

Woolfolk, A. E. (2001). *Educational psychology.* Boston: Allyn & Bacon.

Yinger, R. J. (1979). Routines in teacher planning. *Theory Into Practice, 18*(3), 163–169.

Zenger, W. F., & Zenger, S. K. (1999, April). Schools and curricula for the 21st century: Predictions, visions, and anticipations. *NASSP Bulletin,* pp. 49–59.

Challenges Classroom Teachers Face

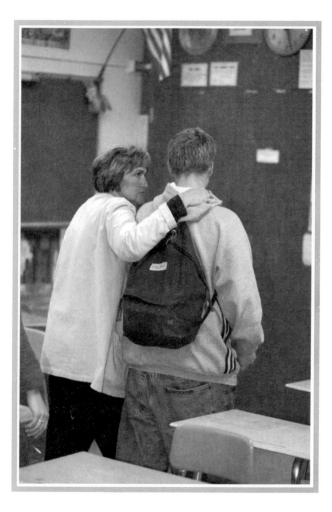

Contents

You probably are entering teaching for one or more of the following reasons:

- you want to serve others, especially helping them to learn
- you enjoy people, especially children
- you like some academic subject and want to teach it
- you know teaching will be challenging yet rewarding.

This chapter is intended to help you successfully meet the challenges of teaching. Herein you will be made aware of the most commonly reported problems that challenge teachers. More importantly, you will learn a process that you can use when facing a problem. Armed with knowledge of the problems teachers report and a problem solving process you can use, you will be better prepared when your turn comes to step up to the plate.

What Is a Problem?

Nearly everyone is challenged or encounters problems. If someone you know does not, they are either very lucky or very skillful. Fortunately, you can avoid most problems, and resolve many others. However, before we get into that, let's consider what a problem is.

The simplest definition of a **problem** is goal-response interference. We need or want to achieve or have something, and we cannot do it (see Figure 14.1). Can you think of something you need or want that is elusive or unattainable? It could be a good part-time or summer job, a particular friend or friends, better living conditions,

FIGURE 14.1 Visual Representation of a Problem

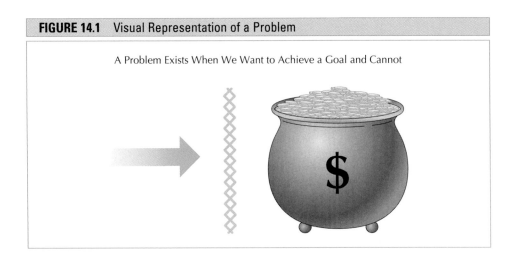

A Problem Exists When We Want to Achieve a Goal and Cannot

or the opportunity to participate in a certain activity. You probably need or want to do well in this class to maintain or increase your grade-point average which, in turn, might affect your student teaching assignment and, ultimately, your ability to obtain a teaching position. Of course, most of you care more about learning to teach than you do about grades. You are intrinsically, or inner, motivated.

You may have noticed we are using the terms *need* and *want*. *Need* designates something that is an absolute necessity to you. You need to breathe. On the other hand, *want* designates something that would be nice to have but is not essential to your well-being. Ice cream is a want. Whether the goal you seek is a need or a want is vitally important, for we must attain a need, whereas we can live without a want. Pursuit of either a need or a want that is elusive or unattainable still designates a problem. The difference is one of kind and degree.

Sources of Problems

Our needs can come from virtually any source. However, they all relate to the pursuit of either primary *biological needs* or secondary *learned needs* (Figure 14.2). Thus, some problems result from the inability to satisfy our inborn biological needs for food, water, and rest. We are driven, or motivated, to meet these primary needs on a regular basis. If you have been deprived of any of these needs for any length of time, you know how devastating it can be. The "machine" breaks down.

Unfortunately, you will see students deprived of these basic needs. Teachers working with students of low socioeconomic status (SES) report that such children frequently come to school without adequate clothing and are often hungry and sleepy. Teachers also report children arriving cold and wet, stealing lunches, and sleeping in class. Be forewarned: Such problems are not peculiar to low SES children. The primary needs of high SES children also may go unmet.

On the other hand, some of our problems and those of our students are fueled by the inability to meet secondary, or learned needs. In the process of growing up, we learn that we "need" to be friendly, to look good, to be successful, and so on. For

Try Incident 1 (Sleepless in Room 221) in Part Four, Unit 3 of the Practice Teaching Manual

14.1 Which needs challenge you most?

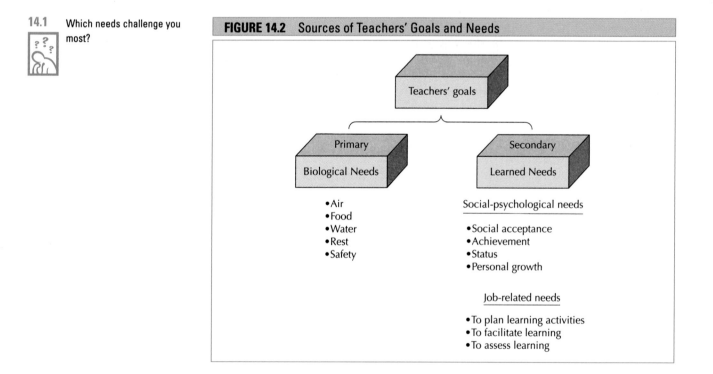

FIGURE 14.2   Sources of Teachers' Goals and Needs

the most part, we hope to please others and ourselves. Inability to satisfy our learned needs is likely to make us feel personally unfulfilled and unhappy. All of us have felt disappointed or discouraged when our efforts to achieve secondary needs are thwarted. Teachers report that students have many problems as a result of their unmet social and psychological needs. They act out, give up, and sometimes break down.

What we do for a living has a direct impact on our ability to meet our primary and secondary needs. Different kinds of work make life easier or more difficult. When our work enables us to satisfy our needs, it hardly seems like work at all. In such cases, we like our job. Conversely, work that is not fulfilling can be killing. Teaching normally is very pleasant work. It enables us to meet our biological needs fairly well, although some teachers in some situations might argue to the contrary. It also has the potential for helping us meet our learned needs. However, that occurs only when we teach well. This brings us to another subcategory of learned needs we will call "job-related." To teach well, we must be good at planning learning activities, facilitating or helping students learn, and assessing learning—activities you have learned about in this book. The end results of teaching well are acceptance, achievement, and personal satisfaction.

What Are the Classroom-Related Problems Teachers Face?

We have been able to determine what the problems or unmet needs of teachers are as they engage in the act of teaching by asking hundreds of K–12 teachers to describe their most difficult problem each day for up to two weeks. When these thousands of teacher-perceived problems were collected and analyzed, we found that there are sixty *common* problems that fall into five larger categories we call "areas of concern": affiliation, control, parent relationships and home conditions, student success, and time (Figure 14.3). Let's look at each area.

14.2 Have you had teachers who seemed to have problems in one or more of the five areas of teacher concern? What were these teachers like?

AFFILIATION

Affiliation is defined as the teacher's need to establish and maintain good relationships with others in the school. This includes students, faculty colleagues, staff, and administrators.

When we ask teachers to describe their day-to-day concerns, they report these problems: liking some or all of their students, getting students to like them, getting cooperation and support from their colleagues and the administration, being professional in their relationships with others in the school, having confidence in

14.3 How important to you is getting along with others?

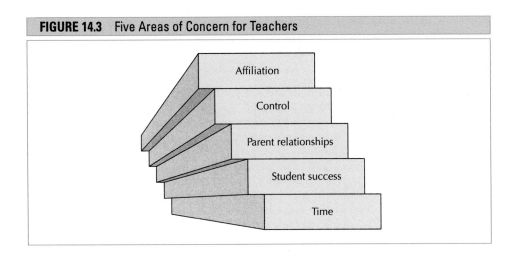

FIGURE 14.3 Five Areas of Concern for Teachers

- Affiliation
- Control
- Parent relationships
- Student success
- Time

14.4 What kinds of affiliation problems do you think you might have?

14.5 How important to you is getting along with students, colleagues, administrators, and staff?

Try Incidents 12 (Getting to the Bottom of Things) and 14 (So Much for Professionalism) in Part Four, Unit 3 of the Practice Teaching Manual

14.6 In what ways do you hope to change so that you might enhance your affiliation with others?

other teachers, and feeling anxious when being supervised (Bainer, 1986; Cruick-shank & Associates, 1980).

Having the comforting acceptance, companionship, and support of others is a very real social-psychological need, as Figure 14.2 indicates. Teachers deprived of human support during their workday feel lonely, unappreciated, ineffective, alienated, and perhaps even rejected. Teachers who report frequent affiliation concerns also report they are dissatisfied with teaching and with the school they are in (Myers, 1980).

The need for affiliation seems to be especially strong in persons who elect to teach. According to Super (1990), when teachers are compared to certified public accountants, engineers, lawyers, and clergy, the teachers value four things more highly: (1) having fellow workers they like, (2) working under pleasant conditions, (3) having the respect of others, and (4) enjoying job certainty. Thus, three of the things teachers prize seem directly related to the need for affiliation. Similarly, when Holland (1997) compared teachers with persons in other occupations using an instrument that measures personality types, he found that they rank highest on the "social" scale.

Affiliation probably is of particular importance to us and more difficult to achieve because of the nature of our work. We are constantly in contact with others. Moreover, at certain times we are required to be leaders, while at others we may be equals or followers. Very few occupations regularly require all three interpersonal roles.

Tracey (1980) provides us with some affiliation-related problems that teachers report:

- I have a problem with a student who swore at me in class. Having had this student in classes for two years, I was disappointed with his lack of respect (p. 78).

- The teachers at my grade level had their weekly meeting. Once again, it was them against me. Everything was decided by them. They didn't even know I was there (p. 78).

- I have heard that my principal said to a colleague of mine that he thinks I do not work hard enough—that I should have more students and teach more classes. I am already working so hard. I can't believe he thinks so little of me when I work so hard (p. 79).

As you can see, affiliation concerns seem directly related to our expectations and to those of our students, colleagues, administrators, and staff. Our inability to meet their expectations, and their inability to meet ours, seem to be the root of the problem. Affiliation concerns also come from our inability to interact effectively. Consequently, we need to be aware of what students, colleagues, administrators, and staff expect of us, and we must know and practice good interpersonal skills such as being sensitive to others and generally trying to assist them in meeting their social-psychological and job-related needs.

Tracey (1980) provides a summary on affiliation:

Affiliation problems, those which involve relationships with students, fellow teachers, and administrators, are troublesome to many teachers. It is important to seek solutions to these problems because the quality of interactions and the degree of affiliation with others greatly affect personal and professional satisfaction. When dealing with an affiliation problem, examine the expectations held by all the people involved. Not meeting expectations of self or others leads to conflict and frustration. . . . Research about [human] interaction provides helpful information. . . .

Affiliation is a critical and complex [area] for teachers. Valuable [related] information can be learned from work in communication, social psychology, psychology, and sociology. There are no simple explanations for human behavior or simple solutions for establishing better affiliation. (pp. 108–109)

The U.S. Department of Education, recognizing that new teachers have problems affiliating, has published *The Survival Guide for New Teachers* (DePaul, 2000). In it veteran teachers offer advice on how to work with other teachers, principals, and parents. The guide is online at www.ed.gov/pubs/survivalguide/index.html.

Web Resource

CONTROL

Control is the teacher need to have students behave well or appropriately. When teachers define *appropriately* they mean students should be reasonably quiet, orderly, courteous, and honest, and they should show respect for others and for property.

14.7 How important is control to you?

Teachers who have participated in our studies report they have several problems: maintaining order, quiet, and control; not knowing how to respond to improper behavior such as swearing and use of obscenities; controlling aggressive behavior; enforcing considerate treatment of property; getting students to use leisure time well; maintaining students' attention; enforcing values such as honesty and respect; removing students who are sources of frustration; and teaching self-discipline (Bainer, 1986; Cruickshank & Associates, 1980).

14.8 What types of control-related problems do you worry about most?

When students do not behave appropriately, two things can happen. First, animosity can develop between teacher and student, resulting also in an affiliation problem. Second, teachers can feel like and be perceived by students, teachers, administrators, and parents as ineffective classroom managers.

To complicate matters, we suspect that many persons who decide to teach are not strongly control-oriented. Remember, mostly we are *socially oriented*. We want to like and be liked. In fact, many teachers believe that the classroom should be "democratic" and that students should be empowered or given authority to decide things and, essentially, to control themselves. Complicating matters even further, many teachers simply don't have a clue about how to establish and maintain any kind of order. After all, they enjoyed learning and presume that their students will, too. When students respond to learning negatively by acting up, many teachers are shocked and stymied.

Novak (1980) provides us with examples of teacher-reported, control-related incidents:

> The same boy, DeWayne, who has been causing all the trouble in one of my classes was off and running again today. He had the girl sitting behind him combing his hair. Later in the period, he threw a paper wad across two rows to a boy. And, he was talking to the boys and girls around him. I think that the time has come for the school authorities to be called in. (p. 115)

Try Incidents 2, 4, 10, and 12 in Part Four, Unit 3 of the Practice Teaching Manual

Chapter 13 contains basic information about organizing, managing, and controlling the classroom that applies to this second area of teacher concern. Novak (1980) provides further help. He proposes five principles that can make control less of a problem (see Table 14.1):

- *Pursue only classroom goals that are truly important and appropriate.* Then make sure the goals are achievable. Thus, when you teach, modify or scale down overly ambitious intentions. In the case of the above control incident Novak provides, it is very important for DeWayne to behave appropriately. However, he and the teacher may have to work at it over time. Therefore, the teacher might modify

TABLE 14.1 Five Principles of Classroom Control
• Pursue only important, appropriate classroom goals • Analyze what may be affecting the problem situation • Use positive techniques for managing behavior • Use punishment sparingly and appropriately • Teach self-control

or scale down classroom goals and ask DeWayne to make an effort to behave appropriately in meeting these easier goals. Rather than expect immediate perfection, the teacher should look for progress.

- *Analyze the factors that may be affecting the problem situation.* Novak reminds us that the more you know about the circumstances of a problem, the more likely you will be able to select and employ effective techniques to resolve it. Therefore, he asks that you analyze the learning task and the students' ability to do it, consider the events that occurred before and during the problem's onset (what led up to the incident?), and consider what happened following the control incident (was there peer laughter, ineffective punishment?). By analyzing the situations DeWayne misbehaves in, you may deduce some clues that can explain his actions.

- *Use positive techniques for managing behavior.* Novak believes that when students do not act appropriately, they must learn new behavior patterns. This requires teaching students what is expected of them and recognizing and rewarding subsequent desirable behavior.

  Students must have a clear understanding of behavioral expectations and of their importance. Some students will simply misunderstand your expectations unless these expectations are absolutely clear and you are doggedly insistent in their pursuit. Other students will need to learn how to behave somewhat differently to what they are accustomed to in other classrooms or at home, where other behavioral expectations often exist. Yet others may have difficulty with you, and you with them, because of some social or emotional shortcoming.

  Novak has specific advice as you work with students who have a difficult time behaving appropriately. *First,* he urges that you single them out when they are doing the right thing and applaud their efforts. *Second,* recognize and reward them only when they engage in desirable behaviors. Do not give in to or reward undesirable behaviors. *Third,* ignore inappropriate behavior as often as possible. Do not allow your attention or the other students' attention to be drawn to it. *Fourth,* make sure that recognition and reward for desirable behavior is indeed rewarding. Not all learners will see better grades, teacher praise, or the assignment of more difficult work as positive. *Finally,* engage students themselves in problem solving. They, too, need to know how to go about resolving problems. Chapter 13 contains information you can readily apply in pursuit of Novak's third principle.

- *Use punishment sparingly and appropriately.* Use only punishment that works, use only as much as necessary, and make certain students know what behavior is inappropriate and, conversely, what is acceptable.

14.9 How important will control be in your classroom?

- *Teach students to manage their own behavior.* Teach them self-control. Notes Novak, "Self-control means having students behave appropriately in the absence of external control" (p. 149). When students know that inappropriate and appropriate behavior have predictable consequences and when they can recognize and respond to important classroom rules, they can exhibit self-control. Rules can include "When directions are being given, it is especially important to listen" and "When you borrow something, return it." Finally, Novak implores, "Don't be too controlling. Seek reasonable control. It is a lot easier to achieve and less stressful to you and your students" (p. 150).

Web Resource

The Master Teacher website (www.disciplinehelp.com/default.htm) offers suggestions for handling over 100 misbehaviors.

PARENT RELATIONSHIPS AND HOME CONDITIONS

We learned in Chapter 2 that most families and caregivers have great influence on children. Therefore, if you are able to involve parents constructively in their child's education, it is more likely that improved attendance, achievement, and behavior will follow (Haynes, Comer, & Hamilton-Lee, 1989; Henderson, 1987; Rich, 1988). Teachers recognize the important role parents and significant others play in the lives of students. Therefore, they want to maintain constructive relationships with them.

Teachers are also aware that the conditions in students' homes impact on their school success. As a result, teachers benefit from knowing what home conditions are like and most teachers would like to influence those conditions positively.

Many teachers who have participated in our surveys tell us that they find it difficult to have good relationships with parents and to find out about and have a positive effect on home conditions. Specifically, they report problems with the following endeavors: improving life for students by correcting conditions both inside and outside school, keeping students away from people and things that may have a bad influence, improving conditions so that students can study better at home, encouraging parental interest in school matters, holding worthwhile parent conferences, understanding the conditions of home and community, and assisting parents who are having difficulty with their children (Bainer, 1986; Cruickshank & Associates, 1980).

Mager (1980) suggests that to achieve constructive parent relationships, teachers and parents or guardians must be mutually supportive. For the most part, this means that teachers must accept and support parental values and behaviors and that parents must do likewise for teachers. Certainly, this is easier said than done, particularly when home and school values and behaviors differ. Mager shares a teacher-written illustration: "I was talking to the class about all the fights they had been getting into. The students told me that their parents tell them to hit anyone who does something they don't like. I suddenly realized that it's the school's no fighting policy versus the parents' don't be a sissy policy" (p. 157).

Perceptions of lack of competence also come into play and thus interfere with good relationships. For example, parents may doubt a teacher's decisions. One teacher writes, "I received a phone call from a parent who questioned the worth of an upcoming field trip. I tried to explain why the trip was worthwhile, but I am plagued by the thought that I was not convincing enough" (Mager, p. 156). Conversely, teachers may question the competence of parents. "I understand why Ellen behaves the way she does. These parents just don't care" (Mager, p. 157).

Failure to achieve mutual support may also result simply because barriers prevent teachers and parents from getting together to talk. Teachers may not have the time and energy. They may perceive that parents are too busy, or they may not want parents to "intrude" into their domain. For their part, parents may not wish to visit with teachers because they lack time or energy, they may not want to intrude, or they may perceive teachers as too busy. Additionally, parents may shy away from interactions with teachers because of unhappy childhood memories they may have of school, feelings of insecurity, or guilt that their child is having problems. Parents and caregivers may also be reluctant to talk with teachers because they have personal or family difficulties, because they may not be the child's birth parent, or because they cannot converse fluently in English.

In discussing the teacher's need to know what students' home and community conditions are like and, relatedly, the teacher's desire to influence them in a positive direction, Mager again points out hindrances. First of all, parents and guardians, not teachers, control home conditions. The following anecdote reveals a teacher's frustration on this count. "Today a student came late to my first hour class for the ninth time in four weeks. The main problem is that most of his excuses are legitimate. His lateness can be directly attributed to his parents. Car won't start, alarm doesn't work, mother got breakfast late, he had to babysit until 2 A.M. and so forth (Mager, p. 161).

Second, home conditions may even be beyond the control of parents. Some parents are forced to live in substandard housing in deteriorating, violent communities. Some parents must raise children without adequate financial and human support.

14.10 How important is getting along with parents and other caregivers?

Try Incidents 11 and 13 in Part Four: Unit 3 of the Practice Teaching Manual

14.11 Which problems in parent-teacher relationships seem most noteworthy to you? Why?

FIGURE 14.4 How to Get Parents on the Educational Express

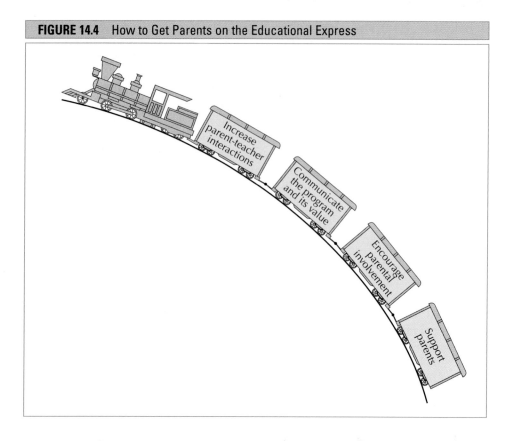

Some children must be left to their own devices. Other parents have limited intellect and/or education. Mager shares another teacher anecdote. "I visited the home of a new seventh grader coming from a rural school. He is having difficulty academically and socially. The purpose of the visit was to obtain permission to have him tested. I have come in contact with many deprived families but this one is very sad. Both parents are extremely retarded as is another child, a sixteen-year-old who has never even been to school. Neither parent can read or write" (p. 162). Unfortunately, these are realities that neither parents nor teachers alone can overcome.

Mager provides suggestions for helping you build mutual support with parents and improve home and community conditions (see Figure 14.4). To achieve mutual support, he argues that you need to increase the frequency and improve the quality of teacher-parent interactions. Such "interactions" can include sending out a classroom newsletter regularly, perhaps monthly; bringing in parent volunteers; forming a mom and/or dad's club, and so forth. To improve the quality of interactions, you need to learn what parents expect of you and you need to share what you expect of parents. Usually, unpleasant interactions are the result of unrealistic or failed expectations.

To achieve the goal of optimal home and community conditions, Mager advises that you take at least two steps. First, recognize that the relationship between home and community conditions and a student's school experience is complex. Avoid simplistic causal explanations such as "Robert would do better if he could move out of that home and neighborhood." That may or may not be true. Second, remember that the nature of the parents or guardians and the quality of the interactions they have with their children are far more important than the material possessions found in the home. Home and neighborhood trappings do not substitute for quality-of-life relationships. Therefore you should not, as the saying goes, "judge the book [home and community] by its cover."

Katz and others (1996) suggest ways to establish a climate conducive to open communication with parents-caregivers:

- Let parents-guardians know how and when they can contact you.
- Have an open-door policy.
- Have an open mind.

- In preparation for a meeting find out what are the parent-caregiver concerns.
- Involve parents in classroom activities.
- Know the school policy for addressing home-school disagreements.

- Use discretion when discussing children and their families.

Source: Lilian Katz and others (no names given). (1996). Preventing and resolving parent-teacher differences. Urbana, IL: ERIC Clearinghouse on Elementary and Early Childhood Education. (ERIC Document Reproduction Services ED 401 048).

Suggestions for preventing or resolving differences with parents are contained in Highlight 14.1.

STUDENT SUCCESS

Student success is defined as the need teachers have to help learners achieve both academically and socially. It is a very important goal because when you are successful in attaining it, you meet your secondary or learned needs for achievement, status, and acceptance in the teaching profession.

Unfortunately, many teachers struggle with student success. In our studies when teachers have described everyday problems, a great many fit into this category of concerns.

Kinds of Success Problems   Teacher-reported student success problems are of three kinds: those related to insufficient student interest, those related to working with students who have special needs, and those related to a teacher's own instructional shortcomings.

Problems related to teachers' perceptions of insufficient student interest include statements such as "I have a problem having students present and on time; getting students to participate; getting them to work up to their ability; prevailing on them to value grades; and overcoming apathy or even dislike of school and learning."

Problems associated with students who face special challenges include helping children with personal problems; helping those with special physical, social, emotional or intellectual needs; overcoming a student's frustration with self; and getting students to feel they are succeeding.

The third kind of student success problem is related to our personal instructional limitations when planning, teaching, and assessing the learning that has taken place. Specifically, teachers tell us they have trouble planning instruction that adds variety to classroom life, creating student interest, providing for individual differences, using different instructional alternatives, assessing learning, promoting students' self-assessment, and extending learning beyond the classroom.

Obstacles to Student Success   Holton (1980) describes four obstacles to achieving student success. First, "Knowledge about teaching is at best sketchy" (p. 205). Although, as we learned in Chapters 11 and 12, knowledge about how to teach is accumulating, we still know less than is needed. If we had what we truly need to know, this text probably would consist of at least five volumes!

A second hindrance to student success is students' individual differences. Recall that Chapter 3 was devoted to student diversity. Holton notes that diversity or individual difference is no cliché. He notes that according to G. W. Beadle, a Nobel

14.12   How important to you is getting students to succeed academically and socially?

Try Incidents 3, 7, and 8 in Part Four: Unit 3 of the Practice Teaching Manual

14.13   Which problems related to student success do you believe may be troublesome for you? Why?

laureate in genetics, if we calculated all possible human characteristics and the resulting permutations, the number of possible different human individuals would be about 2 raised to the 4-billionth power (that is, $2 \times 2 \times 2 \ldots 4$ billion times) (p. 205). So much diversity exists among our students that it is difficult at best to facilitate the learning of everyone (p. 205).

Third, "schools have many, often vague goals and not all of them are consistent with student learning" (p. 205). Some people, Holton notes, want schools to teach "the basics," while others are intent on "developing the whole child." The latter would educate them intellectually, morally, socially, emotionally, and physically. Still others want schools to educate children to change or improve society. Each school of thought about educational goals would have teachers doing different things. Teachers have difficulty working toward student learning if the goals are not well-defined and agreed upon and its character is unclear.

Fourth, says Holton, "Teaching is greater than the sum of its parts" (p. 206). There is some "magic" to it. One can carefully construct lessons and still have them fail; there is no guarantee. Holton attributes this to what he calls the unknown and possibly unknowable *X* factor in teaching. "While we sense the *X*, it has defied our attempts to weigh it, measure it, or catch it. . . . This *X* factor is what makes the successful classroom greater than the sum of its parts" (p. 206). It is the particular genius of knowing how and when to do something that works.

Teacher Behaviors Linked to Student Success   Holton notes that there are important teacher behaviors associated with student academic success. These behaviors are consistent with what appears in Chapters 11 and 12 of this book. He notes that effective teachers are clear, enthusiastic, and businesslike or work-oriented, they use a variety of instructional alternatives and materials, they adjust the material to students' abilities, they recognize the need to arouse interest, they provide adequate opportunity and time to learn, and they help students get the most out of their school experiences.

TIME

Lack of time represents a serious problem for teachers. According to the thousands we have surveyed, teachers do not have sufficient time to prepare for classes, complete the planned work, and diagnose and evaluate learning. Furthermore, constraints on time have increased because of (1) large classes, (2) the number of classes teachers are required to teach, (3) increased emphasis on testing, and (4) the assignment of noninstructional tasks such as bus, lunchroom, and playground monitoring. Finally, they tell us they do not have enough time to do personal tasks because of the amount of work they must take home. Lack of time, then, seems to be a major concern (see Spotlight on Research 14.1).

Unfortunately, there is little likelihood that demands on schools will lessen, and time is not a commodity we can manufacture more of. Rather, for decades, demands have been on the increase—teachers have more rather than less to do. Thus, teacher personal and professional needs seem to be growing inversely in relation to the time available to meet them.

Applegate (1980) suggests that since time is finite, we must learn to use it better, and she offers a number of suggestions. First, *know yourself.* Know your personal and professional needs. Are you spending enough time on the things that are important to you professionally and personally? Know your optimal work times. Are you a morning, afternoon, or evening person? Do you use your "best time" appropriately to get things done? Know your sleep and exercise needs. Are you skimping on or overdoing sleeping or exercising? Have your habits robbed you of vitality?

Second, *know your goals.* Are some in conflict with others, causing you to be counterproductive? For example, do you want both to be a teacher and wealthy?

14.14   What do you think the *X* factor is? Do you think you have or can develop it?

14.15   What personal characteristics and professional abilities do you have that will probably serve you well? What related shortcomings would you like to have help with?

14.16   What kind of time-related problems do you think you may have as a teacher?

Try Incidents 5 and 6 in Part Four, Unit 3 of the Practice Teaching Manual

SPOTLIGHT ON RESEARCH 14.1
Time a Major Concern of K–3 Teachers

Project STAR (Word and others, 1990) sought to find out if there is a relationship between the size of a K–3 teacher's class and his or her self-reported problems. To do so the researchers asked teachers to respond to 60 problem items on the *Teacher Problems Checklist* (Cruickshank and Associates, 1980).

Two findings resulted. Surprise!

Teachers with larger classes had problems that were no more frequent nor more bothersome than did teachers with fewer students. For K–3 teachers regardless of class size, problems related to "time" both occurred more frequently and were more bothersome. Three of the sixty items were consistently top ranked problems both in terms of their

frequency of occurrence and their bothersomeness: (35) "Having enough time to teach and to diagnose learning," (20) "Having enough preparation time," and (5) "Having enough free time."

Source: E. Word, et al. (1990). *Student/teacher achievement ratio (STAR): Tennessee's K–12 class size study. Final report and summary.* Nashville, TN: Tennessee State Department of Education.

Additionally, are your goals realistic and attainable? Are you willing to invest heavily in order to accomplish something fairly remote? Do you want to be "teacher of the year" so badly that you will sacrifice nearly everything?

Third, *know your work environment.* What aspects of teaching can you control in order to use time better? Can you share instructional and other responsibilities with a colleague? Is it possible to eliminate interruptions that detract from instruction? Can you use uninterrupted time more effectively?

Fourth, *plan.* Do you plan in order to maximize your productivity and leisure? Do your plans support the things you consider most important?

Fifth, *learn to set priorities and to say no.* Having decided what is important, do you say no when other things try to intrude? Applegate notes, "When you say no to such a request, you are saying yes to yourself" (p. 277).

Sixth, *know your support system.* Are you aware of the kind of human and material help that may be available to you? Are you willing to ask for and give assistance?

Seventh, *concentrate.* Do you reserve time and space for uninterrupted concentration? Do you fool yourself by taking work home but then fiddle with it or merely bring it back undone? Is your work space uncluttered and amenable to work?

Eighth, *act. Don't procrastinate.* Do you indulge yourself or socialize to avoid work? Do you put things off because they are not rewarding? Many teachers say they do not like to evaluate students' work. By that, they mean they don't like to grade papers. That may be one reason some teachers take so long to return tests and homework.

Applegate's last suggestion is, *follow through. Finish.* Do you follow through on things you begin, or do they often end up incomplete and thus represent wasted effort and time?

14.17 How do you feel about time? Are you in control of your time?

14.18 Which of Applegate's suggestions for using time has the most meaning for you?

Preventing and Resolving Classroom Problems

Try Activity 14.1

At this point we have learned that we have a problem when we need or want something (a goal) but cannot attain it because of obstacles or hindrances. Some of the things we desire we truly need because our biological or social-psychological well-being depends upon our having them. Other goals or objectives, although desirable, are not truly necessary. We merely want them. Additionally, some of our needs are professional, or job-related, such as knowing how to teach well. You are taking this course in large measure because you must learn to teach well in order to get and hold a teaching position. Unfortunately, five categories of problems occur as we engage in teaching. These problems prevent us from teaching as well as we would like. Let's look at how we might prevent these job-related problems from occurring.

PREVENTING CLASSROOM PROBLEMS

How can we avoid problems related to affiliation, control, parent relationships, student success, and time? To be relatively immune to these teacher concerns, we must already possess or acquire specific abilities. Some of the abilities we need in order to prevent problems in each of the five categories are shown in Table 14.2.

Perhaps you are blessed with certain of these attributes already. Most likely those attributes you enjoy are related to affiliation and, to some extent, to time management since you have had years of opportunity to acquire both. Gaining as many of the abilities as possible will put you in an enviable position in any classroom. As the saying goes, an ounce of prevention is worth a pound of cure.

RESOLVING CLASSROOM PROBLEMS

It is doubtful that many, if any, of us have or can acquire all the different kinds of abilities noted in Table 14.2. In our studies, we have come across less than a handful of teachers who claim they have no problems. Unless you are very remarkable or possibly oblivious, you can expect to encounter events that interfere with accomplishing the five major goals teachers share. We can say with assurance that teachers do have problems and that *teaching is tough.* What to do? Obviously, the best way to escape from a problem is to solve it. So let's think about problem resolution.

A problem is solved or resolved only when you are able to either give up the goal (need or want) or get closer to it—while, at the same time, you avoid unpleasant side effects. With the

TABLE 14.2 Abilities That a Teacher Needs to Prevent Problems in the Five Areas of Teachers' Concerns	
If You Have Concerns Related to . . .	**Then You Must . . .**
• Affiliation	• Be accepting, caring, and supportive of others • Be cooperative • Be professional in relationships • Know of and use interpersonal skills • Know of and be able to meet reasonable expectations others have for you
• Control	• Appear to students to have reasonable expectations for work and behavior • Recognize and reward work and behavior that meet your expectations • Get students to monitor and control their own work and behavior
• Parent relationships	• Have good affiliation skills (see above) • Be able to establish a system of mutual support • Get parents and caregivers involved in the student's education
• Student success	• Be able to create and maintain learners' interest • Be able to meet a wide range of individual differences • Be thoughtful and skillful in planning and facilitating learning and assessment • Have the qualities and abilities of effective teachers
• Time	• Concentrate on doing what is most important • Know when during the day you and your learners work best • Plan • Share mutual work and responsibilities with colleagues • Avoid procrastinating and finish what you start

help of extensive literature on problem solving, we have developed a problem-solving approach or regimen that should be advantageous to any teacher in difficulty.

The Problem-Solving Approach (PSA) The PSA consists of five stages and ten steps:

Stage 1: Problem identification and ownership. At the outset, it is essential that the problem, goal, and the ownership of both be clear. The first three steps are to

1. State the problem. What is it that is bothersome to you?
2. Identify the goal(s). What specifically do you need or want to have happen that is not happening?
3. Identify the problem's owner. Who has the problem? Who needs or wants the goal? Obviously, if it is your goal that is blocked, it is your problem.

Stage 2: Value clarification. Once the problem has been identified and its ownership established, the fourth step is to

4. Value the goal. Do you really care so much about the goal to continue to pursue it?

Stage 3: Analysis of the problem situation. Assuming that you have found the goal worthy of pursuit, you now enter the problem analysis stage. The three steps in this stage require that you

5. Identify the obstacles preventing you from accomplishing your goal. What specifically seems to stand between your goal and its accomplishment?
6. Project strategies for removing, overcoming, or circumventing the obstacle(s).
7. For each of the potential solutions, list possible negative side effects or consequences. Remember that it is one thing to "get your way" and another to get it in a manner that harms you or someone else. You could "win the battle but lose the war."

Stage 4: Rating the potential solutions. In Steps 6 and 7, you projected strategies for reaching your goal and identified possible harmful side effects.

8. Rate each proposed solution to arrive at the best one or ones. Remember, *a good solution is one that gains or puts you closer to your goal without causing unpleasant side effects.*

Stage 5: Implementing and evaluating the best solution. In the last two steps of our PSA, you are asked to

9. Decide how you would implement the best solution. What precisely would you do?
10. Decide the extent to which the solution has brought you closer to your goal, thus reducing or eliminating your problem.

Even if you do not have all the abilities necessary to prevent the occurrence of classroom problems, you certainly can learn how to be a better problem solver. Table 14.3 provides an outline of the PSA.

Try Activity 14.2

DEVELOPING A PROBLEM-SOLVING ATTITUDE

No one wants problems, but when faced with one, how do you react and what do you think? Do you consider it a source of irritation and mostly gripe about it? Teachers' lounges are notorious for hosting this activity. Teachers reportedly often stand around and complain to one another. Although this may be a good way to let off steam, it seldom accomplishes much else. Or, do you consider a problem to be a challenge? Do you have a good problem-solving attitude? If so, you may even avoid this use of the teachers' lounge in order to use the time to work toward solving the problem and attaining your goal.

TABLE 14.3 The Problem-Solving Approach (PSA)

Stage 1: Identify the problem and its ownership

1. State the problem. What is it that is bothersome?
2. Identify the goal(s). What specifically do you or does someone else need or want?
3. Identify the problem's owner. Who needs or wants the goal?

Stage 2: Determine the value of the goal

4. Value the goal. After thinking about it, decide whether the goal is of
   ____unquestionable value.   ____little value.
   ____great value.   ____no real consequence.
   ____value but negotiable.

Stage 3. Analyze the problem situation

5. Identify the obstacles to goal achievement.
6. Project ways you might achieve the goal by either getting rid of, overcoming, or circumventing obstacles, or thinking of ingenious creative solutions.
7. List some possible consequences each solution might have.

Stage 4: Rate the proposed solutions

8. Rate each potential solution according to the likelihood it would help reach the goal and cause few, if any, unfavorable side effects.

Stage 5: Implement and evaluate the best solution

9. Decide specifically how to put the best solution to work.
10. Decide to what extent the best solution is working.

14.19 How do you react when you need or want something and cannot readily attain it?

The way you react to problems reveals your problem-solving attitude. As we have talked with teachers, we find those with a positive problem-solving attitude or outlook have certain characteristics. They

- Have a "let's solve this" approach.
- Refuse to blame others for their inability to gain a goal.
- Accept their problems and respond, "I have a problem. How do I solve it?"
- Focus on the present or future rather than bemoan the past.
- Replace natural emotional, visceral reactions to a problem with goal-oriented, thoughtful ones; they "get the problem out of their stomach and into their head."
- Refrain from jumping to conclusions or solutions.
- Search for new approaches, deviate from old habits, and avoid the obvious.
- Expect disagreements and accept and respect the views of others.
- Ask what they themselves can do to reach their goals rather than depending upon others to act on their behalf.
- Accept approximations to a goal: "Half a loaf is better than none."
- Work toward bettering already satisfactory situations to ensure they remain so.
- Consciously make use of available time for problem solving.

14.20 What characteristics of a good problem-solving attitude do you already possess? Which do you need to work on?

Attitude isn't everything, but it counts a lot in terms of whether we face problems feeling action-oriented or immobilized. Be positive. You *can* do it. Just do it!

Some Final Thoughts

Teaching indeed is challenging. However, now you know the five areas of challenge. Now you are aware of a reasoned approach to the problems of practice.

Should you want even greater awareness or practice we have included problems at the end of many chapters and Unit 3 of the Practice Teaching Manual is "Room 221: A Simulation: Solving Classroom Problems."

CHAPTER SUMMARY

- A problem exists when we need or want something and cannot readily attain it.
- Problems result from our inability to achieve primary (*biological*) or secondary (*learned*) needs. Biological needs include air, food, water, rest, safety, and security. Learned needs are social-psychological, and some are job-related. Social-psychological needs include social acceptance, achievement, status, and personal growth. Job-related needs include the ability to plan, teach, and assess learning.
- Teacher problems occur mostly in pursuit of social-psychological and job-related needs. Teachers commonly report about sixty problems that fall into five categories: *affiliation, control, parent relationships/home conditions, student success,* and *time.* Studies provide us with theoretical knowledge that helps us understand the problems in each category.
- It is important both to be able to prevent problems and to be able to resolve them. Teachers with certain dispositions and abilities are likely to have fewer problems. Teachers who employ a problem-solving approach are more likely to resolve classroom problems, and teachers with a positive problem-solving attitude also are more likely to meet their needs.

ISSUES AND PROBLEMS FOR DISCUSSION

1. How legitimate are the five goals teachers share?
2. Which of the five goals are most important?
3. Should teachers be expected to resolve most classroom problems on their own?
4. How can teachers become better problem solvers?
5. Where can teachers find specific pedagogical help related to the classroom problems they face?

THEORY INTO ACTION ACTIVITIES

ACTIVITY 14.1: Talk with a Teacher about Classroom Problems   If you are involved in a field experience, talk with a teacher about classroom problems. You might ask

1. What kinds of problems do most teachers in the school seem to have?
2. What might make teaching easier for one teacher and harder for another?
3. What can I do to minimize and resolve the problems I might have?

ACTIVITY 14.2: Record a Teacher's Problem and Analyze It   If you are in a field experience, ask your mentor teacher if you can record a problem and, with the teacher's help, analyze it.

1. With the mentor teacher's assistance, identify a situation where you or the teacher has a goal in mind and there is difficulty achieving it.
2. Write a detailed account of what happened. In other words, what specifically was the problem?
3. With the teacher's assistance, analyze the problem.
   a. What is desirable that isn't happening?
   b. How important is the goal?

c. What obstacles seem to be in the way of goal achievement?

d. How might the goal be reached with the fewest negative side effects?

REFERENCES

Applegate, J. (1980). Time. In D. R. Cruickshank & Associates, *Teaching is tough* (pp. 257–302). Englewood Cliffs, NJ: Prentice Hall.

Bainer, D. L. (1986). Perceived problems of elementary school teachers related to grade level, teaching experience, and student background. Unpublished doctoral dissertation, The Ohio State University, Columbus.

Cruickshank, D. R., & Associates. (1980). *Teaching is tough.* Englewood Cliffs, NJ: Prentice Hall.

DePaul, A. (2000, May). *Survival guide for new teachers.* Washington, DC: U.S. Department of Education. Office of Educational Research and Improvement.

Haynes, N. M., Comer, J. P., & Hamilton-Lee, M. (1989). School climate enhancement through parent involvement. *Journal of School Psychology, 27,* 87–90.

Henderson, A. T. (1987). *The evidence continues to grow: Parent involvement improves student achievement.* Columbia, MD: National Committee for Citizens in Education.

Holland, J. (1997). *Making vocational choices: A theory of careers.* Englewood Cliffs, NJ: Prentice Hall.

Holton, J. (1980). Student success. In D.R. Cruickshank & Associates, *Teaching is tough* (pp. 199–256). Englewood Cliffs, NJ: Prentice Hall.

Katz, Lilian and others (no names given). (1996). Preventing and resolving parent-teacher differences. ERIC Digests. Urbana, IL: ERIC Clearinghouse on Elementary and Early Childhood Education. (ERIC No. ED401048)

Mager, G. (1980). Parent relationships and home and community conditions. In D. R. Cruickshank & Associates, *Teaching is tough* (pp. 153–198). Englewood Cliffs, NJ: Prentice Hall.

Myers, B. (1980). Relationships between classroom problems, personality, and place of work. In D. Cruickshank & Associates, *Teaching is tough* (pp. 303–321). Englewood Cliffs, NJ: Prentice Hall.

Novak, C. (1980). Control. In D. R. Cruickshank & Associates, *Teaching is tough* (pp. 113–151). Englewood Cliffs, NJ: Prentice Hall.

Rich, D. (1988). Bridging the parent gap in education reform. *Educational Horizons, 66,* 9–92.

Super, D. E. (1990). *Work values inventory.* Boston: Houghton Mifflin.

Tracey, K. (1980). Affiliation. In D. R. Cruickshank & Associates, *Teaching is tough* (pp. 75–111). Englewood Cliffs, NJ: Prentice Hall.

Word, E., Johnston, J., Fulton, B., Zaharias, J., Lintz, N., Achilles, C., Folger, J., Breda, C. (1990). *Student/teacher achievement ratio (STAR): Tennessee's K–12 class size study. Final report and final report summary.* Nashville, TN: Tennessee State Department of Education.

Practice Teaching Manual

PART FOUR

Practice doesn't always make perfect, but it certainly helps. This manual provides an opportunity for you to gain much-needed practice in three important areas. In Unit 1, Microteaching: Practicing Critical Teaching Skills, you can try out your ability to demonstrate the personal attributes and professional skills that are vital to teachers, as discussed in Chapters 11 and 12. In Unit 2, Reflective Teaching: Practicing Being a Thoughtful Practitioner, you have a chance to acquire and practice some of the qualities of reflective or thoughtful practitioners; you learned of these in Chapter 10. Finally, in Unit 3, Room 221: A Simulation: Solving Classroom Problems, you can take on the role of a teacher, encounter real-life classroom dramas, and consider how you would respond to each one.

To our knowledge, this is the first book to incorporate practice teaching experiences such as microteaching, Reflective Teaching, and simulation exercises. We are convinced that engaging in these techniques now will better prepare you for life in the classroom.

In Chapters 11 and 12 you learned that effective teachers possess certain distinguishing characteristics and abilities. This unit is designed to help you practice and improve your use of a few of these qualities and skills through microteaching.

Microteaching is scaled-down teaching. By that, we mean that instead of teaching a complete lesson to a complete class, you teach an abbreviated lesson to a small group of your classmates. An additional feature of microteaching is that your lessons are videotaped, thus allowing you to watch your own teaching performance. Using this approach, you can try out important teaching characteristics or abilities to find out how good you may be at them. For example, in Chapter 11 you learned that effective teachers display enthusiasm, and so in this unit you can develop and teach a short lesson in which you try to demonstrate this quality.

Overview of Microteaching

This unit is organized around four microteaching lessons intended to help you apply and refine your professional attributes and abilities. Each lesson is directed at a different aspect of your instructional performance. Microteaching Lesson One focuses on how well you convey the professional attributes of effective teachers. Microteaching Lesson Two helps you develop your ability to establish set. Microteaching Lesson Three helps you hone your questioning skills. And, finally, Microteaching Lesson Four emphasizes refining your ability to present information clearly.

MICROTEACHING FORMAT

Although each of the four activities is directed toward different skills or abilities, each will follow a similar format. You will (1) read about the activity, (2) review information about the specific skills in earlier chapters, (3) plan a short lesson using the guidelines in Chapter 5, (4) teach the lesson to a group of your classmates while being videotaped, (5) view the videotape in order to assess your performance, and (6) when time allows, replan or revise your lesson and reteach it to improve.

Before we begin with Microteaching Lesson One, it may be helpful to discuss guidelines for each phase of the activities.

Reading about the Activity   Each microteaching activity is described in this unit. It provides information about the skills to be developed, the length of the lesson, and the way in which the lesson will be evaluated. Reading this information will help you focus your planning and instructional efforts to gain the most from the activity.

Reviewing Relevant Information   Remember that these microteaching lessons are intended to help you practice and improve your use of the professional attributes and skills cited in Chapters 11 and 12. Before planning your microteaching lesson, you will be advised to review the sections of these chapters that describe in detail the skills you will be practicing. It will be important that you understand the skill or skills to be developed, the reasons they are important, and the specific instructional behaviors you can use. This information should be used to plan your lesson carefully to help you focus on the specific skills and to remind you to work to incorporate them into your lesson.

Planning the Lesson   When planning your microteaching lessons, you are encouraged to follow the principles and guidelines in Chapter 6 for daily lesson planning. For each lesson you should establish objectives and address each of the lesson plan components. Because the microteaching lessons are short (generally ranging from 4 to 12 minutes), your plan will not be terribly long. However, you should be certain to plan thoroughly for each lesson. This will not only improve your lesson performance but also give you an opportunity to practice your planning skills.

A common problem for teachers in microteaching lessons is that they try to teach a great deal more material than the time allows. In fact, at the end of her microteaching lesson a young English teacher whispered to a friend, "Decide what you think you can teach in the time you have, and then try to teach about one-fifth of it!" Although this may be an exaggeration, you should probably attempt to teach only a portion of the concept or topic that first comes to mind. For example, it would be virtually impossible to effectively teach the entire scientific process in a 5-minute lesson. However, you could select one of the four steps in the process, perhaps on developing hypotheses, and teach a thorough and interesting lesson in 5 minutes. Don't try to teach too much.

Teaching the Lesson   On the day your instructor establishes, you will teach your lesson to a group of your peers. Depending upon the arrangement the instructor prefers, this may range from a relatively small group (four or five students) to the entire class. The lesson will be videotaped to allow you to view your performance later. Remember to teach to your learners, not to the camera.

To help you learn to manage instructional time, each microteaching lesson will be timed. You will be required to conduct some form of valuable instruction for at least a minimum amount of time, and you will not be allowed to go beyond the established maximum time.

When it is your turn to teach, you will have a short amount of time to prepare the room and your materials. You can move the chairs or desks and use overhead projectors, handouts, or other materials. Then your instructor will make sure the video camera is operating and notify you to begin your lesson. When you have met the minimum length for the lesson, the instructor will give you a signal. Then, when you have reached the maximum allowed time, your instructor will have you stop your lesson. When you receive the signal for the minimum time limit, you might want to determine how much more of your lesson you can teach effectively in the time remaining. Often it is better to begin at this point to draw the lesson to an end and achieve closure rather than attempt to hurry through the rest of your planned lesson.

Viewing Your Videotaped Lesson   After you have finished teaching your lesson, you will have the opportunity to view the videotape of your performance. Your instructor may choose to have you do this alone or with a small group of your peers, or in some instances both. It is wise to watch your lesson at least twice. The first time, simply allow yourself to form a general impression of the quality of your performance and to jot down some notes. Then watch the lesson again, this time using checklists or observation forms that allow you to focus on your use of specific desirable behaviors. Then in each activity, you will identify particular aspects of your performance that you should improve, and you will develop specific suggestions for how you might do so.

Reteaching the Lesson   If time allows, your instructor may offer you the opportunity to reteach your lesson to improve your performance. If you are offered this opportunity, you are encouraged to take advantage of it even if your first lesson was satisfactory. Practicing the skills and evaluating how well you use them will help you become even more comfortable and confident.

Microteaching Lesson One: Conveying Positive Personal Attributes

RATIONALE AND OVERVIEW

As previously noted, Microteaching Lesson One gives you the chance to see what you look like as a teacher. Although we all have self-perceptions of what we probably look like when we're teaching, often our actions and words differ from what we imagine. Thus, one of the purposes of this first short lesson is simply to allow you the chance to plan and teach a lesson and then watch yourself on videotape. A more specific purpose is to allow you to compare your teaching "persona" with that of effective teachers. You may remember from Chapter 11 that effective teachers have motivating personalities, are professional, and convey optimism and an orientation toward success. Before you plan your first microteaching lesson, it would be wise to review the personal attributes and characteristics discussed in Chapter 11.

Planning the Lesson   Microteaching Lesson One is to be at least 4 and not more than 5 minutes in length. You may teach your lesson on any topic you wish, but you should select a topic or concept that you can genuinely teach to your classmates. In other words, you should not pretend to teach them a concept that most of them are likely to know. As noted earlier, many teachers make the mistake in this first lesson of trying to teach too much in the time allowed. Select a very small concept or subconcept that you can teach thoroughly in 4 to 5 minutes. Develop an objective for your lesson, and follow the format for planning suggested in Chapter 6.

Teaching the Lesson   Your instructor will tell you when to begin your lesson, when you have reached the minimum time limit, and when you must stop teaching. You should try to follow your instructional plan—but be flexible. When students don't seem to understand, don't keep pressing on just to "get through the content."

Viewing Your Videotaped Lesson   After you have finished teaching your lesson, sit down alone or with some classmates and watch your videotaped lesson. It is probably a good idea to watch the tape twice. Watch it once without stopping, and consider your perceptions of the professional personality you conveyed. After you have watched the lesson, stop the tape and make some notes. If you are watching with classmates, ask them to give you their perceptions. Try to avoid focusing on your hair or clothes, and focus instead on how confident,

For each behavior listed below, rate the quality of the teacher's performance.

Behavior	Quality Rating			
	Excellent	Good	Fair	Poor
1. The teacher conveyed enthusiasm.	4	3	2	1
2. The teacher used humor effectively and conveyed warmth.	4	3	2	1
3. The teacher seemed credible and worthy of trust.	4	3	2	1
4. The teacher conveyed high expectations for him/herself and for learners.	4	3	2	1
5. The teacher was encouraging and supportive of learners.	4	3	2	1
6. The teacher was professional and businesslike.	4	3	2	1
7. The teacher adapted the lesson when time or learner misunderstanding required it.	4	3	2	1
8. The teacher appeared knowledgeable of the topic, of learners, and of pedagogy.	4	3	2	1

Specific suggestions for improvement:

personable, optimistic, and professional you seem to be. Then rewind the tape and prepare to view your performance again using the Observation Form for Microteaching Lesson One to guide your observation (Table U1.1).

Reteaching the Lesson   If time permits, your instructor may allow you to teach another 4- to 5-minute lesson to help you become more comfortable teaching in front of the video camera. If you have the opportunity to do so, you will find that future microteaching lessons seem less intimidating, and you can focus your attention on your professional skills rather than on your nervousness.

Microteaching Lesson Two: Establishing Set

RATIONALE AND OVERVIEW

Microteaching Lesson One focused on your professional attributes and characteristics. Lesson Two now emphasizes your use of professional skills. Specifically, Microteaching Lesson Two focuses on your ability to effectively establish set in a short lesson. Remember from Chapter 12 that effective teachers establish three kinds of set to provide a context for the lesson or lessons they are about to teach. In this short lesson, your goal is to identify one of the three types of set you wish to establish and then to do so in a short lesson. Before going on, you should review the suggestions in Chapter 12 regarding establishing set.

Planning the Lesson   Your Microteaching Lesson Two must be at least 8 minutes and not more than 10 minutes in length. As before, you should build your lesson around the guidelines in Chapter 6. However, because

Microteaching Lesson Two focuses only on establishing set, you do not need to teach an entire lesson. Consider the information in Chapter 12, and then determine a topic that you want to introduce as well as which of the three types of set you will use to do so. Since you may select any topic you wish, be creative and attempt to identify a topic that you can introduce in a meaningful, interesting way in the time allowed.

Teaching the Lesson   You will conduct Microteaching Lesson Two in much the same way as your earlier microteaching lesson. You will have some time to organize your materials; then your instructor will notify you to begin, signal you when you have taught at least 8 minutes, and stop you when you reach the 10-minute limit.

Viewing Your Videotaped Lesson   As before, you should view your videotaped lesson at least twice. The first time, make general notes about the way you established set and compare your perceptions with those of your classmates or peer learners. Then, use the Observation Form for Microteaching Lesson Two to evaluate your performance (Table U1.2). Then, based upon your general notes and ratings on the observation instrument, make a few specific suggestions for improving the way you will establish set in future lessons. Be certain to be specific about how and what you will do to improve.

Reteaching the Lesson   The opportunity to reteach your lesson is probably more important in Microteaching Lessons Two, Three, and Four than in Lesson One. These later activities are focused on professional skills that you can improve relatively easily. Thus, the more opportunities you have to practice them, evaluate your performance, and refine your skill, the more effectively you will be able to use them in the future.

TABLE U1.2   Observation Form for Microteaching Lesson Two: Establishing Set

---

Part I

Circle the number of each of the following behaviors the teacher used in establishing set.

1. The teacher reviewed material from previous lesson(s).
2. The teacher asked a curiosity-provoking question at the beginning of the lesson.
3. The teacher provided an overview of the major points of the lesson.
4. The teacher demonstrated the major concepts or ideas of the lesson.
5. The teacher provided and explained a visual schema depicting the relationships of various aspects or concepts of the lesson.
6. The teacher provided a problem to engage students in processing the concepts to be learned.
7. The teacher pointed out the relevance of the lesson to students' lives and interests.
8. The teacher piqued students' interest or curiosity using a unique or novel question, problem, or scenario.
9. The teacher conveyed interest, enthusiasm, and curiosity about the topic.
10. The teacher informed students of the objectives or goals of the lesson and their responsibilities.

Part II

Rate how well you believe the teacher was able to do each of the following, and use the space below to explain your ratings.

Behavior	Quality Rating			
	Excellent	Good	Fair	Poor
1. The teacher captured students' attention.	4	3	2	1
2. The teacher provided a framework for the lesson.	4	3	2	1
3. The teacher related new information to what students had learned previously.	4	3	2	1
4. The teacher determined students' entry-level knowledge.	4	3	2	1

Specific suggestions for improvement:

Microteaching Lesson Three: Using Questions

RATIONALE AND OVERVIEW

In this activity, you will plan for, use, and evaluate your use of questions in a short lesson. Effective teachers conduct highly interactive lessons and use a variety of questions to keep students engaged, promote higher-order thinking, monitor students' understanding, and introduce variety—among other things. Your ability to use questions effectively is an important but complex skill. Before planning your microteaching lesson, review the discussion of questioning skills in Chapter 12.

Planning the Lesson   Lesson Three is to be between 8 and 10 minutes. In this lesson, you should attempt to include all lesson parts. Thus, address all lesson phases suggested in Chapter 6. Because this lesson is to focus your attention on using questions skillfully, you should not plan a lesson that will require you to present a great deal of information to your learners. Instead, select a topic that allows you to help your learners gain understanding by asking them questions. For example, you

might wish to select a controversial issue that you wish your learners to examine critically. You could build your lesson around questions that would help learners see all sides of the issue, understand various points of view, and appreciate the complexity of the issue. In this type of lesson, you would use questions to guide your learners. Remember as you do your planning to include questions you can use during the lesson closure to help learners draw conclusions about the discussion.

Teaching the Lesson   Microteaching Lesson Three will be conducted just as Lesson Two was. You will have a few minutes to organize the room and your materials, and then your instructor will notify you to begin. When you have taught at least 8 minutes, the instructor will give you a signal and then tell you to stop when you reach 10 minutes.

Viewing Your Videotaped Lesson   As you view your videotaped lesson the first time, focus on how well you used a variety of questions to reach your objective. Did you use many questions? Did the questions seem to guide learners, or did they seem random and unconnected? When

TABLE U1.3 Observation Form for Microteaching Lesson Three: Using Questions

For each behavior below, indicate the quality of the teacher's performance.

Behavior	Quality Rating			
	Excellent	Good	Fair	Poor
1. The teacher asked a question early in the lesson to get students involved.	4	3	2	1
2. The teacher phrased questions clearly.	4	3	2	1
3. The teacher avoided repeating questions unless students didn't understand.	4	3	2	1
4. The teacher used adequate wait time after asking questions.	4	3	2	1
5. The teacher frequently asked appropriate questions.	4	3	2	1
6. The teacher called on all students to respond to questions, not just volunteers.	4	3	2	1
7. The teacher included questions at higher cognitive levels.	4	3	2	1
8. The teacher followed up students' responses appropriately.	4	3	2	1
9. The teacher's questions were clearly directed toward helping learners reach the objectives of the lesson.	4	3	2	1
10. Overall, the teacher used questions effectively.	4	3	2	1

Specific suggestions for improvement:

you asked questions, did you use silence and effective nonverbal behavior to encourage learners to participate? Generally, how do you feel about your use of questioning as you watch the tape? After this first viewing, use the Observation Form for Microteaching Lesson Three to guide your second viewing (Table U1.3). Focus on specific things you did well and on specific aspects of your skill you want to improve; then establish a plan for improving your questioning skills.

Reteaching the Lesson   Using questions effectively is a difficult but important professional skill. Beginning teachers generally are uncomfortable using questions and prefer to teach in an expository and less interactive manner. However, we know that interactive teaching is more desirable. Because it is so difficult to become proficient and comfortable using questions, you are encouraged to take advantage of as many opportunities to reteach your lesson as you can. Each time you reteach, work to plan for and implement questions that integrate the suggestions you made for improving your weaknesses.

Microteaching Lesson Four: Providing Clear Instruction

RATIONALE AND OVERVIEW

In Microteaching Lesson One you focused on your professional attributes. In Lesson Two, you taught a lesson in which you attempted to establish set. And in Microteaching Lesson Three you focused on your use of questions. Now, in Microteaching Lesson Four, you will again attempt to teach a lesson that includes set induction, presentation of content, and closure—a complete lesson. However, in this lesson you will focus on your ability to provide instruction that is clear to learners.

Remember from Chapter 12 that instructional clarity may be one of the most important skills in helping students learn. The specific aspects of clarity can be organized into four categories related to various aspects of the lesson. To make your task more manageable, you will focus on only two of the four areas: (1) introducing and emphasizing content and (2) elaborating on important ideas or concepts. Before going on, return to Chapter 12 and review the discussion of instructional clarity.

Planning the Lesson   Microteaching Lesson Four is to be at least 8 minutes and not more than 10 minutes in length. Your primary goal during this exercise is to plan and teach a lesson in which you help learners come to understand clearly the major points of the lesson. The lesson should include all the aspects of a good lesson described in Chapter 6, and you should plan to maximize the reinforcement of major points by repeating them, writing them on the board, reviewing them, and so on. Thus, in planning your lesson, you must identify the two or three major ideas or points you want your learners to understand, organize them logically, develop explanations and examples of each point, determine questions you may use to ensure that students understand, and determine places in the lesson where you will review. You may also wish to highlight particular terms or points by writing them on the board for your learners.

Teaching the Lesson Microteaching Lesson Four will be conducted very much like Lessons Two and Three. Your instructor will give you some time to organize yourself and your materials and then notify you to begin. When you have reached the 8-minute mark in the lesson, the instructor will signal you. At the end of 10 minutes he or she will ask you to stop. Remember that good lessons include a closure to help learners draw conclusions. When you know you are nearing the end of your allotted time, begin to draw the lesson to a close rather than present new content.

Viewing Your Videotaped Lesson Instructional clarity is "in the eye of the beholder." That's why your learners are in the best position to help you determine whether you provided clear instruction. If at all possible, you should watch this videotaped lesson at least three times—two with your learners and once by yourself. During the first viewing, make notes about how clearly you identified and reinforced major points. Did you treat each major point as equally important? Were major points obvious and distinct from their explanations? Can your learners name the major points? Can they explain them? Generally, did the lesson seem to progress logically and clearly?

In the second viewing of the lesson, use the Observation Form for Microteaching Lesson Four with your learners to focus on your use of some of the specific clarity skills (Table U1.4). Then watch your lesson by yourself using your learners' comments and your own impressions to identify the strengths and weaknesses of your instructional clarity. Remember to identify specific aspects of your performance that you believe need to be improved and to suggest specific ways you will attempt to improve them in future lessons.

Reteaching the Lesson Instructional clarity is a complex skill that requires you to consider and implement a variety of behaviors to help learners reach the instructional objectives. As a result, it is not uncommon for teachers to need several videotaped lessons focusing on their instructional clarity skills. If possible, reteach

---

TABLE U1.4 Observation Form for Microteaching Lesson Four: Providing Clear Instruction

Part I

In the space below, enumerate the major points of the teacher's lesson and provide a brief explanation of each.

Part II

Rate the quality of the teacher's performance of each behavior listed below.

Behavior	Quality Rating			
	Excellent	**Good**	**Fair**	**Poor**
1. The teacher organized and presented the lesson in a logical manner.	4	3	2	1
2. The teacher identified important points.	4	3	2	1
3. The teacher wrote important points on the board or a chart.	4	3	2	1
4. The teacher repeated important points for emphasis.	4	3	2	1
5. The teacher included summaries and reviews within the lesson.	4	3	2	1
6. The teacher clearly explained important points.	4	3	2	1
7. The teacher presented examples to reinforce each major point.	4	3	2	1
8. The teacher pointed out similarities and differences between things.	4	3	2	1
9. The teacher explained unfamiliar words when necessary.	4	3	2	1
10. The teacher used pauses to reinforce important points or to allow learners to ask questions.	4	3	2	1

Specific suggestions for improvement:

your lesson as many times as necessary to enable you to feel comfortable with your performance. When time allows and you have improved your original lesson, try teaching a new lesson to see if you are able to provide clear instruction with a different set of major ideas or points.

Additional Practice

Although this unit has included four microteaching lessons to help you improve your instructional behavior, good teachers are constantly working to improve their skills. In addition to doing the four microteaching lessons, you are encouraged to continue to practice honing your professional abilities. The following suggestions will help you do so.

EXPANDED MICROLESSONS

One of the things you can do to continue developing your professional skills is to expand the microteaching format to include longer lessons and more or different professional skills. For example, a reasonable next step would be to teach a slightly longer lesson, perhaps 15 to 20 minutes, in which you attempt to establish set, provide clear instruction, and use questions effectively. Or you might try teaching several short videotaped lessons in which you work to provide desirable feedback and reinforcement, monitor students' understanding, or use different instructional alternatives. You could develop your own observation instruments for these lessons using the guidelines for each skill included in Chapter 12.

VIDEOTAPING YOUR CLASSROOM TEACHING

Another way to continue your professional skill development is through constant assessment of your classroom behavior and interactions. Even if you feel quite competent in using the professional skills in short lessons to your peers, you may not be so proficient when faced with a classroom of thirty school-age students. By using guided observation and analysis, you can use your classroom teaching experiences as advanced forms of microteaching. First, you can videotape the lessons you teach during your field experiences. Merely set up the camera in the back of the room, turn it on before you begin your lesson, and turn it off when you are done. Then, carefully view your natural classroom lesson just as you did your microteaching lessons. This type of formal self-analysis will be extremely useful in helping you understand your classroom behavior.

You should also attempt to record some of your actual teaching even after you have finished student teaching and have your own classroom. Even skilled, experienced teachers are surprised at their classroom behavior when they see themselves on videotape. They find that they no longer are as effective in using their professional skills as they once were. Most schools have easy-to-use video cameras that teachers can borrow. Every so often, set up the camera in the back of the room for a couple of lessons, and then watch yourself critically. You will be surprised at how some of your professional skills have improved with classroom experience while others have grown less effective. One of the authors videotapes at least one lesson each term—and each time is humbled by the experience. Nevertheless, seeing ourselves on videotape helps us all become more aware of both our strengths and weaknesses.

Teaching is an experience filled with excitement, surprises, frustrations, and delight. By now, you are a step closer to entering this adventure.

Think back over your teacher preparation program thus far. Chances are your instructors have used a variety of experiences to ease you into the act of teaching. What were some of those experiences? Perhaps you have read and discussed biographies about the daily lives of teachers, viewed films or television documentaries about teaching and learning, and observed and analyzed teachers in their classrooms. The next step is to engage you in the act of teaching. Reflective Teaching (Cruickshank, 1991) is a program that allows you to practice the complete act of teaching. It requires you to plan a lesson and to implement those plans. Further, it allows you to find out how well your students learned and how satisfied they were with your teaching. Finally, it provides you with an opportunity to reflect on teaching and learning in order to extend your professional wisdom.

As suggested by the title, Reflective Teaching enables you to practice being a thoughtful or reflective practitioner. In Chapter 10 we pointed out that reflective practitioners are more thoughtful and wise about teaching. This is because they routinely and consciously examine their teaching behaviors, practices, and effectiveness. Their minds are a flurry of questions: Why am I doing what I am doing? What are the consequences of my teaching? How could I have done that differently? How can I improve? As a result of this self-analysis, a reflective practitioner is the ultimate student of teaching.

What Is Reflective Teaching?

Reflective Teaching is a contrived teaching experience carried out on campus rather than in an actual classroom setting. The experience provides you with the opportunity to practice the act of teaching, to evaluate its success, and to gain insights into teaching and learning that should enable you to be even more effective in future teaching episodes.

Although you and a group of friends can independently engage in Reflective Teaching, the program is generally part of a university course. The class is divided into groups of four to six persons. For each Reflective Teaching session, one person from each group is designated as the teacher and provided with the Reflective Teaching Lesson (RTL), which all teachers will

use during the next session. Each designated teacher prepares the lesson independently, considering the best way to achieve the stated objective and to maximize learners' achievement and satisfaction. After instructing, the designated teachers evaluate their lessons by measuring students' learning and satisfaction. Finally, they analyze and reflect on teaching and learning in their small groups and then in an instructor-led discussion engaging the entire class.

As you can see, Reflective Teaching engages you in all four phases of teaching: planning, implementing those plans, evaluating, and reflecting on teaching.

Using Reflective Teaching

Each Reflective Teaching Lesson (RTL) contains a teaching objective, the resources you will need to meet that objective, and a description of ways to measure the learning and satisfaction of your learners. While some RTLs deal with professional education (for example, Clear Teacher Task), other RTLs address a variety of topics. The RTLs included in this chapter represent all three instructional domains (cognitive, psychomotor, and affective) and varied levels of learning within those domains. Further, each RTL focuses on a teacher behavior widely used in classroom situations. For example, in the Origami Task, you practice demonstration skills by teaching your students to fold a paper butterfly.

In order to emphasize evaluation and reflection, the lessons are brief—usually 10 to 15 minutes long. Your Reflective Teaching session, then, should take about 50 minutes:

- Teaching: 10–15 minutes.
- Evaluation: 5 minutes.
- Small-group discussion: 15 minutes.
- Whole-class discussion: 15 minutes.

Although a total of forty-one RTLs are available, six are included in this chapter to help you practice becoming a reflective teacher.

Roles during Reflective Teaching

During a Reflective Teaching session, you will have a variety of responsibilities. These will vary depending on whether you are the designated teacher or a learner.

DESIGNATED TEACHER

When you are the designated teacher, your primary responsibility is to teach an RTL to a small group of your peers. Specifically, you will need to prepare a lesson that will enable your learners to achieve the lesson objective and to gain satisfaction from your teaching. More importantly, you will prepare for and lead your group in reflecting on the teaching and learning that occurred during the lesson.

Although all designated teachers present the same lesson during a Reflective Teaching session, you may teach the lesson using any method you choose. Use Learner Satisfaction Forms to access student satisfaction (see pp. 474 and 475). Your goal, after all, is to select a teaching strategy that you think will maximize students' learning and satisfaction. You must also ensure that all the materials you need for instruction are on hand when you teach. While you should provide materials related to teaching, your university instructor will provide copies of the test used to evaluate students' learning, scoring boxes, and the Learner Satisfaction Forms used to assess student satisfaction. If you need audiovisual equipment or other resources, communicate those needs to your instructor in advance. After all, planning ahead is part of the teaching process!

On the day of the Reflective Teaching session, arrive early to set up your teaching stations and "classroom." Will you seat your students in rows or a circle? How will you display your visual aids? Will you stand or remain seated while teaching? These are all instructional decisions you will need to make as the designated teacher.

When the learners arrive and all the teachers are ready to begin, the university instructor will signal you to begin teaching. Your RTL will specify how long your lesson should be. While you are teaching, the instructor may observe all or a part of your lesson. When the allocated instructional time has expired, the instructor must promptly stop all lessons and provide you with posttests, scoring boxes, and Learner Satisfaction Forms.

By reviewing these forms, you receive immediate feedback that may help you frame reflection and discussion questions. Then turn your attention to leading a discussion with your small group of peers. The questions you pose should focus the group's attention on the *processes* of teaching and learning, rather than on the content of the lesson. During this 15-minute reflective session, use discussion questions such as these:

- As the designated teacher, what knowledge, skills, or attitudes did you need to develop in your learners?
- How did you choose the teaching method to accomplish the lesson's objective? What factors influenced your choice of how to teach the lesson

(for example, content of the lesson, availability of materials, the setting, your experience as a learner, your learning style, and time available for instruction)?

- How well did your teaching method work? Did your lesson go as planned?
- According to the posttests and Learner Satisfaction Forms, how well did your learners learn? How satisfied were they?
- How did the learners feel about their experience? What helped or hindered their learning? What suggestions do they have for improving the experience?
- What specifically did each participant discover about teaching and learning?
- What did you learn about teaching and learning and about yourself as a teacher as a result of this experience?

You may notice that some of these questions address the designated teacher; others are aimed at the learners or addressed to all members of the group. By carefully selecting questions that engage all participants in reflection, you can lead a discussion that will provide you with insights about your teaching.

LEARNER

When you are not assigned to act as a designated teacher, your role will be to receive instruction. It is important for you to be cooperative and available and to be on time. Above all, be yourself; role playing is not usually helpful to the designated teacher or to your learning experience.

When you arrive at class for the Reflective Teaching session, go directly to an assigned teaching station. After the lesson, you will need to complete two evaluations. A posttest will assess how much you learned during the lesson, and the Learner Satisfaction Form will measure how satisfied you were with the lesson. It is most helpful to the designated teacher if you provide honest feedback about how you felt and what contributed to or inhibited your learning and satisfaction.

Following the evaluation, the designated teacher will lead a 15-minute discussion. During the discussion, you should help the designated teacher think openly, honestly, and deeply about the teaching-learning experience. This will provide everyone in your small group with a better understanding of effective teaching.

Following the small group discussion, the entire class will engage in a debriefing led by the university instructor to further inquire into the teaching and learning processes. Your willingness and ability to interact during these reflective sessions will indicate your progress toward becoming a serious student of teaching.

Reflective Teaching Lessons

Following are six sample Reflective Teaching Lessons.* The Clear Teacher Task and Magic Squares Task provide learning experiences in the cognitive domain and enable you to practice teaching behaviors such as designating, describing, and demonstrating. The Bowline Task and Origami Task provide experiences in the psychomotor domain and focus on demonstration. Finally,

in the Time Task and the Honesty Task, you attempt to get students to "change their minds" about people, events, and the content learned. These two tasks are in the affective domain.

REFERENCES

Cruickshank, D. R. (1991). *Reflective teaching*. Bloomington, IN: Phi Delta Kappa.

---

*These six sample lessons are reproduced with permission from Phi Delta Kappa.

THE CLEAR TEACHER TASK

Read each section carefully.

Description of Your Reflective Teaching Task

You are one of several participants chosen to teach this brief lesson to a small group of your peers. The exercise is intended to provide an opportunity for you to experience teaching and then to reflect on the shared teaching and learning. Plan to teach the lesson in such a way that you believe both learning and satisfaction will result.

Your lesson will be taught on _____

INTRODUCTION TO THE LESSON

Teachers sometimes designate and describe—that is, they denote things directly and specifically for learners, and they may tell something of the characteristics or qualities of the things denoted. The following are examples of designating and describing behavior:

1. An elementary teacher designates the planets in the solar system and describes the topographic and atmospheric conditions of each.
2. A social studies teacher designates the various routes fugitive slaves took in their flight to freedom using the Underground Railroad and then describes the perils each route seemed to hold.
3. A music teacher designates the notes of a chord and describes how to play them.

Following is an objective that requires you to designate items to a small group of your peers and then to elaborate on or describe them. The task was selected because your success in accomplishing it probably will not depend on your knowledge of some academic subject or on previous experience you may have had.

YOUR OBJECTIVE

Your goal is to get as many of your learners as possible to list the behaviors that distinguish teachers who are clear from those who are not. You will have a maximum of 15 minutes to accomplish that goal.

MATERIALS

1. Resources: *Behaviors of Clear Teachers* (attached).
2. Test (provided by your instructor).
3. Scoring box (provided by your instructor).
4. Learner Satisfaction Forms (provided by your instructor).

SPECIAL CONDITIONS AND LIMITATIONS

None.

ENDING THE LESSON

When the instructor notifies you that time is up or when your learners are ready to take the test, (you may finish in less than 15 minutes), obtain copies of the test, scoring box, and Learner Satisfaction Form.

Give the learners the test. When the learners have finished the test (allow no more than 5 minutes), read them the correct answers so they can score their own tests, or collect and correct the tests yourself if you like. Enter the learners' individual test scores in the scoring box.

Next, pass out the Learner Satisfaction Forms, and encourage learners to give you maximum feedback. Return the tests and collect the Learner Satisfaction Forms.

Begin to work through the questions for small-group discussion with your learners.

The idea for this RTL was contributed by Donald R. Cruickshank, The Ohio State University, Ohio.

Behaviors of Clear Teachers

According to a series of studies conducted at The Ohio State University, teacher behaviors that comprise clear teaching are numerous and identifiable. If it is necessary or desirable for teachers to be clear, then teachers must know these behaviors and use them in practice. Although there seem to be about 30 in all, several behaviors seem to best discriminate between teachers whose pupils say they are clear and teachers whose pupils say they are unclear. A clear teacher

1. Teaches at a pace appropriate to the topic and to learners.
2. Teaches step by step.
3. Explains things simply, that is, gives explanations we understand.
4. Tries to find out if we don't understand.
5. Stays with the topic until we understand.
6. Repeats things we don't understand.
7. Describes work to be done and how to do it.
8. Asks if we know what to do and how to do it.
9. Explains things, then shows an example.

*Name*_____

List as many behaviors as you can that distinguish clear from unclear teachers.

1.

2.

3.

4.

5.

6.

7.

8.

9.

Directions   Give learners 1 point for each of the attributes of clear teachers. A perfect score is 9.

Learner's Name	Performance Score (0–9)
1	
2	
3	
4	
5	
6	
GROUP AVERAGE SCORE Add all scores and divide by number of learners.	

THE MAGIC SQUARES TASK

Read each section carefully.

Description of Your Reflective Teaching Task

You are one of several participants chosen to teach this brief lesson to a small group of your peers. The exercise is intended to provide an opportunity for you to experience teaching and then to reflect on the shared teaching and learning. Plan to teach the lesson in such a way that you believe both learning and satisfaction will result.

Your lesson will be taught on _____

INTRODUCTION TO THE LESSON

Teachers describe—that is, they tell about something. Teachers also demonstrate—that is, they show how to do something. The following are examples of describing and demonstrating behavior.

1. An elementary teacher describes and demonstrates how to perform division.
2. A chemistry teacher describes and demonstrates how to prepare a solution.
3. An auto mechanics teacher describes and demonstrates how to change a tire.
4. A physical education teacher describes and demonstrates how to do a forward roll.

Following is an objective that requires you to describe and demonstrate something to a small group of your peers. The task was selected because your success in accomplishing it probably will not depend on your knowledge of some academic subject or on previous experience you might have had.

YOUR OBJECTIVE

Your goal is to get as many of your learners as possible to be able to correctly construct a magic square where the number of cells on each side equals seven. You will have 15 minutes to accomplish your objective.

MATERIALS

1. Resources: *An Amusement for Centuries* (attached).
2. Test (provided by your instructor).
3. Answer sheet and scoring box (provided by your instructor).
4. Learner Satisfaction Forms (provided by your instructor).

SPECIAL CONDITIONS AND LIMITATIONS

None.

ENDING THE LESSON

Notify the instructor when your learners are ready to take the test. (You may finish early.) Obtain copies of the test, scoring box, and Learner Satisfaction Form.

Give your learners the test, and when they have finished (no more than 5 minutes), read them the correct answers so that they can correct their own tests. Use the criteria given with the scoring box for scoring.

Next, pass out the Learner Satisfaction Forms. While the learners are completing them, collect the tests and record the scores in the scoring box. Return the tests and collect the Learner Satisfaction Forms.

Begin to work through the questions for small-group discussion with your learners.

The idea for this RTL was contributed by Jerry Mager, Syracuse University, New York.

An Amusement for Centuries

A magic square is one in which the columns, rows, and diagonals all add to the same number. For example, in this square they all add to 15:

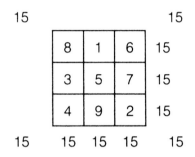

The formation of magic squares has been an amusement for centuries. These boxes were sometimes said to possess magical properties; one particular square was inscribed on a silver plate and carried as a protection against the plague.

You can construct magic squares by trial and error, but the task is very time-consuming. Thanks to a rule De La Loubere discovered in 1693, it is possible to complete odd-numbered squares with ease. There are formulas for even-numbered squares, but they will not concern us at this stage. De La Loubere's rule may be stated as follows:

a. Place the numeral 1 in the middle cell of the top row.

b. Next place the successive numbers moving upwards diagonally to the right. If you have already reached the top row, move to the bottom row as if it were above the top row.

Thus 2 goes to the bottom right-hand corner.

c. If you have reached the right-hand column, move to the left-hand column as if it were to the right of the right-hand column.

	1	
3		
		2

Thus 3 goes to the middle left-hand cell.

d. If, when moving diagonally, you find another number filling a cell, then move to the cell immediately below.

	1	
3		
4		2

Thus 4 goes below the 3.
5 would then go up diagonally to the right from the 4, and 6 up and to the right from 5.

e. When you reach the top right corner cell, place the number directly below.

	1	6
3	5	7
4		2

Thus 7 goes below the 6.

Now you have reached the right column again, so the 8 goes in the top left column as if it were to the right of the right-hand column.

8	1	6
3	5	7
4	9	2

This reaches the top line, so the 9 goes in the middle of the bottom row as if it were above the top row.

The following diagram summarizes the rules:
In general, move diagonally up and to the right.

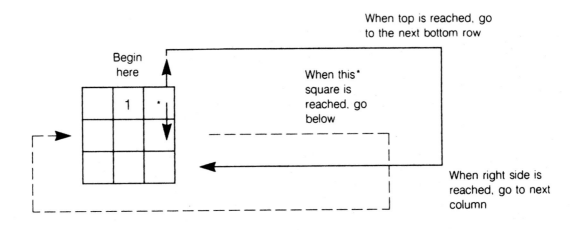

When top is reached, go to the next bottom row

Begin here

When this* square is reached, go below

When right side is reached, go to next column

When any cell already has a number go directly below.
Let us now apply the rule to a five-cell square.

	65					65
	17	24	1	8	15	65
	23	5	7	14	16	65
	4	6	13	20	22	65
	10	12	19	21	3	65
	11	18	25	2	9	65
65	65	65	65	65	65	65

All rows, columns, and diagonals add to 65.

*Name*_____

The square below has an odd number of cells on each side. Use the rules you have learned to construct a magic square.

30	39	48	1	10	19	28
38	47	7	9	18	27	29
46	6	8	17	26	35	37
5	14	16	25	34	36	45
13	15	24	33	42	44	4
21	23	32	41	43	3	12
22	31	40	49	2	11	20

SCORING BOX

Directions   Give each learner 1 point for each number in the correct box. A perfect test score would be 49.

Learner's Name	Performance Score
1	
2	
3	
4	
5	
6	
GROUP AVERAGE SCORE Add learner's scores and divide by number of learners.	

THE BOWLINE TASK

Read each section carefully.

Description of Your Reflective Teaching Task

You are one of several participants chosen to teach this brief lesson to a small group of your peers. The exercise is intended to provide an opportunity for you to experience teaching and then to reflect on the shared teaching and learning. Plan to teach the lesson in such a way that you believe both learning and satisfaction will result.

Your lesson will be taught on _____

INTRODUCTION TO THE LESSON

Teachers demonstrate—that is, they show learners how to do something. The following are examples of demonstrating behavior:

1. A science teacher demonstrates how to light a Bunsen burner.
2. A physical education teacher demonstrates a take-down in wrestling.
3. An English teacher demonstrates how to punctuate independent clauses.
4. A scoutmaster demonstrates how to use a compass and a map to find one's position in the woods.

Following is an objective that requires you to demonstrate something to a small group of your peers. The task was selected because your success in accomplishing it probably will not depend on your knowledge of some academic subject or on previous experience you may have had.

YOUR OBJECTIVE

Your goal is to get as many of your learners as possible to be able to tie a bowline knot. You will have 10 minutes to accomplish your objective.

MATERIALS

1. Resources: *The Bowline Knot* (attached).
2. One 2-foot length of ¼" clothesline for each learner (provided by you).
3. Learner Satisfaction Forms (provided by your instructor).
4. Scoring box (attached).

SPECIAL CONDITIONS AND LIMITATIONS

None.

ENDING THE LESSON

Notify the instructor when you think all your learners can demonstrate how to tie a bowline knot. (You may finish early.) Obtain copies of the Learner Satisfaction Form.

Test each learner one at a time and record the scores in the scoring box. Allow 5 minutes for testing. Only one test is allowed for each learner. Use the criteria given with the scoring box for scoring.

Next, pass out the Learner Satisfaction Forms and collect them when they are completed.

Begin to work through the questions for small-group discussion with your learners.

The idea for this RTL was contributed by John Holton, Appoquinimink School District, Delaware.

THE BOWLINE KNOT

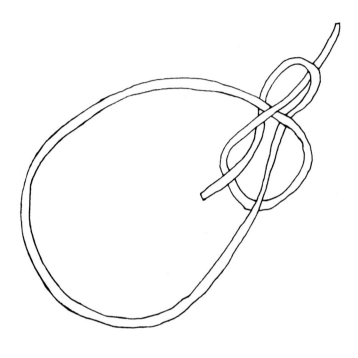

SCORING BOX

Directions   Give each learner 1 point if the knot is tied without error and 0 points if any error is made.

	Learner's Name	Performance Score (0–1)
1		
2		
3		
4		
5		
6		
	TOTAL (add)	

THE ORIGAMI TASK

Read each section carefully.

Description of Your Reflective Teaching Task

You are one of several participants chosen to teach this brief lesson to a small group of your peers. The exercise is intended to provide an opportunity for you to experience teaching and then to reflect on the shared teaching and learning. Plan to teach the lesson in such a way that you believe both learning and satisfaction will result.

Your lesson will be taught on _____

INTRODUCTION TO THE LESSON

Teachers describe—that is, they tell about something. Teachers also demonstrate—that is, they show how to do something. The following are examples of describing and demonstrating behavior:

1. A health education teacher describes and demonstrates how to give mouth-to-mouth resuscitation.
2. A physics teacher describes and demonstrates the phenomenon of centrifugal force.
3. A social studies teacher describes and then engages the class in a demonstration of how a bill becomes a law.
4. A home economics teacher describes and demonstrates the proper way to bathe an infant.

Following is an objective that requires you to describe and demonstrate something to a small group of your peers. The task was selected because your success in accomplishing it probably will not depend on your knowledge of some academic subject or on previous experience you may have had.

YOUR OBJECTIVE

Your goal is to get as many of your learners as possible to make a butterfly from paper using the techniques of origami. You will have 15 minutes to accomplish that goal.

MATERIALS

1. Resources: *The Japanese Art of Paper Folding* (attached).
2. Lightweight square paper for folding—enough for you and your learners (provided by you).
3. Scoring box (provided by your instructor).
4. Learner Satisfaction Form (provided by your instructor).

SPECIAL CONDITIONS AND LIMITATIONS

You may not touch or fold a learner's paper. After teaching the technique, test the learners by having them each fold a butterfly without *any* help from you.

ENDING THE LESSON

Notify the instructor when your learners are ready to take the test. (Your group may finish the task in less than the allotted time.) Obtain copies of the scoring box and Learner Satisfaction Form. Test each learner individually by having them fold a butterfly. Evaluate your learners' butterflies using the criteria given with the scoring box.

Next, pass out the Learner Satisfaction Forms. While the learners are completing them, record the ratings of the butterflies in the scoring box. Collect the Learner Satisfaction Forms.

Begin to work through the questions for small-group discussion with your learners.

The idea for this RTL was contributed by Jerry Mager, Syracuse University, New York.

THE JAPANESE ART OF PAPER FOLDING

The Butterfly

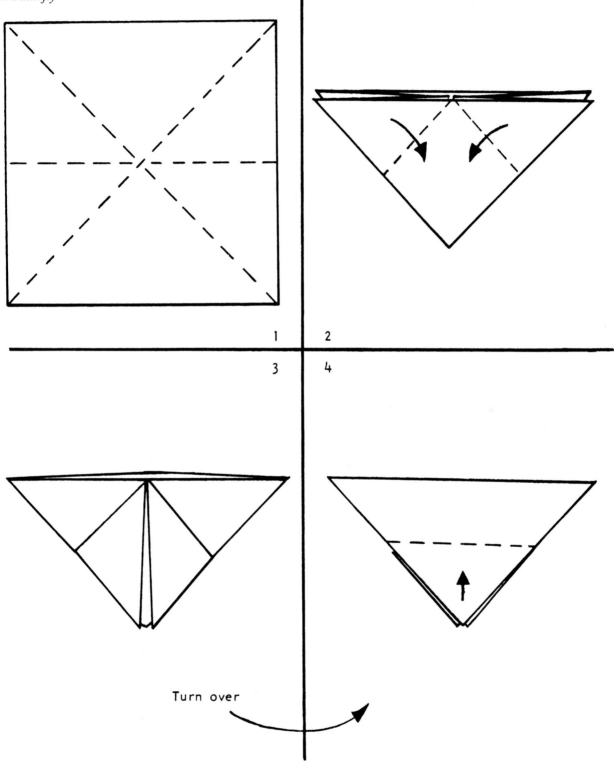

1
2

3
4

Turn over

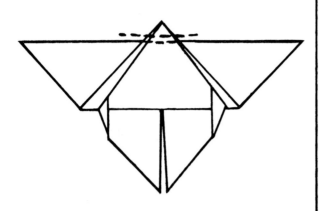

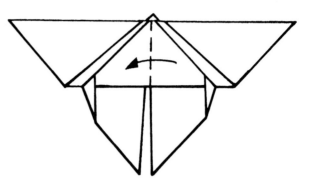

5	6
7	8

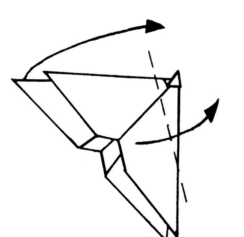

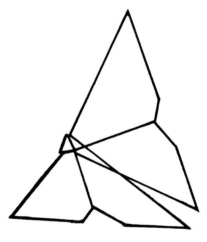

THE BUTTERFLY

Directions   Give each learner's butterfly:

3 points if excellent.

2 points if satisfactory.

1 point if unsatisfactory.

Learner's Name	Rating
1	
2	
3	
4	
5	
6	
AVERAGE SCORE (divide the total rating score by the number of learners)	

Read each section carefully.

Description of Your Reflective Teaching Task

You are one of several participants chosen to teach this brief lesson to a small group of your peers. The exercise is intended to provide an opportunity for you to experience teaching and then to reflect on the shared teaching and learning. Plan to teach the lesson in such a way that you believe both learning and satisfaction will result.

Your lesson will be taught on _____

INTRODUCTION TO THE LESSON

Teachers foster attitude change—that is, they attempt to get students to change their minds about people, events, content to be learned, and so forth. The following are examples of how teachers can foster attitude change:

1. A social studies teacher engages the class in a discussion of how persons of various national origins contribute to present-day American culture.
2. A foreign language teacher shows the class how learning a foreign language will be helpful in their everyday life.
3. A home economics teacher encourages boys to consider assuming responsibility for tasks at home.

Following is an objective that requires you to foster attitude change with a small group of your peers. The task was selected because your success in accomplishing it probably will not depend on your knowledge of some academic subject or on previous experience you may have had.

YOUR OBJECTIVE

Your goal is to get as many of your learners as possible to change their attitude toward the Western notion of time. Specifically, you should try to get your learners to disagree with the following statements, among others:

- Time is money.
- Time waits for no one.
- A stitch in time saves nine.
- Time is of the essence.

You will have 15 minutes to accomplish your goal.

MATERIALS

1. Pretest (attached).
2. Posttest (attached).
3. Scoring box (attached).
4. Learner Satisfaction Forms (provided by your instructor).

SPECIAL CONDITIONS AND LIMITATIONS

Before you begin teaching, obtain a copy of the pretest for each of your learners. Distribute the pretest and have learners respond to it. Collect the pretests before you start.

ENDING THE LESSON

Notify the instructor when your learners are ready to take the posttest. (You may finish early.) Obtain copies of the posttest and the Learner Satisfaction Form.

Give your learners the posttest, and when they are finished (allow no more than 2 minutes), return their pretests and ask them to indicate any changes they may have made from pre- to posttest.

Next, pass out the Learner Satisfaction Forms, and while the learners complete them, collect the pre- and posttests and record the changes in the scoring box. Return the pre- and posttests and collect the Learner Satisfaction Forms.

Begin to work through the questions for small-group discussion with your learners.

The idea for this RTL was contributed by Donald R. Cruickshank, The Ohio State University, Ohio.

*Name*_____

Following are statements about time. Rate each on the basis of whether you agree or disagree with it by placing a checkmark (✓) in one column after each statement. The checkmark must be in a box and not on a line.

STATEMENTS	Strongly Agree	Agree	Disagree	Strongly Disagree
1. Time is money.				
2. Time waits for no one.				
3. A stitch in time saves nine.				
4. Time is of the essence.				

Give yourself:

   0 points for each item checked in the Strongly Agree column.

   1 point for each item checked in the Agree column.

   2 points for each item checked in the Disagree column.

   3 points for each item checked in the Strongly Disagree column.

Total individual pretest score = _____

Name_____

Part A

Following are statements about time. Rate each on the basis of whether you agree or disagree with it by placing a checkmark (✓) in one column after each statement. The checkmark must be in a box and not on a line.

STATEMENTS	Strongly Agree	Agree	Disagree	Strongly Disagree
1. Time is money.				
2. Time waits for no one.				
3. A stitch in time saves nine.				
4. Time is of the essence.				

Part B

Do you think this Reflective Teaching experience has modified your attitude toward time somewhat? (*check one box*)

☐ YES   ☐ NO

Part C

Give yourself:

0 points for each item checked in the Strongly Agree column.
1 point for each item checked in the Agree column.
2 points for each item checked in the Disagree column.
3 points for each item checked in the Strongly Disagree column.

Total individual pretest score = _____

Part D

Total individual posttest score minus total individual pretest score = _____

This represents the amount of individual change. (You may have a negative number.)

When learners have completed the posttest, total the change scores (Part D, posttest) and record below.

Total learners' change	
Number of students with no change (zero change score)	
Number of students with change toward goal (positive change score)	
Number of students with change opposite goal (negative change score)	

From Part B

How many of your learners felt this experience modified their attitudes toward time? _____

Read each section carefully.

Description of Your Reflective Teaching Task

You are one of several participants chosen to teach this brief lesson to a small group of your peers. The exercise is intended to provide an opportunity for you to experience teaching and then to reflect on the shared teaching and learning. Plan to teach the lesson in such a way that you believe both learning and satisfaction will result.

Your lesson will be taught on _____

INTRODUCTION TO THE LESSON

Teachers foster attitude change—that is, they attempt to get students to "change their minds" about people, events, content to be learned, and so forth. The following are examples of how teachers can foster attitude change:

1. Teachers in Montreal, Canada, a community whose history reveals a French-English schism, try to get students to respect and tolerate cultural differences.
2. Teachers try to change low-achieving pupils' attitudes toward learning so that they will have greater school success.
3. An English teacher tries to foster positive attitudes toward reading.

Following is an objective that requires you to foster attitude change with a small group of your peers. The task was selected because your success in accomplishing it probably will not depend on your knowledge of some academic subject or on previous experience you may have had.

YOUR OBJECTIVE

Your goal is to get as many of your learners as possible to change their attitude toward their notion of honesty. Specifically, you should try to get your learners to disagree with the following statements, among others.

- Honesty is the best policy.
- No legacy is so rich as honesty.
- He is wise who is honest.
- Truth will win out.

You will have 15 minutes to accomplish your goal.

MATERIALS

1. Pretest (attached).
2. Posttest (attached).
3. Scoring box (attached).
4. Learner Satisfaction Forms (provided by college instructor).

SPECIAL CONDITIONS AND LIMITATIONS

Before you begin teaching, obtain a copy of the pretest for each of your learners. Distribute the pretest and have learners respond to it. Collect the pretests before you start teaching.

ENDING THE LESSON

Notify the instructor when your learners are ready to take the posttest. (You may finish early.) Obtain copies of the posttest and the Learner Satisfaction Form.

Give your learners the posttest, and when they are finished (allow no more than 2 minutes), return their pretests and ask them to indicate any changes which they may have made from pre- to posttest.

Next, pass out the Learner Satisfaction Forms, and while they are being completed, collect the pre- and posttests and record the changes in the scoring box. Return the pre- and posttests and collect the Learner Satisfaction Forms.

Begin to work through the questions for small-group discussion with your learners.

The idea for this RTL was contributed by Donald R. Cruickshank, The Ohio State University, Ohio.

*Name*_____

Following are statements about honesty. Rate each on the basis of whether you agree or disagree with it by placing a checkmark (✓) in one column after each statement. The checkmark must be in a box and not on a line.

STATEMENTS	Strongly Agree	Agree	Disagree	Strongly Disagree
1. Honesty is the best policy.				
2. No legacy is so rich as honesty.				
3. He is wise who is honest.				
4. Truth will win out.				

Give yourself:

0 points for each item checked in the Strongly Agree column.

1 point for each item checked in the Agree column.

2 points for each item checked in the Disagree column.

3 points for each item checked in the Strongly Disagree column.

Total individual pretest score = _____

*Name*_____

Part A

Following are statements about honesty. Rate each on the basis of whether you agree or disagree with it by placing a checkmark (✓) in one column after each statement. The checkmark must be in a box and not on a line.

STATEMENTS	Strongly Agree	Agree	Disagree	Strongly Disagree
1. Honesty is the best policy.				
2. No legacy is so rich as honesty.				
3. He is wise who is honest.				
4. Truth will win out.				

Part B

Do you think this Reflective Teaching experience has modified your attitude toward honesty somewhat? (*check one box*)

☐ YES   ☐ NO

Part C

Give yourself:

    0 points for each item checked in the Strongly Agree column.
    1 point for each item checked in the Agree column.
    2 points for each item checked in the Disagree column.
    3 points for each item checked in the Strongly Disagree column.

Total individual posttest score = _____

Part D

Total individual posttest score minus total individual pretest score = _____

This represents the amount of individual change. (You may have a negative number.)

When learners have completed the posttest, total the change scores (Part D, posttest) and record below.

Total learners' change	
Number of students with no change (zero change score)	
Number of students with change toward goal (positive change score)	
Number of students with change opposite goal (negative change score)	

From Part B

How many of your learners felt this experience modified their attitudes toward time?   _____

LEARNER SATISFACTION FORM

Name of Designated Teacher _____

1. During the lesson, how satisfied were you as a learner? In arriving at a rating, consider the teaching methods used and how well they met your needs.

4	3	2	1
Very Satisfied	Mostly Satisfied	Somewhat Dissatisfied	Very Dissatisfied

2. What did your teacher do that contributed to your satisfaction?

3. What could your teacher have done to increase your satisfaction?

LEARNER SATISFACTION FORM

Name of Designated Teacher _____

1. During the lesson, how satisfied were you as a learner? In arriving at a rating, consider the teaching methods used and how well they met your needs.

4	3	2	1
Very Satisfied	Mostly Satisfied	Somewhat Dissatisfied	Very Dissatisfied

2. What did your teacher do that contributed to your satisfaction?

3. What could your teacher have done to increase your satisfaction?

One thing is certain, teaching is never dull! That is because each day you face different intellectually and emotionally challenging situations. We thought you might both enjoy and benefit from encountering a few of the more bothersome and frequently occurring situations that teachers report. That's why we have created Room 221: A Simulation: Solving Classroom Problems. This unit contains fourteen incidents that happen to you as a new teacher at Lincoln Park Middle School. Similar incidents occur in elementary and high schools.

The simulation begins as you visit your new school and chat with Pat Taylor, the principal. It continues as you work through all or a selection of the incidents that follow. These incidents, by the way, relate directly to various chapters in this book that deal with student diversity, learning, teaching, assessment, and so forth. They also represent the five major areas of teachers' concerns you learned about in Chapter 14: affiliation, control, parent relationships, student success, and time. The simulation provides a good opportunity to see how well you can apply what you have learned. Have fun—and good luck!

Meet the Principal

My name is Pat Taylor, and I'm principal of Lincoln Park Middle School. I'm so glad you could come in a few days before school starts. This way, you'll have a chance to become familiar with the school and the cumulative record information available for your students.

Let me tell you a few things about our community and school. As you know, we are a suburb of Capital City. Really, the city just grew to us. At one time, we were separated by farms and orchards. We're not what you would call an affluent suburb. Our income level is about average for the state, but it is a little bit lower than most nearby communities. Most of our families have blue-collar jobs, although a number own small businesses, and a few fathers and mothers are professionals.

Seventy percent of our students live with both biological parents, 15 percent live with their mothers, and 4 percent with their fathers. The others live with one parent and a stepparent, with other relatives, or in foster homes. A very few live in a residential care facility for court-referred children. Most people think of this as a community of hard-working people who have high as-

pirations for their children. They tend to expect more than we are able to deliver. But that's all right. It's good to be challenged!

The 750 students in our grade-five-through-eight school score near average on most of the national standardized achievement tests, although they do better in reading than in mathematics. Average daily attendance is high, between 96 and 98 percent, so we must be doing something right. We think it's instruction. Our goal is to make classes so exciting that kids want to be here. Of course, attendance and tardiness are things we work at constantly. We also work at making kids proud of the school, keeping it neat and clean. I would describe Lincoln Park as orderly without being rigid, quiet without being permissive, and focused on the business of learning. In my mind we are the best school not only in the district but in the county. The kids know what is expected of them. And they do the best they can. They do their work, and they treat the school right. Generally, they're cooperative, happy, and proud they go to Lincoln Park.

You probably would like to know a little about your colleagues. There are thirty-nine teachers in Lincoln Park. Thirty are female, nine are male; four are black, or, if you prefer, African American, one is Hispanic, and another, Korean. The majority have been prepared as elementary teachers. Not many middle school teachers are prepared as such, but in our experience, these teachers do really well. In addition, we have an assistant principal, Dale Seymour; a guidance counselor, Merriam Roget; four teachers for exceptional children; a librarian; a home-school coordinator; and a nurse.

Our program reflects newer ideas in middle-level education, including such concepts as team teaching, detracking, and cooperative work. By team teaching, we mean that some teachers from different subject areas plan and sometimes teach together. For example, last year the social studies, English, music, and art teachers planned and jointly taught a unit on Colonial America. By detracking, we are moving toward more cooperative working teams, each consisting of diverse students. We also believe in invitational learning. Perhaps you've read about it in one of your textbooks. I don't want you to think that these are the answers to all education problems, but right now our faculty believes we are moving in the right direction.

One thing the teachers don't particularly like is that Lincoln Park is separated into four separate "houses."

Because of the separation, some of them feel isolated from others they know and like to be with. We have several different "house" teaching arrangements. In the Orange House, which you are in, the classes all are self-contained; that is, one teacher is pretty much in charge of a group of students for the whole day. Most of our new teachers like to start this way and then move into something more challenging. Other "houses" feature team teaching, multiage grading, and block scheduling. That's when, instead of having about eight 50-minute class periods, you have three 2-hour classes every day.

Our parents are pretty satisfied with Lincoln Park School. We did a survey last year, and 87 percent said that we are meeting the children's educational needs well or extremely well. Ninety percent agree that the teachers expect the students to do their best and behave well. We understand that students are vulnerable and sensitive and that they should not be embarrassed. They should be respected.

We collect food and clothing for the needy and occasionally raise money for a worthy community cause. The teachers want students to have a strong sense of community involvement and charity toward others.

The Lincoln Park parents like the idea of having a middle school that is a mixture of both elementary and secondary grades. They see it as starting secondary school earlier but in a warm, protected environment. The students here like to think of themselves as young adults, too old for elementary school.

That's enough for now. I'll let you get on with the things you came in here to do. Dale and I will be around. Give us a nod if you need help.[*]

Fourteen Classroom Incidents

INCIDENT 1: SLEEPLESS IN ROOM 221

For the past hour, your students have been working in small groups on a project they seem to enjoy. However, as you monitor the activity, you notice that Ashley Smith has been somewhat lackadaisical. She has said nothing, and her head is down, resting on her arms. You make a mental note to talk with her later.

At the end of the group activity, you ask the students to return to their seats. As they move about the room, you hear loud laughter in one area. Sharon is repeating, "Wake up, Ashley—Ashley, wake up! You're in my seat." As you approach, Ashley has a dazed look and she rubs her eyes.

---

*The description of Lincoln Park School and community was partly suggested by J. Lipsitz. (1984). *Successful schools for young adolescents* (pp. 27–58). New Brunswick, NJ, and London: Transaction Books.

Later you talk to Ashley about sleeping in class. She tells you that both her parents work a second shift and that she takes care of her younger siblings until they go to bed. Then she watches late-night television because she doesn't like to go to sleep until her parents are home.

You know Ashley can ill afford to miss any class work. She has barely passing grades and has been absent and tardy a number of times. How can you help?

Cumulative Record Information Ashley Smith lives with her mother, stepfather, and four younger school-age siblings in a blended family. Her parents work the afternoon-evening shift in a manufacturing plant. Except for weekends, the children are on their own, with Ashley as their primary supervisor. All the children have absence and tardiness problems. Ashley seems to have average academic ability, although her school achievement has been marginal. She has a slight hearing loss in both ears and has difficulty maintaining personal hygiene. Generally, her peers have little to do with her. She does not seem to have any close friends.

INCIDENT 2: ANGELO FIGHTS BACK

Angelo is a beautiful boy with dark, wavy hair, large brown eyes, and an olive complexion. The girls in class and throughout the school are very attracted to him—probably for his good looks, charm, and talent. He is also an accomplished guitarist, singer, and dancer. Angelo's appeal to the girls annoys the boys. To worsen matters, Angelo is disinterested in sports and other "masculine" activities.

This year Angelo has been the subject of considerable taunting. Occasionally, he has been pushed around. Today, when school began, a group of girls related that Angelo was beaten up on the way to school. Within 15 minutes, Angelo and his older brother enter the classroom, and the older brother shouts at one of the students, "Leave Angelo alone or else." What should you do?

Cumulative Record Information Angelo Carpanian lives with both parents and an older brother and sister. His ethnic background is Gypsy, and his family is part of an extended family living on the edge of the school community. The Carpanians own a used-car business and also operate games and rides at county fairs. They speak their own language and, in public, speak that language with their children. The Carpanians appear happy and reasonably prosperous. Angelo and his siblings have not had an easy time in school. They normally are not permitted to mix freely with the other children, and after school they help their parents.

The girls like Angelo. He is a very handsome, thoughtful boy. He also is quite fun-loving when in their company. He plays guitar and dances.

Angelo's achievement throughout the grades has been very marginal. Mostly, he seems to have been eased upward through the grades. All his teachers agree that he is fun-loving but find him trying as a learner.

INCIDENT 3: SCHOOL IS BORING, BORING!

You really like Tom. He is good natured, laid back, has lots of friends, and never causes a problem. A perfect child? No! Tom doesn't like to learn. You find this strange for a boy who is on time and in school every day.

In school, he putters along, almost keeping up with the task at hand, but when it comes to homework or studying for exams, Tom is almost never ready. You have met with his mother on many occasions. She wants desperately to work with you and has taken all your suggestions including monitoring his efforts and withholding television until work is completed. This proves difficult because she isn't always certain what Tom must actually do; he is unclear, and she is not able to sit with Tom by the hour.

After months of this, you finally get Tom to do more than shrug his shoulders and smile when you ask what's wrong. Today he told you, "School is just plain boring." How do you react?

Cumulative Record Information   Thomas Lindgren lives with his mother, stepfather, and two younger sisters from his mother's second marriage. Tom's natural father left when he was an infant, and Tom has not seen or heard from him. Mrs. Lindgren has tried to find Tom's father in order to obtain child support. Tom has above-average ability according to standardized test results. However, his school achievement is marginal, with grades fluctuating in all subjects. Teachers describe him as an outwardly happy, friendly youngster who needs constant prodding to stay on task both with schoolwork and other responsibilities.

INCIDENT 4: MARNA, MARNA!

You had always dreaded having a student in the class who is regularly disruptive. Unfortunately, she has arrived. Marna is an attention grabber. You name it, she does it: won't stay put, calls out in class, talks constantly with those nearby, pokes others with her pen, takes things without permission, drops books, hums, won't take turns, and so on. You thought it was cruel when other teachers told you they wished one of their students—Marna—would move out of the district! Now you are embarrassed to realize that you are beginning to feel this way, too. The students are alternately annoyed and pleased by Marna: When her actions disrupt *them,* they get angry. When her antics disrupt *you,* they laugh. You think you are becoming paranoid, but you know that your relationship with the class is generally very good. What do you do?

Cumulative Record Information   Marna Wright lives with her parents. She is an attractive girl with above-average academic ability. Throughout school, she has been cited as exhibiting immature social behavior; as early as grade 1, she has been referred to the school psychologist. The psychological reports are more descriptive than useful. They describe Marna as an only child born after her parents had been married 17 years. Both parents are very strict, and Marna presents no problem at home. When the school has contacted Marna's parents, they are chagrined to learn of her school behavior and vow to talk to her. At the same time, they have made clear that this seems to be a school problem and, to that extent, is beyond their control. On one occasion, they raised questions about the competency of Marna's teacher. Pat Taylor, your principal, has had lots of talks with Marna and feels she will eventually grow up.

INCIDENT 5: TEACHERS ARE SUPPOSED TO TEACH!

The class is working quietly on independent study assignments, and you are moving among the students monitoring their efforts, when one of Mrs. Armstrong's students enters the room announcing "Mrs. Armstrong ran out of chalk. Can she borrow some?" This interruption is the second already today and was sufficient to get the students off-task and buzzing.

A few minutes later another student appears at the door and hands you a note from Pat Taylor, the principal. "Please have all students take a recess between 10:00 and 10:30. We have a plumbing problem, and the water will be shut off after 10:30. Thanks."

At noon, you peruse the office bulletin board announcements and are reminded that student health screening will begin tomorrow, student progress cards are to have written comments this marking period, quarterly attendance forms are due, and your assignment for helping with the School Fair is to run the popcorn booth with one of the parents.

You stand there in almost a catatonic state thinking, when will I have time to plan and teach?

INCIDENT 6: HOW CAN I DO THAT?

You have been led to believe that to be a good teacher you must do three things: plan, teach, and assess students' learning. At least that's what you were taught in professional education courses. However, each of these activities takes lots of time. Where does it come from?

Of course, you must teach, and to be very good at it, you must plan. So, understandably, you devote almost all of your time and energy to these tasks. At the same time, you are feeling unprofessional because your assessment activities seem limited to making up and scoring tests. What you don't do very much is "informal assessment" such as systematic observation, use of checklists and rating scales, and collecting and evaluating the everyday work students do. You ask yourself—where will I get the time to do that?

INCIDENT 7: AM I GOOD ENOUGH?

You love teaching. Even before you decided to become a teacher, you thought a lot about the future and about the different ways you could help other people. Teaching seemed a pretty clear choice since you always liked school and enjoyed learning. However, it is becoming increasingly clear to you that some students do not share your attraction to school and learning. Some, like Tom Lindgren, find it boring and say so publicly, which doesn't help. Others are more passive and just doodle their time away, doing only what is required and giving one another sour looks—if they do anything at all. You are reminded of some popular movies and books about teachers who were great. How could you be more like them? Maybe that would make students enjoy learning more.

INCIDENT 8: TEACHING EVERY ONE

If all the students in the class were alike, it would be so much easier to teach. Unfortunately (or fortunately), they are not. The students of most concern to you are those who can't keep up. Andre Harrison is one. Today he sheepishly hands you the following note.

> Dear Teacher:
>
> Please excuse Andre from completing his homework. He worked very hard from the time he had supper until he went to bed. He even missed his favorite TV show. As you know, Andre is not a good reader, but he does try very hard. I know the homework wasn't too difficult, so in no way are we blaming you. We would appreciate any kind of help you can give our son.
>
> Yours truly,
>
> *Mrs. Alberta Harrison*

How can you individualize instruction in order to help more students learn?

INCIDENT 9: CRIME AND PUNISHMENT

One thing you hate to do is to punish students. To you, it is an admission that you haven't done something right—that you may have failed. Nevertheless, sometimes punishment is required. Pat Taylor, the principal of Lincoln Park Middle School, feels it is time to review the school's policy on discipline and punishment. All teachers have been asked to begin by writing a one-page response to the following questions:

1. Under what circumstances are discipline and punishment warranted?
2. What kinds of discipline and punishment should be allowed in our school?

What will you write?

INCIDENT 10: ATTENTION!

You are convinced that movies, MTV, computer software, and the like so dazzle students that it is difficult for teachers to compete for their attention. Certainly, from a student's point of view, school must look pretty bland and colorless—the same thing in the same way day after day. You have decided to make a list of ways to better capture and hold students' interest. What will you put on your list?

INCIDENT 11: PARENTS TO THE RESCUE

The older, more experienced teachers at Lincoln Park Middle School talk constantly of the "good old days." Frankly, you get a little tired of it, but there is probably truth in some of what they say. In fact, the entire staff is bothered by the seeming lack of parental support for school. On many occasions you have heard stories of parents who blame teachers for students' misbehavior, low grades, dislike of school, and so forth. When a child gets in trouble, more than likely the parents will find fault with the school and the teacher. Some teachers excuse this, pointing out that more parents are working longer hours, experiencing rough economic conditions, and having difficulty maintaining satisfying marriages. Accordingly, it is very difficult to get parents to help out when needed.

As a novice teacher, you want to withhold judgment. However, you do want to gain parent support. What can you do to get it?

INCIDENT 12: GETTING TO THE BOTTOM OF THINGS

Assessing students is anything but fun. It takes lots of time to do it well: hundreds of hours evaluating papers and tests, and then more time to figure out the grades for report cards. This marking period was no different, so you felt pretty good when you entered the last mark on the last report card yesterday before leaving school. Looking over your shoulder on the way out the door, you regarded the stack of cards on your desk as a major accomplishment.

Today, the day the report cards were to be distributed, they were nowhere to be found. Later, Don Parsons, a school custodian, entered the room with the cards in his rubber-gloved hand. "I found these in the urinal," he noted in a quiet voice. Several nearby students tittered. Looking back on the incident, you ask yourself—how could anyone do such a thing? What should you do?

INCIDENT 13: CATCH-22

Several of your students work pretty hard, but to little avail. They just don't get it. Although they listen and attend to each assignment, their work is often minimal or incorrect. Your heart goes out to these kids, and you are caught in a catch-22. If you give them passing grades, you are deceiving both them and yourself. If you fail them, they will likely give up. You say to yourself, there must be a solution. You decide to send home midterm failure notices. The next morning one child's mother confronts you in the hall and demands, "Are you prejudiced against my son?" How would you react?

INCIDENT 14: SO MUCH FOR PROFESSIONALISM

You believe that teachers are professionals. It has been disheartening for you to hear and see teachers criticizing one another, making personal remarks about their students, gossiping, complaining about the principal, joking about parents, and taking sick days when they aren't sick. You vow never to go into the faculty lounge again. But you can't do that. What can you do?

ONE MORE INCIDENT: WHAT TO DO?

Recall a teacher dilemma you have witnessed. Write it down and share it with your peers.

Praxis III is a system for assessing the skills of beginning teachers. At this time, it is used in 38 states. For those interested in preparing for the Praxis III assessment, here is a list of Praxis III criteria and reference to where related material can be found in *The Act of Teaching*.

Criterion A1: Becoming familiar with relevant aspects of students' background knowledge and experience.

- See Chapter 2: The Changing Nature of Childhood and Youth.
- See Chapter 3: Student Diversity.
- See Chapter 5: Getting to Know Your Students and Motivating Them to Learn.

Criterion A2: Articulating clear learning goals for the lesson that are appropriate to students

- See Chapter 4: Cognitive Approaches to Teaching and Learning; The Behavioral School of Thought.
- See Chapter 6: Writing Specific Objectives; When Are Objectives Good; The Nature of Learners; Preparing Lesson Plans.

Criterion A3: Understanding the connections between the content that was learned previously, the current content, and the content to be learned

- See Chapter 4: Beliefs about Long-Term Memory; Reception Learning; and Behavioral School of Thought.
- See Chapter 8: Constructivism.
- See Chapter 12: Establishing Set.

Criterion A4: Creating or selecting teaching methods, activities, materials appropriate to students and aligned with lesson goals

- See Chapter 4: Cognitive Approaches to Teaching and Learning; Humanistic Approaches to Teaching; Behavioral Approaches to Teaching.
- See Chapter 7: Presentation, Discussion, Independent Study, and Individualized Instruction.
- See Chapter 8: Cooperative Learning, Discovery Learning, Constructivism, and Direct Instruction.

Criterion A5: Creating or selecting evaluation strategies appropriate for students and aligned with lesson goals

- See Chapter 6: Parts of a Lesson Plan: Assessment.
- See Chapter 9: Teacher-made Assessments.

Criterion B1: Creating a climate that promotes fairness

- See Chapter 1: How Gender Influences Our Teaching; How Student Differences Affect Our Teaching.
- See Chapter 3: Student Diversity.
- See Chapter 11: Encouraging and Supportive.

Criterion B2: Establishing and maintaining rapport with students

- See Chapter 2: The Changing Nature of Childhood and Youth.
- See Chapter 11: Warmth and Humor; Credibility; Encouraging and Supportive.
- See Chapter 13: Planning the Psychological Environment.
- See Chapter 14: Affiliation.

Criterion B3: Communicating challenging learning expectations to students

- See Chapter 11: High Expectations for Success.

Criterion B4: Establishing and maintaining consistent standards of classroom behavior

- See Chapter 13: Establishing Classroom Rules and Routines; Monitoring Students' Behavior; Holding Students Accountable; Reacting to Misbehavior.
- See Chapter 14: Control.

Criterion B5: Making the physical environment safe and conducive to learning

- See Chapter 13: Establishing the Physical and Psychological Environment.

Criterion C1: Making learning goals and instructional procedures clear to students

- See Chapter 7: Good Presentations; Good Discussions; Good Independent Study; Good Individualized Education Programs.
- See Chapter 8: Good Cooperative Learning; Good Discovery Learning; Good Direct Instruction.
- See Chapter 12: Providing Clear Instruction.

Criterion C2: Making content comprehensible to students

- See suggestions for Criteria A1, A3, and A4 above.
- See Chapter 12: Providing Clear Instructions.

Criterion C3: Encouraging students to extend their thinking

- See Chapter 6: Kinds and Classifications of Learning Outcomes.
- See Chapter 8: Discovery Learning.
- See Chapter 12: Using Questions.

Criterion C4: Monitoring students' understanding, providing learners with feedback, and adjusting learning activities

- See Chapter 11: Adaptable/Flexible.
- See Chapter 12: Ensuring Student Understanding; Monitoring Students' Progress. Providing Feedback and Reinforcement.

Criterion C5: Using instructional time effectively

- See Chapter 12: Using Instructional Time Efficiently.
- See Chapter 13: Establishing Classroom Rules and Routines.
- See Chapter 14: Time.

Criterion D1: Reflecting on the extent to which learning goals are met

- See Chapter 6: Parts of a Lesson Plan: Assessment, Evaluating Lesson Plans.
- See Chapter 10: Characteristics of Reflective Practitioners, Benefits of Reflecting on Teaching.

Criterion D2: Demonstrating a sense of efficacy

- See Chapter 11: Orientation Toward Success.

Criterion D3: Building professional relationships and so forth

- See Chapter 6: Cooperative or Team Planning.
- See Chapter 14: Affiliation.

Criterion D4: Communicating with parents-guardians

- See Chapter 2: The Changing Family.
- See Chapter 14: Parent Relationships and Home Conditions.

Glossary

The following terms include selected boldfaced words and concepts defined in the text as well as some words and concepts used but not defined in the text.

academic games Instructional alternative where learners compete with each other, one-to-one or team-to-team, to determine which individual or group is superior at a given academic task (including spelldowns, anagrams, and so forth).

academic instruction time Actual amount of time the teacher is conducting instruction.

academic learning time (ALT) Amount of academic instruction time during which students are actively and successfully engaged in learning.

accountability The idea that teachers should be held responsible for what and how much students learn.

achievement tests Tests that measure what a student knows in a subject area (for example, mathematics) compared to what other, like students know.

action research Process of conducting school-based research to improve teaching and learning.

action zone The triangular area, defined by imaginary lines across the front and down the middle of the classroom, where most student-teacher interaction occurs.

active listening When a teacher permits or encourages a learner to provide information or express some feeling and then paraphrases what the learner has said.

active teaching Instructional method containing five instructional phases: the opening, development, independent work, homework, and review.

activity reinforcers Special privileges given to students when they behave appropriately in order to increase the likelihood that they will repeat the behavior.

activity routines Classroom routines established to minimize problems related to such things as the location of materials and acceptable behaviors.

advance organizer A tool that prepares learners for new information to follow (for example, a video clip, an anecdote, or an illustration).

affective domain The area of learning that deals with students' feelings, interests, attitudes, appreciation; focuses on the attitudinal, emotional, and valuing goals for learners. Five subdivisions of this domain (arranged hierarchically from simple to complex) are receiving or attending, responding, valuing, organization, and characterization.

affiliation need Teacher's need to get along with students, parents, other teachers.

allocated time Amount of mandated time intended or scheduled for academic activities.

alternative responses Part of a series of multiple-choice questions that offer possible solutions to the stem.

American Agenda Report of the Forty-first President of the United States regarding poverty and the underclass.

analysis The process of breaking down material into component parts so it can be understood.

anecdotal comments Brief, teacher-written descriptions about students, usually found in school records.

anticipatory set An introductory activity that will capture students' attention, help them see the purpose and value of what they are to learn, and relate what they are to learn to what students already know.

applied behavioral analysis (ABA) Based on principles of operant conditioning. Teachers reward or reinforce learners when they do the right thing.

aptitude tests Tests that measure a student's general potential to learn. They provide information about students' comparative ability to deal with abstractions and to solve problems. Some aptitude tests measure the potential to learn in specific fields

such as music, while others predict how well one would do generally in college.

artifact Any object produced by the student or teacher related to the schooling experience.

assessment Process of collecting, synthesizing, and interpreting information to aid in decision making.

at-risk students Students most likely to experience school failure. Profiles of such students indicate that recurring at-risk factors include living with a single parent, being at home alone for long periods of time, having parent(s) with low levels of education or income, having low English language facility, and/or having a sibling who is a school dropout.

attention deficit disorder (ADD) Disorder that prevents certain children from maintaining their attention on learning tasks.

baseline Information about how often a specified student presently performs a desired behavior. Used in applied behavioral analysis.

basic practice Teaching method employing much supervised student practice and teacher provision of corrective feedback.

behavior disorders Conduct disorder, anxiety-withdrawal disorder, and immaturity.

behavior modification Systematic attempt to change behavior by using rewards or adversive stimuli that are linked to those behaviors.

behavioral learning theory School of thought that attempts to explain why we behave as we do. Behaviorists are interested in finding out how external or environmental stimuli cause behavior and how behavior can be changed by modifying what happens in a learner's environment.

behaviorists Advocates of behavioral learning theory.

block plans Daily plans that clearly show the scope and sequence of a learning unit as well as general objectives, learning activities, evaluation, and resources.

brainstorming Instructional alternative where learners are asked to withhold judgment or criticism while they produce a very large number of ideas for something such as how to resolve a problem.

case study Written document that pieces together all kinds of information to obtain a more complete and articulated picture of a student.

centers of interest Classroom displays used to interest learners in themes or topics.

Chapter 1 compensatory education Federally funded program that, among other things, provides monies to improve student performance in reading and math.

child abuse A problem affecting many children at some time during childhood. Classifications include emotional/verbal, sexual, or physical abuse and neglect.

Children's Defense Fund Organization that advocates on behalf of America's children. Engages in research, public education, monitoring of federal agencies, litigation, child health, adolescent pregnancy prevention, child mental health, and so forth.

clarity See instructional clarity.

classical conditioning Learning that occurs when we already have an established connection (contiguity) between a stimulus and a response, and then a new stimulus is paired with the original stimulus long enough to evoke the same response when the original stimulus is absent.

classroom management Using the provisions and procedures needed to create and maintain an environment in which teaching and learning can occur.

climate Sociopsychological dimensions of the classroom including the emotional tone and the comfort level students feel with the teacher, with learning tasks, and with one another as a social group.

cognitive development Piaget suggests cognitive/intellectual development evolves through four stages: sensorimotor, preoperational, concrete operational, and formal operational.

Most developmental theorists agree that all children proceed through all stages but at different rates.

cognitive domain Area of educational objectives that contains objectives related to intellectual tasks such as recalling, comprehending, applying, analyzing, synthesizing, and evaluating information.

cognitive learning theory School of thought that attempts to explain what goes on in the brain when we are learning; focuses on information processing (how we take in, store, and retrieve information) and meaningful learning (how to organize, structure, and teach information so that it might be best used).

cognitive style The consistent ways an individual responds to a wide range of perceptual learning tasks.

cognitivists Advocates of the cognitive learning theory.

colloquium Instructional alternative in which a guest or guests are invited to class to be interviewed about their interests or activities.

completion item Type of test item that requires students to supply missing words in a statement or a short phrase that answers a question posed in a stem.

computer-assisted instruction (CAI) The use of computers to present programmed instruction or to assist learners with specific learning tasks. Most programs require learners to complete drills and practice exercises.

conceptual tempo Style of learning based on usage of time; one's conceptual tempo falls between impulsive and reflective.

concrete operational stage Piaget's third stage of intellectual development (approximately 7 to 11 years of age). Children become capable of logical thought and learn to solve specific problems and think logically about concrete experiences.

conflict resolution A method used in Teacher Effectiveness Training to encourage teachers to establish open and honest communication in the classroom in order to resolve problems.

constructivism An approach that asserts that for learners to gain deep understanding, they must actively come to know (construct) concepts for themselves.

contiguity Simple stimulus-response pairing or connection. When one stimulus is regularly associated with another, a response (S-R connection) is established. If two events occur together repeatedly they will eventually become associated, so that even if only one of the events occurs, the response will occur with it.

contracts Written agreements students and teachers enter into that describe the academic work the student is to accomplish at a particular level in a particular period of time.

control need Teacher's need to have others behave well or appropriately.

convergent thinking Style that predisposes people to think in conventional, typical ways by encouraging them to look for a single, local answer to a given problem. Contrasts with divergent thinking.

cooperative learning Instructional procedures whereby learners work together in small groups and are usually rewarded for their collective accomplishments.

created response items Test questions that require students to develop or create a response in their own words.

criterion-referenced scores Student raw scores that are compared to a specific preestablished standard or criterion.

cumulative record A personal record kept for each school enrollee that contains personal information, home and family data, record of school attendance, school grades, standardized test scores, and teacher anecdotal comments.

day care programs Programs that provide child care services for children too young to attend school. Originally begun as a service to working parents, programs have expanded rapidly. Many have incorporated a child development and/or education program.

debates Formal discussions in which a few students present and contest varying points of view with regard to an issue.

demonstrations Form of presentation whereby the teacher or learners show how something works or operates or how to do a particular task.

development Orderly changes that occur in a person over time from conception to death. Includes physical, emotional, or cognitive changes across time.

developmental stages Erikson's comprehensive theory of emotional and social development suggests that there are eight critical stages, each leading to a positive or negative outcome—trust vs. mistrust, autonomy vs. shame and doubt, initiative vs. guilt, industry vs. inferiority, identity vs. role confusion, intimacy vs. isolation, generativity vs. stagnation, and integrity vs. despair.

dialogue journal A journal recording a running conversation that expresses thoughts, questions, and problems related to the roles, responsibilities, and practices of teaching.

differentiated instruction See **individualized instruction.**

direct teaching or instruction (expository teaching) An approach in which teachers control instruction by presenting information, giving directions to the class, and using criticism; associated with teacher-centered, teacher-controlled classrooms; an instructional procedure for teaching content in the most efficient, straightforward way.

disabled or challenged children Students with special needs. May be mentally or physically challenged, emotionally disturbed, learning disabled, or have communication or behavior problems.

discovery learning Learning that occurs when students derive their own meaning from experiences and experiments.

discussion Occurs when students, or students and a teacher, converse back and forth to share information, ideas, or opinions, or to resolve a problem.

disengaged children Those who are inattentive, disinterested in school. Also called reluctant learners.

distance education When instruction is provided for persons off-campus through the use of computers, telephone, printed materials, and so forth.

divergent thinking Style that predisposes a person to think in independent, flexible, and imaginative ways; often equated with creativity. Divergent thinkers can come up with different ideas for accomplishing a task or solving a problem. Contrasts with convergent thinking.

dyslexia Reading impairment; often the result of genetic defect or brain injury.

economically disadvantaged children Children whose parents fall below a governmentally determined poverty line.

Estimated to include 13 million children, 500,000 of whom are homeless.

educationally disadvantaged children Children who do not perform well academically, who are more often identified as retarded, who drop out of school at a higher rate, and who are more likely to enter school with experiential defects. Such children tend to live in communities and states that spend less on education and have fewer well-paid teachers.

efficacy Having a sense of control over one's circumstances.

emotional intelligence (EQ) The ability to get along with others.

established structure The class rules and routines that effective teachers establish and enforce.

establishing set What teachers do at the beginning of a lesson to provide a context for the lesson and the instruction.

evaluation Process of making a qualitative judgment based on collected measurement data.

evaluative set The knowledge that a teacher establishes regarding what students already know about a topic.

exceptionality The special physical, social, emotional, or mental needs or gifts certain children have. Exceptional children may be considered either disabled or gifted. Both types of children may be less than successful students unless certain adaptions are made for them.

executive planning routines Classroom routines that help a teacher to manage personal time and to fulfill the many roles of teaching, such as completing paperwork and clerical chores, grading papers, and planning.

explicit instruction Teaching method whereby teachers review and check homework, present new content/skill, guide students' practice, provide feedback and correctives, move to independent practice, and conduct regular reviews.

expository lesson A lesson in which the teacher presents facts, ideas, and explanations.

expository teaching (direct instruction) Occurs when teachers present information and direction to students. Teacher-centered, goal-oriented, structured approach to teaching.

extended response items Test questions that do not place any restrictions on

student responses, thus allowing greater creativity and flexibility of response.

extinction The elimination of minor misbehavior by ignoring it (as long as it is not dangerous or distracting to other students).

feedback Information teachers provide to inform students of their progress and to help them learn to monitor themselves and improve their own learning.

field dependent Cognitive style of a person who sees the larger picture but not its specifics or details. Field-dependent learners "see the forest" rather than the individual trees.

field independent Cognitive style of a person who sees the specifics or details of something but not the larger picture. Field-independent learners "see the individual trees" rather than the forest.

field observation Observations made or work carried on in a natural setting. Also referred to as fieldwork or field trips.

follow-up Phase of the questioning process where the teacher reacts to the student's response to a question.

formal curriculum What the state and school district expect will be taught and learned.

formal interview A structured, face-to-face meeting with the explicit purpose of obtaining specific information about the interviewee's experiences, views, likes, and so forth.

formal observation Carefully planned observational efforts to obtain specific information about a target student or students.

formal operational stage Piaget's fourth stage of intellectual development, beginning at about age 11. At this level, children are more able to deal in abstractions or perform activities mentally.

formative assessment Ongoing student assessment conducted during the course of instruction.

gender roles Male/female roles learned early in life. The current tendency is to hope children acquire a gender role that combines traits traditionally thought unique to each gender.

generativity The ability to have and nurture children and/or be involved with future generations. Productivity and creativity are essential features.

Gifted and Talented Act (Public Law 95-561) Provides federal funding for gifted education.

gifted and talented children Children who possess outstanding abilities or potential in the areas of general intellectual capacity, specific academic aptitude, creative or productive thinking, leadership ability, visual or performing arts, and psychomotor ability.

grade equivalent scores Scores that describe the pupil's level of performance in comparison to pupils in a particular grade.

group alerting The process of keeping the students' attention and of holding them accountable for their behavior and learning.

Head Start program Preschool program intended to counteract negative environmental effects for economically disadvantaged 3- and 4-year-old children.

higher-level cognitive skills The intellectual ability to analyze, synthesize, and evaluate information.

humanistic learning theory School of thought emphasizing the development of the learner as a psychologically healthy person. Advocates of this theory desire to make children feel better about themselves and be more accepting of others.

hurried children Children whose caregivers hurry or pressure them to excel and/or to grow up.

hyperactivity Behavior disorder characterized by abnormal amounts of movement, inattentiveness, and restlessness.

identity The organization of the individual's drives, abilities, beliefs, and history into a consistent self-image.

impulsive learning/thinking style Cognitive style of responding quickly but often inaccurately. Persons with this learning style tend to act without serious forethought and to do poorly in school tasks requiring analysis of details. (Not everyone who works fast is impulsive, however). Contrasts with reflective learning style.

independent study Any school-related assignment done more or less alone by students.

indirect teaching or instruction (learner-centered instruction) Occurs when teachers provide students with experiences or information and then ask students for their observations and conclusions. Contrasts with direct instruction or expository teaching.

Individualized Educational Plan (IEP) A learning program that teachers, parents, a qualified school official, and perhaps the student help develop for a student with special learning needs. It sets forth goals, services, and teaching strategies for that student. IEPs are mandated by the Education for All Handicapped Children Act.

individualized instruction Instruction that attempts to tailor teaching and learning to a learner's unique strengths and needs.

Individuals with Disabilities Education Act (Public Law 105-17) Law requiring that students with disabilities be placed in the least restrictive, or most normal school environment they can succeed in.

informal interview A face-to-face meeting that is more like casual conversation, allowing talk to flow naturally and spontaneously in more or less any direction.

informal observation Casual, unplanned observation of a student(s).

information processing Efforts to understand how we take in and store new information and how we retrieve it when it is needed.

inquiry-oriented teaching The highly individual process of reflecting on one's teaching in order to make rational, deliberate decisions about teaching and learning.

instructional alternative Any teaching approach that can be used to facilitate student learning and satisfaction.

instructional clarity A quality of effective instruction that helps students come to a thorough and accurate understanding of the material.

instructional objective Statement of concepts, attitudes, or skills that students are expected to achieve by the end of some period of instruction.

instructional planning Process by which someone (usually a teacher) decides how best to select and organize a learning experience to maximize both teacher and student achievement and satisfaction.

instructional routines Routines or procedures teachers regularly follow when they teach such as the formats for giving directions, monitoring student work, and questioning students.

intervention A reinforcement given to students every time they perform a desired behavior in order to encourage them to behave appropriately more often. Used in applied behavioral analysis.

invitational learning Occurs when teachers communicate to learners that they are "responsible, able, and valuable" people.

inviting classroom An appealing, positive place that provides a sense of physical and emotional safety for both students and the teacher.

Inviting School Success A program developed to get teachers to communicate to learners that they are "responsible, able, and valuable" people.

laboratory experiences Scaled-down teaching experiences carried out on campus, often with a small group of peers, rather than in an actual classroom setting.

latchkey children Children between about 6 and 13 years of age who do not have adult supervision for some part of the day.

latchkey programs Before- and after-school programs for children who otherwise would be without adult supervision.

learning abilities Classified by Sternberg as memory, analysis, creativity, and application.

learning module A self-contained package of individualized learning activities that guides students to know or to be able to do something.

learning style A consistent pattern of behavior and performance an individual uses to approach learning experiences. Includes how a person learns best; the person's learning personality; and the learner's tendency to use different sensory modes to understand experiences and to learn (visual, auditory, kinesthetic).

learning theory-based direct instruction The sequence of events followed by teachers who are guided by what is known about learning.

least restrictive environment A school setting that is as normal as possible given a child's special problems and needs. Often involves placing a child with disabilities into a regular classroom for all or part of the day. Mandated by the Education for All Handicapped Children Act.

long-term memory Seemingly limitless and permanent storage system where we keep information for a long time. Retrieval of long-term memory information is most effective when the information has been related to something we already know.

mainstreaming Placing a challenged or handicapped child in as many activities as possible within regular classrooms.

management routines Classroom routines used to organize the classroom and direct student behavior; nonacademic routines.

mandated time Formal time scheduled for school or academic activities.

mastery learning Allows students to study academic material at their own pace until they learn it. All students might be expected to reach a certain level of proficiency, and they are given time and corrective instruction until they master the material.

matching items Test questions that ask students to match items in one column with related items in another.

meaningful learning Occurs when information is effectively organized, structured, and taught so as to maximize its usefulness.

measurement Process of gathering objective, usually quantitative, information or data about student performance.

momentum The flow of activities and the pace of teaching and learning maintained in a classroom.

moral development A progressive increase in the capability for moral reasoning. Piaget suggests that moral development/reasoning evolves through two levels: morality of constraint and morality of cooperation.

moral education Akin to character education, values education, and citizenship education. Moral education is intended to help learners develop more responsible behavior both in school and out.

morality of constraint The first of two levels in Piaget's stages of moral reasoning. At this stage, children regard rules as sacred and unchangeable, and punishment as inflexible.

morality of cooperation Piaget's second stage of moral reasoning. At this stage, individuals regard rules as flexible, believe there can be exceptions to them, and believe that punishment must take into account the circumstances surrounding the misbehavior.

multiethnic education Educational practices that encourage learners to revere their roots and culture, as well as the cultures of others.

multiple-choice items Test questions that each consist of a stem, which presents a problem or asks a question, followed by several alternative responses. Students are expected to select the alternative that offers the best solution to the problem or best answers the question presented in the stem.

negative reinforcement Encouraging desirable behaviors by removing or omitting an undesirable or aversive stimulus.

nonnegative affect A manner teachers have that ensures that learners feel psychologically safe and secure.

norm-referenced scores Raw scores of an individual student compared to those of other students who took the test; indicate how well a student's achievement compares with that of other students in the class, school, district, state, or nation.

normal curve Bell-shaped graph depicting the frequency with which particular scores are expected.

norming group The class-, school-, district-, statewide-, or national group of students standard scores are compared to.

observational learning Also called social learning. Occurs when learners learn by watching; in order for observational learning to be effective, learners must attend to someone's behavior, retain what they observed the "model" do, imitate or reproduce the behavior they saw, and experience reinforcement or satisfaction as a consequence.

operant conditioning Learning facilitated through reinforcement. Behaviors are strengthened or weakened depending upon the reinforcement or punishment received.

oral reports Instructional alternative whereby individuals or groups of learners are given or choose topics and present the researched topic to the rest of the class.

orientation set A new instructional activity that engages students' attention.

overcorrection The compulsory practice of appropriate behavior as a result of undesirable behavior.

overlapping Teacher's ability to attend to more than one classroom activity or episode at a time.

parent relationships and home conditions need Teachers' need to maintain constructive relationships with parents and to be aware of the impact of home conditions on school success.

pedagogy The art and science of teaching; instruction in teaching methods.

percentile rank (PR) score Indicates what percentage of people taking the test scored at or below a given score.

perceptual modality preferences Learner's tendency to use different sensory modes to understand experiences and to learn (visual, auditory, kinesthetic). (See **learning style**.)

performance differences The way students vary with regard to school performance. Some students do well at most things, others do poorly at most things, but most students demonstrate an unevenness within a range of school activity.

physical environment Those aspects of the classroom that are concrete, easily identifiable, and exist independent of the people who inhabit the classroom.

physically challenged or impaired Having orthopedic handicaps, epilepsy, cerebral palsy, or other physical challenges.

portfolio A collection of artifacts collected during schooling, selected as representative of the student's experience, and reflected upon to show links to academic, skill, or behavioral objectives.

positive expectations The desire effective teachers show for the academic progress and success of each student.

positive reinforcement Giving students praise, rewards, or a positive reaction when they choose to behave appropriately.

precision teaching Overlearning through continued practice.

preoperational, prelogical stage Piaget's second stage of intellectual development, lasting from approximately 2 to 7 years of age. Young learners at this stage develop knowledge from personal experience, explore and manipulate concrete objects, and learn the three Rs and other basic knowledge and skills. In this stage youngsters also begin to use symbols to represent ideas.

presentation Informative talk a more knowledgeable person makes to less knowledgeable persons.

proactive management Classroom management that focuses on preventing problems from arising in the classroom by eliciting student cooperation and involving students in educationally relevant activities.

probing Asking additional questions of the responding student to help expand or raise the level of the student's response.

problem Goal-response interference.

problem solving Requires learners to consider how they would attain a goal. A major goal of education is to assist learners in becoming better problem solvers. Different types of problems include well-structured problems (subject matter–related) and ill-structured problems (life-related).

process approach An approach to instructional planning that results in a general rather than precise plan.

product approach An approach to instructional planning that results in a precise rather than a general plan.

programmed instruction (PI) Instruction whereby the material to be learned is usually presented in small parts (called frames) so students can teach themselves. Learners respond to the information; if their responses are correct, they receive positive reinforcement and the next step or frame is presented.

project method Form of individualization that allows learners to choose and work on projects and activities.

protocols Original records of some important event that learners study to try to understand the event or its consequences.

proximity Amount of space between teacher and students. Proximity can influence students' behavior and keep them alert.

psychological environment The social and emotional climate of the classroom, including the emotional tone and how students feel about the teacher, learning tasks, and one another as a social group.

psychomotor domain The area of learning that deals with students' physical abilities and skills. It includes behaviors such as handwriting, typing or keyboarding, swimming, sculpting, and so forth. According to Simpson, there are seven divisions of this domain: perception, set, guided response, mechanism, complex or overt response, adaptation, and origination.

psychosocial development Erikson's theory of development that describes the relationship between the individual's needs and the social environment. Suggests that adult personal and social characteristics are a result of the life stages in which individuals resolve various dichotomies (for example, trust vs. mistrust, autonomy vs. shame, industry vs. inferiority).

Public Law 93-247 A law defining abuse and neglect as "physical or mental injury, sexual abuse, negligent treatment, or maltreatment of a child under 18 by a person who is responsible for the child's welfare under circumstances which indicate that the child's health or welfare is harmed or threatened thereby."

Public Law 94-142 (Education of All Handicapped Children Act) Law requiring that students with handicaps be placed in the least restrictive (most normal) environment.

Public Law 95-561 (Gifted and Talented Act) Provides federal funding for gifted education.

punishment Something undesirable, painful, or discomforting that is applied to a student as a result of misbehavior and that is intended to weaken the probability that the inappropriate behavior will recur.

reactive management Classroom management that focuses on reacting to students' misbehavior.

reception learning Takes place when teachers present students with carefully organized and structured new information.

reciprocal teaching Occurs when the teaching function is slowly and systematically given over to students.

recitation Learning activity in which students are given information to study independently and then recite what they have learned when the teacher questions them.

recognition need The need to obtain positive attention; the need to be praised and recognized.

redirecting When teachers ask another student to answer the same question.

reflection Learning from experience through the ongoing process of critically examining and refining teaching practice. Takes place by considering the personal, educational, social, and ethical aspects of schooling.

reflective learning style Cognitive style of responding slowly, carefully, and accurately. (However, not all slow responders give accurate responses.) Contrasts with impulsive learning style.

reflective teaching A laboratory experience in a supportive environment that allows one to teach a lesson that serves as a basis for subsequent analysis and introspection.

reinforcement A principle of learning that recognizes that learners are more likely to do things when they feel good about doing them, usually by receiving some reward or recognition.

reinforcement menu A list of reinforcers that are effective with a particular student or group of students.

reinforcement theory The idea that a teacher can influence student behavior by rewarding desirable behaviors and ignoring or discouraging undesirable behaviors.

reliability The quality of providing consistent measurement results over time; a measure of how well a test evaluates what it is meant to evaluate from one situation to the next.

reliability coefficients Statistical indications of the reliability of tests; range from .00 to 1.00, with zero representing no reliability and 1.00 indicating perfect reliability.

remediation Help for students who did not master the material the first time.

rephrasing When teachers restate the same question in different terms to help a student understand it.

research-based direct teaching or instruction The sequence of events followed by teachers who are more effective in bringing about student learning.

resilient children Children who are able to overcome negative circumstances and achieve successes.

resource unit A plan for teaching something in the curriculum available from a source such as the state education department.

restricted response items Created response test questions that set explicit parameters students are to respond within.

role confusion Having an inconsistent image of self with respect to one's drives, abilities, beliefs, and history.

role playing An activity in which learners take on the role of another person to see what it would be like to be that person.

routines Established procedures whose main function is to control and coordinate movement and events in the classroom.

rubric A matrix or table of indicators characteristic of particular levels of student performance; used to evaluate student work, usually projects or performances.

scheduling Changing the frequency of reinforcement based on students' behavior.

score band Range of scores that includes the student's actual score (usually at the middle of the band) and indicates how far above or below that score the student might have performed on a different day.

selected response items Test questions that require students to select or choose a correct response from a list of possible answers.

self-esteem Feelings of personal worth.

self-fulfilling prophecy When a person gets what he or she expects or achieves at the level he or she expects to reach.

self-referenced grading system When grades are determined by comparing a student's current performance with past performances. The grade is based upon improvement.

sensorimotor stage The first of Piaget's four stages of intellectual development, lasting from approximately 0 to 2 years of age. During this stage, the intellect develops primarily through the use of senses and motor activity.

set The context for the lesson and instruction to follow.

set induction Planning an introductory activity that will capture students' attention, help them see the purpose and value of what is to be learned, and relate what they are to learn to that which they already know.

short-term memory Severely limited storage system that holds only a small amount of information for merely seconds. Also referred to as working memory.

simulation games Specially designed competitive games that mirror some aspect of life.

simulations Experiences intended to give the appearance or have the effect of some situation in order to provide "firsthand experience" with how that situation works.

smoothness Moving students through a lesson with few interruptions.

social learning Also called observational learning. Its chief theorist, Bandura, states that for observational learning to be effective, learners must attend to someone's behavior, retain what they observed the "model" do, imitate or reproduce the behavior they saw, and experience reinforcement or satisfaction as a consequence.

social reinforcers Positive messages, either verbal or nonverbal, given to a student who behaves appropriately so as to increase the likelihood that the behavior will be repeated.

socioeconomic status (SES) Sociological term used to describe variations in wealth, background, and prestige of individuals in society.

sociogram Diagrammatic representation of the social relationships that exist within a group at a particular point in time; shows frequency of nomination; attractions.

sociometry Technique used to obtain information about the social acceptability of individuals within a group.

speech impairment The inability to produce effective speech because of difficulties in articulation, stuttering, or voicing.

standard deviation Indication of how widely the scores vary from the mean; small standard deviation indicates that scores do not differ greatly, most being very near the mean; large standard deviation indicates much variation in the scores.

standard scores Norm-referenced scores that report a student's performance in relation to the mean and standard deviation of the norming group.

standardized tests Tests that have controlled, consistent administration, scoring, and interpretation procedures. These tests allow a given student's score on a specific test to be compared with scores made by a very large number of similar students who have taken the same test.

standardized test score Score that shows how one student's performance compares to others.

stanine scores A nine-value scale that reports standardized test results; 5 is the midpoint or mean and each standard deviation is 2. Stanine scores are more easily interpreted than z scores and T scores because stanine scores are less precise.

stem The part of the multiple-choice question that presents a problem or asks a question.

student cooperation and accountability In direct instruction, holding students accountable for their academic work and for assisting each other and sharing materials.

student success need The need of teachers to help learners succeed both academically and socially.

summative assessment Assessment conducted after instruction is completed; used to make final judgments about a student's learning and to summarize a student's achievement or progress.

sustained expectations Teacher-held expectations that do not accurately reflect the student's ability. These expectations come about because some teachers stubbornly refuse to adjust their initially inaccurate expectations of students.

synthesis The ability to put component parts together in a new and different way.

T score Score scaled to the normal curve which uses 50 as the midpoint (mean) and sets each standard deviation at 10 points; all scores are positive; eliminates negative numbers and decimal places.

tangible reinforcers Concrete objects given to a student who behaves appropriately to increase the likelihood that the behavior will be repeated.

task orientation Characteristic of direct instruction that places the primary emphasis on academic learning.

taught curriculum What is actually taught by teachers. Includes the formal curriculum and whatever is done to supplement or complement it.

teachable moment Taking advantage of something that happens unexpectedly and learning about it. For example, a thunderstorm.

teacher centrality Characteristic of direct instruction whereby teachers exert strong instructional direction and control.

team teaching When teachers collaborate and jointly teach a group of students.

test blueprint Matrix that depicts the relationship between instructional objectives or topics covered, cognitive levels, and items on a test; used as a guide to developing teacher-made tests.

test sophistication The degree to which a student is comfortable and knowledgeable about how to complete tests efficiently.

theory of multiple intelligence A theory that suggests that intelligence includes many different kinds of skills and abilities.

time need The need to have sufficient time to do what needs to be done.

time on task Time when students are actively engaged in academic tasks.

time-out Removing the student from the situation and from attention and rewards in order to reduce unwanted student behavior.

transition set Information that helps students understand how new material relates to what they learned previously.

transitions Points in an instructional interaction when the context changes in some way, for example, when moving from one activity to another.

tutoring Form of individualization whereby either a teacher or a fellow student provides a learner or small group of learners with special help.

unit plan A plan for learning a major section or topic within a course. Usually learned over a period of weeks and limited to one topical area.

valence and challenge arousal Ability to engender students with curiosity and enthusiasm and get them involved in independent work.

validity The degree to which a test measures what it was intended to measure.

values clarification Methods whereby learners (1) identify how they feel or what they believe about something; (2) value that feeling or belief; and (3) if valued, act on it.

variety and challenge The ability to identify and assign independent study assignments that are different enough to be interesting and challenging enough to maintain attention.

visually impaired Having poor vision or considered educationally blind.

wait time The pause between teacher question and student response and the pause between student response and teacher reaction.

withitness The ability of a teacher to communicate to students that he or she is aware of student behavior throughout the classroom at all times, even when the teacher is not nearby or looking directly at the students.

z score Most basic type of standard score; mean is 0 and each standard deviation is 1. The larger the z score, the more the raw score differs from the mean; z scores are reported to two place values.

Visual Credits

p. 5 Ford Button, *Recess Time: The Best Cartoons from the Kappan,* Kristin Herzog (ed.), Phi Delta Kappa, Bloomington, IN, 1983, p. 79.

p. 12 Martha Campbell (January 2001). PHI DELTA KAPPAN, Vol. 82, No. 5, p. 383.

p. 21 Chuck Morman, *The Student Body: Great Cartoons from the Kappan,* Carol Bucheri, Terri Hampton, and Victoria Voelker (eds.), Phi Delta Kappa, Bloomington, IN, 1991, p. 81.

p. 31 James Estes (January 1999). PHI DELTA KAPPAN, Vol. 80, No. 5, p. 363.

p. 53 Robert Hageman (March 1994). PHI DELTA KAPPAN, Vol. 75, No. 7, p. 511.

p. 67 Martha Campbell, *Scholarship: More Great Cartoons from the Kappan,* Kristin Herzog and Mary Miller (eds.), Phi Delta Kappa, Bloomington, IN, 1985, p. 90.

p. 68 Martha Campbell, *Recess Time: The Best Cartoons from the Kappan,* Kristin Herzog (ed.), Phi Delta Kappa, Bloomington, IN, 1983, p. 29.

p. 69 Martha Campbell, *Recess Time: The Best Cartoons from the Kappan,* Kristin Herzog (ed.), Phi Delta Kappa, Bloomington, IN, 1983, p. 18.

p. 77 Ford Button, *Recess Time: The Best Cartoons from the Kappan,* Kristin Herzog (ed.), Phi Delta Kappa, Bloomington, IN, 1983, p. 74.

p. 90 Randy Glasbergen, *The Student Body: Great Cartoons from the Kappan,* Carol Bucheri, Terri Hampton, and Victoria Voelker (eds.), Phi Delta Kappa, Bloomington, IN, 1991, p. 57.

p. 98 Dave Carpenter, *The Student Body: Great Cartoons from the Kappan,* Carol Bucheri, Terri Hampton, and Victoria Voelker (eds.), Phi Delta Kappa, Bloomington, IN, 1991, p. 78.

p. 140 Frank Cotham, *Recess Time: The Best Cartoons from the Kappan,* Kristin Herzog (ed.), Phi Delta Kappa, Bloomington, IN, 1983, p. 68.

p. 143 Glen Dines, *Recess Time: The Best Cartoons from the Kappan,* Kristin Herzog (ed.), Phi Delta Kappa, Bloomington, IN, 1983, p. 69.

p. 194 Glen Dines, *Recess Time: The Best Cartoons from the Kappan,* Kristin Herzog (ed.), Phi Delta Kappa, Bloomington, IN, 1983, p. 58.

p. 201 Martha Campbell (March 1989). PHI DELTA KAPPAN, Vol. 70, No. 7, p. 511.

p. 213 Fred Thomas, *The Student Body: Great Cartoons from the Kappan,* Carol Bucheri, Terri Hampton, and Victoria Voelker (eds.), Phi Delta Kappa, Bloomington, IN, 1991, p. 105.

p. 214 Frank Cotham, *Recess Time: The Best Cartoons from the Kappan,* Kristin Herzog (ed.), Phi Delta Kappa, Bloomington, IN, 1983, p. 55.

p. 242 Fred Thomas (1995, December). PHI DELTA KAPPAN, Vol. 4, No. 1, page 315.

p. 252 Kathy Cruickshank Grossart

p. 252 Bo Brown (1995, September), PHI DELTA KAPPAN, Vol. 77, No. 1, p. 61.

p. 273 Fred Thomas, *The Student Body: Great Cartoons from the Kappan,* Carol Bucheri, Terri Hampton, and Victoria Voelker (eds.), Phi Delta Kappa, Bloomington, IN, 1991, p. 55.

p. 278 Dave Carpenter, *The Student Body: Great Cartoons from the Kappan,* Carol Bucheri, Terri Hampton, and Victoria Voelker (eds.), Phi Delta Kappa, Bloomington, IN, 1991, p. 64.

p. 284 Bo Brown, *The Student Body: Great Cartoons from the Kappan,* Carol Bucheri, Terri Hampton, and Victoria Voelker (eds.), Phi Delta Kappa, Bloomington, IN, 1991, p. 36.

p. 293 Randy Glasbergen, *The Student Body: Great Cartoons from the Kappan,* Carol Bucheri, Terri Hampton, and Victoria Voelker (eds.), Phi Delta Kappa, Bloomington, IN, 1991, p. 22.

p. 299 Art Bouthillier, *The Student Body: Great Cartoons from the Kappan,* Carol Bucheri, Terri Hampton, and Victoria Voelker (eds.), Phi Delta Kappa, Bloomington, IN, 1991, p. 53.

p. 334 Francis H. Brummer, *The Student Body: Great Cartoons from the Kappan,* Carol Bucheri, Terri Hampton, and Victoria Voelker (eds.), Phi Delta Kappa, Bloomington, IN, 1991, p. 104.

p. 337 Art Bouthillier, *The Student Body: Great Cartoons from the Kappan,* Carol Bucheri, Terri Hampton, and Victoria Voelker (eds.), Phi Delta Kappa, Bloomington, IN, 1991, p. 115.

p. 343 Art Bouthillier, *The Student Body: Great Cartoons from the Kappan,* Carol Bucheri, Terri Hampton, and Victoria Voelker (eds.), Phi Delta Kappa, Bloomington, IN, 1991, p. 85.

p. 352 James Estes, *The Student Body: Great Cartoons from the Kappan,* Carol Bucheri, Terri Hampton, and Victoria Voelker (eds.), Phi Delta Kappa, Bloomington, IN, 1991, p. 12.

p. 354 Martha Campbell, *The Student Body: Great Cartoons from the Kappan,* Carol Bucheri, Terri Hampton, and Victoria Voelker (eds.), Phi Delta Kappa, Bloomington, IN, 1991, p. 9.

p. 363 Frank Cotham, *The Student Body: Great Cartoons from the Kappan,* Carol Bucheri, Terri Hampton, and Victoria Voelker (eds.), Phi Delta Kappa, Bloomington, IN, 1991, p. 68.

p. 405 George Abbot, *The Kappan,* Vol. 74, No. 2, October 1992, p. 171.

Photo Credits

Name Index

Subject Index

AAAS; *see* American Association for the Advancement of Science

ABA; *see* Applied behavioral analysis

Academic games, 212

Academic instruction time, 354

Academic learning time (ALT), 354–355

Accountability in education, influence on teaching, 13

Achievement standards, influence on teaching, 32–33

Achievement tests, information in cumulative record about, 91

Action research, 319

Action zone, in seating arrangement, 384–385

Active teaching, 253–254

Activity reinforcers, 400

Activity routines, 394

Adaptability, of effective teachers, 341–342

ADD; *see* Attention deficit disorder

ADHD; *see* Attention deficit/hyperactivity disorder

Advance organizers, types of, 70; *see also* Set induction

Affective domain, educational objectives in, 149

Affective education; *see* Humanistic education

Affiliation, as teacher problem, 425–427, 434

Allocated time, 354

ALT; *see* Academic learning time

Alternative-choice items; *see* True-false items

Alternative responses, 286

American Agenda, 42

American Association for the Advancement of Science (AAAS), 146

Anecdotal comments, 91–92

guidelines for writing, 91–92

information gained from, 92

Anticipatory set, 162

Applied behavioral analysis (ABA), 80

Aptitude, student, 53

Aptitude tests, information in cumulative record about, 90–91

Artifacts, teaching, 318

Assessment, of student performance

classroom, 271

evaluation in, 271–272

formative, 275–276

grading and, 297–301

information accuracy in, 273–275

Assessment, of student performance—*Cont.*

information sources for, 272

measurement in, 271–272

observational, 291–297

pencil-and-paper tests, 282–292

reliability in, 274–275

standardized testing and, 276–282

summative, 276

synthesis of information in, 301–303

validity in, 274

At-risk children, 29–31

Attention, 67; *see also* Set induction

guidelines for gaining and holding learners', 67

and variety in teaching, 351–352

Attention deficit disorder (ADD), 55

Attention deficit/hyperactivity disorder (ADHD), 55

Attitude change, reflective teaching lessons on, 466–473

Auditory learners, 52

Authentic assessment; *see* Observational assessment

Autobiography, gathering student information with, 97

Baseline, 80

Basic practice model, 252

Behavior modification, 80

Behavioral theory of learning, 76–81

classical conditioning and, 77

contiguity and, 76

operant conditioning and, 77

principles of, 78

social learning and, 77–78

teaching approaches of, 78–80

Beliefs, influence on teaching, 6

Bilingual Education Act, 44

Block plans, 160, 167

sample, 160

unit plans and, 160

Bloom's taxonomy of educational objectives, 148–150

writing objectives using, 153

Boredom, student, 31–32

Brainstorming, 212

Bullying, 407

Businesslike character, of effective teachers, 339–341

Busywork, independent study and, 194, 197

CAI; *see* Computer-assisted instruction

Case approach, 98–99, 100

data needed for, 98–99

example of, 100

Case studies, by students, 212

Centers of interest, 212

Challenged children, 49–50

Character education, as teaching approach, 75

Checklists, in observation assessment, 293–294

Child abuse and neglect, 28–29

Child care; *see* Day care

Childhood and youth, changing nature of, 26–32

abuse and neglect, 28–29

at-risk children, 29–31

disengaged children, 31–32

economically disadvantaged children, 27

hurried children, 31

inadequate supervision, 27–28

Children's Defense Fund, 42

Chunking information, 68

CIRC; *see* Cooperative integrated reading and composition

Citizenship education, as teaching approach, 75

Clarity; *see* Instructional clarity

Class size

influence on teaching, 10–11

and teacher problems, 433

Classical conditioning, behavior theory of learning and, 77

Classroom environment

equipment and materials, 386

organization in, 390

physical environment, 383–387

psychological environment, 387–390

room arrangement, 386–387, 388

seating patterns, 383–384

task orientation in, 390

tone of, 387–390

Classroom management; *see also* Classroom environment

definition of, 382

and discipline, 381

first day of school and, 396–397

group alerting, 398–399

momentum, 398

overlapping, 397–398

proactive, 382, 390

proximity, 398–399

Mandated time, 353
Maslow's hierarchy of human needs, 388, 389
Mastery learning, 79–80, 214
Mastery teaching program, 258–259
Matching items
    characterized, 287–288
    examples of poor and good, 289
Material and equipment availability, 12, 386
Meaningful learning theory, 66, 69–74
    problem solving, 71–73
    reception learning, 69–70
    reciprocal teaching, 70–71
Measurement, of student performance, 271–272
Memory, 66–67, 68–69
    long-term, 67, 68
    short-term, 66–67, 68
Methods, teaching; see Instructional alternatives
Microteaching
    definition of, 440
    individual practice lessons, 441–446
    steps in, 440–441
Mild desists, and student misbehavior, 407
Minority population
    distribution of, 20
    growth of, 19–20
Minority students, teaching, 44–45
Misbehavior; see Student misbehavior; Student misbehavior interventions
Momentum
    in classroom management, 398
    and instructional time, 356
Monitoring student progress
    forms of, 368–369
    tips for, 369
Moral development, 48
    Kohlberg's theory of, 48
    Piaget's theory of, 48
Moral education, as teaching approach, 75
Morality of constraint, 48
Morality of cooperation, 48
Motivating students, 102–103, 104
Multiethnic education, 44–45, 75
Multiple-choice items
    characterized, 286–287
    guidelines for, 288
Multiple intelligence, theory of, 53–54
Music Educators National Conference, 146

National Board for Professional Teaching Standards (NBPTS), xv
National Coalition for the Homeless, 42
National Council of Teachers of English, 146
National Council of Teachers of Mathematics, 146
National imperatives
    accountability and, 13
    influence on teaching, 13

NBPTS; see National Board for Professional Teaching Standards
NCE; see Normal curve equivalent scores
Negative reinforcement, 402
Nongraded schools, individually guided education and, 206
Nonnegative affect, in direct instruction, 251
Norm-referenced grading, 299–300, 302
Norm-referenced test scores, 278–279
Normal curve equivalent scores (NCE), 281

Objectives; see Instructional objectives; Learning outcomes; Lesson objectives
Observation of students, 92–93
    checklist for, 93
    formal and informal, 93
Observational assessment, 292–297
    checklists in, 293–294
    portfolio assessment in, 297
    rating scales in, 294–295
    rubrics in, 295–296
Observational learning, behavioral theory of learning and, 77–78
Operant conditioning, behavioral theory of learning and, 77, 79, 80
Oral reports, 214
Orientation set, 350
Overlapping, in classroom management, 397–398

Panel discussion technique, 186
Parent involvement
    gathering student informaton from, 97–98
    and relationship with teacher, 428–431, 434
    student achievement related to, 24–25
Pedagogical preparation, influence on teaching, 9
Pencil-and-paper tests, 282–292
    administering, 291–292, 293
    completion items, 289–290
    created response items, 282, 283–285, 286
    extended response items, 283, 284–285
    guidelines for constructing, 292
    matching items, 287–288, 289
    multiple-choice items, 286–287, 288
    reliability in, 291
    restricted response items, 283, 284
    selected response items, 282, 283, 285–290
    test blueprint, 291
    true-false items, 288–289
    validity in, 291
Percentile rank (PR), 280
Perceptual modality
    auditory learners, 52
    kinesthetic learners, 52
    tactile learners, 52
    visual learners, 52
Performance assessment; see Observational assessment

Personal characteristics, influence on teaching, 3–6
    age and experience, 5
    beliefs, 6
    gender, 4–5
    personality, 5–6
Personality, influence on teaching, 5–6
Physical environment, of classroom, 383–387
PI; see Programmed instruction
Piaget's theory
    of cognitive development, 47–48
    of moral development, 48
Planning, instructional; see Instructional planning
Population changes, and teaching, 19–20
Portfolio assessment, in observational assessment, 297
Portfolios, teacher, 318–319
Positive expectations, in direct instruction, 251
Positive reinforcement, 399
PR; see Percentile rank
Praise, effect on students of, 401
Praxis III requirements, xv, 481–482
Precision teaching, 80
Preoperational, prelogical stage, 48
Presentations, 7, 69, 175–183, 214; see also Direct instruction; Reception learning
    characteristics of, 176–177
    closure of, 180–181
    concept, 180
    definition of, 176
    delivery of, 179
    effective presentations, characteristics of, 177–181, 183
    explanations and, 181
    good presenters, characteristics of, 177, 181
    handouts, 180
    preparation for, 178–179
    pros and cons of, 182–183
    purposes of, 176–177
    reflective teaching lessons in, 454–465
    sample lesson for, 182
    Socratic technique and, 176
    visual aids and, 179
Proactive management, of classroom, 382, 390
Probing, when questioning students, 363–364
Problem-solving method of learning, 71–73, 214
    ill-structured problems and, 72–73
    well-structured problems and, 71
Problems
    definition of, 423
    sources of, 424–425

Standard scores, 279
Standardized tests, 276–277
  administering, 277
  criterion-referenced scores in, 279
  grade equivalent scores in, 281
  information in cumulative record
      about, 90
  normal curve equivalent scores in, 281
  norm-referenced scores in, 278–279
  percentile rank in, 280
  preparing students for, 278
  raw score in, 278, 279–280
  score bands for, 281
  stanine scores in, 281
Stanine scores, 281
Statewide adoption of textbooks, 147
Stimulus-response pairing, behavioral
    theory of learning and, 76
Student cooperation and accountability,
    in direct instruction, 251
Student diversity, influence on teaching, 10
Student misbehavior
  academic engagement and, 382
  bullying, 407
  causes of, 404
  definition of, 403
  teacher reaction to, 404–405
Student misbehavior interventions
  extinction, 406–407
  mild desists, 407
  punishment, 409–410
  reprimands, 408
  time-out, 408–409
Student success
  kinds of problems regarding, 431
  obstacles to, 431–432
  teacher behaviors associated with, 432, 434
Student-team learning; see Cooperative
    learning
Student teams, achievement divisions
    (STAD), 231, 233–235
Subject knowledge; see Content knowledge
Subject matter
  curriculum standards, sources of, 146
  Internet resources for, 168
  unit plans, 158
Success, student; see Student success
Summative assessment, 276
Supportiveness, of effective teachers,
    337–339
Survival Guide for New Teachers, 427
Sustained expectations, teachers', 336

T scores, 279
Tactile learners, 52

TAI; see Team-accelerated instruction
Tangible reinforcers, 400–401
Task orientation, in direct instruction, 251
Taught curriculum, 147
Teachable moments, 143
Teacher centrality, in direct instruction, 251
Teacher education, influence on teaching, 9
Teacher expectations
  in direct instruction, 251
  effect on student learning of, 335–337
  high versus low, 338
  information about students and,
      101–102
  self-fulfilling prophecy and, 336
  sustained expectations, 336
Teacher-pupil planning, 166
Teacher-team planning, 166
Teacher's age, influence on teaching, 5
Teaching experience, influence on
    teaching, 5
Teaching methods; see Instructional
    alternatives
Teaching practice, influences on; see
    Influences on teaching practice
Teaching styles
  direct, 7
  expository, 7
  indirect, 7–8
  influence on teaching, 7, 8
  male vs. female, 4
Teaching unit plans, 158
Team-accelerated instruction (TAI),
    231–232
Team-assisted individualization, 231–232
Team teaching, and presentations, 176
Teams, games, tournaments (TGT), 231
Technology use in teaching
  classroom routines and, 393
  digital content use and development,
      216–217
  preparation for, 217
  software selection, 215–216
  Web use, 216
Television, effect on children of, 31
Test blueprint, 291
Test construction, 292
Test sophistication, 278
Testing
  pencil-and-paper, 282–292
  reliability in, 274–275
  standardized, 276–282
  and student assessment, 273
  validity in, 275
Textbooks, use in determining curriculum
    of, 147

TGT; see Teams, games, tournaments
Time; see also Instructional time
  individualized instruction and, 204
  as teacher problem, 432–433, 434
  use of, in planning, 155–156, 167
Time on task, 353
Time-out, and student misbehavior,
    408–409
Transition set, 350
Trial-and-error approach to teaching,
    versus reflective practice, 315
True-false items
  characterized, 288–289
  guidelines for, 289
Tutoring, 215
  individualized instruction and, 206

Unit plans, 158–160, 167
  benefits of, 160
  block plans and, 160
  experience, 158
  integrated, 158–159
  resource, 158
  sections of, 159
  subject matter, 158
  teaching, 158

Unstructured problems, problem-solving
    method and, 72–73

Validity in testing and assessment, 274, 291
Values clarification, as teaching approach, 75
Values education, as teaching approach, 75
Variety in teaching, holding attention by,
    351–352
Visual aids, presentations and, 179
Visual learners, 52

Wait time, questioning students and,
    360–362
Warmth, of effective teachers, 332–334
Web site, development by teachers and
    students, 217
Web (World Wide), use in teaching, 216
Weighted scores, 302–303
Well-structured problems, problem-solving
    method and, 71
Winnetka plan, 205
Withitness, in classroom management, 397
Work groups, cooperative learning and, 229

Yale Child Study Center, 53

Z-scores, 279